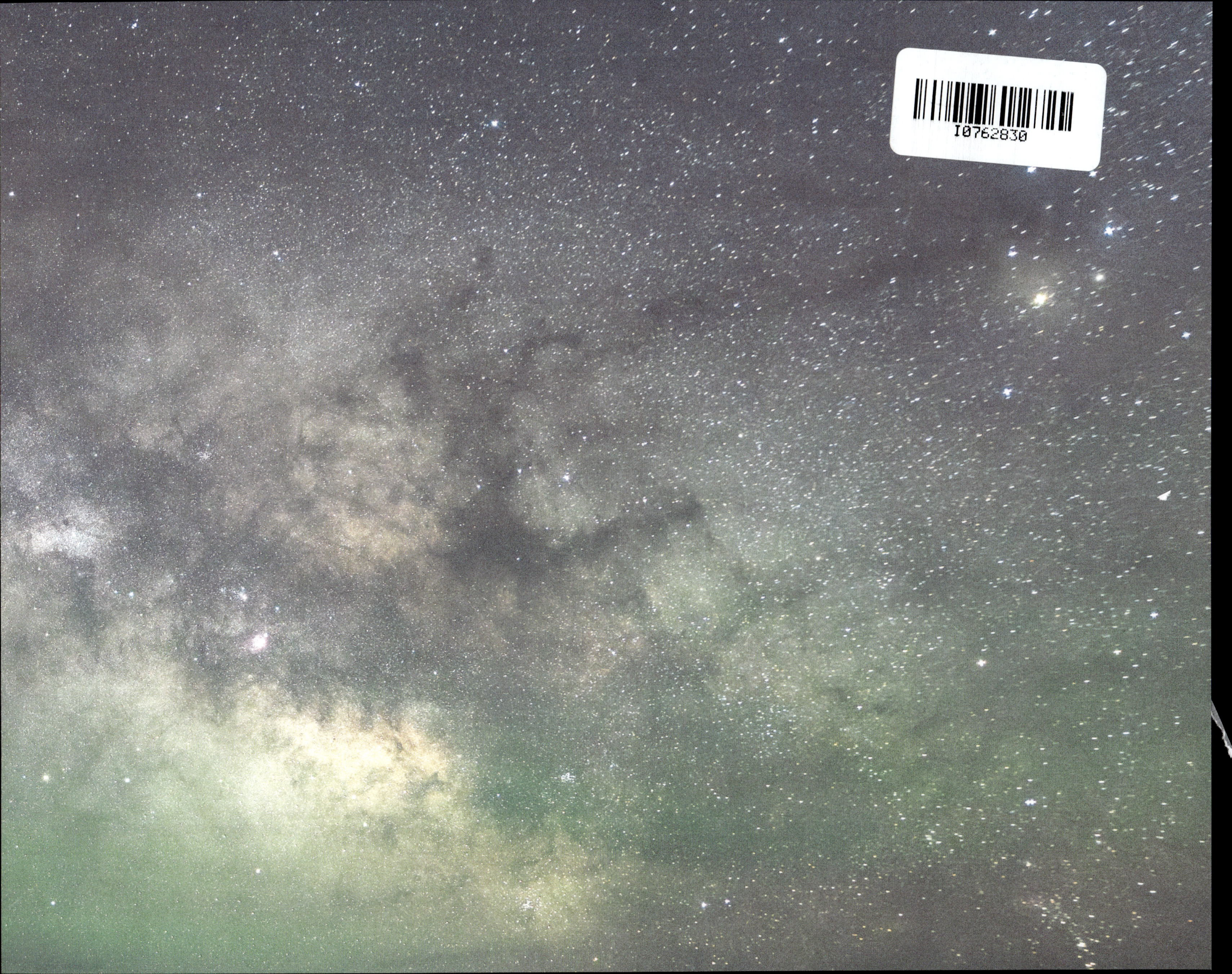

I0762830

MIDNIGHT ON CAPE COD

A Starlit Journey Across the Cape and Martha's Vineyard

Timothy Little

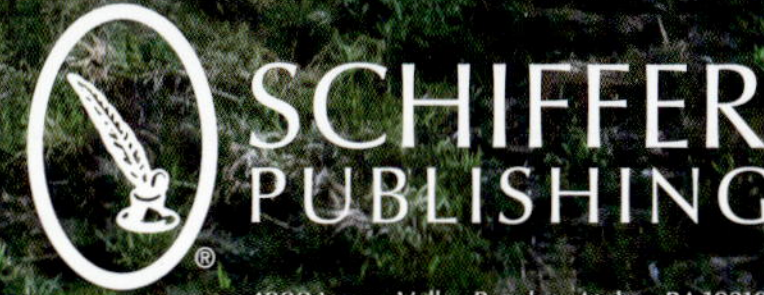
SCHIFFER PUBLISHING
4880 Lower Valley Road • Atglen, PA 19310

For anyone who thinks you can't, you can.

Other Schiffer Books by the Author:
Cape Cod Nights: A Photographic Exploration of Cape Cod and the Islands After Dark, 978-0-7643-4293-6

Other Schiffer Books on Related Subjects:
Art from above Cape Cod, Christopher Gibbs, 978-0-7643-5747-3
Easy Astrophotography: Shooting the Night Sky, David Skernick and Brian Valente, 978-0-7643-6684-0

Library of Congress Control Number: 2025930179

Edited by Ann K. Charles
Designed by Alexa Harris
Cover design by Danielle D. Farmer
Type set in Baskerville Display / Corporate S

ISBN: 978-0-7643-7029-8
ePub: 978-1-5073-0617-8

Printed in China

10 9 8 7 6 5 4 3 2 1

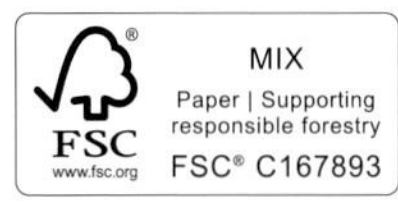

Published by Schiffer Publishing, Ltd.
4880 Lower Valley Road
Atglen, PA 19310
Phone: (610) 593-1777; Fax: (610) 593-2002
Email: info@schifferbooks.com
Web: www.schifferbooks.com

For our complete selection of fine books on this and related subjects, please visit our website at www.schifferbooks.com. You may also write for a free catalog.

Schiffer Publishing's titles are available at special discounts for bulk purchases for sales promotions or premiums. Special editions, including personalized covers, corporate imprints, and excerpts, can be created in large quantities for special needs. For more information, contact the publisher.

CONTENTS

If it weren't for these blackout curtains, I would never sleep.

PREFACE

I am writing this in 2024; more than a decade has passed since I penned the preface for my last book, *Cape Cod Nights: A Photographic Exploration of Cape Cod and the Islands After Dark*. It was a collection of moonlit, long-exposure images I had captured over hundreds of hours, and represented everything I had photographed up to my deadline in late 2012.

But not long after, I got hooked on another type of night photography. On the other end of the spectrum, far away from the light of the moon, was astro-landscape photography. Starry skies became nature's only source of light. And it was a new way for me to shoot some of my favorite locations under completely different conditions but still after dark.

Now I was photographing nearly all month long, weather and time permitting. At the expense of sleep, I began to log more hours roaming Cape Cod after dark than I had ever done before. Whether it was moonlight, starlight, or the occasional field of fireflies, I was out there.

This book took twelve years to make, and the journey was no less precarious than my last. Coyotes, mosquitoes, slippery rocks, steep sand dunes, and high winds all were, and continue to be, part of the adventure. There is something magical about photographing at night. It's something I've never grown tired of experiencing for myself or sharing with others who venture into the darkness with me to learn all about how it works. I'm thankful to be able to pursue this passion, and I'm happy you've chosen to join me for the journey laid out for you on the pages ahead. I hope this book finds a prominent place in your home and that you refer to it often when you need a few moments of peace or want to revisit Cape Cod.

ACKNOWLEDGMENTS

Supporting someone who vanishes into the darkness can be a lot to ask. Although many of these activities are a practice in solitude, I always carry the support of those who care enough to check in with me the next morning and verify I made it home safely.

Despite me being well into my forties, my parents are always interested to know how last night went. I don't know where they envisioned their son going in his life, but I am pretty sure this wasn't it. What I do know is that they are okay with it. My mother carries my business cards around with her, handing them out to anyone who might listen. Like the time she noticed that the local bank was being remodeled, and passed my info along in consideration for artwork. Less than a year later, two of their offices would be furnished with my photography. Or my father, who keeps a copy of my book on a stand in his living room and frequently shares my images across social media. He also bought me my first planetarium, astronomy book, and telescope. He has only himself to blame.

Besides providing me with the opportunity to create art, becoming a night photographer has connected me with some truly amazing people. This community of like-minded artists is one of the kindest, most supportive I've ever encountered, and I am a better person and artist for it.

Ken Lee and Mike Cooper are two of the best photo buddies a guy could have. We've logged thousands of miles exploring all sorts of weird places under the light of the moon, and I know we've got many more miles to go. Steve McIntyre, whom I met at a workshop more than a decade ago, became an annual travel partner who mixed night photography with sidesplitting, late-night laughter as we set course for West Coast burger joints and abandoned cars. I hope there are more of those weeks ahead too.

George, thanks for designing the light that illuminates my nights and for your friendship. I enjoy our chats while waiting for long-exposure dinosaur images to finish.

If it weren't for having discovered Troy Paiva's visionary night photography, along with his willingness to educate others, I doubt I'd even own camera equipment. I will happily acknowledge him in any book I am lucky enough to produce, and I know many others who feel the same.

To Nicole, who listens to me yammering about all things night photography and has adjusted her life to accommodate all the weirdness that comes with it. Thank you for worrying about me until those blackout curtains get drawn.

When I started writing this book in March 2024, I wrote that my beagle, Sunny, "will be seventeen years old in November and has kept me moving and entertained every day. I've done some of my best thinking on our daily 3-mile walks. I bet you have too. And thank you for sleeping as late as I do." But in May, he passed due to a sudden medical issue. For sixteen and a half years I came home at all hours to him patiently waiting, and I could tell he couldn't truly go to bed until I did. He was the perfect conclusion to those nights out, and I am so thankful to have had him in my life for all that time. As pet owners know, it is never long enough. Night night, my friend. See you tomorrow.

I'm eternally grateful and humbled to those of you who purchased one of my prints to display in your home. Whether the art ended up on Cape Cod or in Italy, Australia, or points in between, the map is always growing, and it never ceases to amaze me as to how far it travels. My art has been to more places than I have!

And, finally, I must recognize each and every person who has ever attended one of my group adventures or a night photography tour. To you, my sincerest thanks. You are the best part of this journey, and I sincerely hope our time together is a good memory and a source of creative inspiration. You are appreciated and remembered always.

INTRODUCTION

I have terrible night vision. But so do you. So does everyone. We're just not made to see that well at night. Your eye is made up of two main types of receptors: rods and cones. Rods help you see in dimly lit environments, at the cost of depth and color. Cones help you see color but need a lot of light to work. So therein lies the problem—you're not going to see much color at night, which is an absolute shame.

Color doesn't go away just because your cones aren't working—much like how ultraviolet light and infrared light continue to exist even though you can't perceive them. Did you know there is a creature called a mantis shrimp that scientists believe can see ten times more color than a human eye can resolve? They have sixteen color receptors, while you and I have three. What would the world look like with that ability? And, more importantly, why does a shrimp get to see better than me?

Night photography is about revealing the "non-cone-friendly" world around us. Camera equipment does not suffer from these limitations and can easily become our window into the darkness, as you will see in the pages ahead.

While on some nights the moon casts its silvery and pale light across the landscape, a moonless sky becomes a blank canvas. In very dark areas, the sky may reveal the soft green tones of atmospheric airglow, a natural phenomenon caused by the recombining of oxygen atoms in the upper atmosphere that were previously ionized by the daytime sun. Stars of different colors can sprinkle the sky from horizon to horizon with red, yellow, and blue. A meteor could streak the darkness with orange. The camera can see all this, and more.

To the average eye, the northern lights may appear to be a faint, sometimes colorless glow, but to the camera, the sky is awash with ribbons of greens, pinks, and purples. Here on Cape Cod, we do occasionally have the opportunity to see it or, more accurately, to photograph it despite it being so dim you may not even notice. I have been surprised, more than once, by an aurora appearing in one of my images. Even when I know there's a chance of one occurring, I have to go on faith that it will appear in the photograph when I can't see it with my eyes alone.

Another advantage for a camera is the continual collection of light. This is known as "exposure time." Think of the camera sensor as a barrel, the shutter as the cover, and the light as rain. In this case, we leave the shutter open until we feel like enough light has trickled in, slowly compounding with every passing second. Like the rain barrel, it continues to fill. Too much water and the bucket overflows. Too much light and the image is washed out. While overexposing an image under night conditions is very unlikely, capturing too much movement of the sky can be an issue. In some cases, very long exposures can reveal the apparent movement of the stars over time. Compositionally, this can work really well. But when capturing the Milky Way, minimizing that motion is key. *It is a delicate balance between light, movement, and intention*. It's the most enjoyable part of the process.

All of the images in this book were captured with this idea in mind, and every one of them required a tripod. Complete stillness of the camera is essential for capturing sharp long-exposure images. The simplest tap or a sudden gust of wind sabotages the moment.

In 2013, I began photographing with a Canon 6D DSLR, and in 2017 I moved to a Pentax K1, which I am still using as of 2024. At least two-thirds of the images you will see here were shot with the newer camera, the rest with the 6D, and a few with the camera responsible for my first book, the Canon 7D. Many cameras in the last decade can achieve similar results depending on the lens attached and the conditions in front of it. I've always believed that the most important piece of gear available to you is your artistic mind. If you're confident in that, the camera is far less important than you might think. The best compliment you can pay a photographer is "You have a great eye." Complimenting the camera is like applauding the oven after a great meal. I suspect the chef would have something to say about that.

Whether obvious or not, many of the photographs benefit from a technique called light painting. While this can be defined in many ways, for the purposes of my work this is the process in which I use handheld lighting to enhance a subject in real time. Maybe the foreground was going to be too dark if I was exposing for just the sky alone. Or perhaps some element of the foreground needed a splash of color. You'll know it when you see it!

The technique itself is quite simple. The difficult part is figuring out from what position to light, how high to hold the light, and for how long. In dark conditions, only a few seconds of lighting will be needed, since it quickly burns into the image and will remain. In others, it may need to shine longer to overpower some other interfering source, such as a streetlamp. It's even possible to light from multiple directions in a single image. Light painting helps bring out texture, guides the eye, and balances a subject. It's a powerful, organic tool that physically connects a photographer with the final image. Long-exposure photography is the only type that provides enough time for this opportunity—another reason why it is so enjoyable and immersive.

But what about moonlit nights? Yes, they are here as well. During these adventures, the camera's sensitivity is reduced so that time can let the moon slowly illuminate the landscape. This process allows passing clouds to stretch, star trails to grow, and light sources, such as cars or trains, to streak. It is the very essence of capturing time in an image, another ability outside that of the human eye. Light painting here is trickier. The moon is an eraser of light painting, meaning I can work only within the shadows—the areas untouched by moonlight. This is useful for the shady sides of buildings, interiors, or the dark sides of trees.

What I am getting at by telling you all of this up front is that *these images are organic*. I chose to shoot these compositions based on the time of year, the position of the Milky Way, or the direction of the moonlight at a given hour. The colors, the stars, the lighting—all are as they appeared in front of the camera. Nothing here is staged; the sky is as it was that night. The camera's ability to see what you cannot, whether that be in the form of color or time, simply gives you added insight into this nighttime world. These locations are real.

Over the last decade, social media has bombarded us with photography. Some of it is authentic; some of it is not. And it is getting harder to tell the difference. No matter where that goes, it will never replace the moods and the moments a photographer experiences by packing up the equipment and trekking to an interesting location. In my world, the photographs are the bonus to a good night out. Enjoying the night sky was the goal. I hope this is conveyed to you as you move ahead.

Cape Cod Nights: A Photographic Exploration of Cape Cod and the Islands After Dark was a journey from the canal to the outer Cape and then to the islands. *Midnight on Cape Cod* is a bit different. Here, we will travel together not based on locations alone, but rather moods. We'll venture through the darkest of nights with a dazzling Milky Way overhead, to the moonlit shores and landscapes during the weeks of the full moon, and even to snowy main streets on blustery winter nights. And if you've never seen the Vineyard at the holidays, you're in for a treat. You'll learn about the astronomy side of these images, and I will share with you details on how I captured some of my more complex compositions. I also relay some wacky stories about the inevitable situations a night photographer finds himself dealing with alone in the dark. In my last book, I was a bit reserved about sharing these tidbits, but, as I have learned over the years, what makes a lot of these images even more interesting is hearing about what the camera didn't capture. It will ensure you get the full picture. Pun intended.

Having Cape Cod as my foreground is an amazing opportunity I appreciate more with every passing year. Beaches, lighthouses, harbors, and the soft sounds of wind and waves at night come together to create an ambience that is hard to convey. Before I left the corporate world to pursue this as a full-time endeavor, I would use these nights out to decompress and disconnect from that daytime world. Nature can do that for you. Nature at night does this even more. Now, I frequently find myself showing a student what this world is like and hoping they can find solace with these places under the stars.

Much has been written about Cape Cod, as described through the thousands of authors sharing their own unique perspectives of what the area means to them and how it has impacted their lives. If you have been here before, you know. And if you haven't been here before, you should come. I hope this book inspires you to do so or reconnects you to a favorite Cape Cod memory. Each one of these images represents a great memory for me.

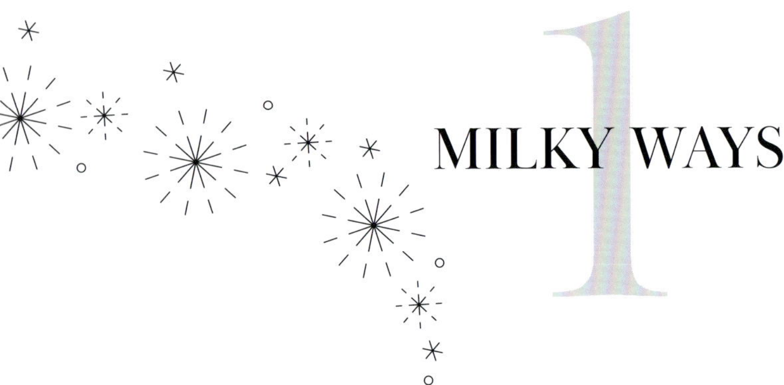

1 MILKY WAYS

We're not downtown. We're not uptown. We're in that part of the suburb where if you look out the kitchen window on a clear night, you can see the distant skyscrapers of the city.

That's our place in the Milky Way. I thought it would be important to give you that perspective so that you have a better understanding of what it is you're seeing when you're looking at many of these images.

The Milky Way is the name of our home galaxy. Our sun is one of billions of stars that circle the galactic center. Our galaxy loosely resembles a pancake. We're closer to the outside edge of our galaxy than we are to the core. This means that when you look at the night sky on a moonless night and you see what appears to be this soft glowing band across the sky, you're looking at our galaxy. On Cape Cod in the summer, if you follow that band overhead and then down along the southern part of the sky, it gets wider. This area is known as the galactic core, and this is the center of our galaxy. It contains a high concentration of stars just like our sun. It is the brightest part of the Milky Way. But between us and that, there is a lot of space dust, gases, and other yet-to-be-discovered mysteries. This tends to obscure much of the light coming from the core and also creates what appears to be rivers of dark patches against the light. These are commonly referred to as dust lanes, because—you guessed it—they are made mostly of dust.

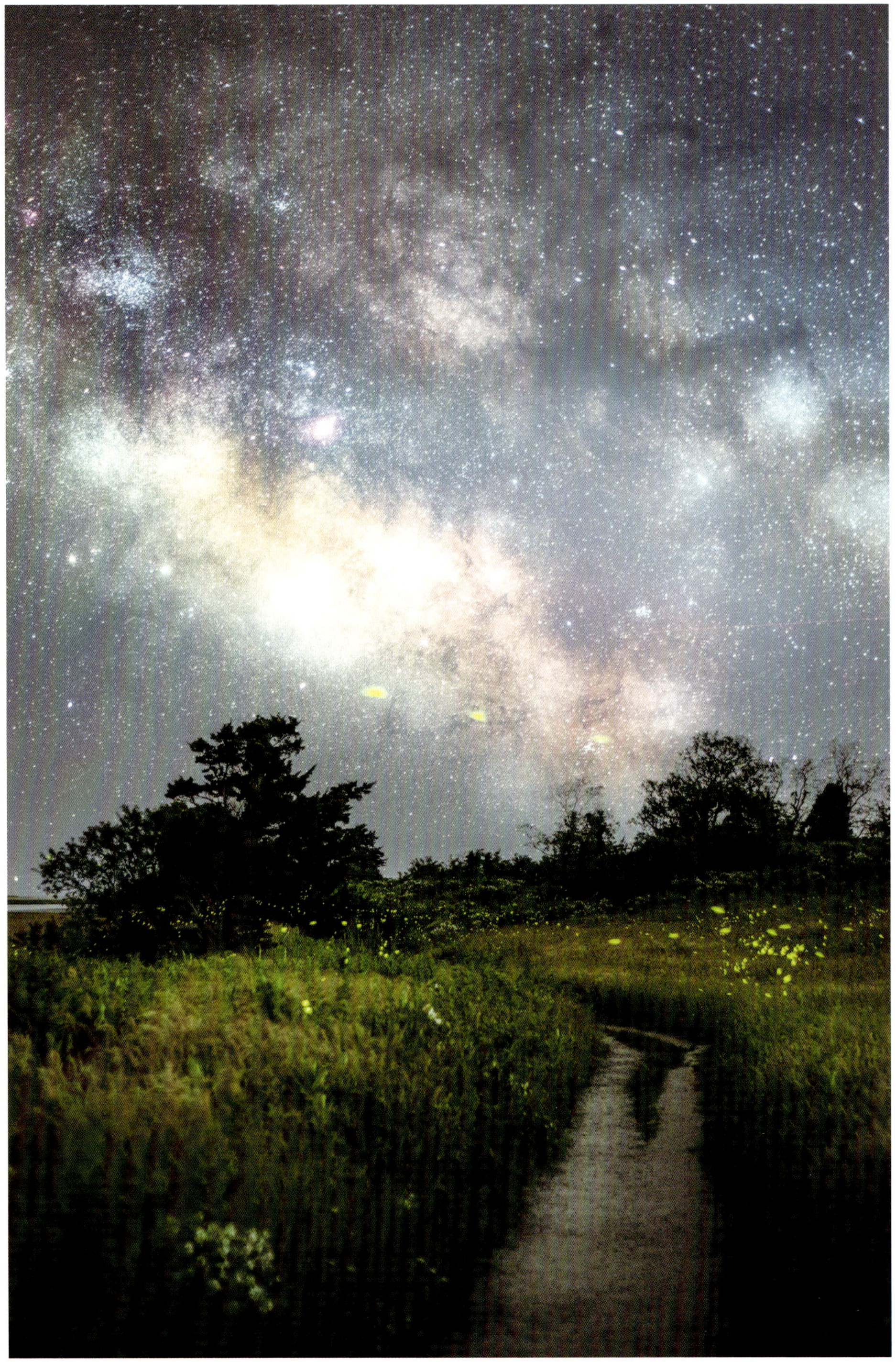

Visit Fort Hill in Eastham during the moonless weeks of June, and you may be lucky enough to be surrounded by fireflies. A vintage 50 mm lens causes the starry backdrop to be compressed with the foreground, making it appear larger. A soft lime-colored light was used to enhance the nearby grass and to match the glow from the fireflies. It took several attempts to capture this photograph, because one pesky firefly continued to pass very close to the lens, resulting in big, green dashes each time. In essence, I was being "photobombed" by a firefly. Like shooting stars, fireflies are hard to capture at lower ISO settings or smaller apertures.

The bulk of the Milky Way core is approximately 26,000 light-years away from Earth. A light-year is a measurement of distance, not time. I know that might sound confusing, but bear with me and I promise it will make sense in a minute. For example, let's say "Nocturnal Bob" can walk 1.5 miles in a full hour; we could now refer to that distance as a "Nocturnal Bob hour" instead of a "boring" 1.5 miles. And so, something 3 miles away would be "two Nocturnal Bob hours" distant. On such a small scale, this type of measuring isn't all that useful. When it comes to the great unexplored mass of the galaxy, this is far easier than presenting a number that has so many zeros after it.

A light-year is the distance that light can travel in a year at a speed of 186,000 miles per second. To calculate this, multiply that number by the sixty seconds in a minute, by the sixty minutes in an hour, by the twenty-four hours in a day, and by the three hundred sixty-five days in a year. It's a big number. Doesn't one light-year sound better?

When light reaches your eye, you are seeing the source as it appeared when the light left it. Jupiter, for example, is between 35 and 52 light-minutes away from Earth, depending on where it and we are in our orbits. When you see Jupiter, you're seeing it as it appeared by that amount of time in the past. The sun is 8 light-minutes away, so you're seeing it as it appeared eight minutes ago (don't look at it!). Yes, that means that the beautiful Cape Cod sunset you just enjoyed really happened eight minutes earlier. Weird!

As you gaze upon the galactic core, you're seeing it as it appeared 26,000 years ago! That may be a blink of an eye to the universe, but that's a lot of time for humans. Some of the stars you're seeing don't exist anymore, and none of them are in the same place they appear to you now. Looking into the night sky is always a look into the past. Next time you have a look at the moon, just know it is 1.3 light-seconds away.

The Milky Way core has a seasonality to it. With each passing day, it appears to rise earlier and earlier, until it rises and sets during daylight hours. In late January, just before dawn, you can wake up early and make a trip out to the Cape Cod National Seashore, where you'll get a glimpse of the rising core to the east before the sun pops up just behind it. By the time summer comes along, it is immediately visible high in the sky at the very last fading of the sun's light, known as astronomical twilight. With the changing colors of the fall leaves, you may catch a brief glimpse of the galactic core to the west just after sunset. But being on the East Coast means that much of our light pollution is on the western horizon, which quickly gobbles up our last views of the Milky Way for the season come November.

The key to good viewing or photography is to, of course, find a dark location and plan ahead. As the world seemingly gets brighter with every year, this can be quite challenging, but there are resources available to help!

The Bortle Dark-Sky Scale is a tool that provides an assessment of the night sky's brightness at any given location. It has nine levels, with the lower number being the best opportunity for dark-sky enjoyment. For reference, Cape Cod is mostly a level 4. As you will see in the pages ahead, you can still observe quite a bit at that level, even though it's almost halfway through the scale. Currently, the very best you could hope for on Cape Cod is a level 3, beginning just south of Truro, and transitioning to a level 4 north of Highland Light. Downtown Hyannis peaks at level 6, while Falmouth averages level 5. Contrast this with Boston, which hovers between 8 and 9, or southern Oregon, which achieves a level 1. You can assess your area's level by using resources such as www.lightpollutionmap.info or via countless astronomy apps.

Will you see, with your own eyes, the Milky Way exactly as it appears in the pictures featured ahead? Not quite. Remember, the camera is designed to see better than you and me. But, given the right conditions, you'll see the unmistakable glowing haze of the Milky Way band. Just be patient. Give your eyes at least ten full minutes to adjust. Avoid looking at your phone screen or nearby lights. If you need any light to help see the terrain around you, use a red-capped light. Red helps preserve your night vision. Keep it at low power and use it sparingly. And don't forget to look straight over your head. You may see the galactic band there, and then you can trace it down to the center.

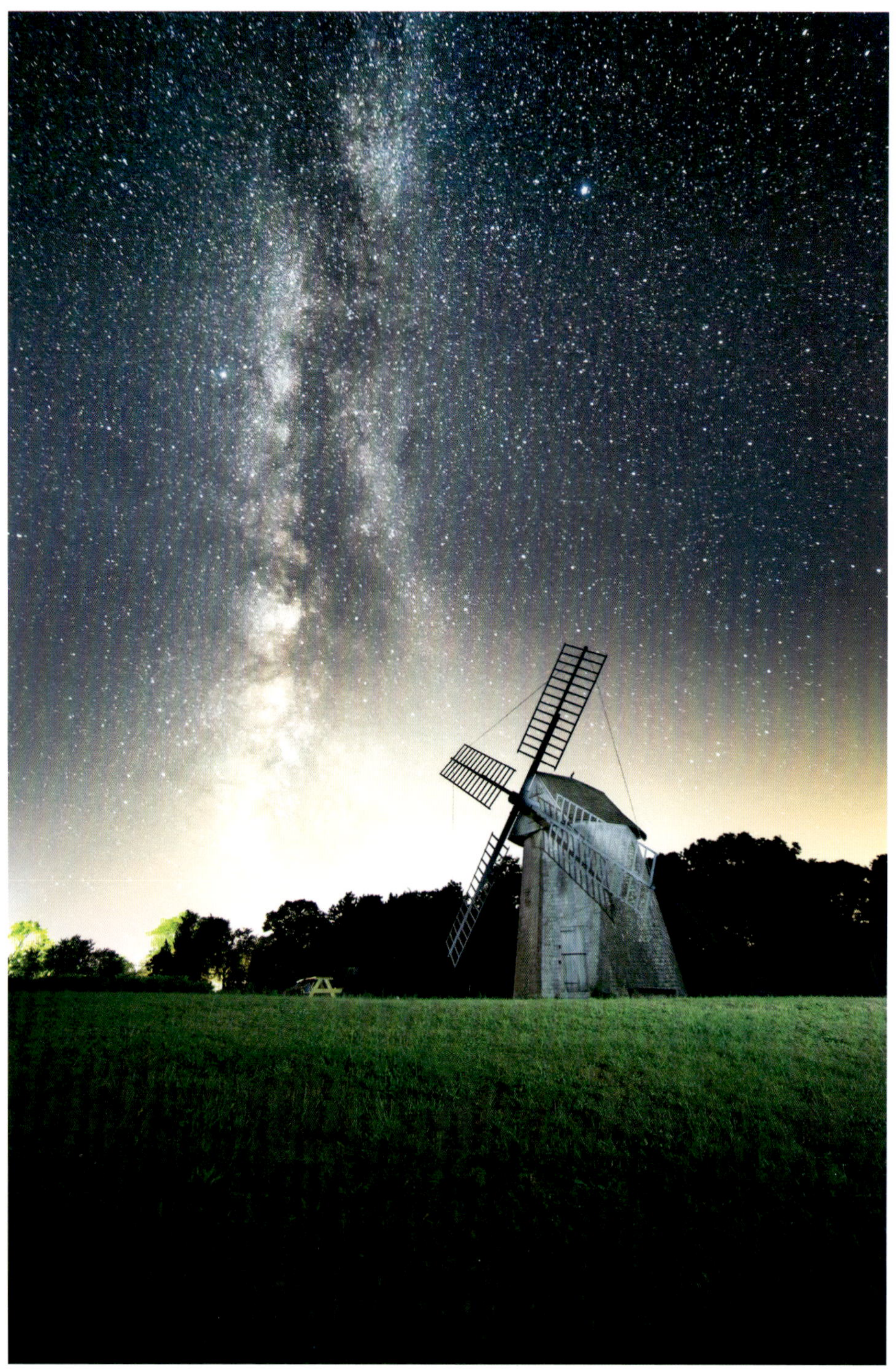

QUICK TIPS FOR CAPTURING THE MILKY WAY

Want to capture the Milky Way with your camera? Try these settings after placing your camera on a sturdy tripod.

ISO 3200

f/2.8 (or as low as your lens will allow, down to this aperture)

20 seconds

Always shoot in your camera's RAW file format. This captures the most picture information and gives you the most flexibility in editing later. You've probably heard of JPEG, which should be reserved only for saving your fully edited image later.

Remember to disable all image stabilization. Keeping it turned on can have the opposite effect when the camera is attached to a tripod, and your pictures will appear blurry as if they were out of focus.

Speaking of focus, do not rely on autofocus. Switch to manual, either on the lens or in your camera's settings. Use your live view screen to digitally zoom in on a portion of your subject, using magnification functions, and manually focus on light sources or on an area that you illuminate with a flashlight. On touchscreen cameras, you can pinch to zoom. Almost all cameras have a physical magnifying button. Do not zoom in optically, focus, and then zoom out, since not all lenses will maintain focus throughout their zoom ranges. Use digital magnification only.

Some cameras come with a function called *focus peaking*, which is used to assist in showing which areas of the subject are in focus while looking at the camera's live view. During the day, it is quite reliable. It can be helpful at night but not as certain. Try out yours to see if it helps, but don't rely on it alone.

In any situation, review the image after you've taken it before proceeding with your next shot. Digitally zoom in on your subject to verify that you focused successfully. I highly recommend you refocus every time you move your camera,

An August Milky Way sets the backdrop for this windmill at Drummer Boy Park in Brewster. Since the structure was in complete darkness, I slowly waved a wide-beamed light across it and the ground. This is how painting with light can easily balance the exposure between foreground and the sky.

even if shooting distant landscapes. Vibrations from walking can cause a lens to lose focus. Temperature changes will also impact focus.

By default, your camera may have noise reduction enabled. This is the process in which the camera automatically takes a second exposure immediately following the first and then blends them both together to reduce digital noise, which can often be seen when you're using higher ISO settings or long exposures. You'll know if your camera is doing this if you cannot review your first image immediately after it has been taken. I recommend disabling all noise reduction functions. You can apply this later by using postprocessing software to your preference. If you allow the camera to do it, you cannot undo it later. Sometimes this can result in stars being identified as noise or the foreground losing detail. Wherever possible, don't let the camera make decisions for you.

Your eyes have likely adjusted to the darkness, and any image that pops up on the back of your camera will appear much brighter in that moment than it actually is. Please, don't use your camera's screen or viewfinder to assess the picture's brightness.

Or don't do any of that! Just grab a chair and go sit outside and look up at the night sky!

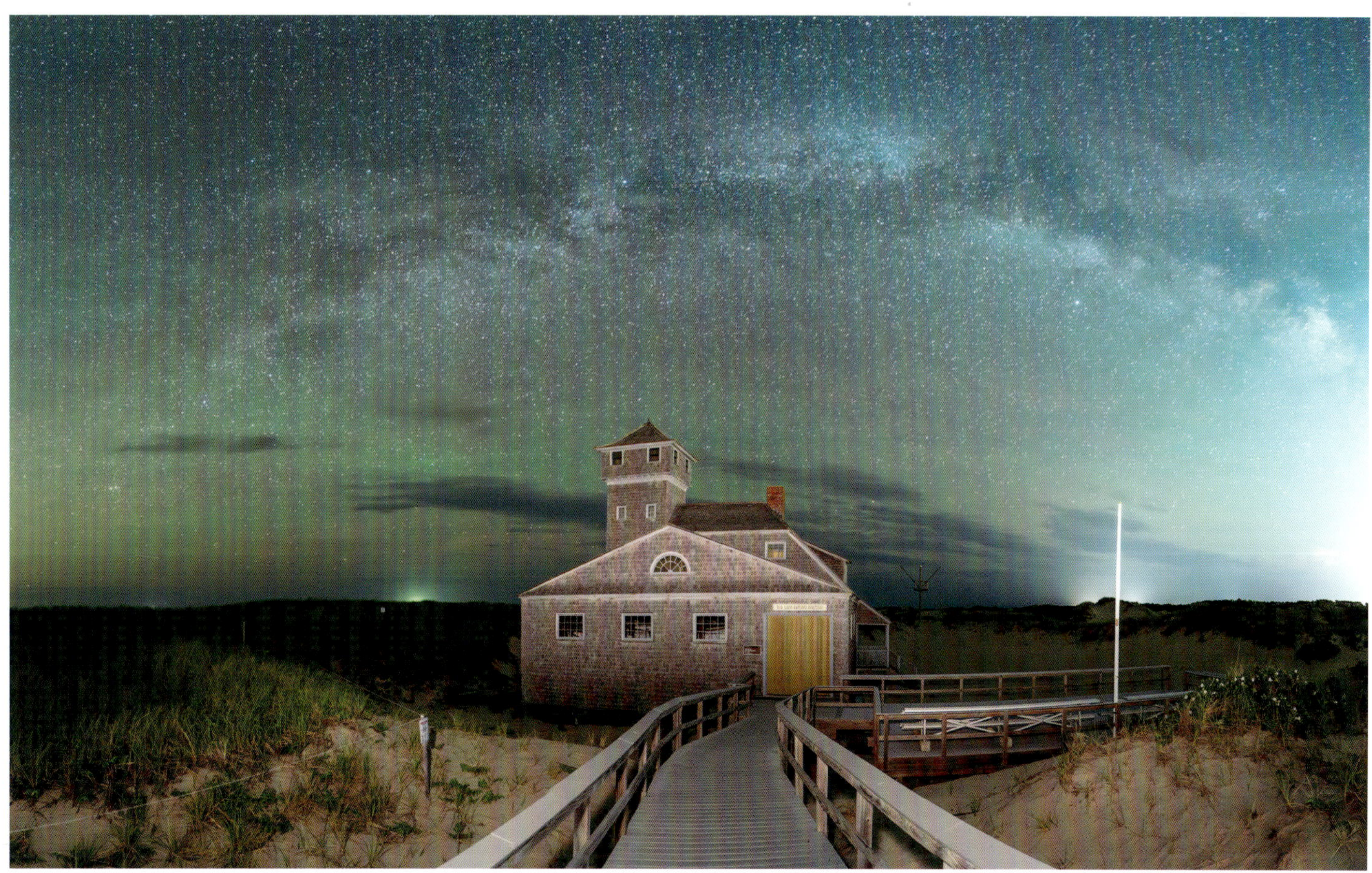

The Life-Saving Station located at Race Point Beach in Provincetown. The final image was created from several vertical shots, allowing for a panoramic sky. I used a handheld light on the foreground and duplicated the technique for each of the images. I later used software to "stitch" the images together to complete the final photograph.

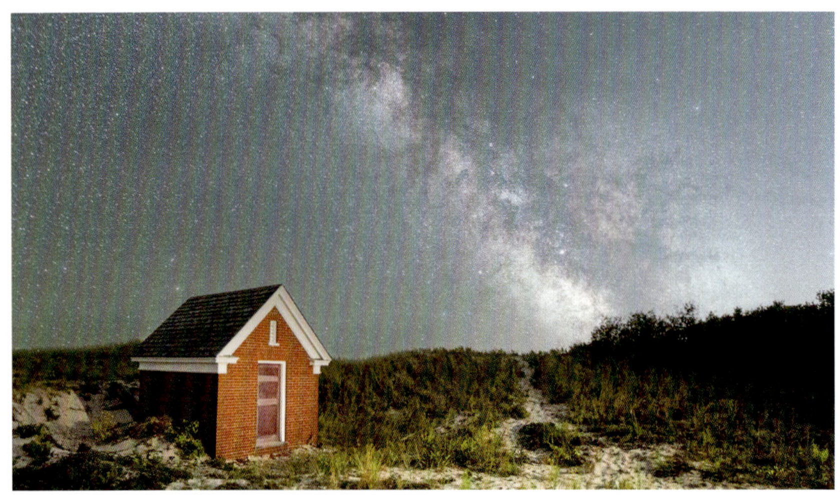

A small brick shack adjacent to Sandy Neck Light. Structures like these were often used to store supplies such as the whale oils needed to power the lanterns. When visiting lighthouses anywhere, look for them or the foundations that remain.

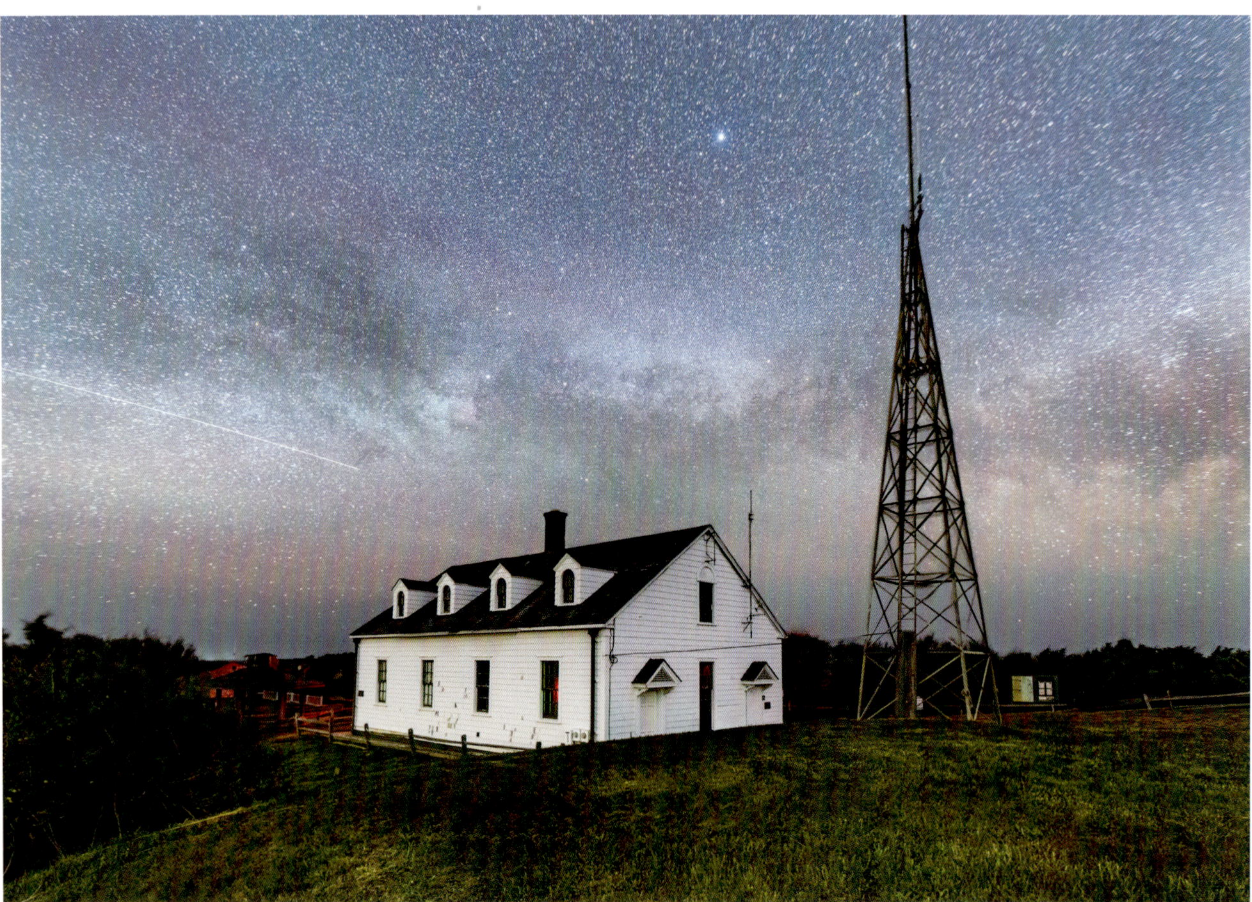

This property is now owned by the National Park Service and serves as a bathroom, changing area, and shower for visitors of the nearby beach. It is also located on one of the best properties to view the rising Milky Way in the spring. While this image was being taken, a surprise visitor began to traverse the skies over the structure. Look for the white trail cutting across the starfield. This is the International Space Station.

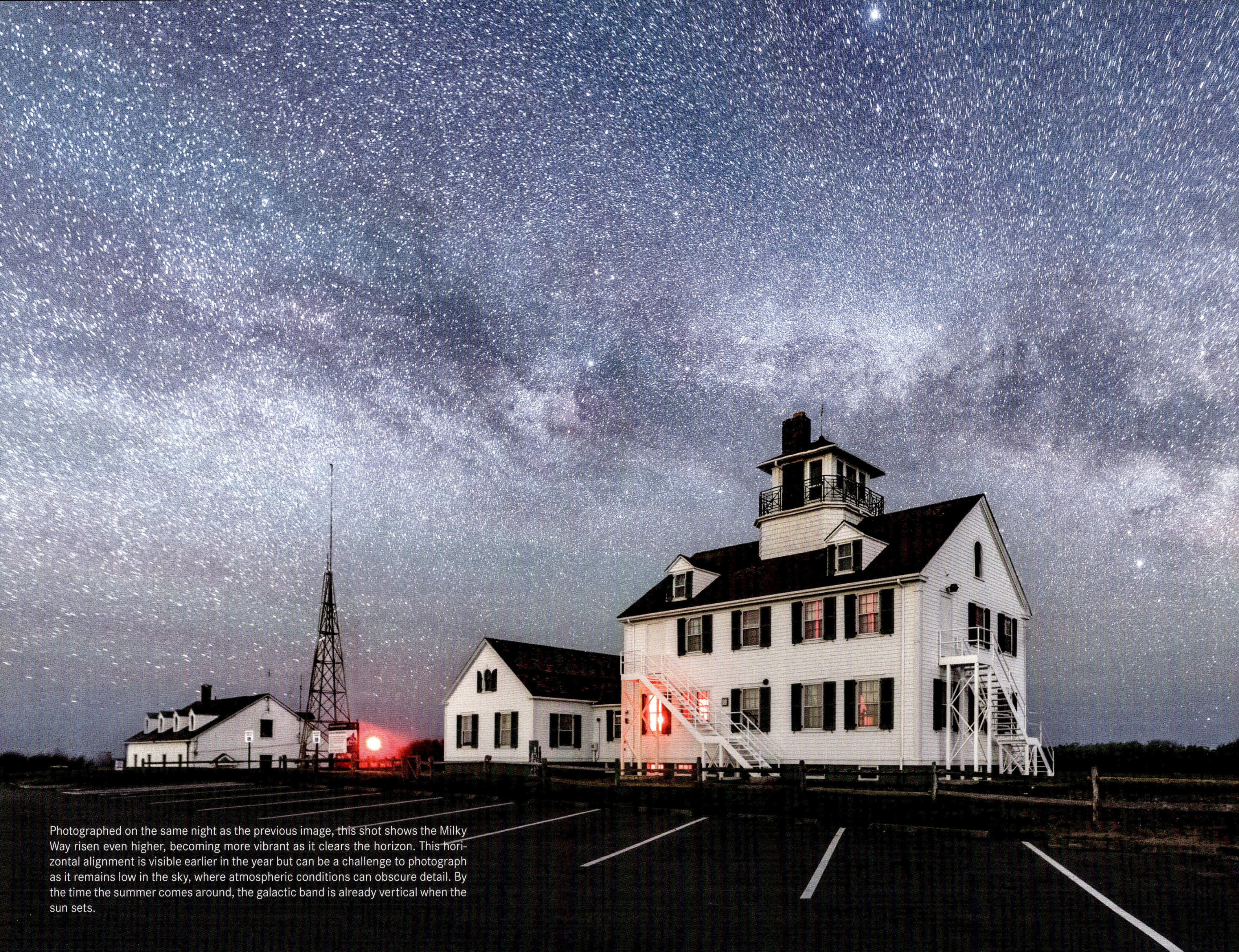

Photographed on the same night as the previous image, this shot shows the Milky Way risen even higher, becoming more vibrant as it clears the horizon. This horizontal alignment is visible earlier in the year but can be a challenge to photograph as it remains low in the sky, where atmospheric conditions can obscure detail. By the time the summer comes around, the galactic band is already vertical when the sun sets.

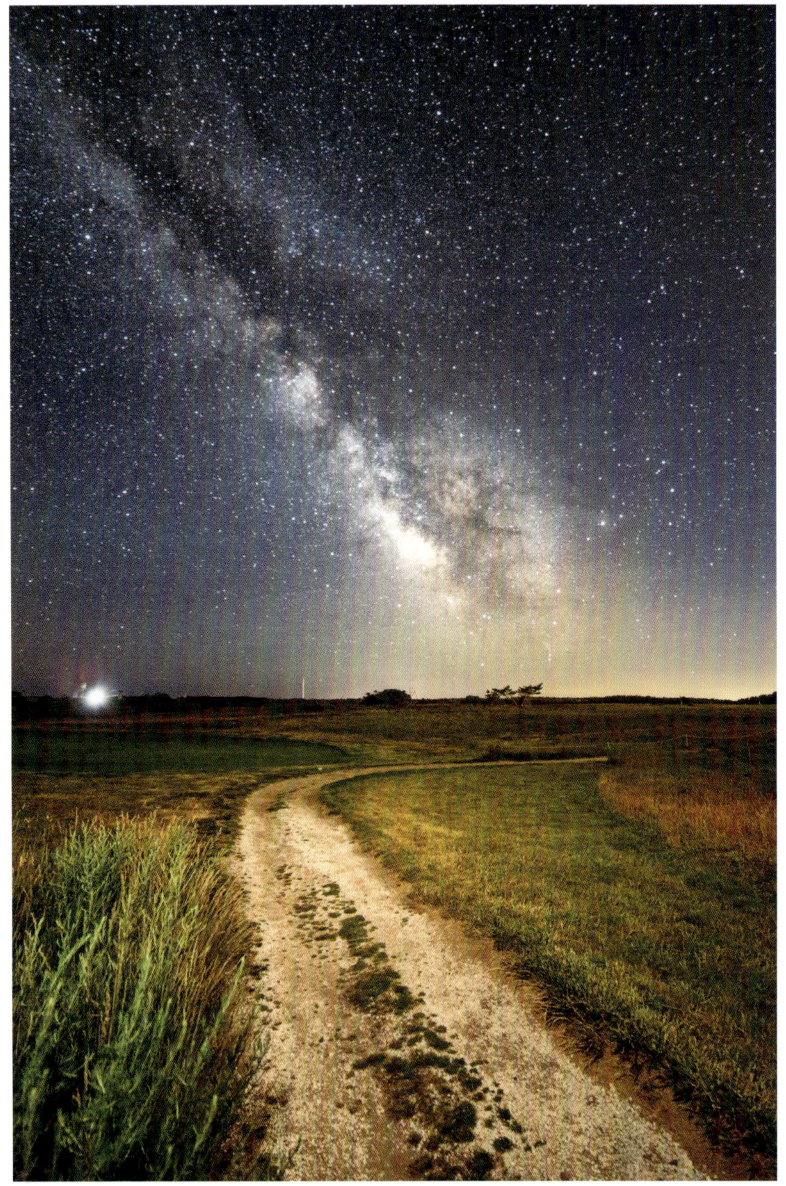

The Milky Way meets the horizon along the Highland Links golf course in Truro. The foreground is a golf cart path, which was illuminated with a handheld light at the time of the exposure. This allowed me to get the entire image in one take. Without the light, it would have taken two images to complete the composition: a short one for the sky and a long one for the foreground. Lighting the path during a shorter exposure kept the stars sharp. I returned the following night to photograph the small pine trees on the hill just under the Milky Way core.

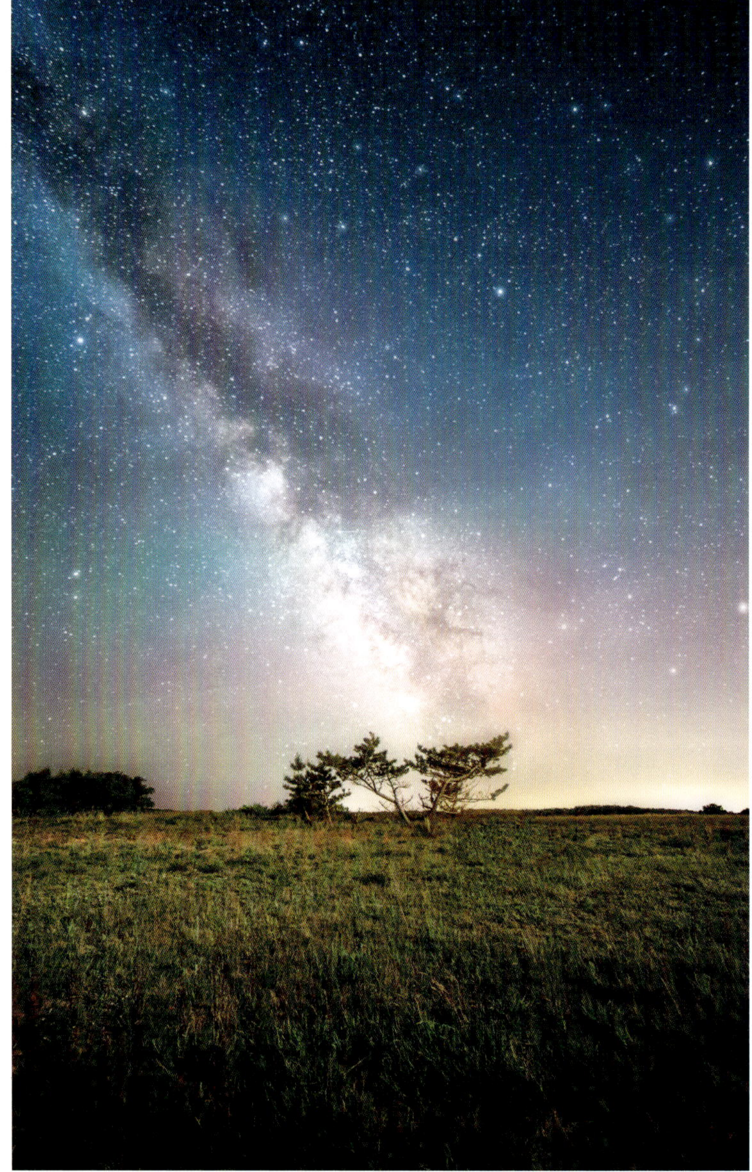

A small pine cluster grows near one of the golf greens. They reminded me of a type of tree you might see on an African safari. The warm glow from the nearby lighthouse illuminates the foreground. Sadly, not many of these trees remain due to the relentless wind and weather they have experienced over the years.

Walking back from Nauset Light on a July evening in 2014, I spotted this alignment of the Milky Way across the roofline of the shack. The beam from the lighthouse would periodically sweep the old building, so a flashlight was needed to soften the shadows being projected by the nearby trees. It wasn't until I returned home that I spotted the shooting star across the top and center of the image.

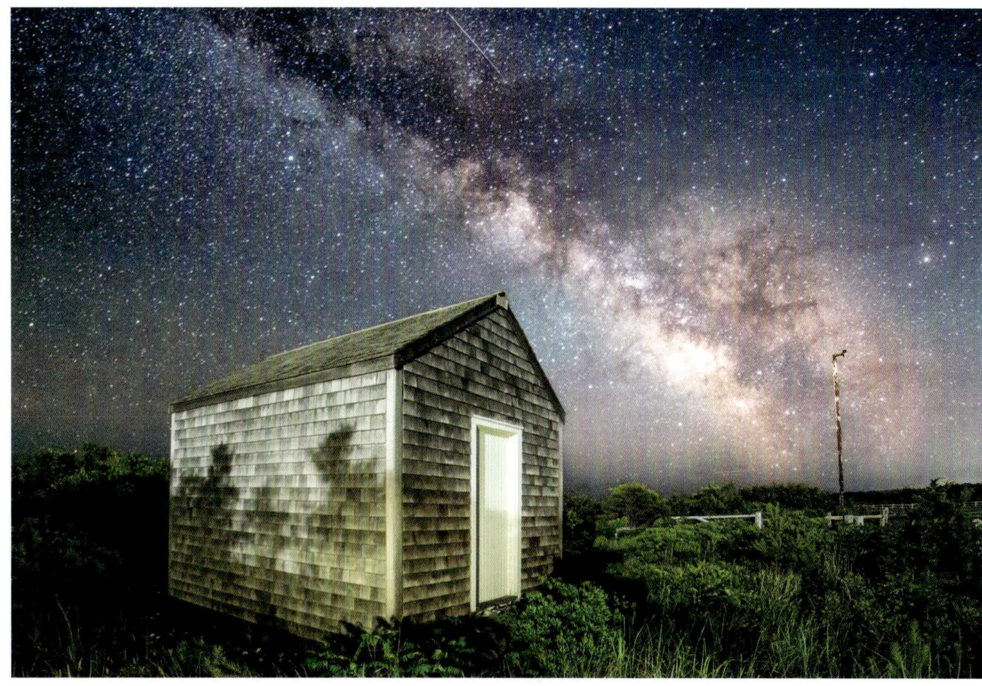

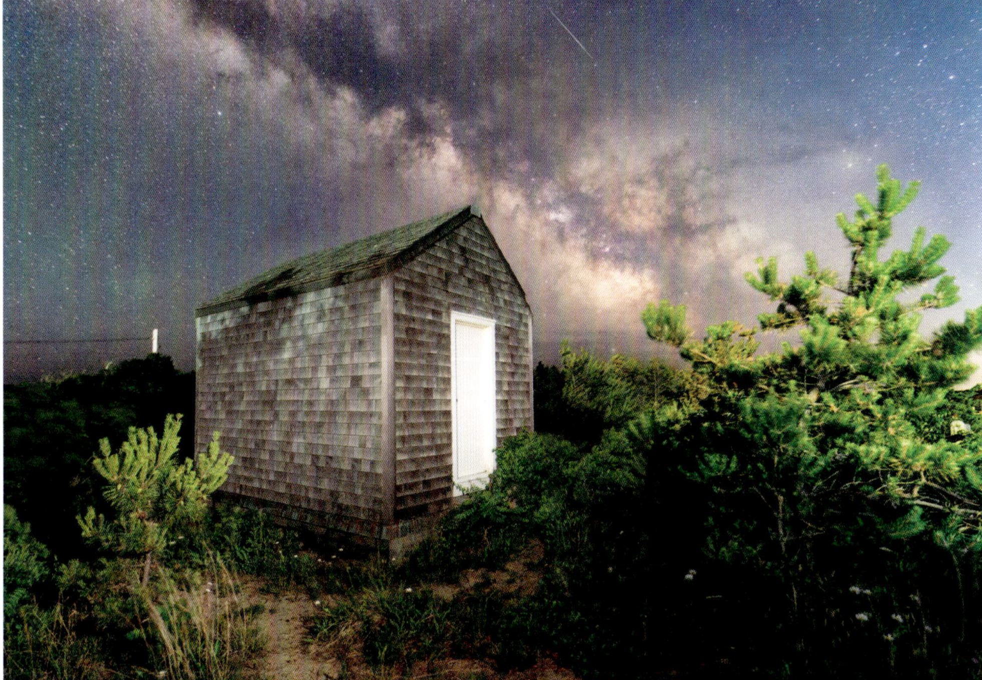

In July 2022, I found myself at the same location with a nearly identical alignment of the Milky Way. I rarely reshoot the same subject but decided to try it again with newer camera equipment and processing techniques. In the eight years since my last visit, the vegetation had grown tall, but the shack remained unchanged. Once again, it wasn't until I returned home that I spotted the shooting star across the top and center of the image . . . in the same place! What were the chances of this?

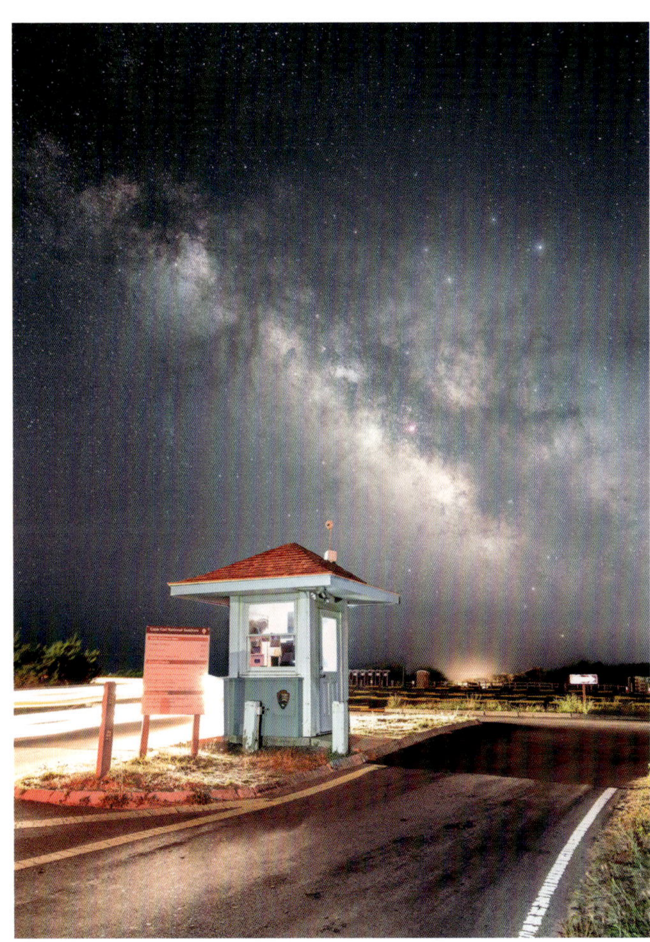

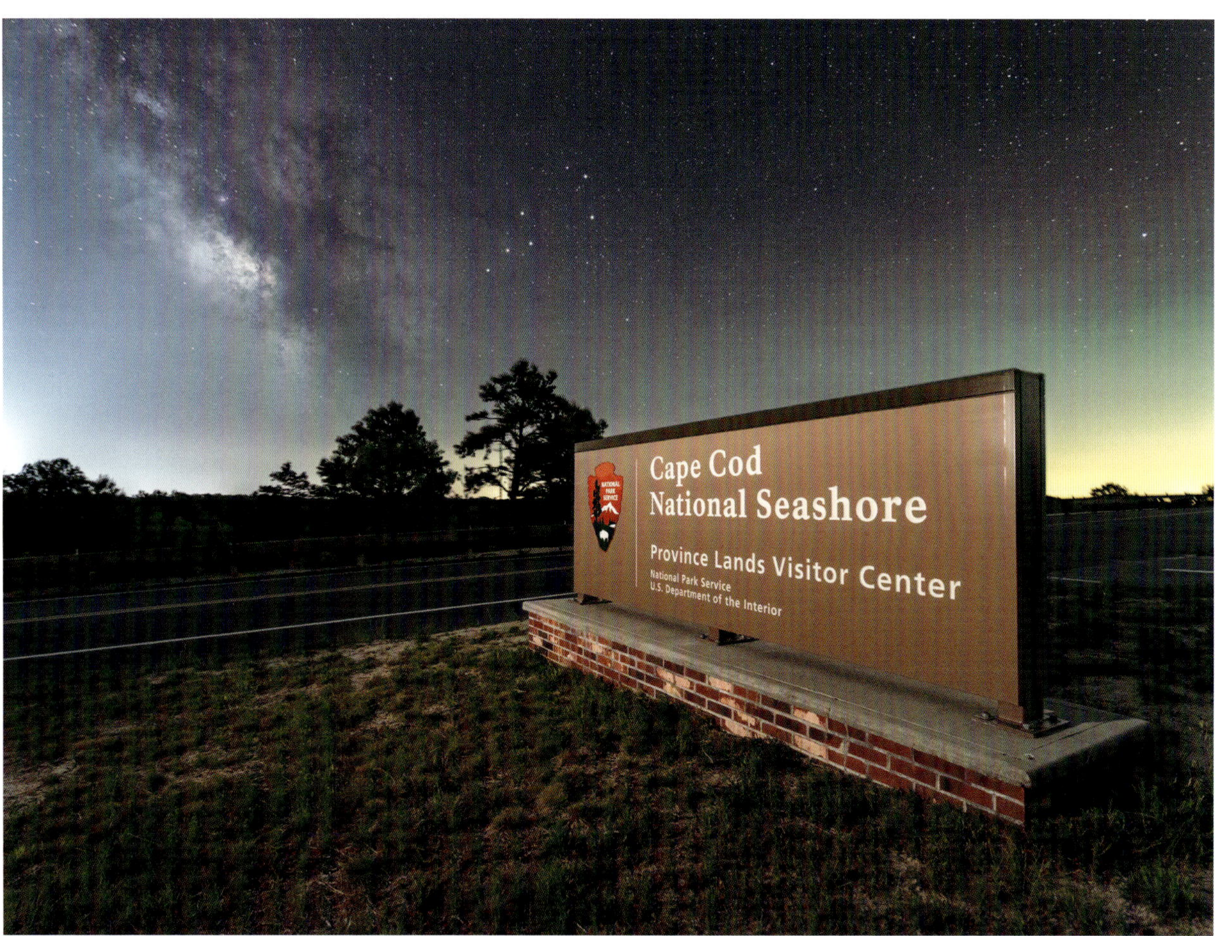

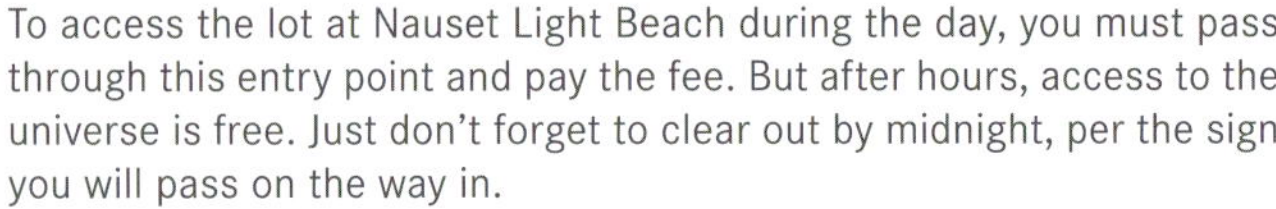
To access the lot at Nauset Light Beach during the day, you must pass through this entry point and pay the fee. But after hours, access to the universe is free. Just don't forget to clear out by midnight, per the sign you will pass on the way in.

The Province Lands is where you will find a visitor center, Race Point Beach, and a lighthouse, along with many hiking trails and sand dunes. But watch out for the endangered bird known as the piping plover. Their beach sand nests result in the closure of surrounding areas to ensure they stay safe from people and pets.

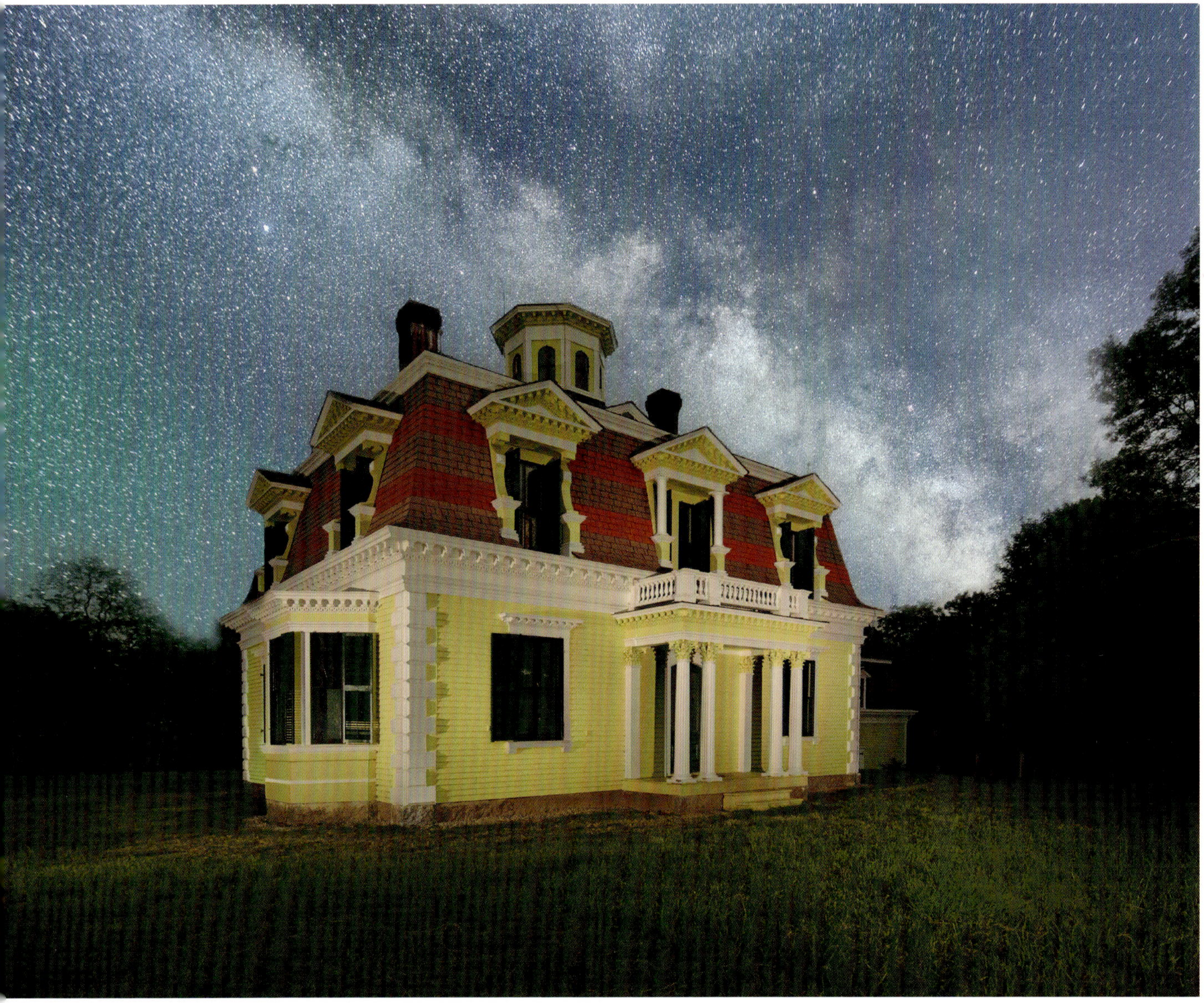

The Captain Penniman House is located on the way to Fort Hill and was built in the mid-1800s for use by the whaling captain's family while he was at sea. It is now managed by the National Park Service. On most nights, it is completely dark, making it a great subject beneath starry skies.

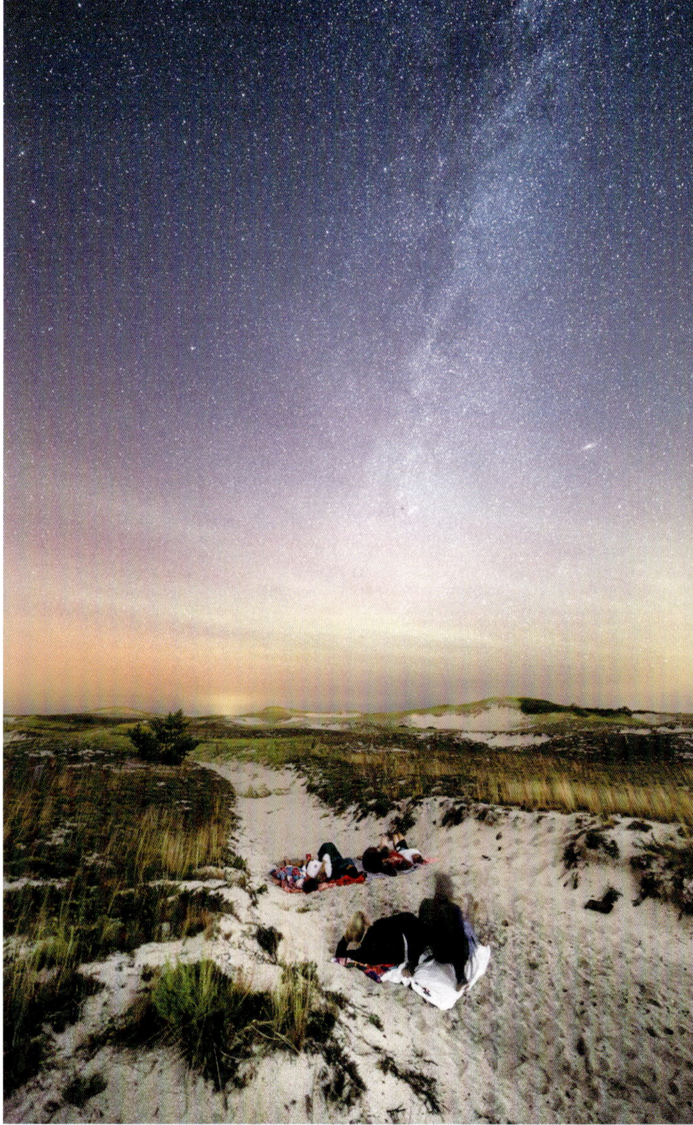

Visitors staying at the Sandy Neck Light property were treated to the perfect night for stargazing. The fuzzy disc in the sky, *right of center*, is the Andromeda galaxy.

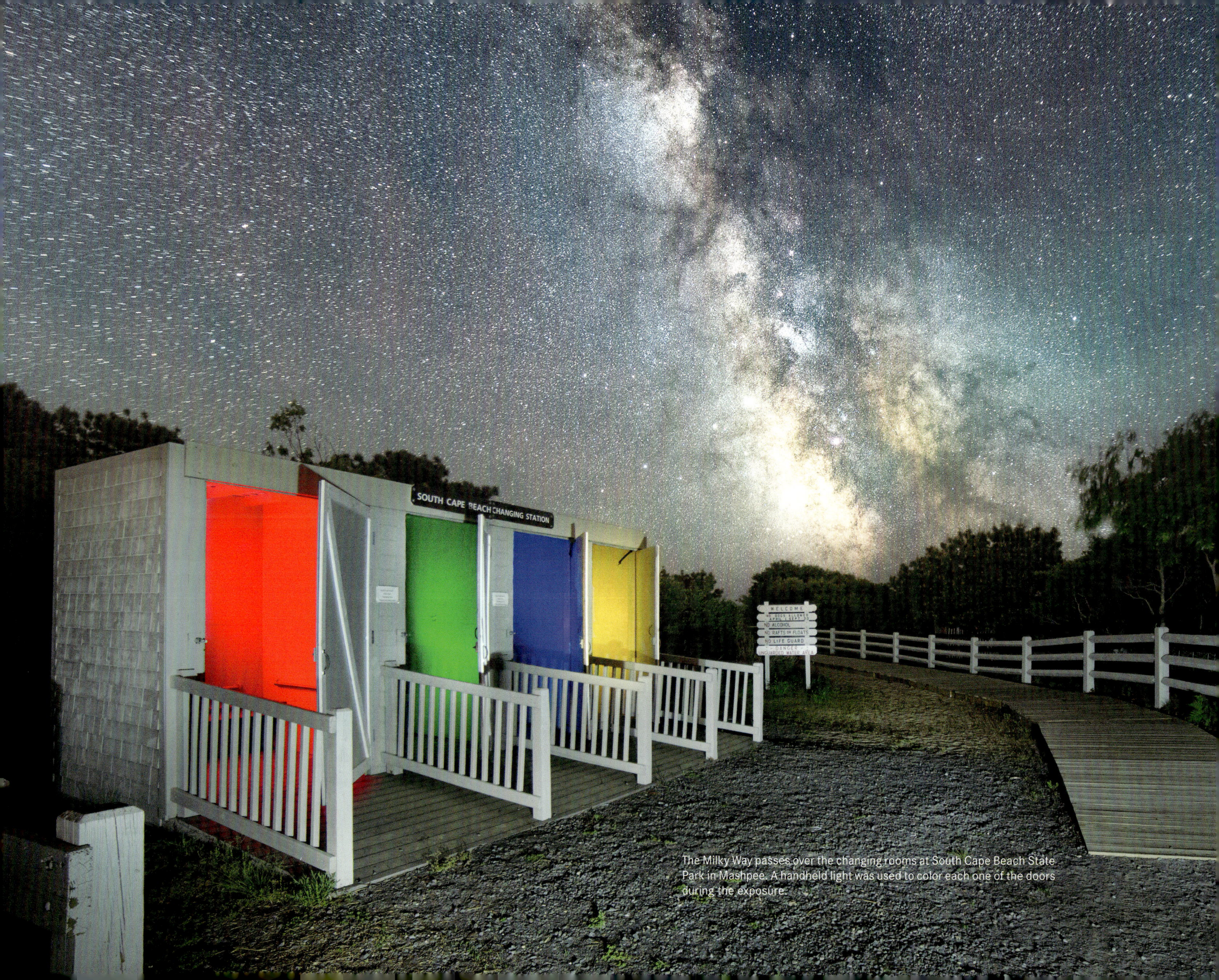

The Milky Way passes over the changing rooms at South Cape Beach State Park in Mashpee. A handheld light was used to color each one of the doors during the exposure.

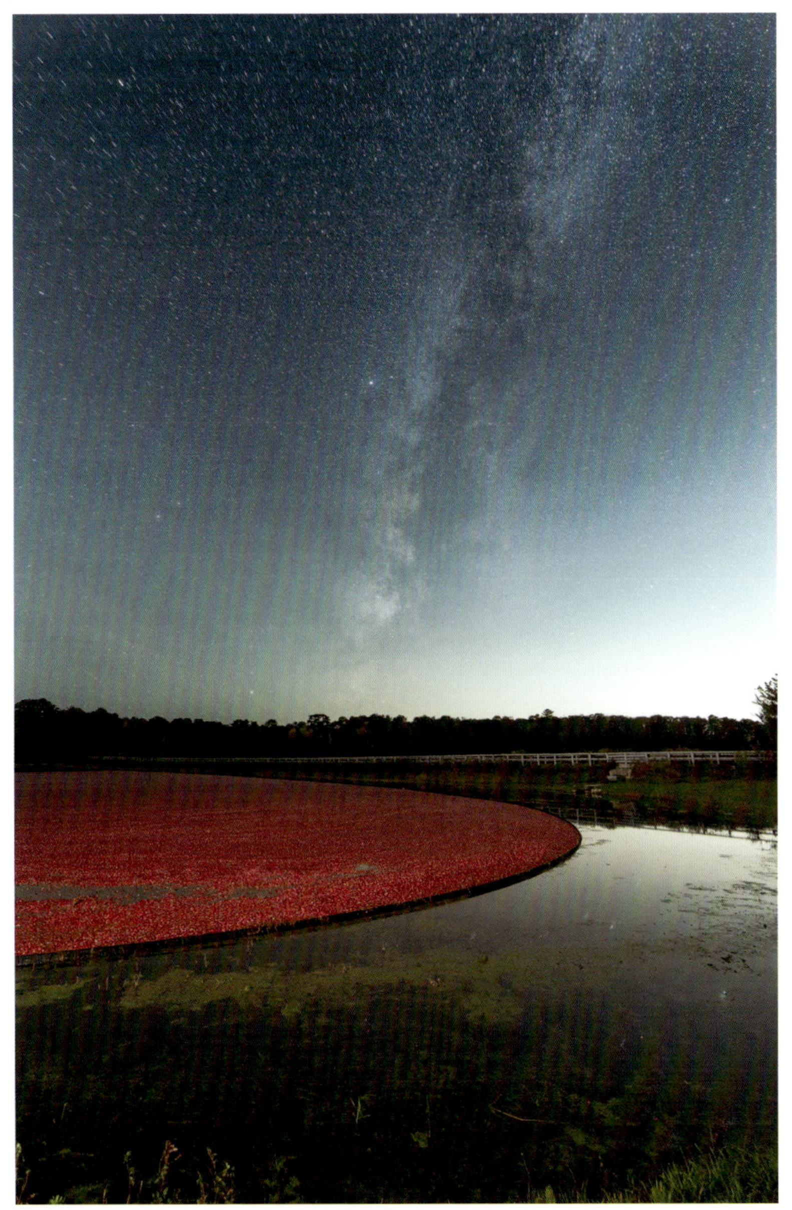

A rare combination of a cranberry harvest and an October Milky Way in Falmouth. To collect the berries, the bogs are flooded, forcing the berries to float. Then, they are corralled and scooped into large nets, dropped into nearby trucks, and transported to a facility that will turn them into juice and other edible delights. The entire harvesting lasts only a day or two, and the timing of this occurring with a moonless night was pure coincidence.

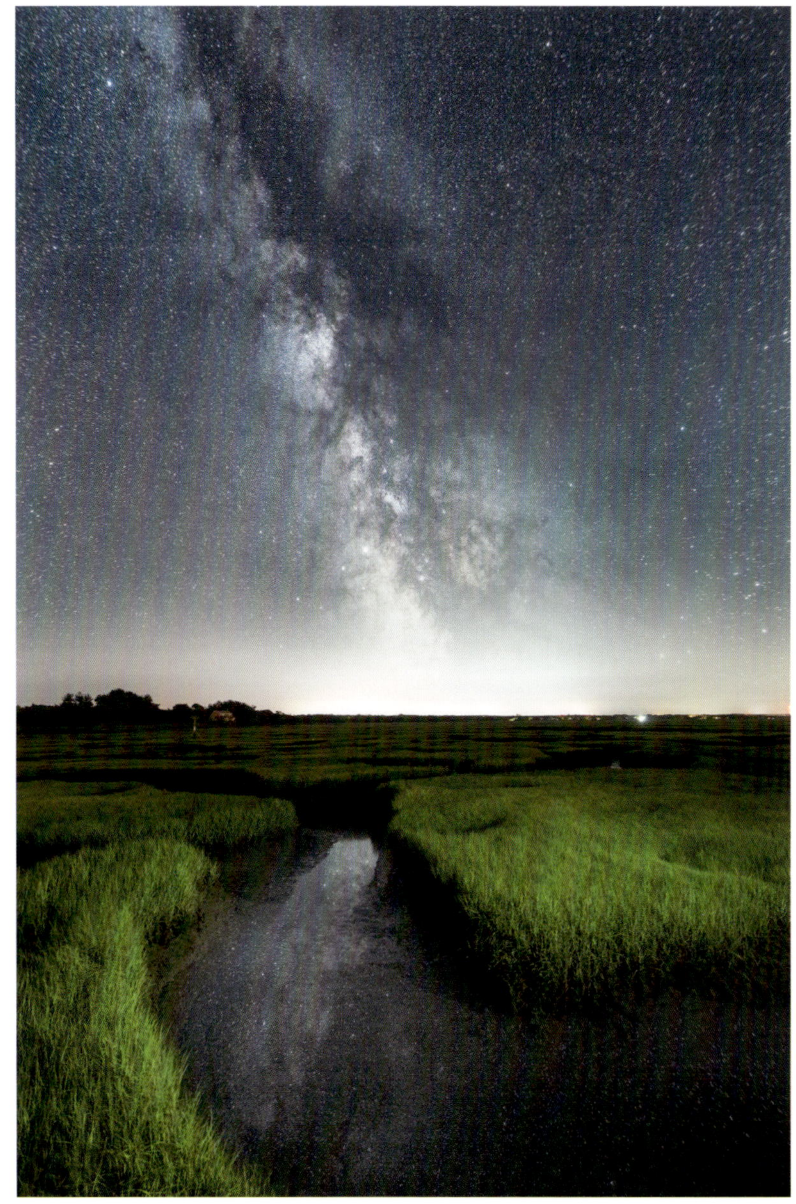

The never-ending channels cut through the marsh at Gray's Beach in Yarmouth and bustle with sea creatures such as fiddler crabs and horseshoe crabs, while hungry ospreys nest nearby. When the tide comes in, the habitat fills up, providing temporary protection from predators. As it moves out, the residents scurry for cover in mudholes and under rocks. You can hear signs of life at nearly any hour in the form of the occasional splash or a distant squawk. It's a great place to see the night sky or a sunset—but do bring your bug spray.

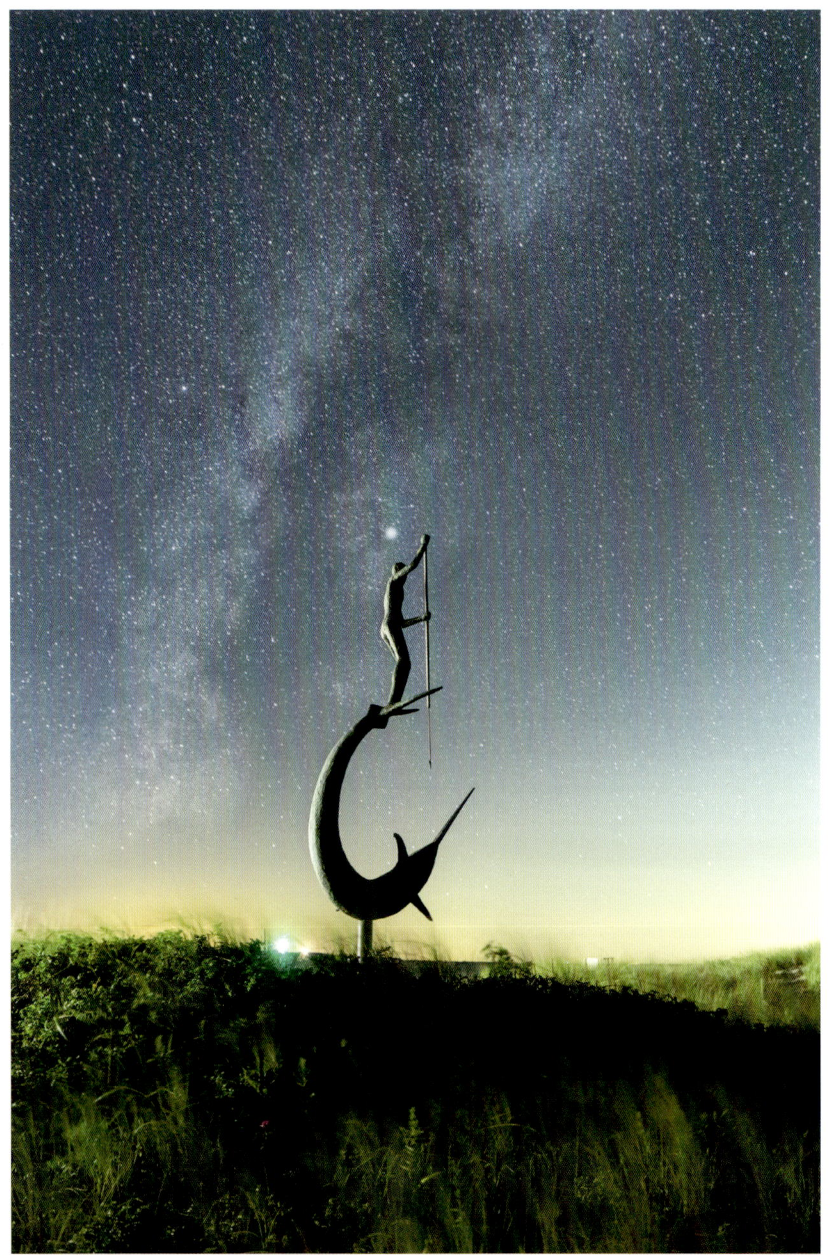

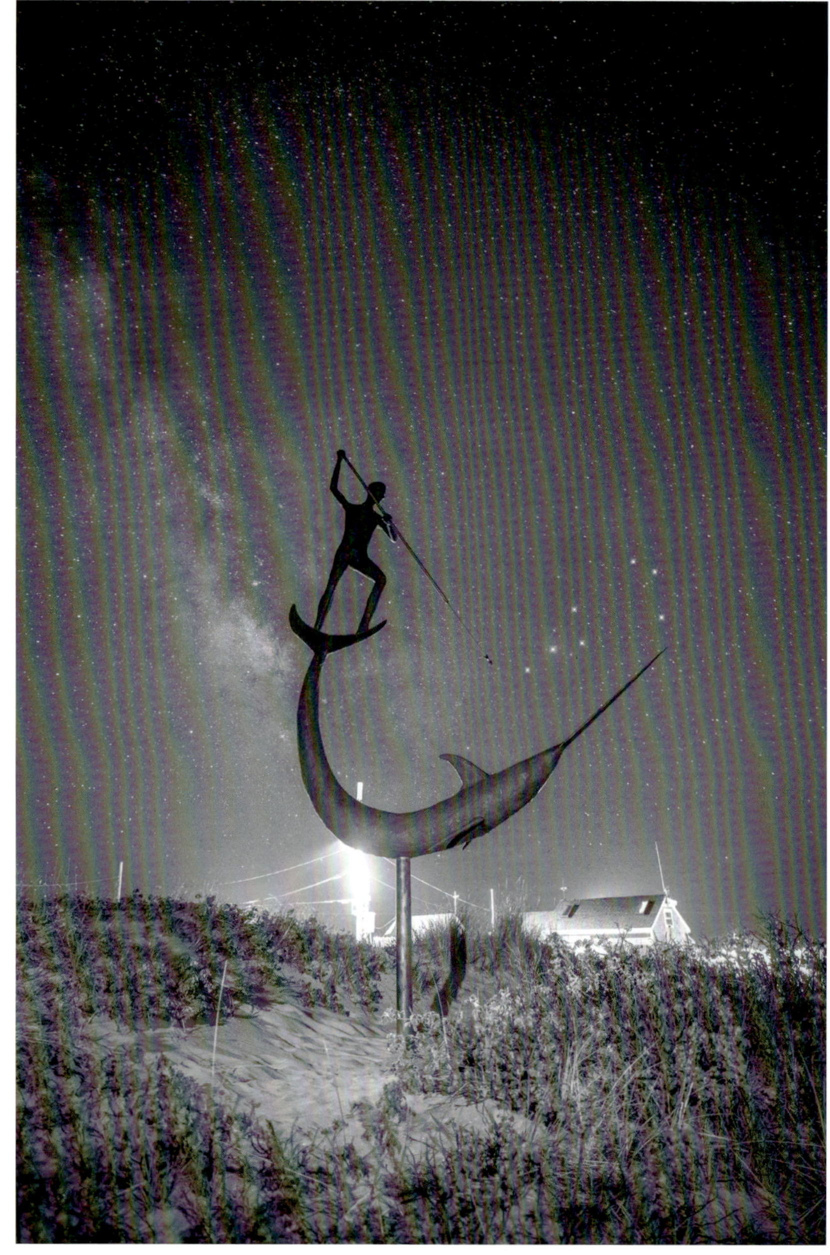

Ever harpooning this swordfish, the sculpture is easy to spot when driving into the Menemsha area on Martha's Vineyard. The first version was installed in 1994 to celebrate the tricentennial of Chilmark, but it eventually had deteriorated due to the elements and was removed. After a year of restoration, it returned in 2017. Although a bright light shines on one side, clever photographers can find relief in nearby dunes and still capture it along with starry skies.

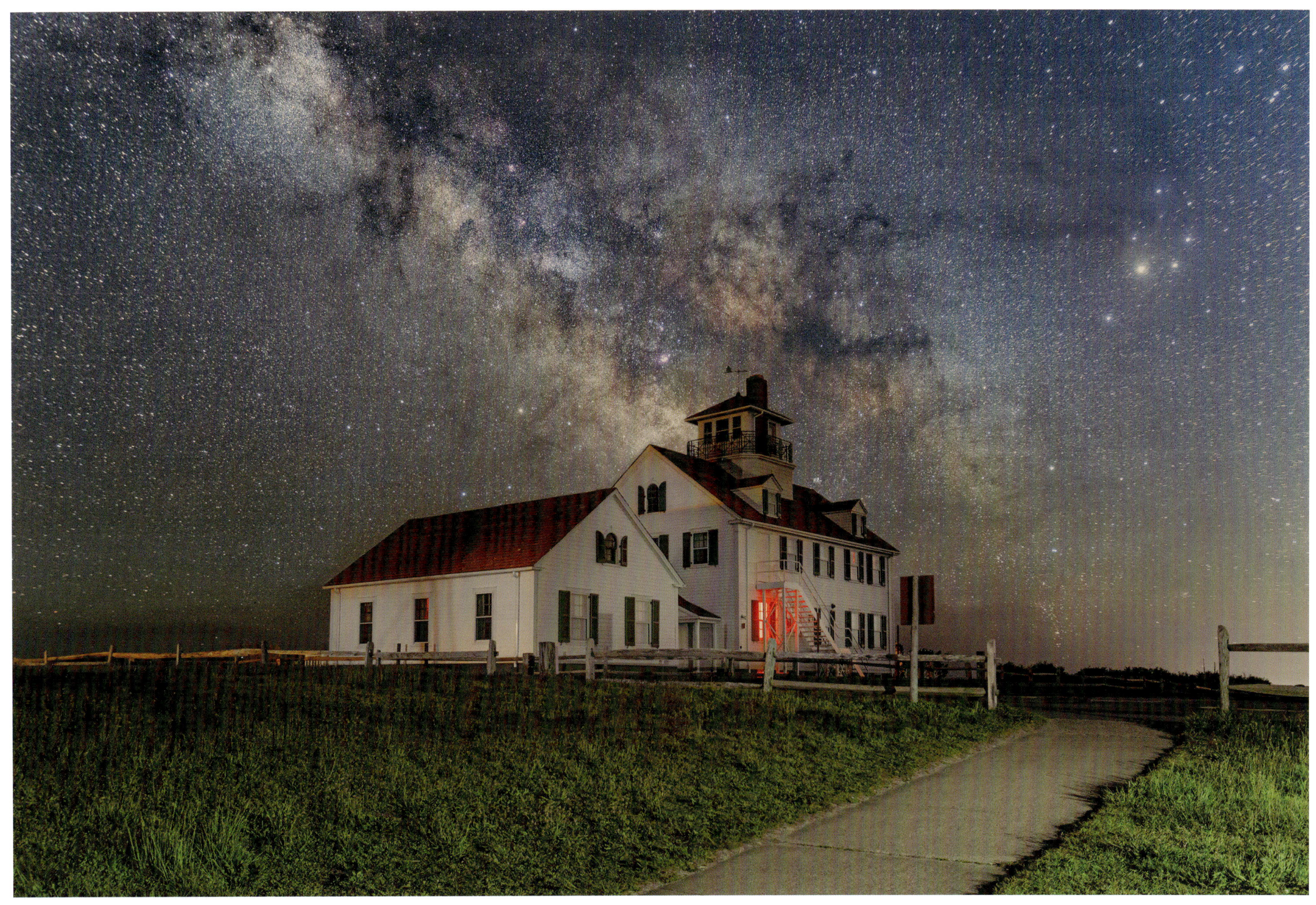

The Milky Way begins to take on a vertical profile in the late hours of a May night. The red glow that appears in the front window is caused by an "Exit" sign.

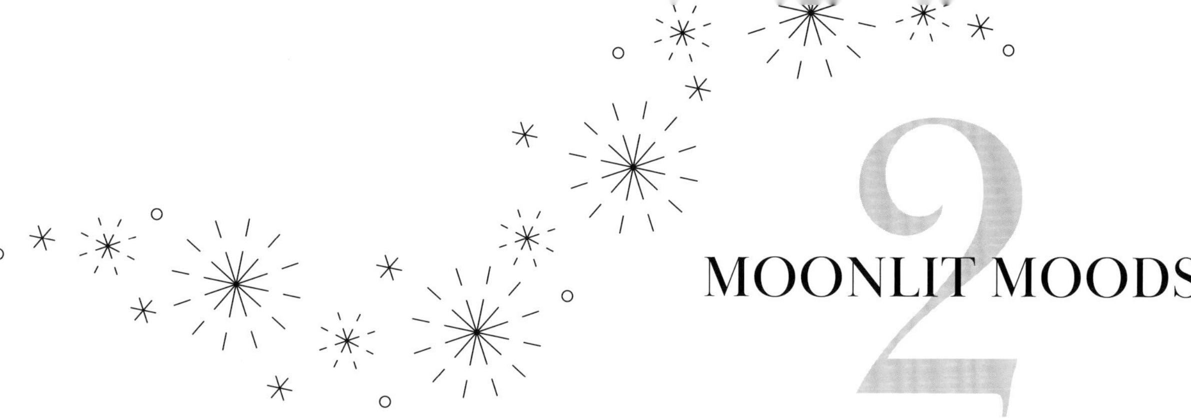

2 MOONLIT MOODS

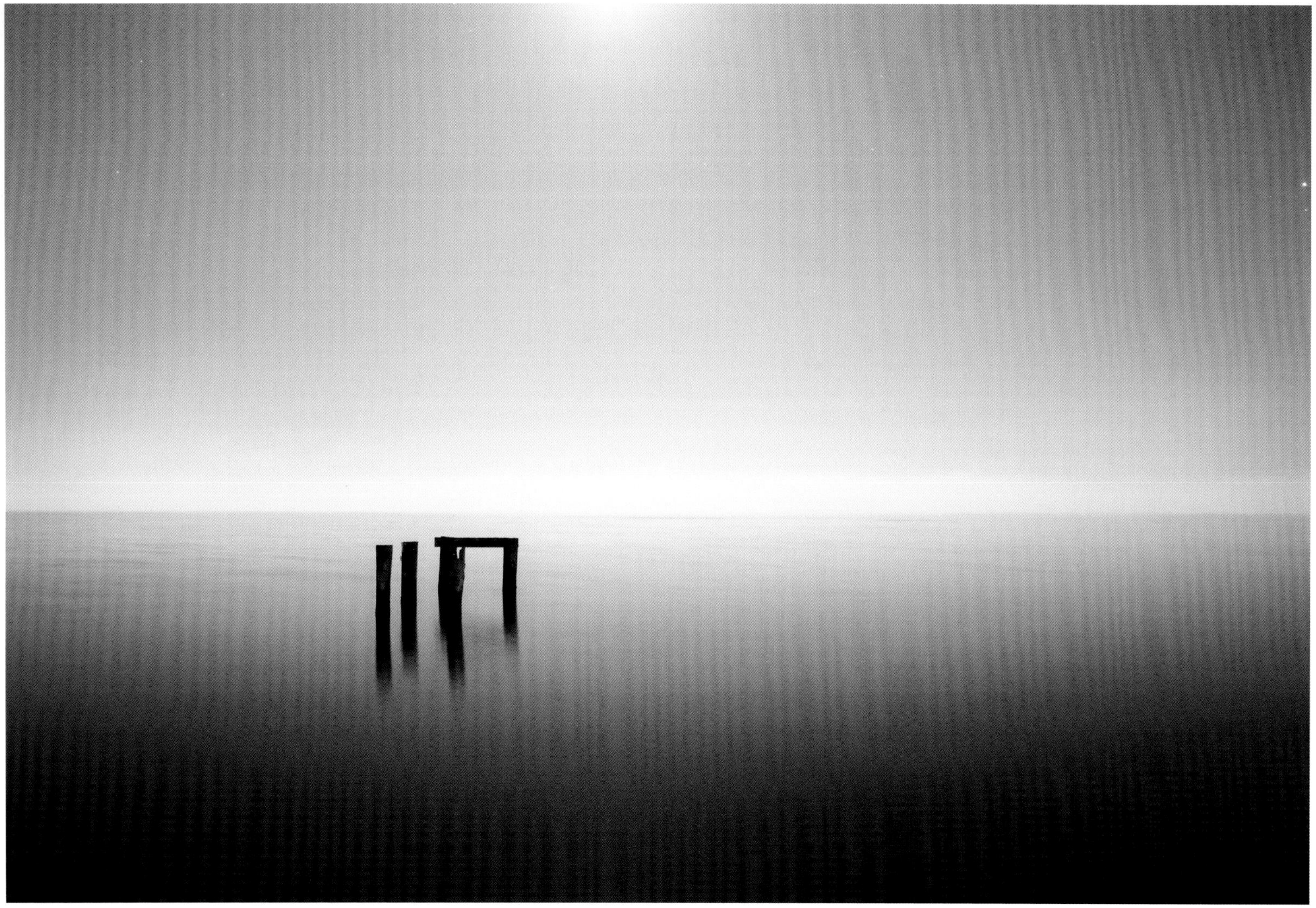

The remnants of a pier at Old Stone Dock in Falmouth sit isolated in the water as moonlit fog rolls across the horizon, obscuring the view of Martha's Vineyard. It was quiet here at two o'clock in the morning—just the occasional sound of a distant buoy bell and the very faint lap of small waves on the rocks below my feet.

Some quick moon facts before we get started! The moon is a giant reflector for the sun. The moon's phases change depending on where the moon is in its orbit around Earth. Each month has a full moon, and some have two, depending on the year! When that happens, this second full moon is called a blue moon (which might be a little disappointing for those of you who might have thought that the moon would actually appear blue). Despite rumors, current scientific data also suggest that the moon is not made of cheese. Although I cannot verify this, I think it to be accurate.

For the purposes of my night photography, the moon is my light source rather than my subject. Just a giant lightbulb floating across the sky. From the vantage point of our own eyes, the moon moves its own width every two minutes. During a long exposure, the moon will blur as it travels, and it will also appear overexposed. For me, that's okay because it is the foreground I am more concerned about. If trying for a detailed moon image, the exposure would be very short, at just a fraction of a second. In this case, the moon would look great! But everything else would be entirely underexposed.

There are few times when you can capture both a detailed moon and a properly lit foreground. Most often, this involves bright subjects such as cityscapes or lighthouses. This can also occur just after twilight or just before sunrise, when the moon is still aglow but residual sunlight is dimly illuminating the landscape.

If you ever see an image that contains both a sharp moon and star trails (or headlight trails from passing cars), this is a composite. This is a technique used to combine two or more images together. There is no natural way that star trails and a sharp, detailed moon surface would appear together above the landscape in a photograph.

Some composites like this are done better than others. The most common mistake you will encounter is an image that has a dark ring around the edge of the moon where it meets the brighter sky around it. No part of a full moon is ever darker than the light it is producing. In a carelessly edited image, you will notice that a moon overwater casts no reflection or light upon the water's surface. I call this the "Vampire Moon," unable to see itself. You can add that to other moons you've heard of such as Harvest Moon, Blood Moon, or Strawberry Moon. The difference is that while those three are natural, the Vampire Moon is just bad editing.

In my own long-exposure shots, I welcome star trails and the recording of the movement of clouds. I lower my camera's sensitivity so I can slowly bake the light into the scene. By doing this, the camera can produce very sharp, clean images without any digital grain or noise often seen by using higher ISO settings. If done right, they require almost no processing when completed. This is one of the easiest types of night photography out there. Just dial in your settings, stand back, and enjoy the night. Isn't that why we do it?

QUICK TIPS FOR MOONLIGHT PHOTOGRAPHY

A low ISO of 400, an aperture of f/8, and two minutes of exposure time is a good place to start. This will provide clean, noise-free images and a good depth of field and will help make any lights in your foreground look like small starbursts. Time is the wild card. A good rule of thumb is to start with a two-minute exposure. Remember, don't let your "nighttime-adjusted" eyes convince you that your image is too bright. A histogram could help here.

The previous chapter's tips regarding focusing, image stabilization, and file format all apply here as well.

Be sure you have a very sturdy tripod and avoid using the center column to get a higher angle. Center columns introduce a lot of instability, which can sabotage a long exposure relatively quickly under even a slight breeze. Ensure that the tripod head is tight and that the camera does not shake on it. Verify that every knob is locked down. There are a lot of great tripods on the market at good prices. The best ones for night photography are usually not the ultralight travel models. The heavier, aluminum ones, such as the Benro Adventure series or the Slik Pro 700DX, provide a lot of stability. They're also quite a bit cheaper than the lighter, carbon fiber alternatives.

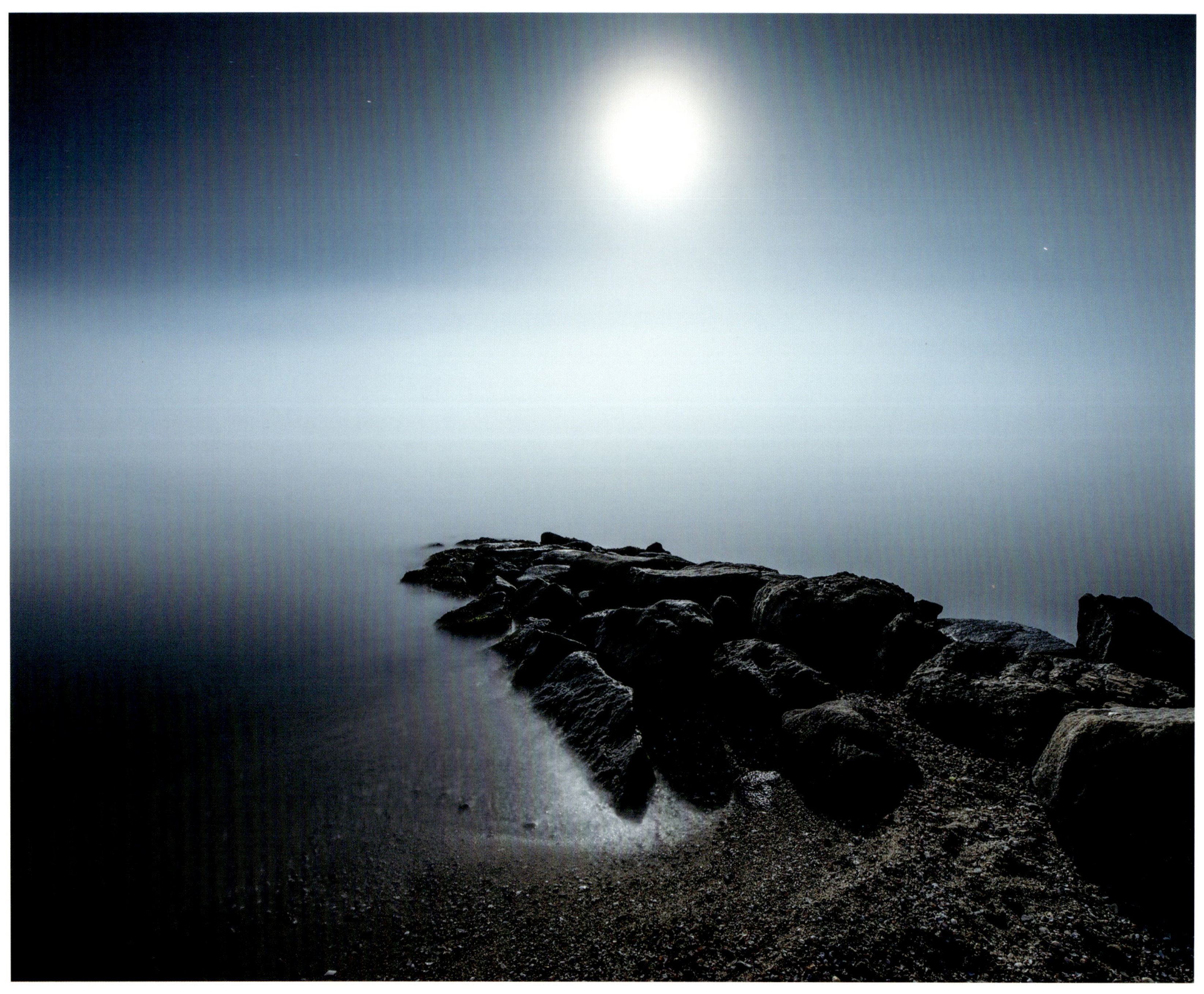

A view into what appears to be the edge of the earth, lit by the moon, in May 2018.

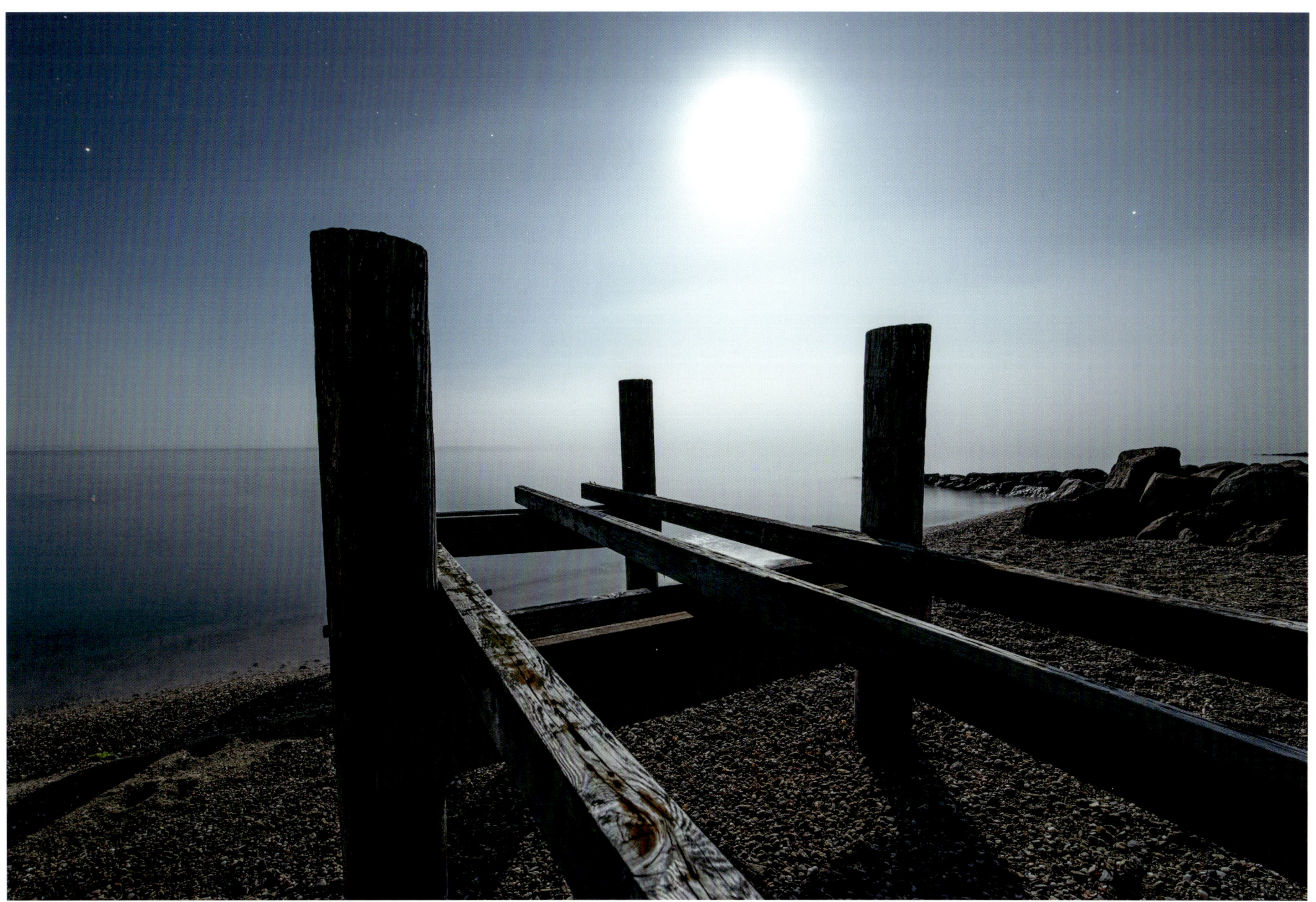

This old dock in Falmouth has seen better days. It appeared, in much better condition, under moonlit skies on the back cover of my last book, *Cape Cod Nights: A Photographic Exploration of Cape Cod and the Islands After Dark*. But time and weather have stripped away much of the planks, leaving just the frame behind.

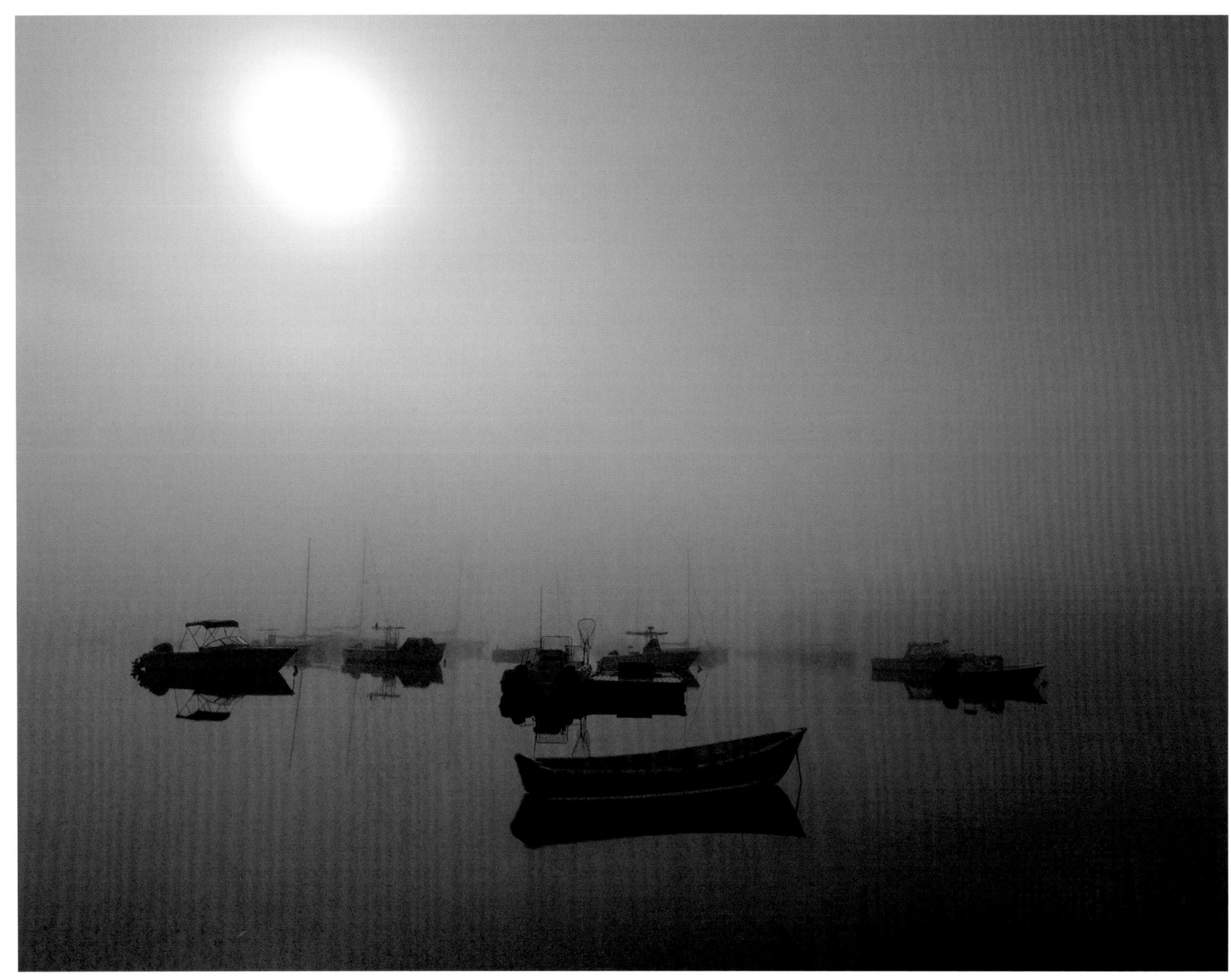

Fog is a sign of calm air and calm waters. In the spring, fog like this at Quissett Harbor will appear offshore and wait patiently for nightfall, when the ground cools and clears the way for it to move in.

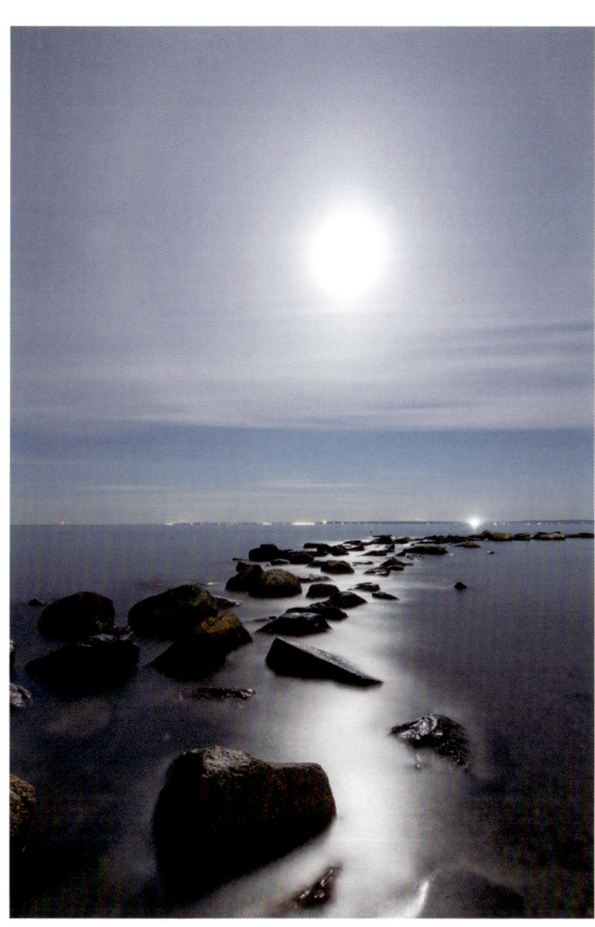

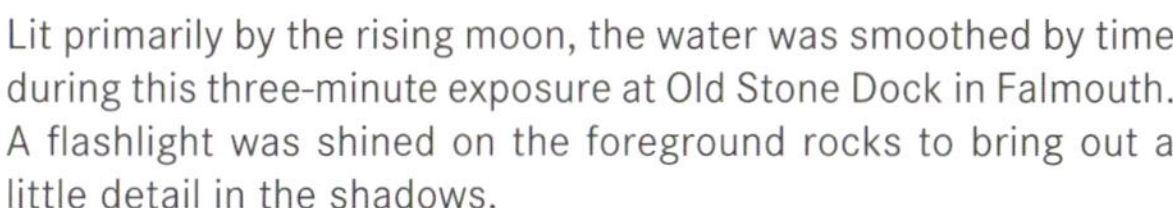

Lit primarily by the rising moon, the water was smoothed by time during this three-minute exposure at Old Stone Dock in Falmouth. A flashlight was shined on the foreground rocks to bring out a little detail in the shadows.

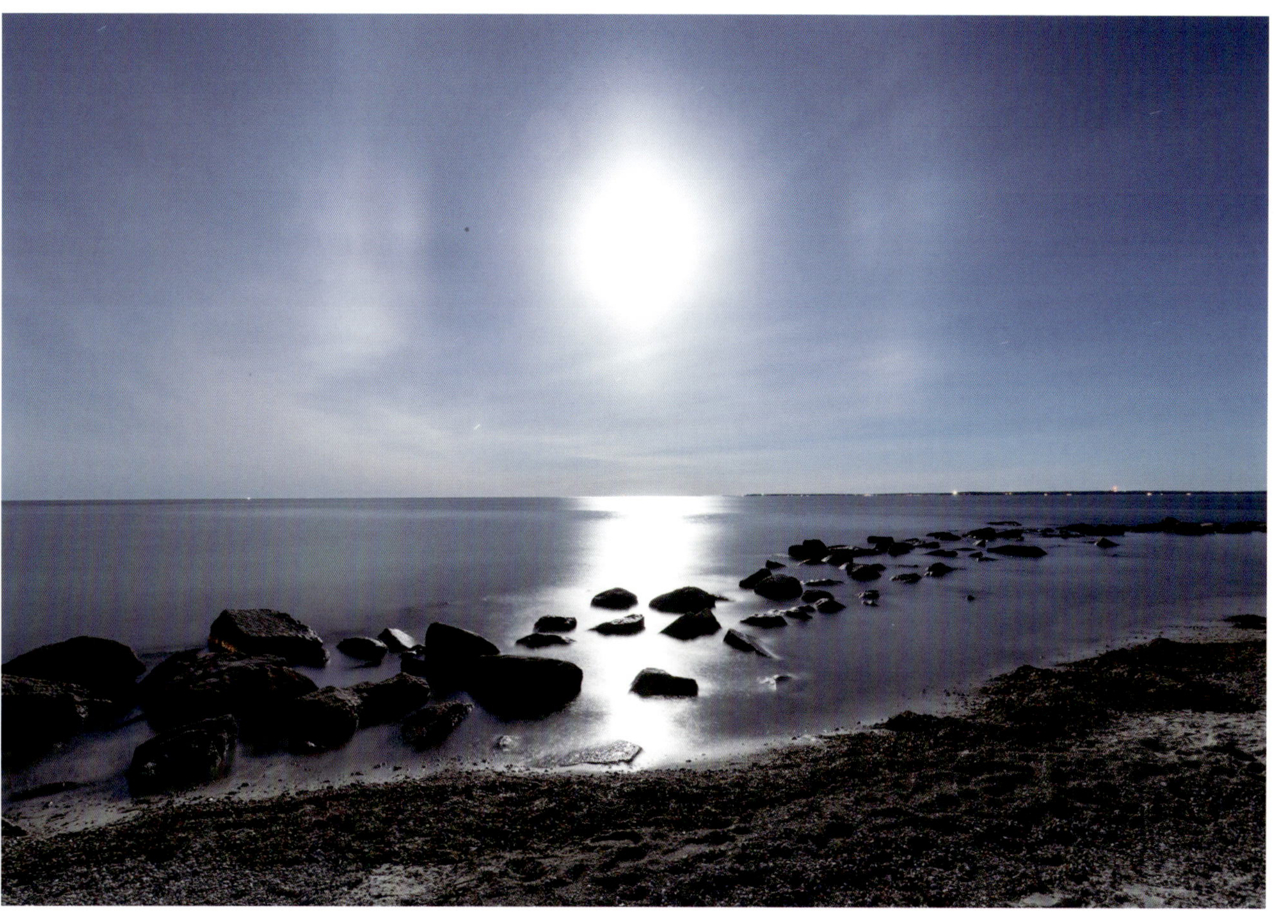

Shoreline barrier rocks stretch into the moonlit waters of Vineyard Sound. At low tide, these rocks are easy to navigate, and local fishermen can frequently be seen casting their lines.

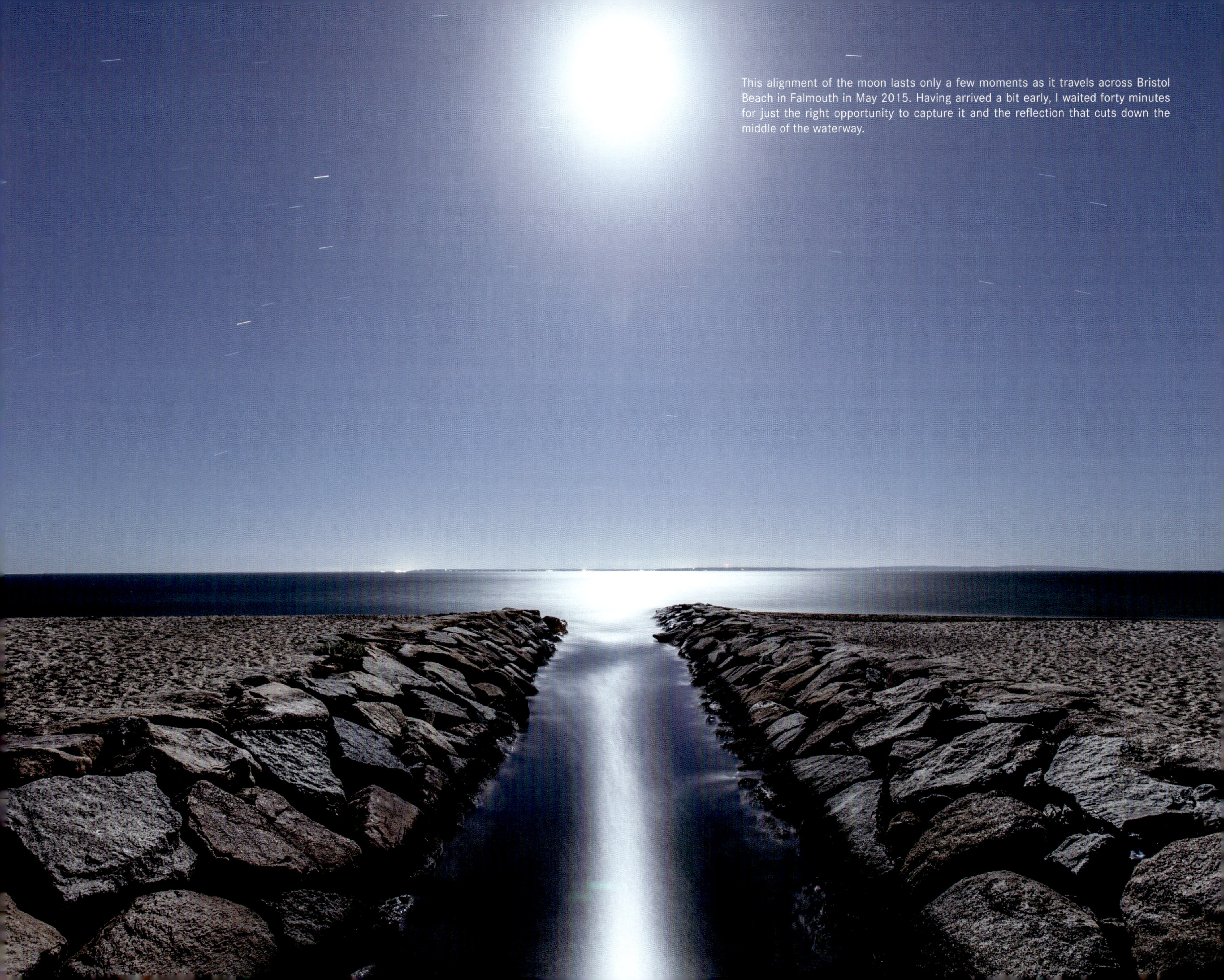

This alignment of the moon lasts only a few moments as it travels across Bristol Beach in Falmouth in May 2015. Having arrived a bit early, I waited forty minutes for just the right opportunity to capture it and the reflection that cuts down the middle of the waterway.

Forty-five minutes of exposure time led to this surreal starry backdrop along Surf Drive in Falmouth. Stars appear to circle the North Star during long exposures like this, revealing north to be located toward the top left corner of this image. While the camera clicked away on this cold winter night, I sat warmly in my truck across the street.

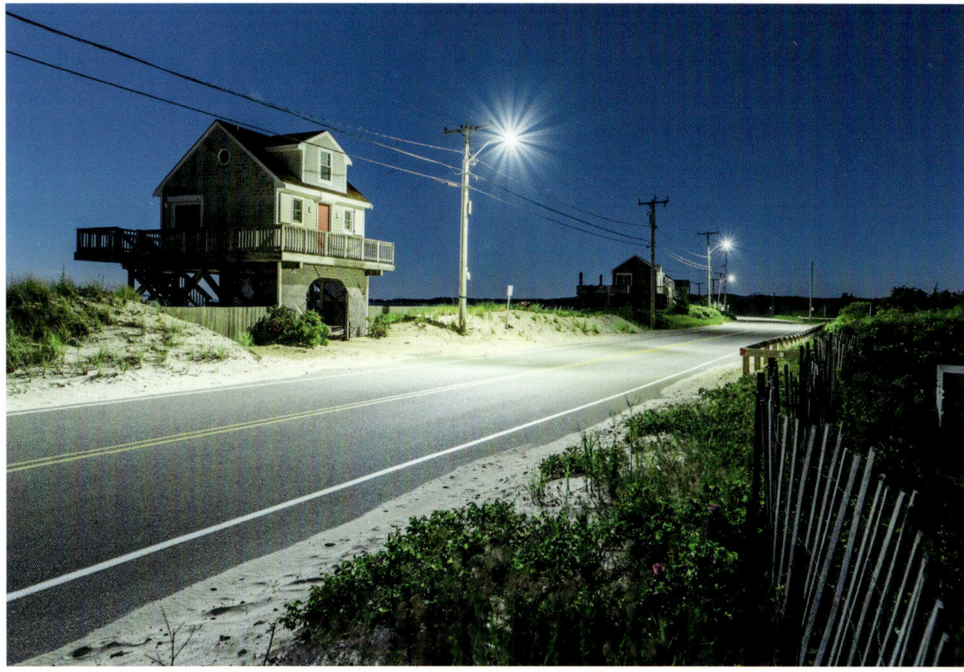

These shacks in Falmouth are instantly recognizable thanks to their stilt foundations. This was a requirement after Hurricane Bob's visit on August 19, 1991. Houses that survived were allowed to remain on their original foundations. It was stilts for the rest!

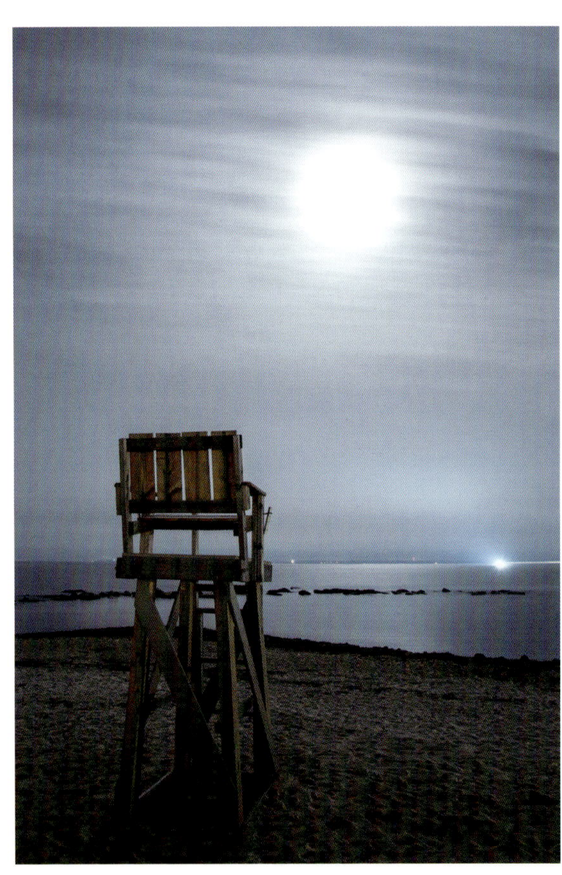

This Falmouth lifeguard chair is a great spot to watch a rising moon over Martha's Vineyard. People can frequently be seen enjoying the elevated view here after dark.

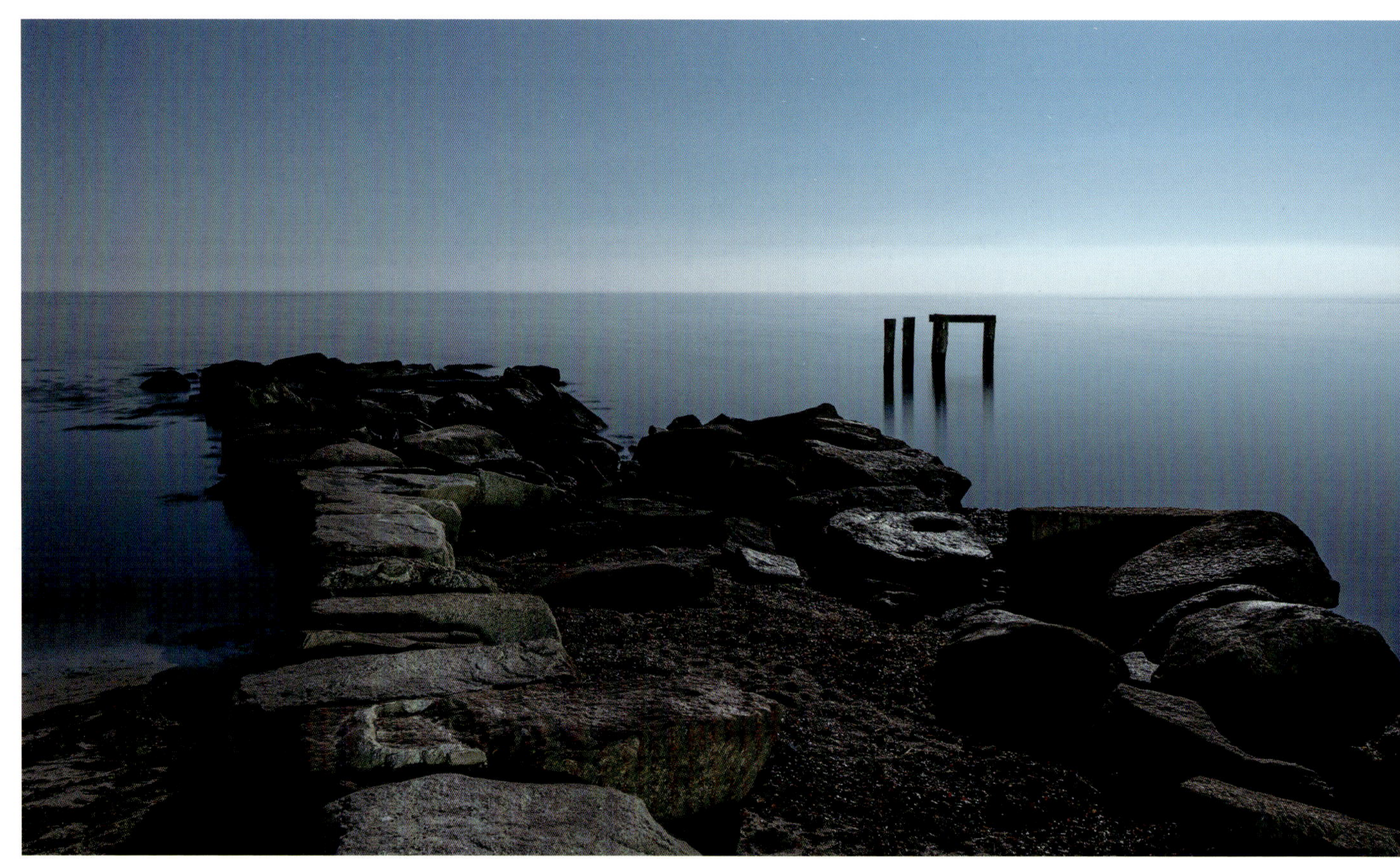

More than one photographer has fallen victim to these slippery rocks when trying to get the perfect shot of the old wood pilings.

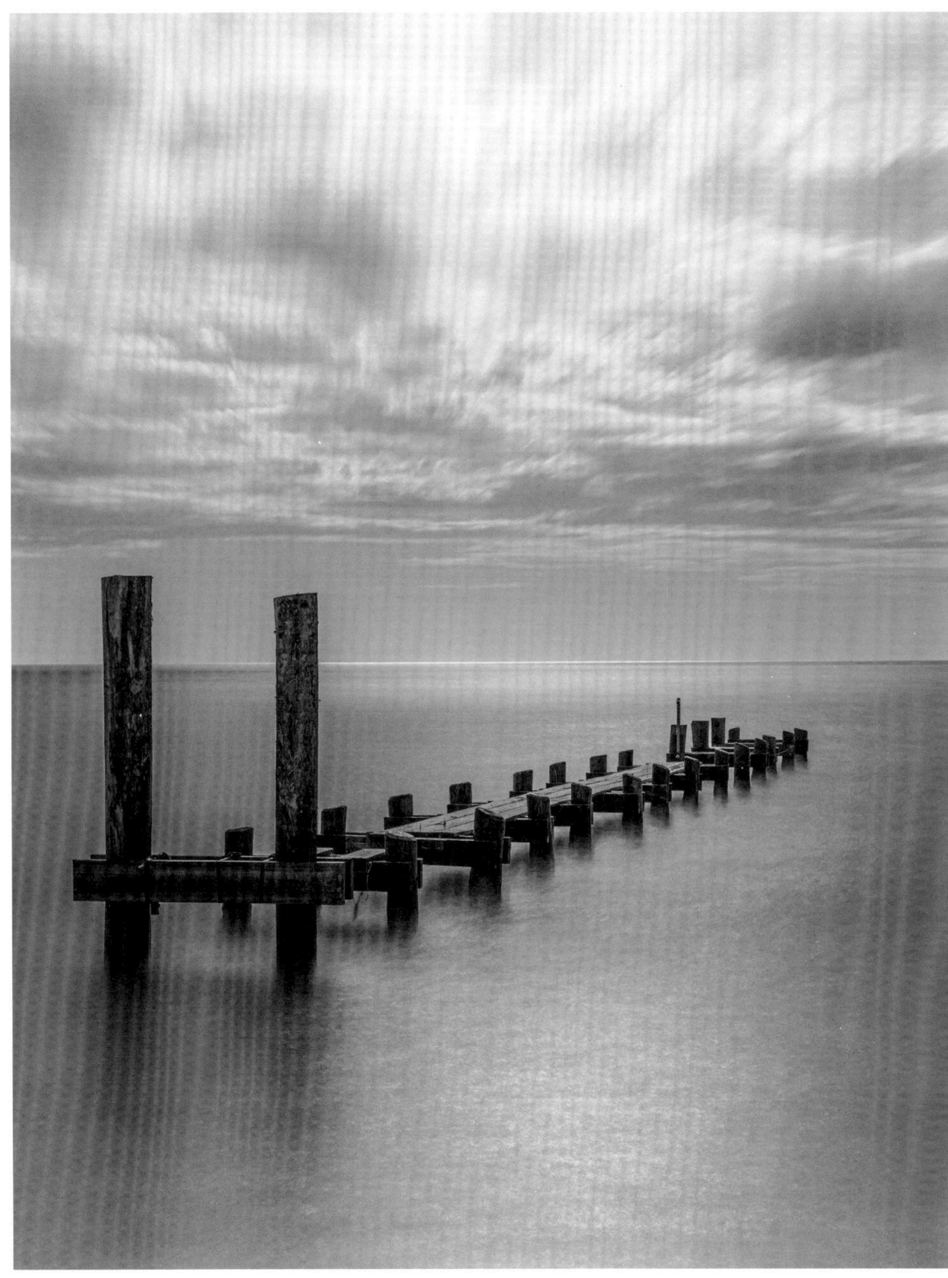

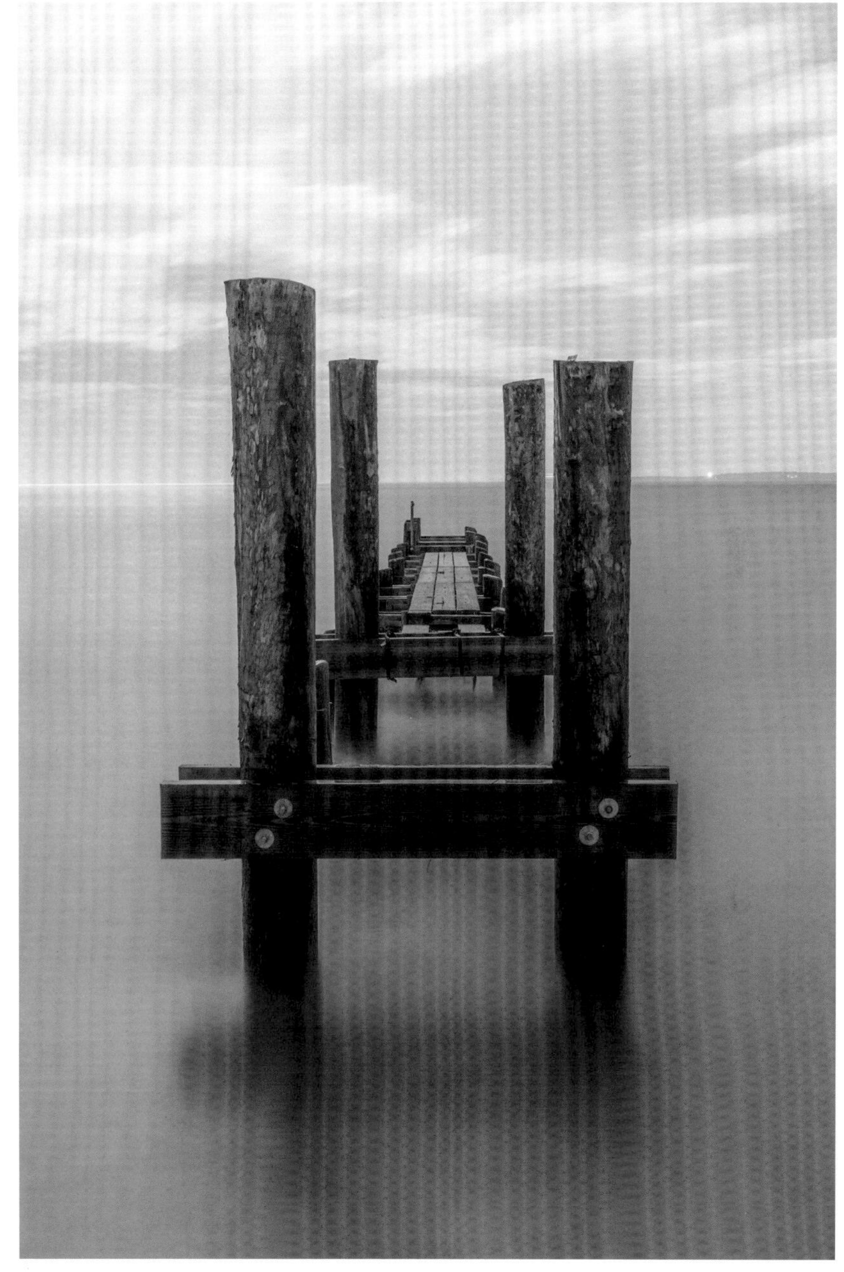

Remnants of old docks, or those freshly damaged by weather, line the shores of Cape Cod. Despite each being of similar design, no two look alike, thanks to the elements. This one sits in the waters of Vineyard Sound along Nobska Road in Falmouth and is disconnected from the shore on a moonlit night.

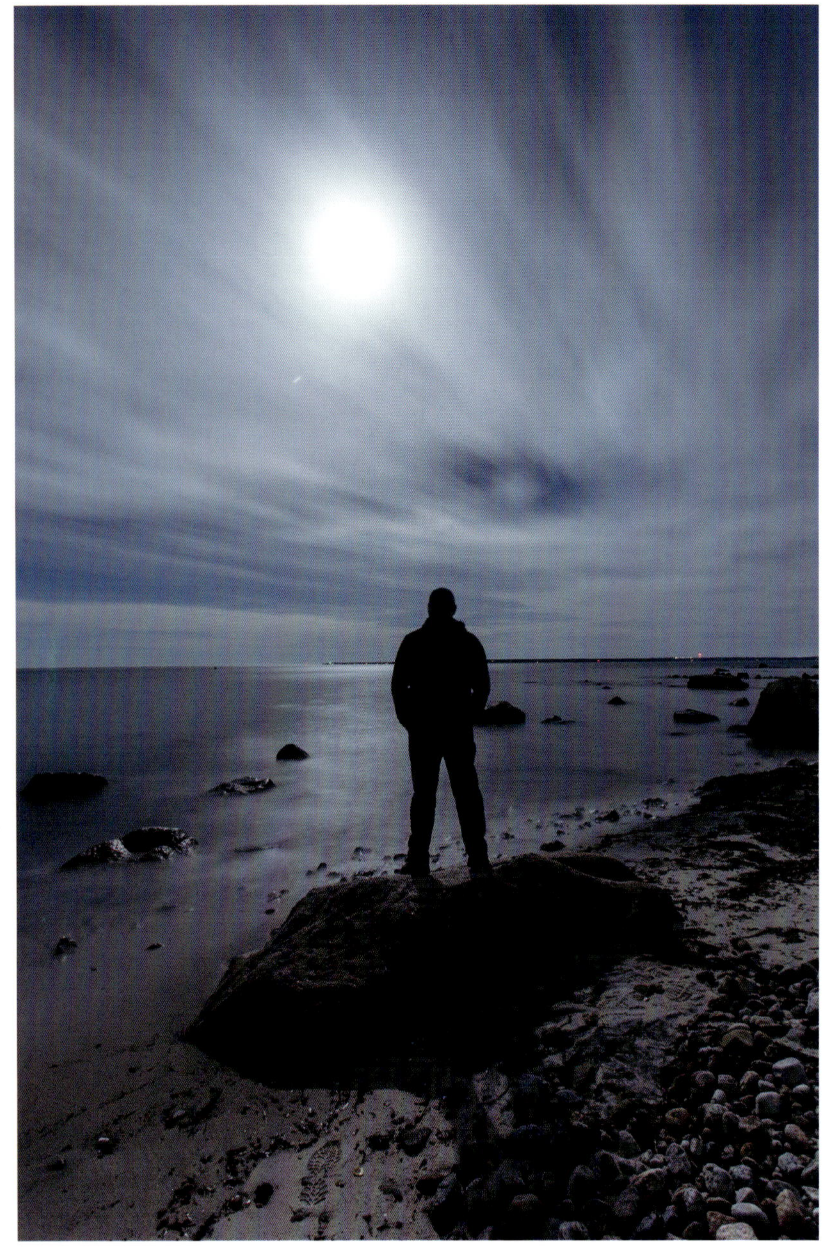

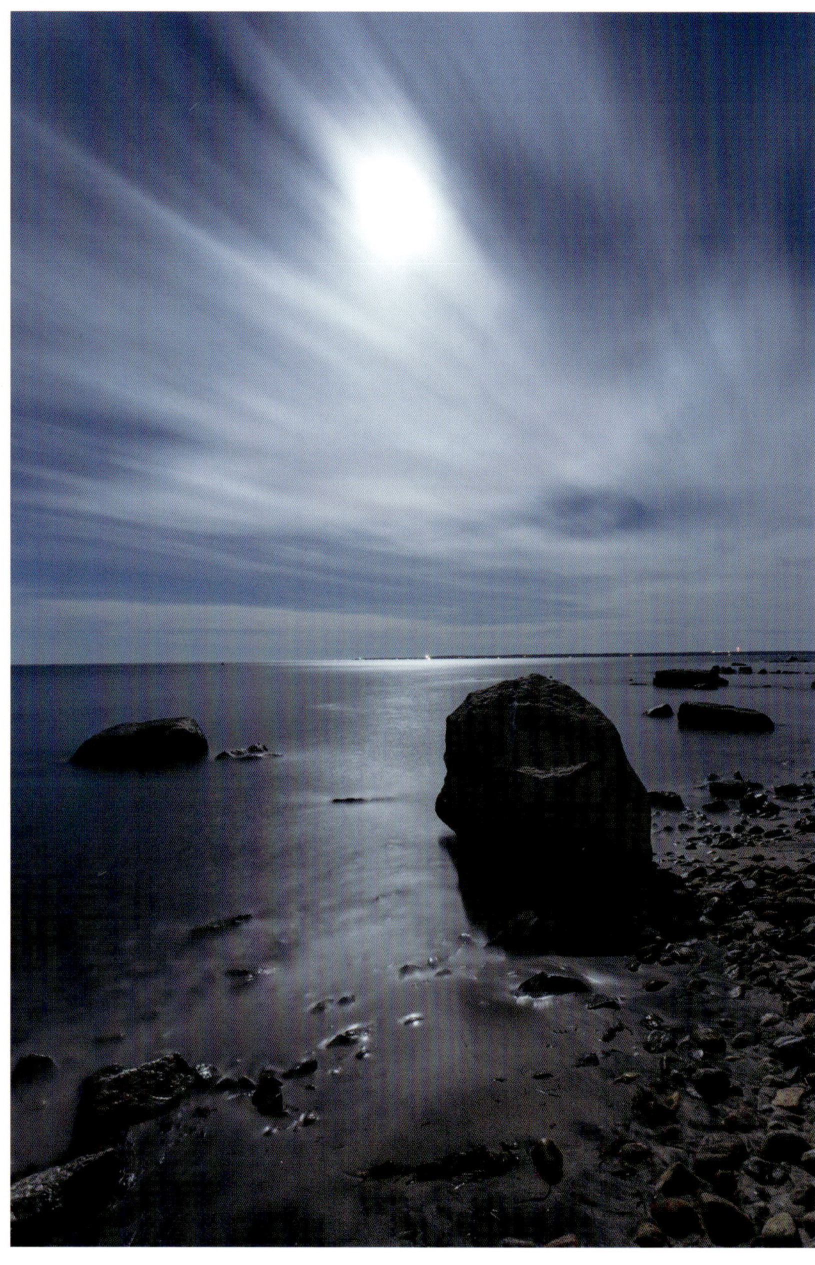

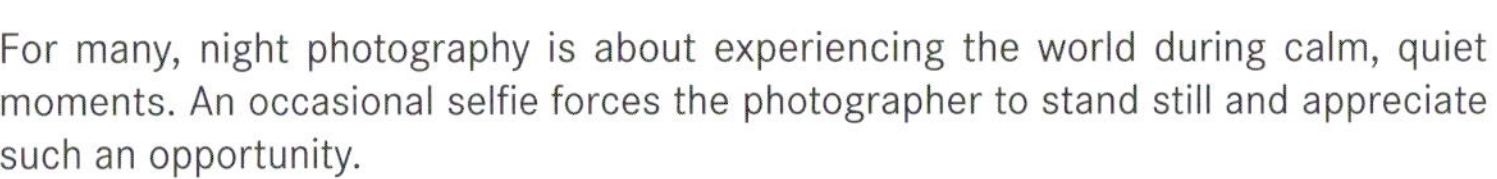

For many, night photography is about experiencing the world during calm, quiet moments. An occasional selfie forces the photographer to stand still and appreciate such an opportunity.

The shores near Nobska Point are unusually rocky compared to the rest of the area. Much of this is visible from the road approaching Nobska Light via Falmouth. During low tide, many more boulders are visible.

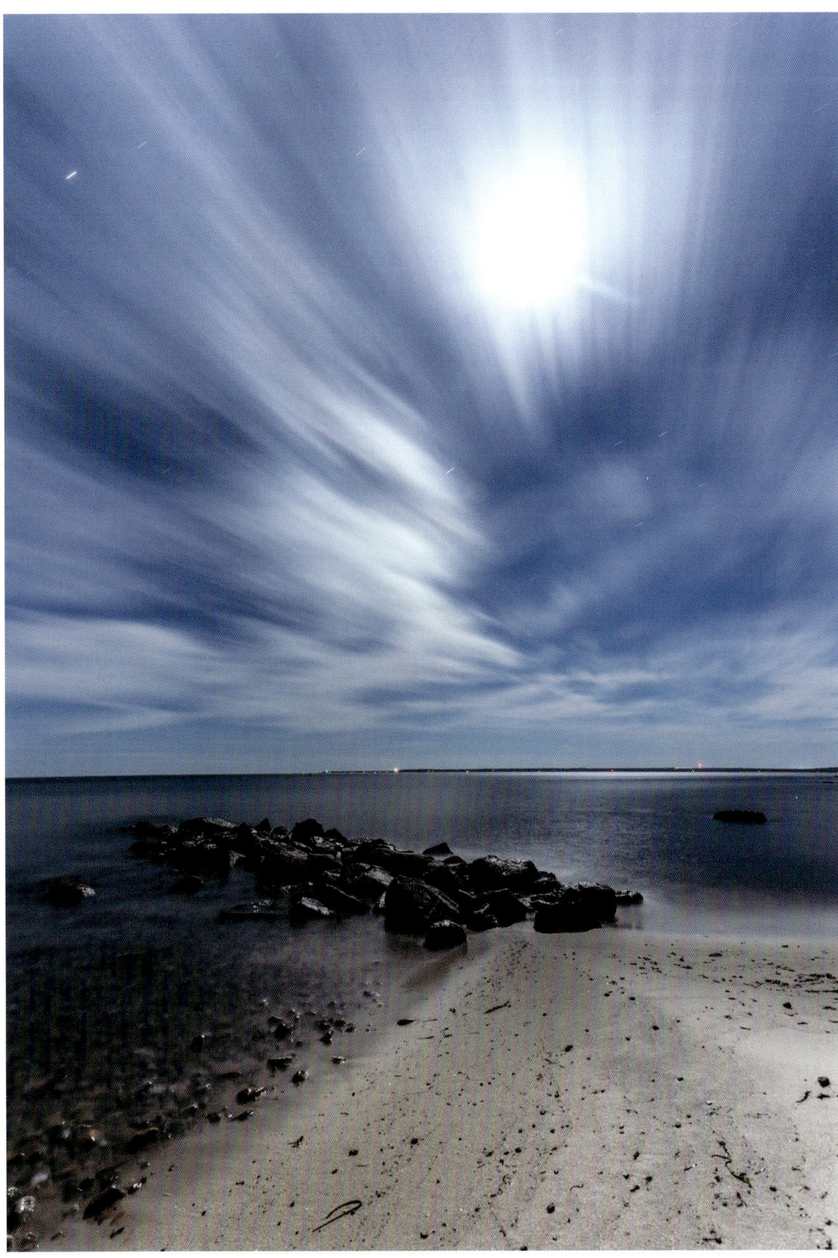

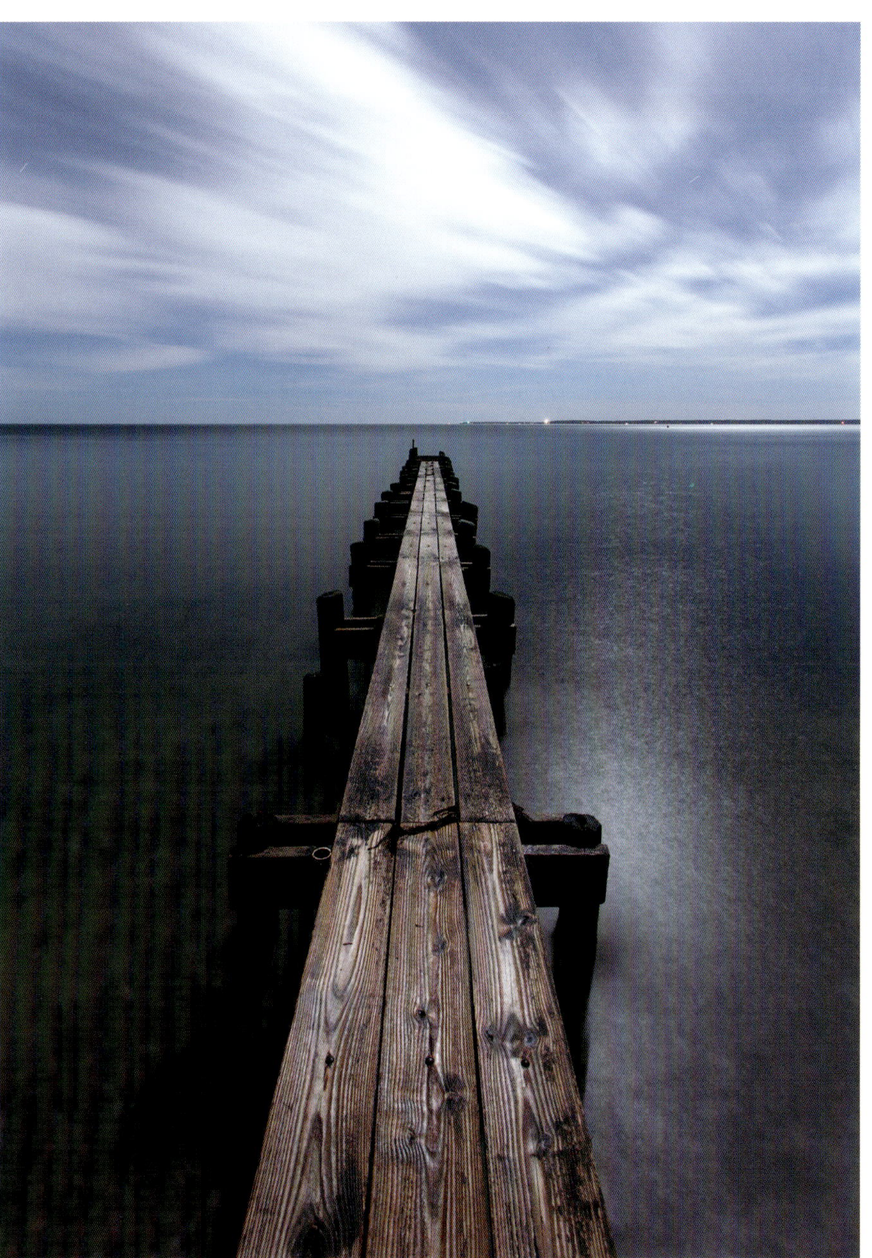

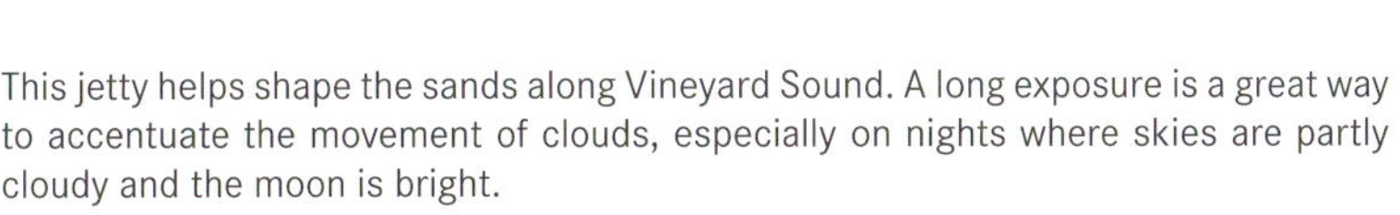

This jetty helps shape the sands along Vineyard Sound. A long exposure is a great way to accentuate the movement of clouds, especially on nights where skies are partly cloudy and the moon is bright.

This narrow, moonlit dock reaches out into Vineyard Sound as if it could almost connect Falmouth to Martha's Vineyard. But, as is the case with life, it is all about perspective.

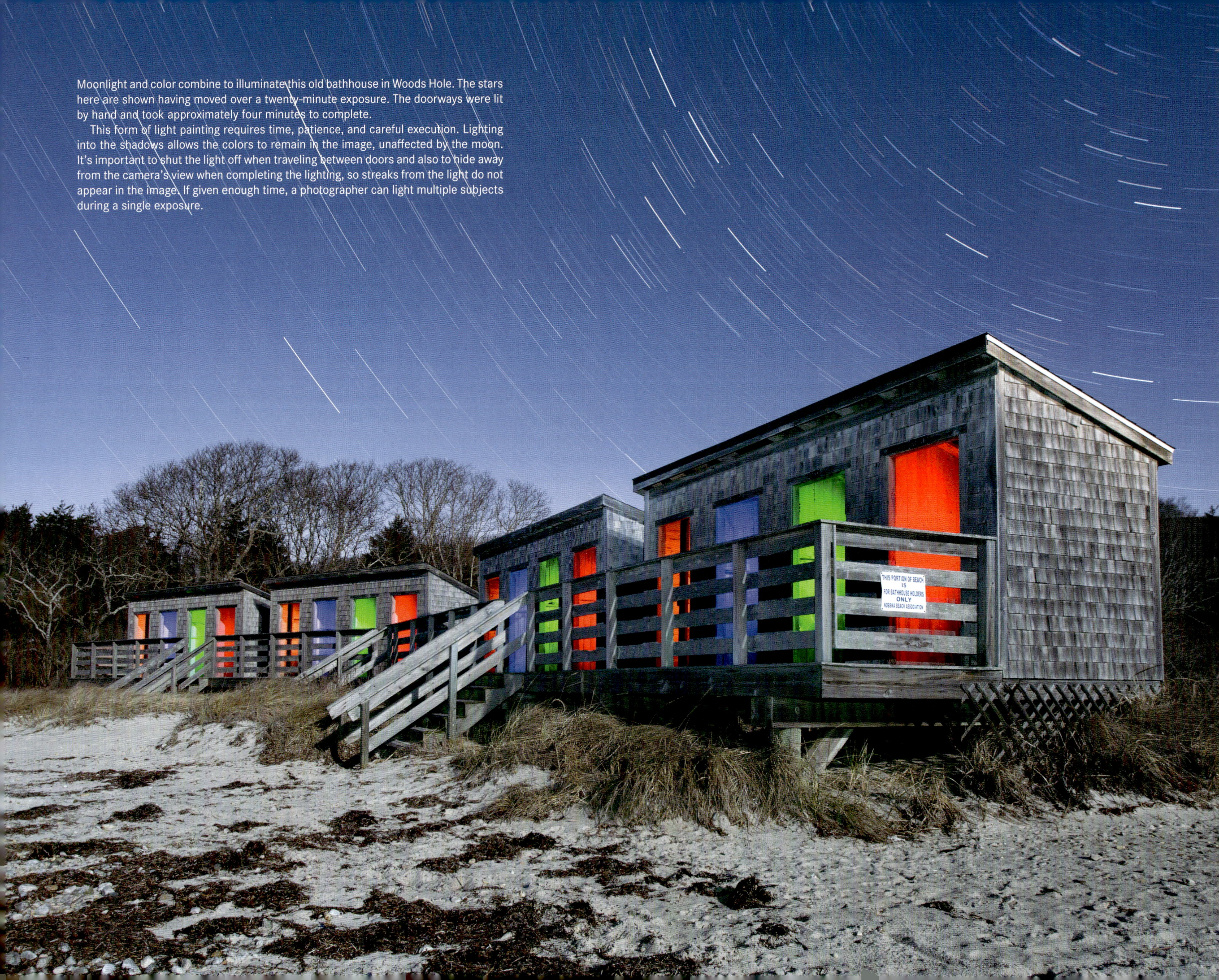

Moonlight and color combine to illuminate this old bathhouse in Woods Hole. The stars here are shown having moved over a twenty-minute exposure. The doorways were lit by hand and took approximately four minutes to complete.

This form of light painting requires time, patience, and careful execution. Lighting into the shadows allows the colors to remain in the image, unaffected by the moon. It's important to shut the light off when traveling between doors and also to hide away from the camera's view when completing the lighting, so streaks from the light do not appear in the image. If given enough time, a photographer can light multiple subjects during a single exposure.

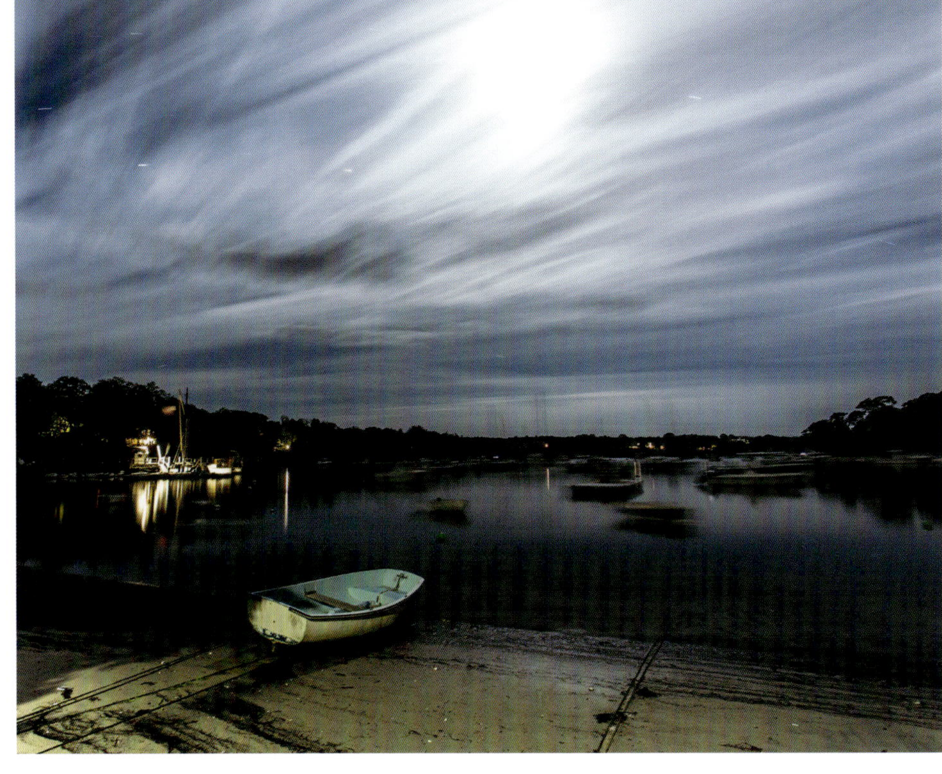

Clouds at different altitudes move along different paths, as is shown here in the skies above Quissett Harbor. A bright moon helps illuminate their movement over this three-minute exposure.

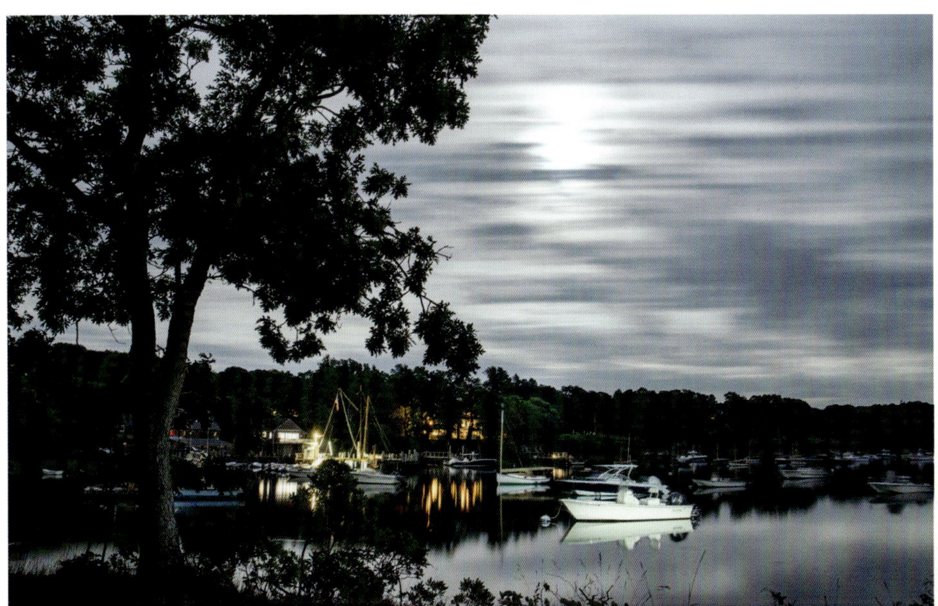

Summertime is the best time to see the boats at Quissett Harbor. Briefly shining a flashlight helps to freeze them in the photograph and minimize their apparent movement during a long exposure. Calm waters are a big help too.

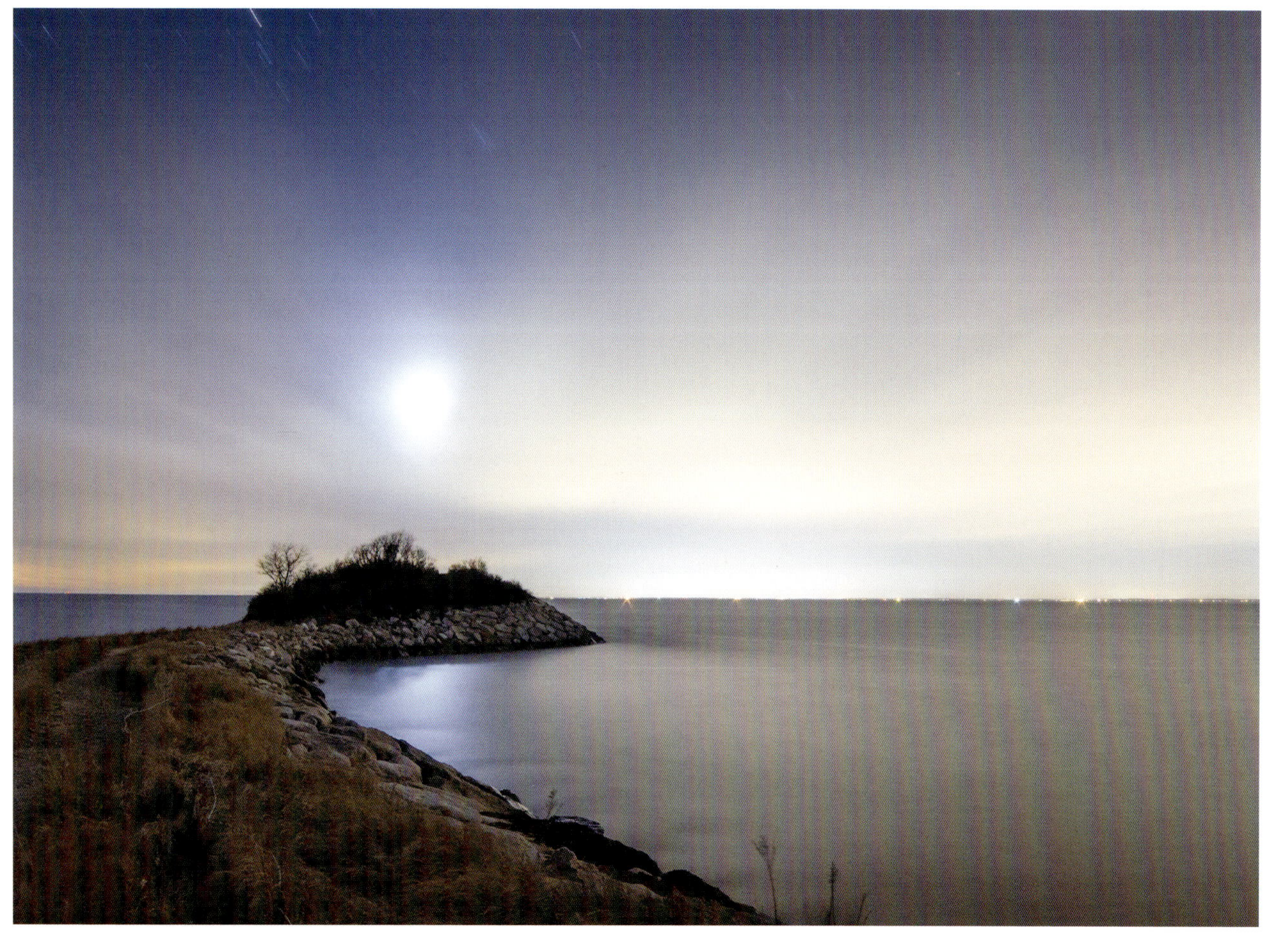

The moon sets over the Knob near Woods Hole. This is a popular place to visit for sunset views via a short and easy hike. Photographers frequent this area for portrait backgrounds, and more than a few engagements have begun here.

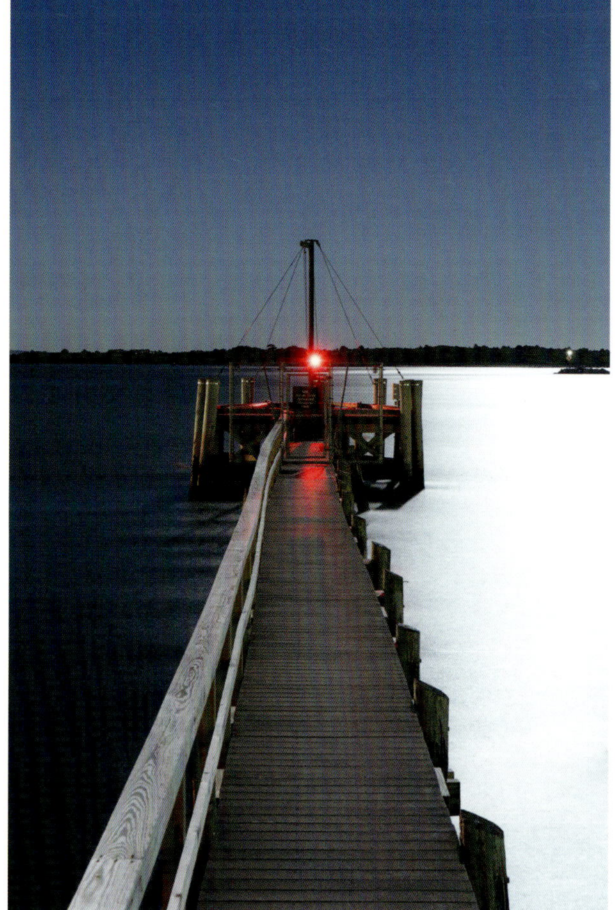

A dock belonging to the Marine Biological Laboratory in Woods Hole splits the moonlight on a cloudless night in 2019.

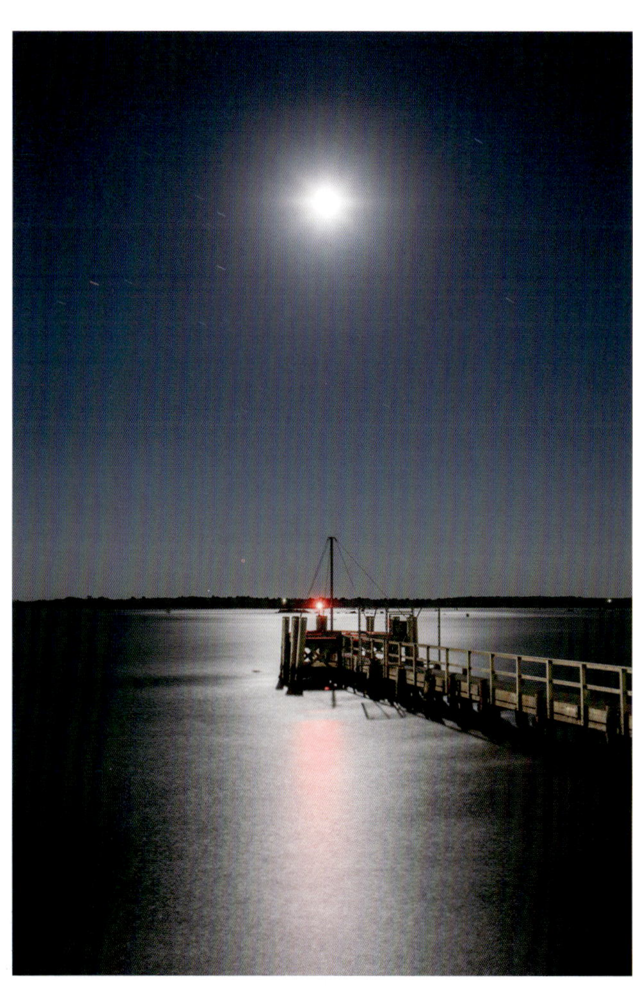

The moon sets over the Knob near Woods Hole. This is a popular place to visit for sunset views via a short and easy hike. Photographers frequent this area for portrait backgrounds, and more than a few engagements have begun here.

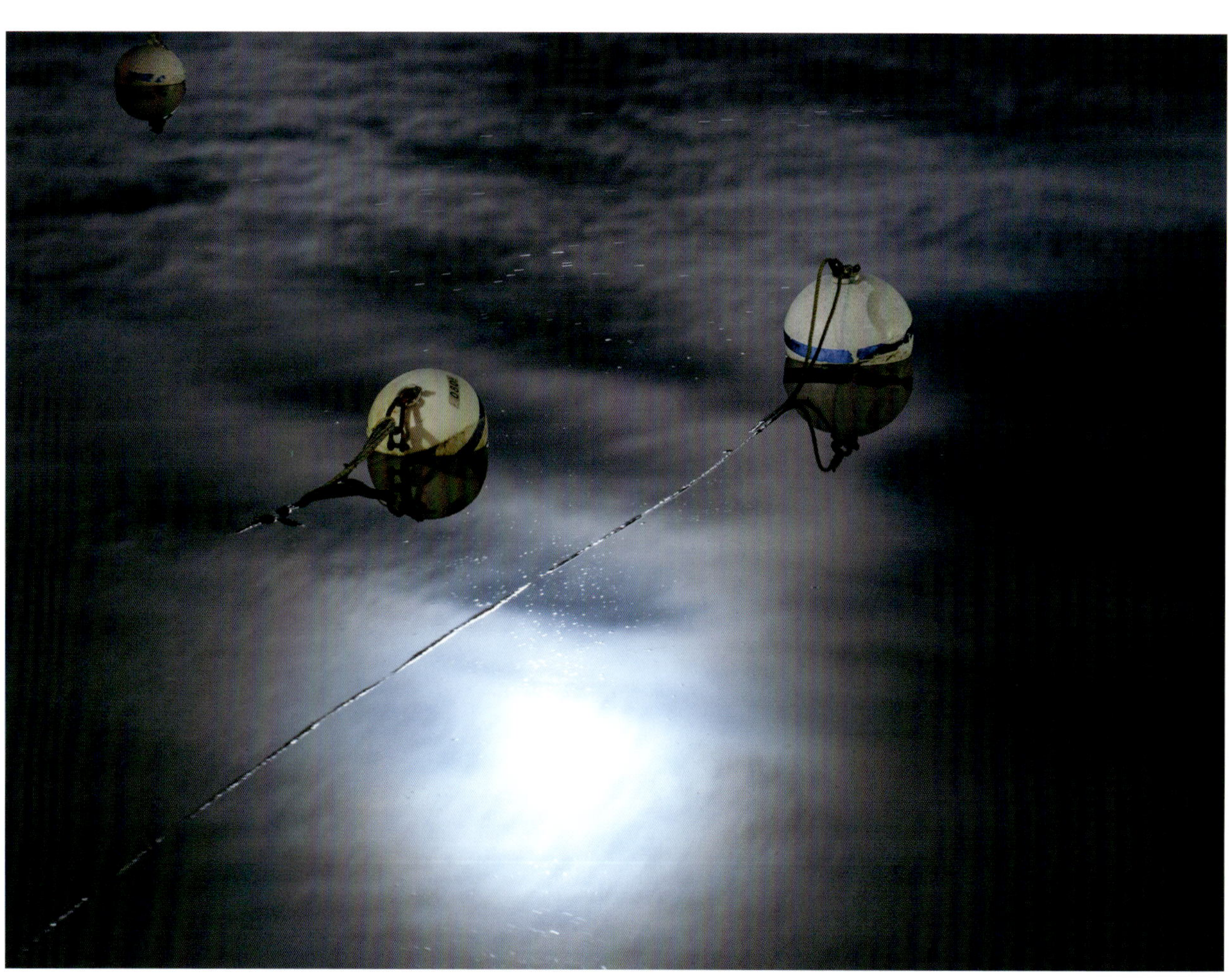

Unused in the winter months, these buoys sit quietly waiting for the boats of summer to return to Eel Pond in Woods Hole.

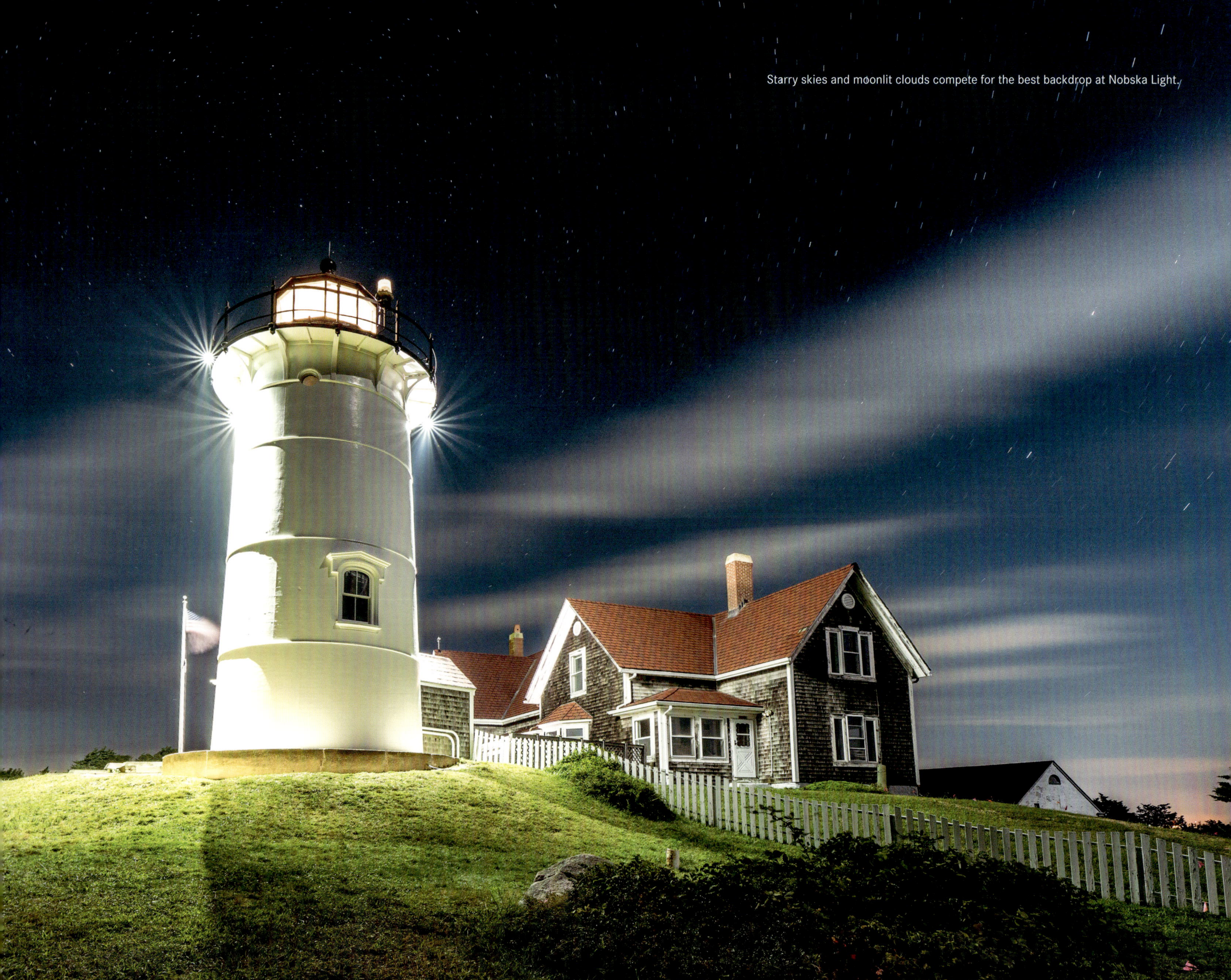

Starry skies and moonlit clouds compete for the best backdrop at Nobska Light.

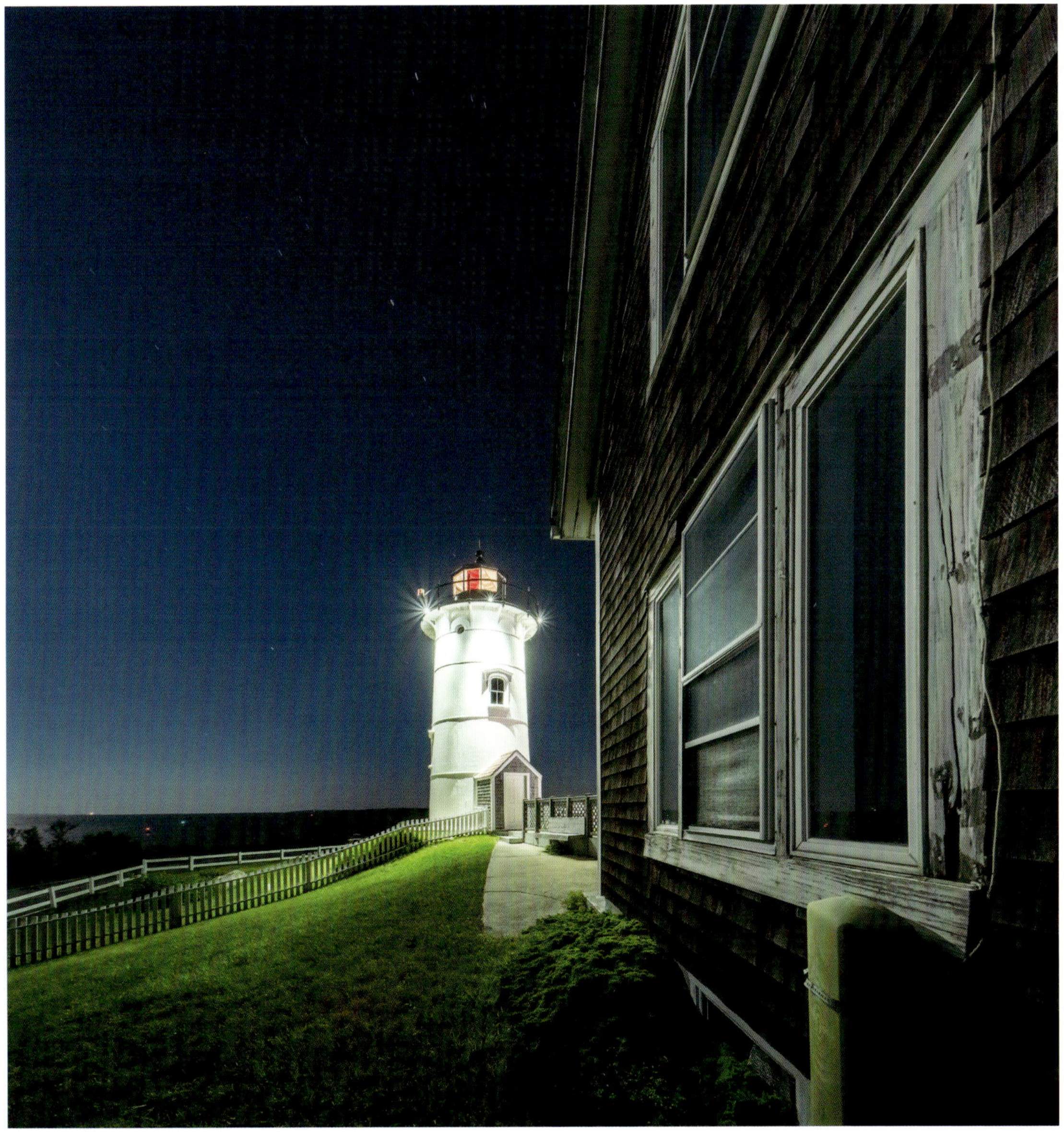

Visitors to Nobska may not notice the red pane of glass on this side of the tower. Seeing it from the water tells of danger. Keep moving parallel to the shoreline until the red glass is no longer visible before turning toward land.

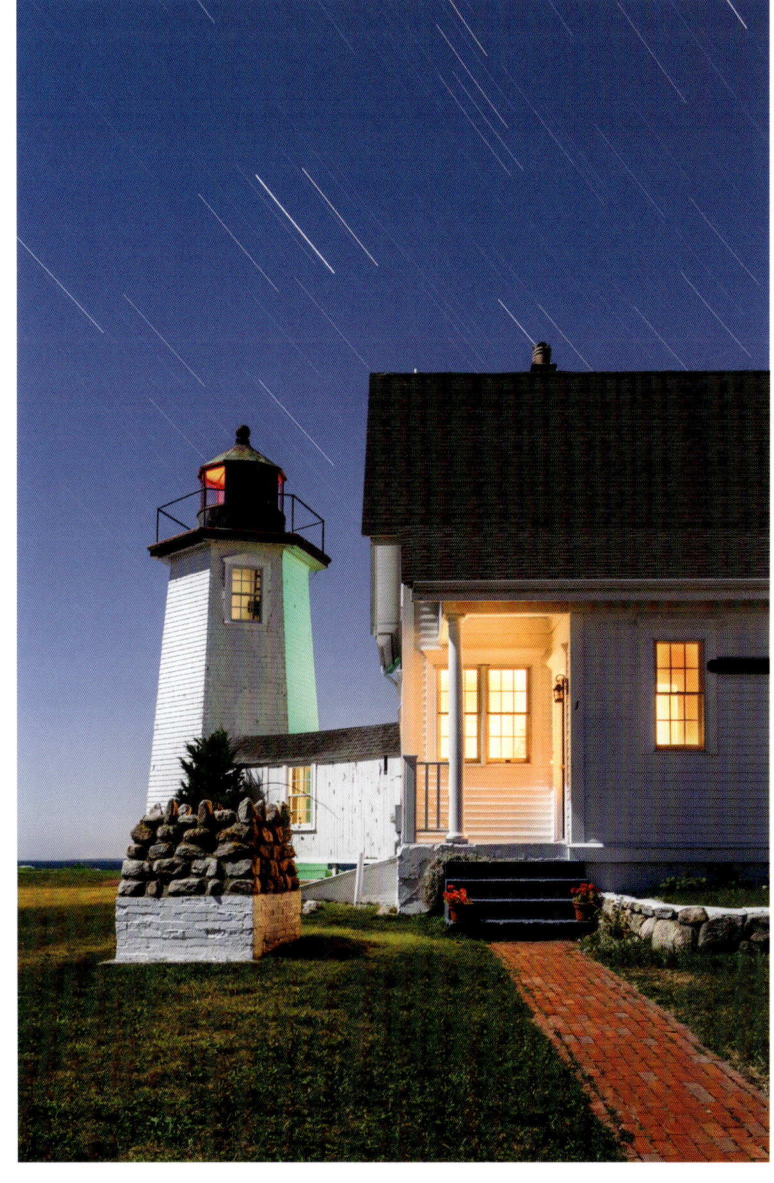

An email request to photograph this property was all that was needed for unrestricted access to Wings Neck Light. The tower was lit with a flashlight as it no longer had a functioning beacon system. The stars reveal approximately twenty minutes of exposure time.

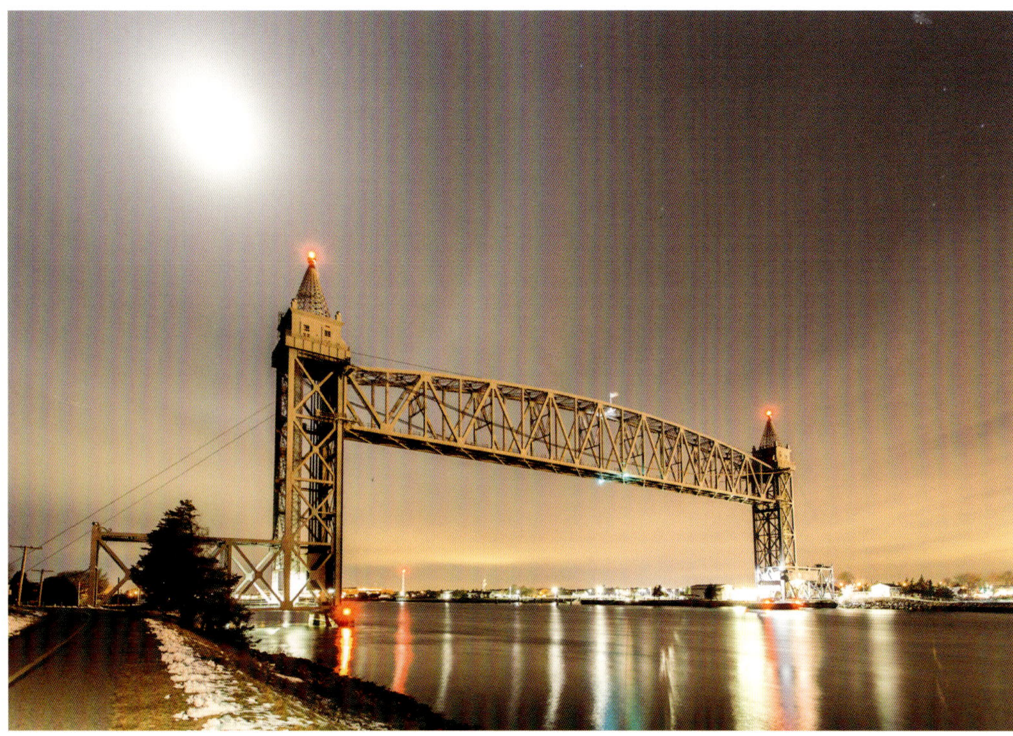

A halo around the moon or sun appears when light is refracted through high-altitude ice crystals. This is a common occurrence over Cape Cod during the winter months and is most easily seen on the nights close to a full moon.

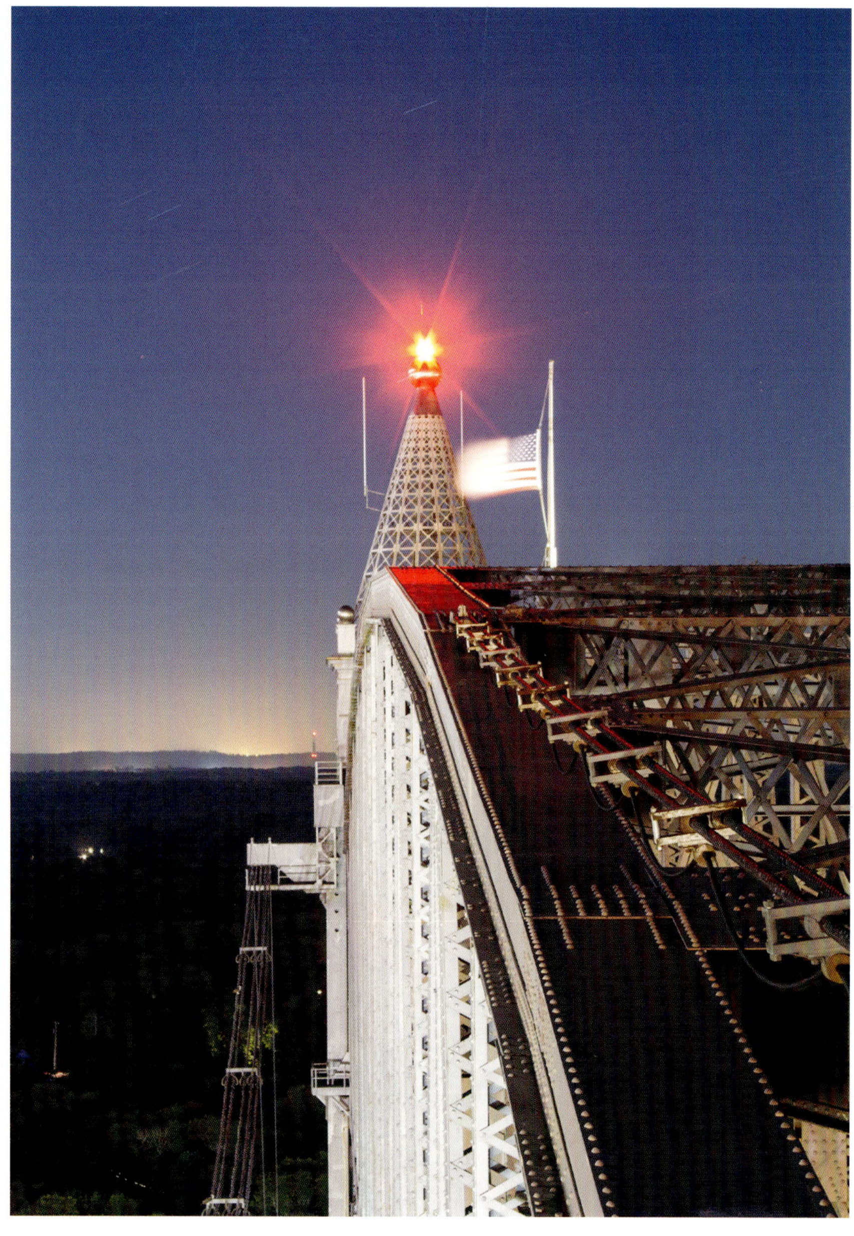

After a short ride on the tiny bridge elevator, I emerged from the door at the top of the railroad bridge to this view, on a windy evening in the summer of 2013. The structure measures 271 feet in height but felt quite a bit higher from this vantage point.

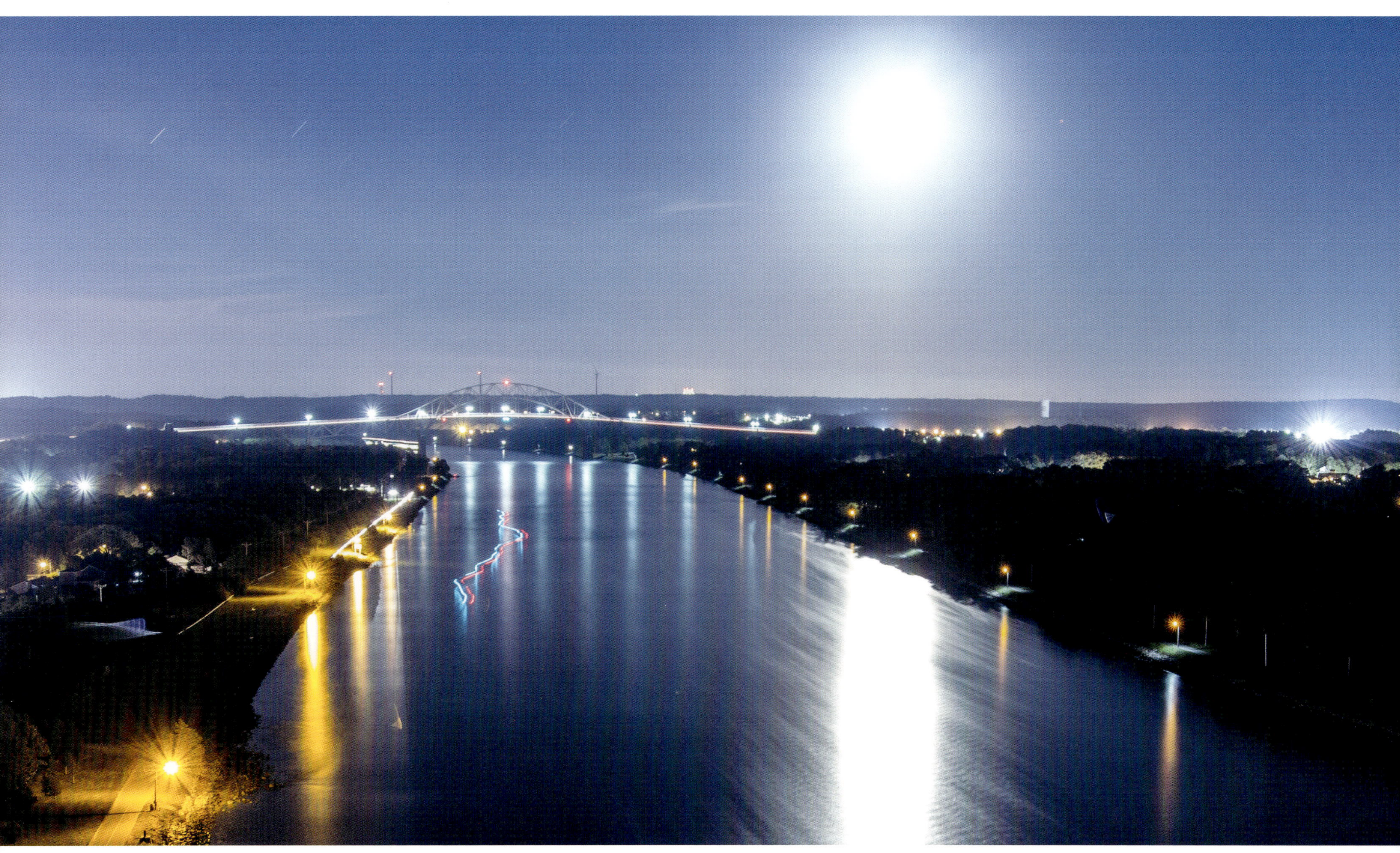

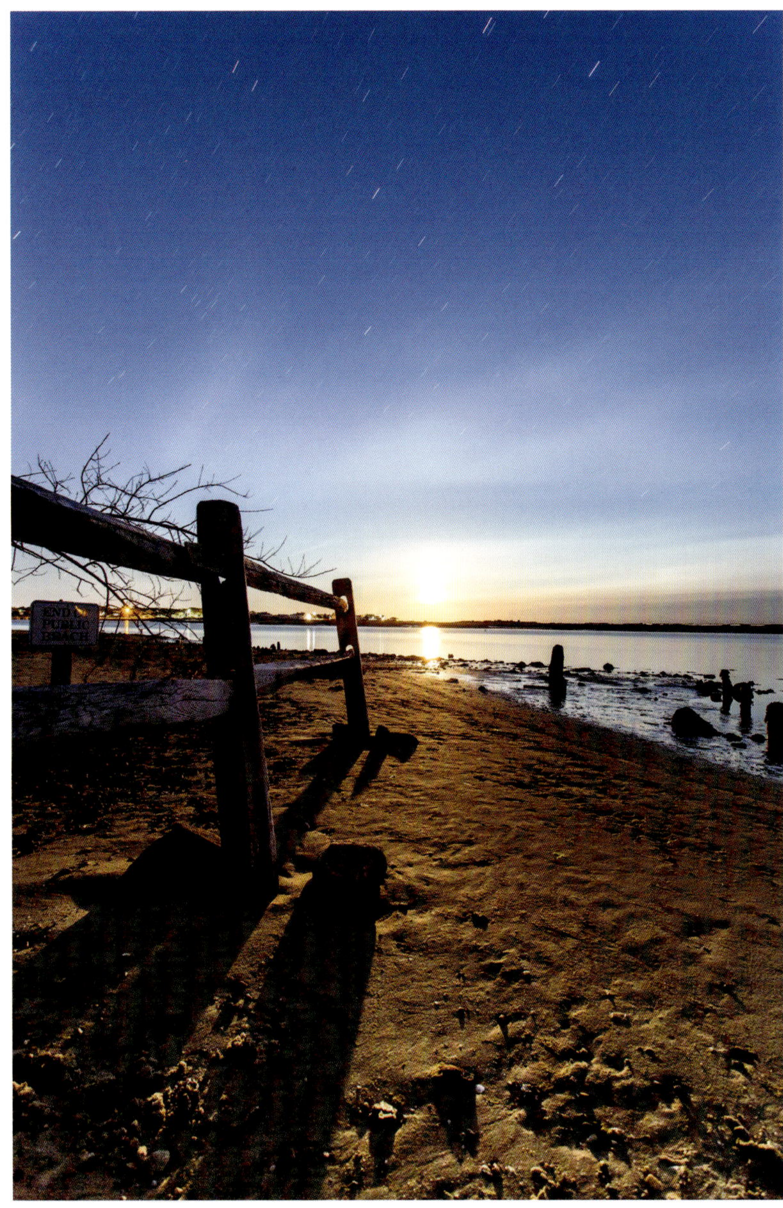

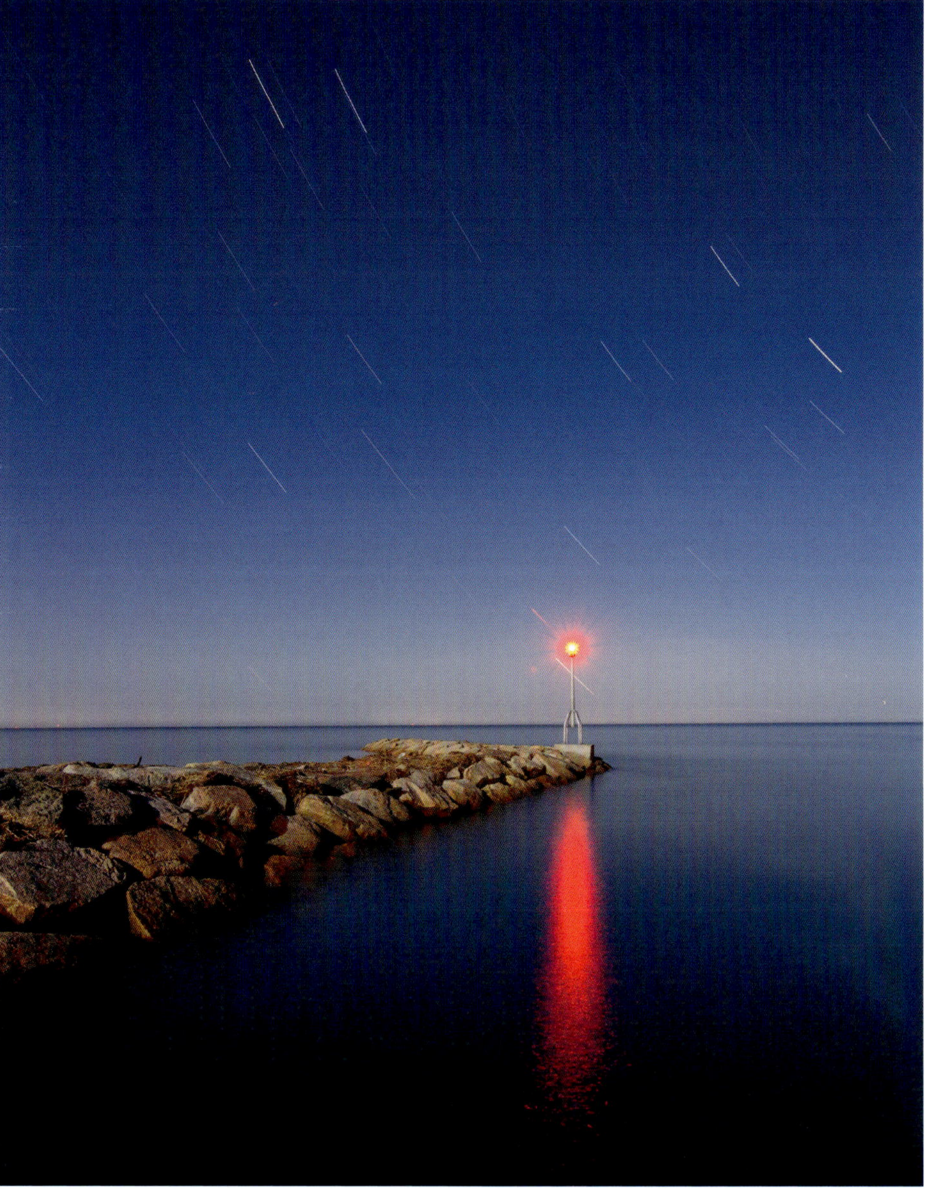

Yellow or orange moons are typically caused by dust, smoke, and particulates in the air. It is more pronounced when the moon is closer to the horizon, since this is where the atmosphere appears thickest. As the moonlight travels through this, blue light is filtered out, leaving only the warmer tones to shine. On most nights, the moon becomes a pale white as it reaches overhead, where the atmosphere is the thinnest. Long shadows grow across these golden shores at Windmill Beach along Bass River.

A boat ramp at Rock Harbor was the perfect setting for this star trail shot, until a rising tide lapping at the base of the tripod forced the exposure to be cut short.

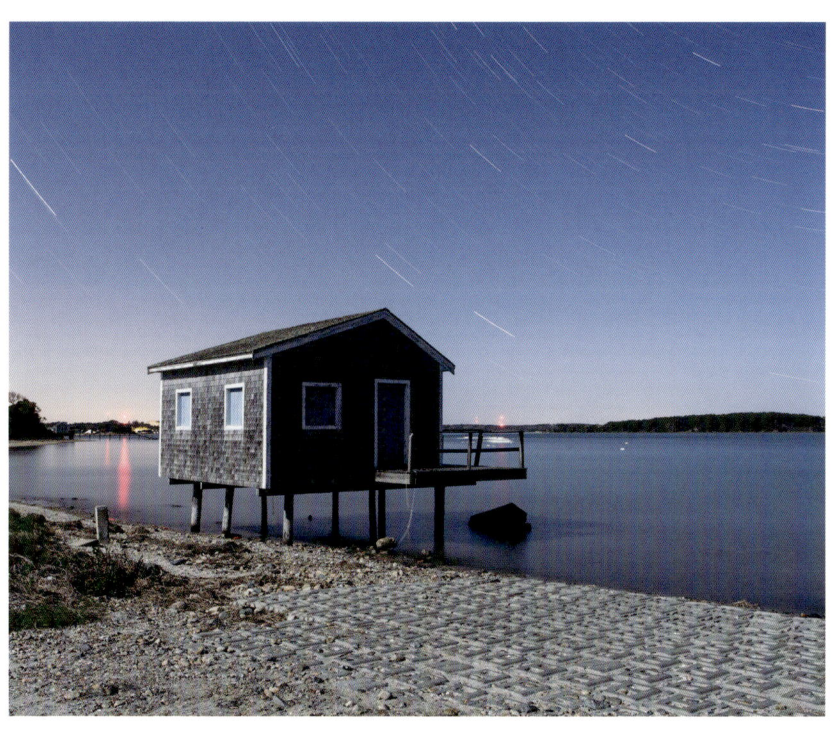

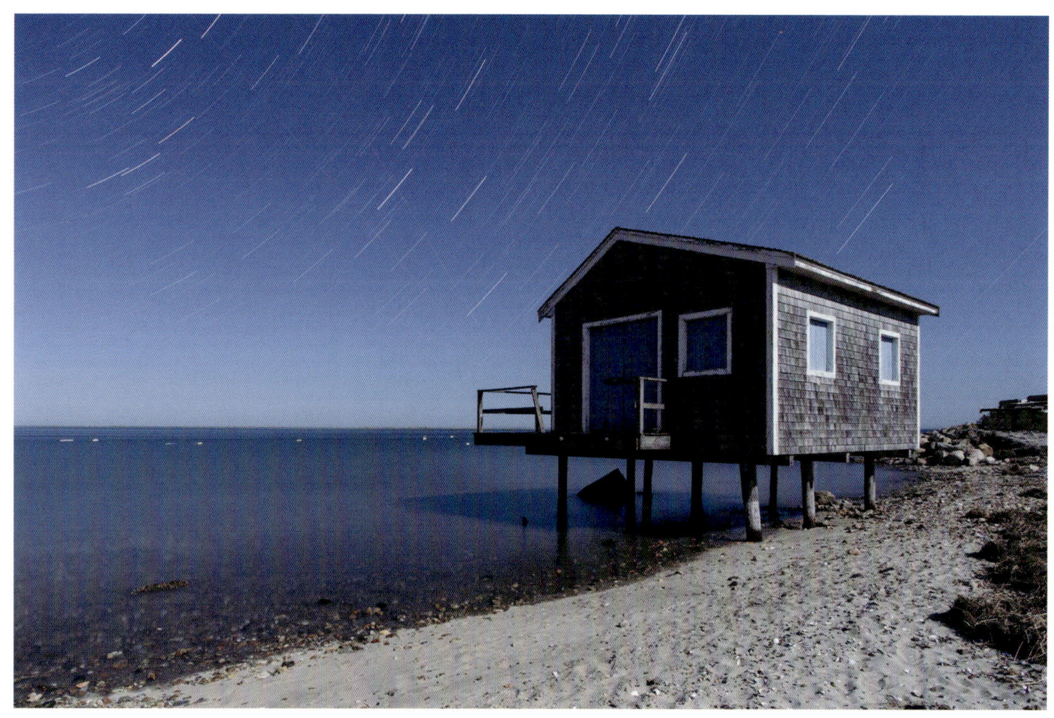

A private boathouse bathes in moonlight as the stars streak the skies over Chatham. The faint white lines of passing aircraft can be seen heading from the horizon. I photographed this location in 2014, and I was hopeful to photograph it again for this book. While researching this location, I was surprised to learn that the structure was gone. Presumably, it was destroyed by a coastal storm. In 2024, only the support pillars remained.

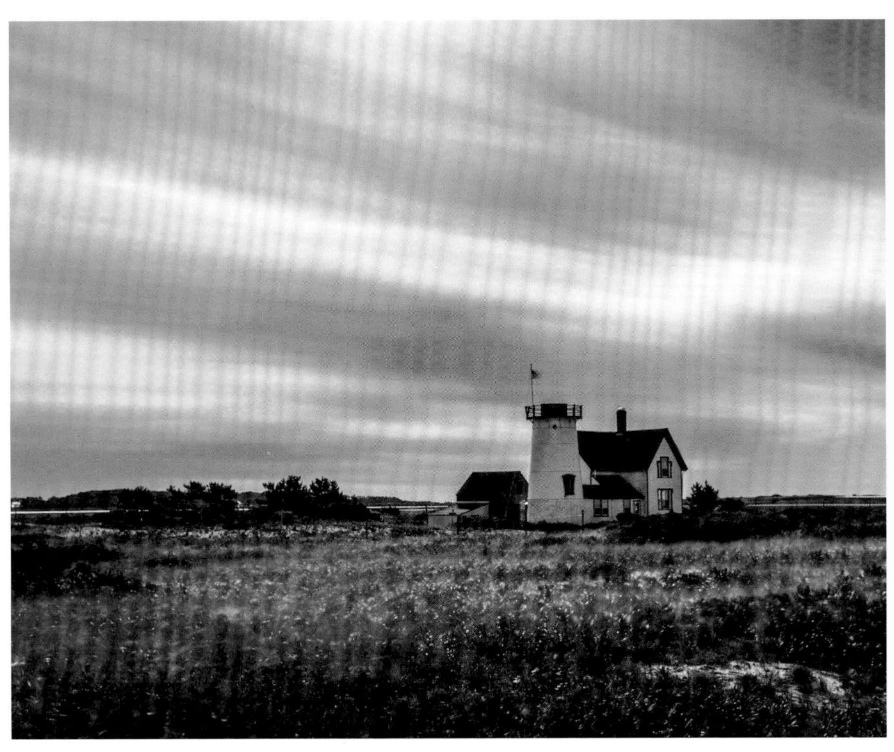

Moonlight glistens across windblown dune grass at Stage Harbor Light. It can take around twenty minutes to walk out to the lighthouse from the Hardings Beach parking lot. It's not a difficult hike, but it can be a minor workout with a camera bag and tripod in tow.

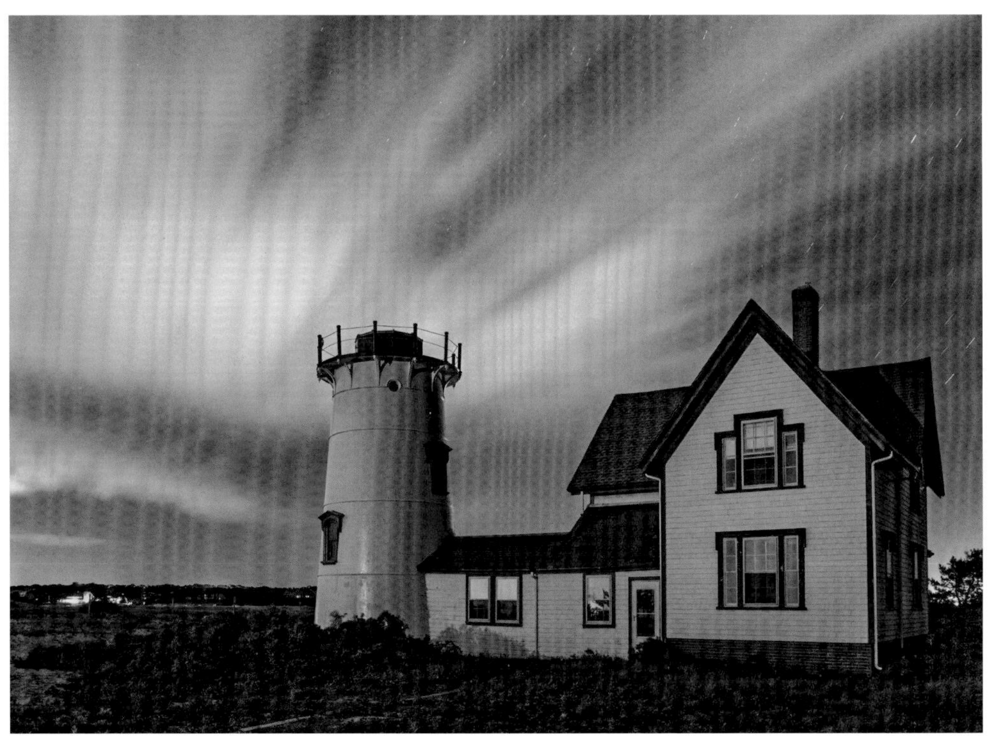

The white light from a nearby channel marker illuminates the front of Stage Harbor Light while the glow of nearby towns defines the fast-moving clouds.

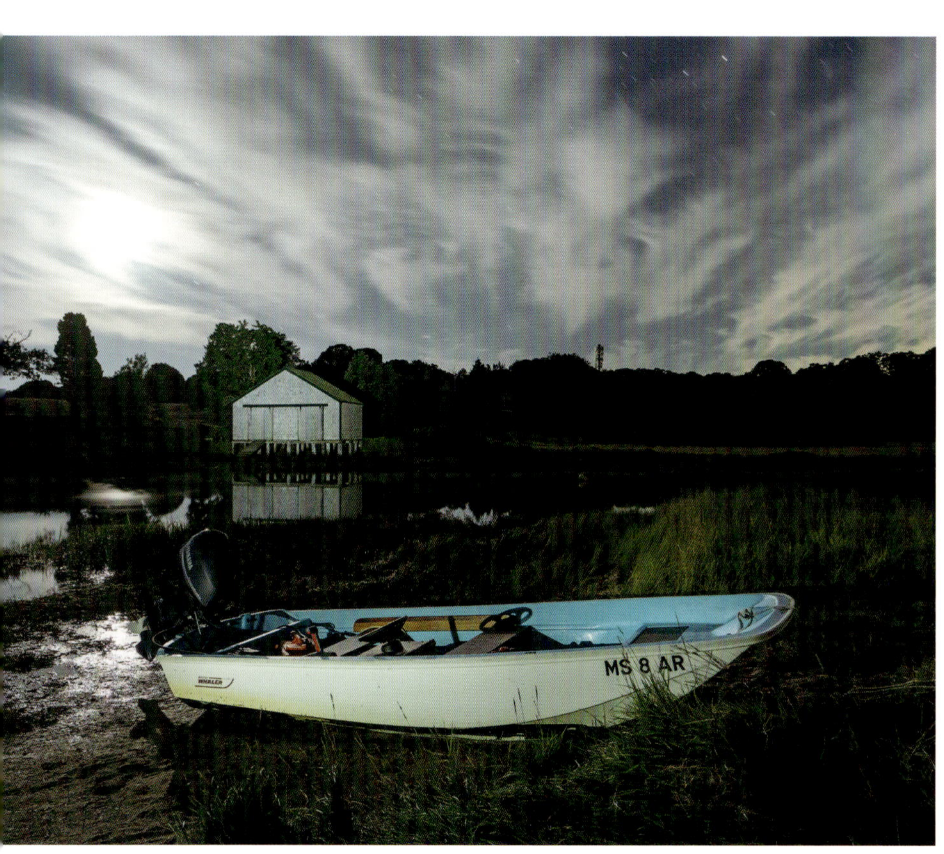

This "whaler" spends most of its time floating in the waterway leading into Salt Pond in Eastham, but on this night it got to enjoy a break on the shoreline's soft grass.

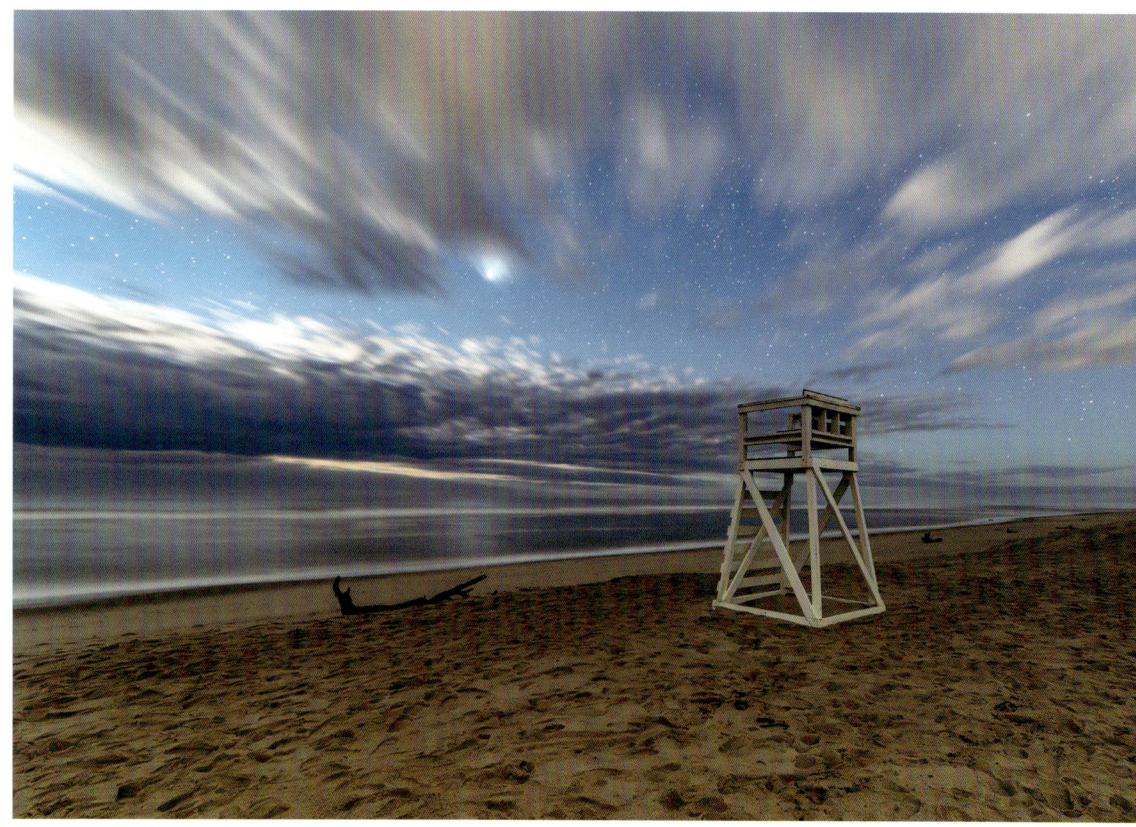

Skies begin to lighten thanks to a rising moon shining through broken clouds. Even Jupiter is bright enough to light the waters along the sands of Coast Guard Beach.

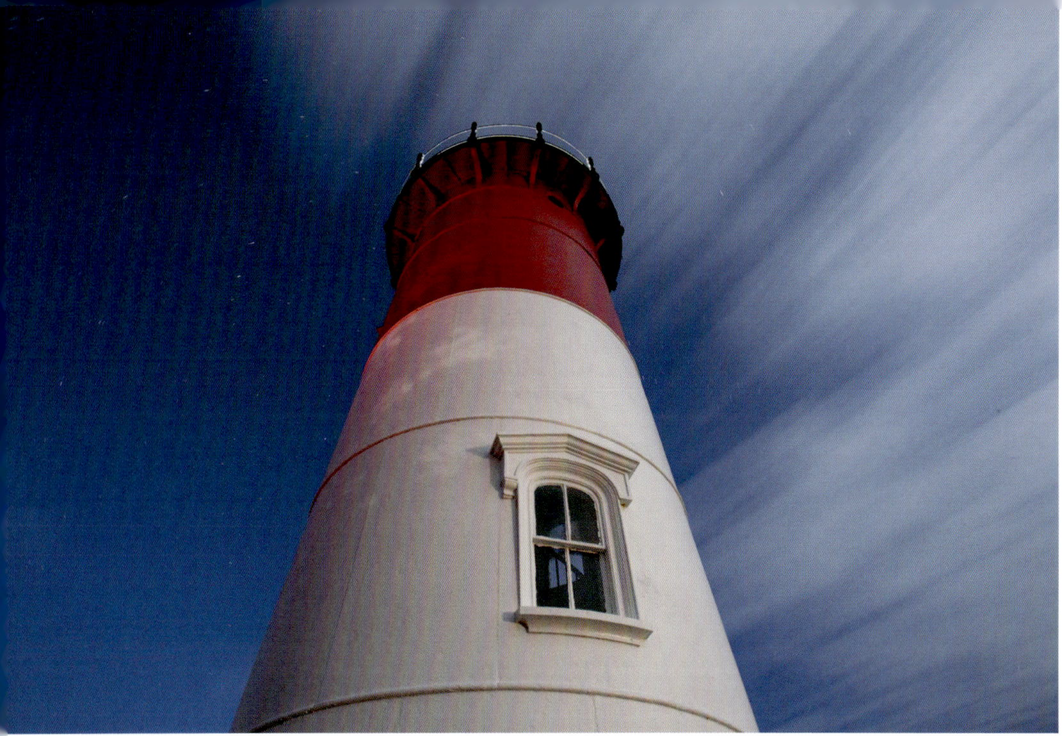

From this angle of the Nauset tower, you can look through one window and out another. In between, the silhouette of a spiral staircase railing can be seen.

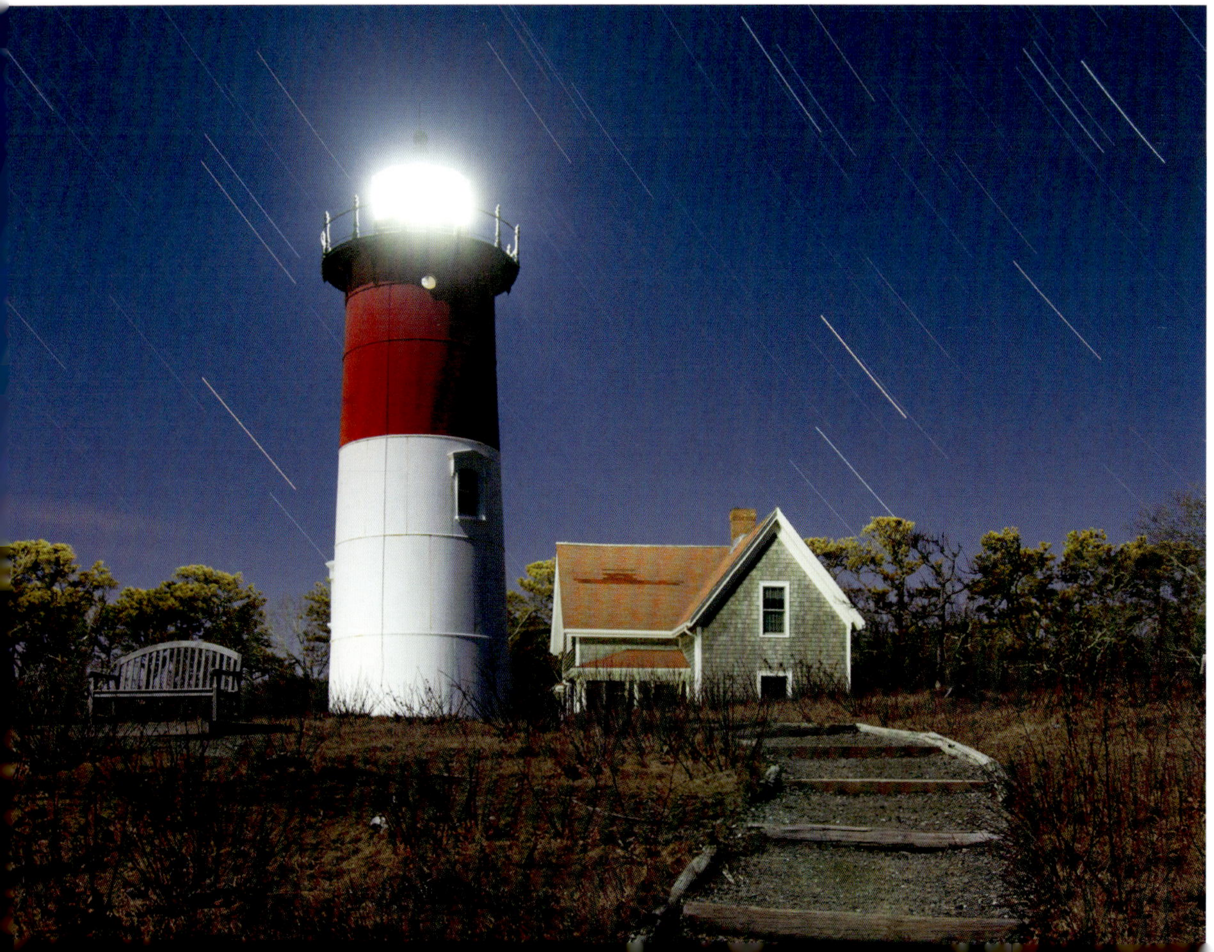

A March full moon shines brightly across the eastern face of the tower and house while westerly stars travel the sky during this twenty-minute exposure. Sitting on the bench of this elevated property provides visitors with the perfect vantage point to watch a sunrise or a moonrise over the Atlantic Ocean. This lighthouse is featured on a certain potato chip bag, but the artwork places the water on the wrong side.

On October 9, 2022, the public was invited to tour the lighthouse under the light of the full moon. The weather could not have been better, as the skies were clear from horizon to horizon. A zigzag line of hundreds stretched from the parking lot, down the road, up the stairs, and into the tower. Small groups were led up the spiral staircase to the level just below the beacon room, where they could view the moonlit ocean through the circular portholes. And, although they couldn't enter the beacon room itself, visitors could climb the ladder and poke their heads through the floor to see the spinning mechanism.

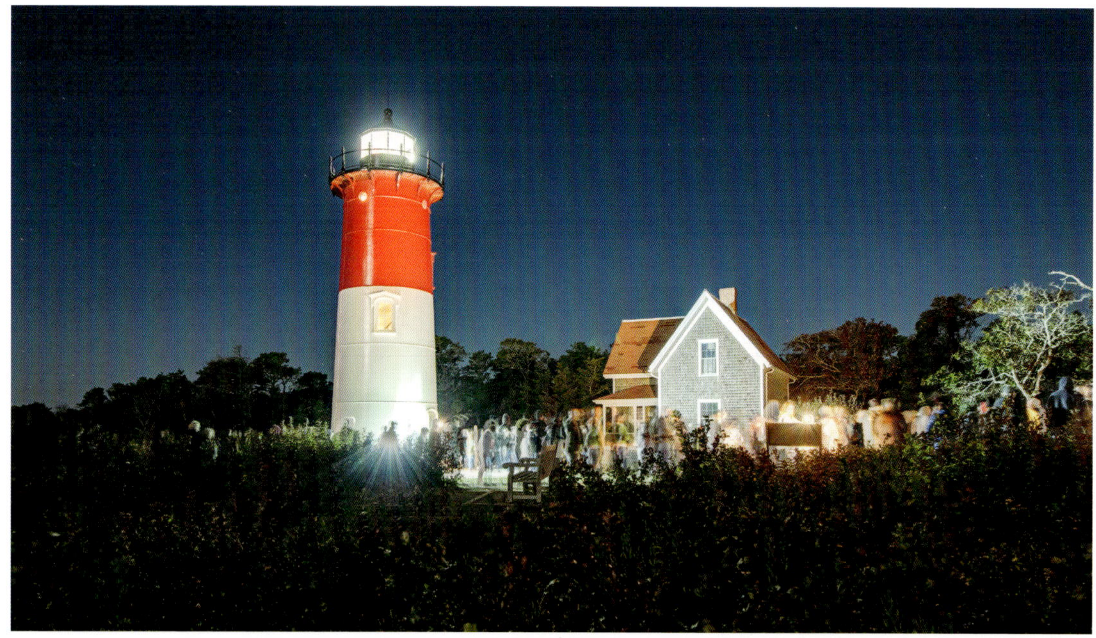

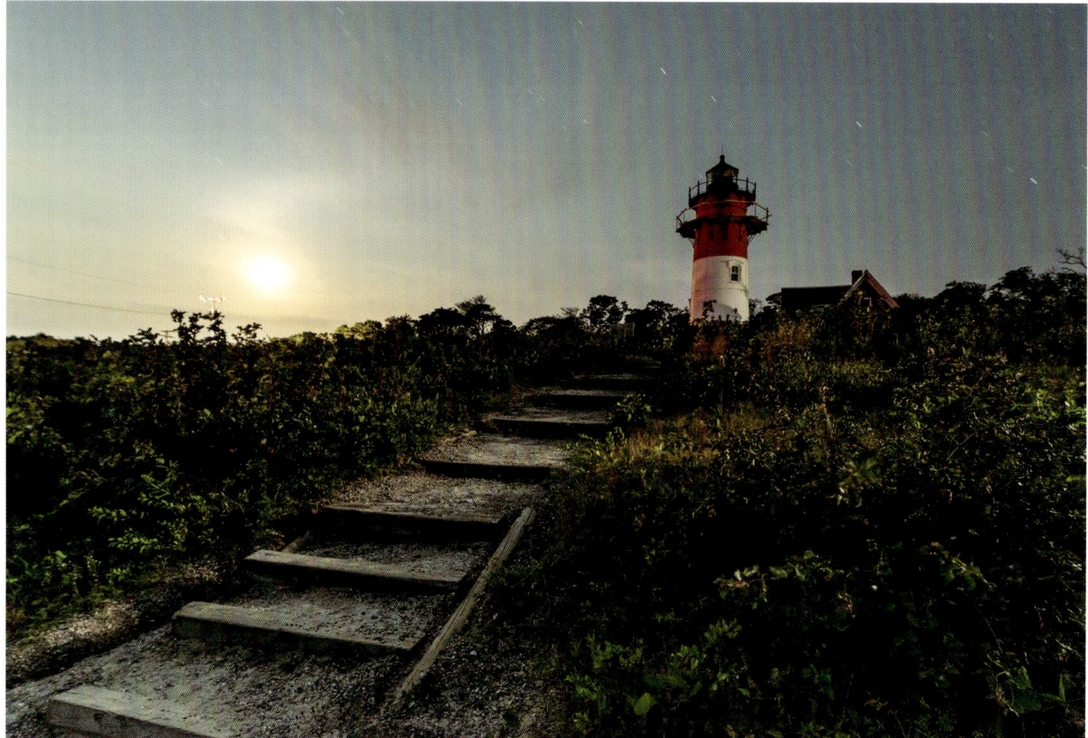

A well-deserved fresh coat of paint had been ordered in the fall of 2021, resulting in the temporary shutdown of the lighting mechanism on a moonlit week. The red tower paint had faded, and the telltale sign of rust began to streak down the sides. Cape Cod weather is not very forgiving when it comes to metal lighthouses.

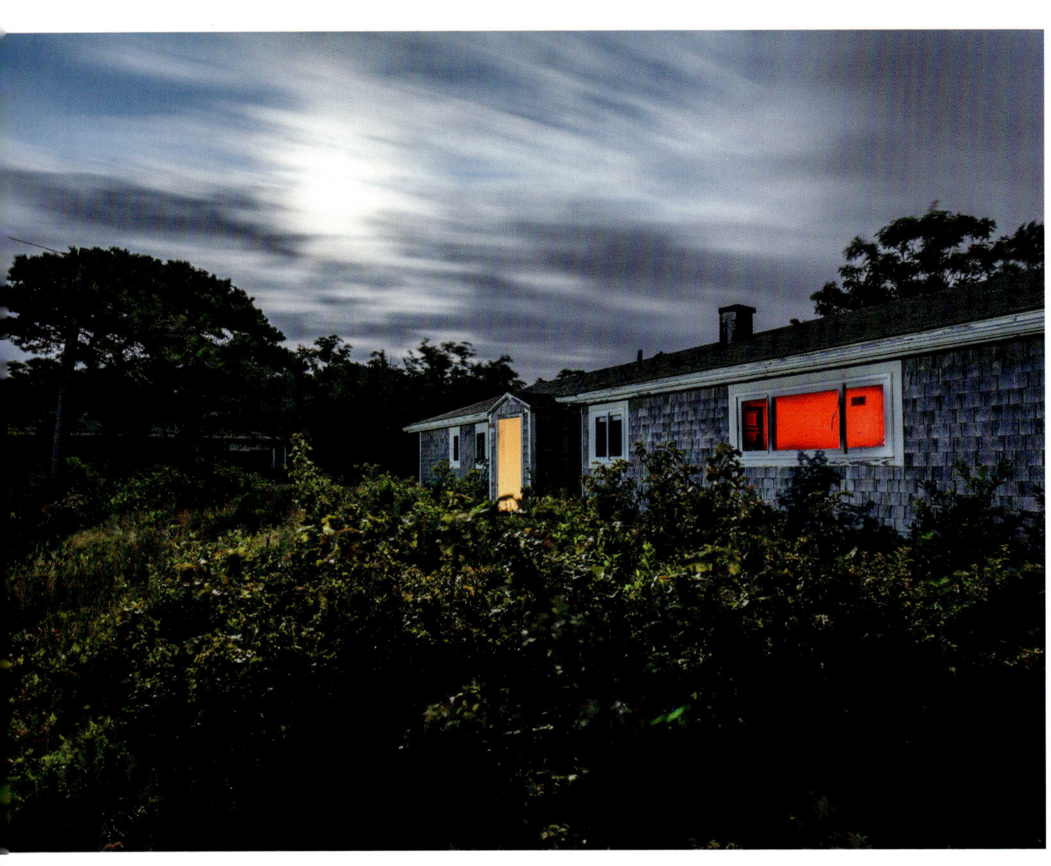

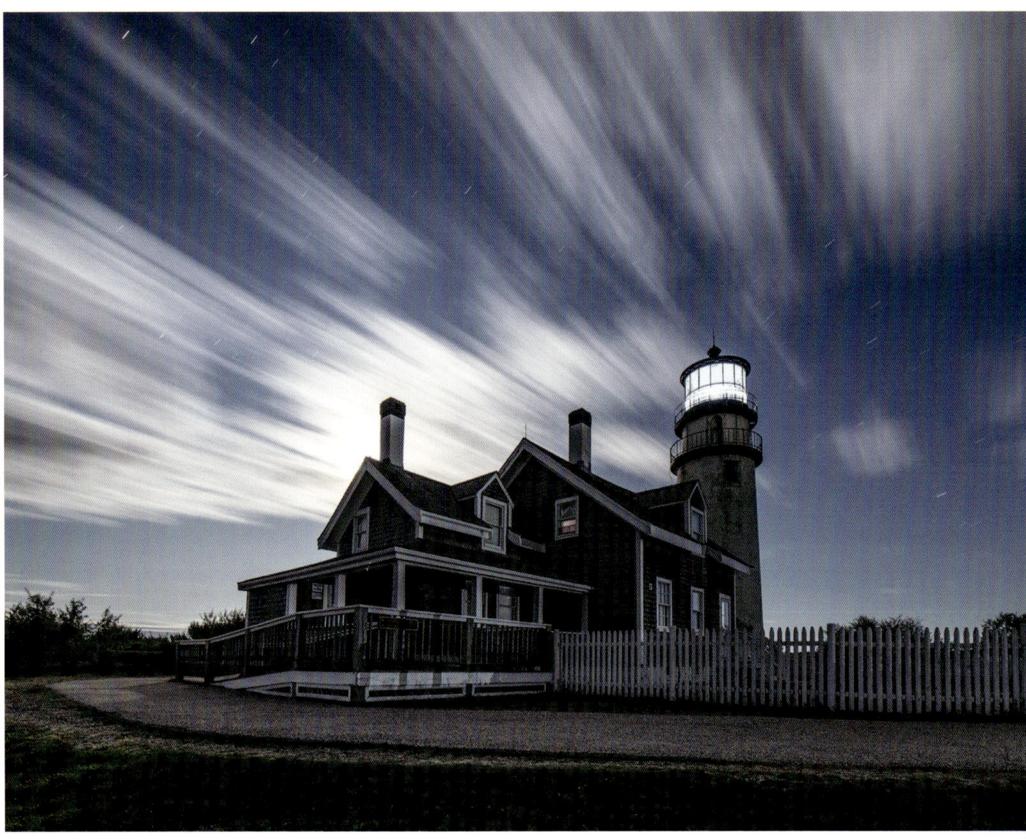

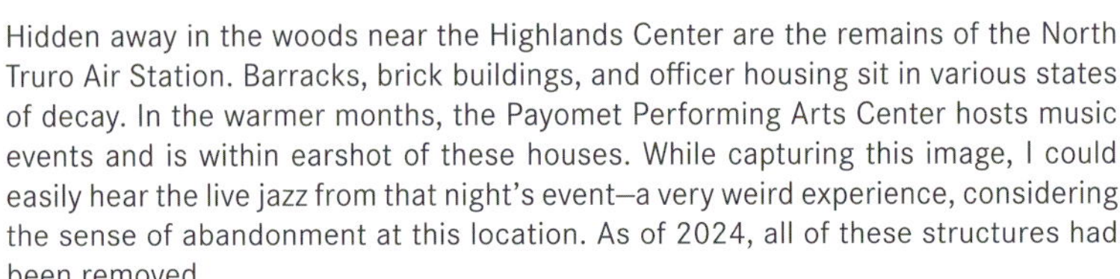

Hidden away in the woods near the Highlands Center are the remains of the North Truro Air Station. Barracks, brick buildings, and officer housing sit in various states of decay. In the warmer months, the Payomet Performing Arts Center hosts music events and is within earshot of these houses. While capturing this image, I could easily hear the live jazz from that night's event—a very weird experience, considering the sense of abandonment at this location. As of 2024, all of these structures had been removed.

Three minutes of exposure time allows for the clouds to streak the skies on an early September night. This lighthouse is photogenic from any angle, but this corner is rarely photographed.

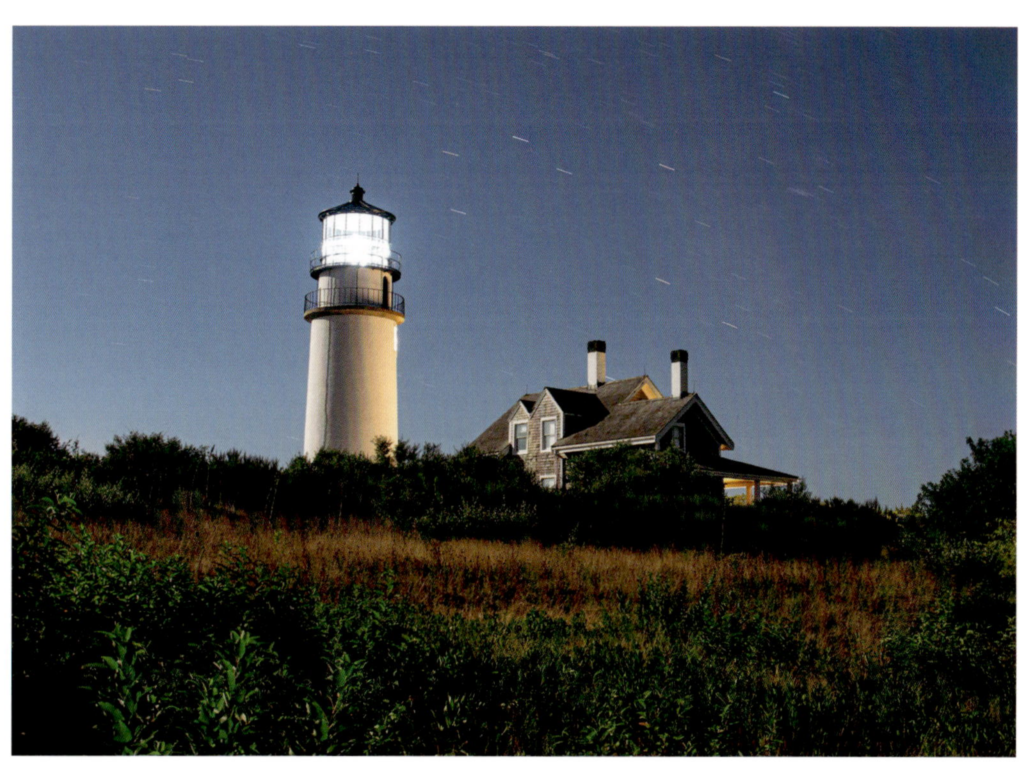

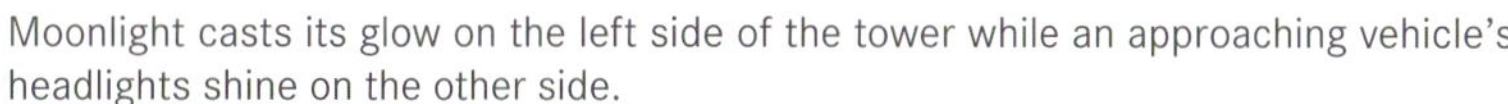

Moonlight casts its glow on the left side of the tower while an approaching vehicle's headlights shine on the other side.

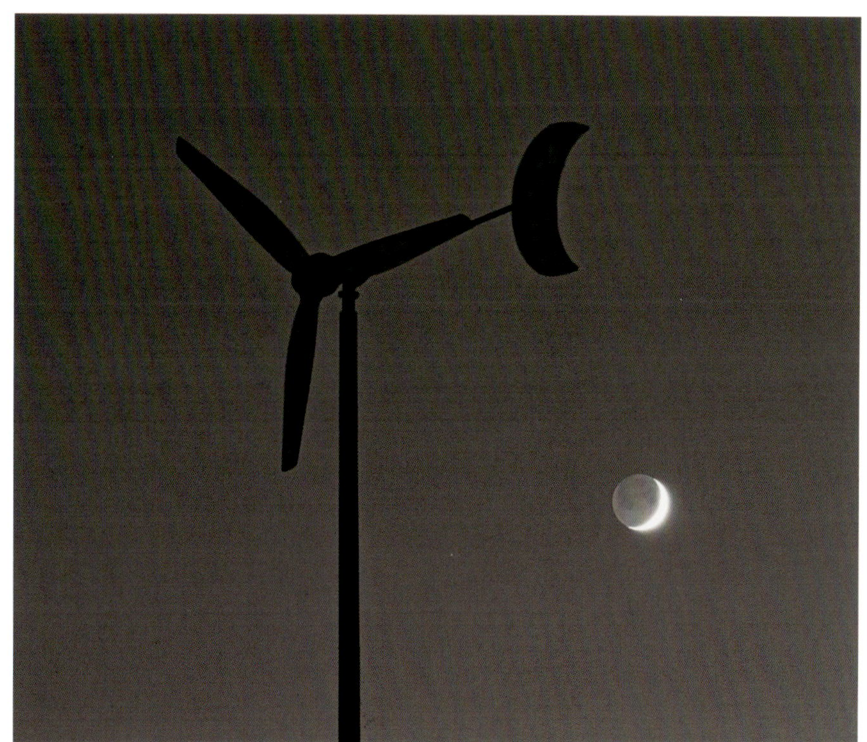

This unique weathervane is located next to the Whistle House at Race Point Light. It paired well with the setting moon on this night.

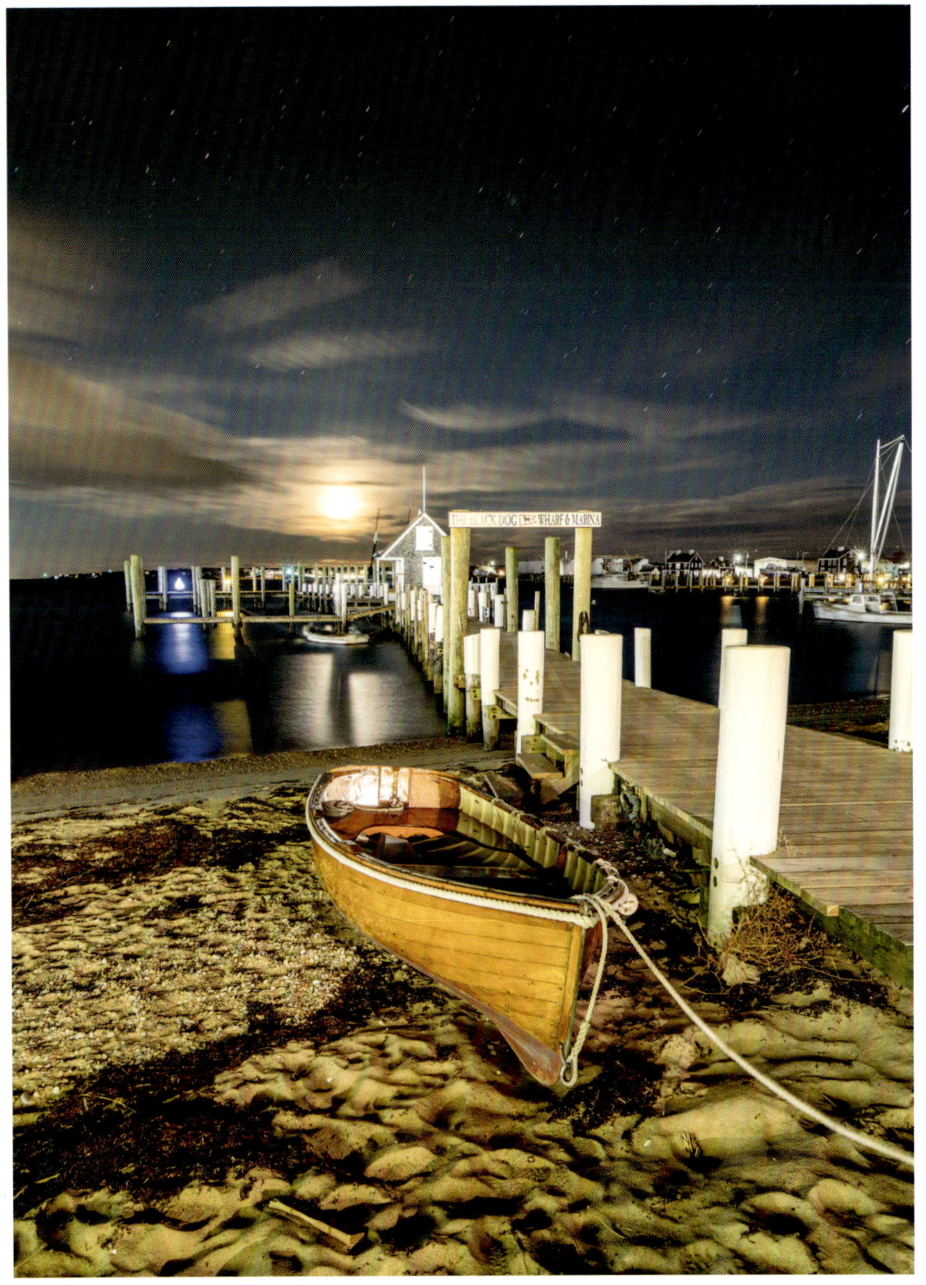

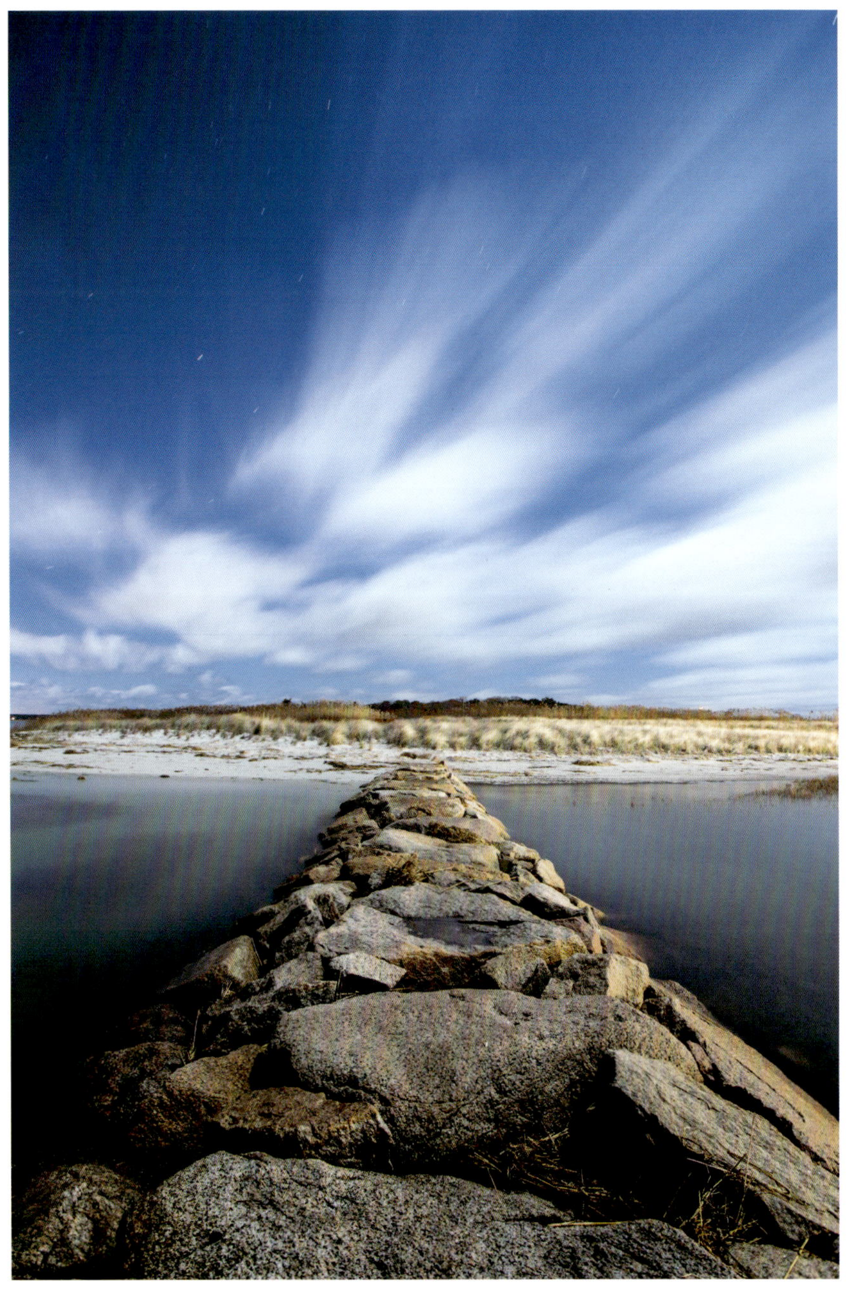

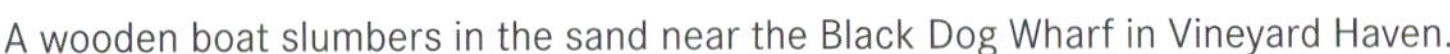

A wooden boat slumbers in the sand near the Black Dog Wharf in Vineyard Haven.

The moon provides all the light that was needed to capture this two-minute exposure at Rock Harbor in Orleans. What you can't see here was the curious seal that popped its head up behind me as I was waiting for this to complete.

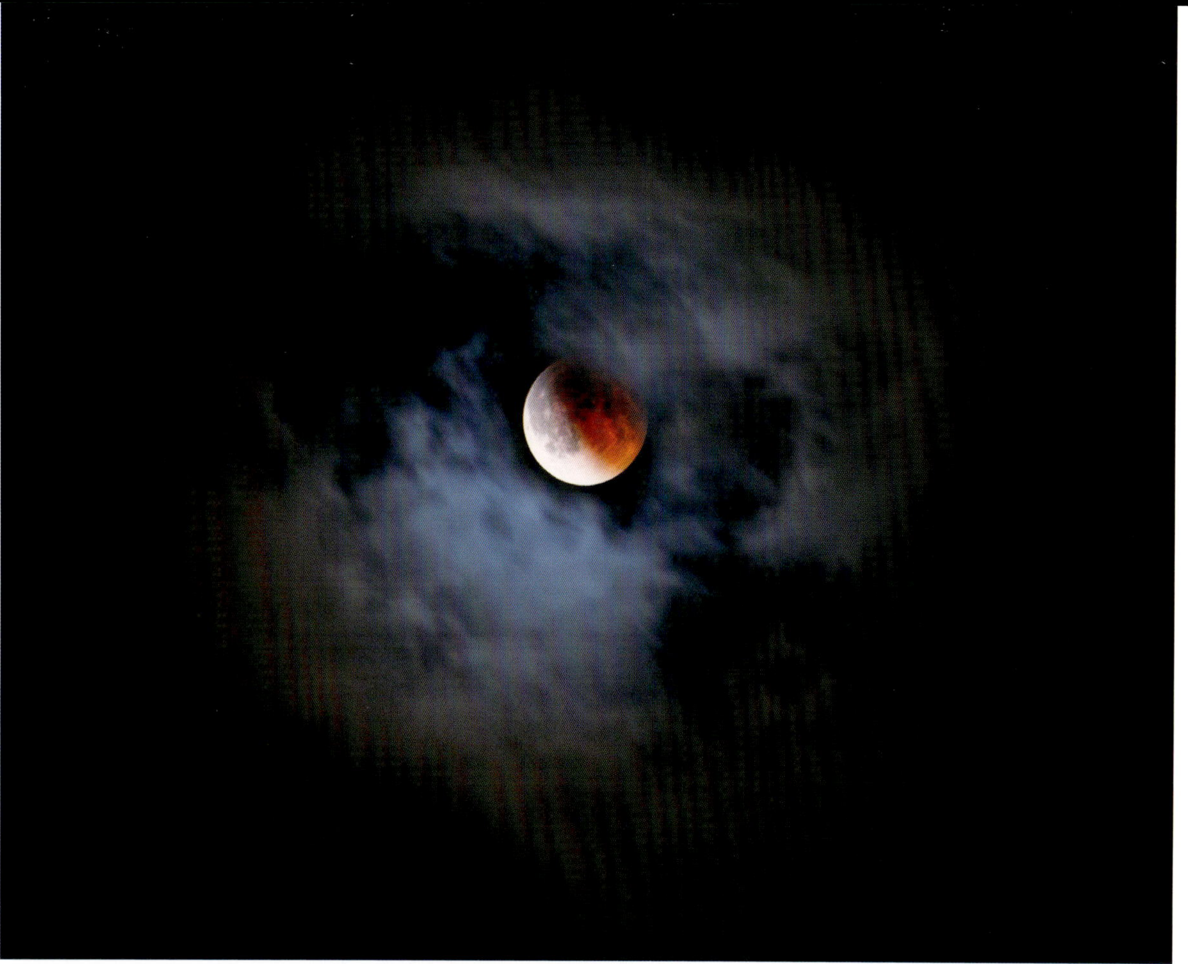

A lunar eclipse as seen from the shores of Falmouth in the overnight hours of September 27 and 28, 2015. These eclipses occur when the earth sneaks between the sun and the moon. Blue light is filtered out by the earth's atmosphere, leaving only red, some of which makes its way to the moon. This is why lunar eclipses often peak with a deep red glow. You may hear this referred to as a "blood moon."

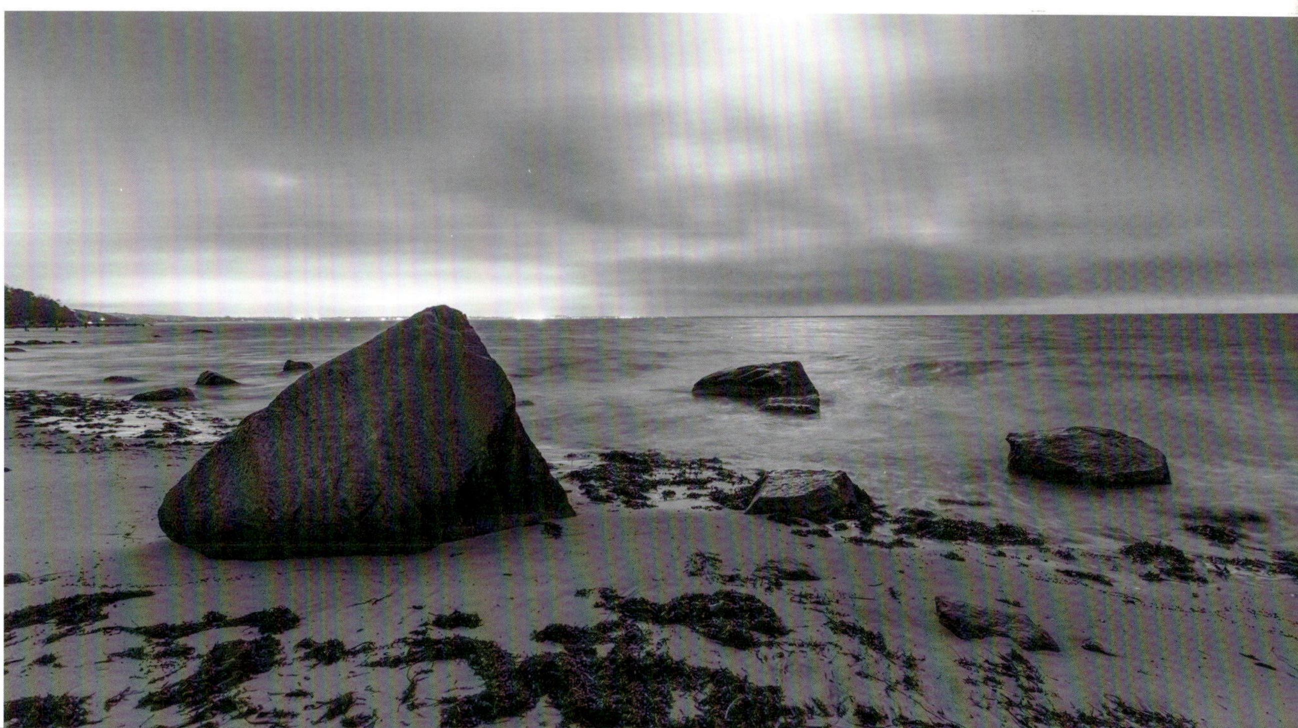

This is the most recent image taken for this book, photographed on December 16, 2024. It's also the second shortest in exposure time, at just two and a half seconds. This allowed the camera to capture the water's texture and the position of the clouds. The moon provided just enough light to pull it off.

3

STARRY SHORES—THE BEACH AS A WINDOW TO THE UNIVERSE

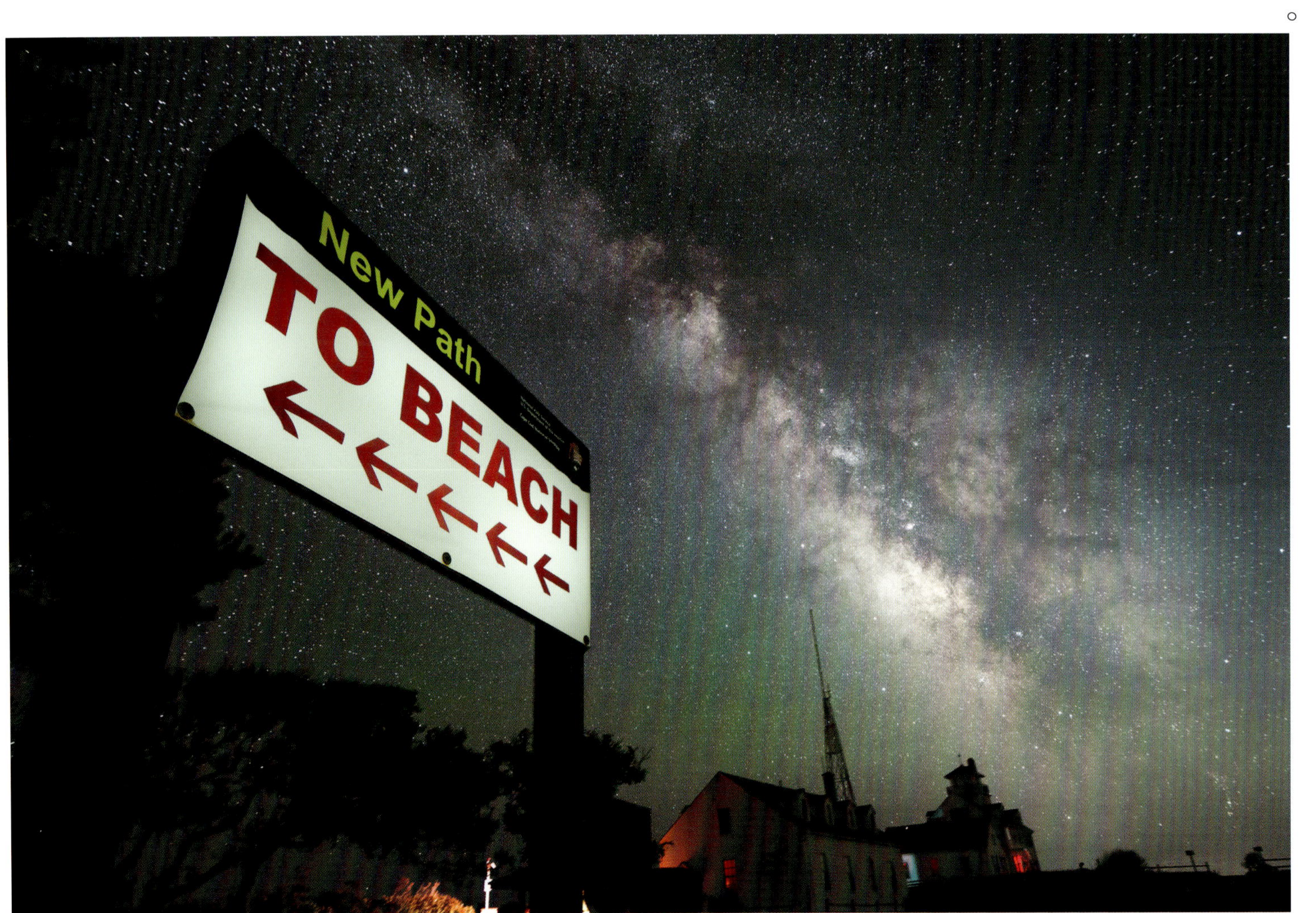

Coast Guard Beach is a great place to visit at night. Fishermen, photographers, stargazers with telescopes, and people looking to relax can be spotted here at just about any hour of the evening when skies are clear. If you are lucky enough to be in the area during a meteor shower, this is the place to be.

The Cape and the Islands offer some of the darkest skies in New England. With a little bit of planning, it is easy to find yourself standing on the sands of any number of easily accessible beaches.

At the Cape Cod National Seashore, late winter leading into spring provides the best times to catch a rising Milky Way as it appears along the horizon across the waters of the Atlantic Ocean. Here, you will have no light pollution to contend with, save for the occasional passing ship.

As the year progresses, areas south and southeast of the seashore become the best vantage point. Hardings Beach, South Cape Beach, and even the shoreline in Falmouth along Vineyard Sound can offer easy views of the galactic core.

Just remember, no camera required! If you find yourself with a clear night and some time, make the journey to your local beach. Let your eyes adjust to the darkness, listen to the waves, and relax. Capturing a photograph is simply a bonus to an already great moment and a lesson of which many photographers should take note. You do yourself no favors by viewing the wonders of the universe through the back of a camera alone.

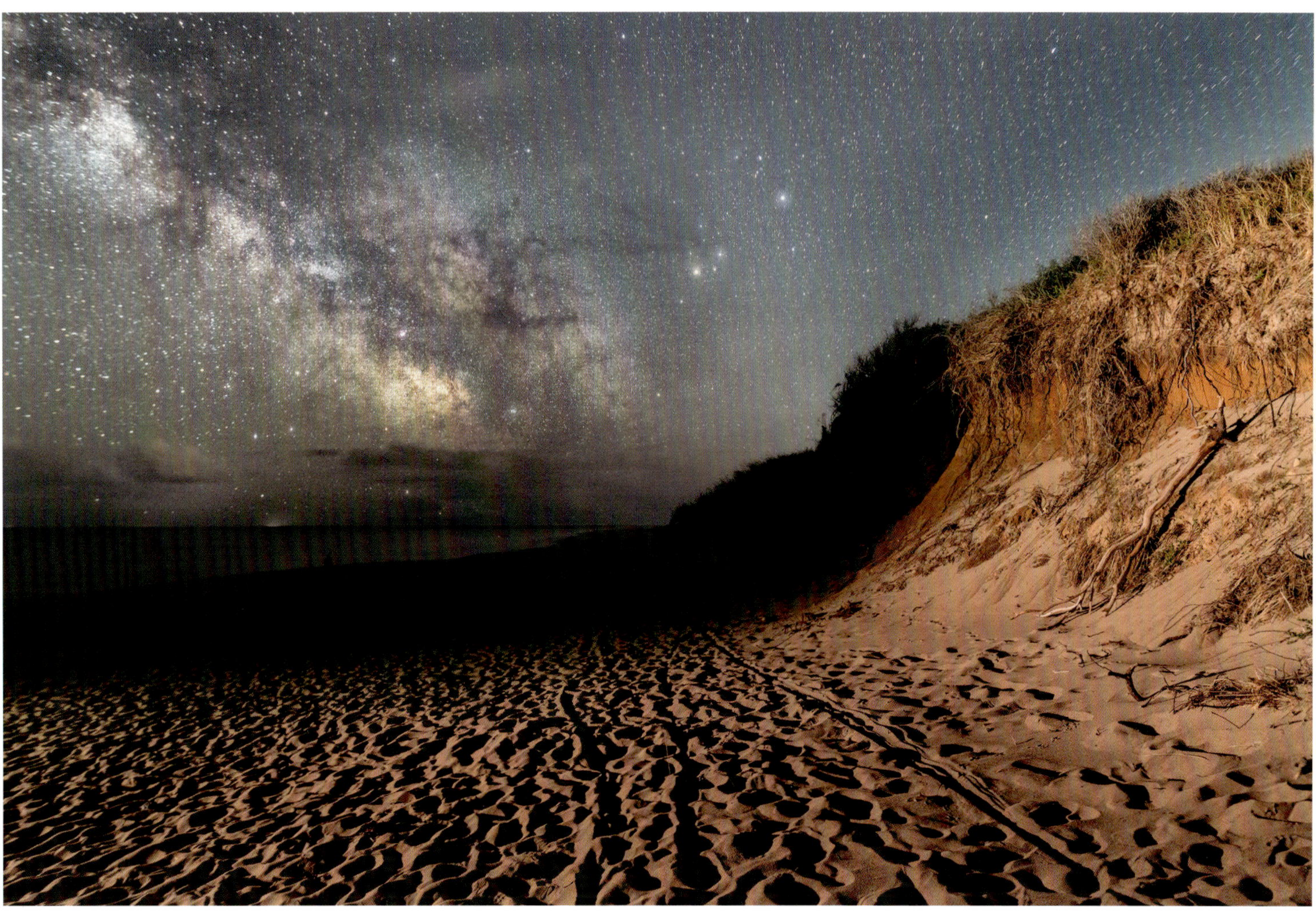

Coast Guard Beach at night is very dark, since the cliff face obscures the glow from both Eastham and any cars that happen to be passing through the area. I spotted this alignment while hosting a night photography tour in May 2020 and decided to return the next night for a chance to capture it. After setting the camera on a timer, I ran down toward the water and held the light over my head to clear the sloped beach and light the cliff.

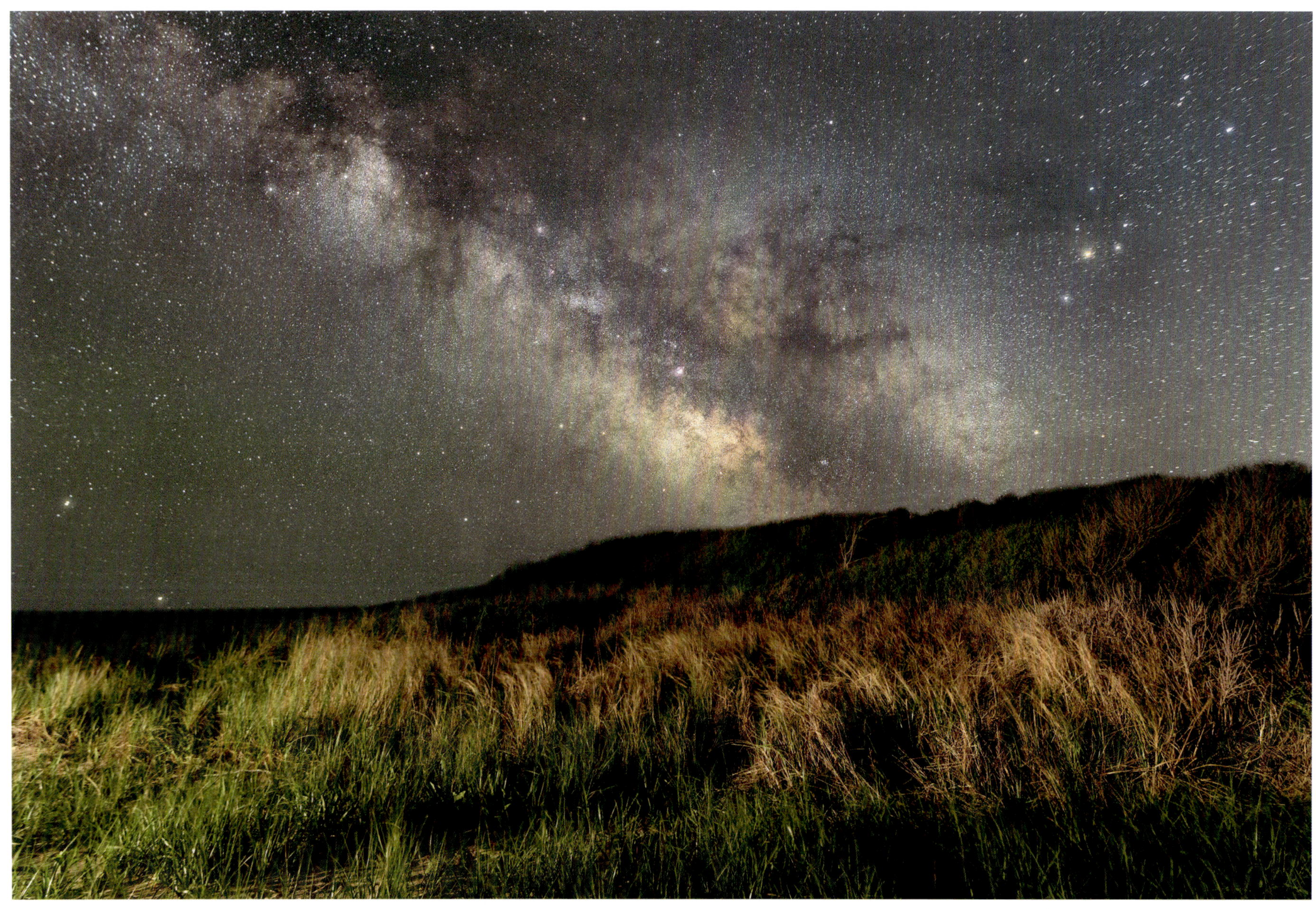

Dune grass blows across a hillside at Coast Guard Beach. The purple glow of the Lagoon Nebula can be seen in the center of the galactic core. There's a lot of color in the night sky, and the right camera settings can reveal this even when your eyes can't. A low-ISO tracking technique was used to capture the sky, which is what brings those colors out. A pass of warm light was used to bring out the various greens and tans of the landscape.

There is no darker view of the night sky than what can be seen along the eastern shorelines of Cape Cod. Save for the occasional passing cruise or container ship, the next source of light pollution in this direction is Europe, and you won't be seeing that from here. This image was photographed at the Nauset Light parking lot.

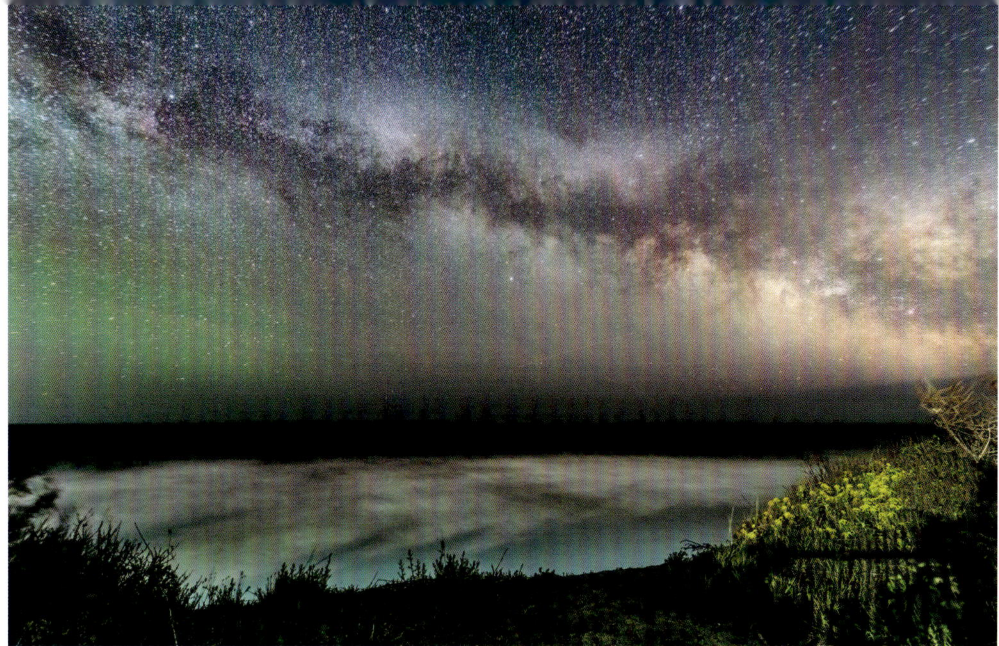

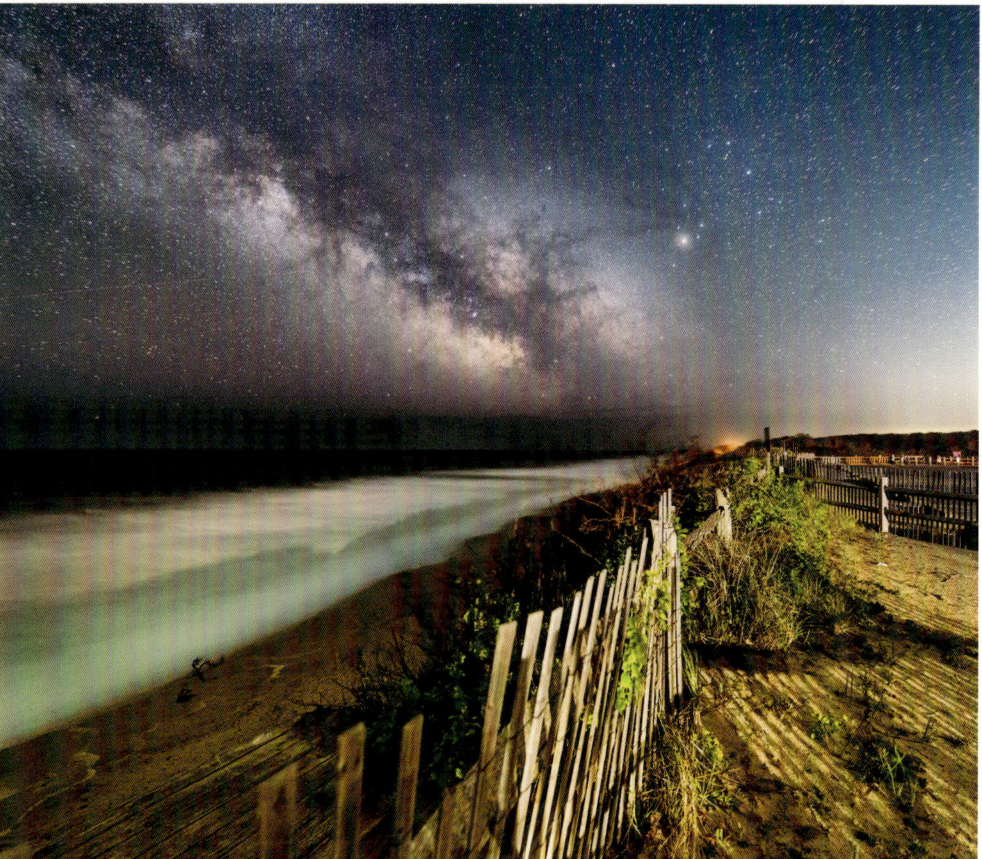

In photography, there is a term known as the vanishing point. This is where leading lines converge in a way that draws the viewer's eyes to a point that seems beyond the horizon. Here, this is accomplished via the fence, the shoreline, the horizon, and the slope of the Milky Way. All this leads to a point obscured by the small orange light in the distance, possibly from a bonfire or a streetlight.

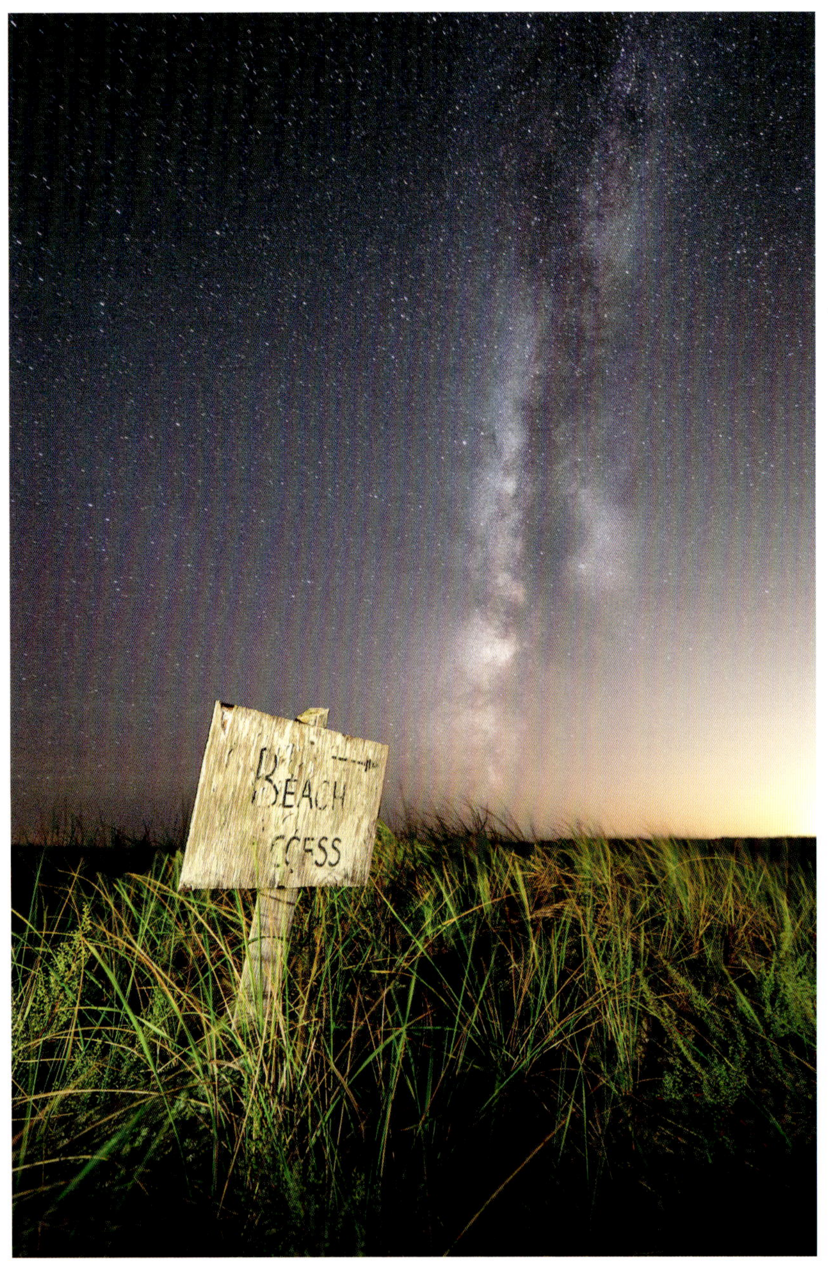

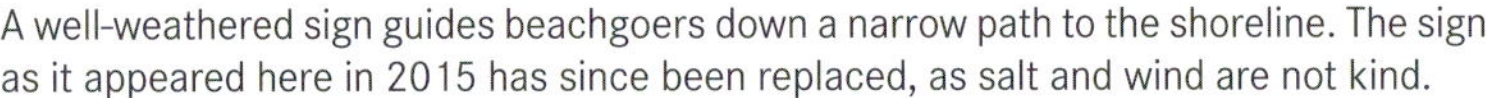
A well-weathered sign guides beachgoers down a narrow path to the shoreline. The sign as it appeared here in 2015 has since been replaced, as salt and wind are not kind.

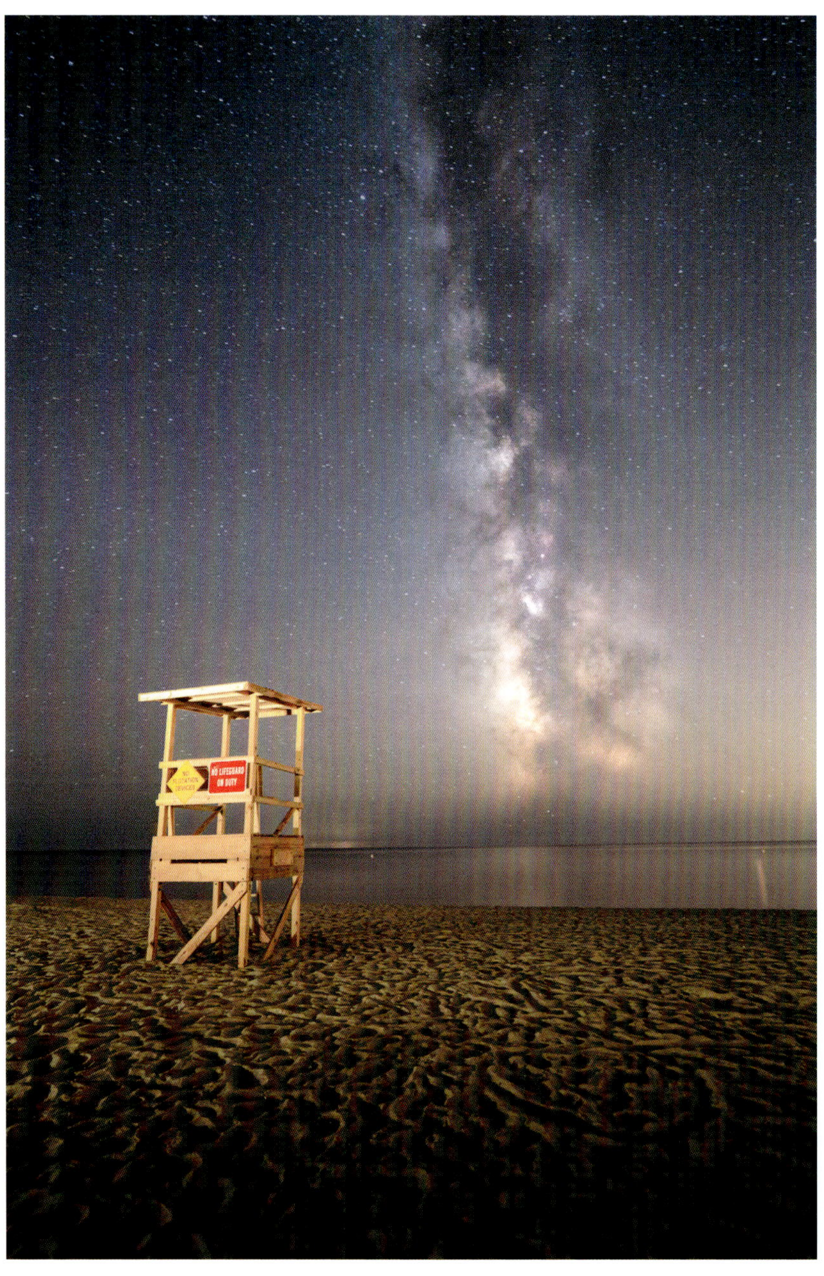

Cape Cod has an assortment of lifeguard chairs, each beach offering a different design from the next. This one, located at Hardings Beach, provides a front-row view of a summertime Milky Way. The soft glow along the horizon just to the right of the chair is from Nantucket. Around the Fourth of July, fireworks from the island are visible just above the waterline.

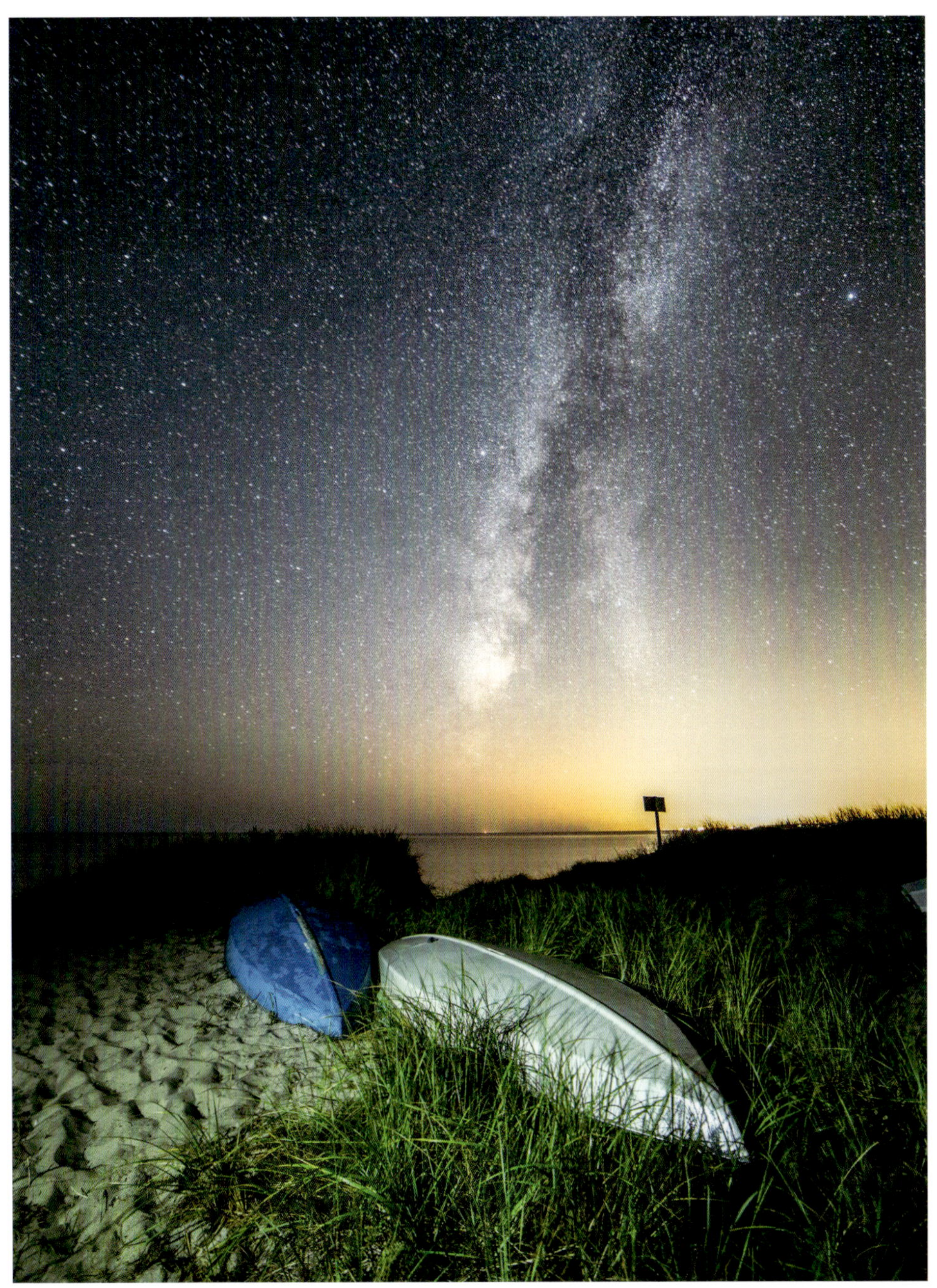

These boats are almost always here, lying in the sand dunes of Hardings Beach. Occasionally, they appear as though they have been moved. Are they abandoned? Someone knows.

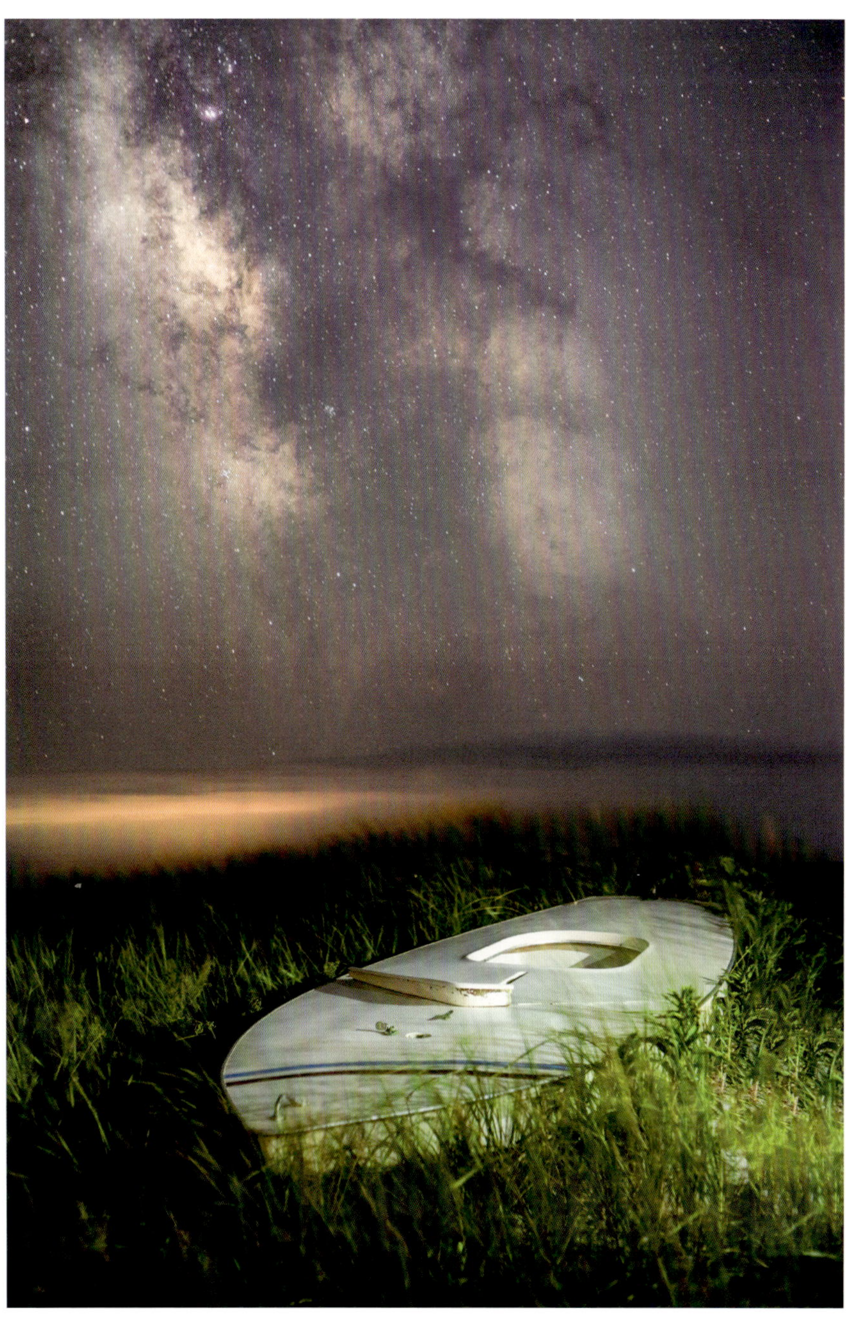

A small sailboat remains hidden in tall dune grass in Harwich. You never know what you might find if you take the time to look around.

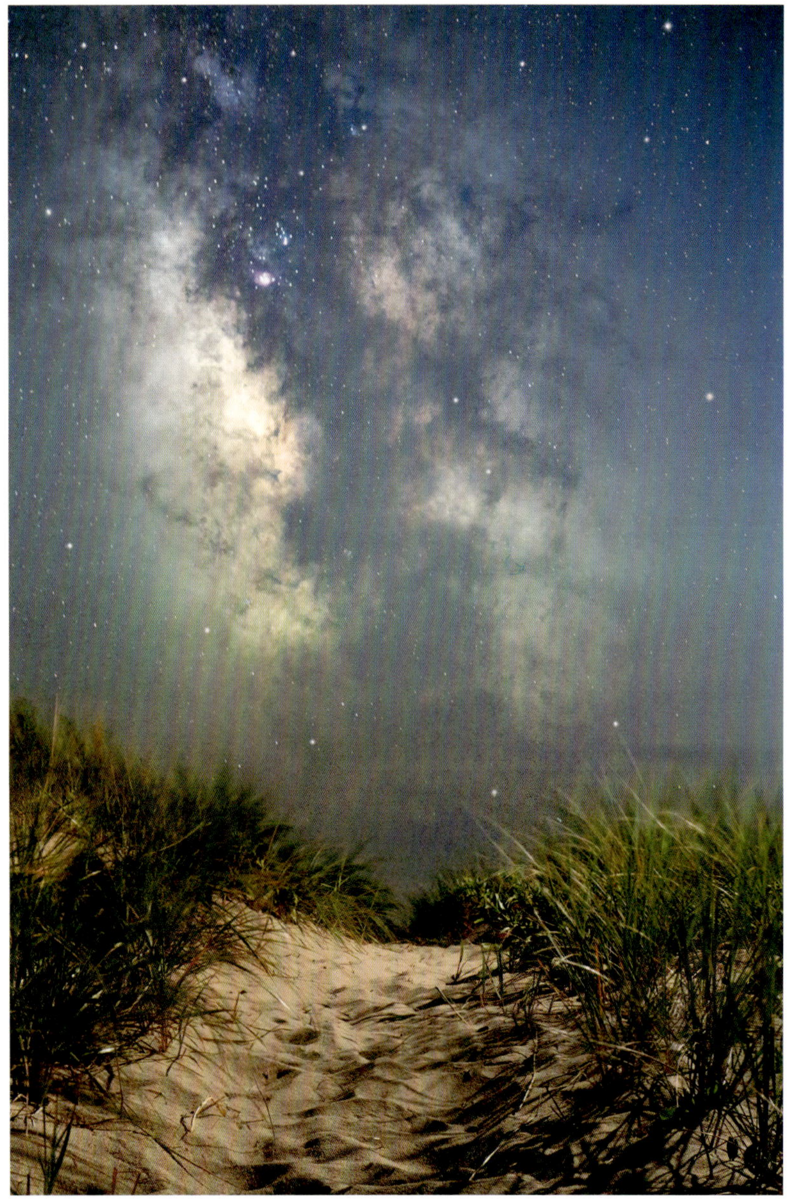

It took four photographs to accomplish this final image. Three of them were to capture just the foreground, using a technique called "focus stacking." Each image was focused on a different portion of the foreground, starting closest to the camera and then moving toward the horizon, and they all had to be lit the same. They were blended together during postproduction to bring the entire foreground into focus. The fourth photograph was for the Milky Way. The blur of the grass was due to the summer breeze.

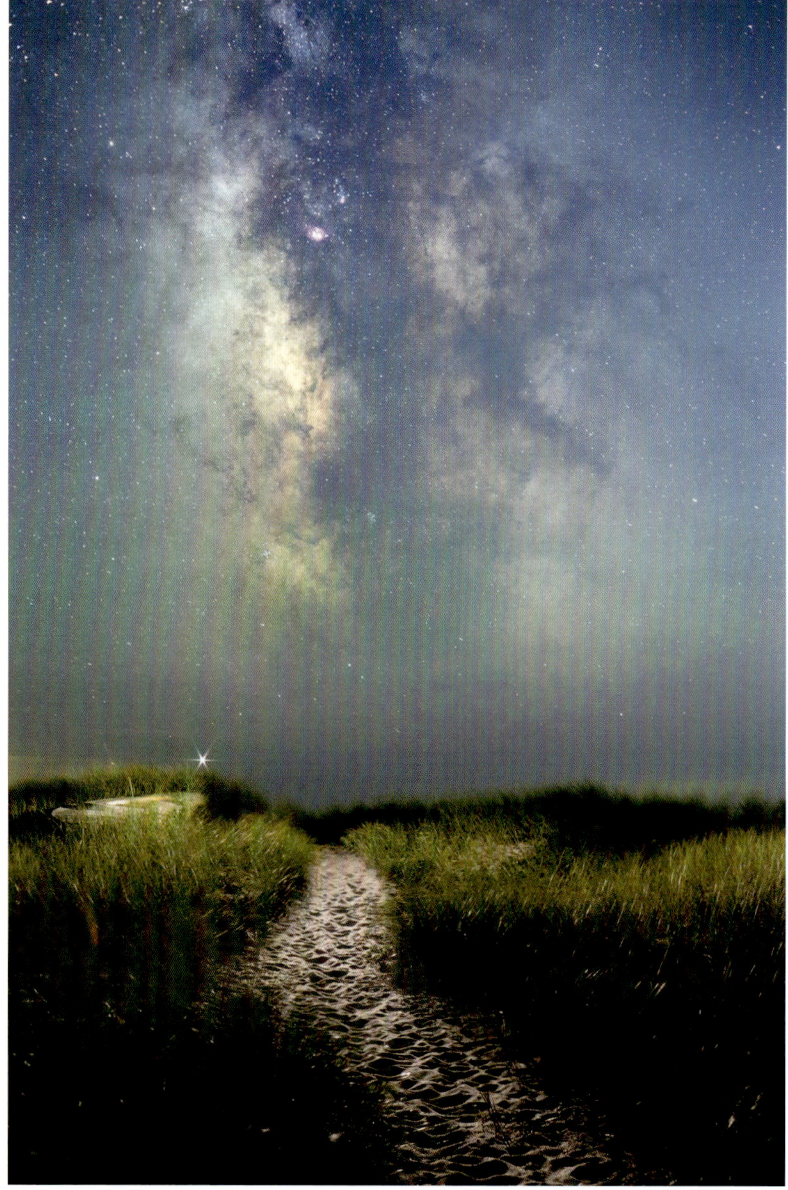

This image was taken on the same night as the previous image. The white light peeking over the grass is from the top of a boat mast, just offshore. The foreground was lit by a light held over my head after I found the right spot on a nearby hill. Aligning the slope of the Milky Way with a sandy path or woodsy trail always makes for a great composition.

Exploring the far ends of Salt Pond in Eastham is rewarding for anyone willing to make the hike, but be careful. High-tide cycles can flood the path behind you. At the end of the trail, leading around the left side of the pond, is this shed. In June the sky can be seen as it appears here.

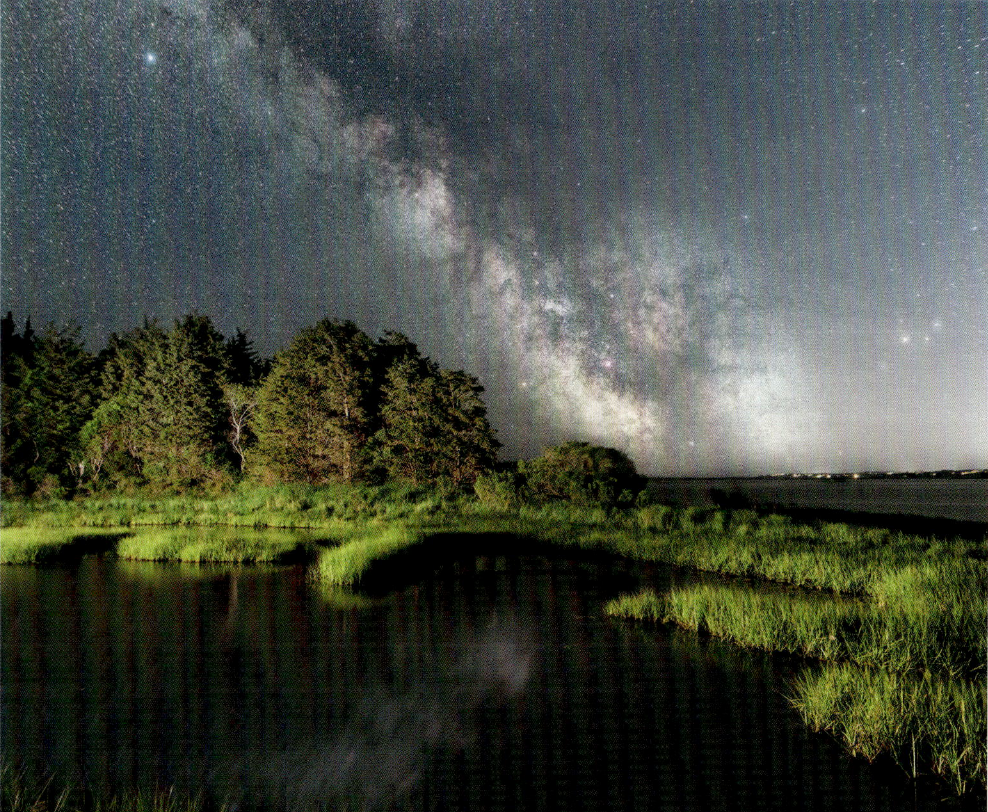

A little farther beyond the shack is this inlet. It is a squishy walk to this hidden gem, often missed by photographers. The foreground was lit from two locations. The purple glow of the Lagoon Nebula is easily seen at the center of the Milky Way core.

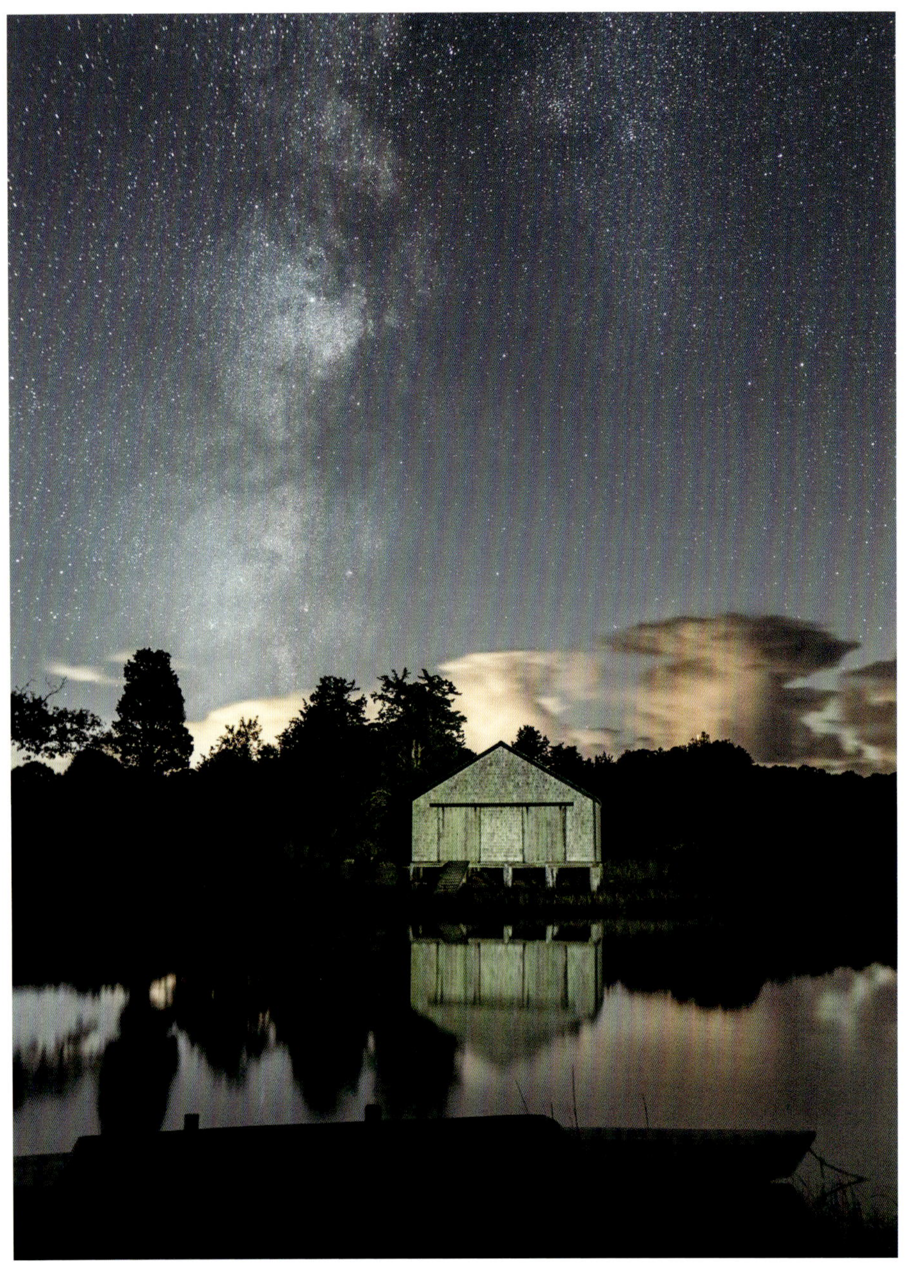

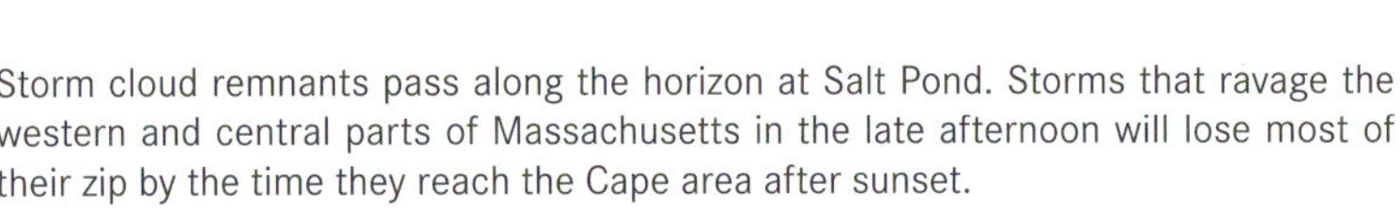

Storm cloud remnants pass along the horizon at Salt Pond. Storms that ravage the western and central parts of Massachusetts in the late afternoon will lose most of their zip by the time they reach the Cape area after sunset.

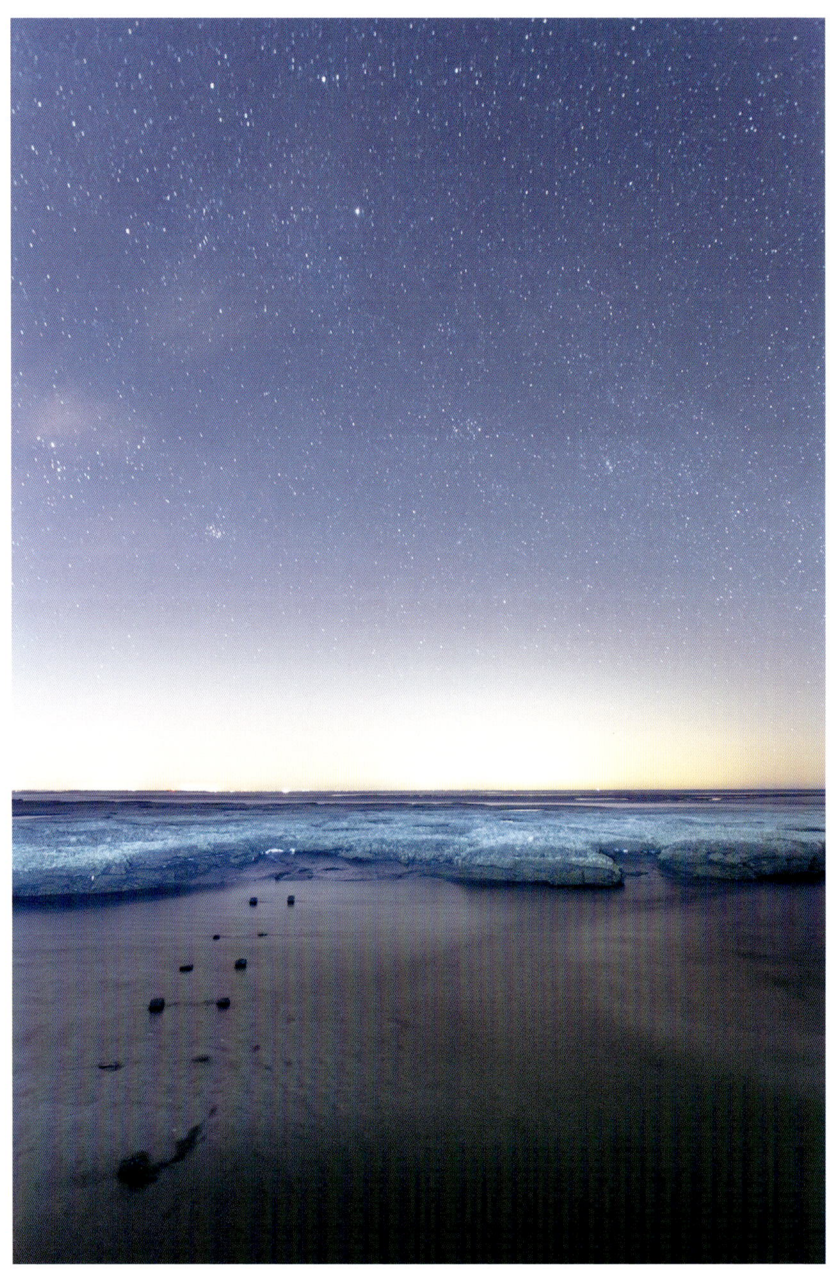

A chilly night at the end of the Bass Hole Boardwalk. The “ice” was simulated by waving a cool-white light across the top of the sea grass. The glow in the distance is not sunset, but rather the lighting from Plymouth. Light pollution is frequently visible when photographing toward the west from this location along Cape Cod Bay.

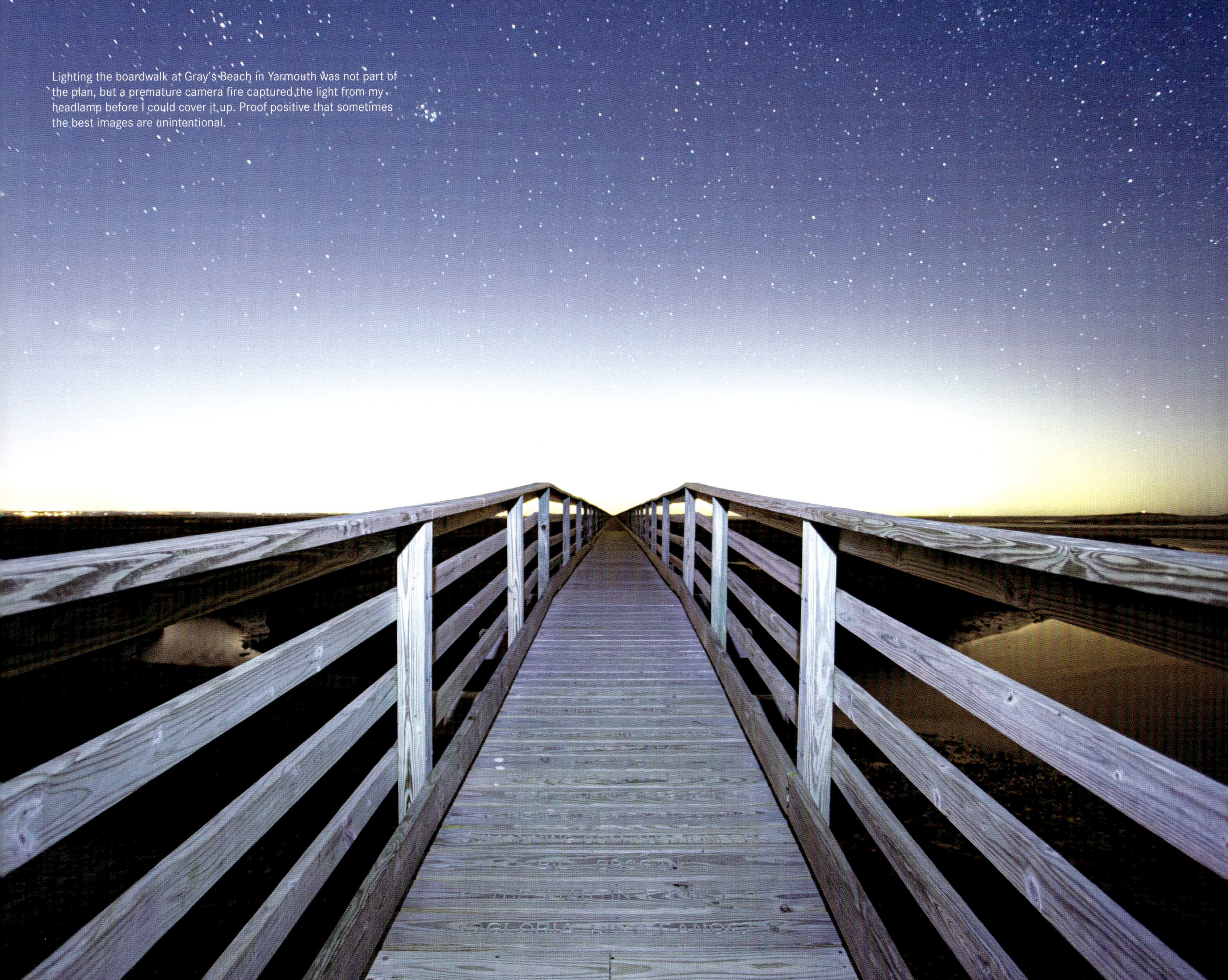

Lighting the boardwalk at Gray's Beach in Yarmouth was not part of the plan, but a premature camera fire captured the light from my headlamp before I could cover it up. Proof positive that sometimes the best images are unintentional.

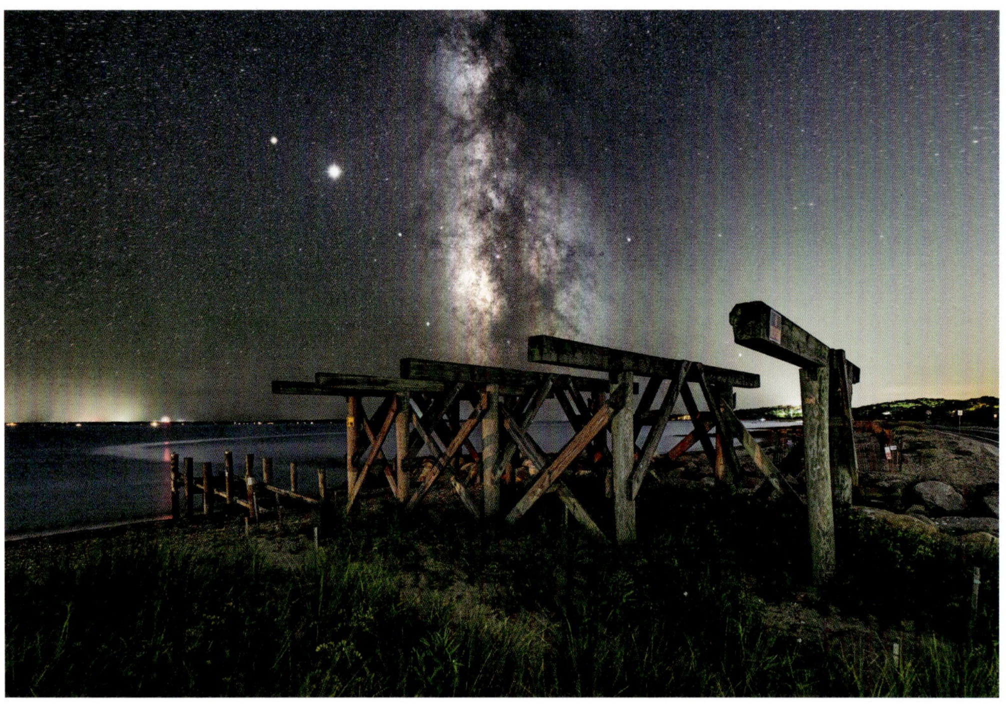

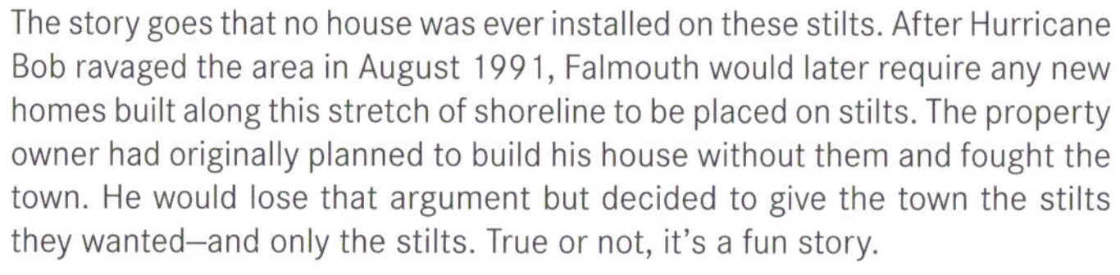

The story goes that no house was ever installed on these stilts. After Hurricane Bob ravaged the area in August 1991, Falmouth would later require any new homes built along this stretch of shoreline to be placed on stilts. The property owner had originally planned to build his house without them and fought the town. He would lose that argument but decided to give the town the stilts they wanted—and only the stilts. True or not, it's a fun story.

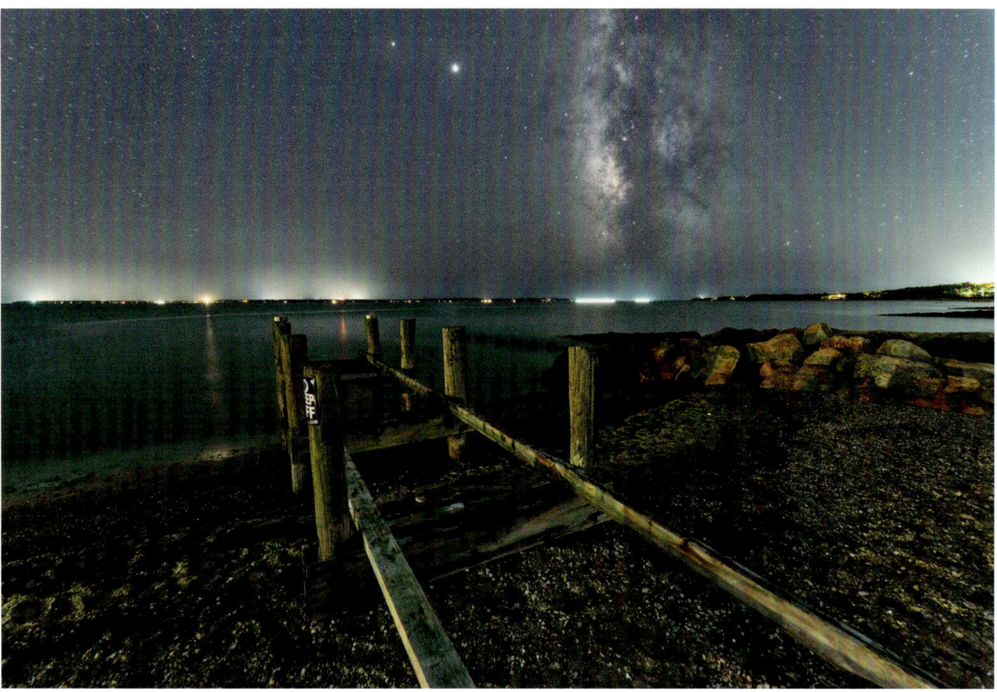

The leftovers of the dock behind the old stilts. Year after year, the horizontal planks were washed away. Now, it occasionally serves as a nighttime fishing spot or a photo opportunity for passersby. More often, it is just a place for birds to perch and to judge beachgoers.

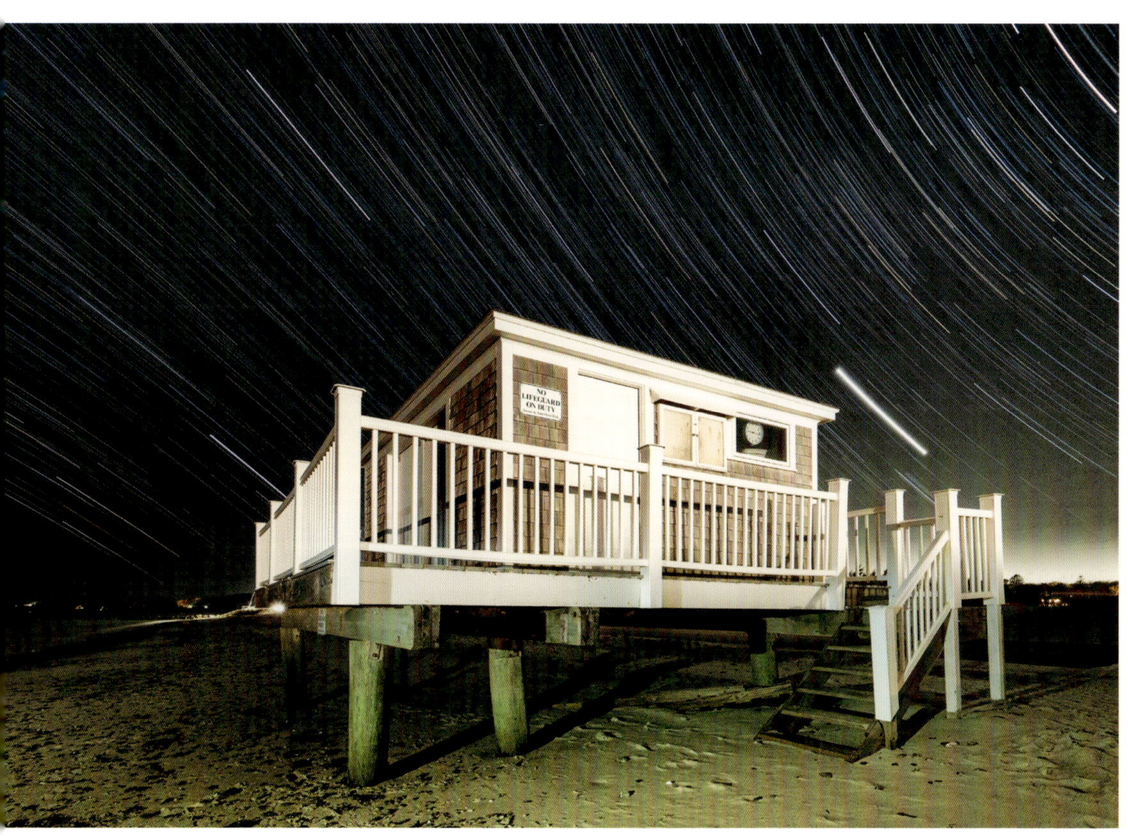

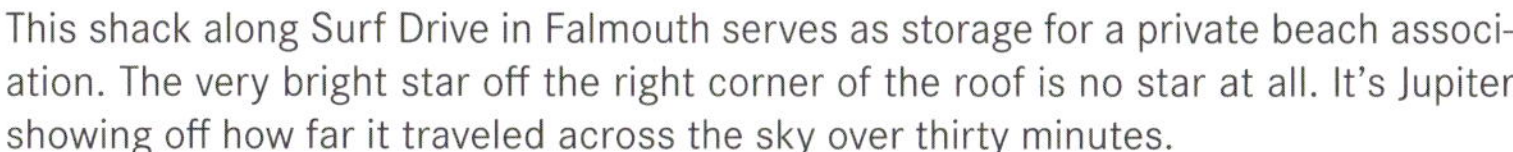

This shack along Surf Drive in Falmouth serves as storage for a private beach association. The very bright star off the right corner of the roof is no star at all. It's Jupiter showing off how far it traveled across the sky over thirty minutes.

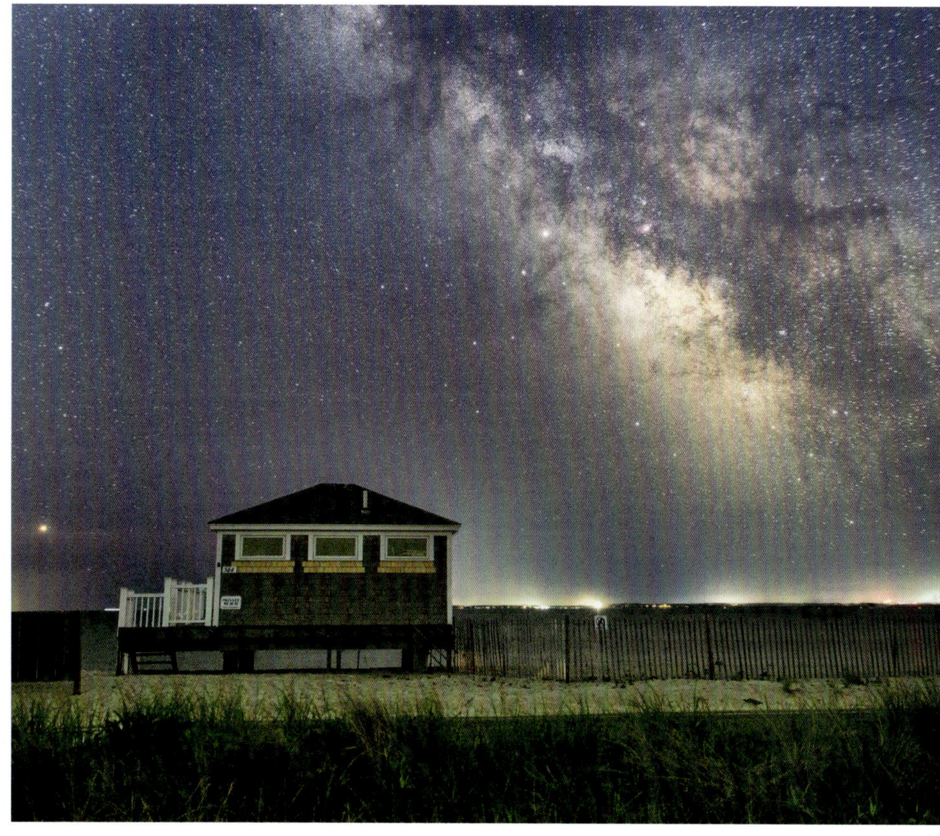

The same cabin on a different night, making a great foreground for the Milky Way as it travels over the Vineyard in the distance. Despite the late hour, many cars passed by as drivers enjoyed the starry view of the sound. Surf Drive is where you go when you want to enjoy your convertible, motorcycle, or bike.

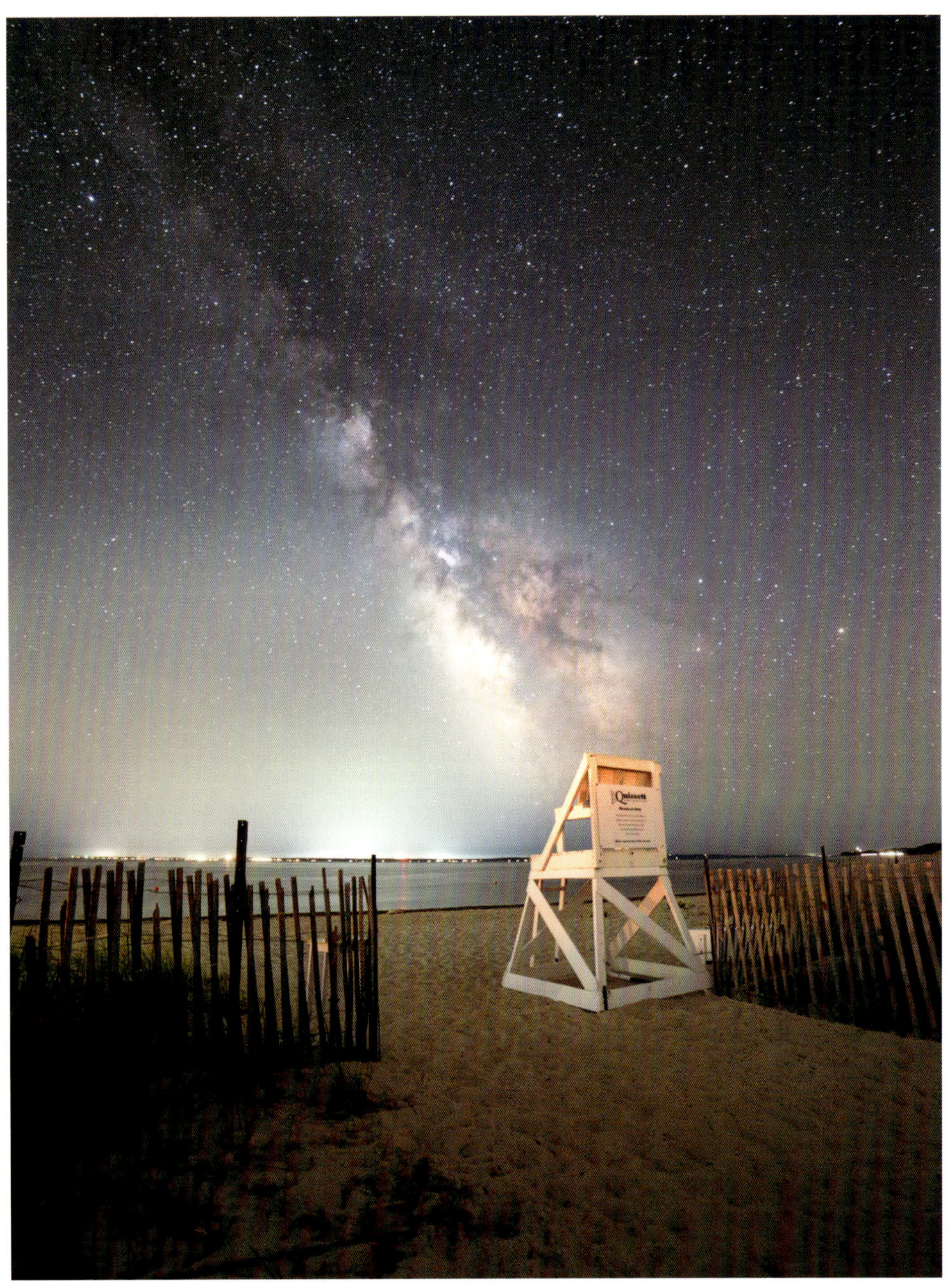

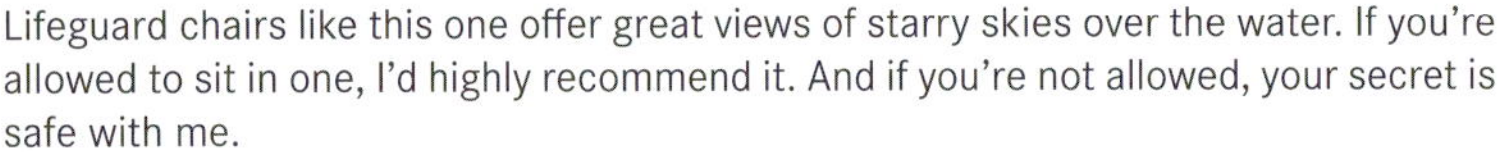

Lifeguard chairs like this one offer great views of starry skies over the water. If you're allowed to sit in one, I'd highly recommend it. And if you're not allowed, your secret is safe with me.

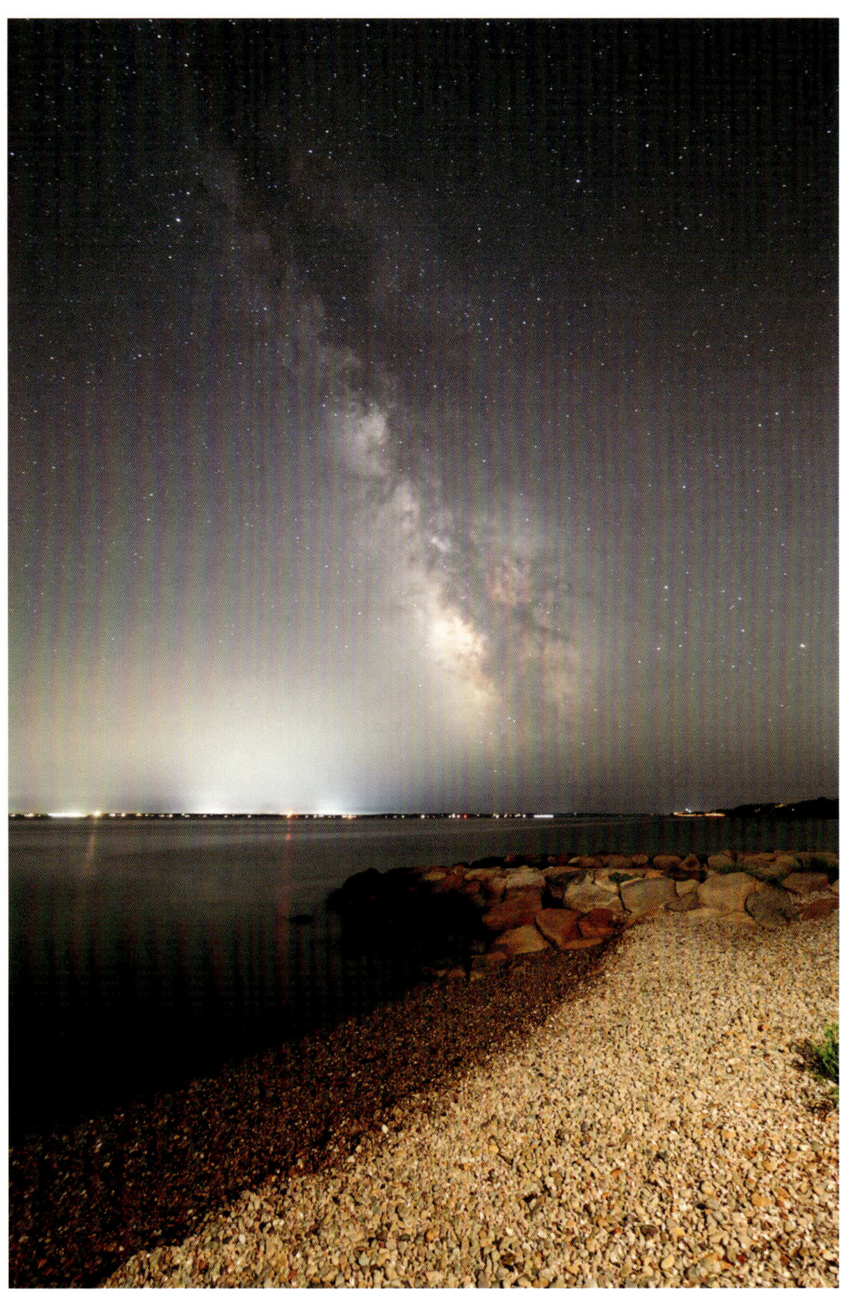

The shoreline in Falmouth can offer spectacular views of the Milky Way throughout the late winter and into June. Despite rumors to the contrary, photographing starry skies here is entirely possible. Although not as dark as the Cape Cod National Seashore, give it a chance to impress you anyway.

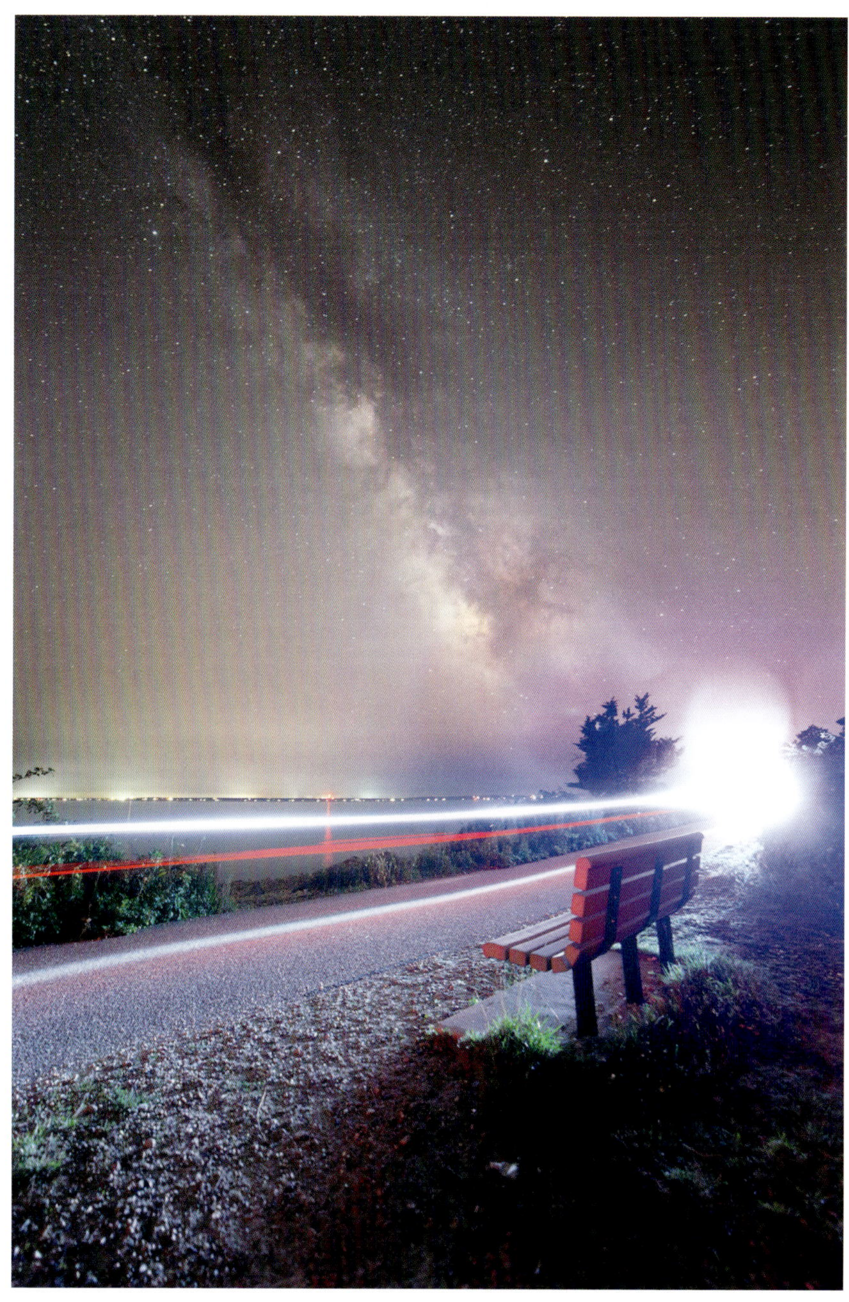

A Milky Way shot along the Shining Sea Bikeway sabotaged by a bicycle with head- and taillights! Despite the late hour, it is common for bikes to whiz by as workers from Woods Hole return home.

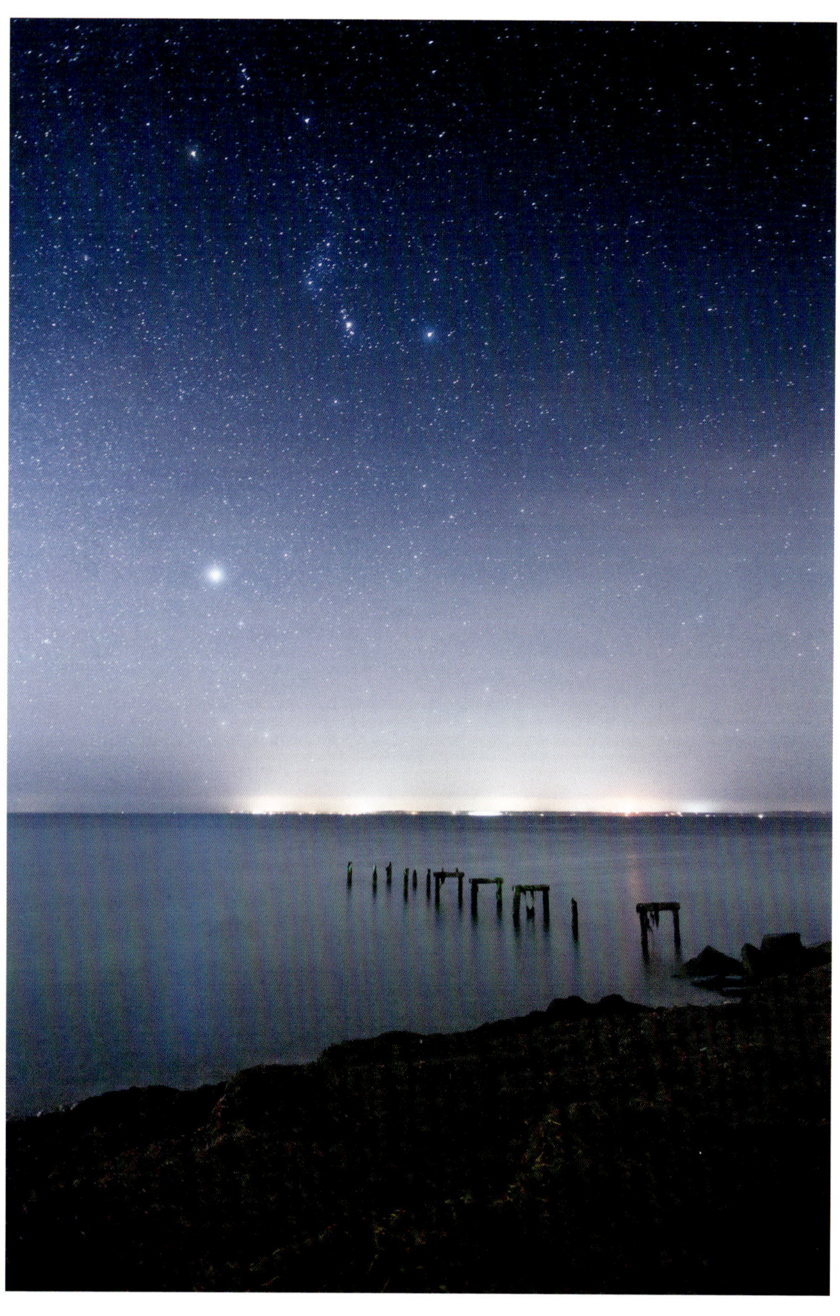

Old dock pilings greet the constellation of Orion as it appears over Martha's Vineyard. The bright star low to the horizon is known as Sirius and is the brightest star visible from Earth, besides our own sun. See them both during the winter months from anywhere on Cape Cod.

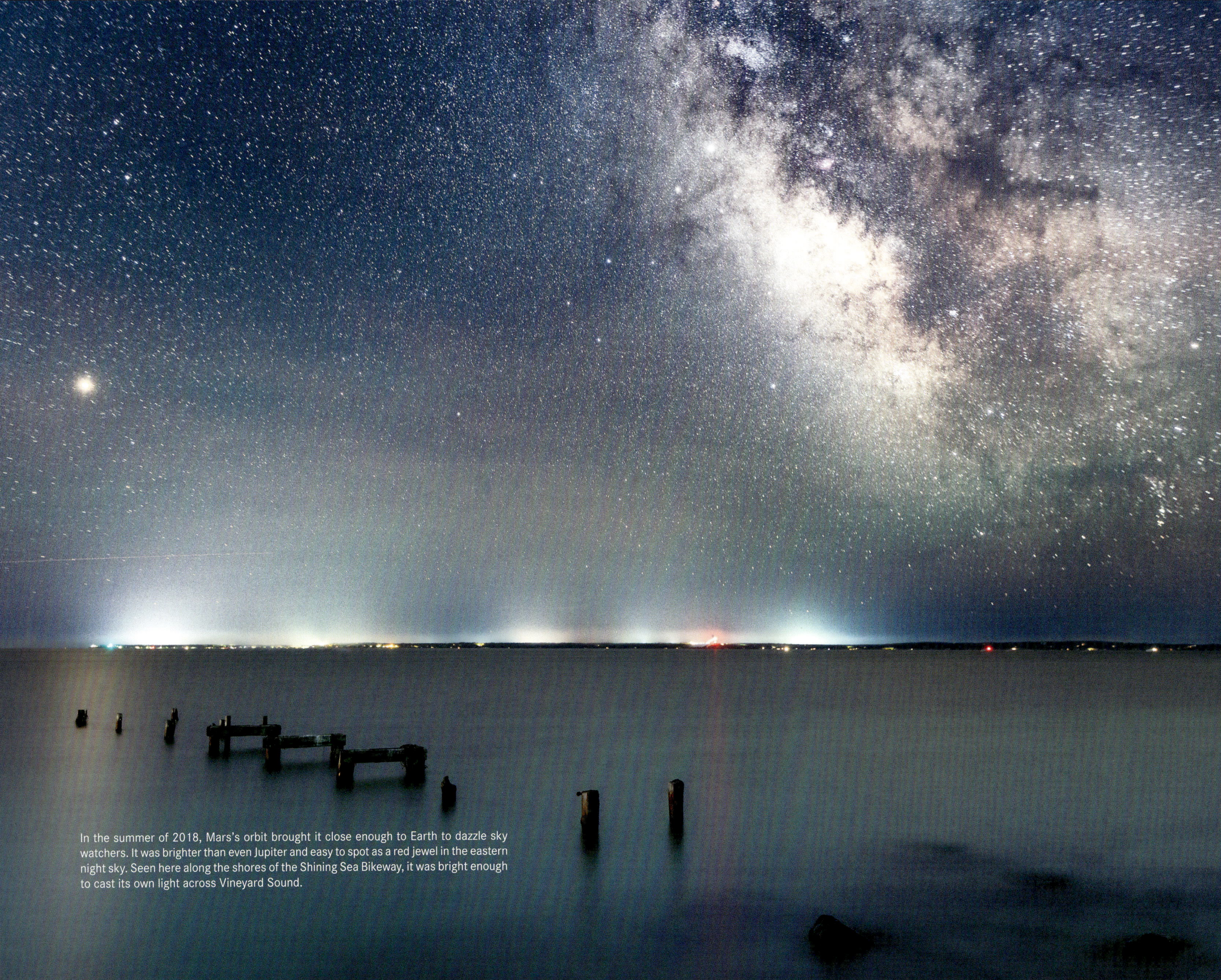

In the summer of 2018, Mars's orbit brought it close enough to Earth to dazzle sky watchers. It was brighter than even Jupiter and easy to spot as a red jewel in the eastern night sky. Seen here along the shores of the Shining Sea Bikeway, it was bright enough to cast its own light across Vineyard Sound.

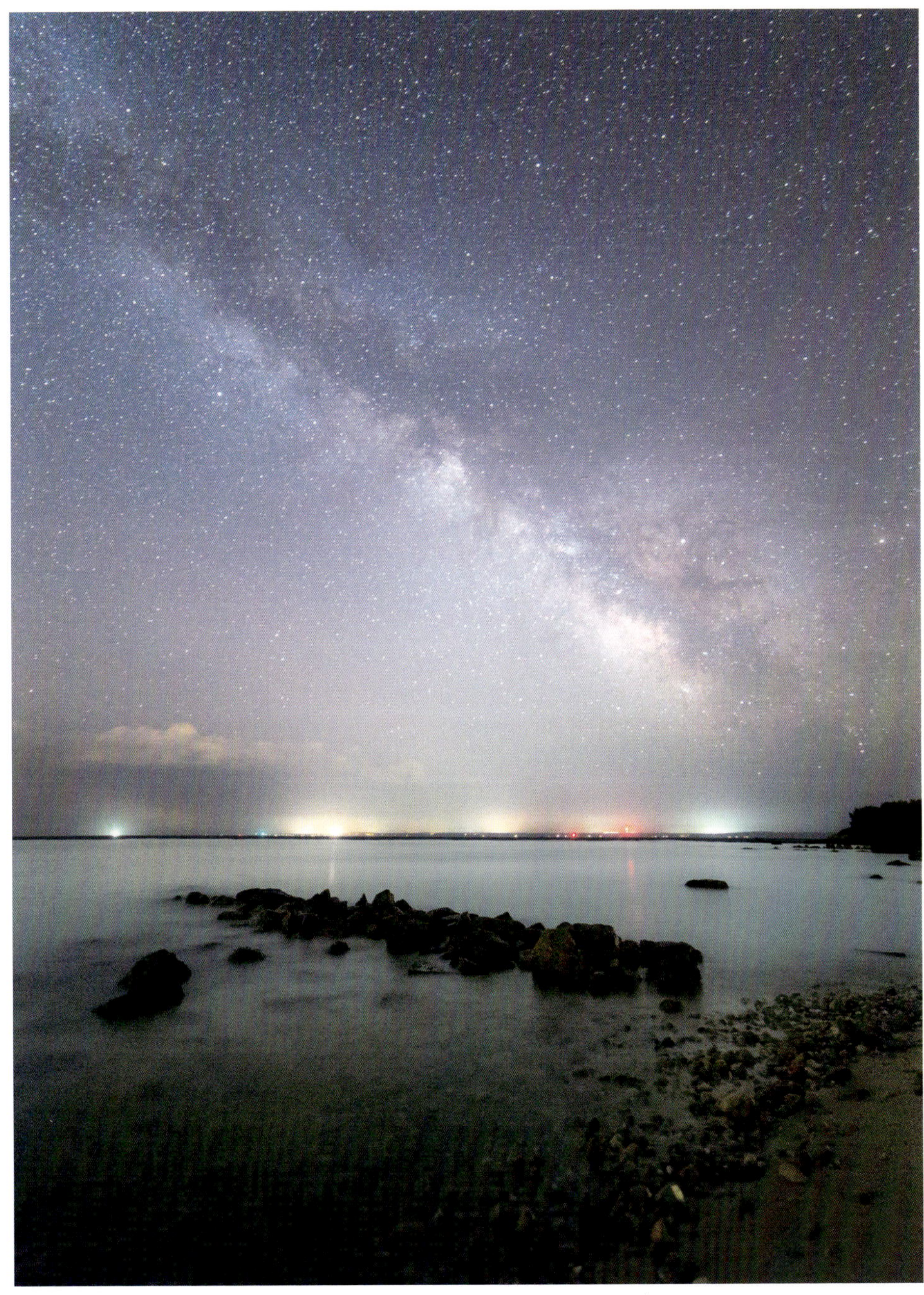

A rocky shore gives way to an old jetty under starry skies.

A little help from a flashlight helps reveal the shoreline in Falmouth as clouds push away from a summertime Milky Way.

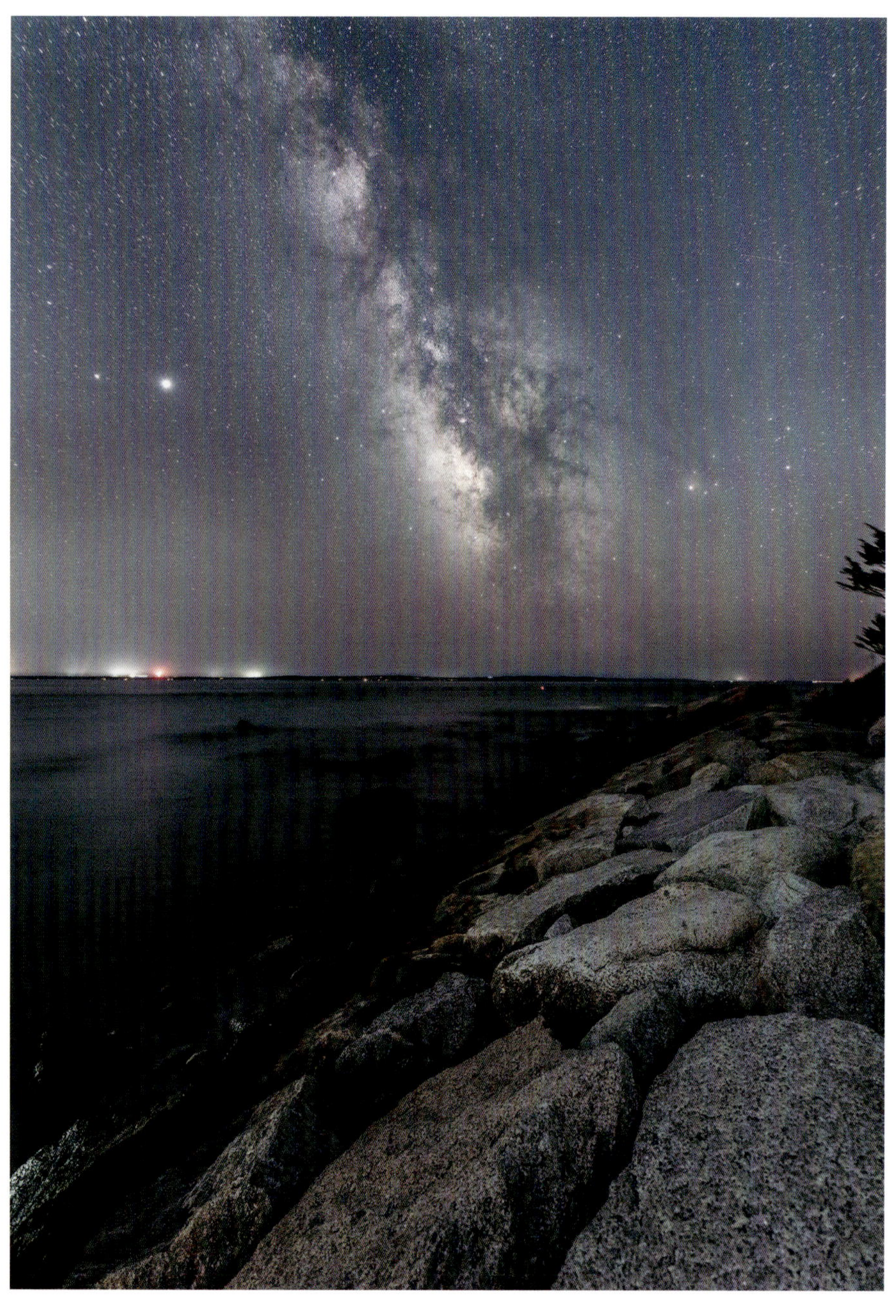

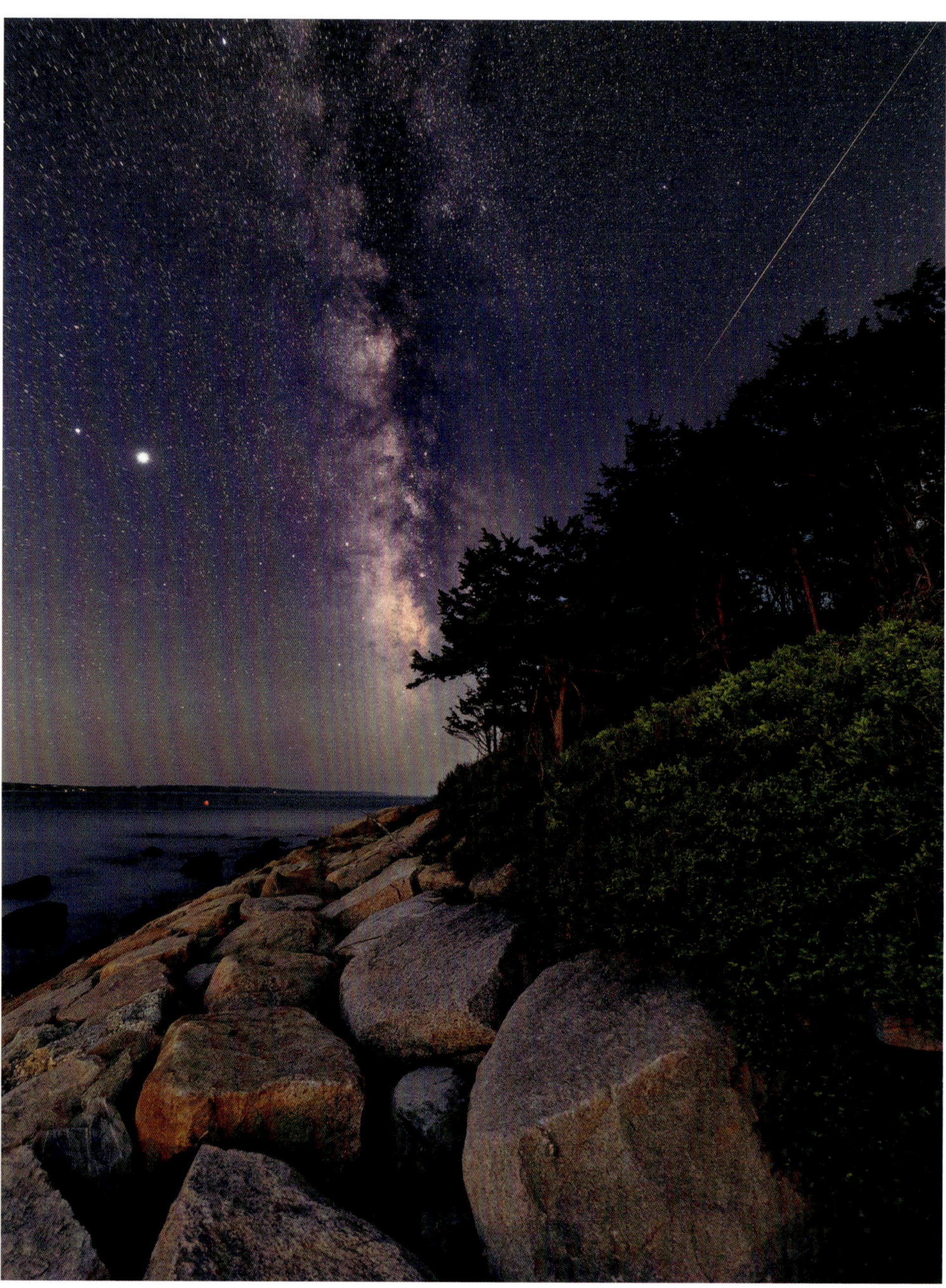

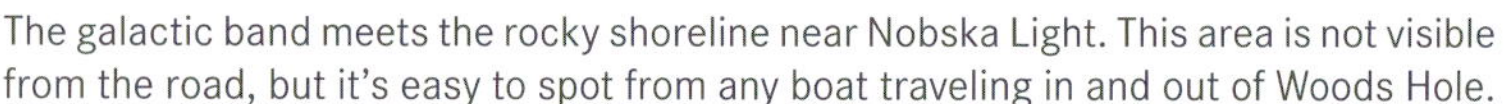

The galactic band meets the rocky shoreline near Nobska Light. This area is not visible from the road, but it's easy to spot from any boat traveling in and out of Woods Hole.

A little while later, the dawn caught up with me. The warm morning glow of twilight began to slowly change the color tones of the sky before the Milky Way would disappear. The line seen streaking across the sky is caused by sunlight reflecting from the International Space Station.

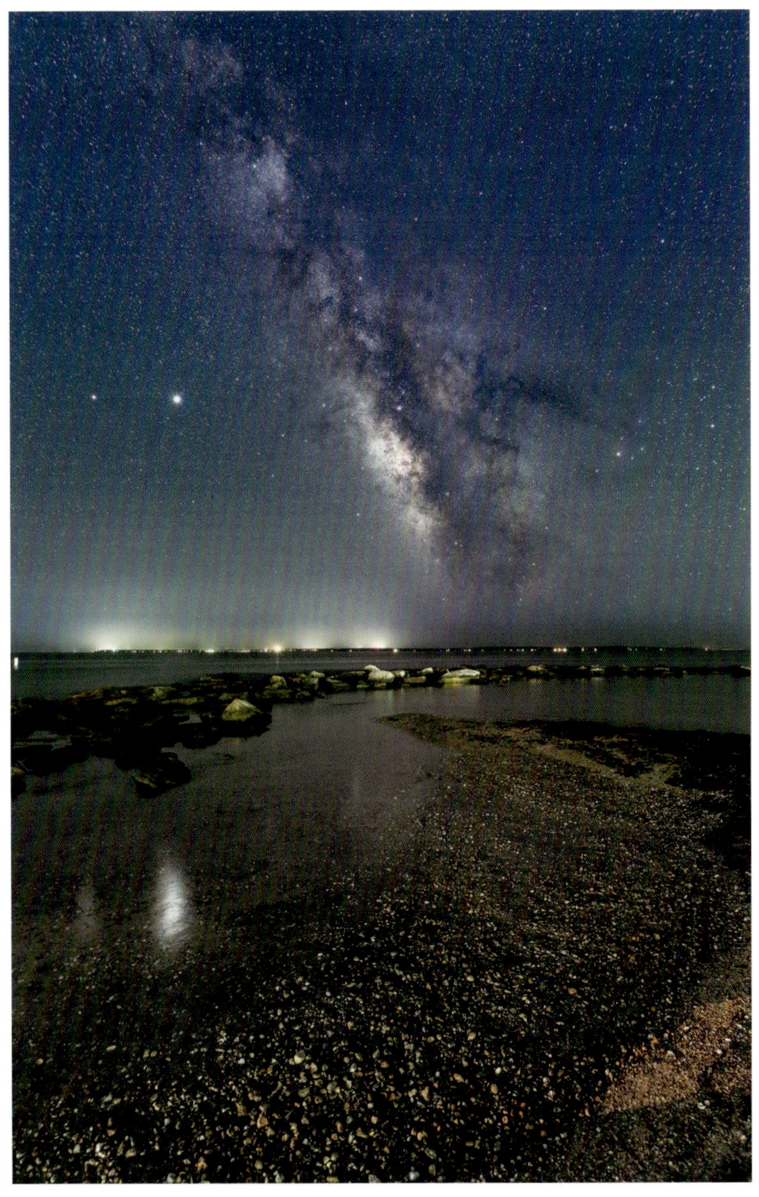

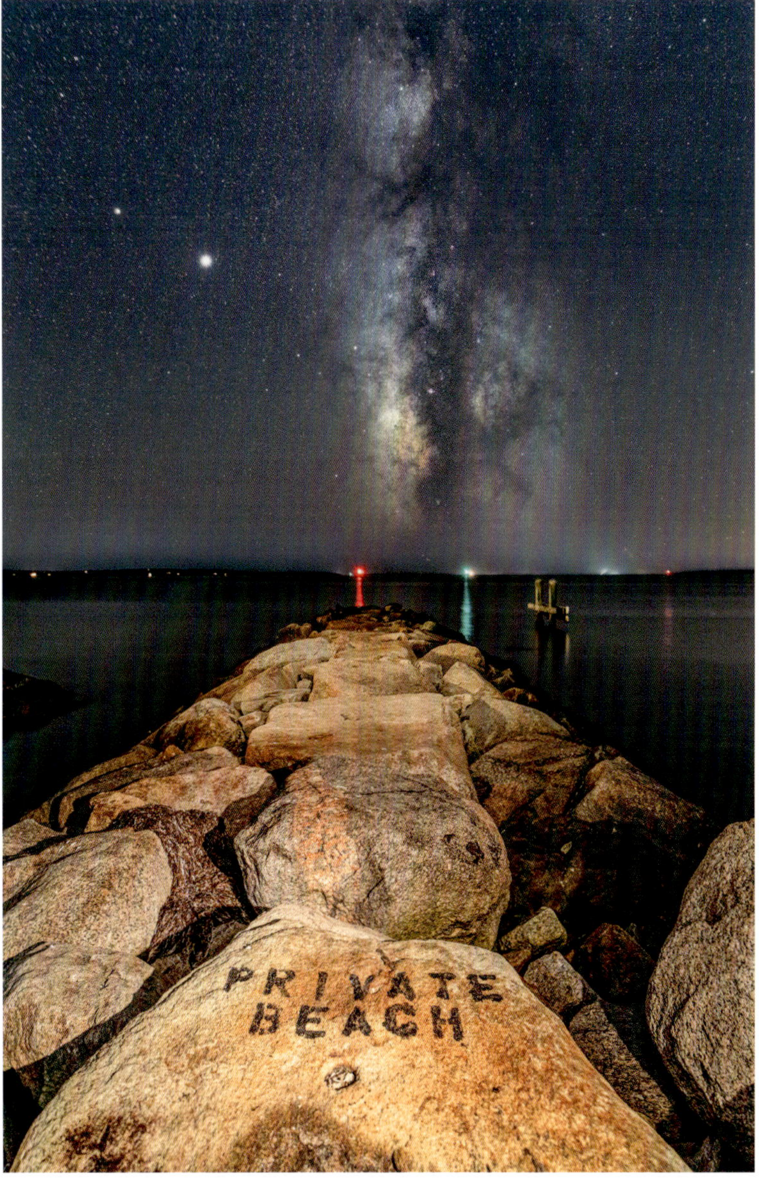

Many photographers have insisted that you cannot get a good shot of the Milky Way from the shores of Falmouth. By now, you know that's not true, as further evidenced here in this image from 2020. Also making an appearance are two bright points to the left of the Milky Way core. You may see these in other images taken that year. The brighter of the two is Jupiter; the other is Saturn. Over the course of 2020, these two planets appeared to get closer and closer, until a rare convergence on December 21 created what some considered a single, bright Christmas star. I waited all year to see it. We had mostly cloudy skies that night.

Photographic evidence that one night an image of the Milky Way, with Jupiter and Saturn in hot pursuit, was captured on a rock jetty marked private. Let's just keep that between us.

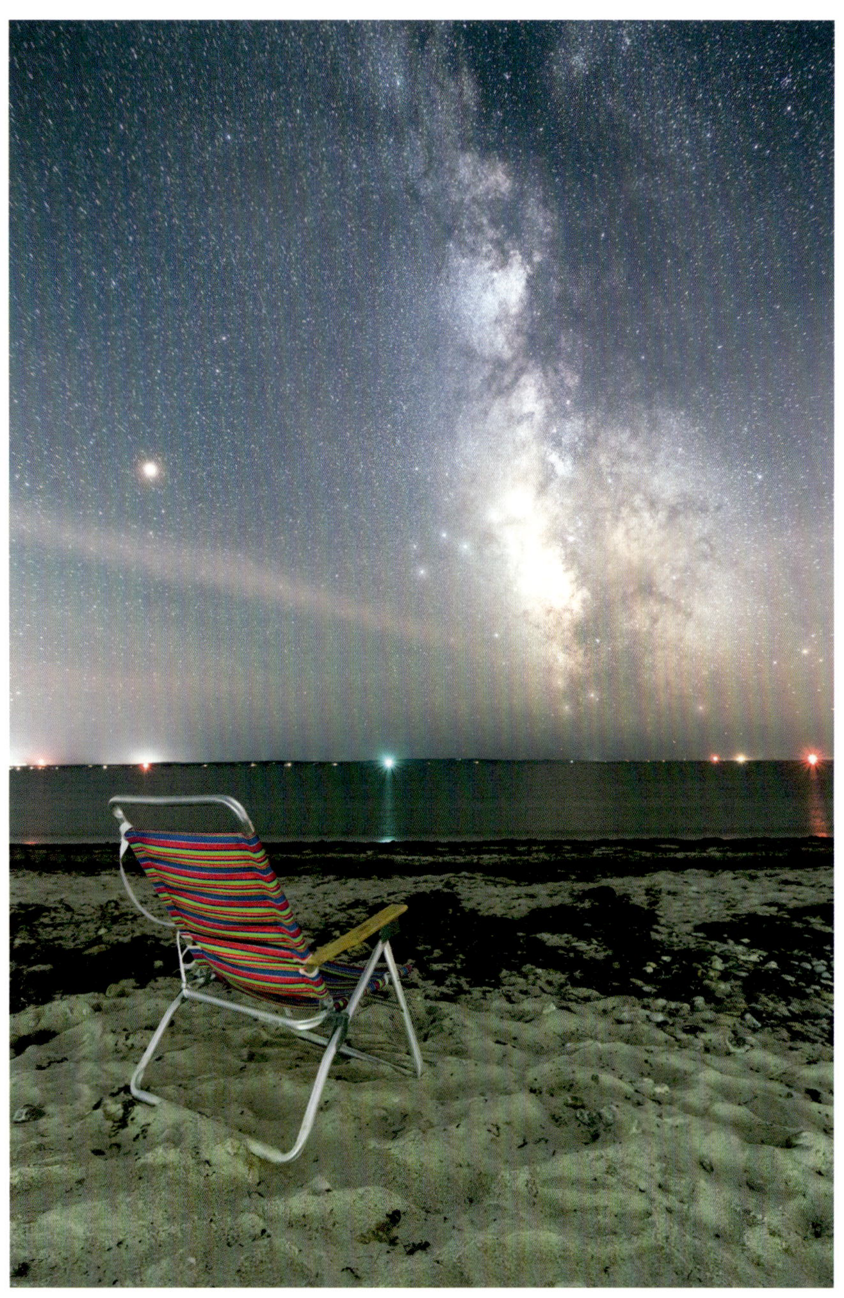

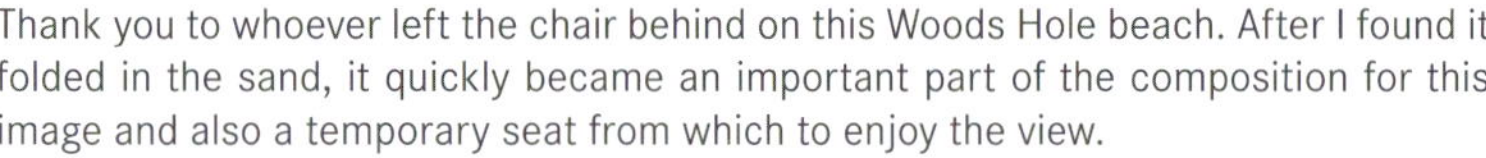

Thank you to whoever left the chair behind on this Woods Hole beach. After I found it folded in the sand, it quickly became an important part of the composition for this image and also a temporary seat from which to enjoy the view.

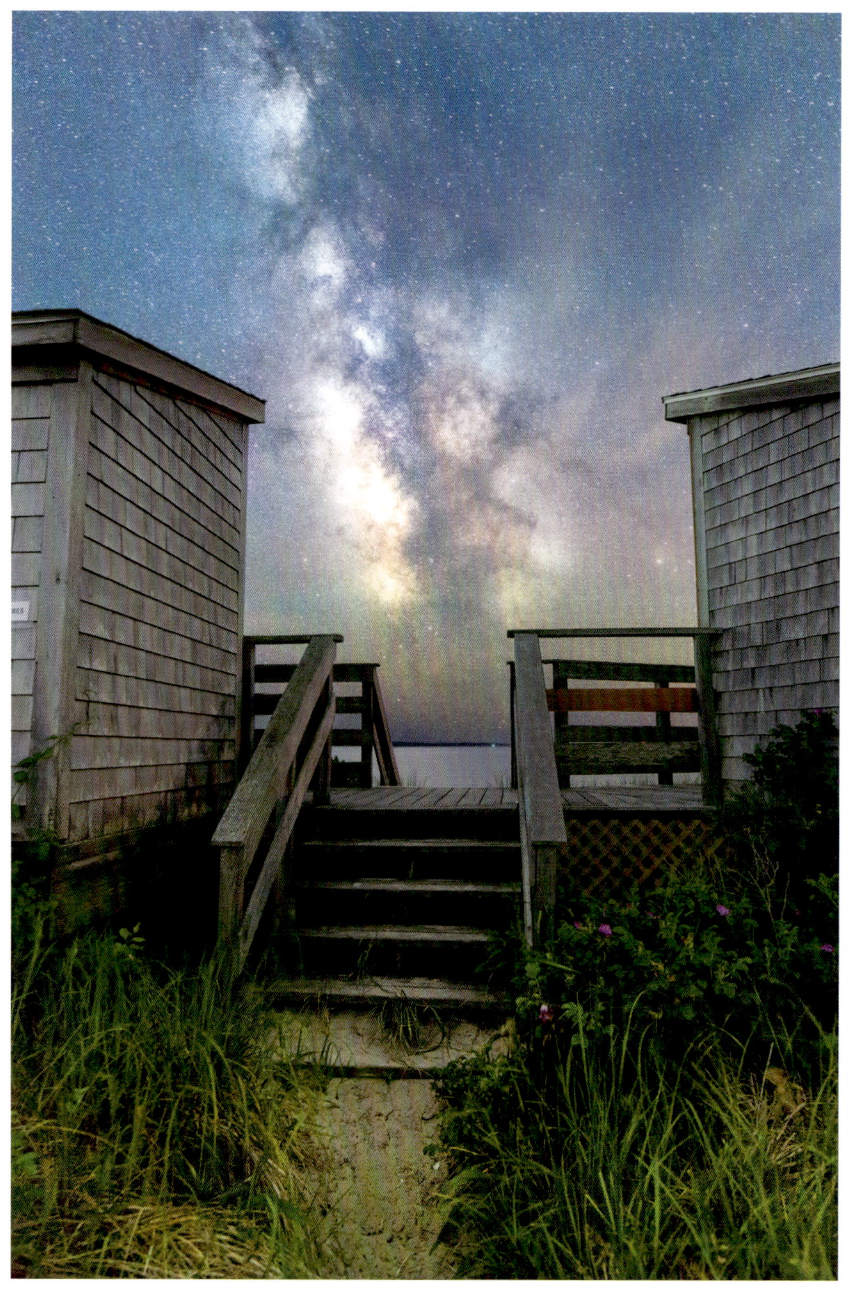

For a brief few moments, the galactic core aligns just right with these steps to a private beach in Woods Hole. Planning and patience can reward you with an organic opportunity like this.

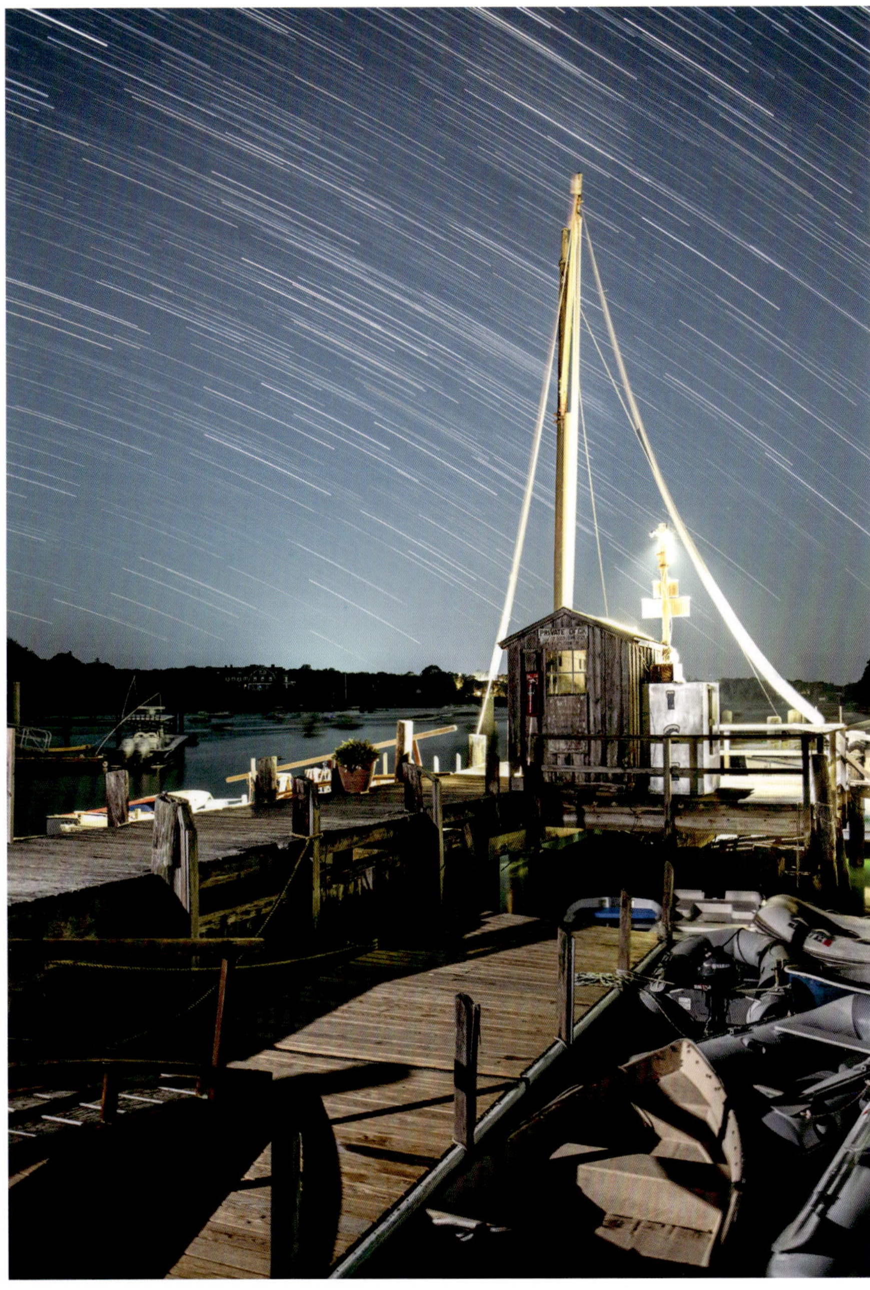

A south-facing view of the dock near the Quissett Harbor Boatyard. On a quiet night, you will often hear fish jumping out of the water and maybe even see the distant light of a kayaker's headlamp.

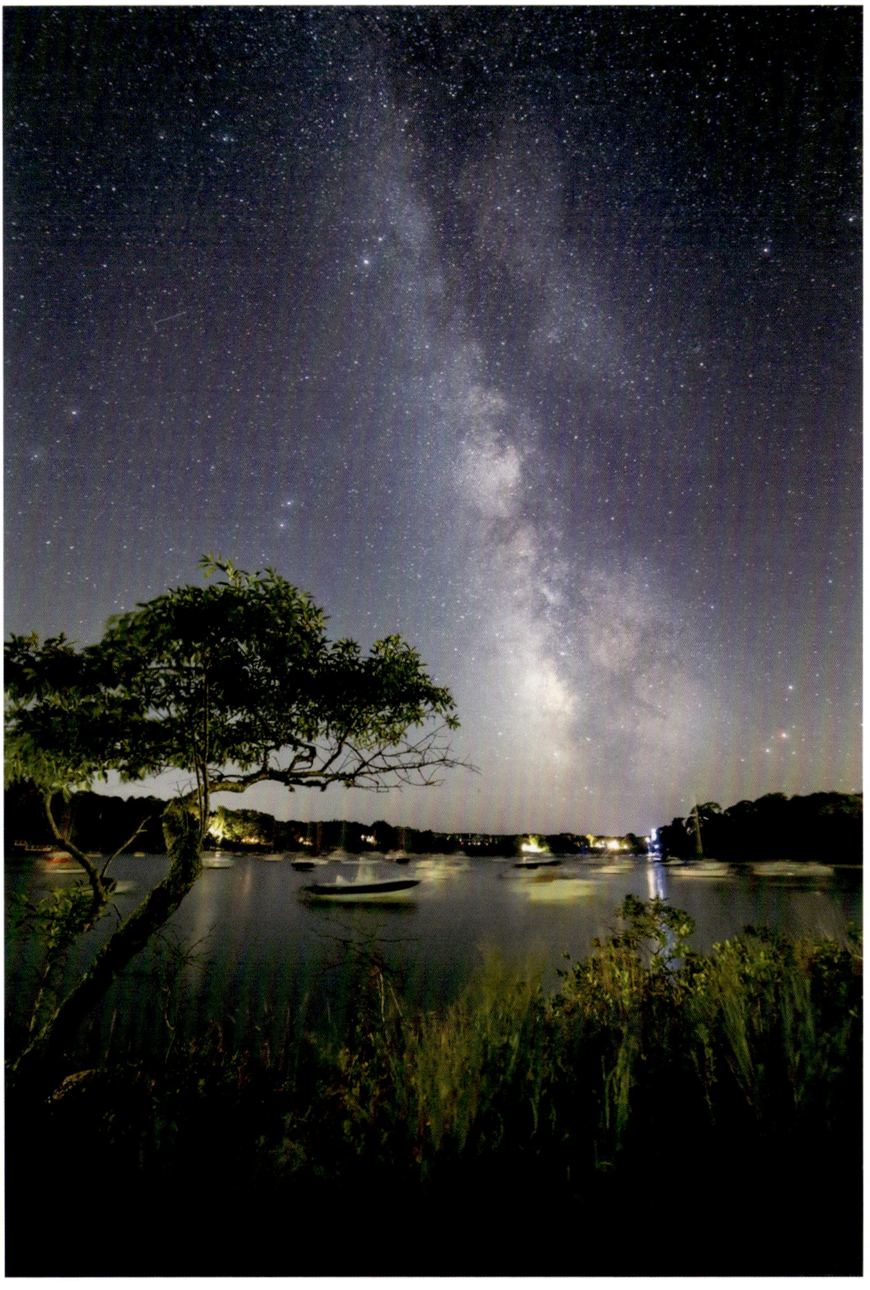

This tree at Quissett Harbor always seemed a little out of place. Wind can affect the shape and growth direction of a tree, and this is most obvious around harbors and near beaches. They make great foreground elements for starry nights.

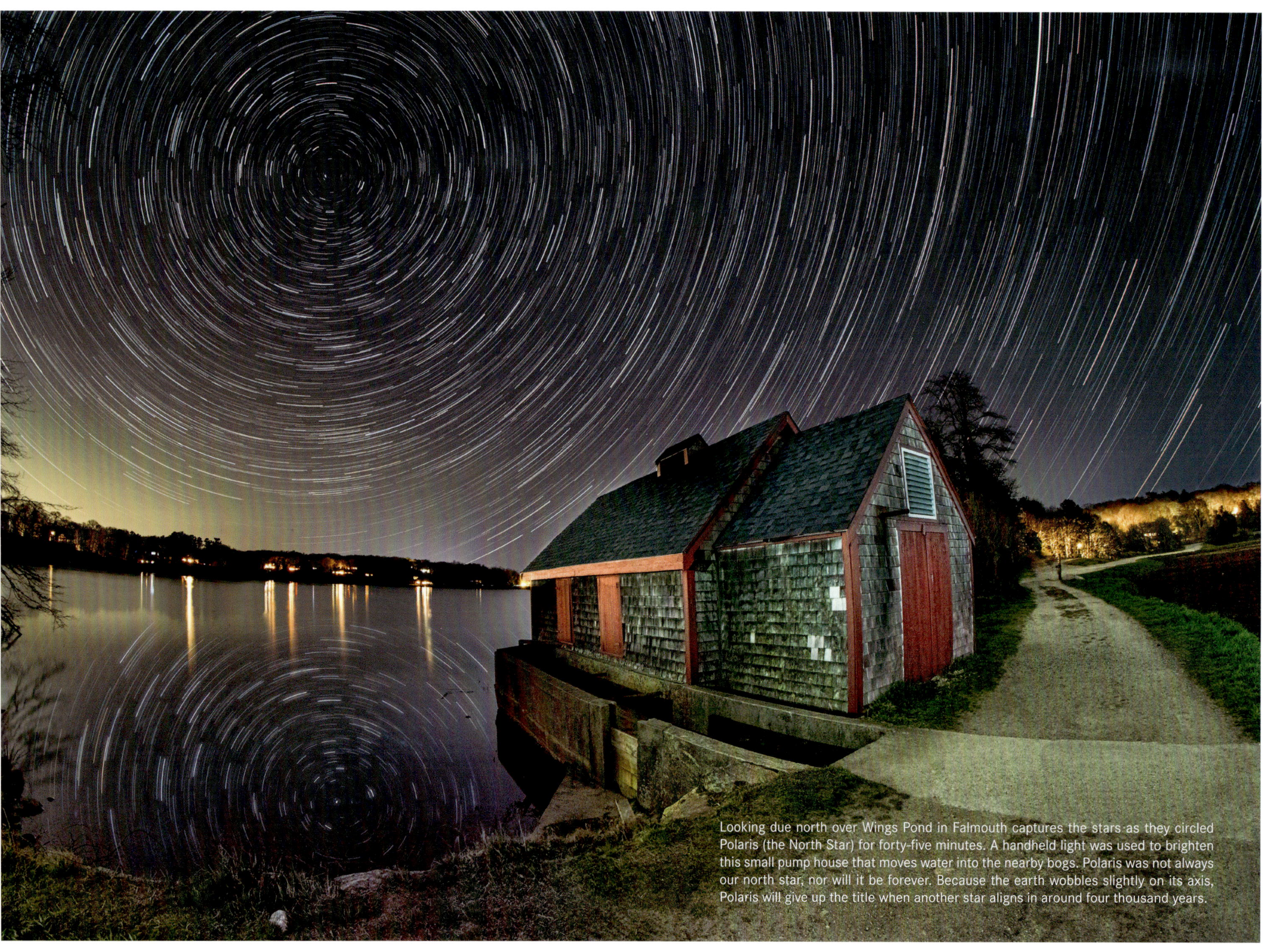

Looking due north over Wings Pond in Falmouth captures the stars as they circled Polaris (the North Star) for forty-five minutes. A handheld light was used to brighten this small pump house that moves water into the nearby bogs. Polaris was not always our north star, nor will it be forever. Because the earth wobbles slightly on its axis, Polaris will give up the title when another star aligns in around four thousand years.

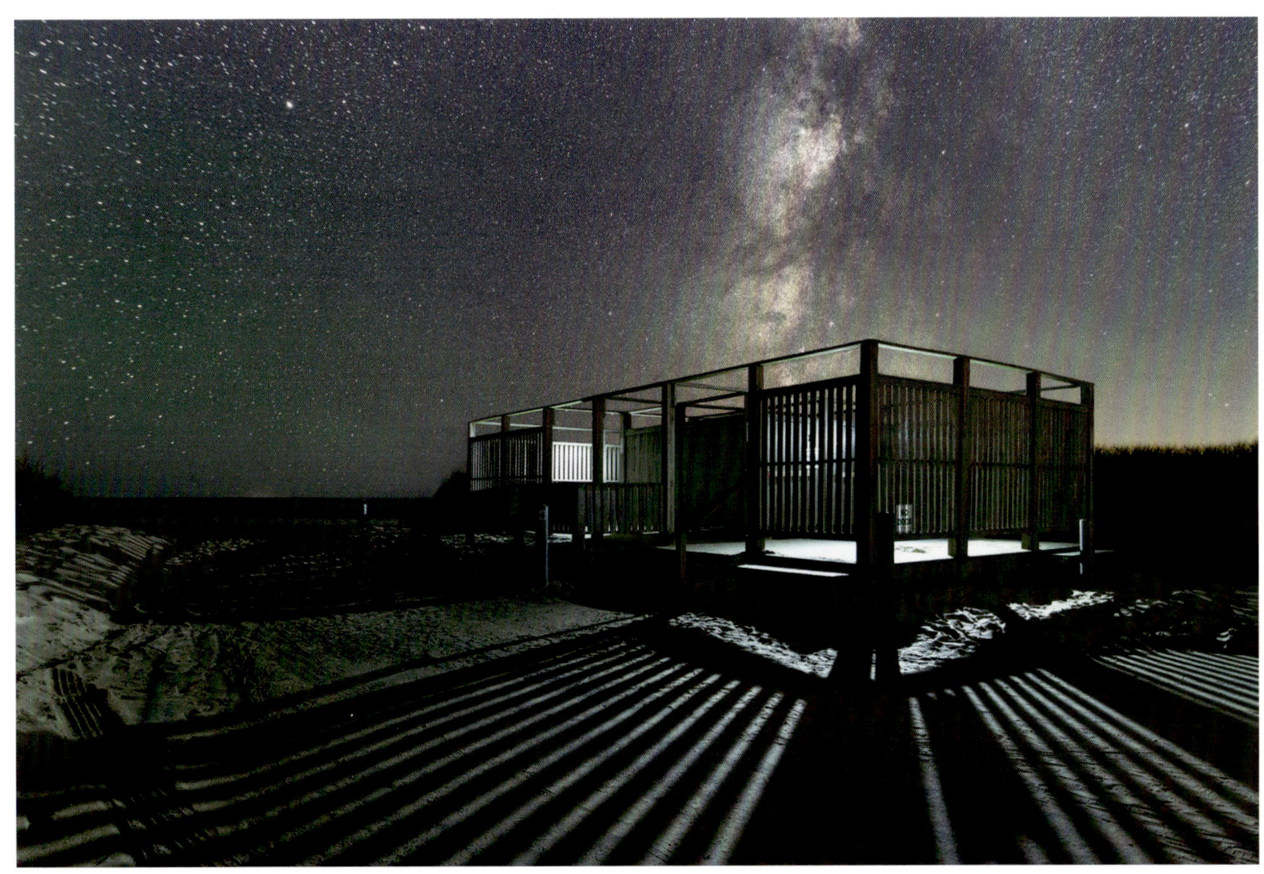

Many area beaches have structures like this serving as a place to change on the way in or out. Katama is part of Edgartown and is quite dark, making it a great place for stargazing. The lighting effect was completed by shining a flashlight from two positions and slowly sweeping it across the scene to project the shadows. Around the same time, I could hear a group of girls approaching the area. They hadn't seen me until I started shining my light, at which time I heard a scream, and then they ran away!

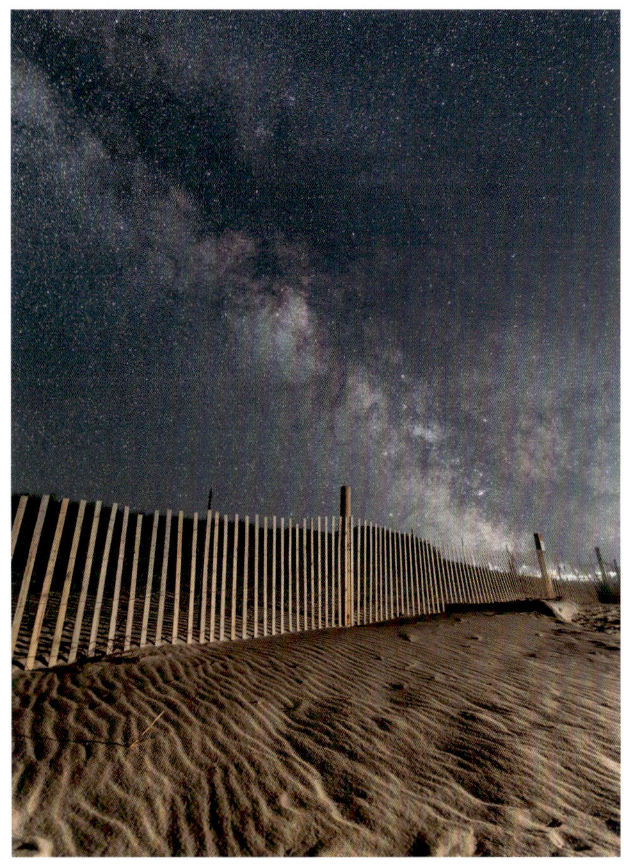

Wind can create interesting patterns in beach sand, which can be further enhanced with the right lighting. Here, a fence helps keep the sand from pushing farther inland and beachgoers off the dunes in Menemsha.

If you've ever looked through photographs of the beaches of Martha's Vineyard, there is no doubt you have seen an image or two from Lucy Vincent Beach in Chilmark. For a time, one of its photographic wonders was a particular rock formation that was reminiscent of a column and sat along the shoreline. But a storm eventually wiped it out. Still, this beach and others nearby are peppered with interesting boulders, driftwood, and cliffs. Best of all, the view from this beach faces out into the great abyss of the Atlantic Ocean, uninhibited by the city lighting, making it the perfect place to set up a camera on a moonless night.

In the spring of 2024, I made a last-minute decision to hop the ferry and grab a rental car for what would turn into an all-night photography session, much of it taking place along this beach. The forecast was promising, the moon phase was right, and the Milky Way would be rising just before midnight. Since it was May, it would be very quiet there. This is a "residents only" beach during the summer months, so this would also be my last legal opportunity to park and photograph there until around September.

Driving down a narrow, windy road whose entrance is easy to miss, I dodged potholes and divots, eventually emerging into a surprisingly large dirt parking lot. From here, you can't quite see the beach yet. Instead, you must pass through a small wooded area before emerging onto the sand, at which time you are immediately greeted by a rather expansive shoreline.

To the right, a small cliff obscures your immediate view of the beach. To the left, the sands stretch for a few hundred feet before meeting taller cliffs, boulders, and (at least on this evening) driftwood in the form of tree trunks.

I had visited the beach a few years before with a group of photographers I was hosting for a night photography event, but it was cloudy so we didn't stay long. Since then, wind turbines had been constructed in the waters south of this shoreline, adding a soft glow to the horizon and a peppering of red warning lights—not so bright that they would affect the view of starry skies, but noticeable in any image I shot from this location.

I began photographing just after midnight, starting with a nearby cliff face and working my way east toward the larger, towering cliffs. I didn't have a real plan other than to find some interesting foregrounds and go from there. The amount of time I had set aside for photographing this beach was about an hour, since there were a few other locations I wanted to visit. Morning twilight would begin to appear shortly before 4 a.m. However, this beach was rich with subjects, and each aligned perfectly with the galactic core. It would be nearly three hours before I sped off to the next stop in Menemsha—and even then I could have remained much longer.

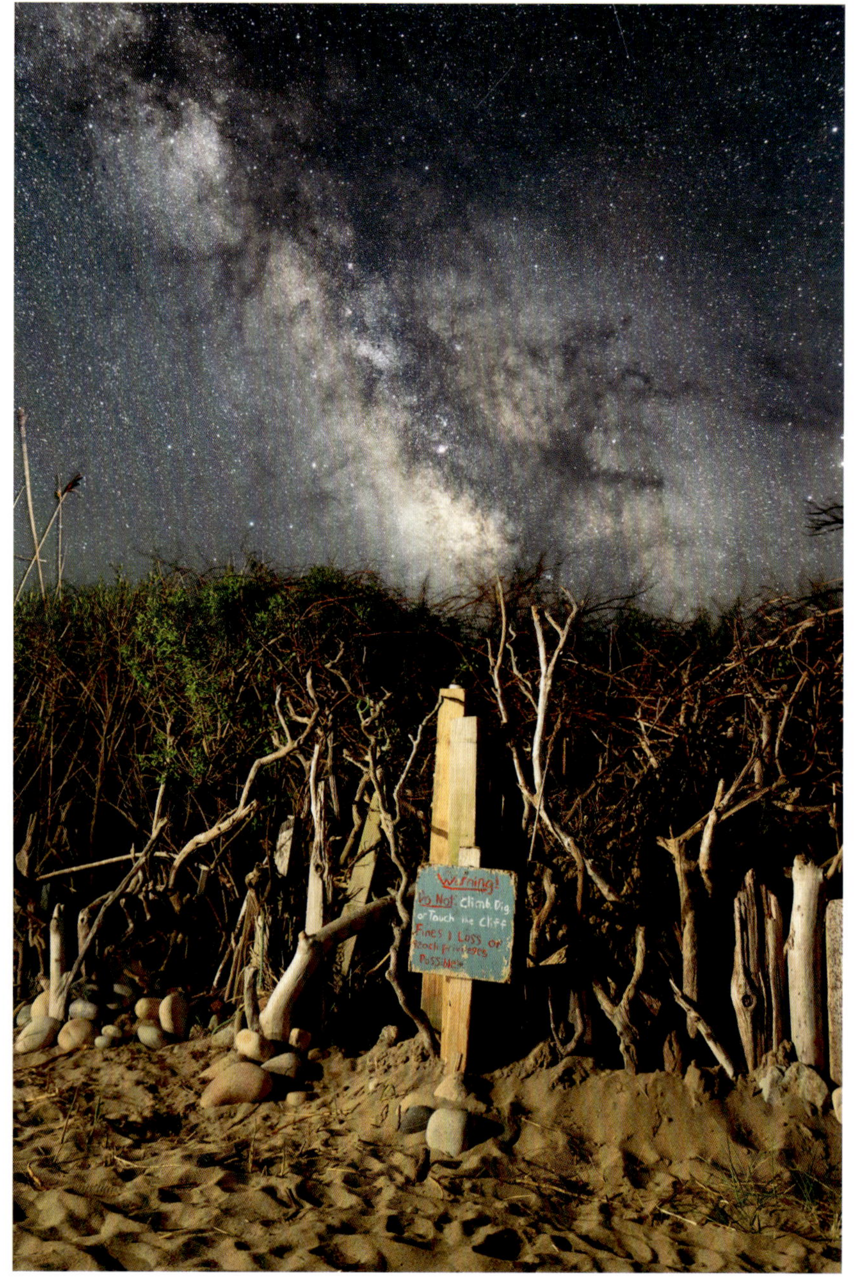

Warning! Do not climb, dig, or touch the cliff. Fines and loss of beach privileges possible. Now you know the rules should you visit Lucy Vincent Beach in Chilmark, and, since you must pass this sign when walking to the beach, there is no excuse for not knowing!

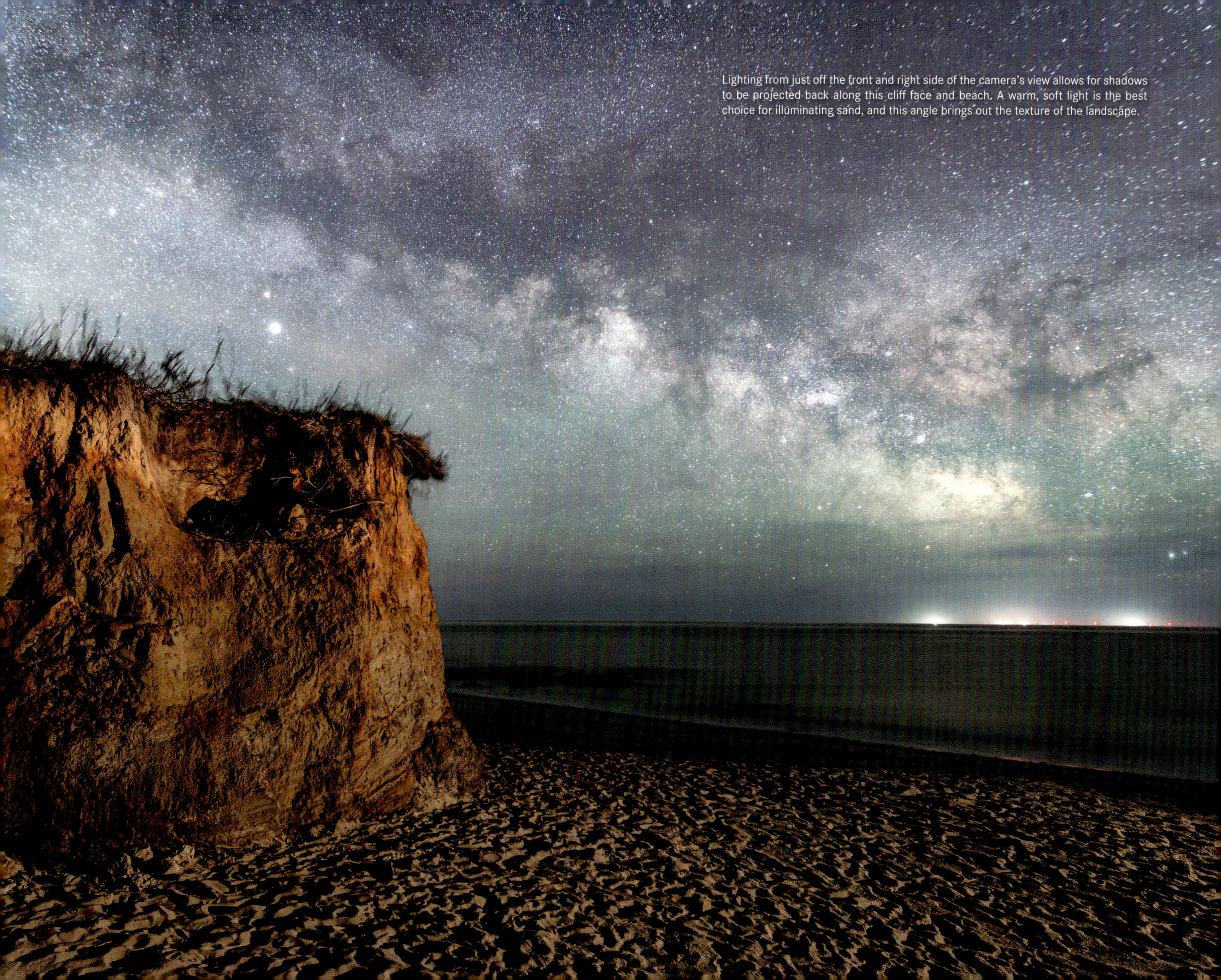

Lighting from just off the front and right side of the camera's view allows for shadows to be projected back along this cliff face and beach. A warm, soft light is the best choice for illuminating sand, and this angle brings out the texture of the landscape.

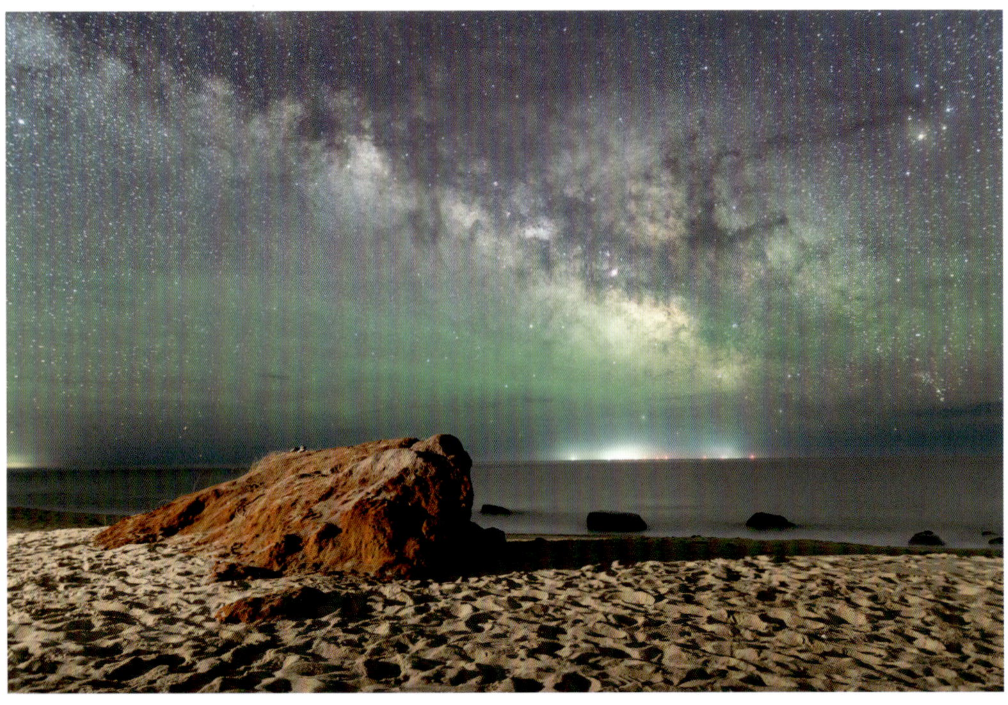

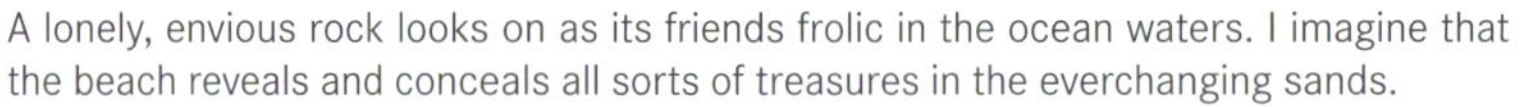

A lonely, envious rock looks on as its friends frolic in the ocean waters. I imagine that the beach reveals and conceals all sorts of treasures in the everchanging sands.

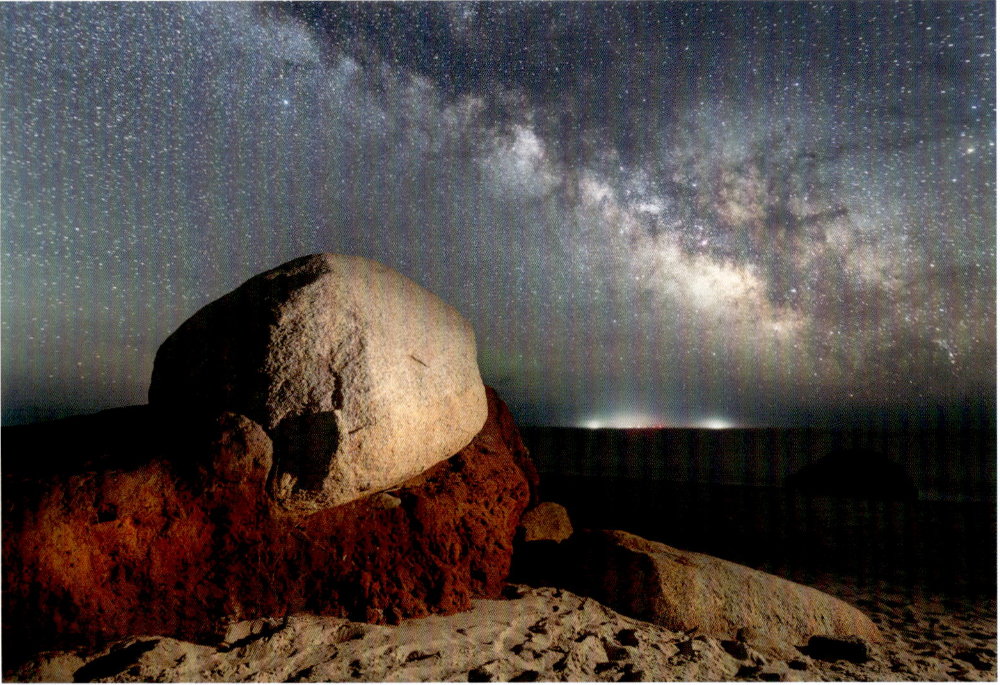

This rock looks like it was simply placed atop another. The geology of Lucy Vincent Beach seems like a great merging of multiple landscapes.

A massive tree trunk has arrived, and it does not appear to be of a type native to the Vineyard. What caused this tree to be washed out to sea? How many miles did it travel before washing ashore? The mysteries of driftwood are unsolvable.

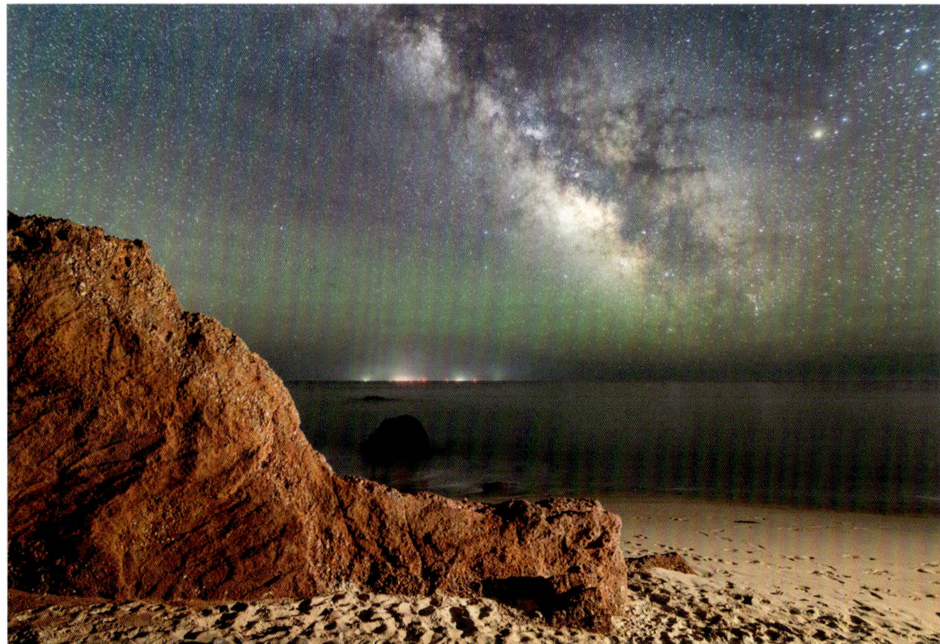

A rock wall provides some protection from ocean waves. This is attached to a much larger cliff where many birds have made their homes. I would have photographed here a little longer, but the tide was coming in and I wasn't sure if my route back to the main beach area was going to be cut off if I waited too long. After ten minutes, I exited this alcove in favor of safer sands.

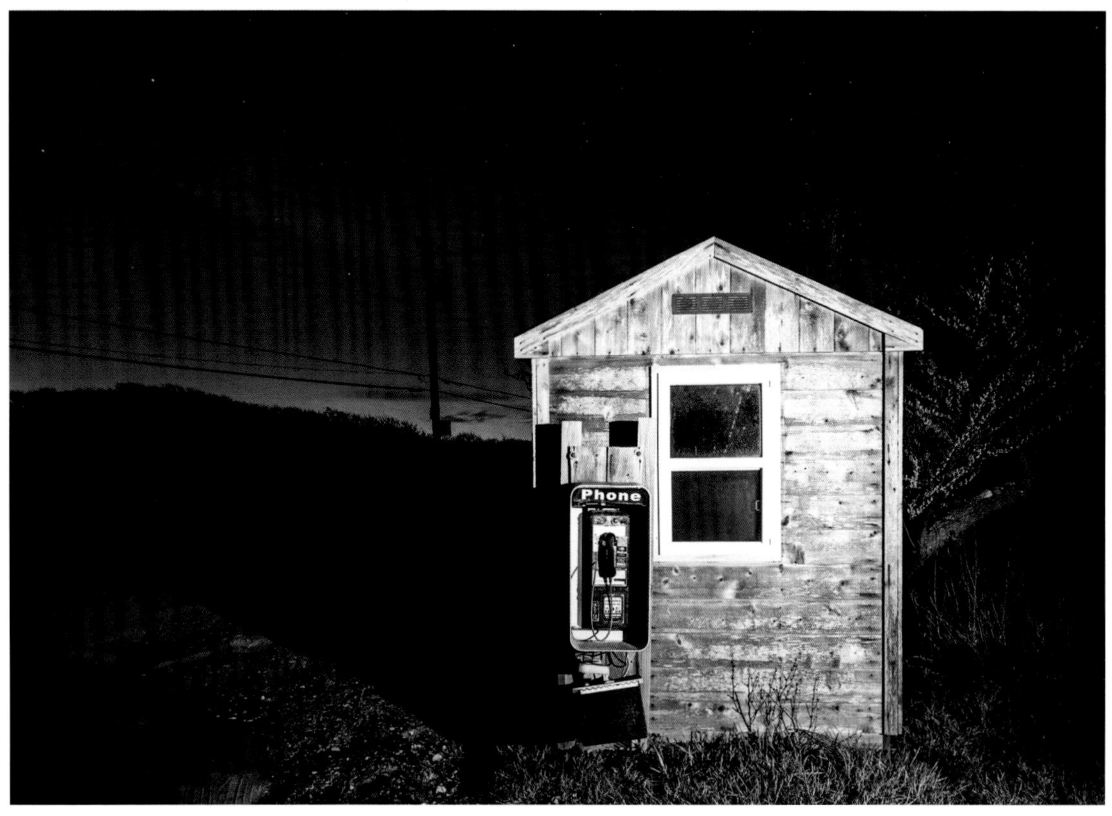

WILL YOU ACCEPT THE CHARGES?

Racing against morning twilight, I stopped at the Gayhead Town Beach, not far from the lighthouse and the cliffs. I had high hopes for this location, but upon exiting the car I could see that blue hour had begun. This is the time before sunrise or after sunset when the sun's light begins to filter into the sky at a blue wavelength. Some photographers love this time, but for me it means either I started photographing too soon after sunset or my overnight shoot has ended and I need to get to bed!

But, first, perhaps there was still one more wacky composition I could pull off. I had forgotten about having seen this completely intact pay phone a few years back. It was still there, looking as good as ever. Even the old phonebook binder dangled below, just like some of us remember.

One way to trap a photographer is to put a pay phone in the middle of nowhere. There is no better example of the juxtaposition of technology and solitude. A photographer will always gravitate toward capturing such a pairing and often cannot resist the temptation to photobomb their own image.

Here, a small panel light was set up on a tripod to the left of the camera. The tricky part of photographing anyone during a long exposure is keeping them still. Even the slightest sway will cause the subject to blur. Having something to lean against, such as a pay phone, prevents this. Thanks to the light panel and the morning twilight, the exposure time on this image would be comparatively shorter than anything else I had photographed on that evening, at just 1.3 seconds.

As of this writing, I can count on one hand the amount of times I purposely appeared in one of my own night images. Even though this was a last-minute decision, the composition didn't seem quite right without having someone in it. My favorite part isn't my contribution—it's the telephone pole in the background carrying wires past this disconnected, forgotten line.

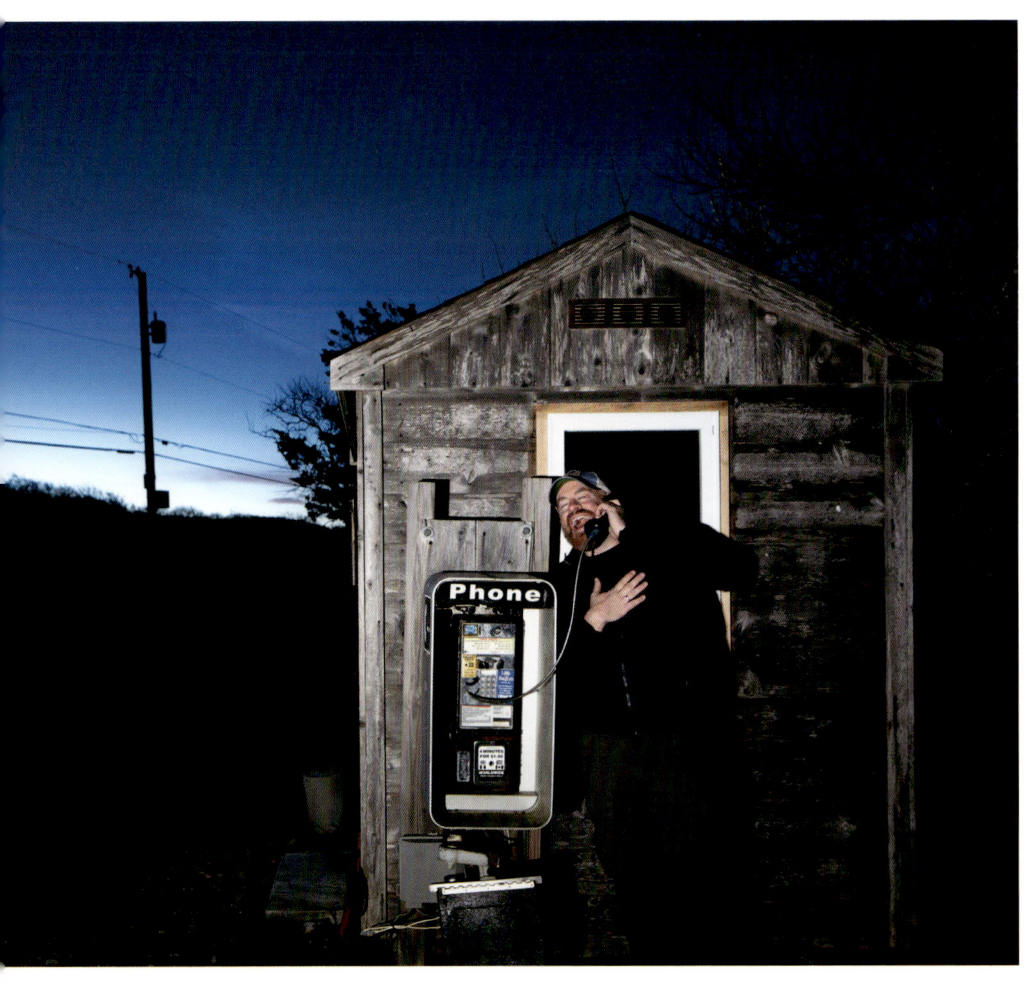
Phone

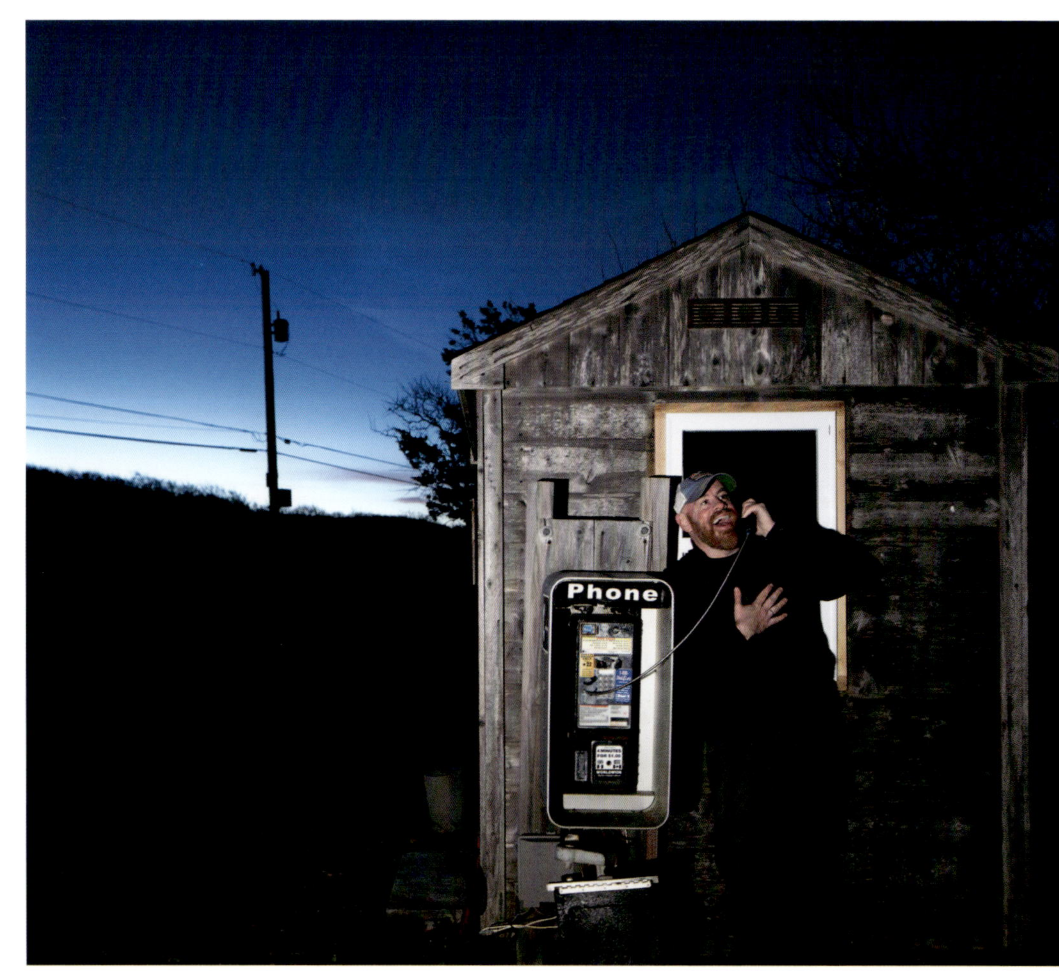
Phone

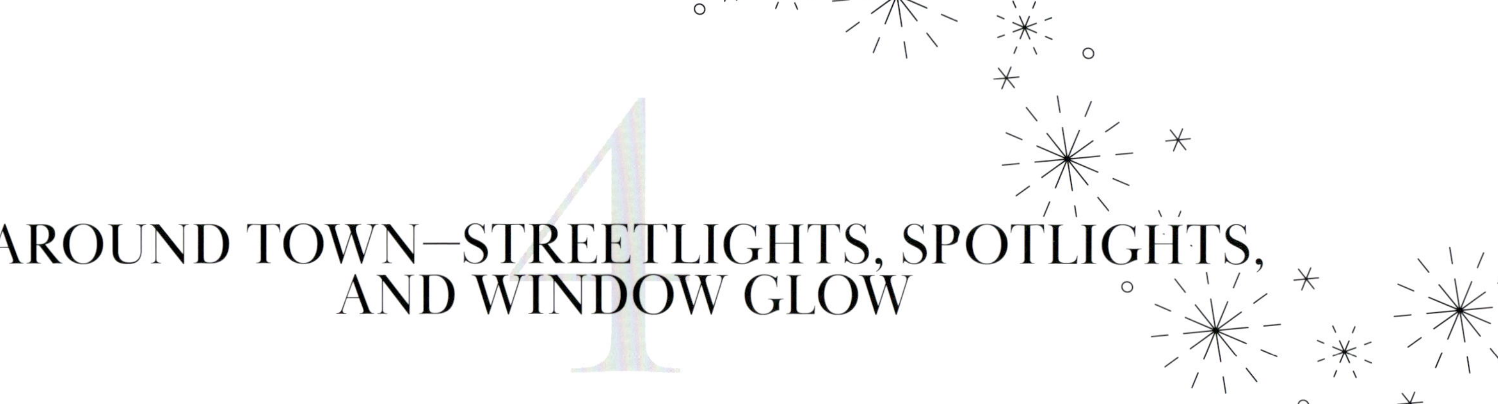

4
AROUND TOWN—STREETLIGHTS, SPOTLIGHTS, AND WINDOW GLOW

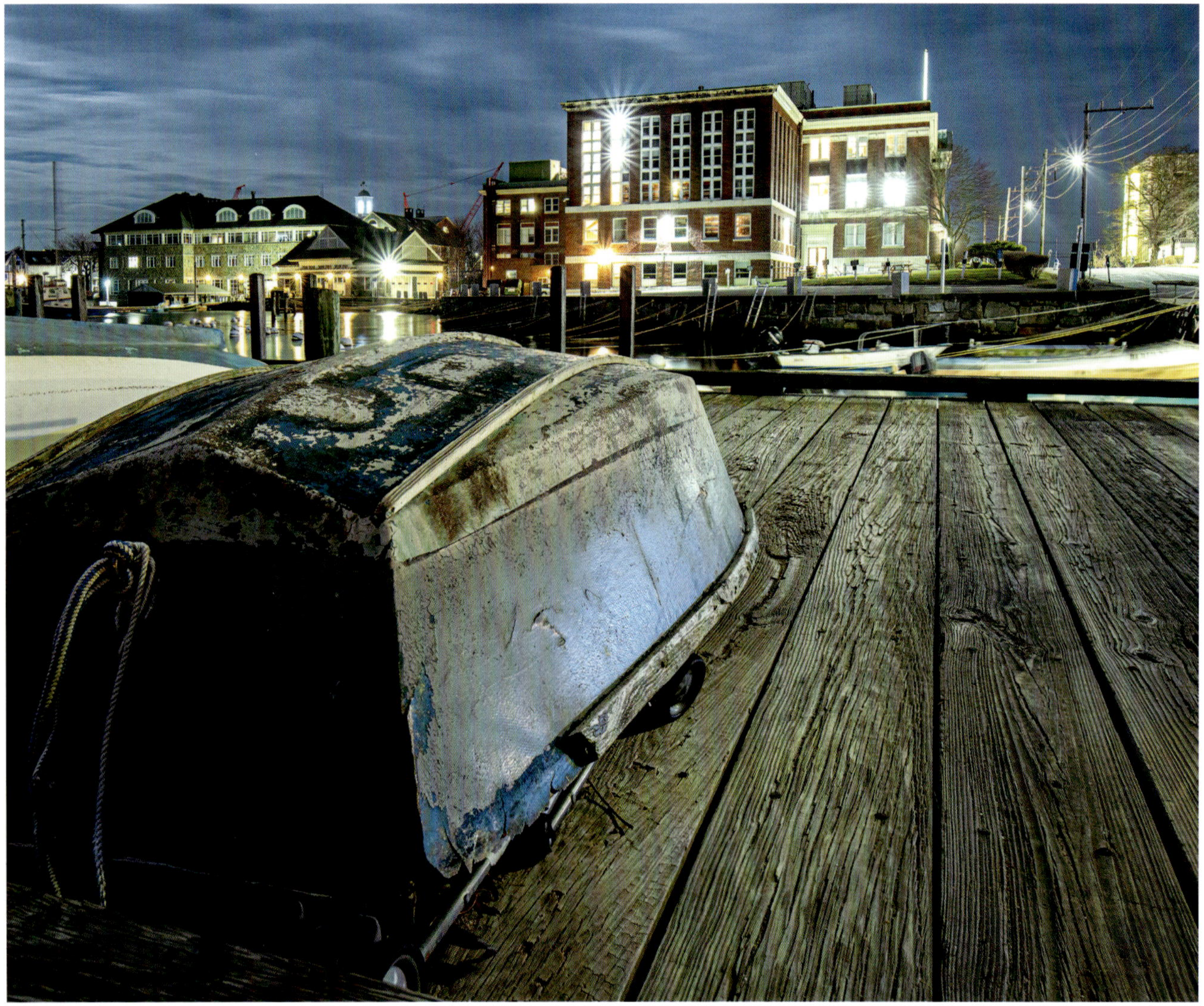

This dock near the MBL properties in Woods Hole is frequently lined year-round with multiple small boats like this one, waiting to transport you out to one of the tall-masted sailboats resting within the safe waters of Eel Pond.

Lights are everywhere. Streetlights, headlights, lights on radio towers, channel marker lights, lights on boats, lights in houses, neon lights, and lights on bikes. You just can't avoid them.

Night photography comes in many forms. Whether it's starlight, moonlight, or streetlights, each environment has its own challenges and rewards. And anyone you ask to define the term will have their own answer.

On Cape Cod, the canal is one of the most picturesque places to photograph at night, despite all the lights nearby. This is mostly because of the bridges, all of them having their good angles and opportunities. And now more than ever, it is the best time to shoot the Bourne and Sagamore Bridges, as their days are numbered. As this book is being written, decisions are being made on how to replace them, since they have nearly reached the end of their operational lives. Someday in the not-too-distant future, new bridges will connect the Cape to the mainland, and no one quite knows what that will look like. Will they follow the design lineage of the ones they are replacing, or will they be an entirely new design? I'm happy to memorialize these old but iconic bridges within the pages of this book and my last.

What about the railroad bridge? Well, worry not, dear reader. There are no plans to replace that one anytime soon. It remains the second-longest vertical-lift bridge in the United States. I would hope that it would be historically preserved.

Besides the bright lights of the canal, there are many well-lit harbors and main streets throughout Cape Cod. The most photogenic are the ones that still feature streetlamps housing old incandescent bulbs, like what you might see in Edgartown. Second best are those that have transitioned to the newer LED streetlights, which provide a more natural color tone. The ones to avoid are the older-style sodium vapor lights, which cast a terrible orange glow on everything nearby.

The pages ahead feature subjects lit primarily by artificial light sources.

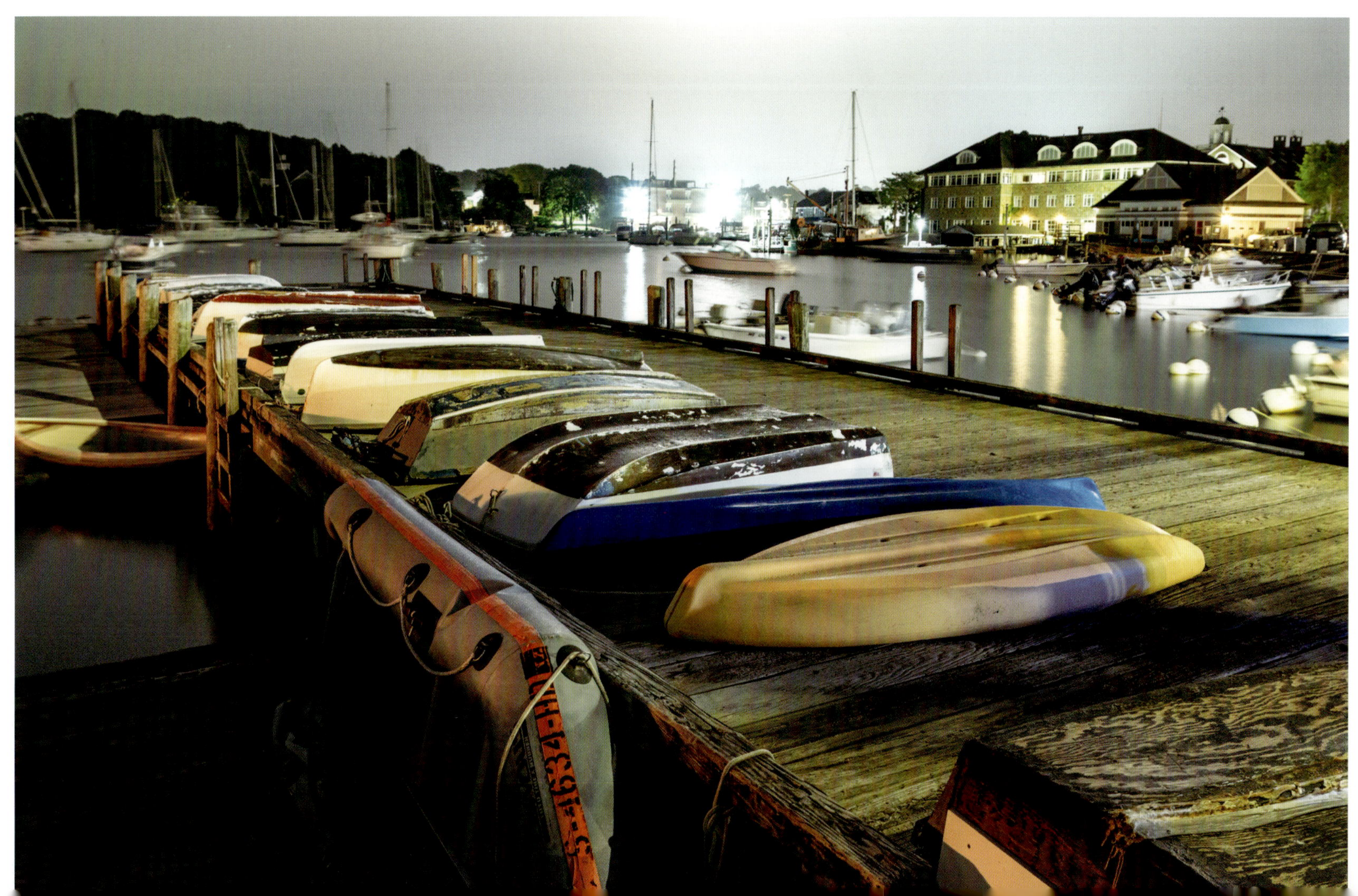

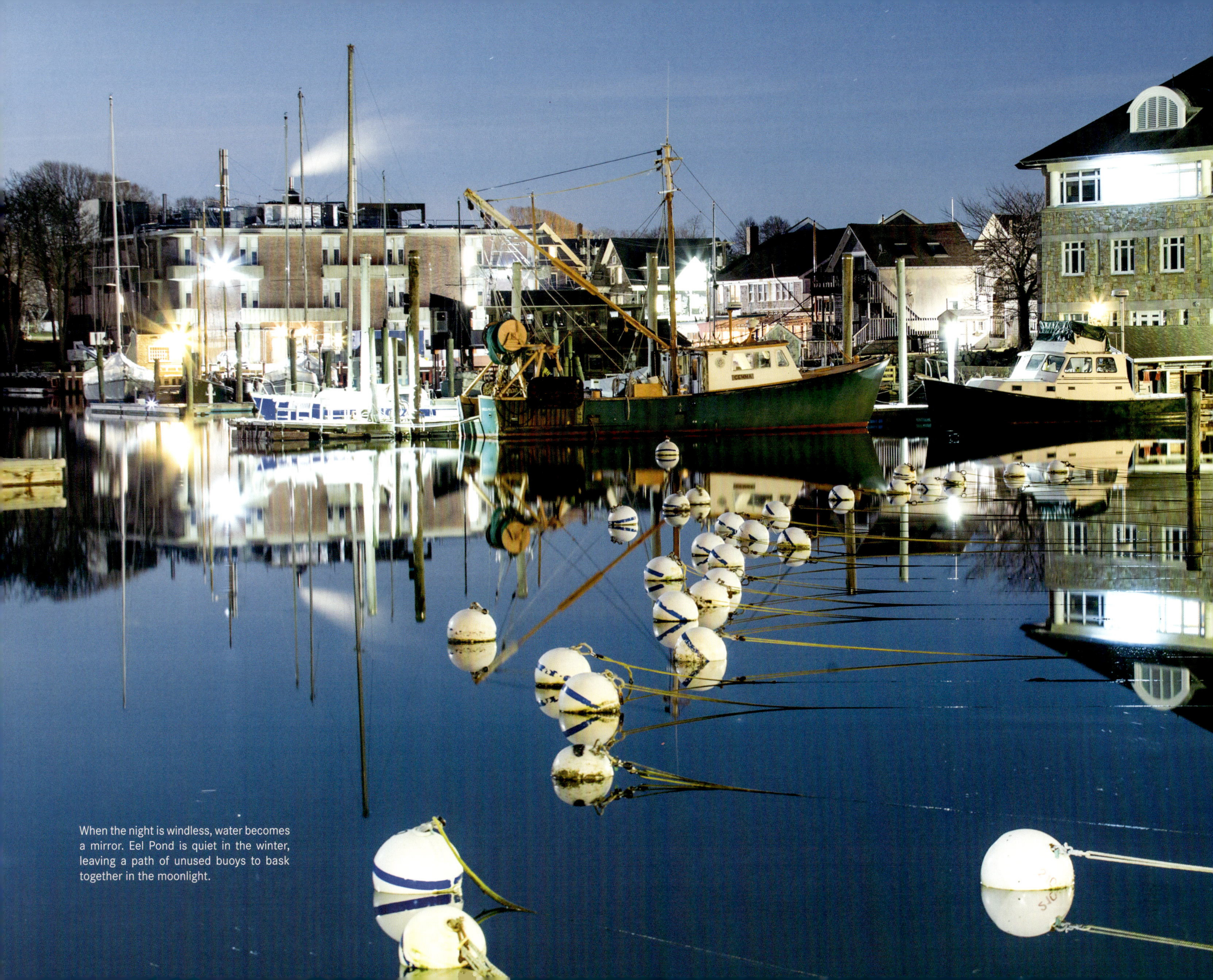

When the night is windless, water becomes a mirror. Eel Pond is quiet in the winter, leaving a path of unused buoys to bask together in the moonlight.

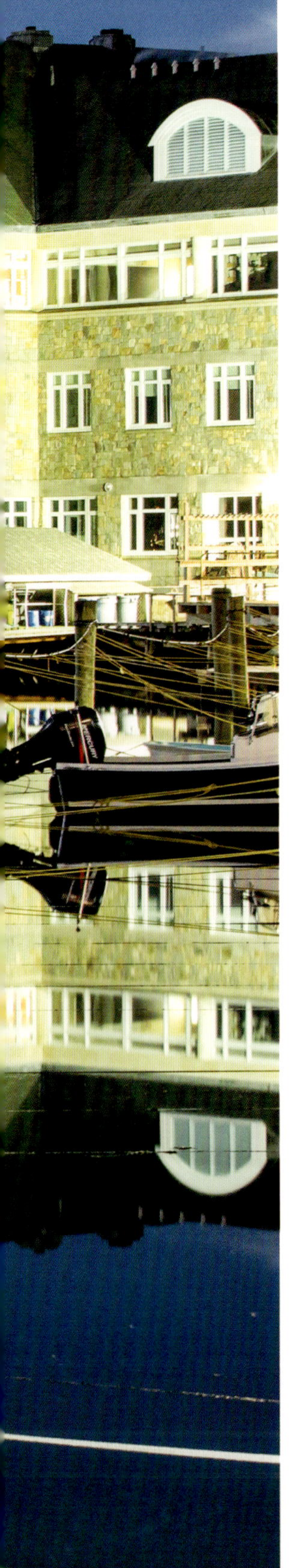

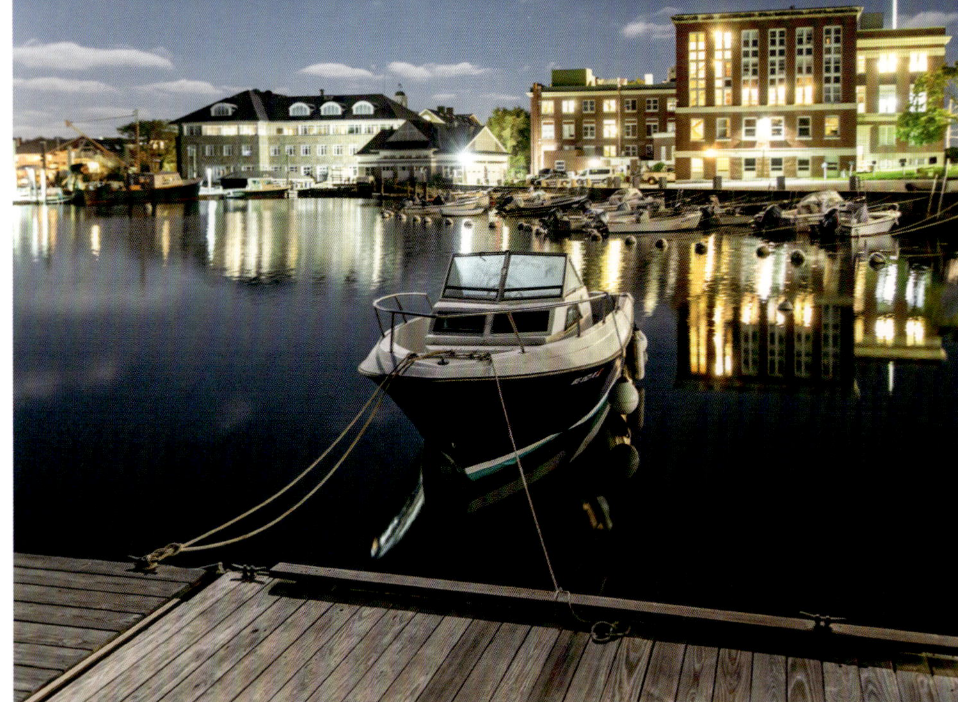

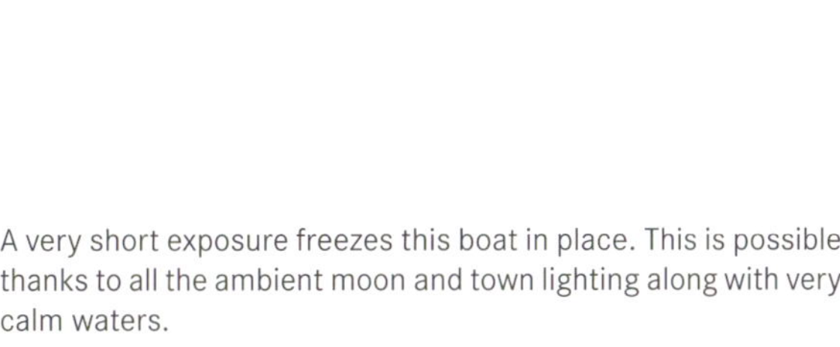

A very short exposure freezes this boat in place. This is possible thanks to all the ambient moon and town lighting along with very calm waters.

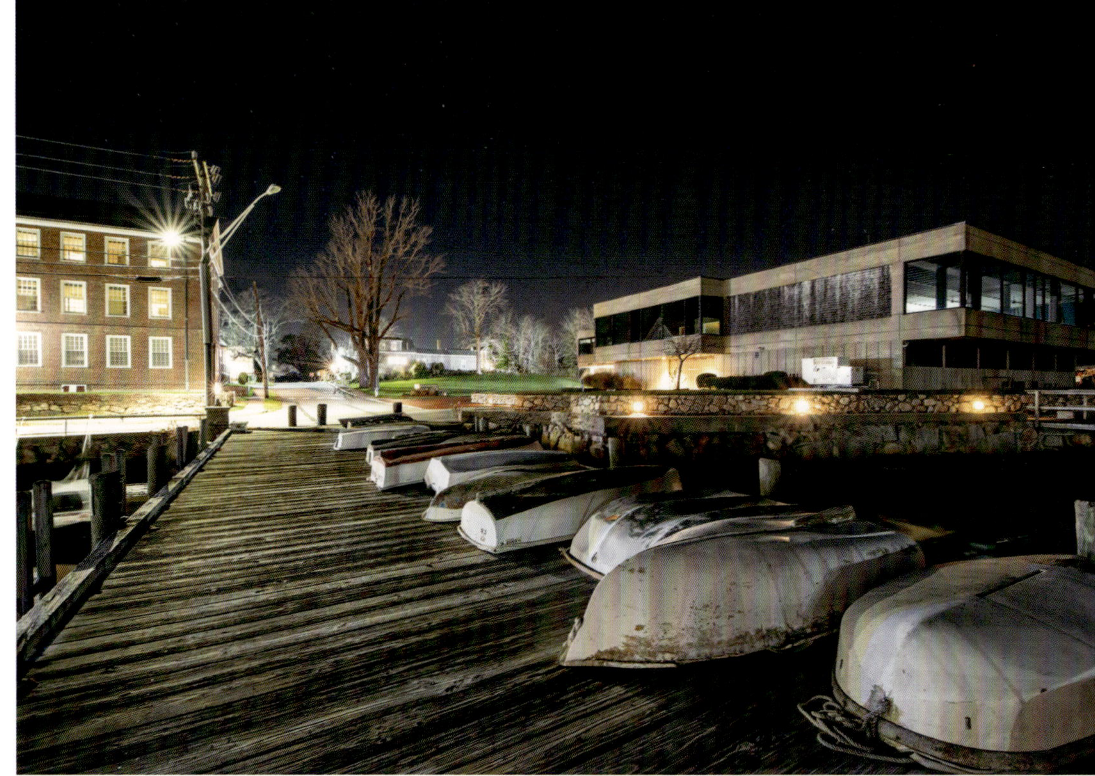

Park along MBL Street in Woods Hole to visit this dock. If you can't visit in person, at the time of this writing there was a live camera pointed right at it that you could enjoy from home.

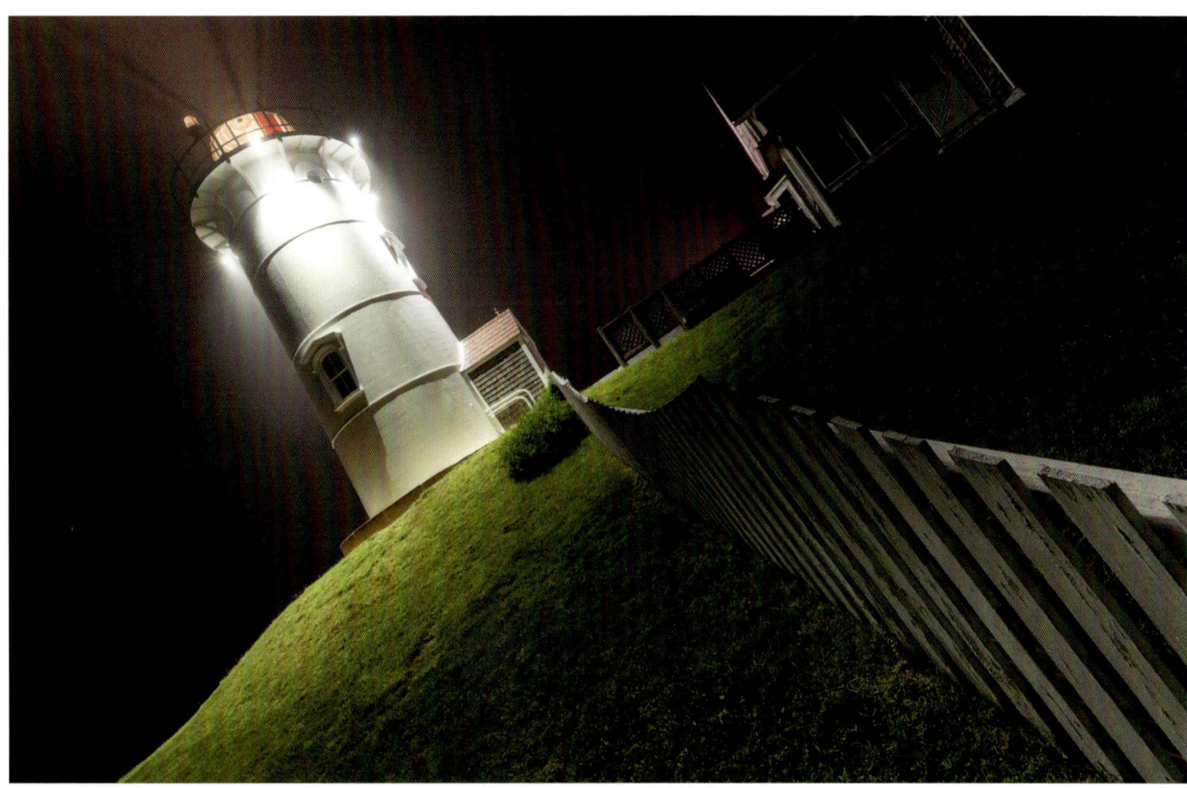

This old fence was removed as part of a recent property refurbishment. Fences create great leading lines in any composition.

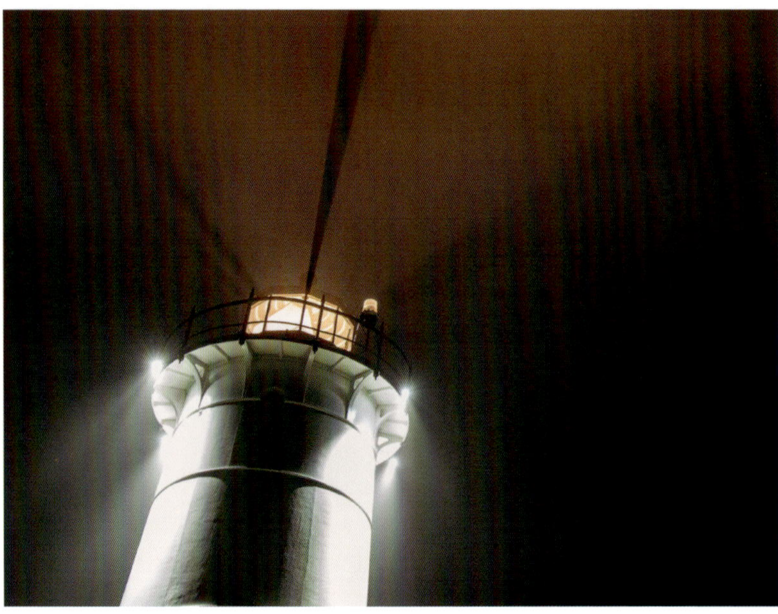

The mist enhances the beam from Nobska Light. The bright white, downward-facing lamps were part of the tower's refurbishment but were replaced with warmer-toned lights, presumably to simulate the earlier system. The shadows in the beam are caused by the window panes.

In May 2024, I was invited to meet up with a visiting workshop group at Nobska Light. After exchanging a few emails with lighthouse volunteers, I was able to get the majority of the external lighting shut down, leaving unusually dark conditions. Still, the green glow of the interior exit signs remained. Converting the image to black and white helped address this. About ninety seconds of exposure time was required, and the clouds created a mysterious vibe.

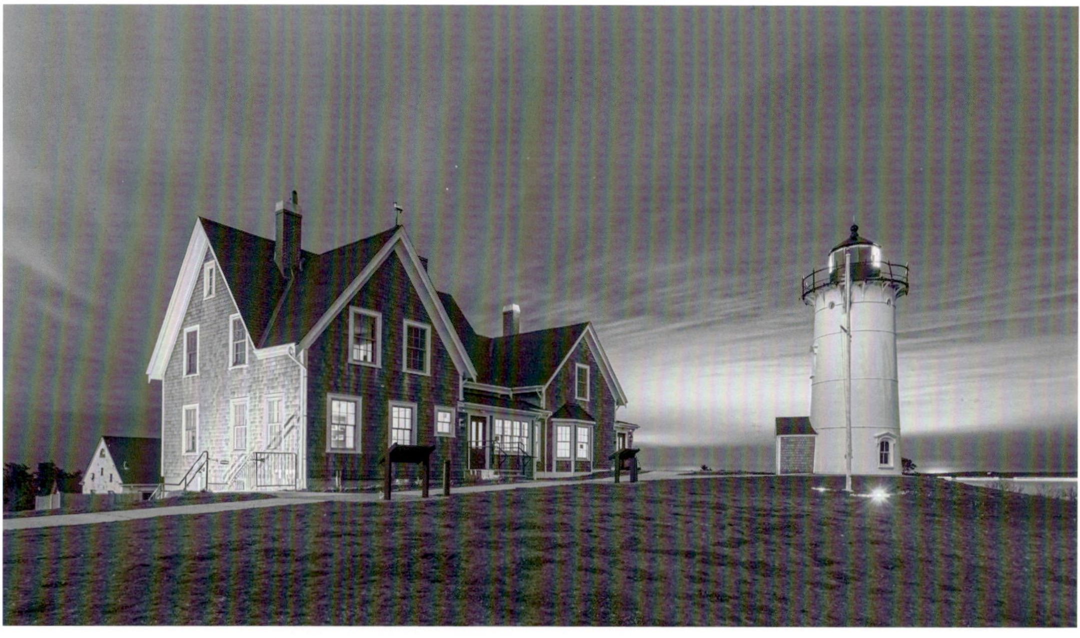

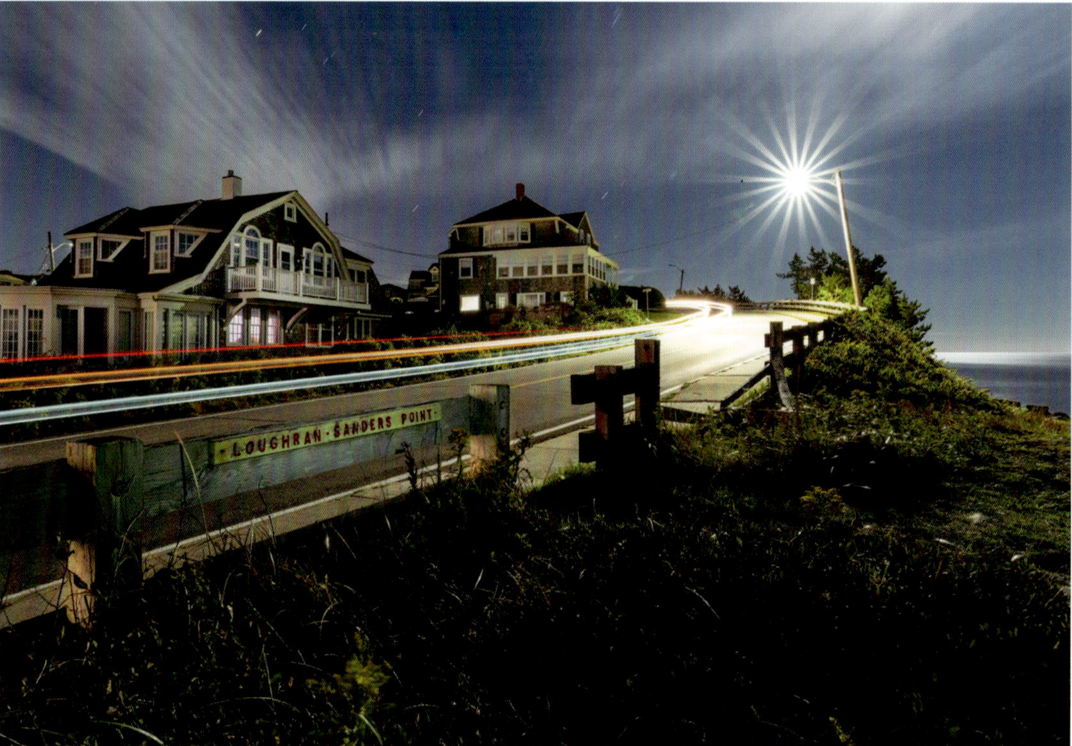

Whether a moonlit night in May or a sunny July afternoon, Grand Avenue along Falmouth Heights is a popular route to cruise at any time.

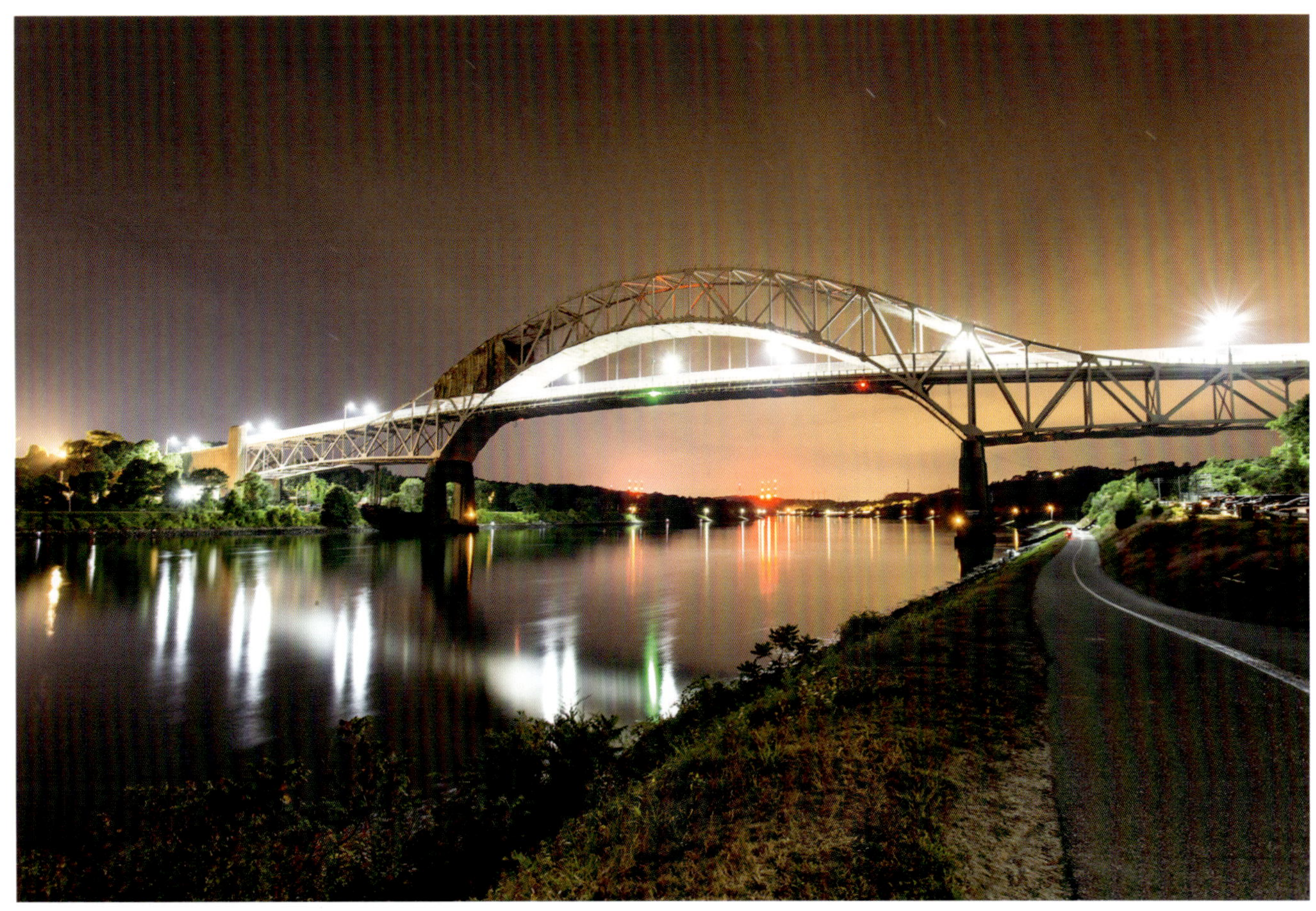

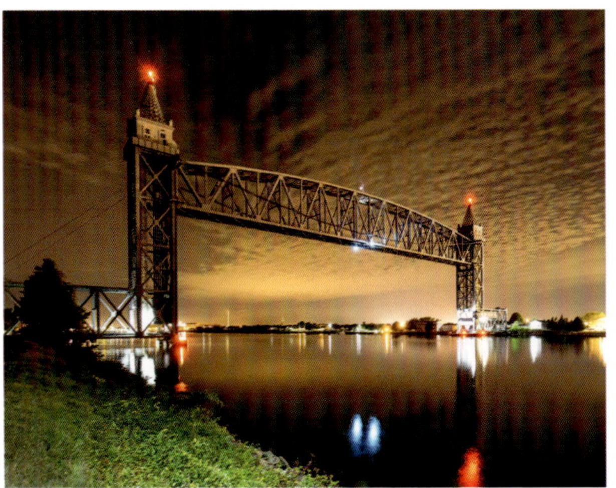

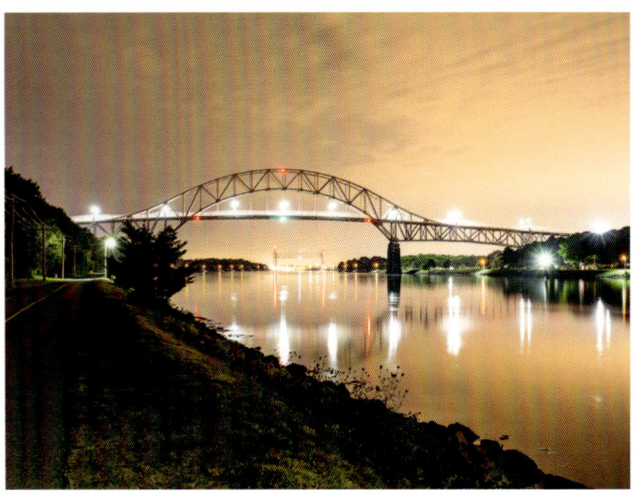

Low clouds reflect nearby town lighting, creating a warm glow from one end of the canal to the other. These three images were taken within an hour of each other, beginning at the Sagamore Bridge, followed by the Bourne, and then the railroad bridge. The result was a trio connected by tone.

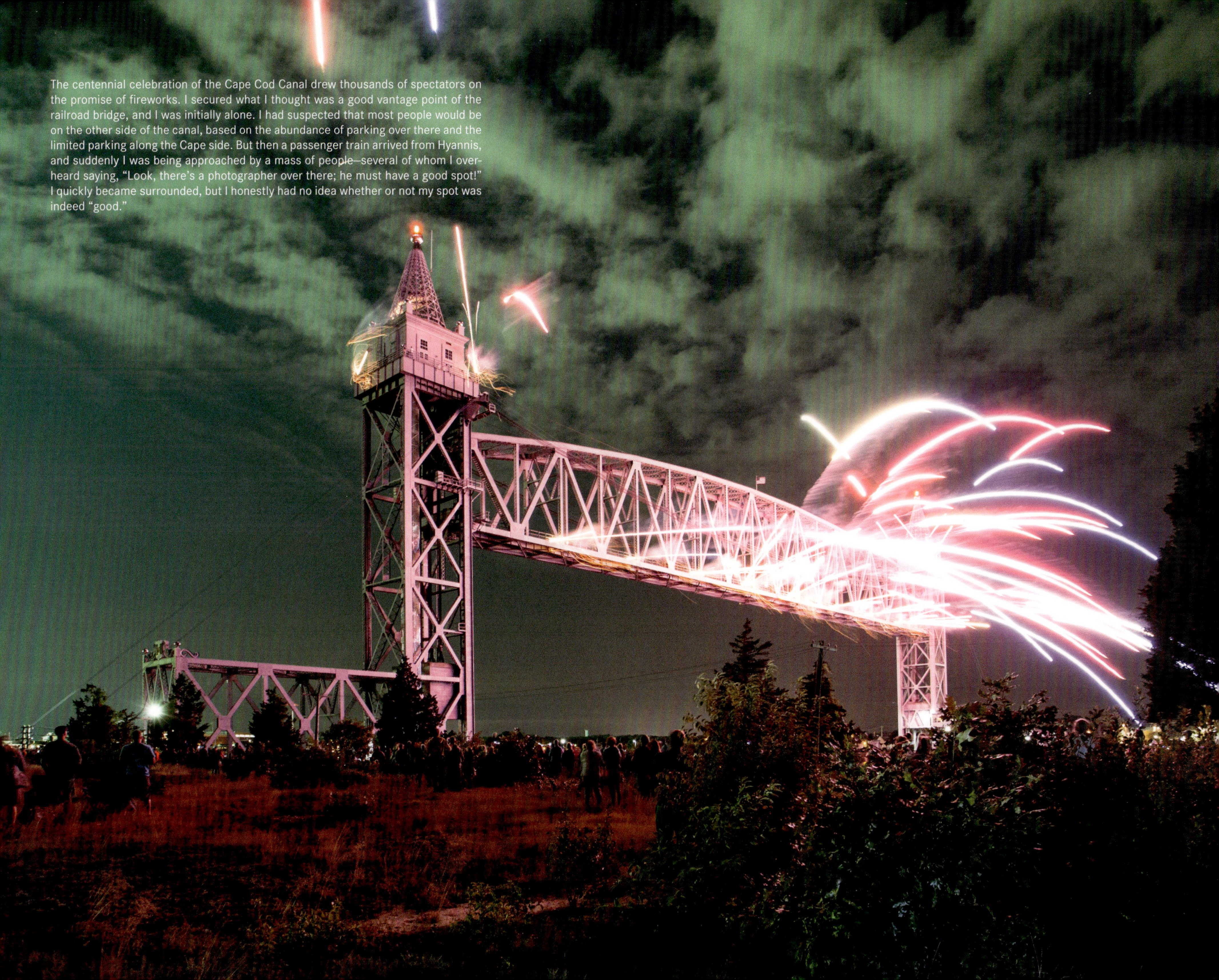

The centennial celebration of the Cape Cod Canal drew thousands of spectators on the promise of fireworks. I secured what I thought was a good vantage point of the railroad bridge, and I was initially alone. I had suspected that most people would be on the other side of the canal, based on the abundance of parking over there and the limited parking along the Cape side. But then a passenger train arrived from Hyannis, and suddenly I was being approached by a mass of people—several of whom I overheard saying, "Look, there's a photographer over there; he must have a good spot!" I quickly became surrounded, but I honestly had no idea whether or not my spot was indeed "good."

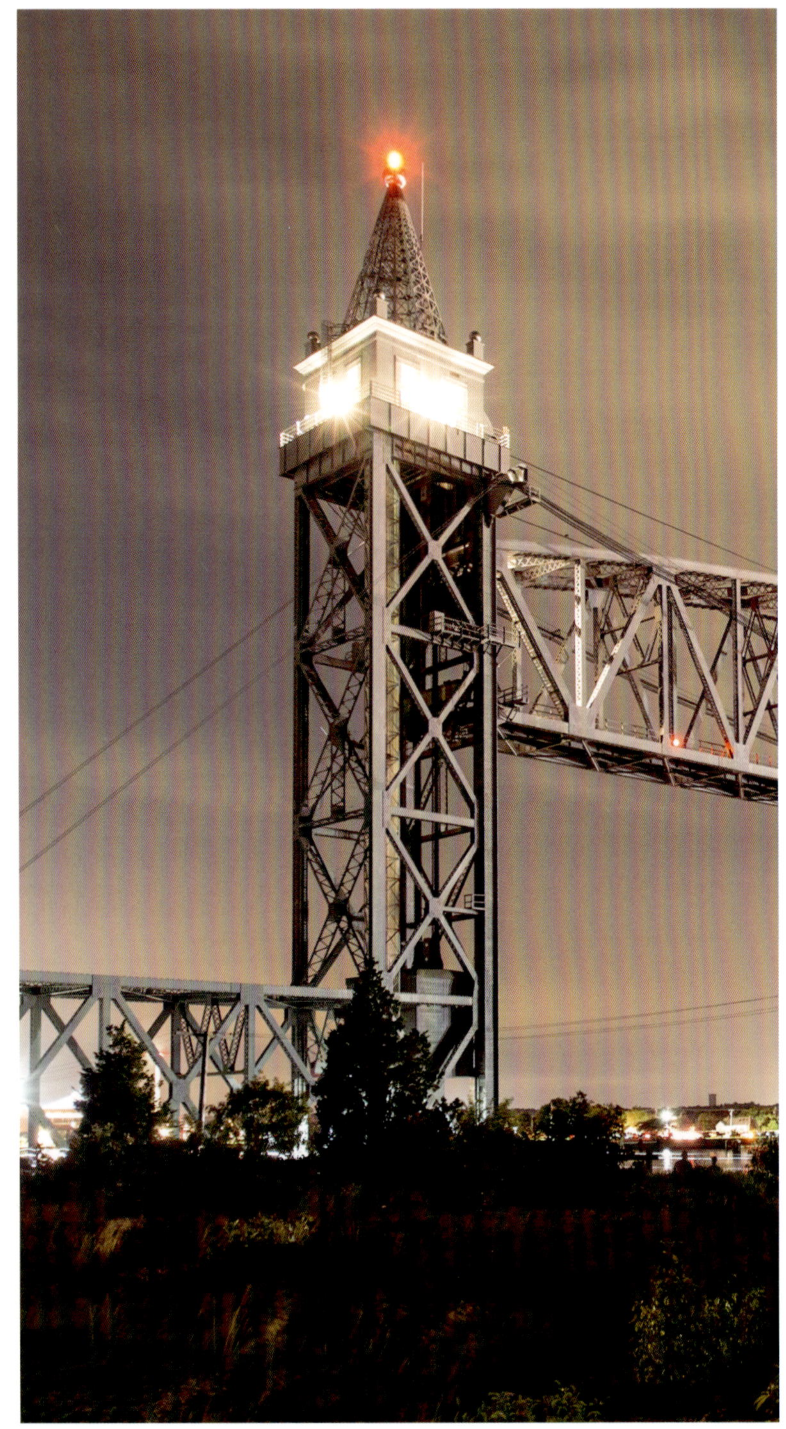

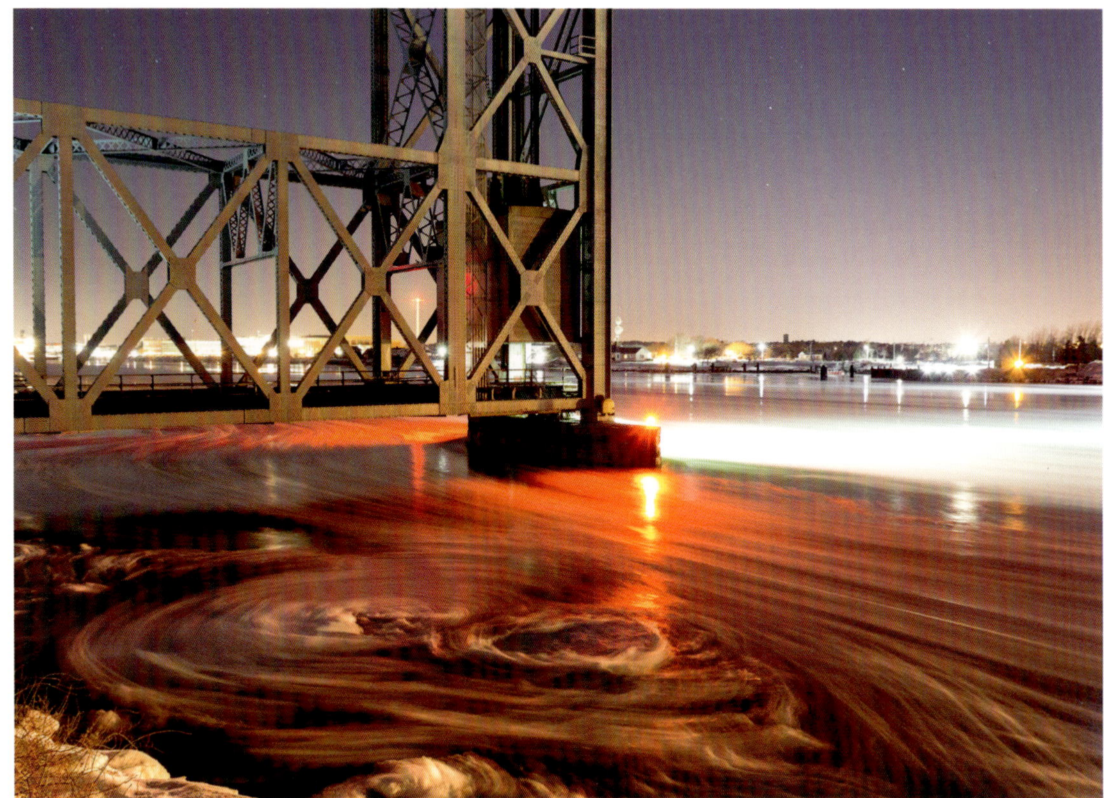

Locals were presented with a winter mystery in 2015, when large pieces of freshwater ice began to wash up on local beaches and travel through the canal. Here, several chunks of ice had been caught in a vortex at the base of the railroad bridge. The long exposure smooths out their motion as they endlessly circle this watery trap.

The Cape-side support of the canal railroad bridge. The metal sides of the bridge often take on the same color tones as the sky and reach a height of 271 feet. It is fairly rare to see the windows in the upper rooms lit.

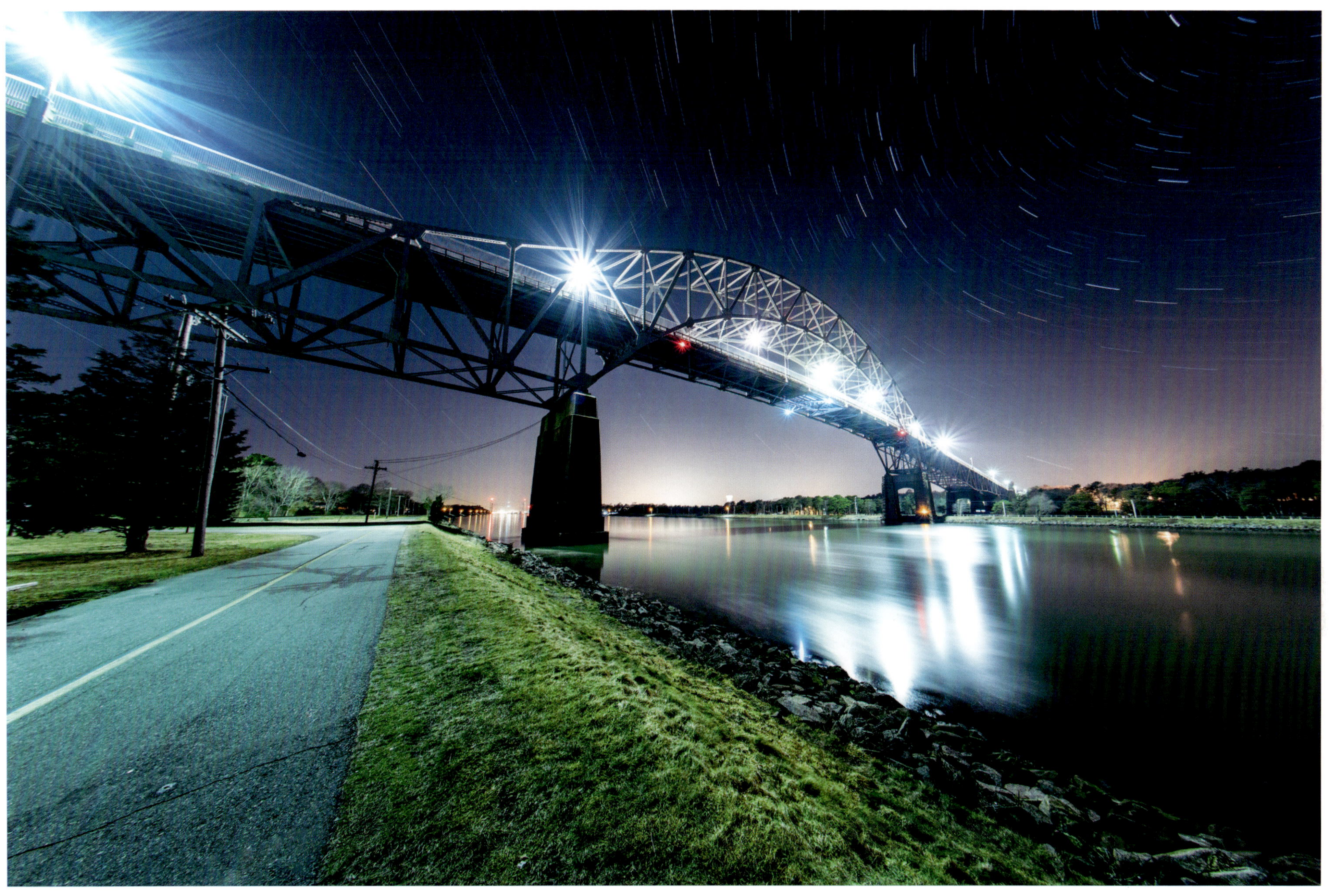

A fish-eye lens helps exaggerate the span of the bridge. It took twenty minutes to complete this image, allowing the stars to make their own trip across the canal.

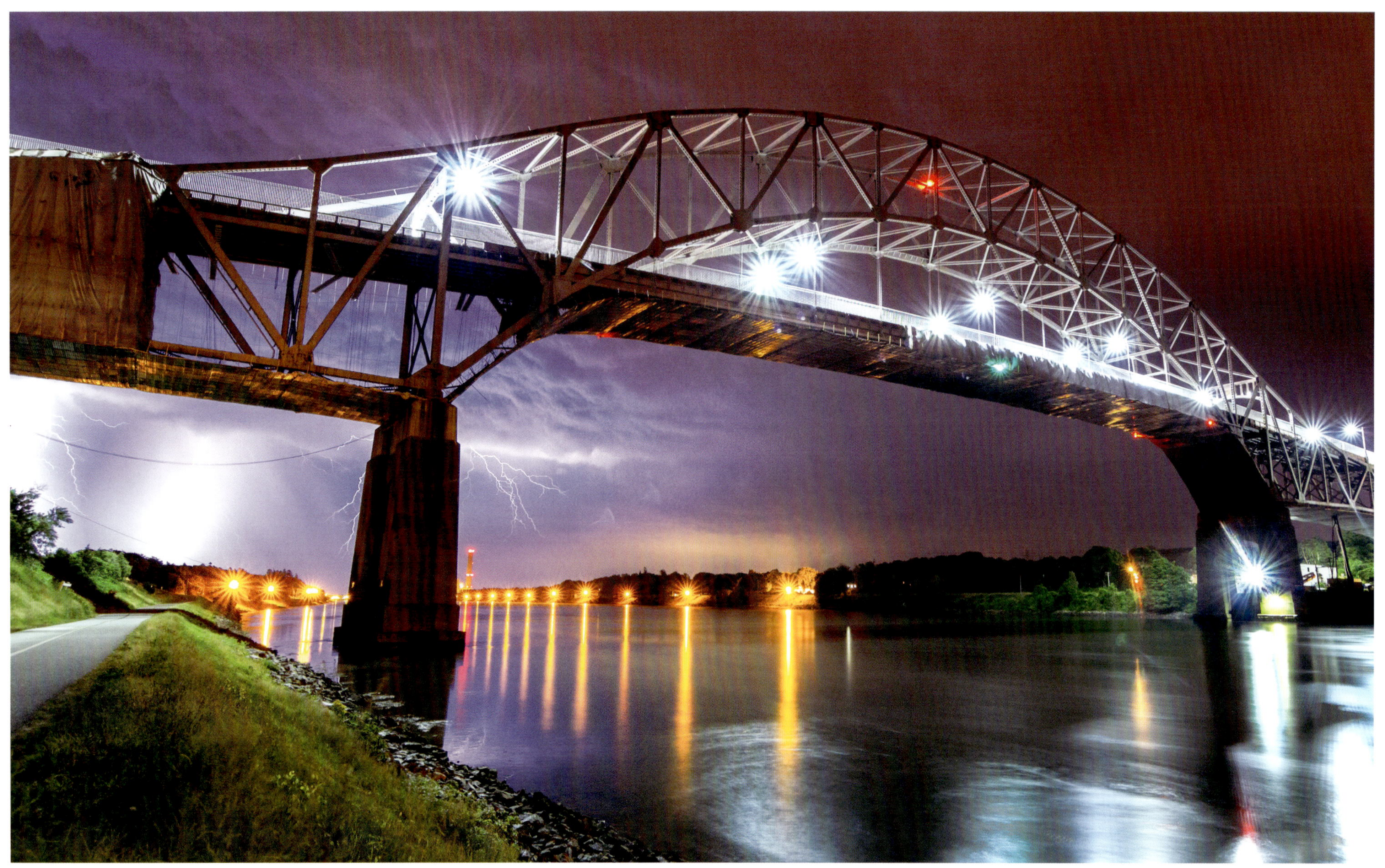

A fast-moving lightning storm dazzles the canal. I was traveling home with a trunkful of camera equipment after hosting a night photography workshop in the Berkshires. It seemed like I was chasing this storm as I approached the Cape, and I decided to risk a few shots of the Sagamore Bridge. Less than an hour later, the storm had mostly cleared, revealing a rising moon. Cape Cod weather often changes this quickly, which is why I rarely look at a forecast outside twenty-four hours.

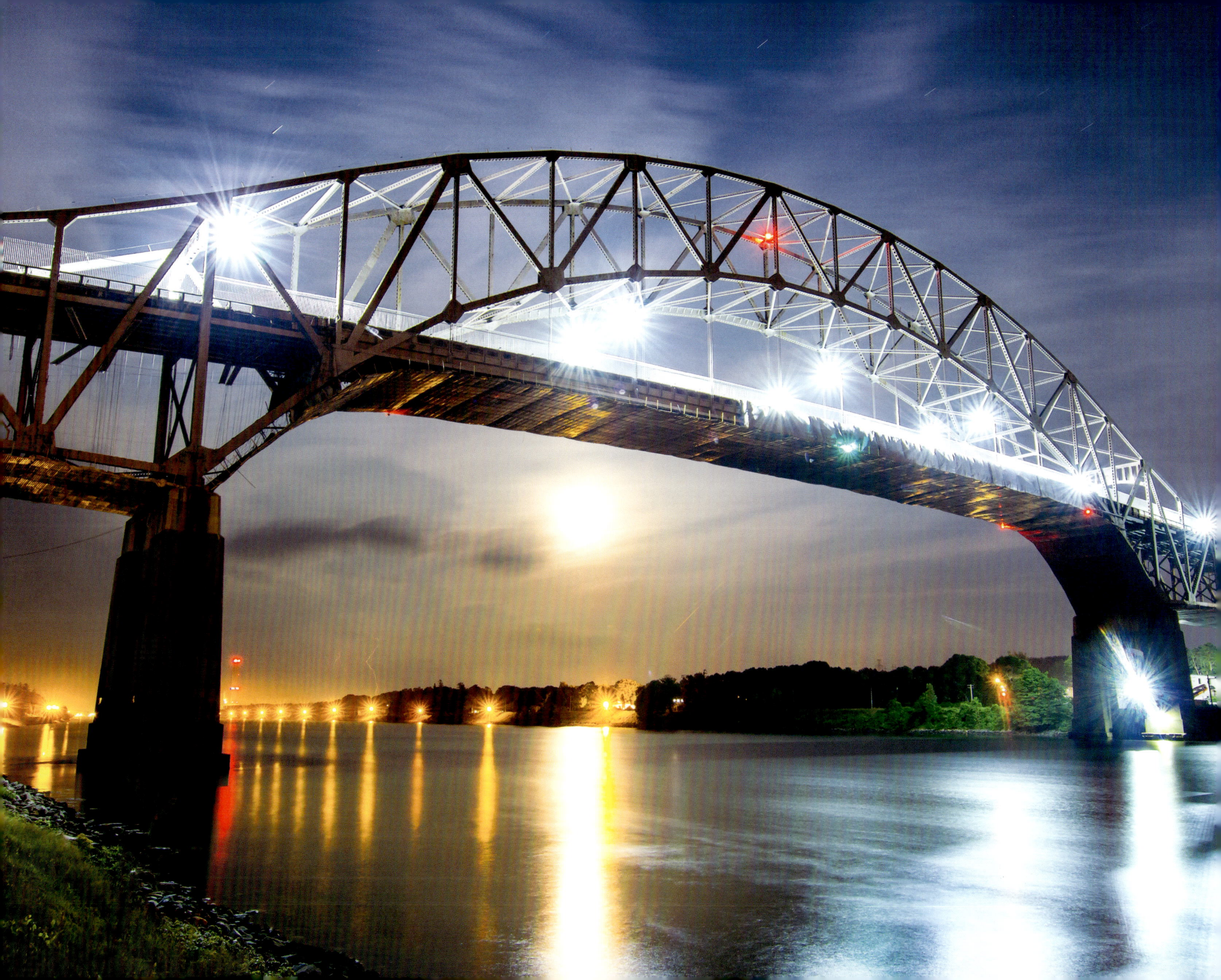

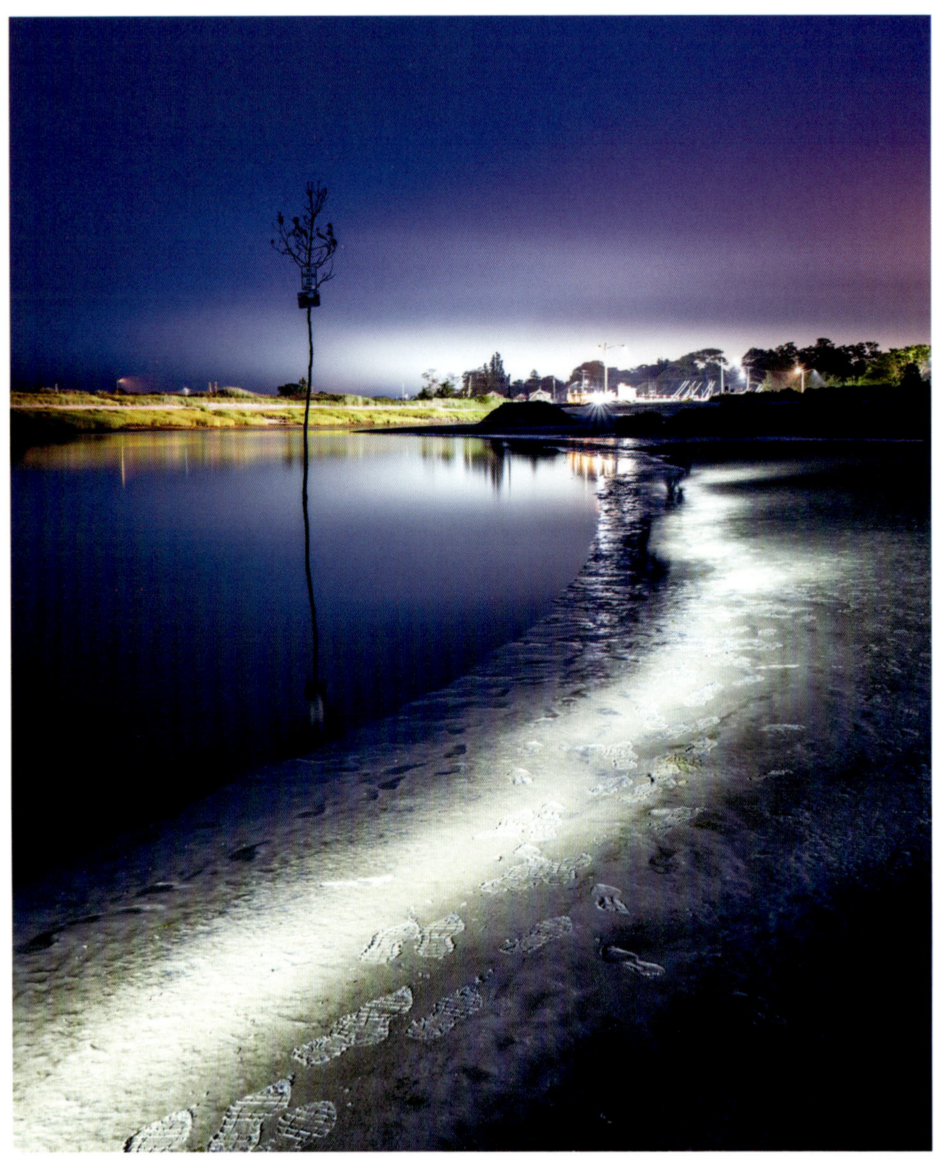

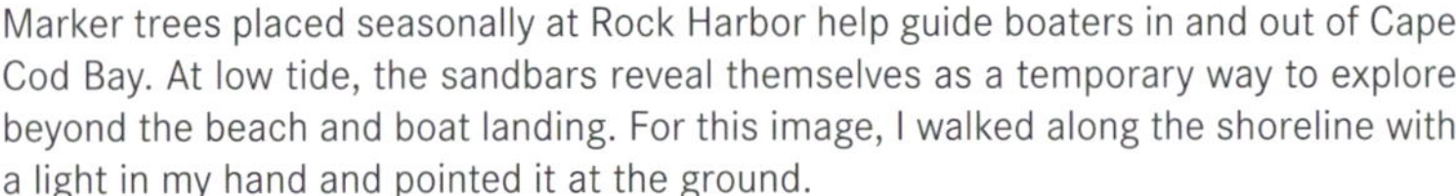

Marker trees placed seasonally at Rock Harbor help guide boaters in and out of Cape Cod Bay. At low tide, the sandbars reveal themselves as a temporary way to explore beyond the beach and boat landing. For this image, I walked along the shoreline with a light in my hand and pointed it at the ground.

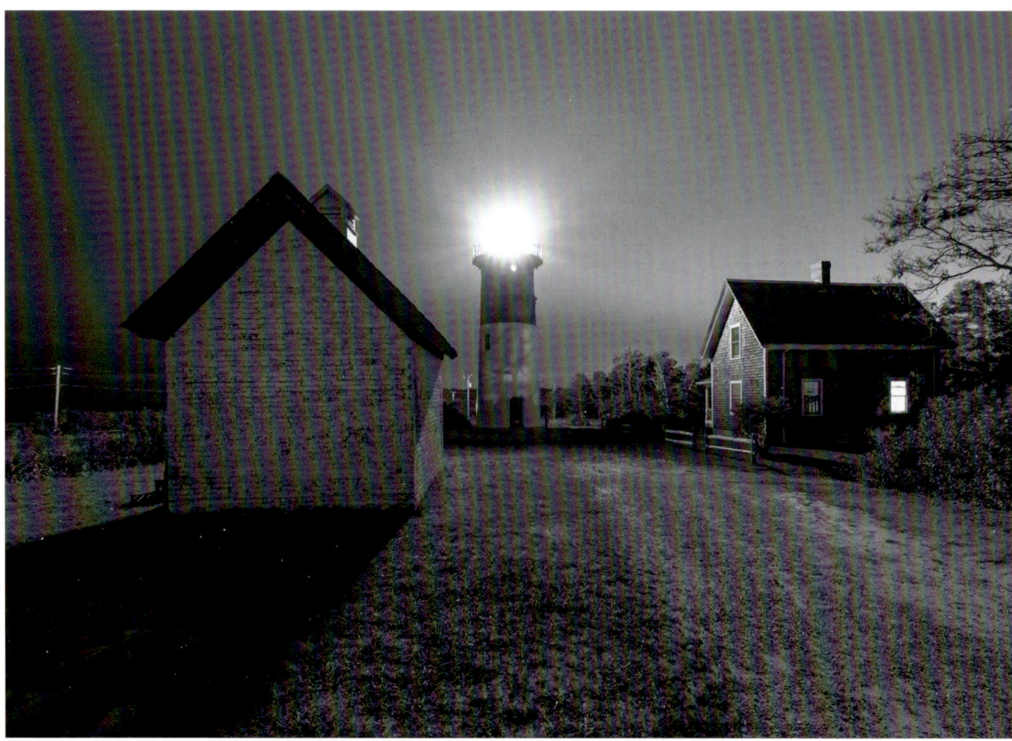

The old oil house now serves as a mini museum occasionally open to the public. Inside, visitors will discover the history of Nauset and a beautiful light-up map that details the lighthouses, marker buoys, and channels of Cape Cod.

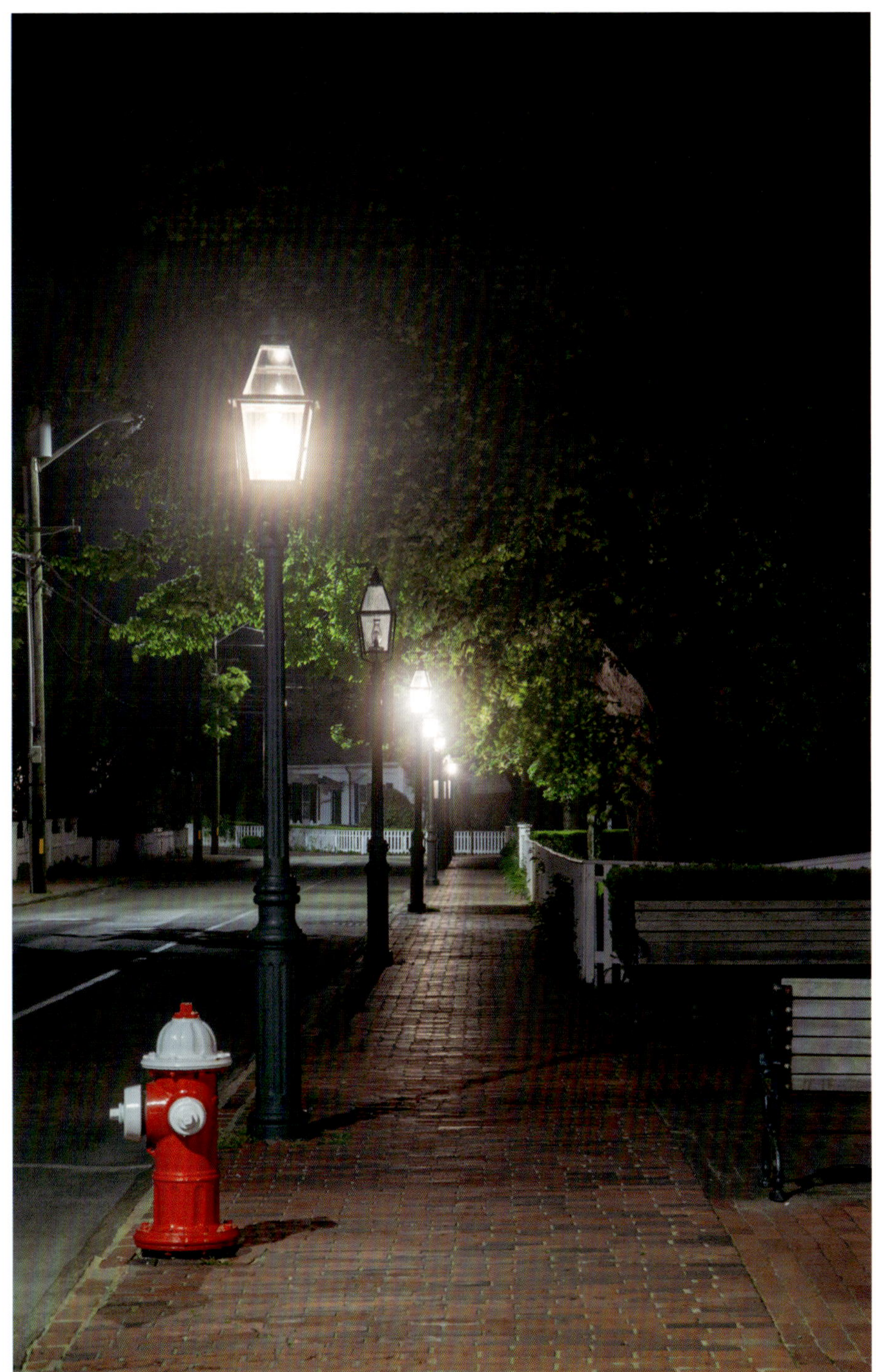

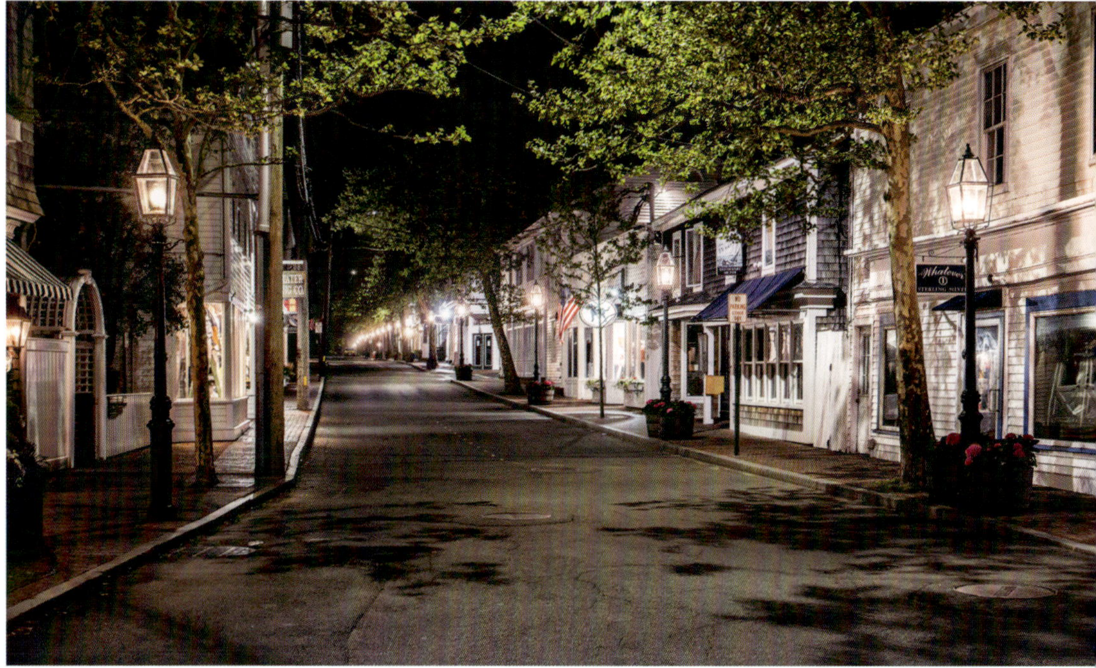

Main Street in Edgartown appears empty in the late hours of a May night. Here, I could photograph safely in the middle of the road for as long as I wanted without worrying about traffic. I was, however, surprised by a skunk—which was also taking advantage of the quiet evening—running by me and to the end of the street.

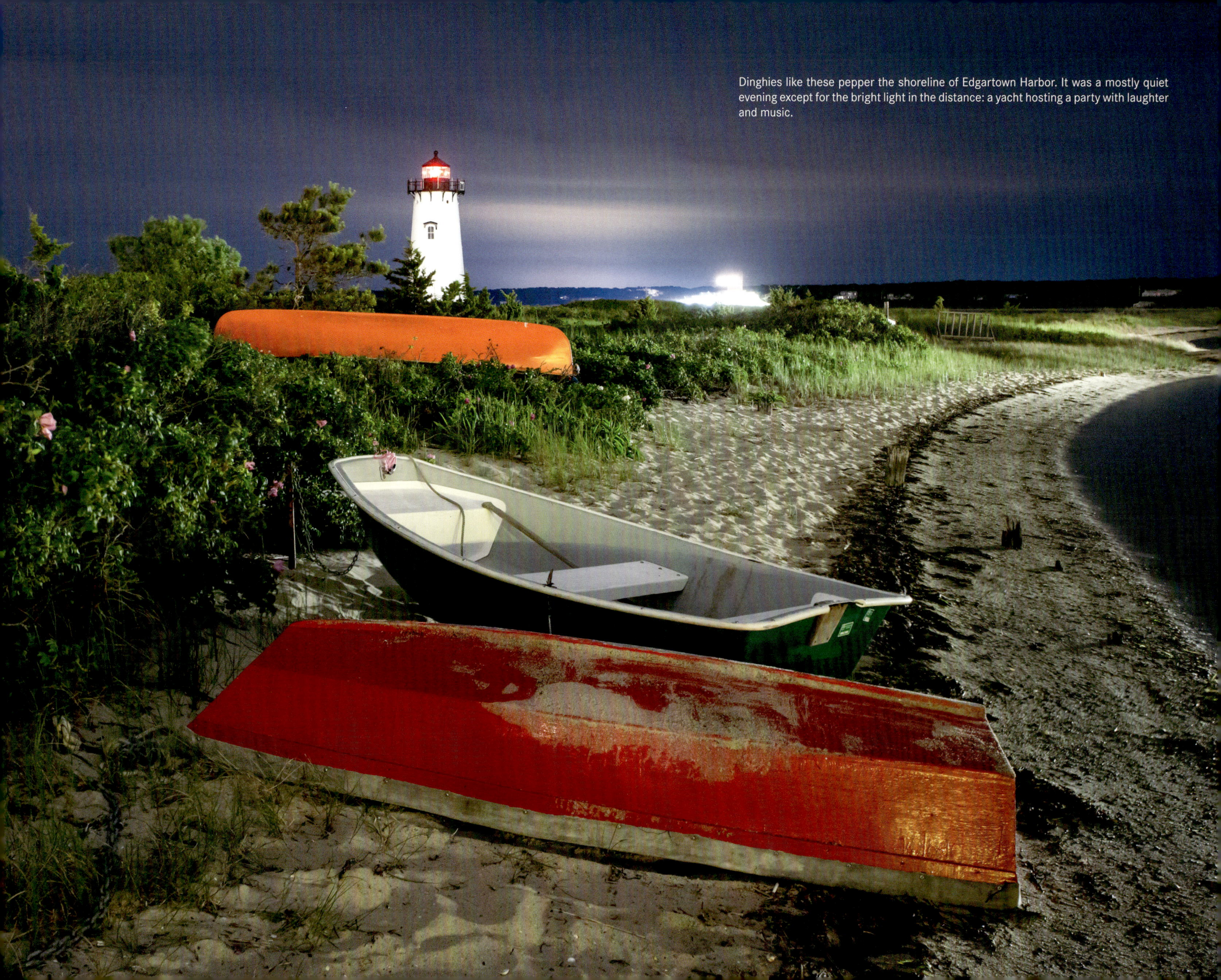

Dinghies like these pepper the shoreline of Edgartown Harbor. It was a mostly quiet evening except for the bright light in the distance: a yacht hosting a party with laughter and music.

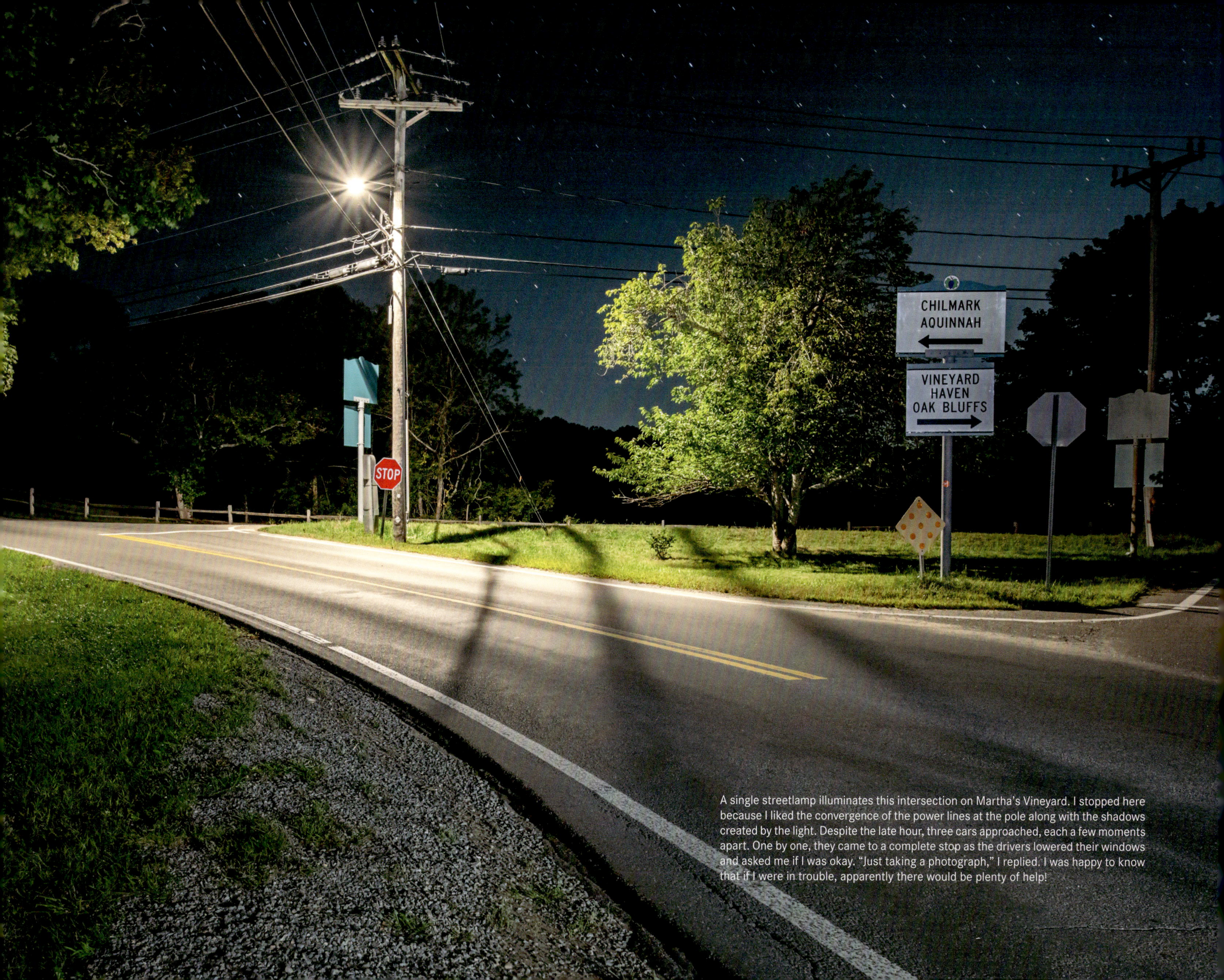

A single streetlamp illuminates this intersection on Martha's Vineyard. I stopped here because I liked the convergence of the power lines at the pole along with the shadows created by the light. Despite the late hour, three cars approached, each a few moments apart. One by one, they came to a complete stop as the drivers lowered their windows and asked me if I was okay. "Just taking a photograph," I replied. I was happy to know that if I were in trouble, apparently there would be plenty of help!

5 STAR LIGHTS—BEACONS IN THE NIGHT

Cape Cod has no shortage of lighthouses. Several of them are easily accessible, while others require a bit of a hike. They make amazing subjects for artists of all mediums. Visit any art gallery on the Cape, and you will see lighthouses featured in paintings, sculptures, and photographs. No trip to the Cape would be complete without taking time to see one of them in person. One such lighthouse, Nobska Light (*opposite*), is a very accessible property with great views of the waters near Woods Hole.

When it comes to night photography, capturing a lighthouse can be a challenge. In most cases, a lighthouse is doing the thing it is meant to do, which is to put out a lot of light. Sometimes, there are ways around this. I classify every lighthouse into one of two categories: *blinkers* and *spinners*.

Spinners are the difficult ones. You've seen these before. They feature a continuously glowing light with some sort of rotating mirror contraption that projects a beam across the landscape. Unless they have a mechanical failure or a bulb burnout, they are constant and relentless. They are my nemesis.

Blinkers are much friendlier. They love to be photographed and welcome night photographers like me with a constant but forgiving blinking pattern. In the case of Highland Light (also known as Cape Cod Light), the period between blinks is about five seconds. This works out great when you know the timing, because there are at least four full seconds of complete darkness. Does that mean you can capture only a four-second exposure? Nope. If you have rhythm, you can capture dark skies around a lighthouse by simply covering the lens every five seconds. Do it right by not allowing any light to leak through, and the camera sees only the other four seconds in the cycle. Repeat this throughout your exposure and you've got yourself a dark lighthouse with beautiful, unaffected skies. If you want a little bit of light to shine, let one or two blinks through.

Highland Light used to be a spinner. It had one of the most aggressive spinning systems I had ever seen. There were multiple sides to the rotating mechanism within the light's beacon room, which created what I can only describe as a wagon wheel effect. There were several narrow beams constantly spinning around the landscape. It was a halogen light, which also created a warm color cast everywhere. I could work with this depending on what my expectations were and where I positioned my camera, but it left a lot of options off the table.

In 2017, I arrived to a surprising change: That wagon wheel system had been replaced with a much dimmer, bluish-white blinking LED. The future was here and so were a lot of new image opportunities. Over the next several years, I racked up many new shots until the lighthouse went into scaffolding for structural repair. Based on the public notification sign posted outside the museum, this was a job that was supposed to take several months but ultimately stretched into a few years thanks to the pandemic.

In the spring of 2023, I had just completed a photography tour with a nice couple from Australia. We had made Highland Light our last location. It was a cool, clear, perfectly starry night. The Milky Way core was just starting to rise as we wrapped up. I make a habit of never capturing my own images while hosting guests unless it is for demonstration purposes. But since I was here and we were all parting ways, I said goodbye and then hiked back up to the lighthouse from the parking lot.

Early season compositions are unique in that if you don't get the Milky Way alignment then, you won't be able to again until the following year. I knew this would be my only chance based on conditions and timing, so I set up in a spot I had envisioned a little earlier while hosting the tour.

The Milky Way was over the top of the museum and behind the tower as seen from the front. Facing east offers the darkest skies we can get here on the Cape Cod National Seashore. After all, in that direction, the next source of light pollution is Europe. In other words, light pollution is not a problem.

As I often will do, I angled the camera and looked through the live view screen, moving the tripod a few feet back and a little to the right. Little by little I figured out the perfect spot and began to dial in my settings.

I've been doing this a long time, and I am generally pretty aware of what is going on around me. This includes keeping track of animal sounds, avoiding pricker bushes, or staying concealed from drunk teenagers howling in the night as they run up the path with their iPhones, trying to get amazing night images and then wondering what went wrong.

And yet, on that midweek night in April, I think I let my guard down a little, because I had no expectations of anyone other than myself being there at two in the morning. Needless to say, I was quite startled by the sound of footsteps just 20 or 30 feet away. I immediately hit the offender with the beam of my flashlight and quickly realized I had just blinded some poor photographer who probably also thought he was alone.

I apologized, saying something like "Sorry about that; you kind of snuck up on me. I am a photographer."

He said he was planning on doing the same thing and that he had come up from New Jersey hoping to photograph this lighthouse. He then said something that somewhat took me by surprise.

"Your voice sounds familiar," he said, not being able to see my face in the darkness, nor I his.

"It does?" I asked.

"Yeah. Do you have a YouTube channel?"

"I do, actually," I answered back from the darkness.

"No kidding? I saw your video on this lighthouse. That's why I'm here."

What were the chances of that? I wished him good luck and happy shooting on his visit, and he carried on with his mission, as did I. Within ten minutes or so, I had gotten what I needed.

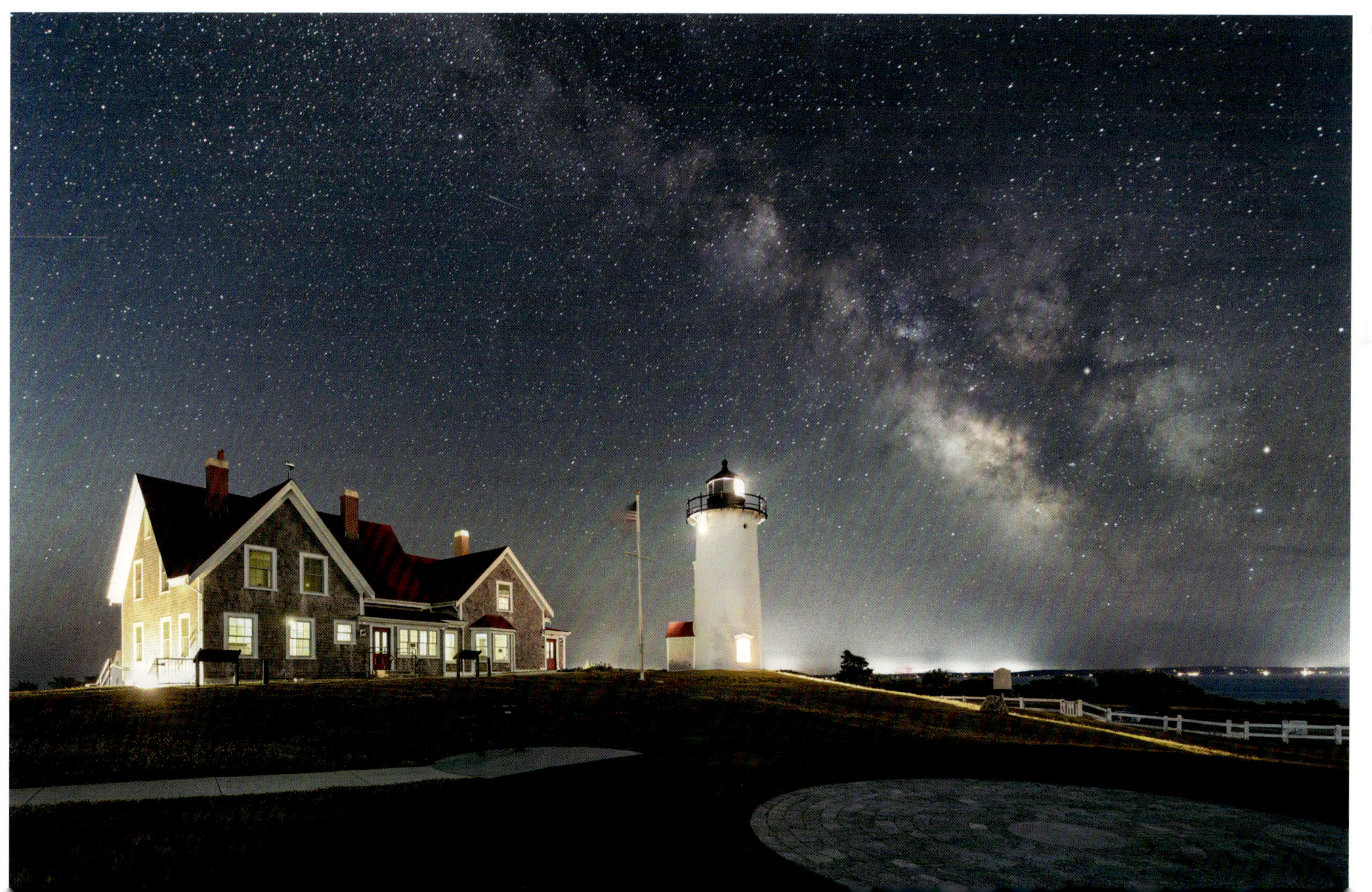

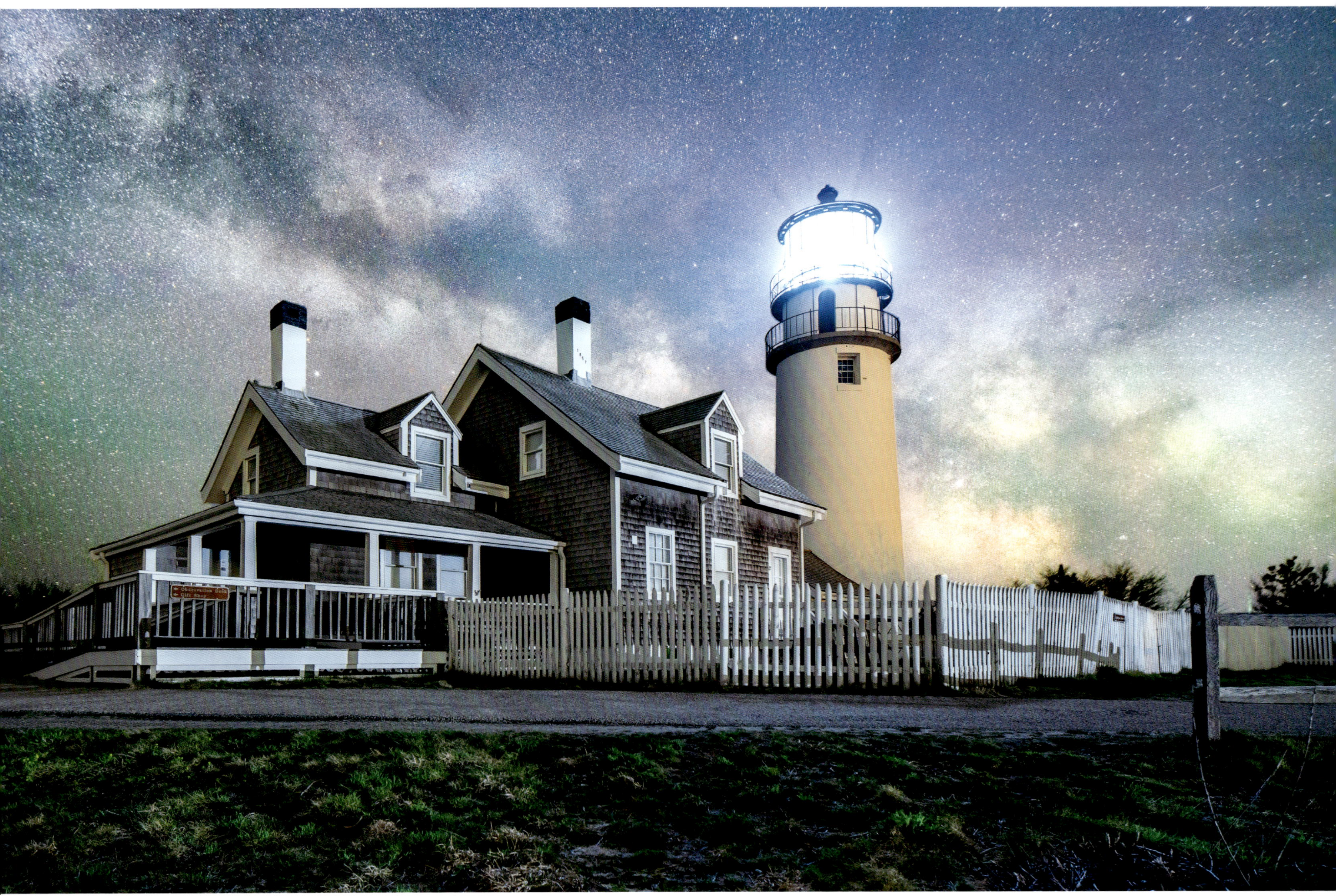

QUICK TIPS FOR TRACKING

Tracking is a technique that involves moving the camera at the same speed and direction as the night sky to avoid star trails. Why would you want to do this?

Most photographers will use the settings I offered in chapter 1. It's quick and easy. Throw a little light in the foreground, and you've got it all done in one take. But there are drawbacks. The higher ISO settings often result in grainy images that get worse with older cameras. Photographing with wide apertures often requires expensive lenses. We do both of these things because time is working against us. If the exposure is too long, the stars will begin to trail and the Milky Way will begin to blur.

A tracker overcomes that problem entirely. It converts time from a liability to an asset. It also eliminates the need for wide-aperture lenses while allowing images to be captured at lower ISO settings. This results in images with better color and more flexibility in editing shadows and highlights later. It opens up even very old digital cameras and their kit lenses to become great Milky Way shooters.

A small tracker can be mounted between the tripod and the camera. After a calibration that usually takes less than ten minutes, the tracker knows where it is and how to move to ensure you get what you need. There is one challenge, however. Since the sky is being tracked, the foreground blurs with the movement. A second, untracked image will have to be captured to ensure a sharp foreground and then combined with the tracked sky image in editing later. But the results speak for themselves. All techniques come with trade-offs. Deciding what technique fits your skill level and equipment capability is the most important thing to consider here. For this image (*opposite*), I used a Pentax K1, which has a proprietary function called Astrotracer. Rather than move the entire camera, the sensor alone will track the night sky. This can give you up to five minutes of tracking, which is more than enough for me. There's no external tracker needed, and faster calibration time. It may not be ideal for deep-sky-object astrophotographers who require longer tracking periods, but for this type of work, it is more than enough.

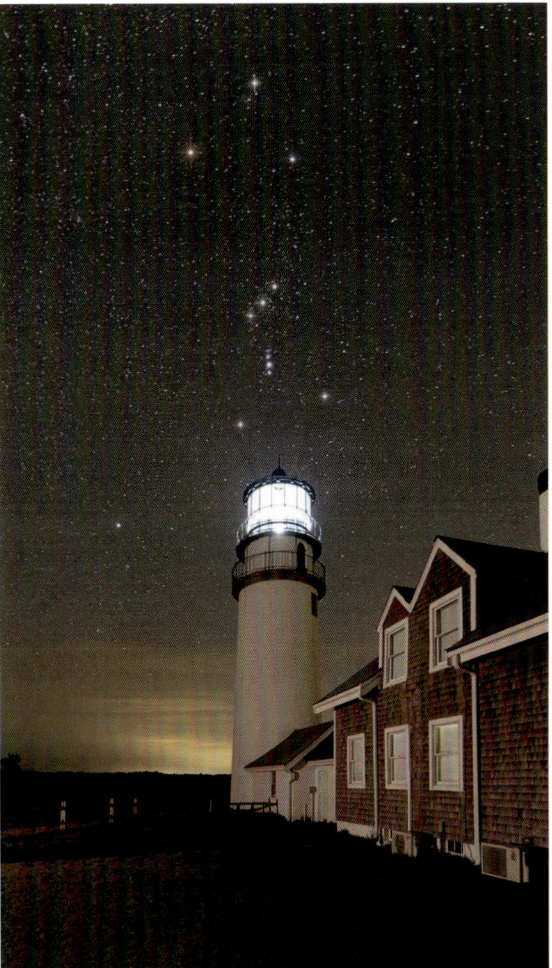

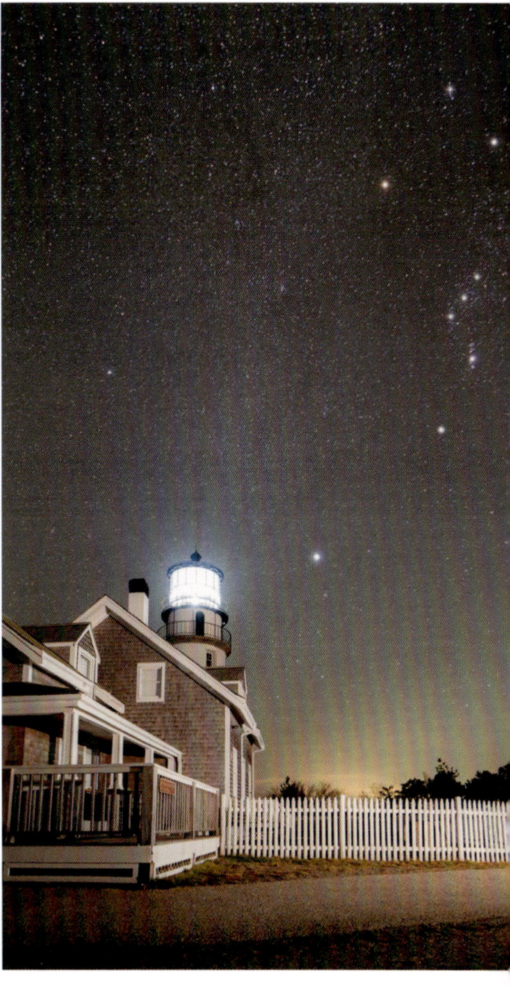

Orion is known as a "winter" constellation and is one of the easiest ones to spot over Cape Cod. For astronomers, it's rich with interesting objects such as nebulae and ancient stars. Early morning risers can see it in the east just before dawn in September, and high in the sky by the end of the year. Here it is seen visiting Highland Light.

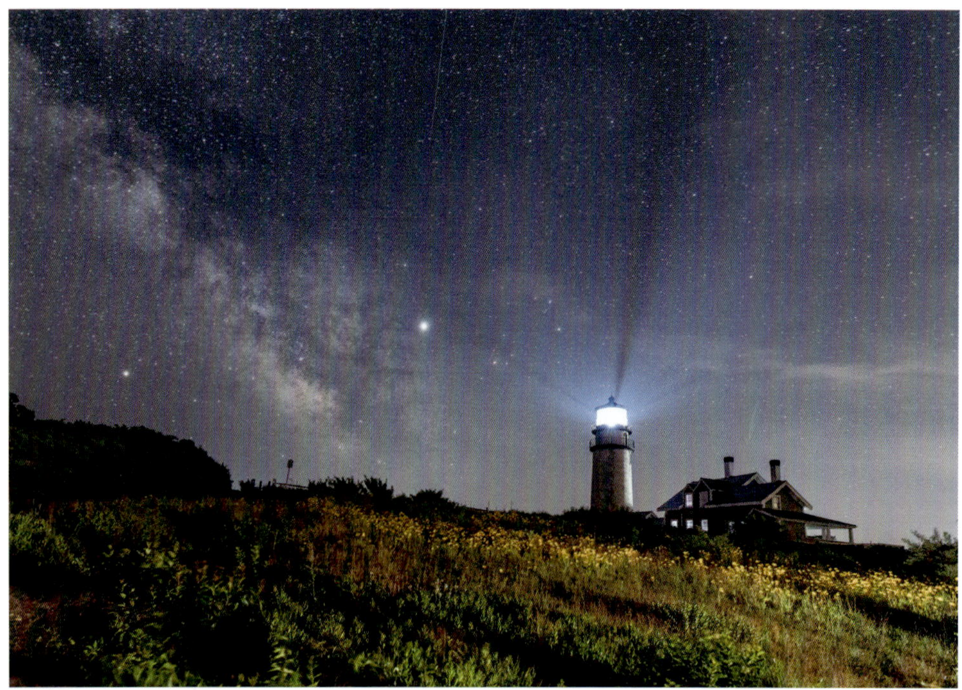

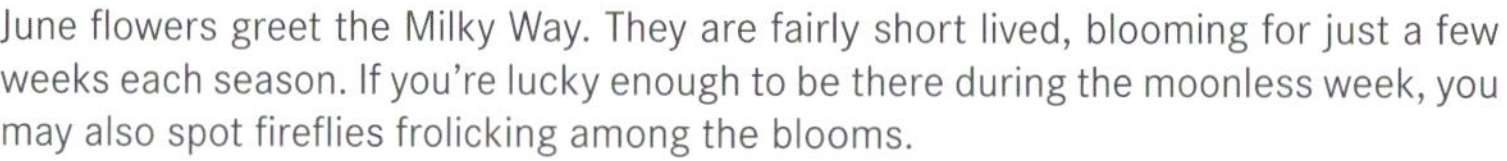

June flowers greet the Milky Way. They are fairly short lived, blooming for just a few weeks each season. If you're lucky enough to be there during the moonless week, you may also spot fireflies frolicking among the blooms.

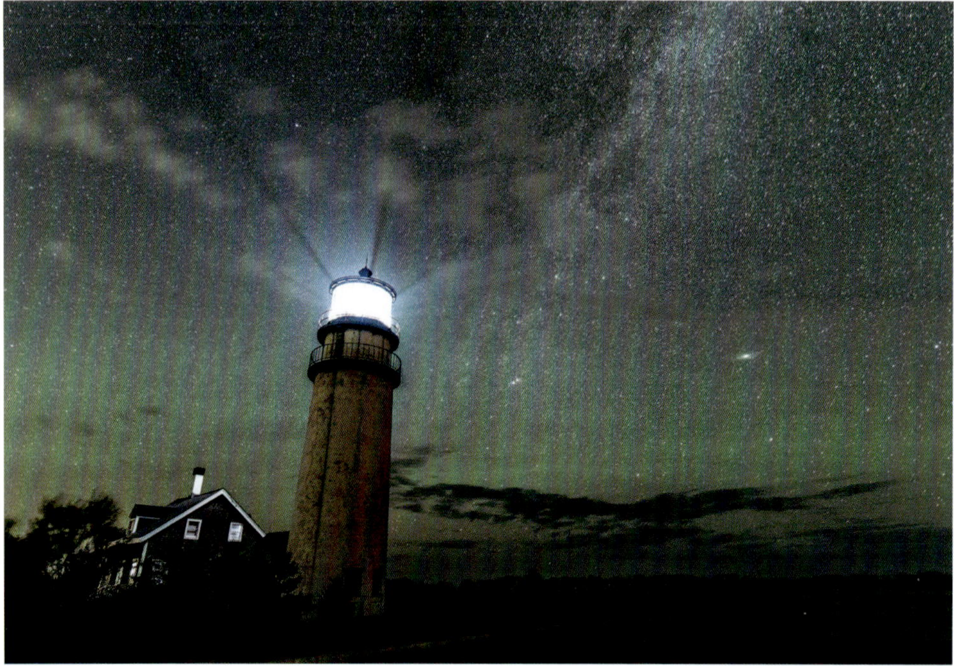

This is the most intense example of airglow I had captured to date. Barely visible to the unaided eye, the green glow is caused by oxygen atoms recombining after having been ionized by the daytime sun. It is not related to the northern lights and can be photographed with dark enough conditions anywhere on Earth. On this night, I could see the silhouette of the clouds, which hinted that airglow was present. The National Seashore, facing east, provides the best opportunities to experience it on Cape Cod.

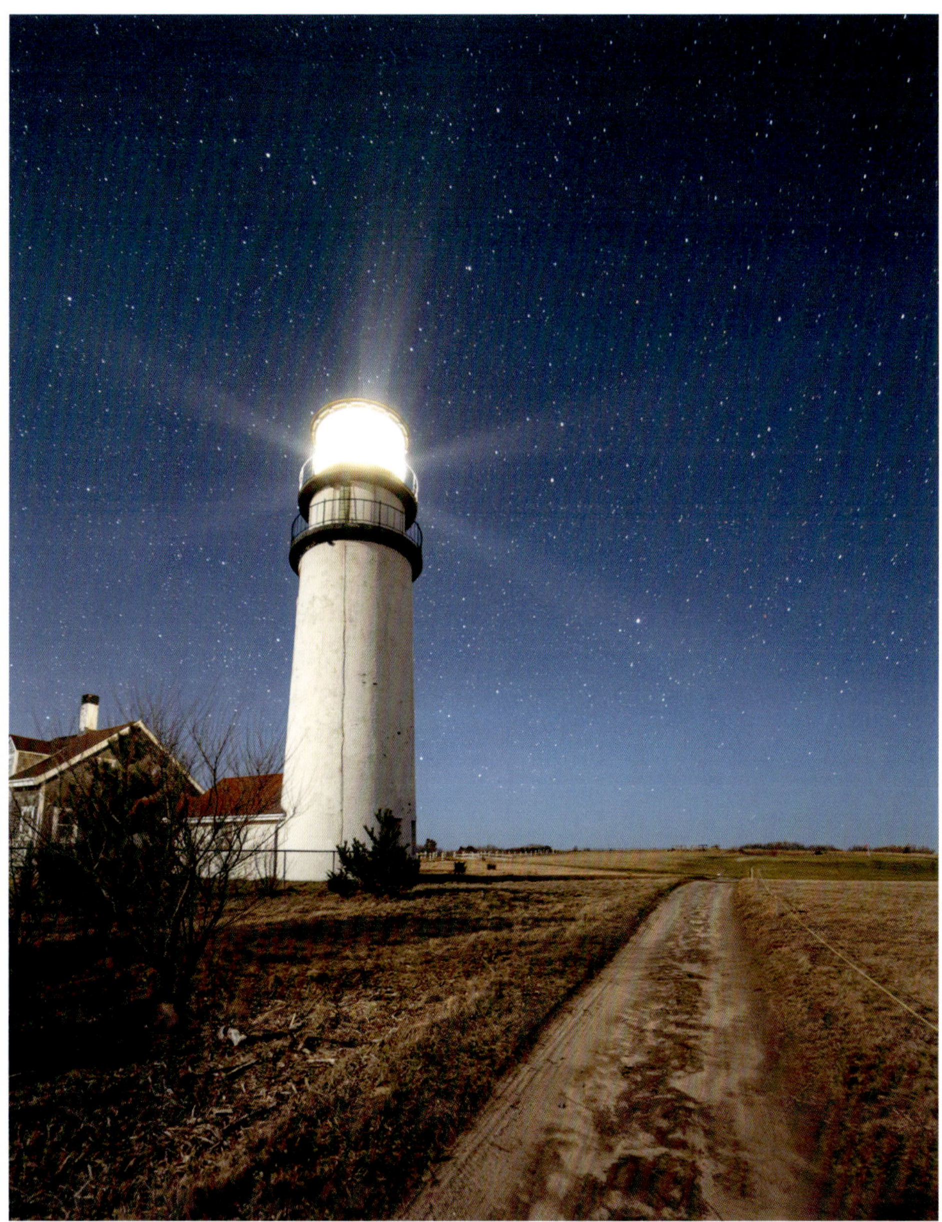

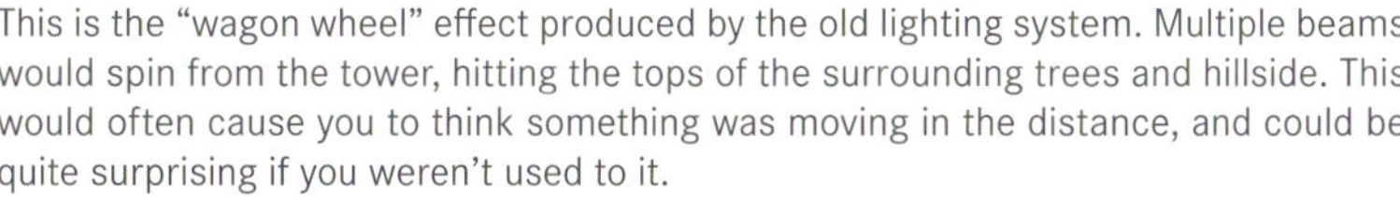

This is the "wagon wheel" effect produced by the old lighting system. Multiple beams would spin from the tower, hitting the tops of the surrounding trees and hillside. This would often cause you to think something was moving in the distance, and could be quite surprising if you weren't used to it.

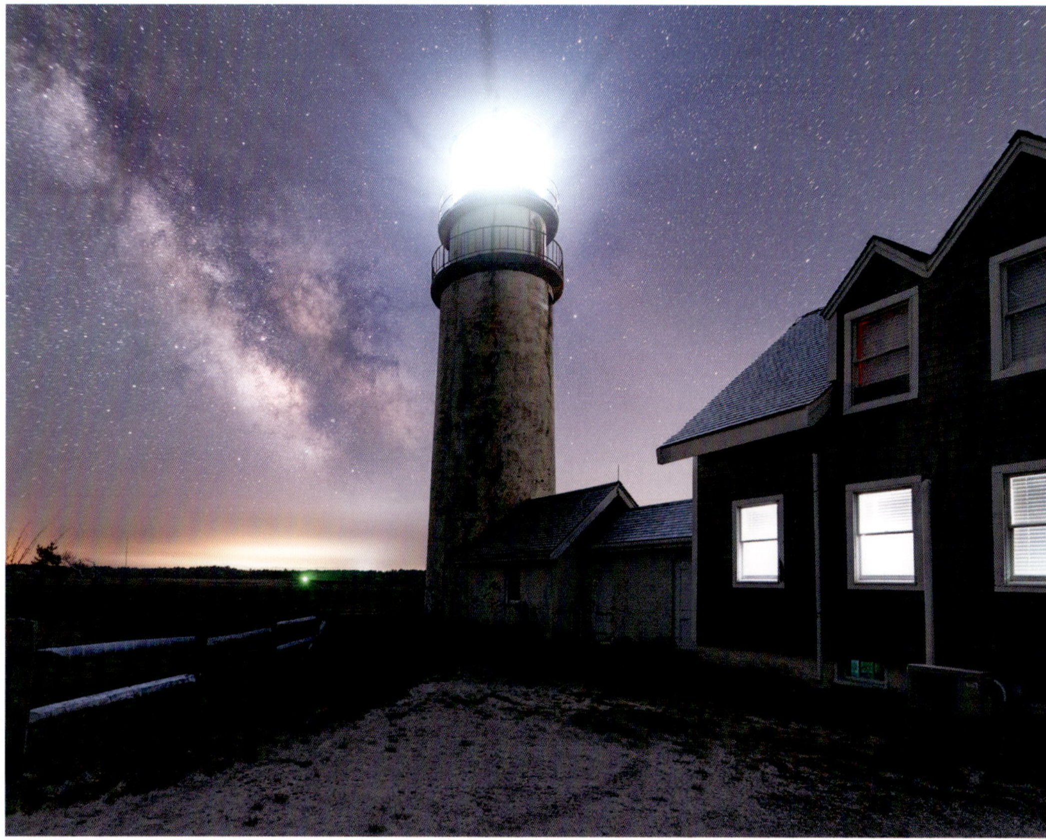

For years I wondered what that little green light on the horizon was. It appeared in many of my images. I knew that the light was on the nearby golf course, but I was frequently too far away to determine the source. At last, I finally made the walk out there for the sole purpose of solving the mystery. Turns out, it tells golfers that the hole ahead, which is not visible from the tee, is clear of players. Golfers press a button to change it to red, proceed with play, and then press a button to switch it back to green on the other end.

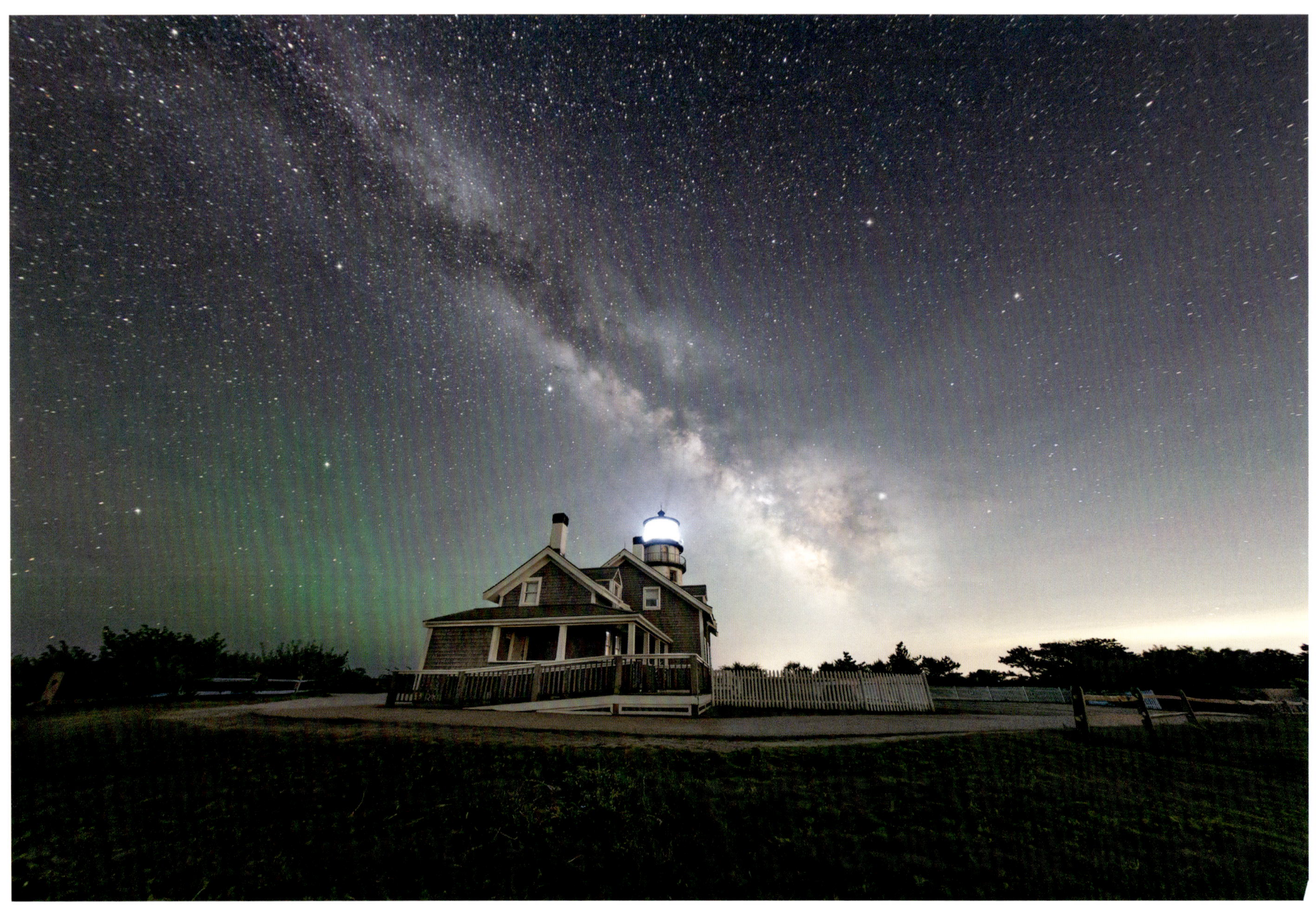

A fish-eye lens captures the expansive skies over Cape Cod / Highland Light. Such a lens is a great way to make a small area look large. Despite how it appears, there is not much room to photograph from this side of the lighthouse. A vertical galactic band is best viewed after sunset in the summer months. Unless you like to get up early in the spring! The green sky to the left of the building is atmospheric airglow.

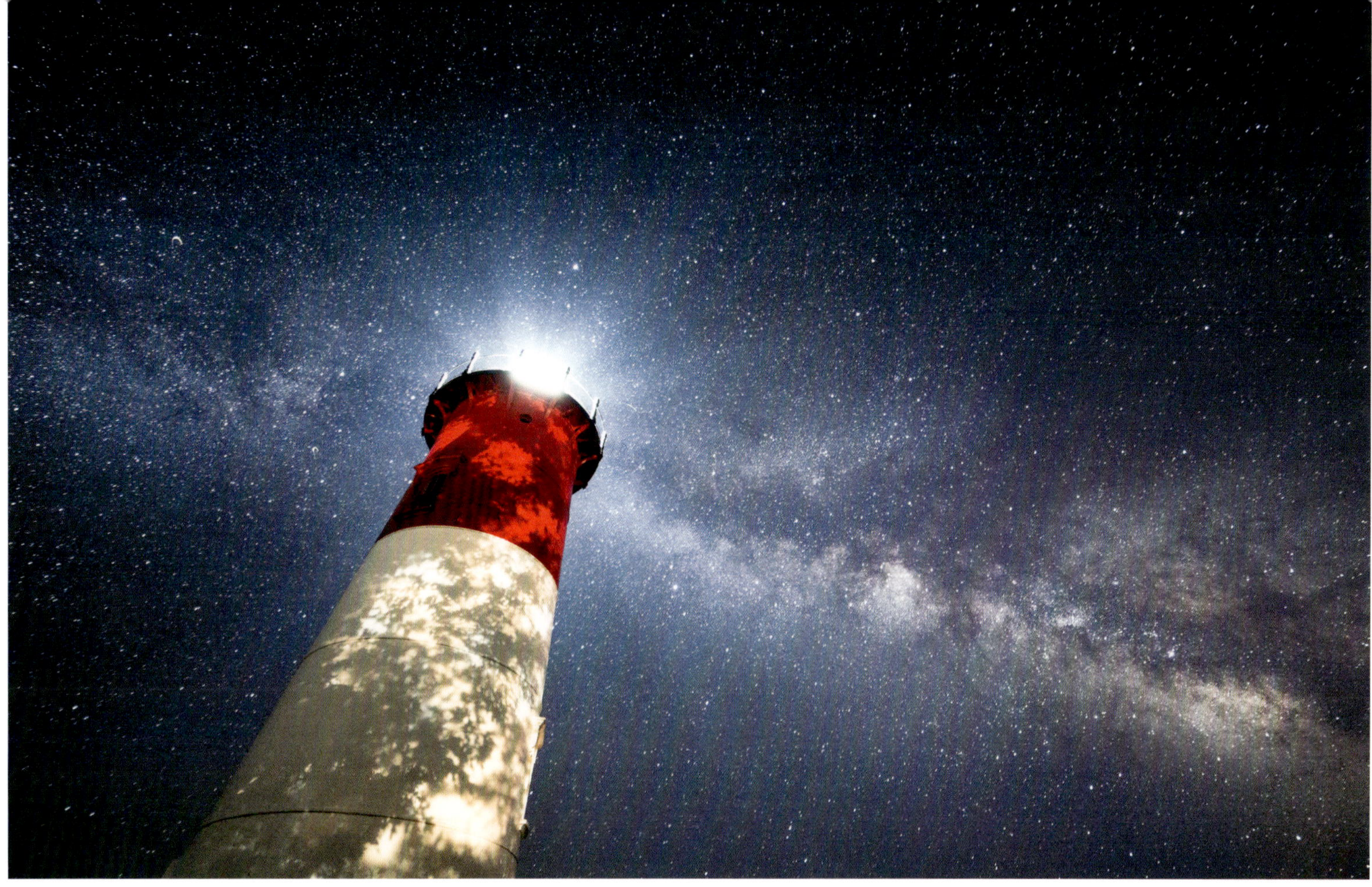

INTO THE SHADOWS

Nauset Light is one of those dreaded *spinners* that I mentioned earlier. Although I had captured several long-exposure images of Nauset over the years, as of 2014 I had not been able to capture a Milky Way photograph. As far as I could tell, no one had up to that point. Earlier that year I had obtained my first ultrawide aperture lens with just such a shot in mind. But how to approach Nauset Light, or any spinner for that matter, was elusive.

In July 2014, I decided to make the trip there. By the time I arrived, the Milky Way band was high overhead, as is the case through the dark weeks of the summer months. Scouting around the area and thinking about trying to solve this problem, I figured out that a starry shot might be possible but would require very specific positioning. So specific, in fact, that I would have to lie on the ground at the base of the lighthouse tower.

To defeat a spinner, you must photograph from the "shadow zone." Most lighthouses have a shadowy parameter at the base of the tower where the main light source is obscured by a catwalk or some other design element of the lighthouse. If you can find a composition within this zone, on a night without mist or humidity to enhance the beam, you too may be able to get a shot like this.

Since the camera sees much better than the human eye, it sometimes will reveal something that was otherwise entirely invisible. After taking the first few images, I noticed an odd pattern on the tower structure. I thought my camera was malfunctioning, so I repeated the image again and again but garnered the same result. After zooming in on the camera screen, I realized that what I had captured was the glow of a floodlight, shining through the trees of a nearby home. The patterns resulted from the perfectly projected leaf shadows on a windless night.

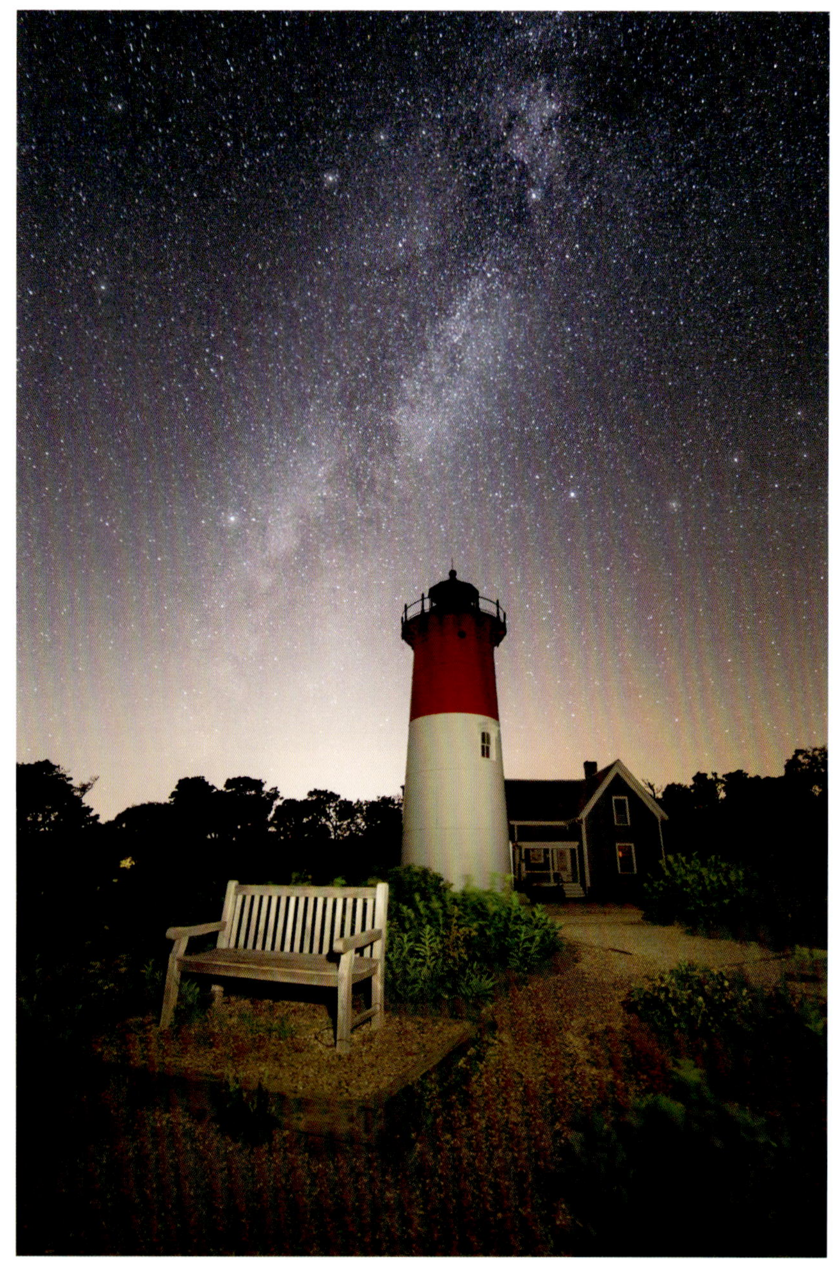

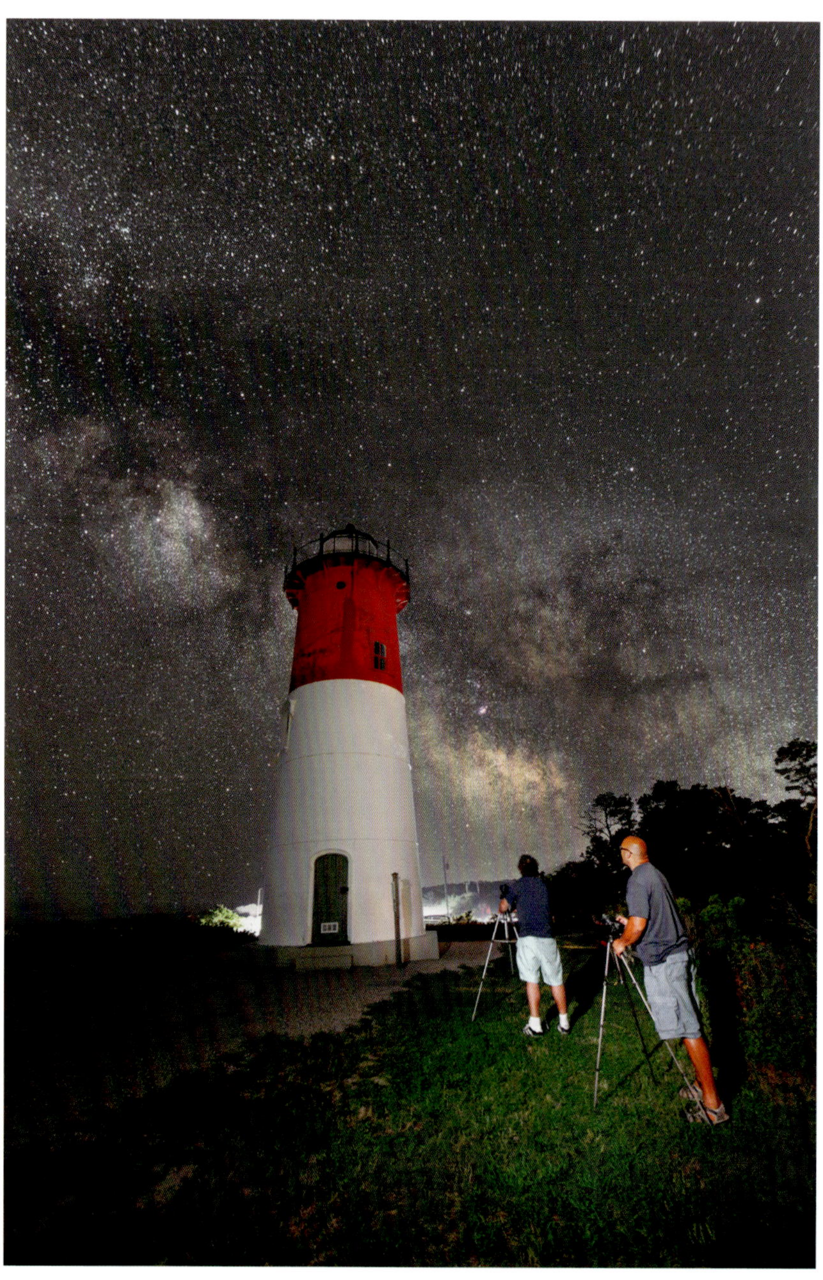

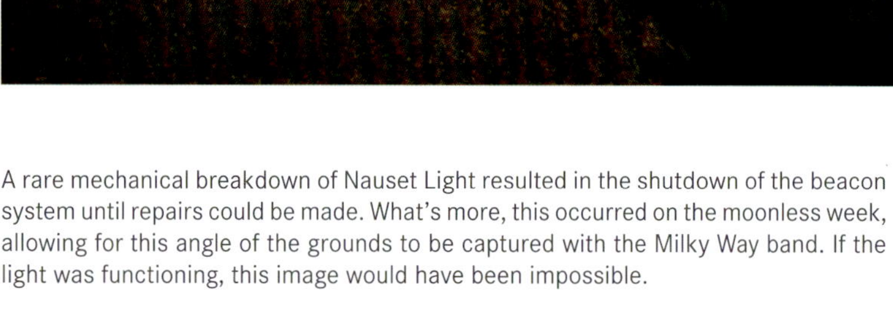

A rare mechanical breakdown of Nauset Light resulted in the shutdown of the beacon system until repairs could be made. What's more, this occurred on the moonless week, allowing for this angle of the grounds to be captured with the Milky Way band. If the light was functioning, this image would have been impossible.

Meet Chris and George, two brothers who sometimes book a night photography tour with me. They were lucky enough to experience the dark conditions from Nauset Light's temporary shutdown.

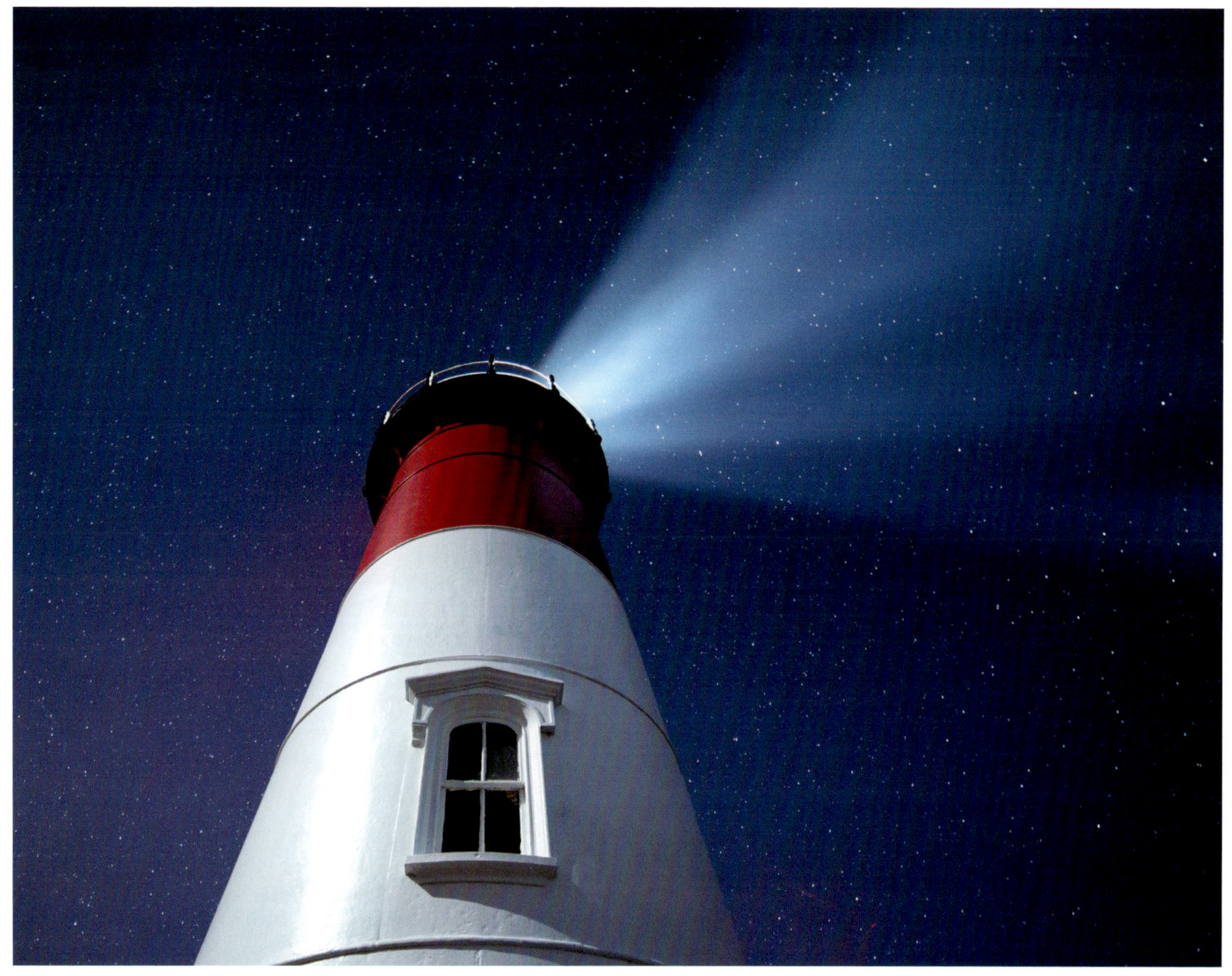

A setting crescent moon provides just enough light to reveal the left side of Nauset Light. This is a thirty-second exposure, and a hand was placed over the camera lens until the spinning beam approached the right-side corner of the composition. The hand was then lifted for a few seconds and then dropped again. This "froze" the beam in place; otherwise the entire sky would have been washed out by the rotating beam. This was repeated five times while the shutter was open. It's an organic, in-the-field trick to help shape the light. You could also use a lens cap, a piece of cardboard, or even a hat—anything that fully covers the lens and is easily removable.

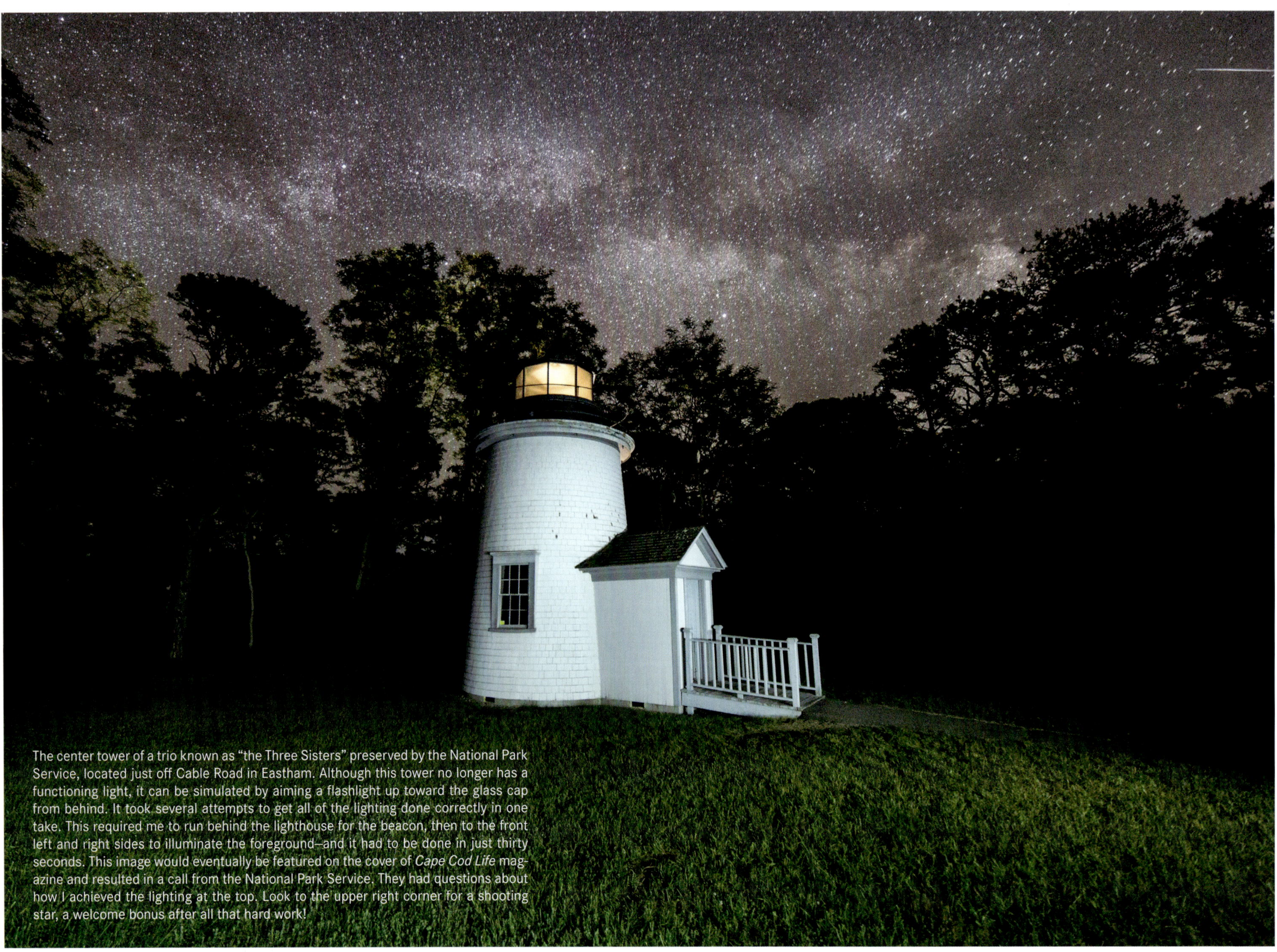

The center tower of a trio known as "the Three Sisters" preserved by the National Park Service, located just off Cable Road in Eastham. Although this tower no longer has a functioning light, it can be simulated by aiming a flashlight up toward the glass cap from behind. It took several attempts to get all of the lighting done correctly in one take. This required me to run behind the lighthouse for the beacon, then to the front left and right sides to illuminate the foreground—and it had to be done in just thirty seconds. This image would eventually be featured on the cover of *Cape Cod Life* magazine and resulted in a call from the National Park Service. They had questions about how I achieved the lighting at the top. Look to the upper right corner for a shooting star, a welcome bonus after all that hard work!

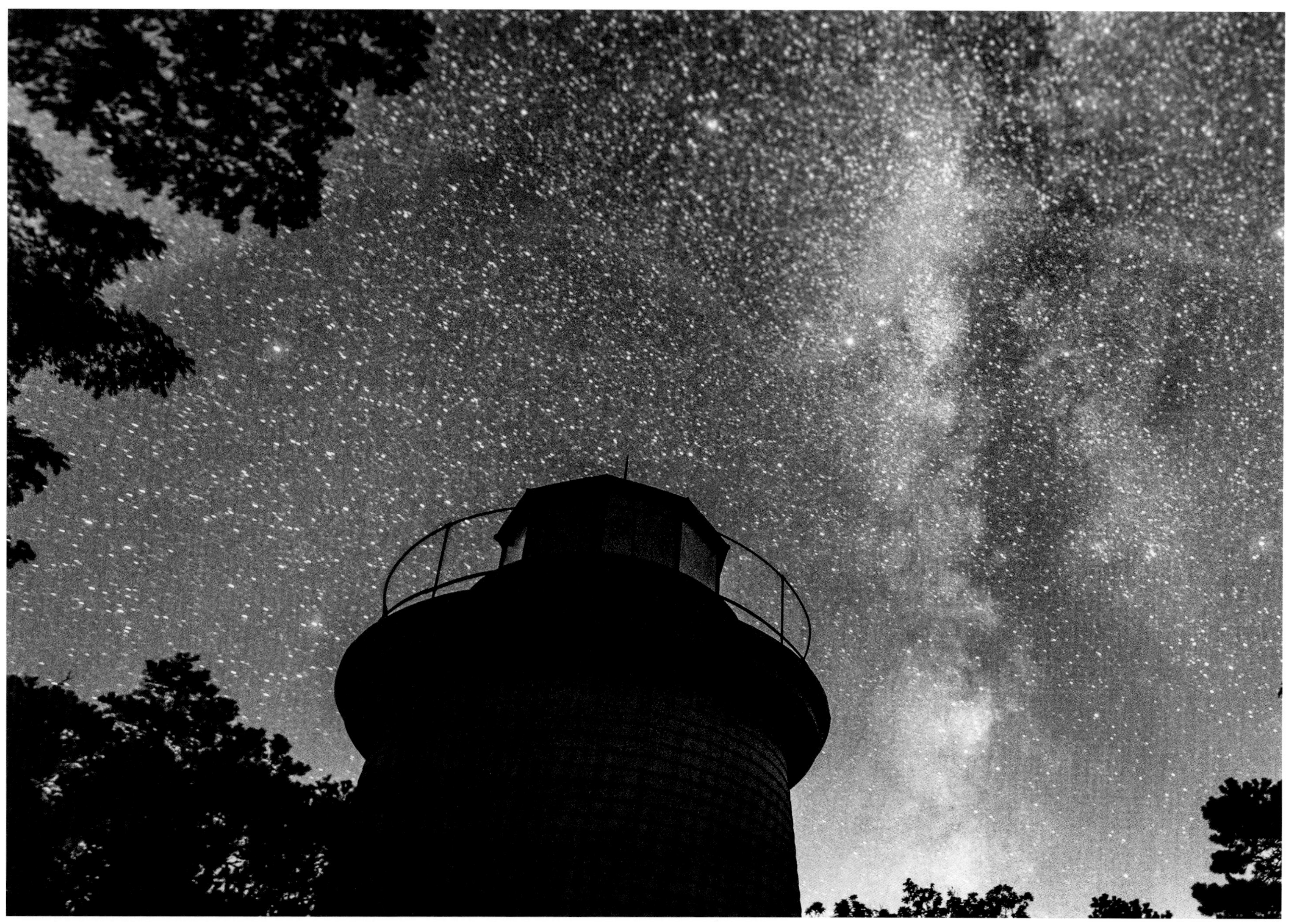

A starry night above the same center tower.

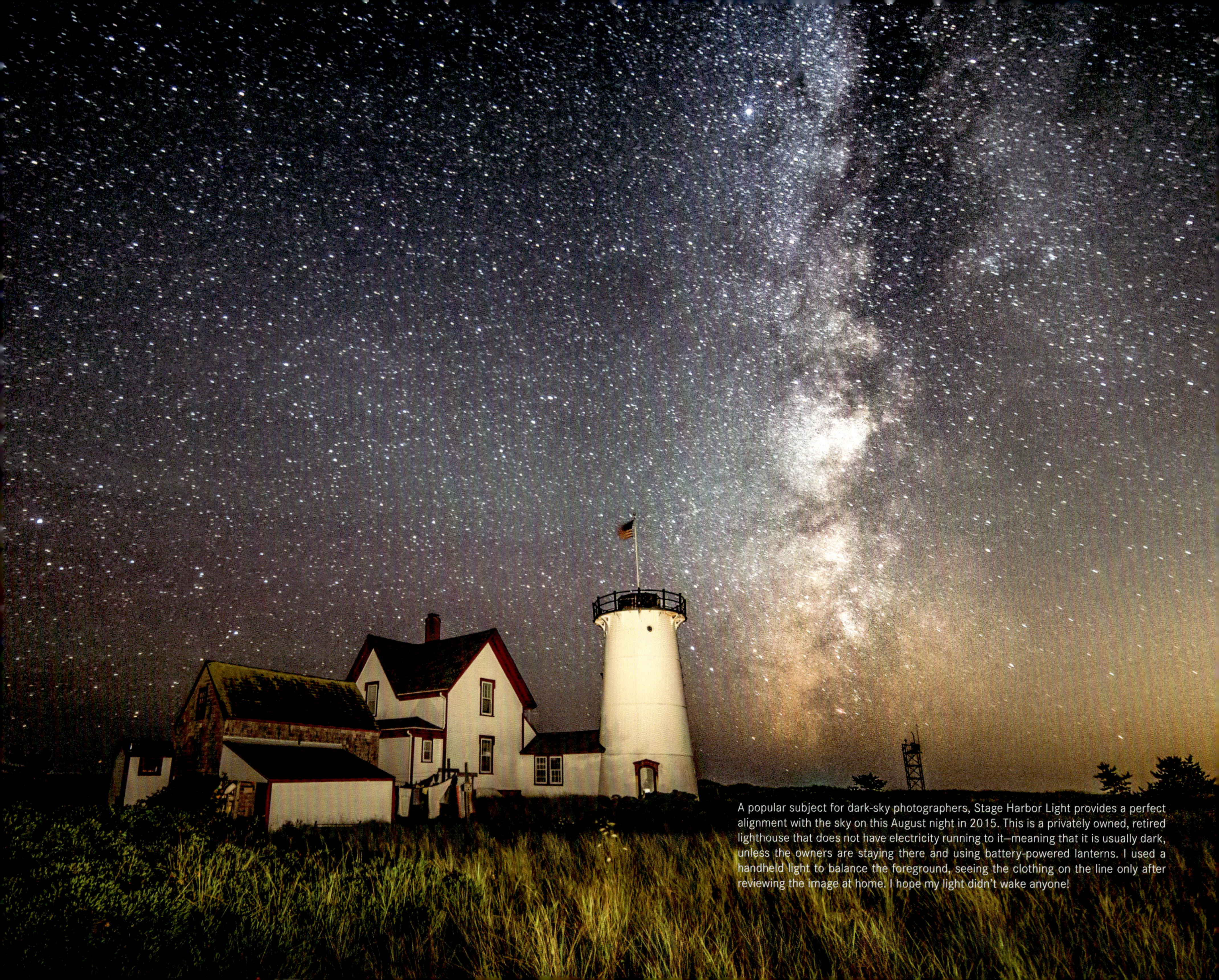

A popular subject for dark-sky photographers, Stage Harbor Light provides a perfect alignment with the sky on this August night in 2015. This is a privately owned, retired lighthouse that does not have electricity running to it—meaning that it is usually dark, unless the owners are staying there and using battery-powered lanterns. I used a handheld light to balance the foreground, seeing the clothing on the line only after reviewing the image at home. I hope my light didn't wake anyone!

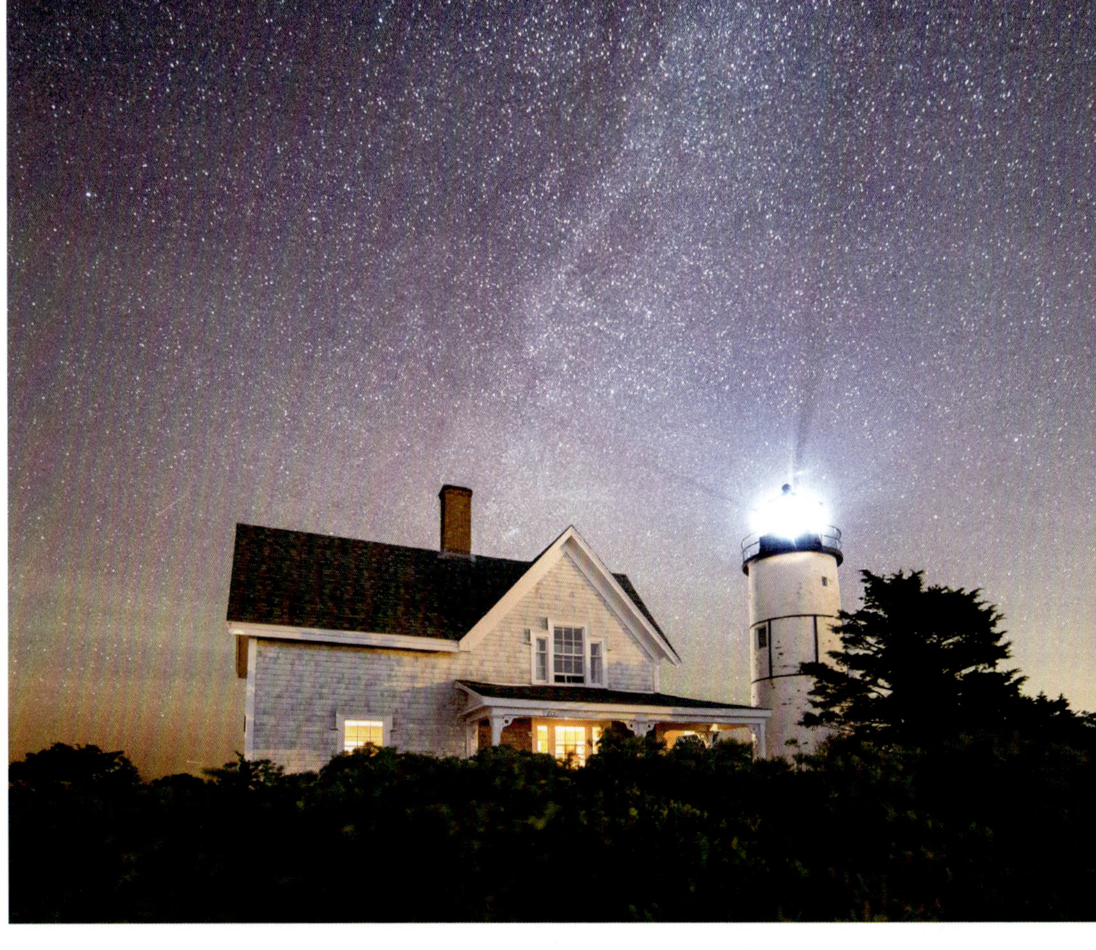

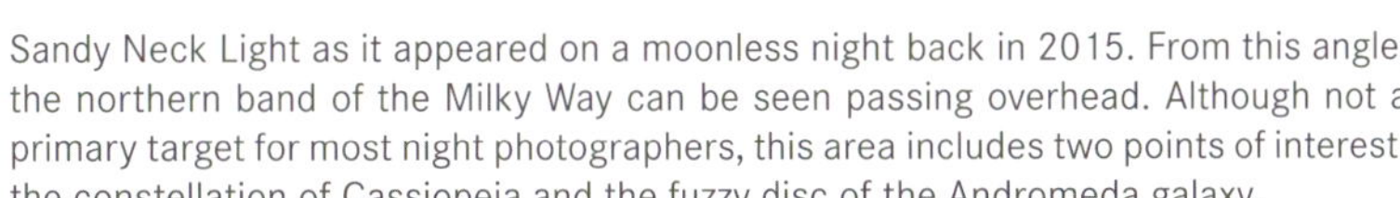

Sandy Neck Light as it appeared on a moonless night back in 2015. From this angle, the northern band of the Milky Way can be seen passing overhead. Although not a primary target for most night photographers, this area includes two points of interest: the constellation of Cassiopeia and the fuzzy disc of the Andromeda galaxy.

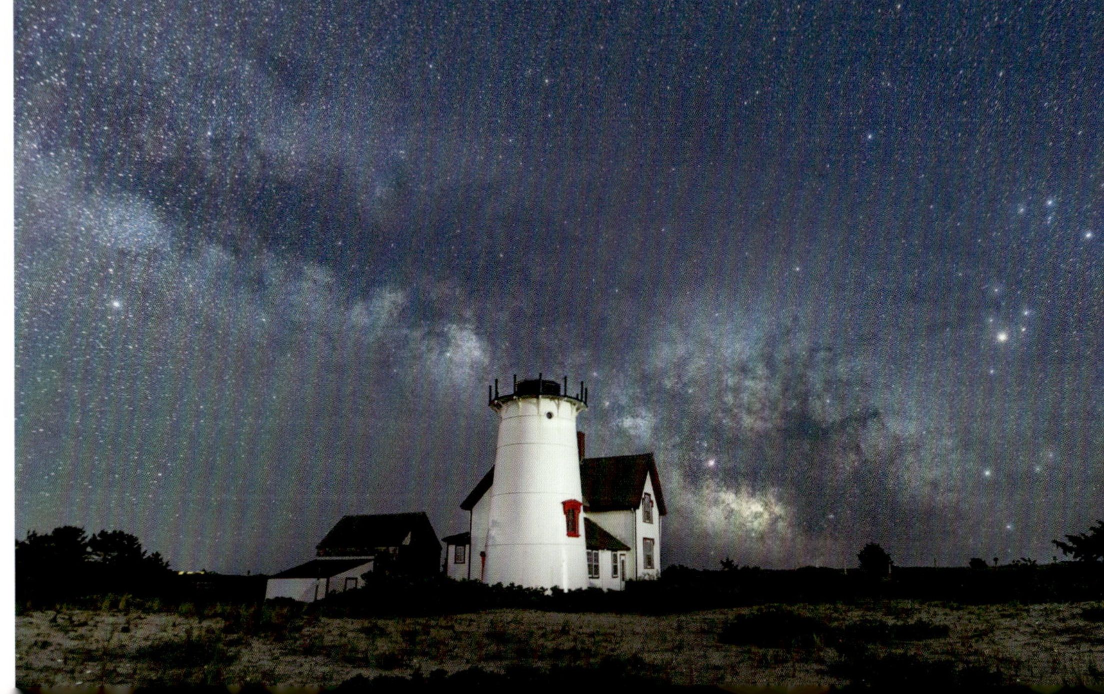

The last glow of a setting moon provides just enough ambient light for the foreground without obscuring the rising galactic core. It also results in a touch of blue being added to the sky. A visit here earlier in the year is the best time to see the Milky Way and the lighthouse together from this vantage point.

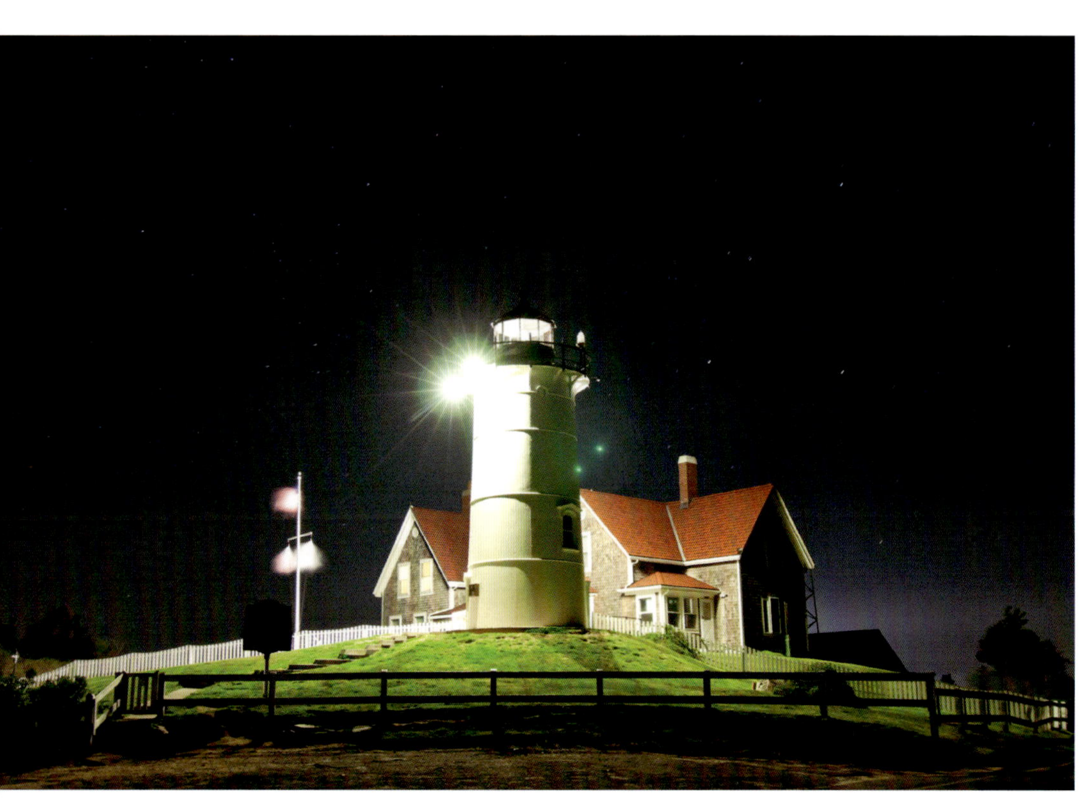

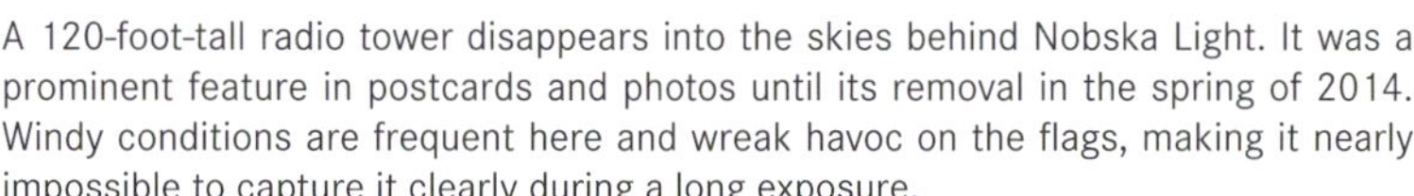

A 120-foot-tall radio tower disappears into the skies behind Nobska Light. It was a prominent feature in postcards and photos until its removal in the spring of 2014. Windy conditions are frequent here and wreak havoc on the flags, making it nearly impossible to capture it clearly during a long exposure.

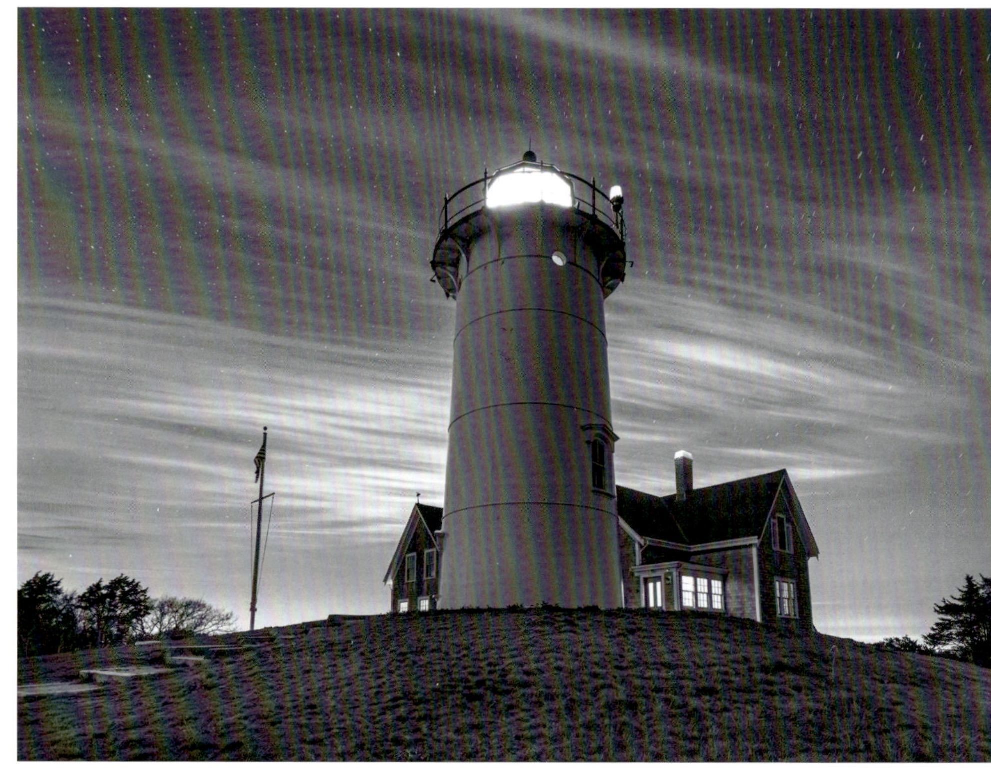

The downward-facing tower lights make Nobska a difficult subject to shoot. In spring of 2024, I made a request to the Friends of Nobska, asking if the tower lights could be turned off for the evening. As you can see, the request was granted, which gave me the opportunity to photograph this lighthouse under better conditions. The wispy clouds, lit by Falmouth, were a welcome addition.

On July 2, 2024, I had the rare opportunity to photograph the summertime Milky Way band and the lighthouse together. Up to this point, I had never been able to accomplish this due to the aforementioned tower lights. One thing to contend with was the green glow on the cement walkway, which was cast from the exit signs inside the nearby house. I was able to reduce this during image processing.

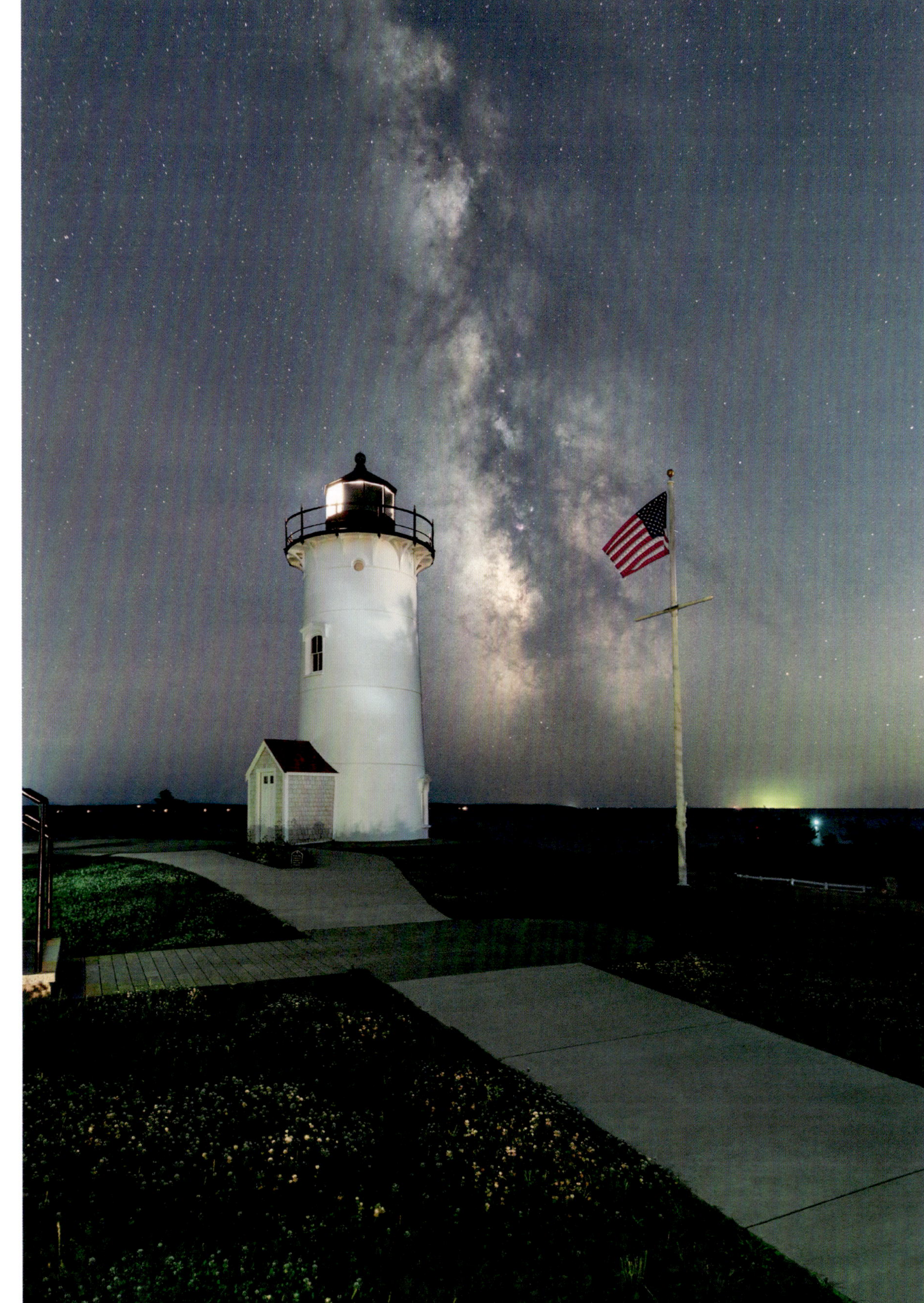

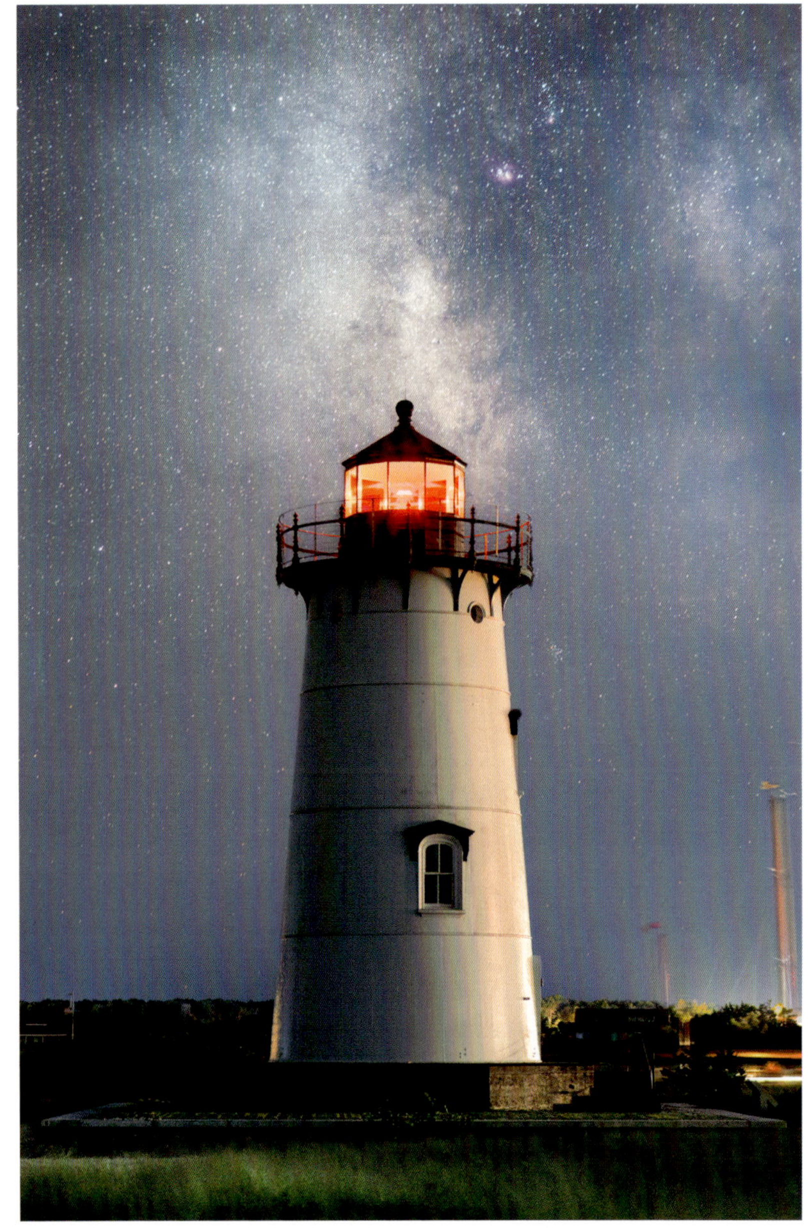

Nearby town lighting creates a glow along the right side of Edgartown Light. Look to the skies overhead to see the faint purple glow of the Lagoon Nebula, which always appears in the "big" part of the Milky Way. It's located over 4,000 light-years away from Earth. This means that it took the light, traveling at 186,000 miles per second, four thousand years to reach my camera on that night.

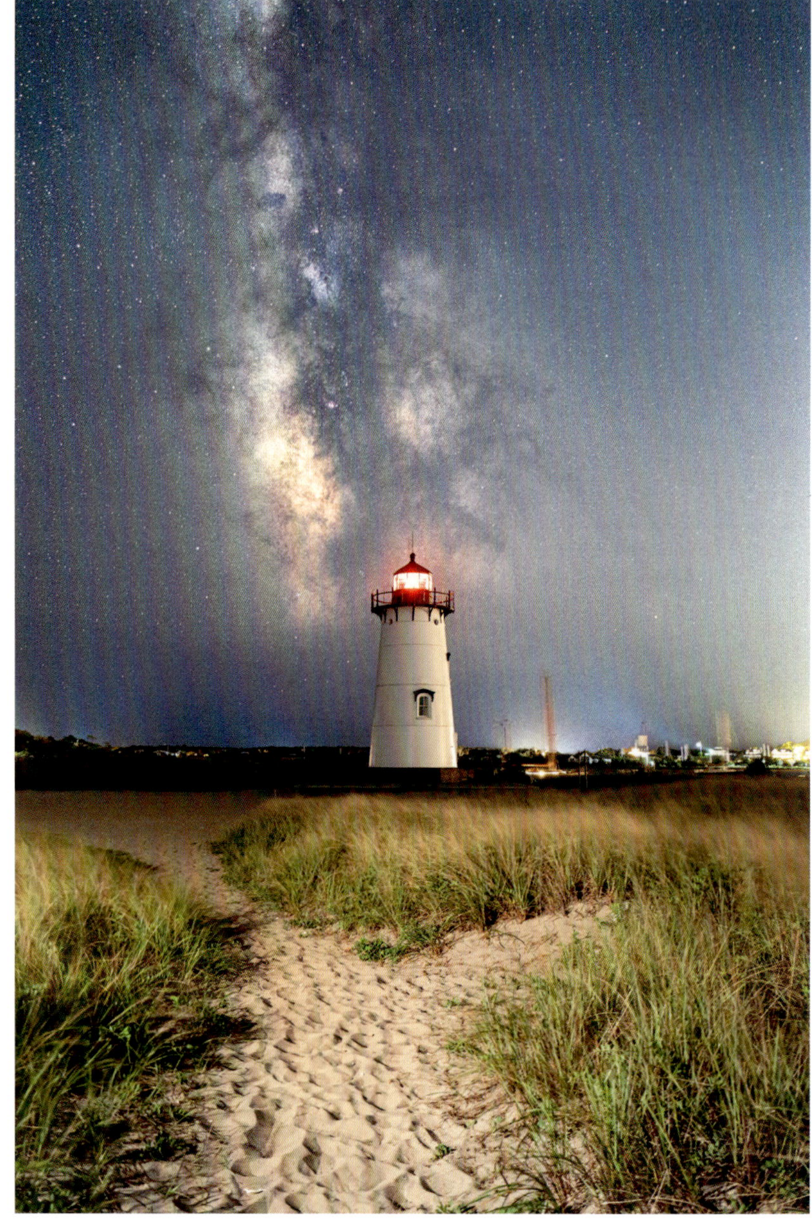

The galactic core leads to the tower on a quiet weekday evening. The path was lit at an angle to bring out the texture created by the footprint divots. In the distance, swaying masts wave back, which is inevitable when creating long exposures near harbors.

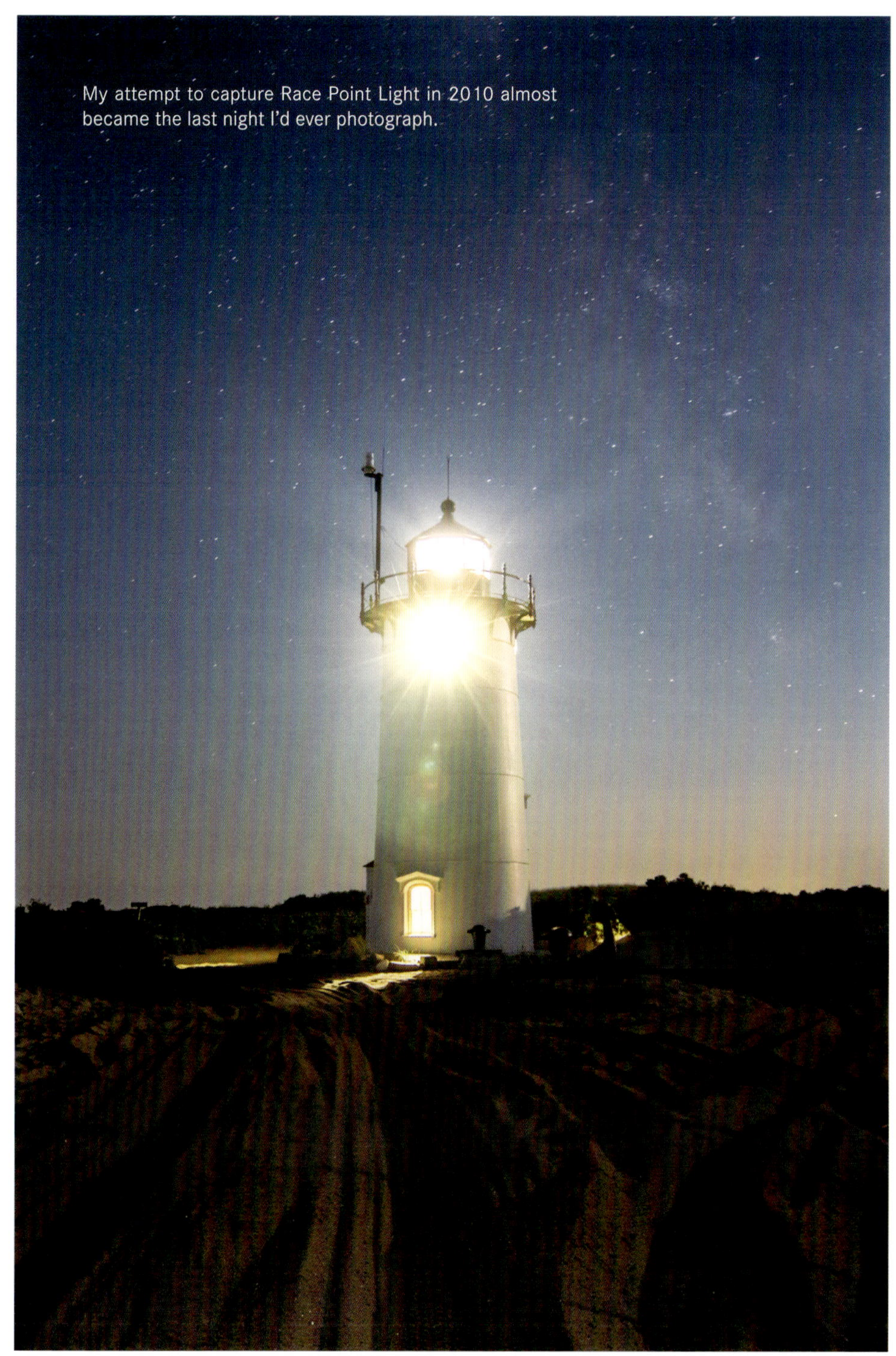

My attempt to capture Race Point Light in 2010 almost became the last night I'd ever photograph.

MY EVENING AT RACE POINT

I was confident I was going to die. So much so that I was thinking, "Well, if this is the way I am going to go, at least it was doing something I loved." Poor planning led me to this point.

When I had started my walk to Race Point Light in Provincetown in 2010, I knew I would make it. My destination didn't seem that far, at least from what I could tell based on the online map I reviewed before making the ninety-minute drive to my starting point.

The walk began as I had expected. I planned to park at the beach lot and walk the shoreline until it hooked around and eventually connected with the lighthouse. It was the summer, a moonlit night, and around 75 degrees Fahrenheit. It was also quite humid, and before long I started sweating thanks to the sandy hike and the bag of camera gear strapped to my back.

I had been walking for what seemed like an eternity. I could see the soft puff of light over the dunes from Race Point lighthouse every five seconds or so, but I still wasn't seeing the actual tower. The moon was getting lower in the sky, almost directly ahead of me, and I started to wonder if I had made the wrong choice by not tackling the over-the-dune trail that led directly to my destination instead. I read that it was a grueling, tiring walk, and it was the last thing I had wanted to do with a backpack and a tripod.

Lost in thought about this decision, I noticed I was coming up to a point where I couldn't go any farther. The sand was narrowing; water was on both sides of me. None of this made any sense until I realized my error: Somehow, in the dim moonlight, I had managed to walk myself out to a sandbar, leaving the main beach behind me. What's more, apparently that sandbar materialized only during low tide—and since that had already passed, the water was starting to slowly flow in behind me. It wasn't going to be long before I was on an island that would also soon disappear.

I turned around and began jogging back with my equipment. I reconnected with the beach in a few minutes, but after all of this I was sweaty, tired, and cranky. I also had to work the next day. Eventually, I found a break in a sand dune, which revealed the lighthouse to be just a few more minutes' walk. Sweat was pouring down my face and into my eyes, mosquitoes were buzzing all around me, and I was exhausted. Did I mention I was also terribly out of shape?

By the time I reached Race Point Light, I had decided to get a few images for the sake of making the walk worth it and then head back. It was close to midnight by now, and thinking about the hour-long walk back, followed by a ninety-minute drive, wasn't helping. I took the images and left.

This time, I decided I would walk the dune trail back. I knew it would be shorter but more difficult. I figured I could use what little energy I had left and just power through it. I was wrong. Dune after dune after dune and I still couldn't see the parking lot. How long was this trail? I didn't know because I had no cell phone service. I just had to keep walking. After about thirty minutes of this, I had to sit down. Boy, I sure wished I had brought some water. That's right, I made this whole journey without bothering to pack any water. So there I was, sitting alone in the dark on a sand dune with no water, and I started to feel something I had never felt on a night photography trip before: panic.

I mustered up some energy after sitting for a few minutes and made it over one more dune. Still no parking lot. By now, I couldn't even see the lighthouse behind me. The moon was very low, and the shadows were getting long. Only the tips of the dunes were now lit. What I wouldn't have done for some water. Ironic, since not 100 yards away was the sound of crashing waves.

After one more dune, I stopped, and that's when I thought, "I'm done; this is where it ends." I wasn't capable of going any farther. No one was going to be coming by at that hour; I couldn't call for help. What a dumb decision this whole night was. I had overestimated my fitness level and had underestimated the distance.

The trail I was walking on was a wide one. With a permit, you can take a four-wheel-drive vehicle out to the lighthouse. During the day, someone probably would have passed me. At the beginning of my walk back, someone had, but I just got out of the way because I figured I'd be fine. I didn't need any help.

I pulled myself up and shined my flashlight around the area to see what the terrain looked like and whether or not I had any bright ideas on how to get myself out of this mess. Lots of beach grass, sand, tire tracks . . . and something else. I could just make it out because it was partially covered in sand. I really couldn't believe what I was seeing, because if it was what I thought it was, this would be my ticket back to the parking lot.

I left my camera bag on the dune and scurried down toward the item on which I had trained my flashlight. I knelt down and held the flashlight in my mouth as I brushed the sand away from this surprising find with both hands like Indiana Jones uncovering a lost tablet.

It was a treasure in the sand, the only treasure someone in my situation would care about: a bottle of water. Yes, I found a bottle of water in a sand dune in the dark at one o'clock in the morning. It was the best water I've ever had. Make of it what you will. I drank that entire bottle in one breath.

Twenty minutes later, I was emptying the sand out of my shoes before getting into the car and beginning my drive back. I didn't love the pictures I got that night. They were okay. To me, they were more of a minor prize after everything that had happened. I vowed someday to go back, more prepared and in better shape. Ten years later, I did.

In the summer of 2020, I received a message via social media from another photographer I had met online. He said he was heading to Race Point and was wondering if I would want to meet up. As you may or may not recall, there were some things going on in 2020, and a lot of people weren't really meeting up in the traditional sense. But outside, on a hike, wouldn't be much of an issue. It just so happens that I had spent the last several months losing 40 pounds via diet, walking, and a whole lot of treadmill time. If ever there was going to be a time to conquer this hike, it would be then.

Unlike the first trip out, this was going to be a moonless night. I would be photographing the Milky Way there, and I was really looking forward to it, despite the fact that my newer camera equipment was a bit heavier than the last. I made that hike out there like it was a walk around the neighborhood. Quite honestly, when we got to the lighthouse, I thought to myself, "That's it?" Sure, it still took me over all the same dunes, but there's something to be said about exercise and bringing your own water.

We spent several hours there before my hiking partner had to head back. I loved what I captured there that night. So much so that I went back again the following month on my own. One "bonus" to the environment was that, due to the pandemic, the bed-and-breakfast located next to the lighthouse was closed for that year, which meant that it was much darker around the area than it normally would have been. It was a great comeback from a miserable experience!

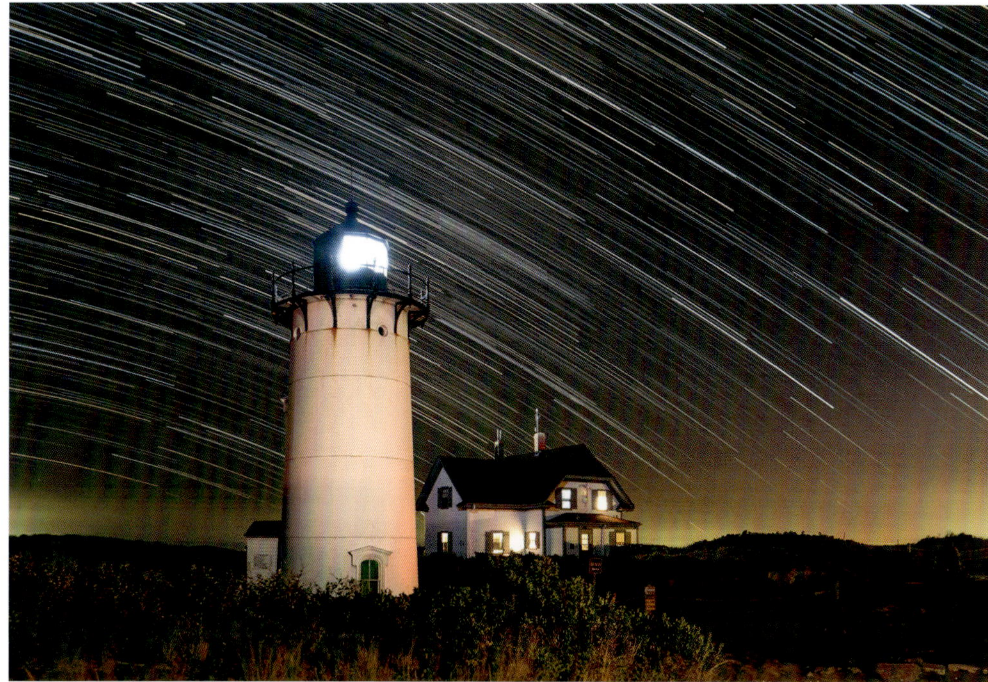

The stars appear to curve away from each other when aiming east or west because of how the camera captures the split of the Northern and Southern Hemispheres. Sixty shots, each lasting thirty seconds, were combined to create the apparent movement of the stars over a thirty-minute period. In one image, the tower was lit with a handheld light.

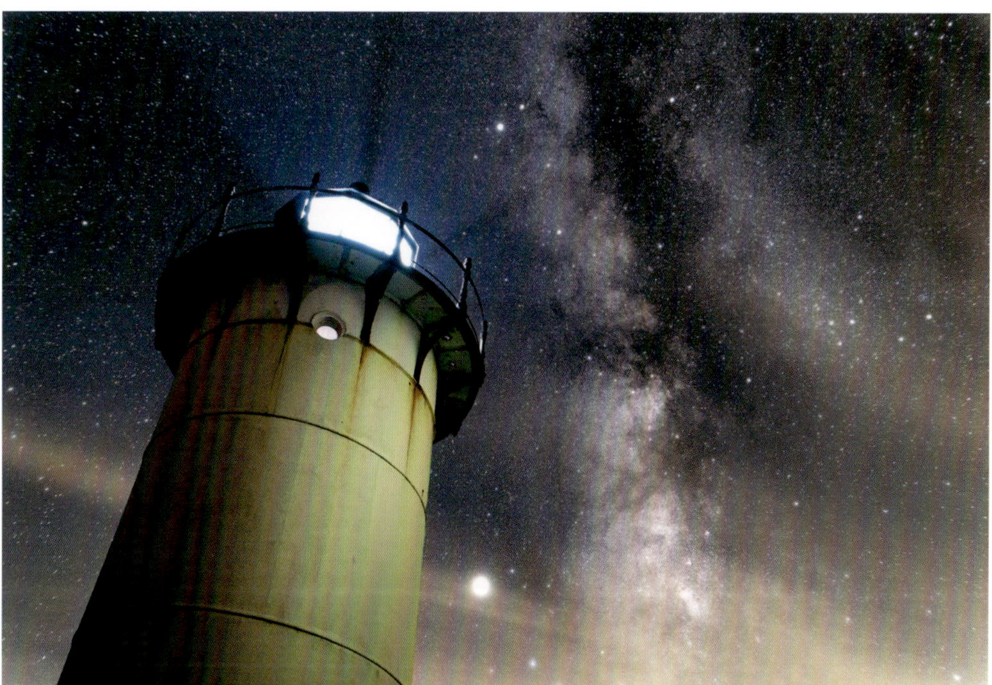

Hazy skies give way to the galactic core over Race Point Light. The bright glowing orb just to the right of the lighthouse is Jupiter, enhanced by the haze.

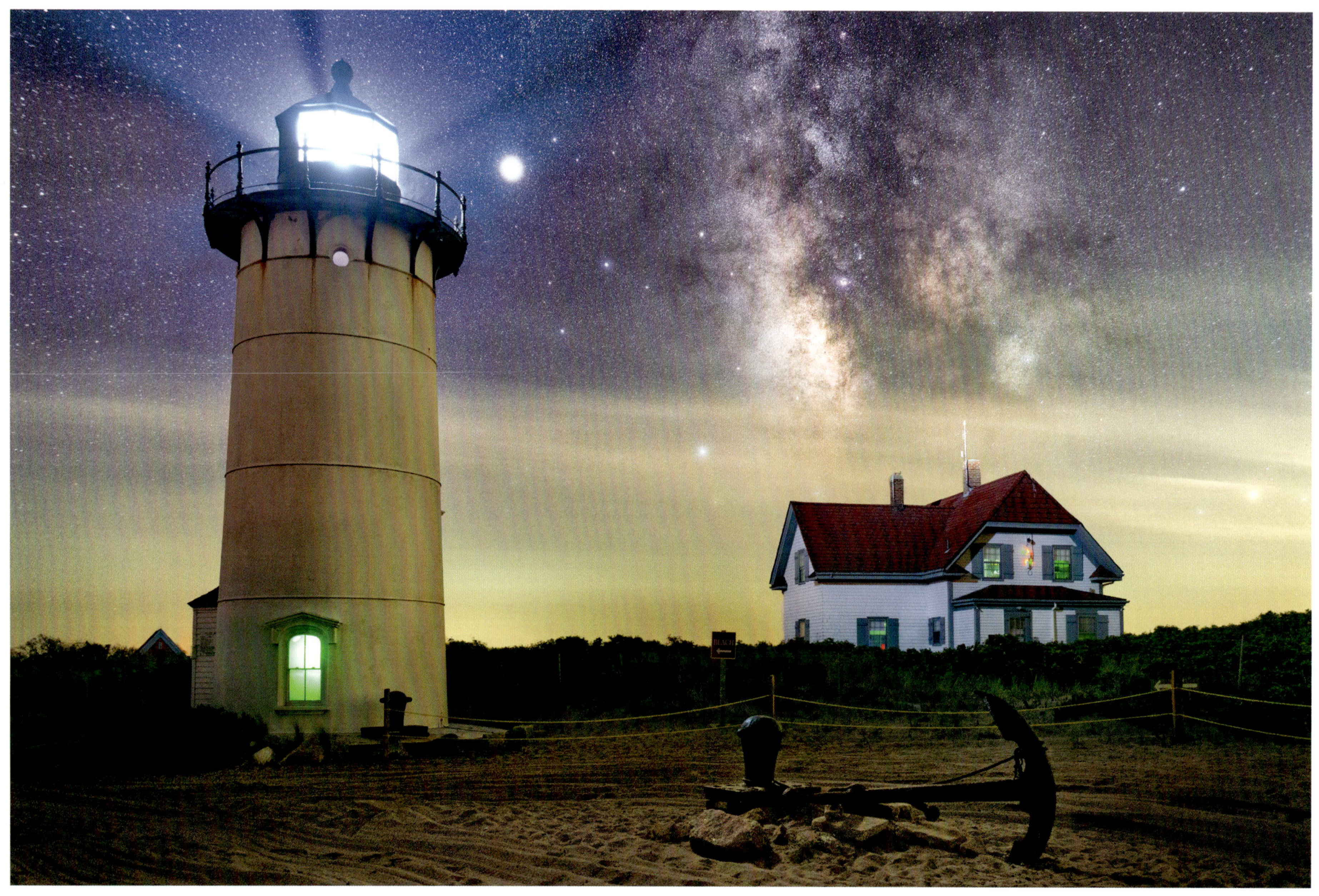

Driving the dune road from the Race Point Beach parking lot will lead you to this view as you approach the lighthouse. Be careful not to hit the anchor! The road sneaks to the left of the tower and brings visitors out to the beach. If you'd rather skip the hassle of getting a permit and letting the air out of your tires, you can grab a dune tour out of Provincetown and let someone else do the driving.

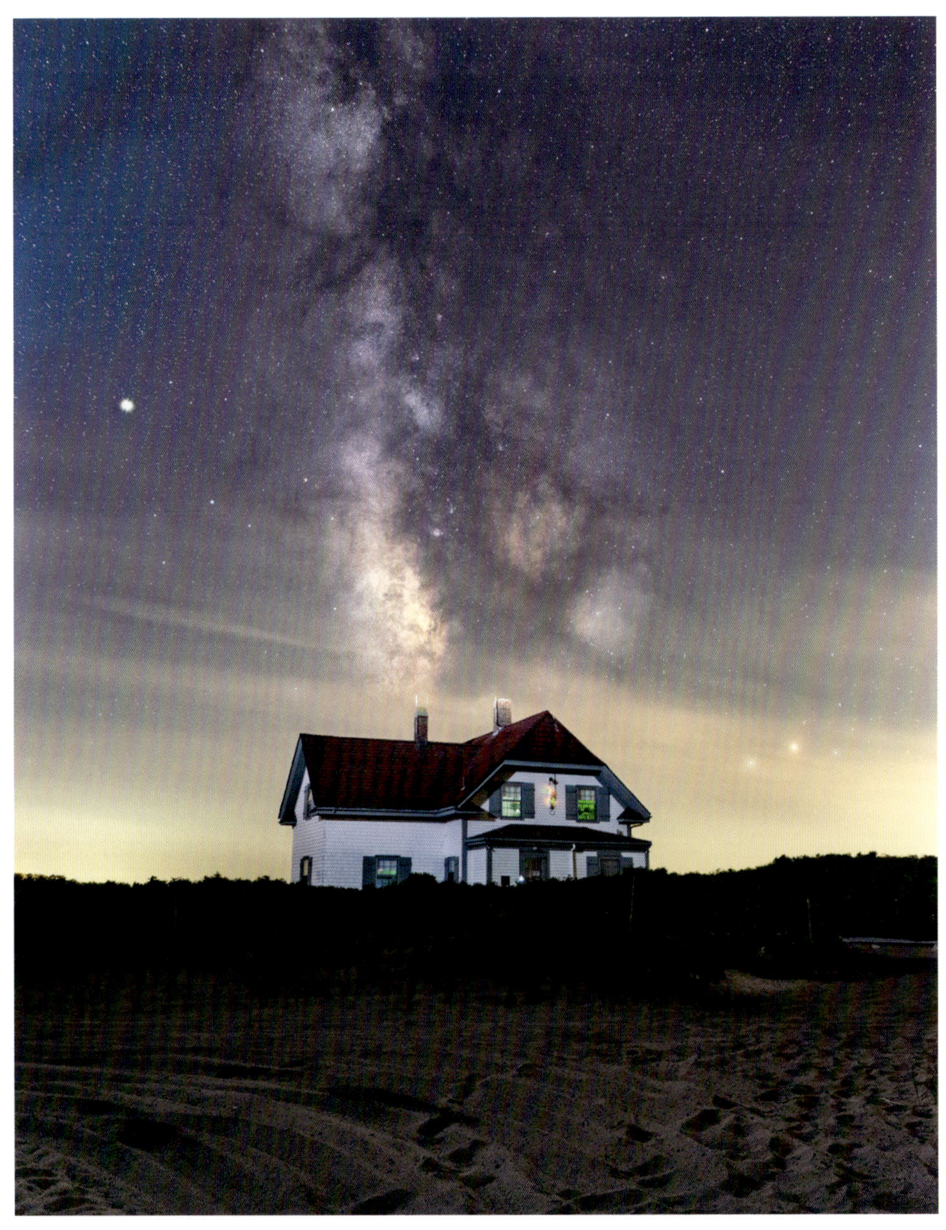

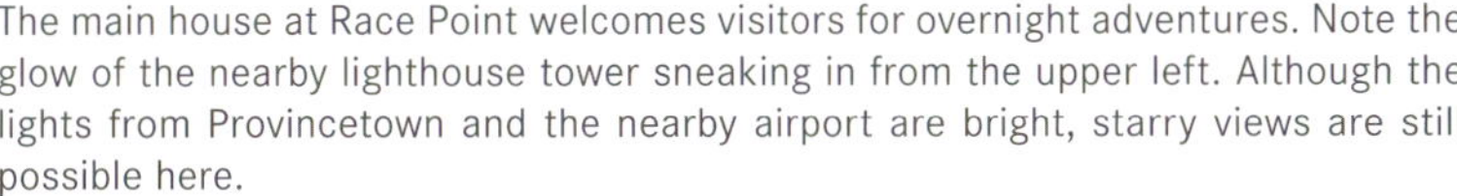

The main house at Race Point welcomes visitors for overnight adventures. Note the glow of the nearby lighthouse tower sneaking in from the upper left. Although the lights from Provincetown and the nearby airport are bright, starry views are still possible here.

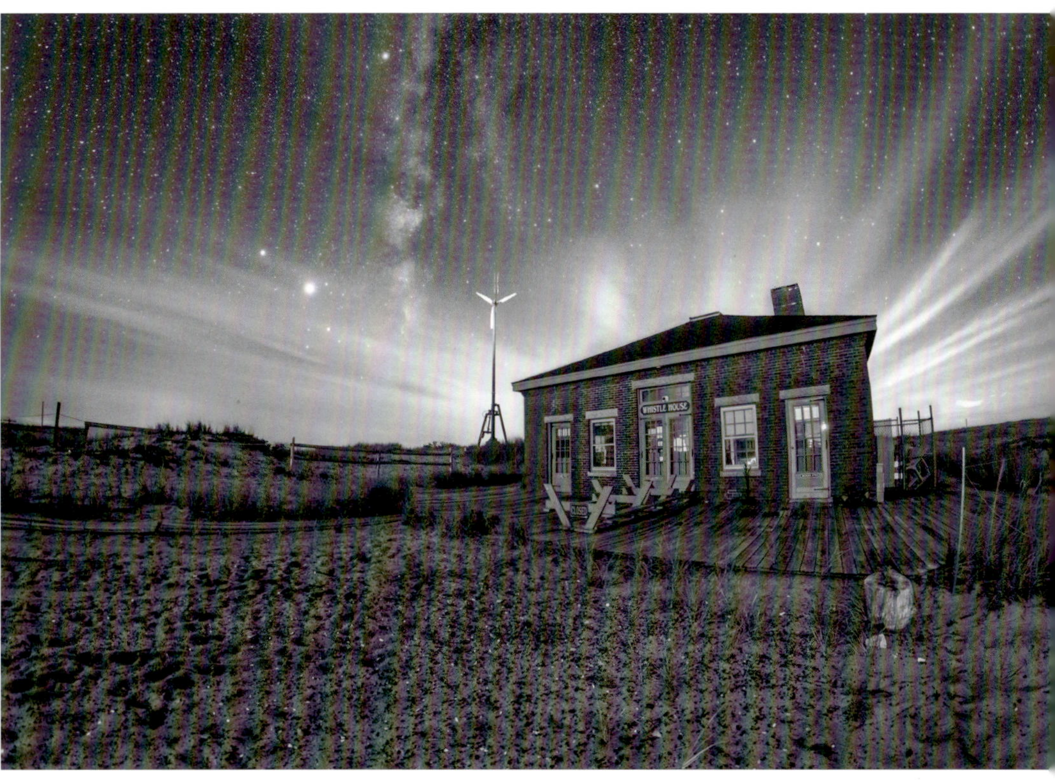

This brick building offers seasonal accommodations near Race Point Light. Approaching clouds stretched by the camera's long exposure are poised to obscure the Milky Way. The image was converted to black and white as a way to address the very orange light pollution from Boston being reflected off the clouds.

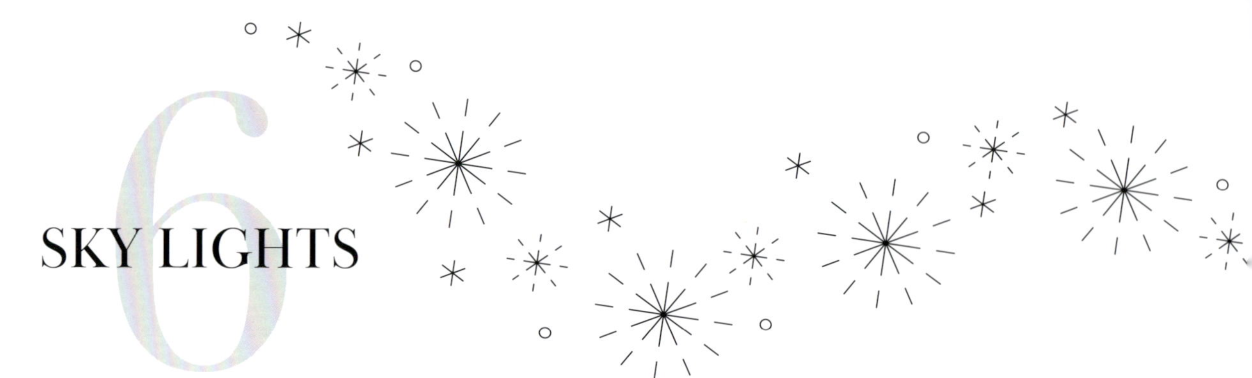

6 SKY LIGHTS

Sometime in 2019, the decision was made to begin extensive repairs on the tower at Highland Light. Over the years, it had developed a rather large crack, and the National Park Service had secured funding to repair it. This would involve building extensive scaffolding around the tower for the workers to complete the task. For a time, the lighthouse would be less photogenic than most of us were used to. Meanwhile, somewhere in the solar system, something never before seen was heading in our direction.

In March 2020, a comet named NEOWISE was discovered. Astronomers were hopeful that it would put on a show unlike anything we've seen from Earth in a very long time. And it did not disappoint.

Photographing the comet meant aiming to the north. I had made the decision early on to photograph it at Highland Light. Wide-open skies would mean multiple opportunities to get good alignments, even if the tower was under repair.

Arriving just after twilight, I set up the camera and waited anxiously for the comet to begin to appear as skies got darker. I experimented with a few settings to see what might work best during this transition to night. Soon, the comet began to appear in my images—well before my own eyes could resolve it in the sky.

Not long after darkness fell, patchy clouds began to roll in, bouncing the orange glow from Provincetown back toward the camera. I waited patiently for gaps in the clouds to appear. They were few and far between. I managed to get a few images before the comet became completely obscured.

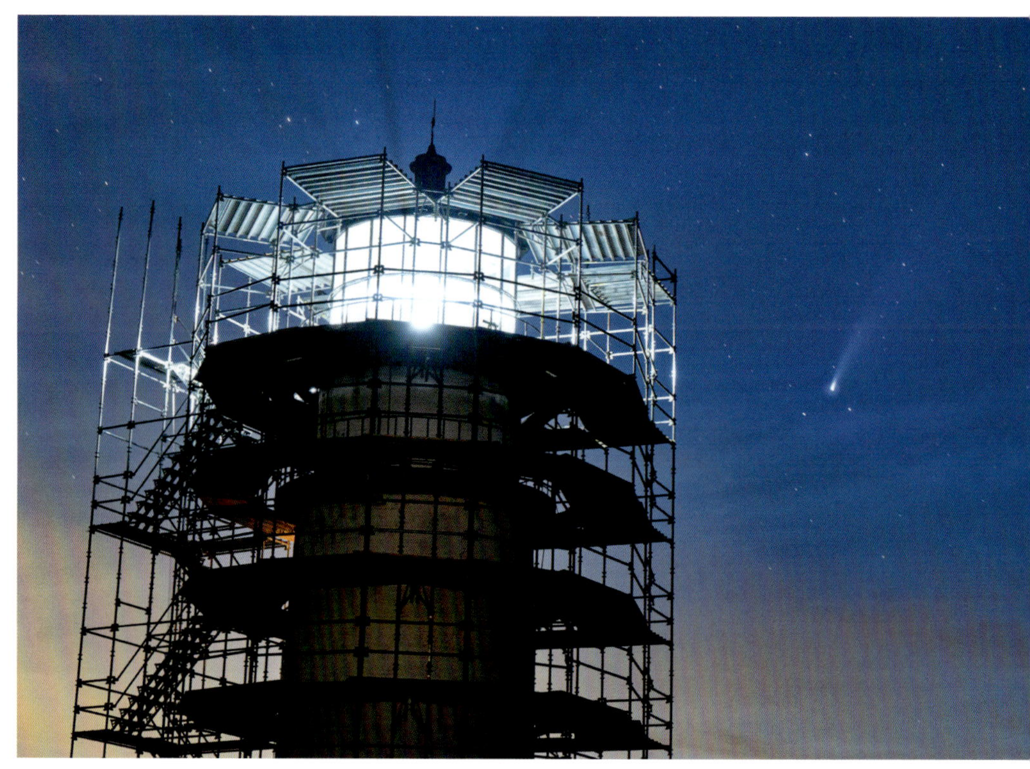

Comet NEOWISE shares the sky with the last glow of twilight and the beacon at Cape Cod Light.

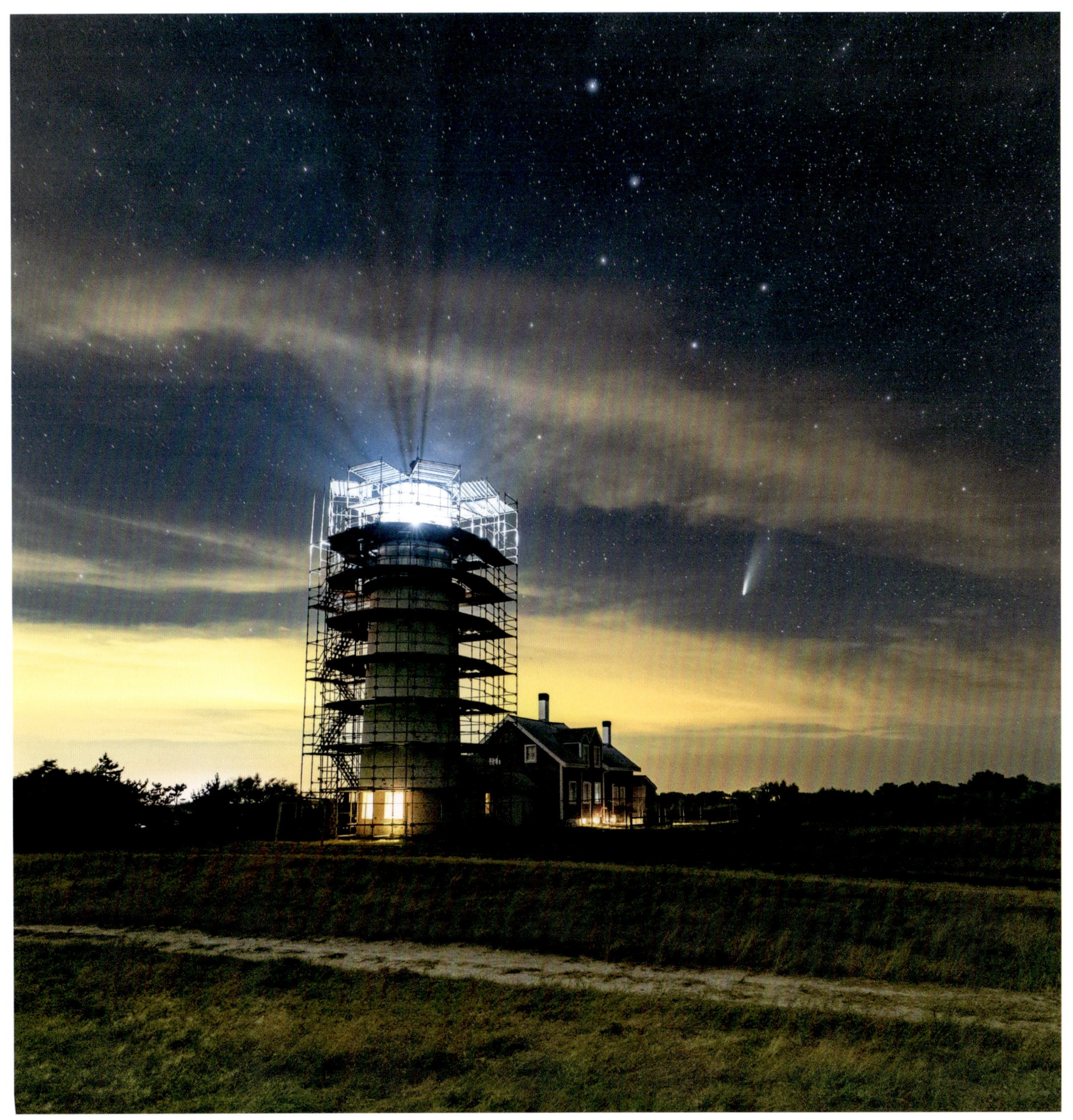

Partly cloudy skies didn't spoil another opportunity to capture Comet NEOWISE over Cape Cod / Highland Light. Nearly every night's forecast called for these conditions. As bands of clouds would move across the sky, the comet would peek out as it continued to set. Locating the Big Dipper and looking just below it was the easiest way to find the comet.

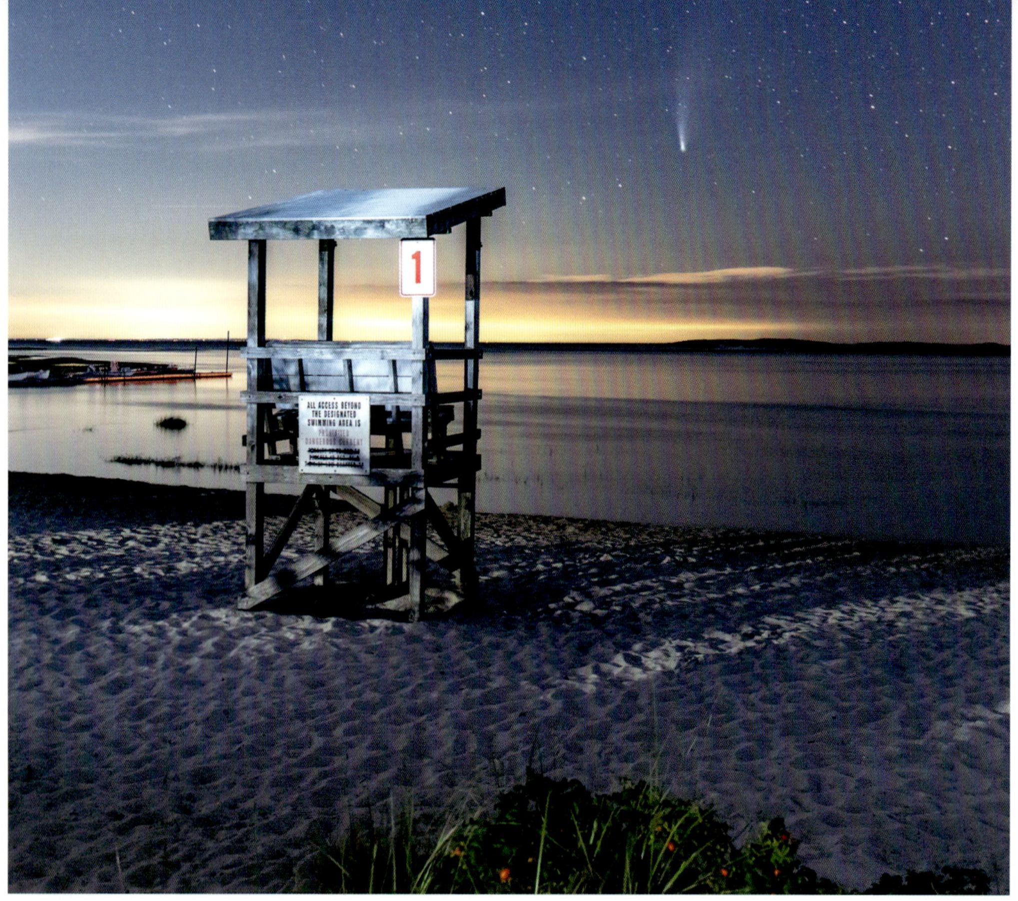

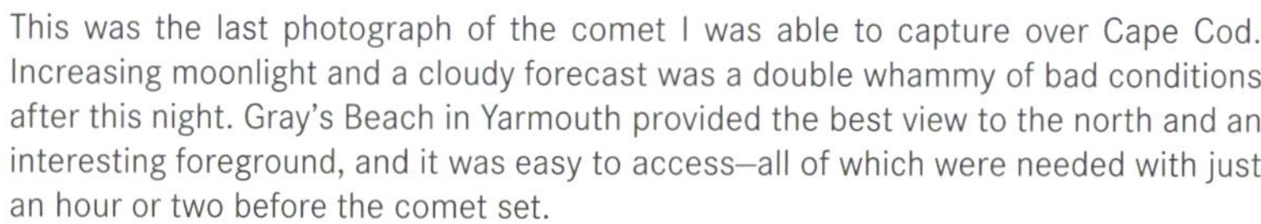
This was the last photograph of the comet I was able to capture over Cape Cod. Increasing moonlight and a cloudy forecast was a double whammy of bad conditions after this night. Gray's Beach in Yarmouth provided the best view to the north and an interesting foreground, and it was easy to access—all of which were needed with just an hour or two before the comet set.

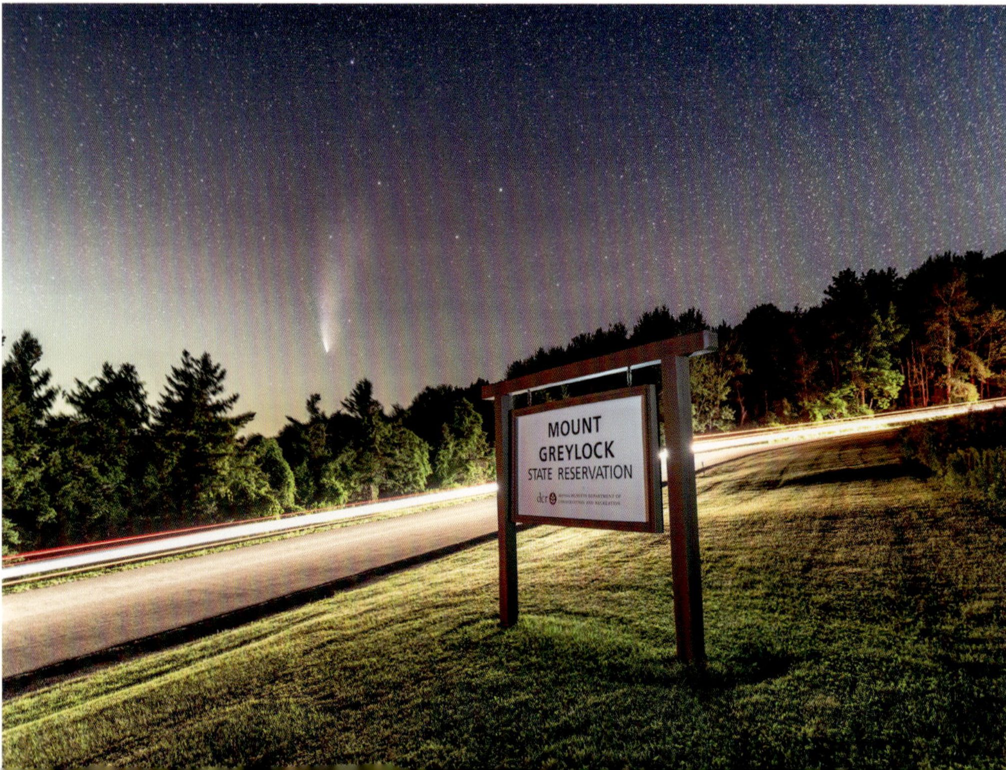

Having run out of clear nights but still wanting to photograph the comet, I scoured the forecasts throughout Massachusetts and discovered that the Berkshires would enjoy clear skies the night after my Gray's Beach shoot. I made a quick run out there in the late afternoon and captured it near the Mount Greylock State Reserve. Although the location isn't part of Cape Cod, I wanted to make sure you had a few more chances to see the comet just like I did.

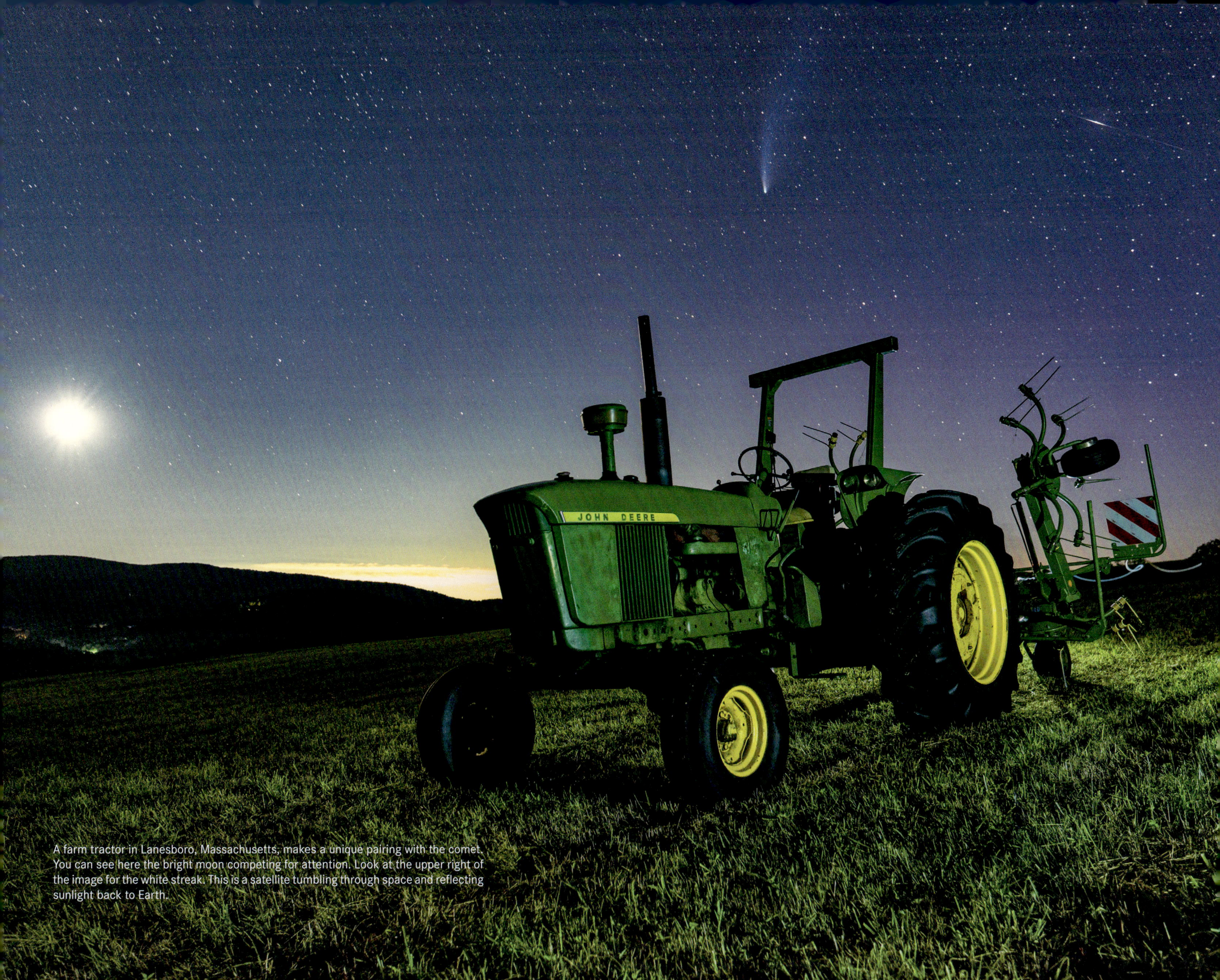

A farm tractor in Lanesboro, Massachusetts, makes a unique pairing with the comet. You can see here the bright moon competing for attention. Look at the upper right of the image for the white streak. This is a satellite tumbling through space and reflecting sunlight back to Earth.

The northern (and southern lights) are caused when particles from the sun slam into Earth's magnetosphere. The shape of the magnetic field focuses these particles over the poles, resulting in a colorful interaction that often does not extend far from these points. But a strong storm can light the skies even down to the equator—not unlike one I witnessed on a winter night back in the mid-nineties, well before I had the skill to capture such an event. More often than not, a camera will see the lights before your eyes can detect them. I've seen some occasional pinks from weak storms appear in my images, but they've been nothing more than a soft glow on a distant horizon.

The forecast didn't look too great. I had scheduled a night photography workshop event for May 2024 because I knew there would be some good Milky Way alignments with great local vistas. But I also knew that I would potentially be up against a lot of springtime uncertainty. Would we have clear nights or would the fog roll in?

I had people coming in from all over New England and even Canada. I scheduled our shoots to take place over four nights, to maximize the chances that one of them would reveal starry skies.

Throughout the afternoon before our first shoot, there were rumors swirling that a strong solar storm was heading our way. If conditions were right and it was as strong as the forecasters believed it to be, we'd have an exceptionally rare opportunity to see the northern lights. The weather forecast said it would be partly cloudy, but we could work with that.

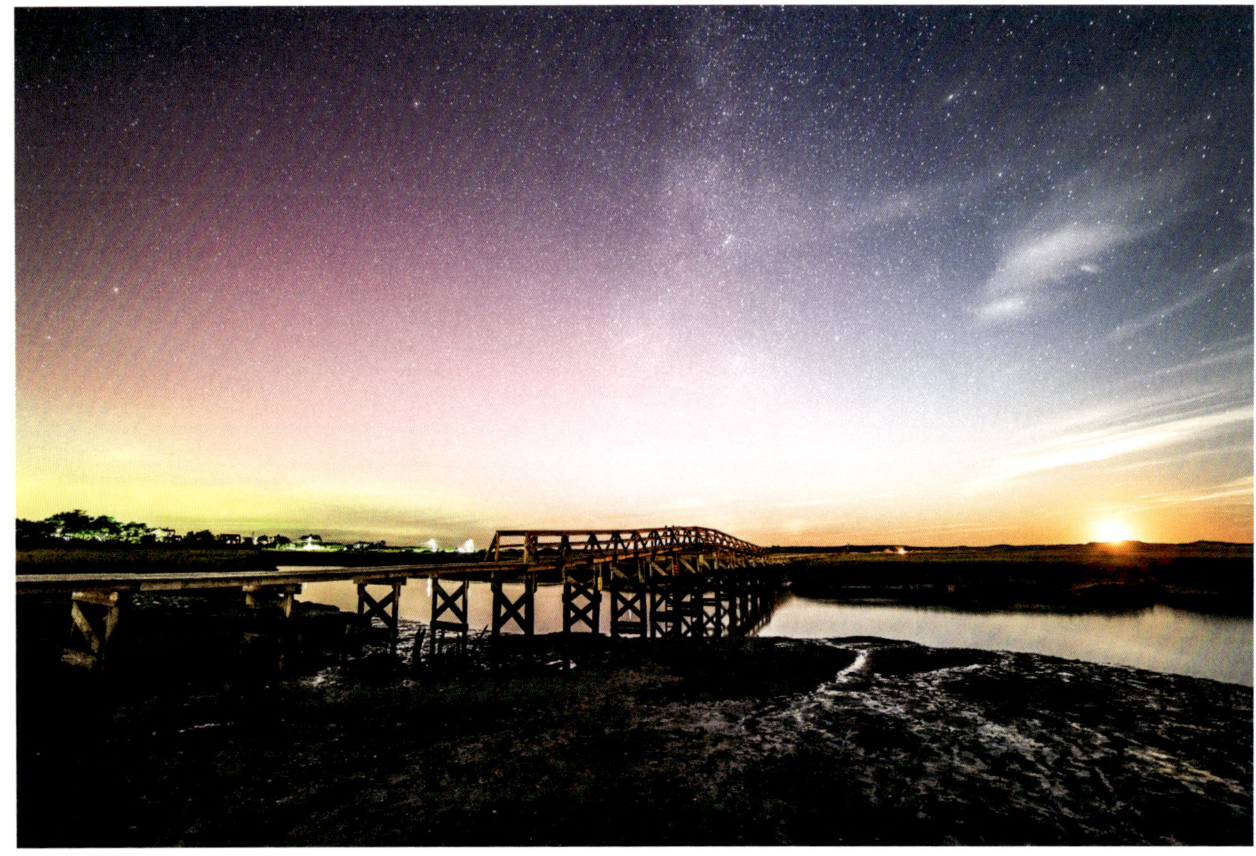

Under normal conditions, this is usually about the best one could expect when attempting to capture the northern lights as far south as Cape Cod. Here, a rising moon at the Sandwich Boardwalk is ready to all but erase the faint pinks and greens.

A few hours later, the group arrived at Nauset Light. Within a few minutes of firing up the cameras, one of the participants, Brian, aimed his camera to the north and said he was starting to see some color peeking through the gaps in the passing clouds. It took only a few minutes more for the intensity to increase, and I quickly advised the group to move to the other side of the lighthouse tower so that we could put Nauset in front of the potential aurora. What we saw was nothing short of amazing. Shades of green, pinks, and purples began shimmering through the sky and were bright enough to backlight the clouds.

On this night, we could see the colors with our own eyes, so we knew we had found ourselves in the middle of a once-in-a-lifetime event on Cape Cod. What's more, it was happening not only to the north but in all directions, including behind us to the south. I reached out to a friend who was in West Virginia that night, and he confirmed that he too was seeing some color.

We spent two hours at Nauset before the clouds got far too thick to see the colors, and then packed up for Highland Light. We arrived there thirty minutes later and found that the aurora was strong and better seen from this location's clearer skies.

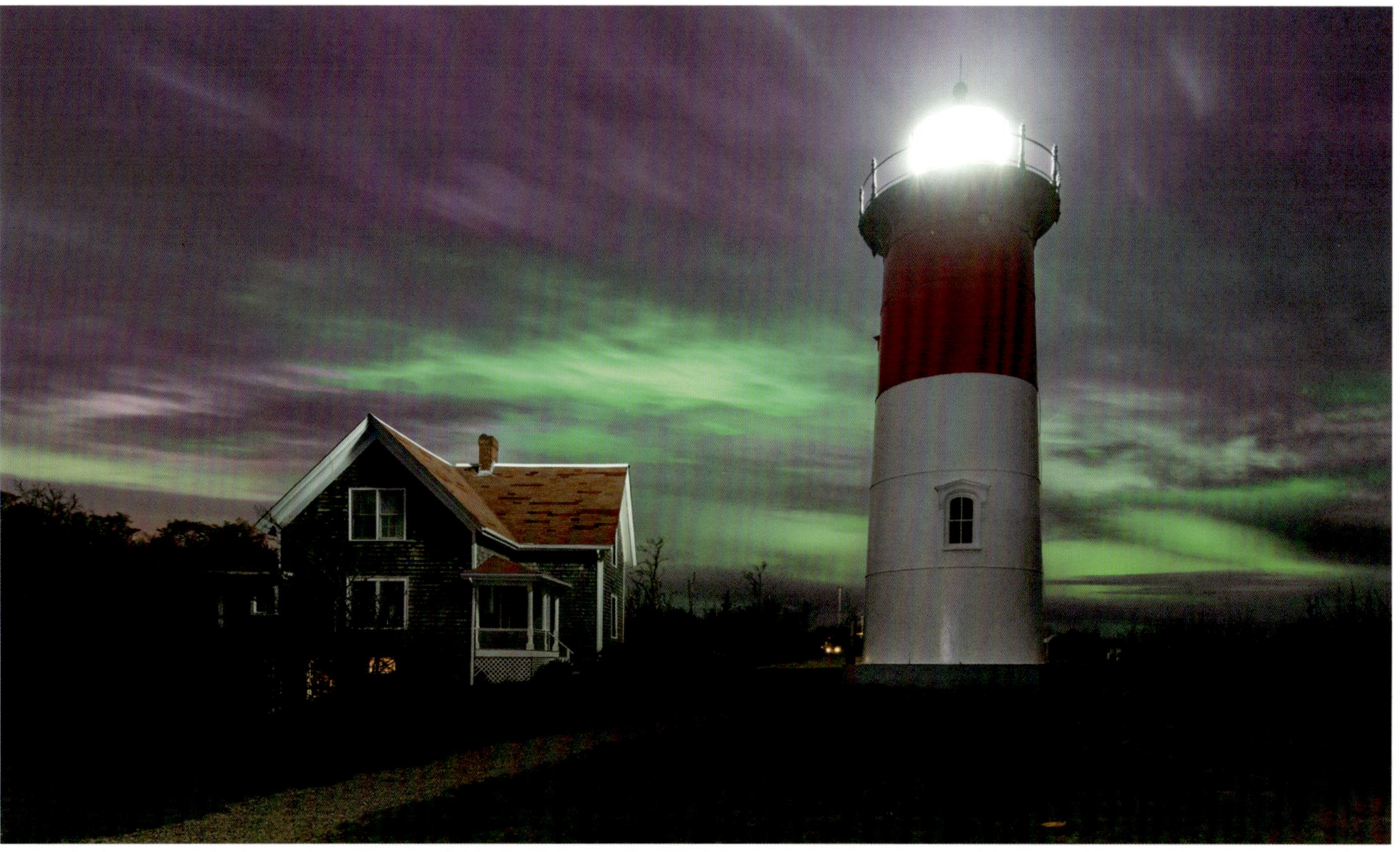

This is how the evening started on May 10, 2024. Cloud breaks revealed shifting greens, purples, and pinks above Nauset Light. The display was so bright that it was backlighting the clouds.

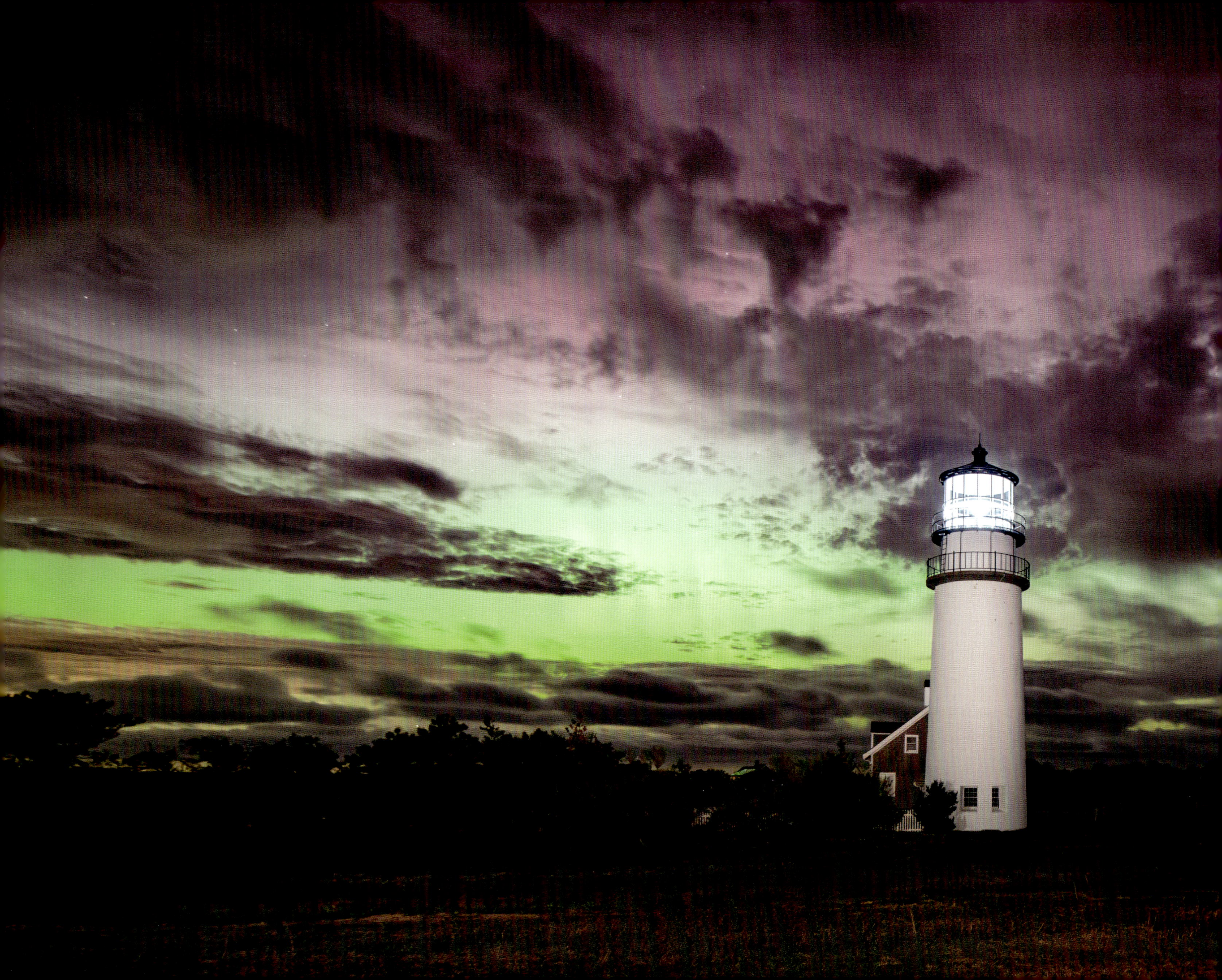

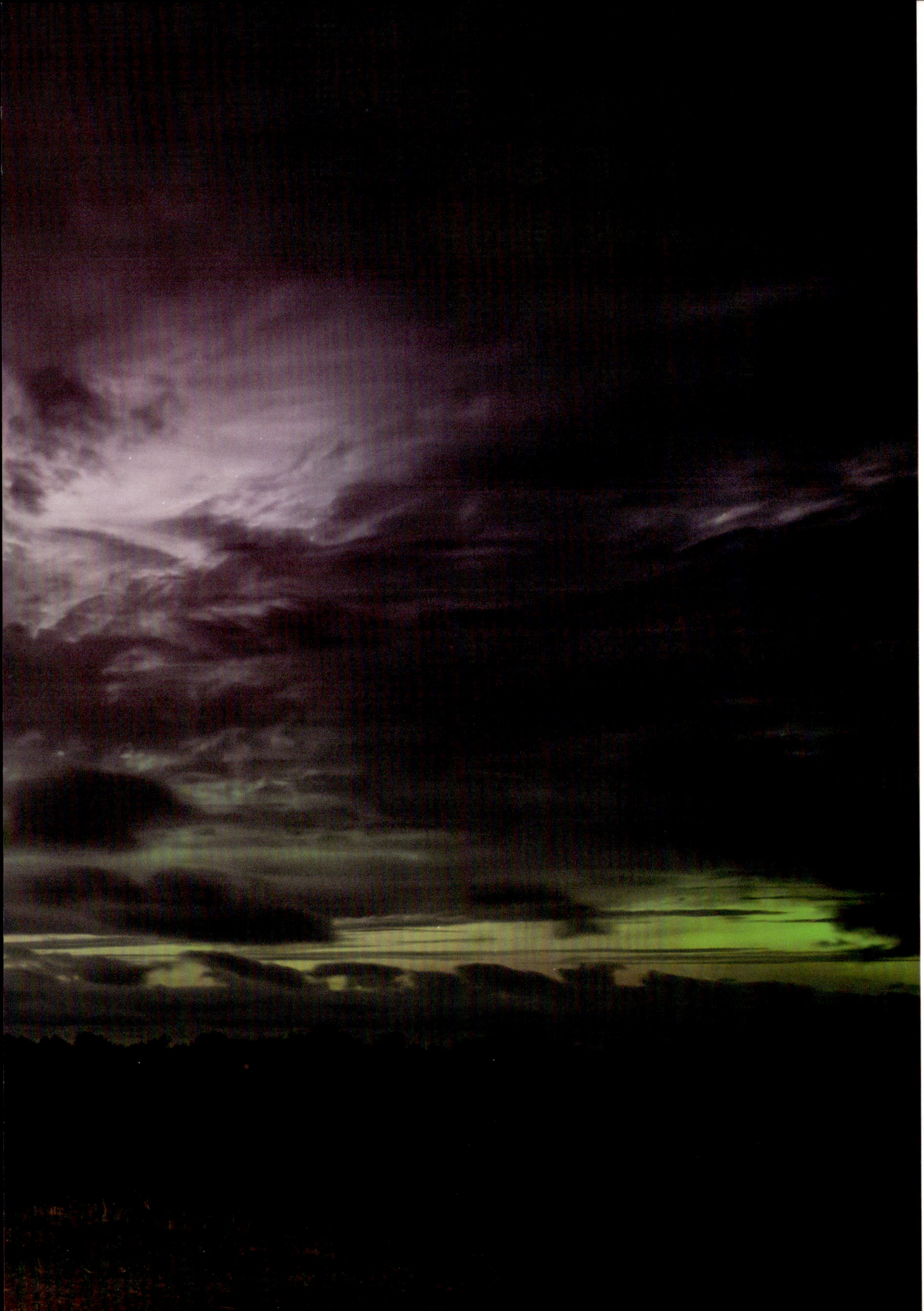

If I hadn't seen this with my own eyes, I would not have believed this picture was possible on Cape Cod. I can only imagine what this scene would have revealed had there been less cloud cover. Still, the clouds add an interesting dynamic to an already incredible sky. Look at the green patch to the left of the tower to see the columns of light. These columns moved slowly back and forth and would return briefly the next night.

You can experience this aurora by scanning the QR code. You'll be brought to a YouTube video featuring a short time-lapse video of this very event!

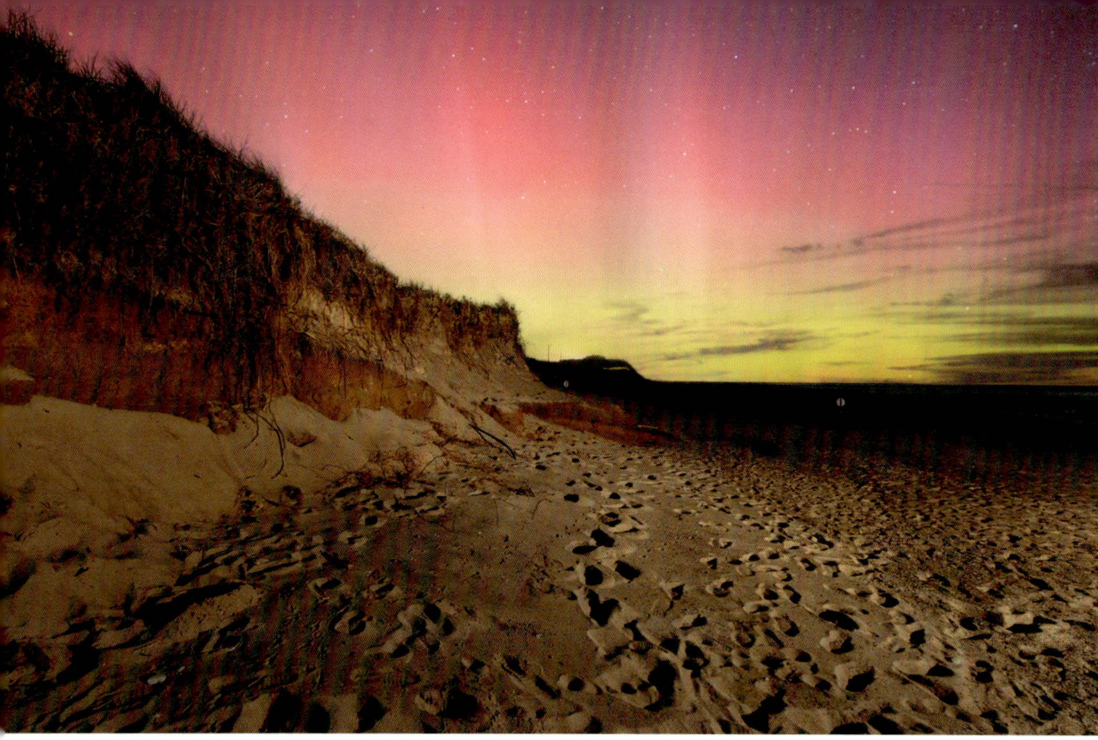

Skies were clear on May 11, but the aurora seemed to have all but disappeared. We waited patiently at Coast Guard Beach, watching many people come and go, hoping to catch what they had missed out on the previous night but leaving disappointed. Suddenly, just after midnight, the aurora returned and filled the north with greens and pinks. The intensity lasted only fifteen minutes, but it was enough time to get a few great images.

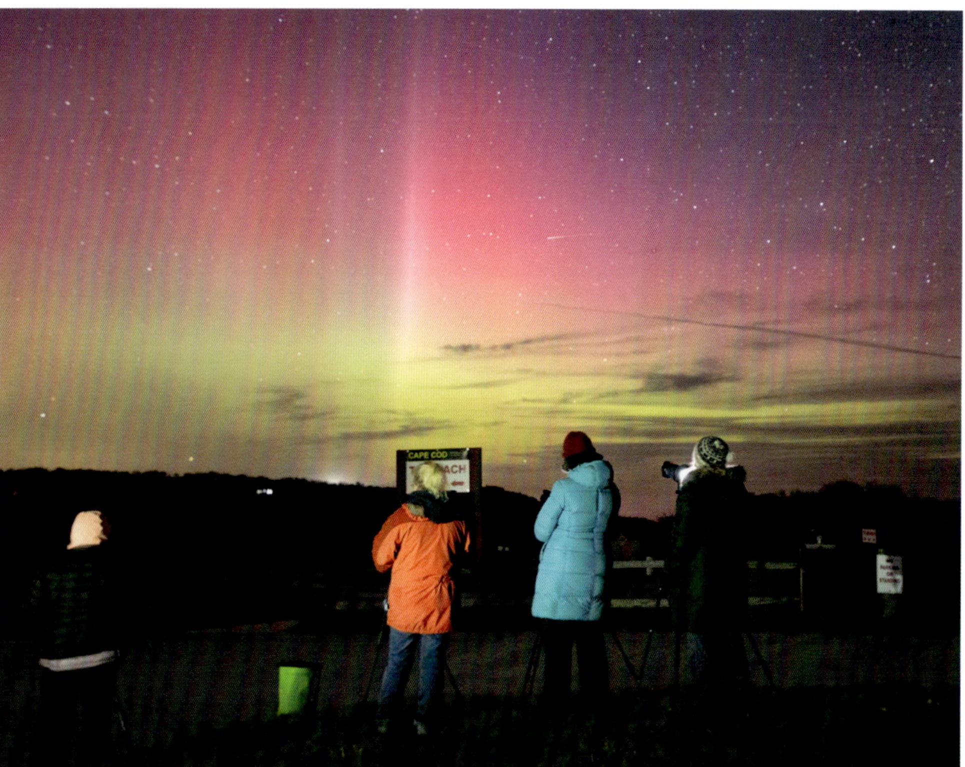

My photography group had little time to swing their cameras around and start photographing. As we were clicking away, each shot revealed a rapidly changing sky. The flare-up disappeared as quickly as it had arrived, leaving behind a faint pink glow on the northern horizon. I was thrilled that the group had this unexpected opportunity.

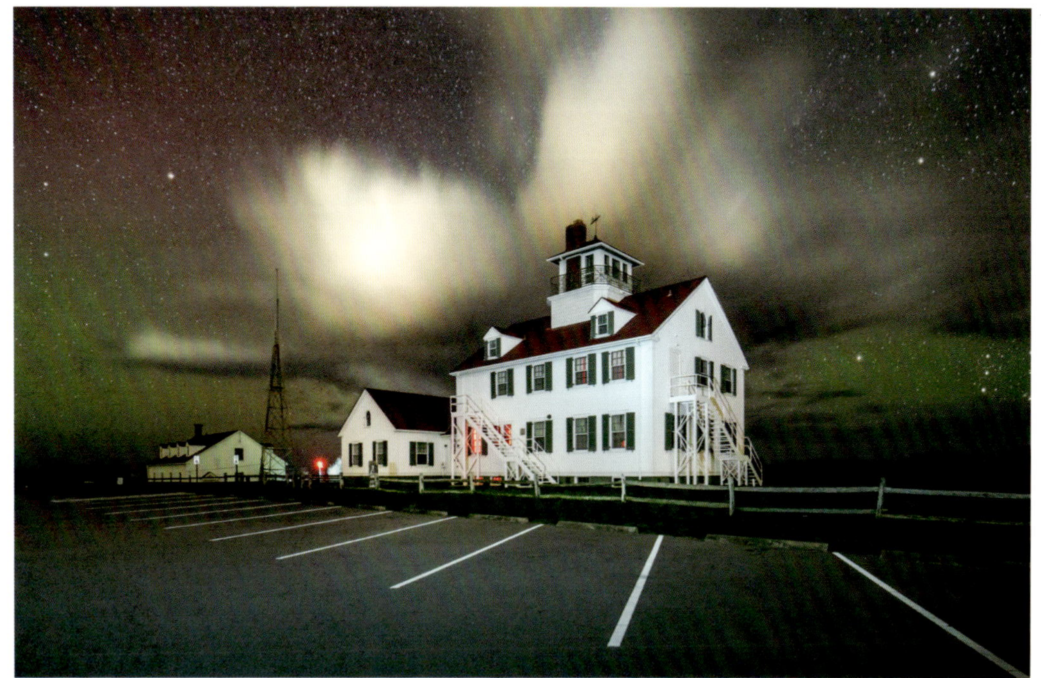

A single cloud photobombs a barely visible aurora glow over Coast Guard Beach in Eastham.

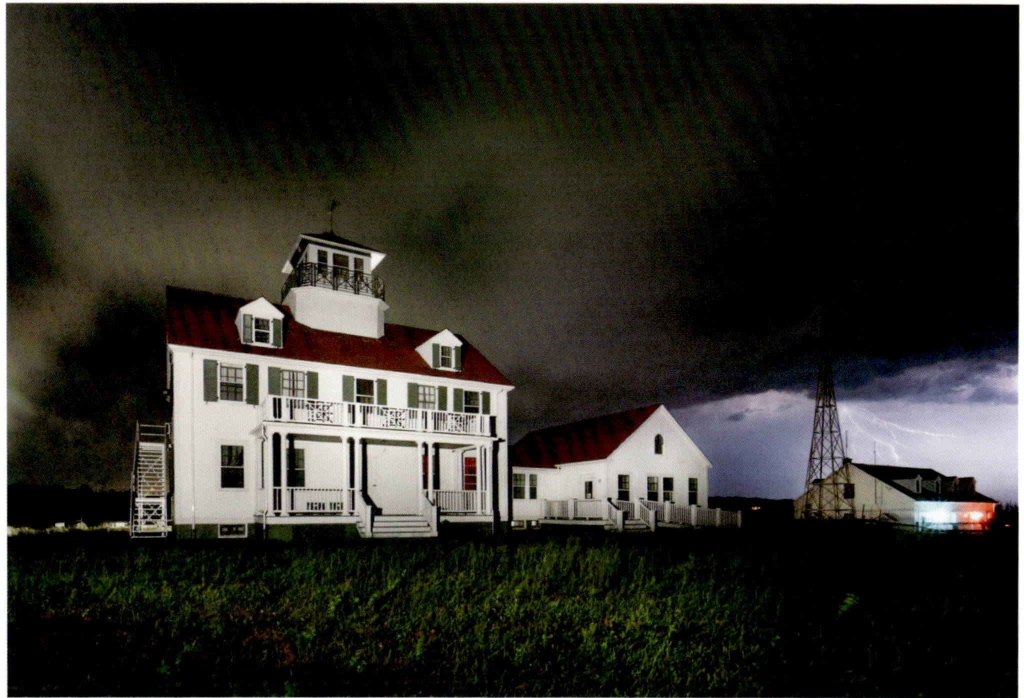

Not a cosmic visitor but no less impressive, a strong thunderstorm strikes the Cape as it heads out to sea.

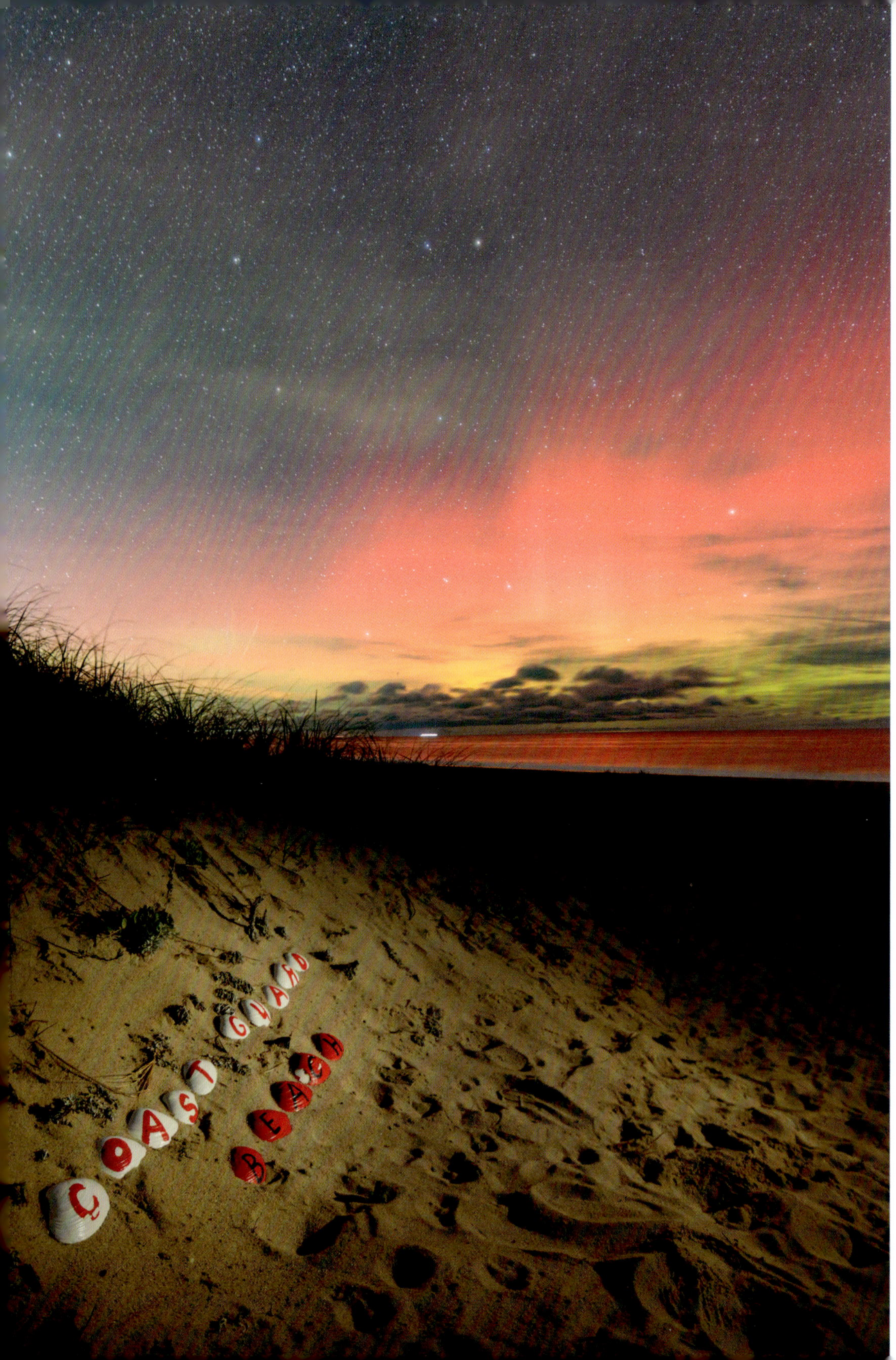

Rumors of a minor aurora flare-up led me to the other Coast Guard Beach in Truro, just down the road from Highland Light. I arrived just in time to see the end of a momentary peak in the lights. I remained there for about an hour, photographing subjects with a northern backdrop.

Scan this QR code to see the time-lapse video captured while photographing this beach on October 6, 2024.

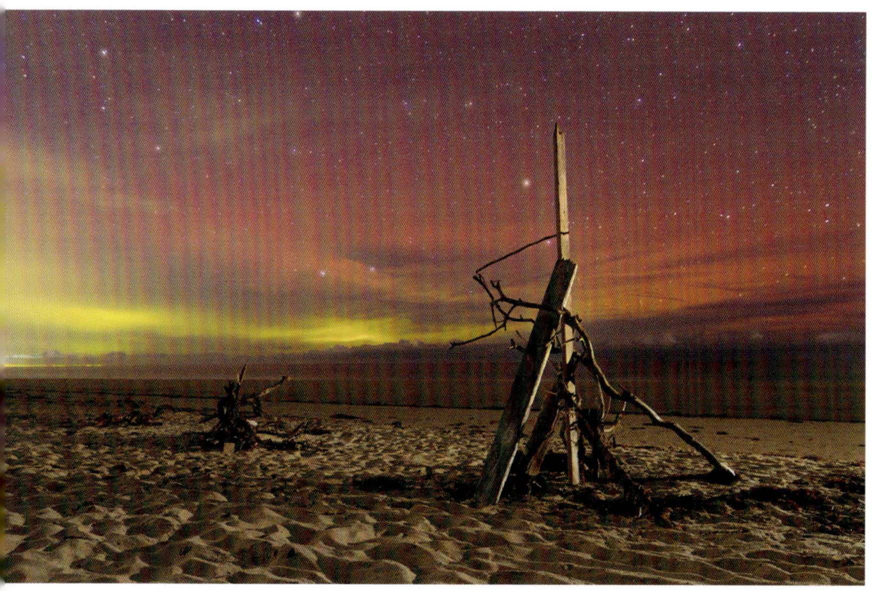

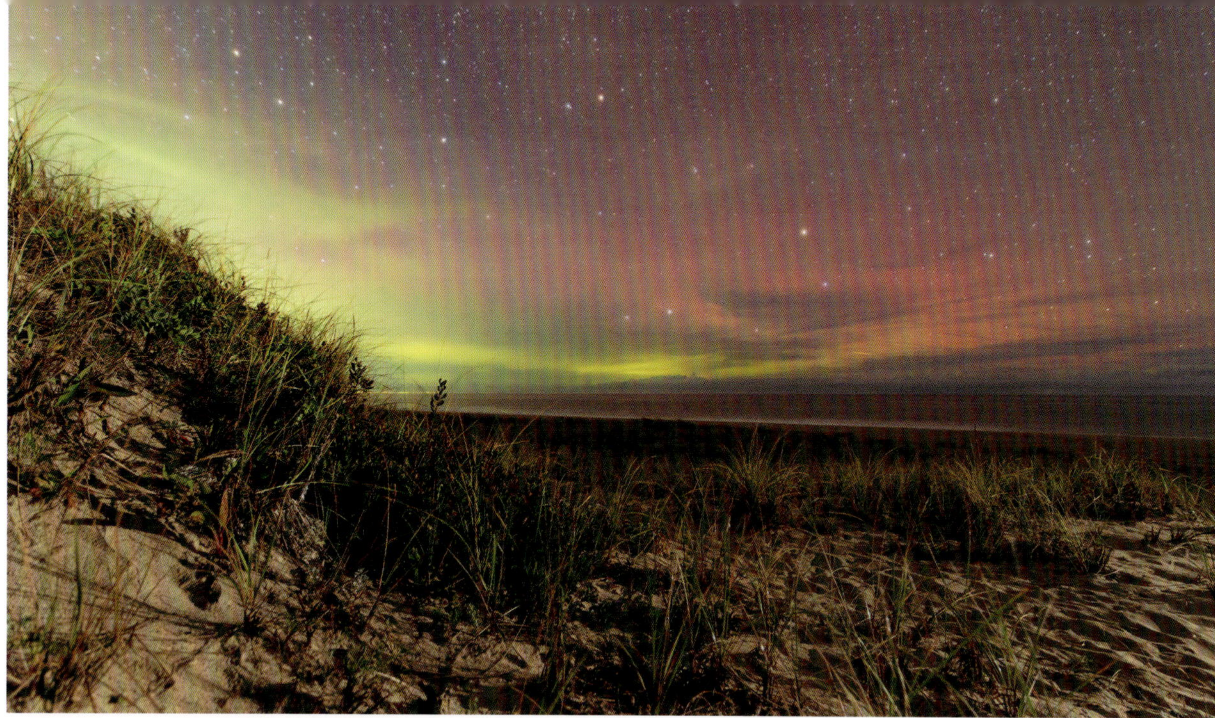

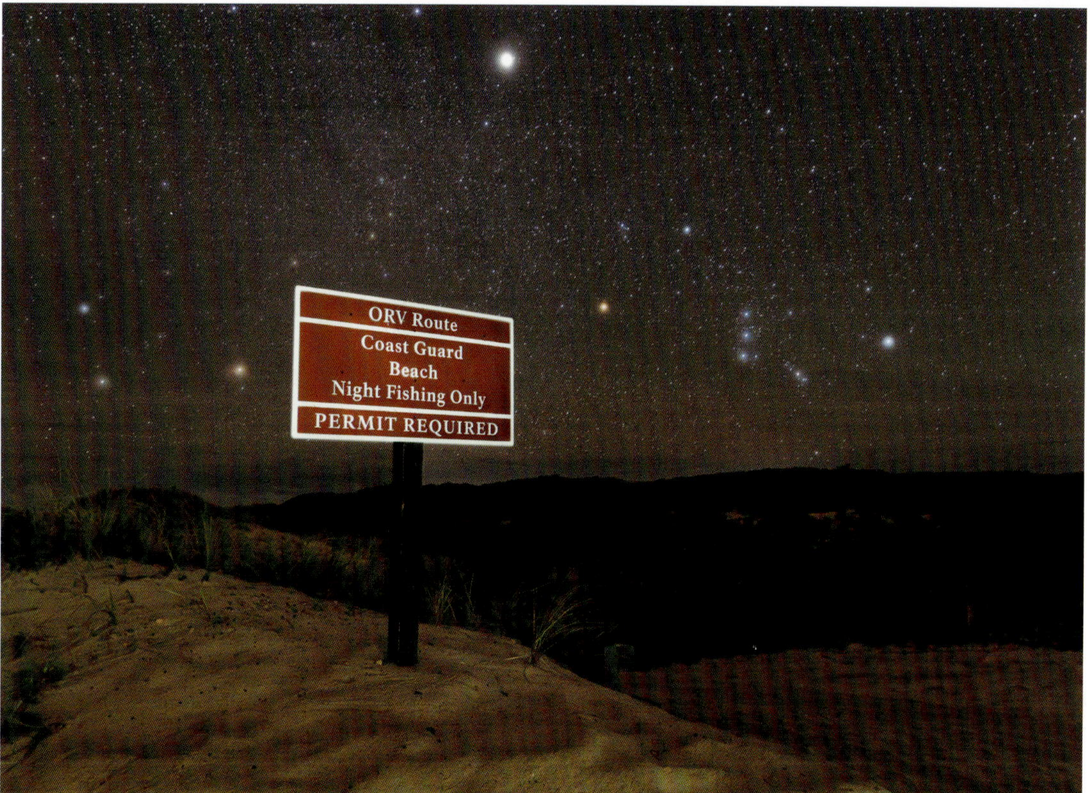

Before heading back home for the evening, I spotted the telltale sign of winter in the form of the constellation of Orion. It is one of the most recognizable constellations in the night sky and makes a great compositional element when low to the horizon.

A MAGICAL THURSDAY

Five months to the night after the April 2024 display, Cape Cod would be treated to another incredible display of the northern lights. News outlets had been buzzing on October 9, 2024, about the high potential for a strong solar storm event hitting on the evening of Thursday, October 10. The KP index numbers were predicted to be potentially stronger than that of the previous May's storm.

Sure enough, and as early as 8 p.m., we started to see a pink aurora so strong that it was casting light across the ground. I quickly started a one-hour drive to the Cape Cod National Seashore, hoping that it would hold up long enough for me to get out there and begin photographing.

My first stop would be the dunes at Marconi Beach. From there, I had a wide-open view of the ocean and several great foregrounds from which to photograph. Pinks, greens, and the occasional purple danced across the sky. I would have been happy with just an hour of this. But as the night wore on, the show continued.

By the time 5 a.m. had arrived, I could count Three Sisters Lights, Nauset Light, Coast Guard Beach, and Gray's Beach as successful destinations from which I photographed this aurora. I arrived home just before dawn, exhausted and thrilled. Had sunrise not threatened to end my evening, I'd have pushed ahead for several more hours, not knowing when next I would have this opportunity.

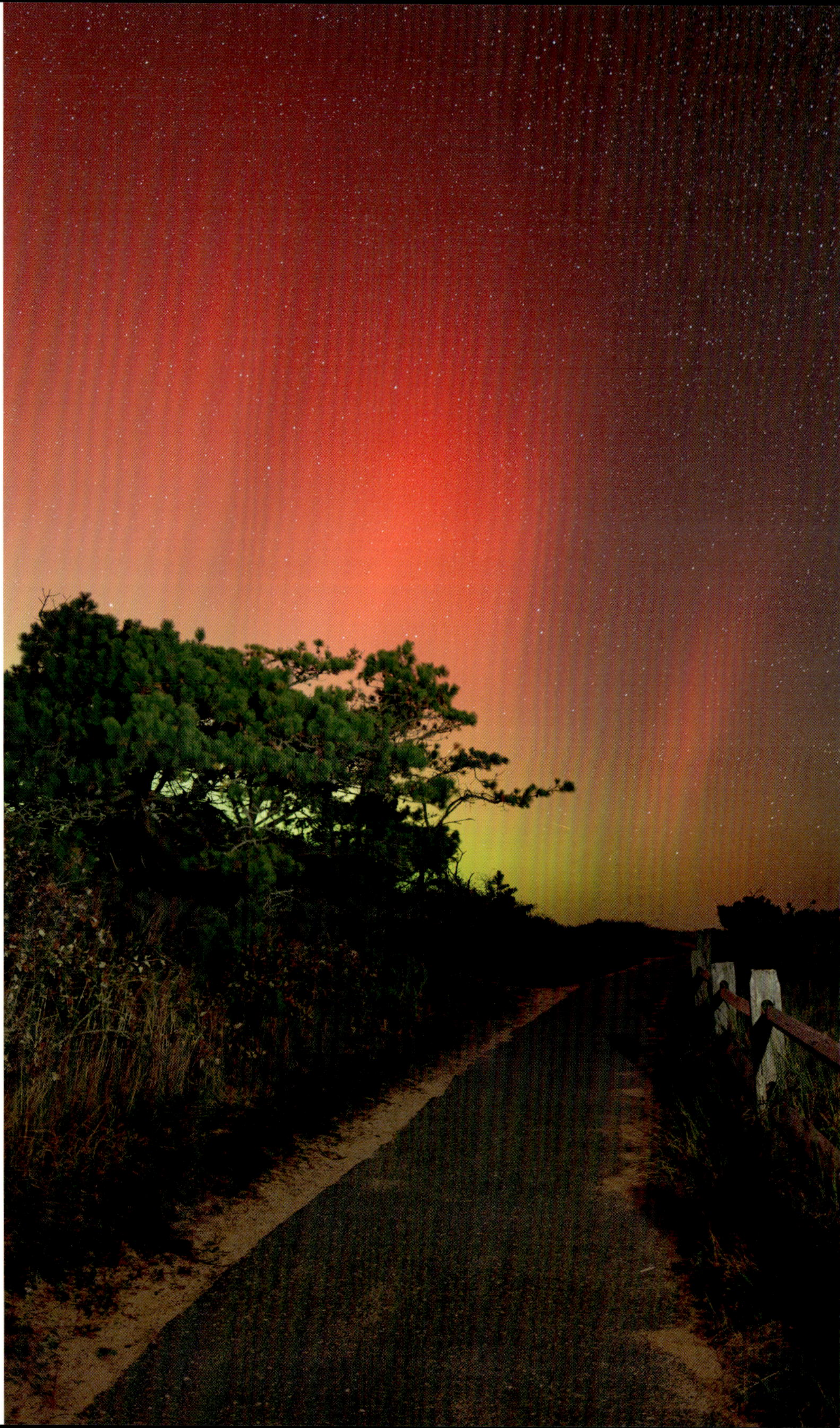

The pathway to the Marconi Beach overlook also leads to the night's aurora show and the best direction from which to photograph it.

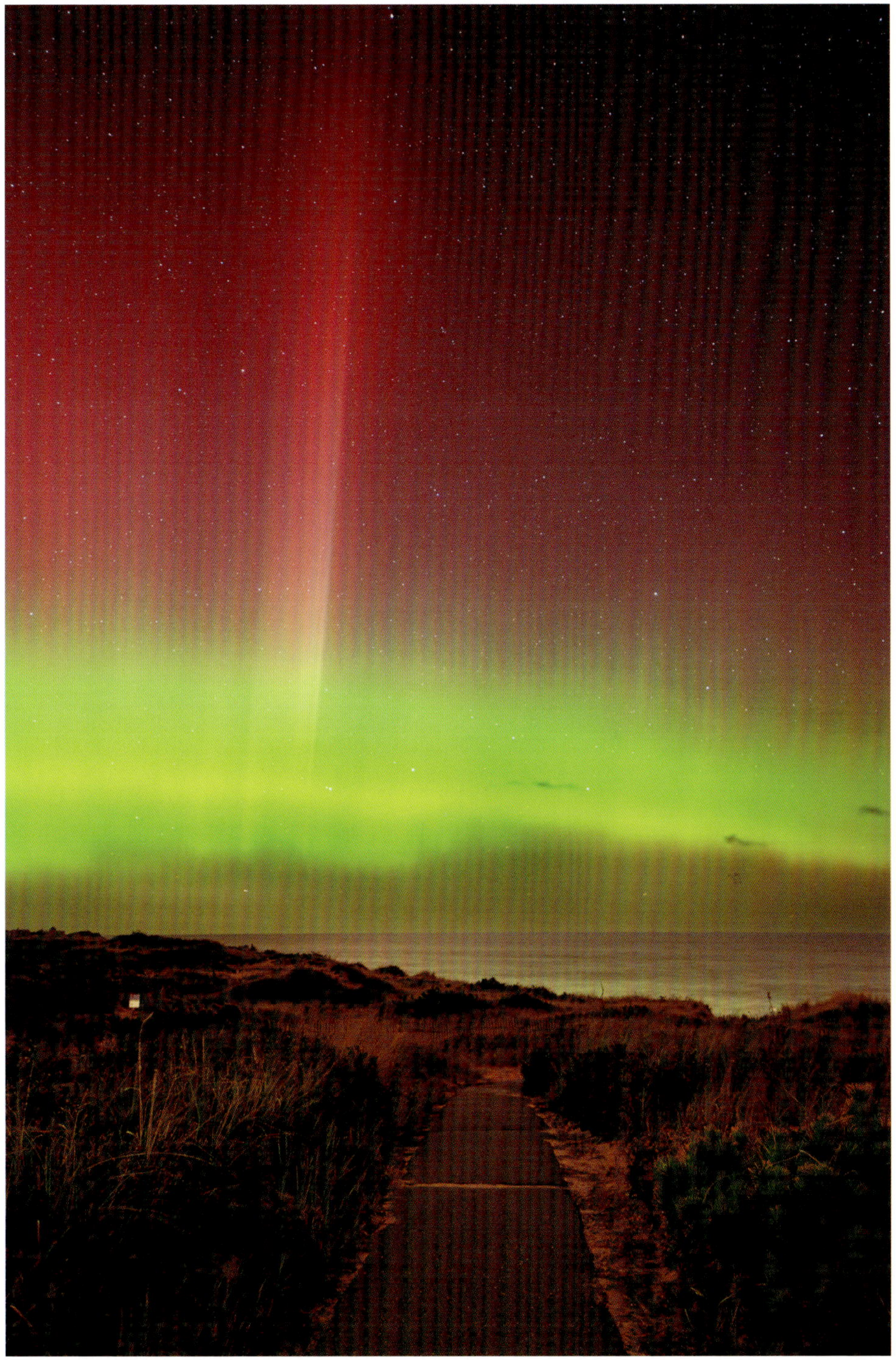

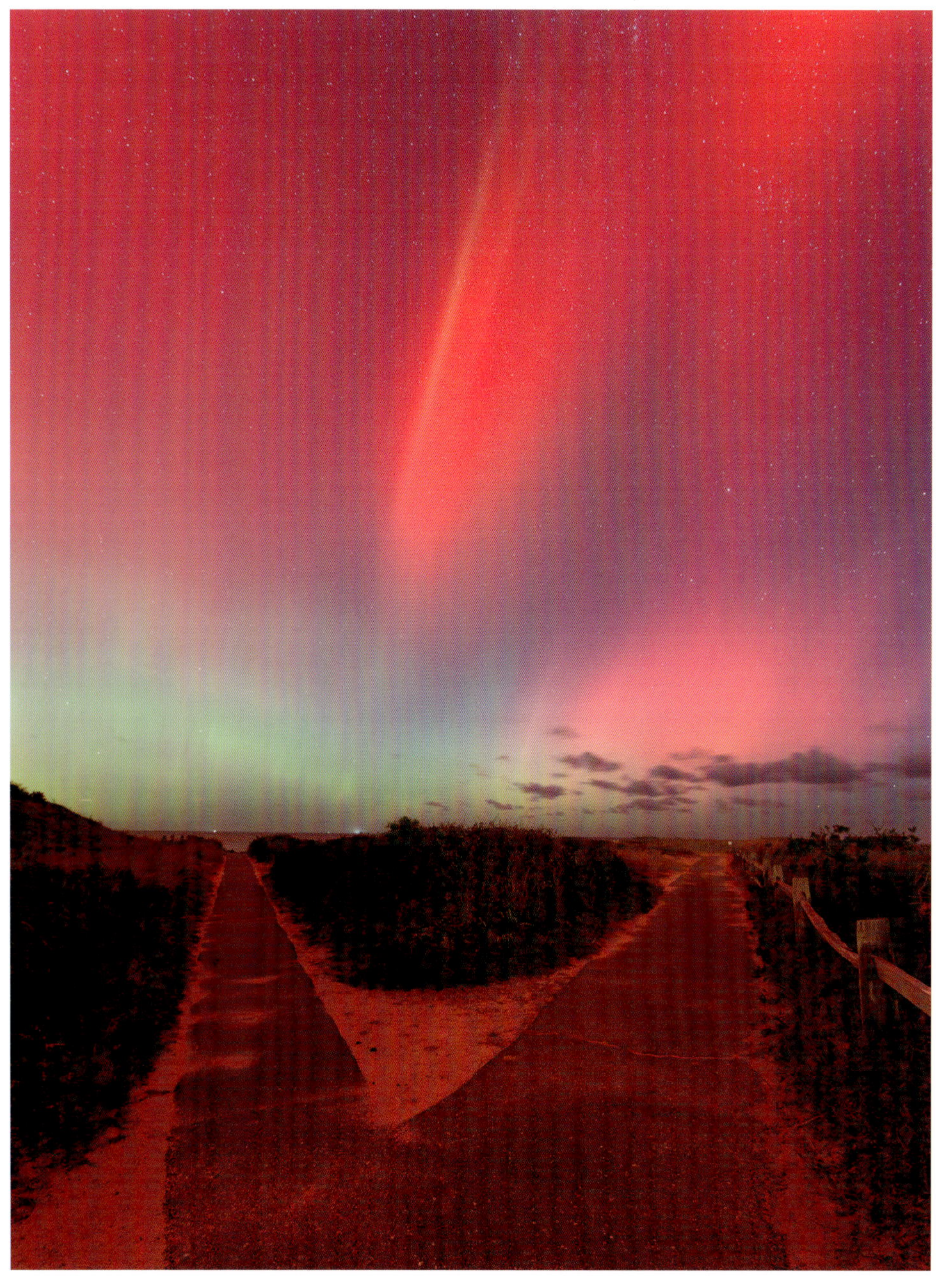

This image best shows the natural pink glow across the path and nearby environment. The camera could see this far better than I, but the fact that I could see it at all was a testament to the strength of the storm.

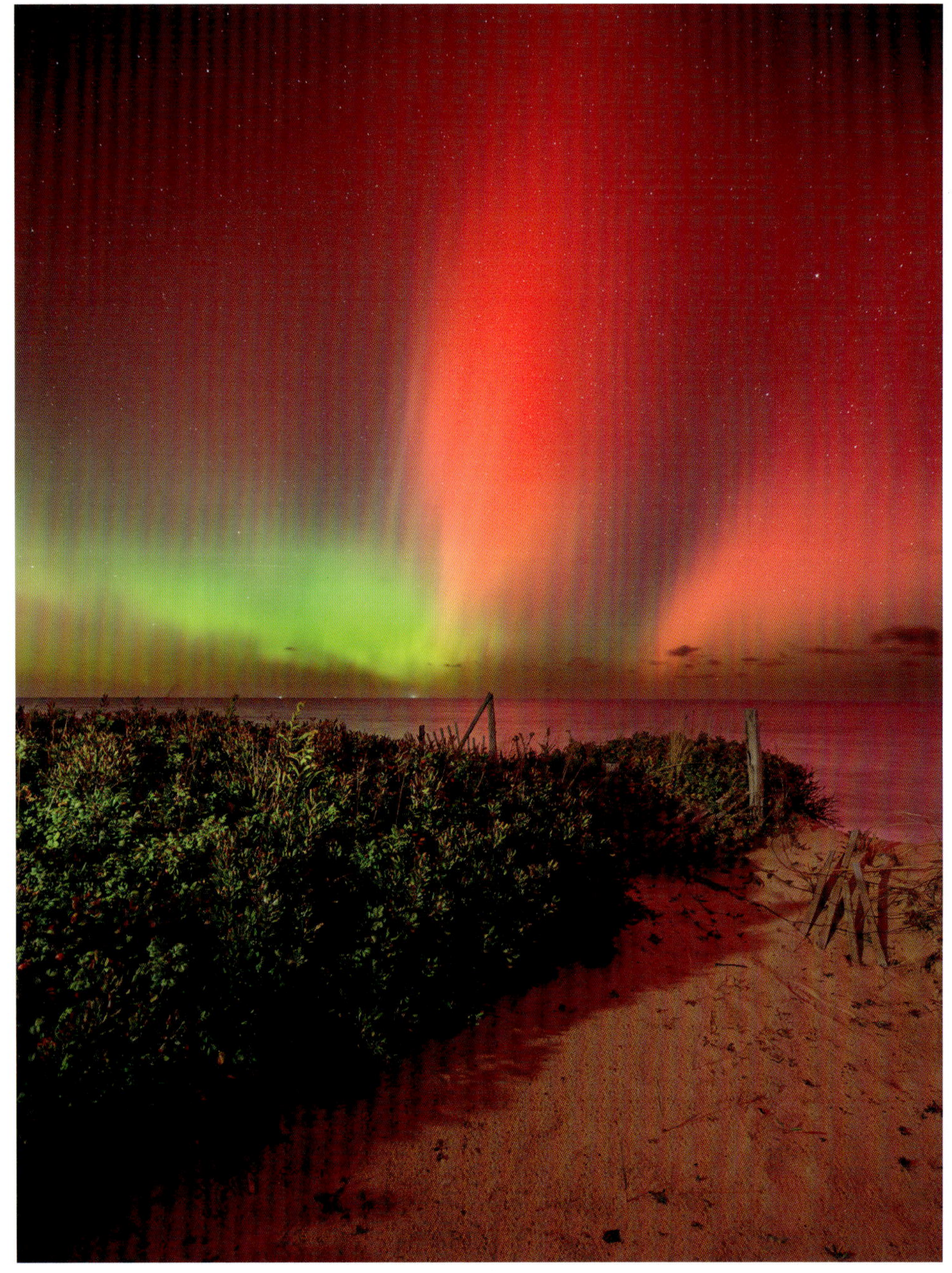

Columns of aurora push across the eastern horizon and light the waters below. The foreground was illuminated by hand while the pink aurora glow fills in the shadows.

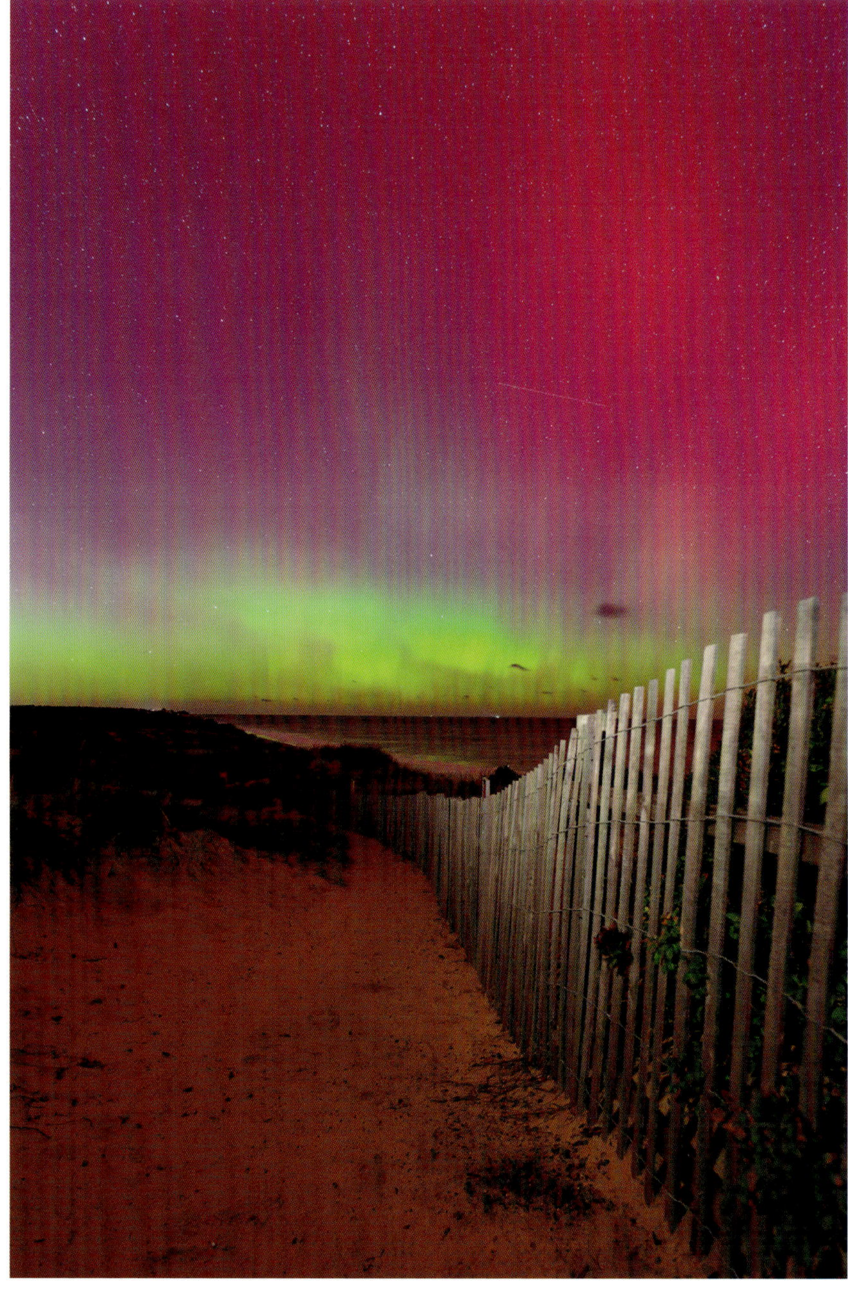

Deep pinks and purple fill in the skies to the north along a dune fence at Marconi Beach.

Here's Jeremy. I didn't know him prior to this night, but seeing him photographing atop this nearby dune gave me an opportunity to showcase the scale of what I was seeing. I later climbed the hill and exchanged information so I could get him this image. From what he showed me on his own camera, he was also having a successful night.

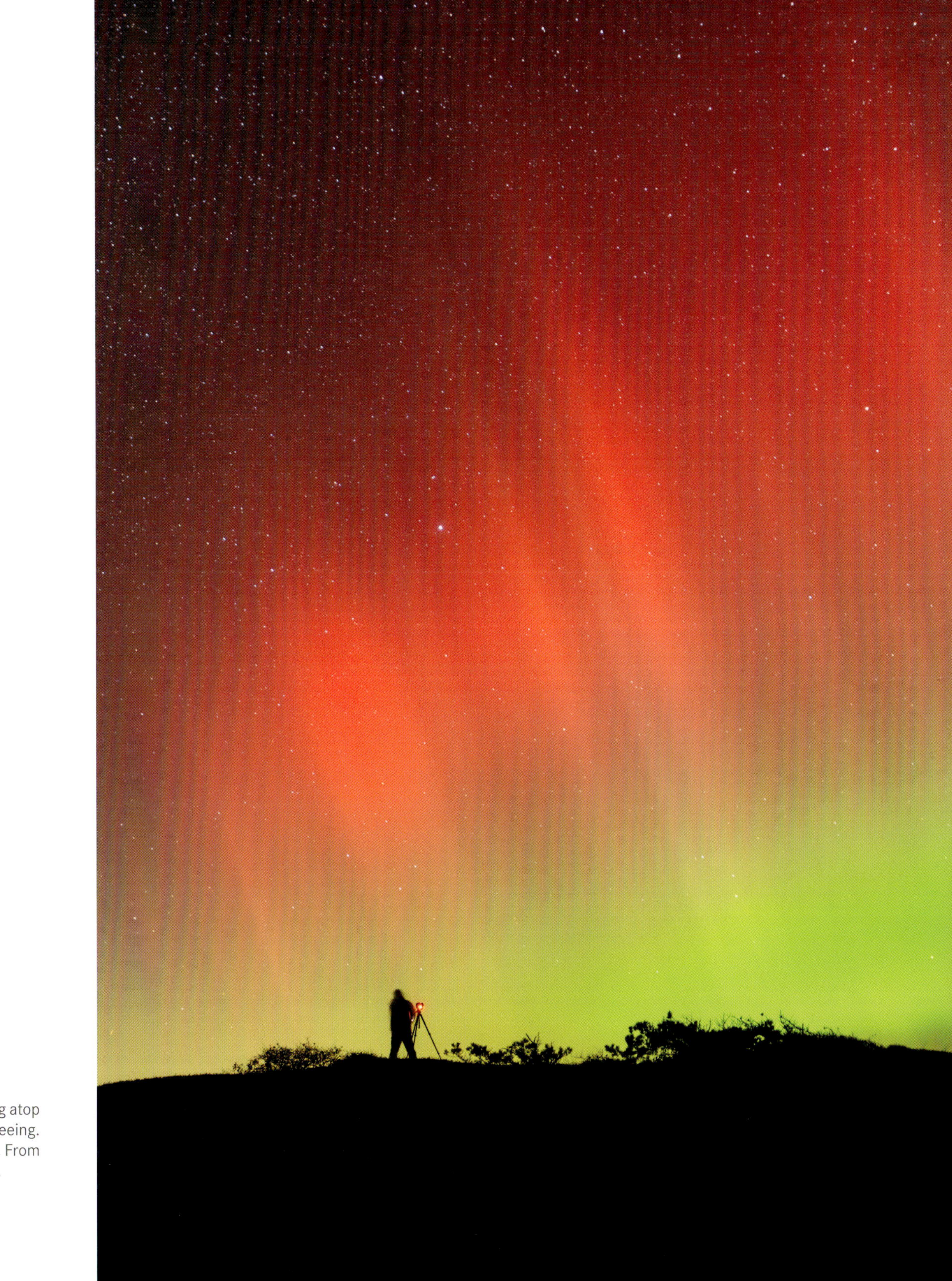

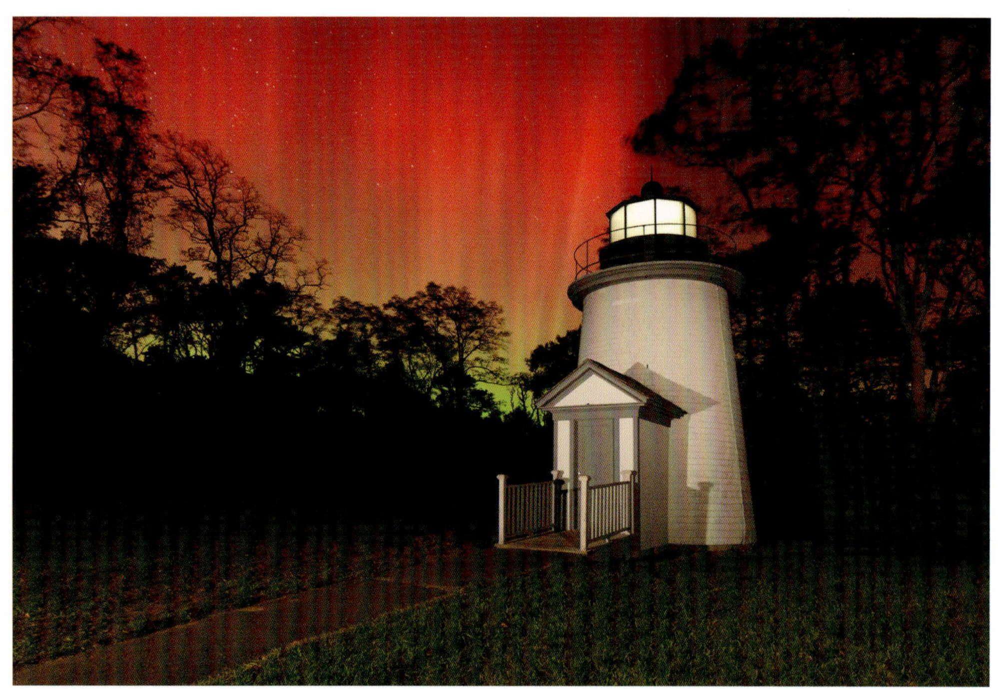

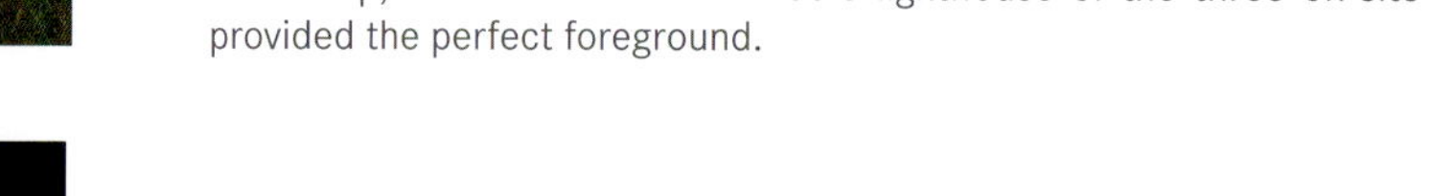

Next stop, Three Sisters. The middle lighthouse of the three on-site provided the perfect foreground.

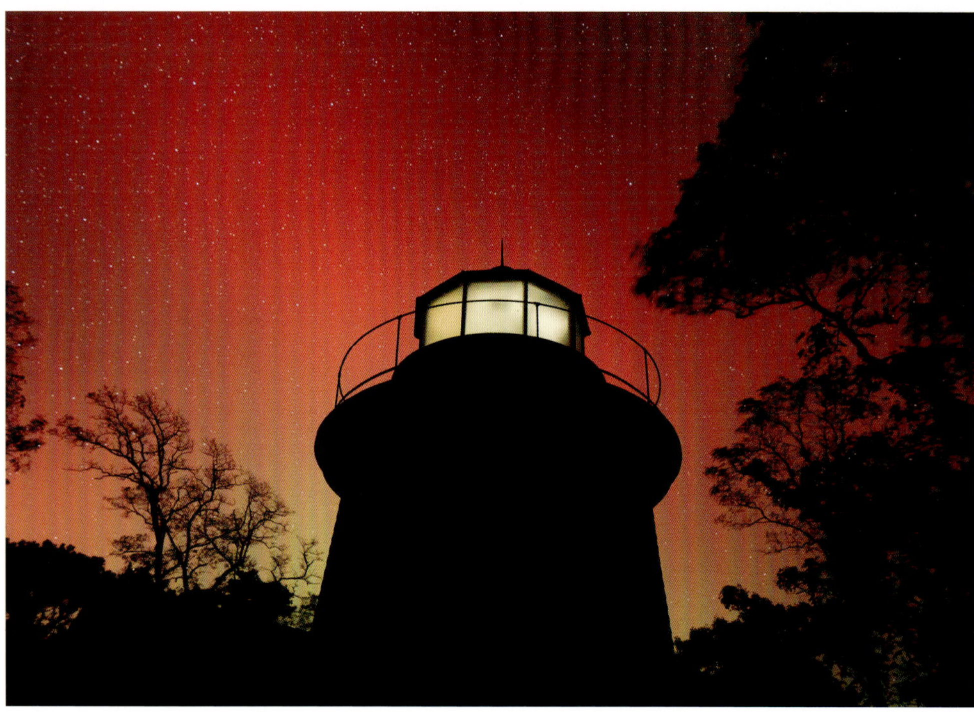

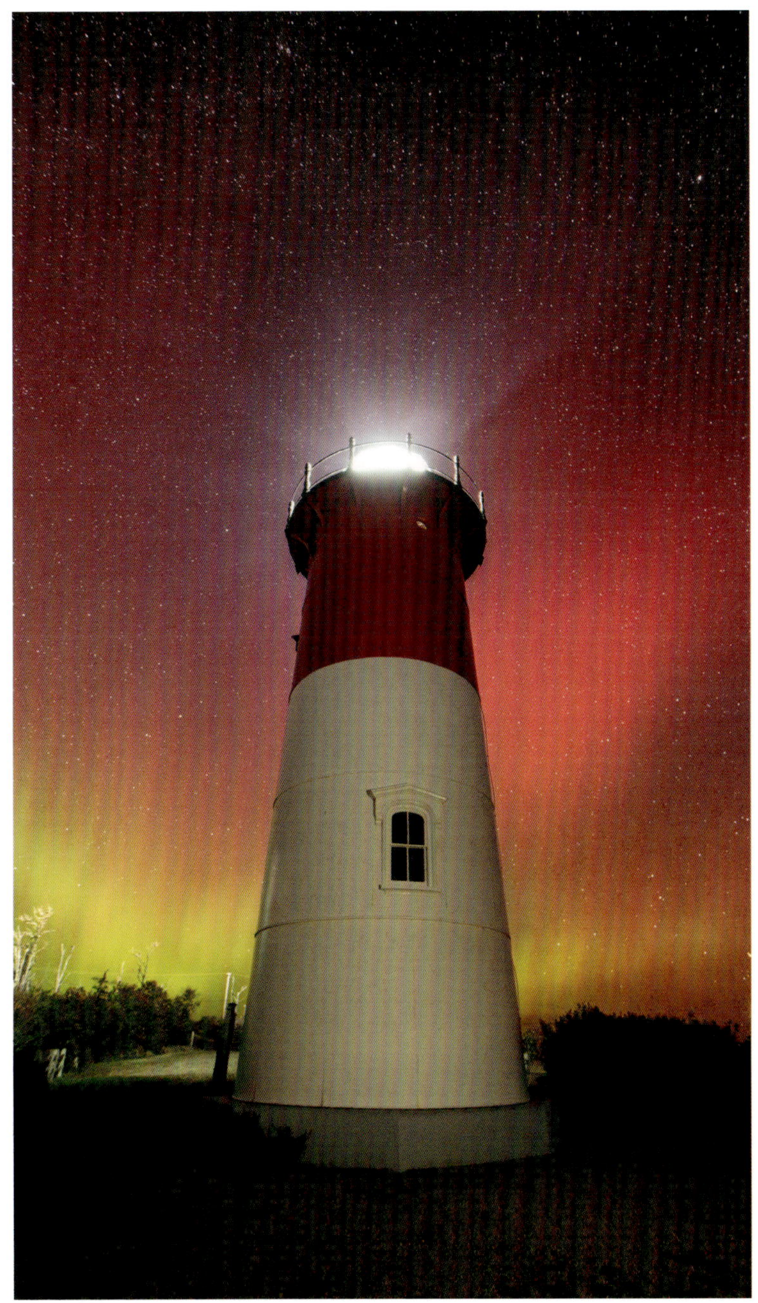

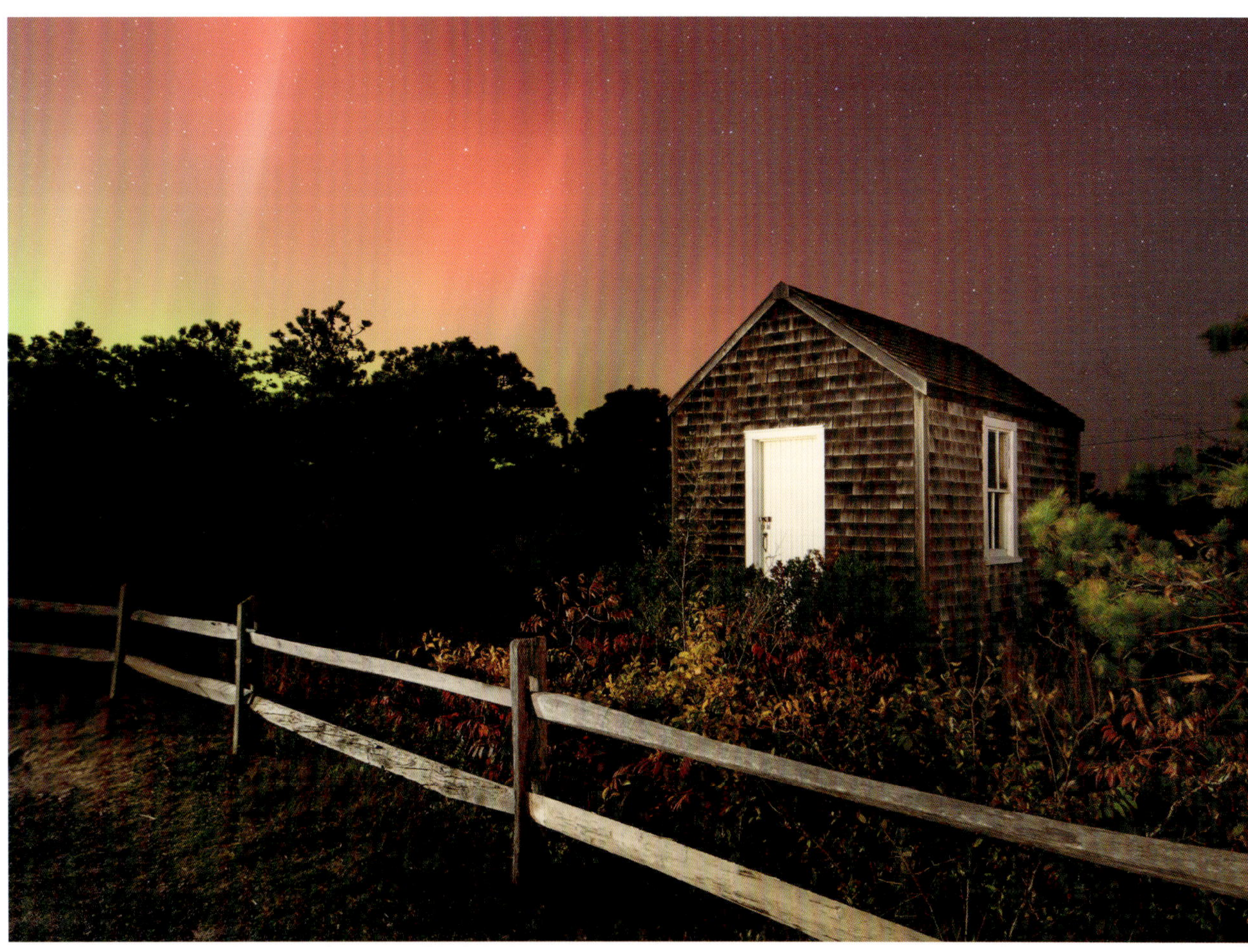

Of all the images captured that night, this one is my favorite. You may recognize this shack from earlier in the book. Having previously photographed the Milky Way over it, I welcomed the chance to get a new angle with a new sky. A light was used on the foreground, accentuating the subtle fall colors.

During my May visit to Nauset Light, cloudy skies obscured most of the aurora, but on this night in October the skies were crystal clear.

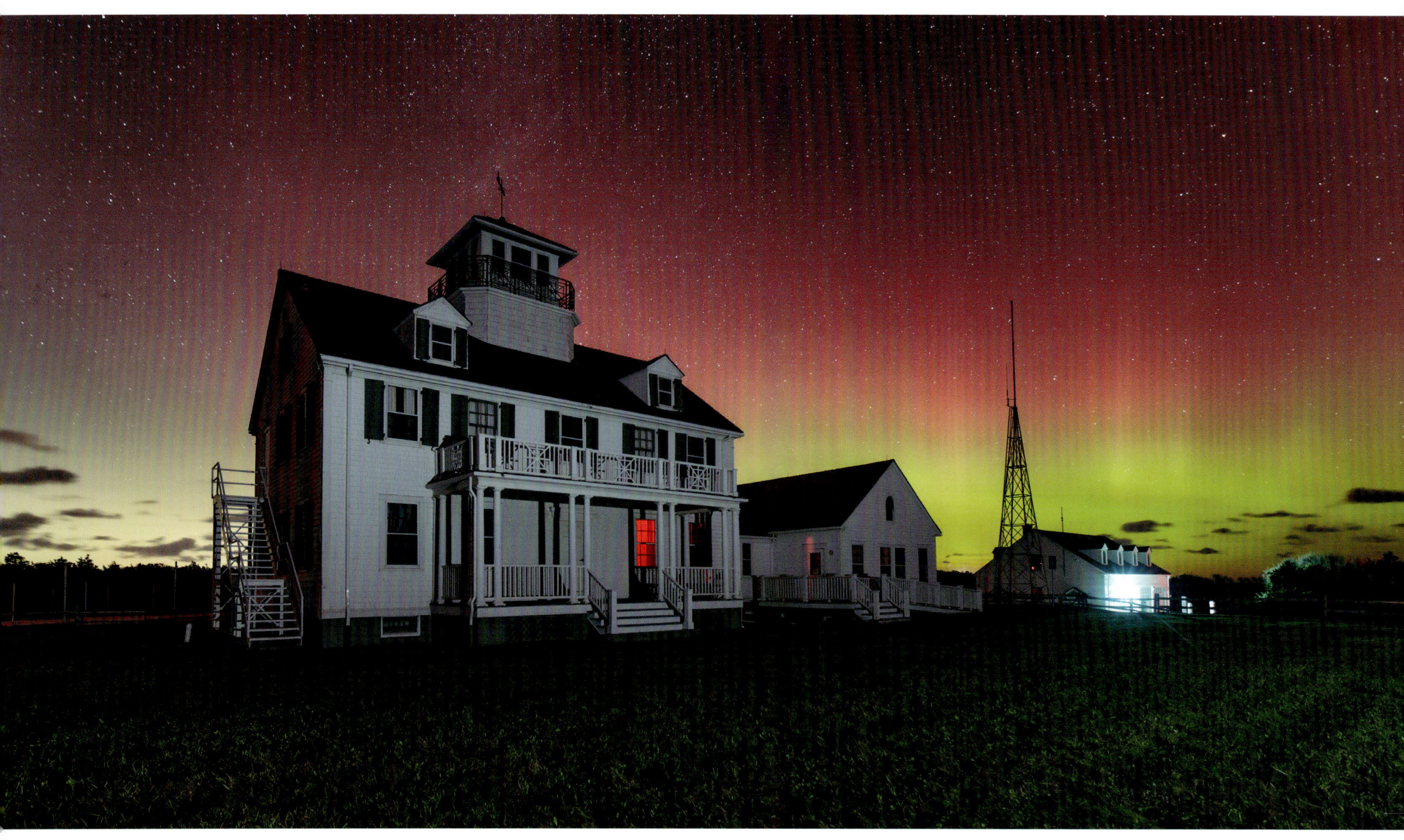

Just a few minutes away from Nauset Light was another opportunity to photograph the buildings at Coast Guard Beach.

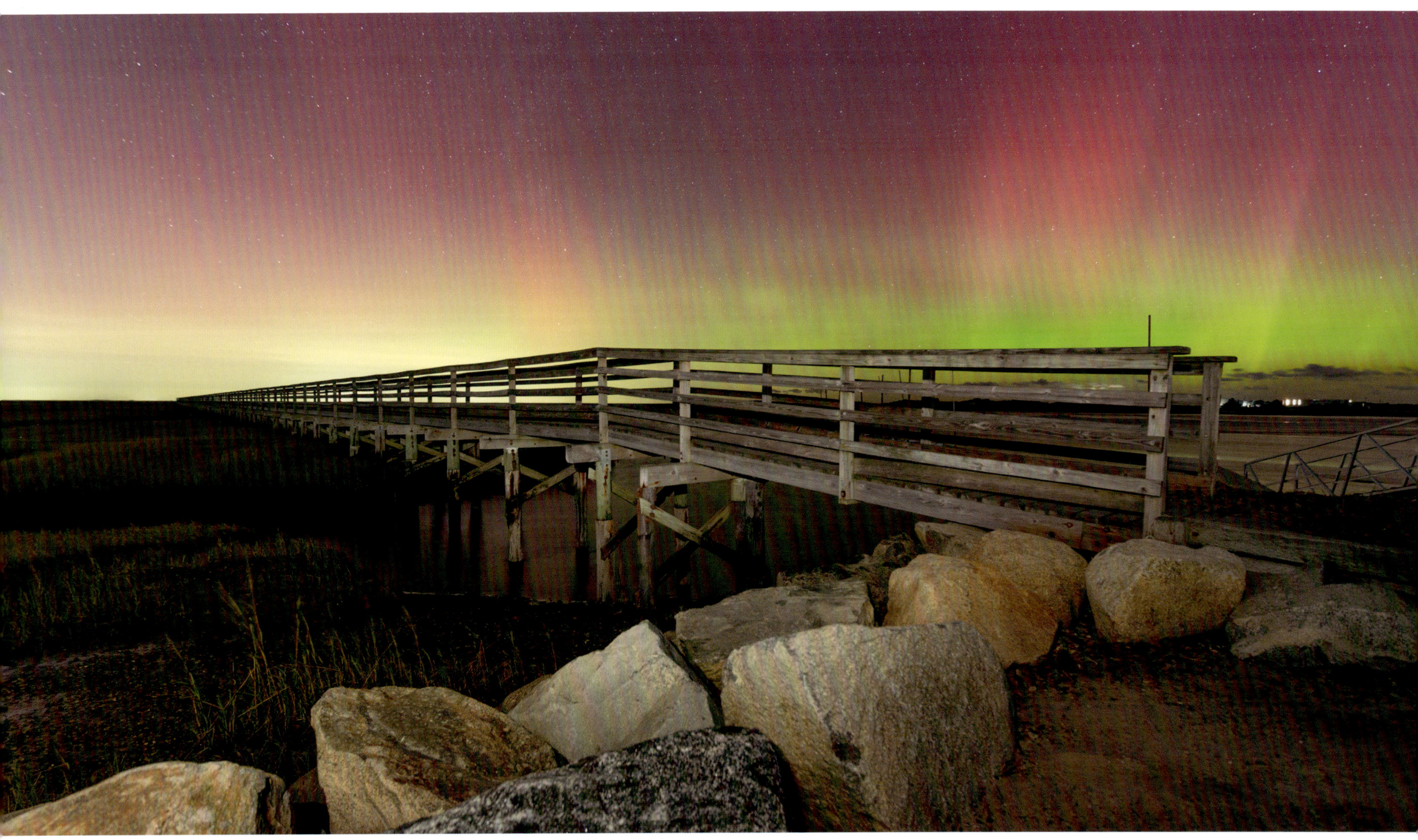

Bass Hole Boardwalk provides an excellent view to the north and, with it, this night's aurora. The air temperature had been bearable at every other location up to that point, but here it was quite windy. I spotted at least one other photographer. Counting Jeremy from earlier, this was only the second person I had seen all night.

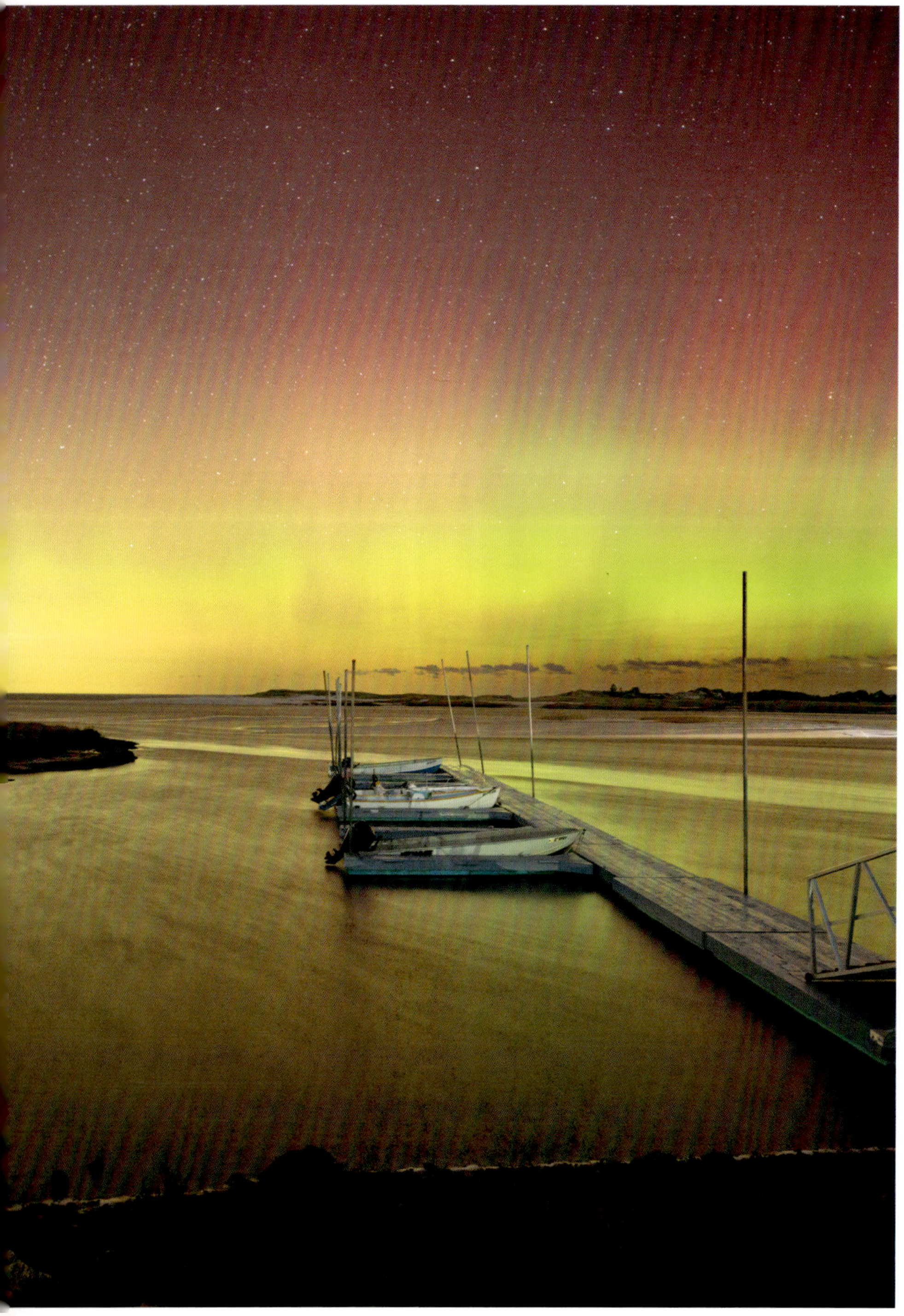

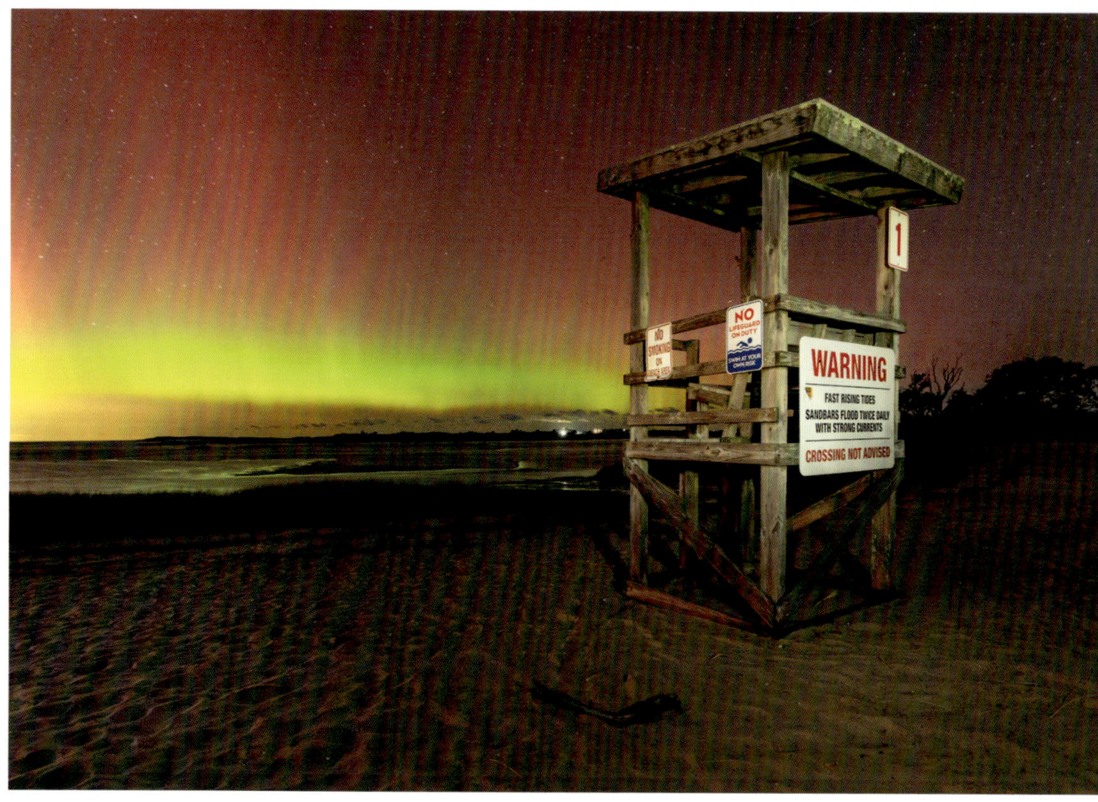

The permanent lifeguard chair at Grays Beach was available to anyone who wanted a front-row seat to the October 10 aurora.

The distance from the earth to the moon is around 239,000 miles. This truck has driven more than 350,000 miles, which means it could have made it there. Look closely elsewhere in the book for far less obvious appearances of my "moonrover." Here it is seen under the early October aurora in 2024.

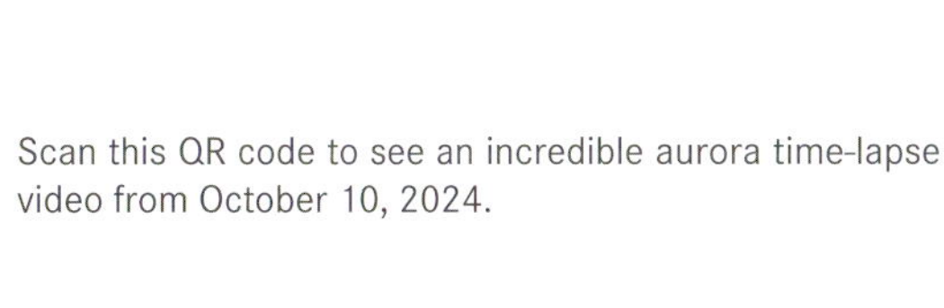
Scan this QR code to see an incredible aurora time-lapse video from October 10, 2024.

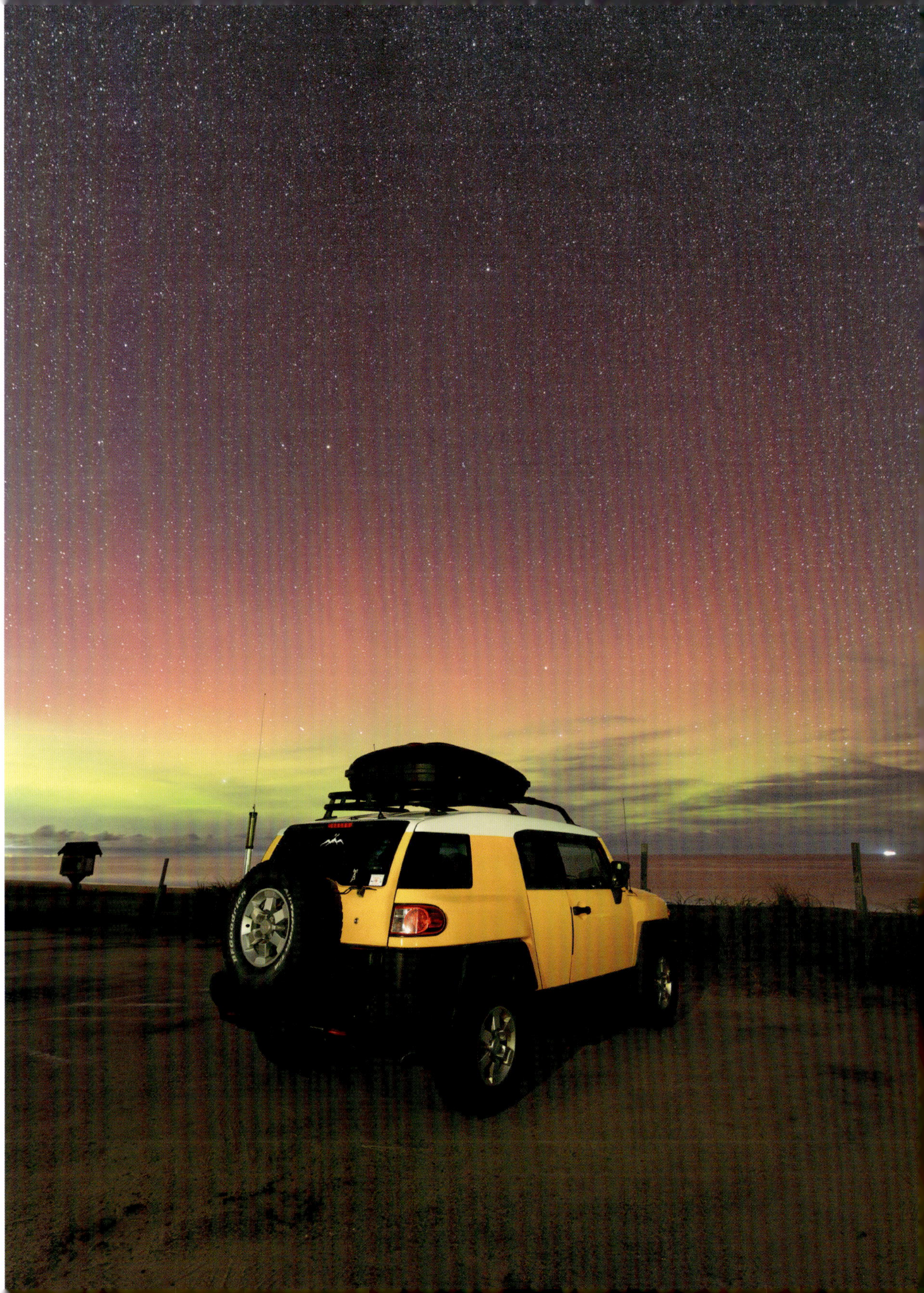

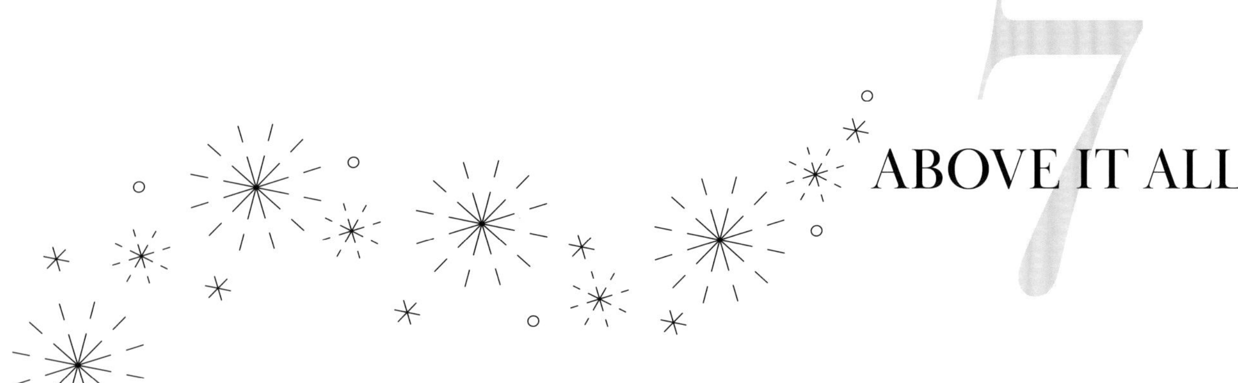

7 ABOVE IT ALL

The second *Back to the Future* film revealed that by the year 2015, we'd all be enjoying flying cars. As you may have noticed, this wasn't quite accurate. Even as late as 2011, had you told me that ten years later I'd own a flying camera, I would have thought your prediction to be equally inaccurate. And yet, in 2021, I purchased my first flying camera!

Initially, I had planned to use it only for daytime photography and video. At that time, night photography with a drone was possible, but the results were somewhat lacking. Many drones couldn't expose long enough to capture a night image, and those that could weren't able to remain steady enough to avoid blurring.

But drone technology had begun to advance exponentially. In 2023, I purchased an even more advanced drone, and I was finally able to start photographing from the sky after dark, albeit under very specific conditions. Many drone photographers were having success photographing brightly lit city streets and skylines, but no one was attempting night photography outside that environment. Challenge accepted.

I learned pretty quickly that there was a window each month, around the nights of the full moon, that could provide enough light on the landscape to pull it off. I began to practice night flying. Unlike with ground-based photography, where I could simply plant my tripod in the sand and get going, this process required very calm conditions. Even the slightest breeze would cause the drone to drift and ruin the exposure. I needed still air and moonlight on the same night. Up until this point, I had never realized how rare such a pairing could be on Cape Cod.

In May 2023, I finally had my first window. I decided to set my sights on Nobska Light, which was both a relatively short drive from home and is self-illuminated. A little extra light would certainly help. This image is from that evening. It was truly exciting! Imagine having access to a 100-foot tripod. It was a whole new way to capture the night.

I carefully aligned the moon so that it would reflect off the water and light the sky behind the foreground. Capturing the moon itself would not be important. I used a "bracketing" process to ensure I got the best possible image data. This means taking multiple images at different exposure levels to properly capture the lit areas of the scene. For example, one short image for the tower and house lighting, a longer exposure to capture the dimmer ground lighting and water, and an even longer exposure for the sky and the distant horizon. These three images are then combined later, balancing everything out.

After a successful shoot, I was able to take this process to other locations and get similar results. The sky was now truly the limit!

As of this writing, however, I think it will be quite some time before we are able to see aerial Milky Way photographs. This is because the sensors aren't quite able to recover that dim starlight without the benefit of extra time. I am hopeful that someday this will be possible as sensor technology for drones improves.

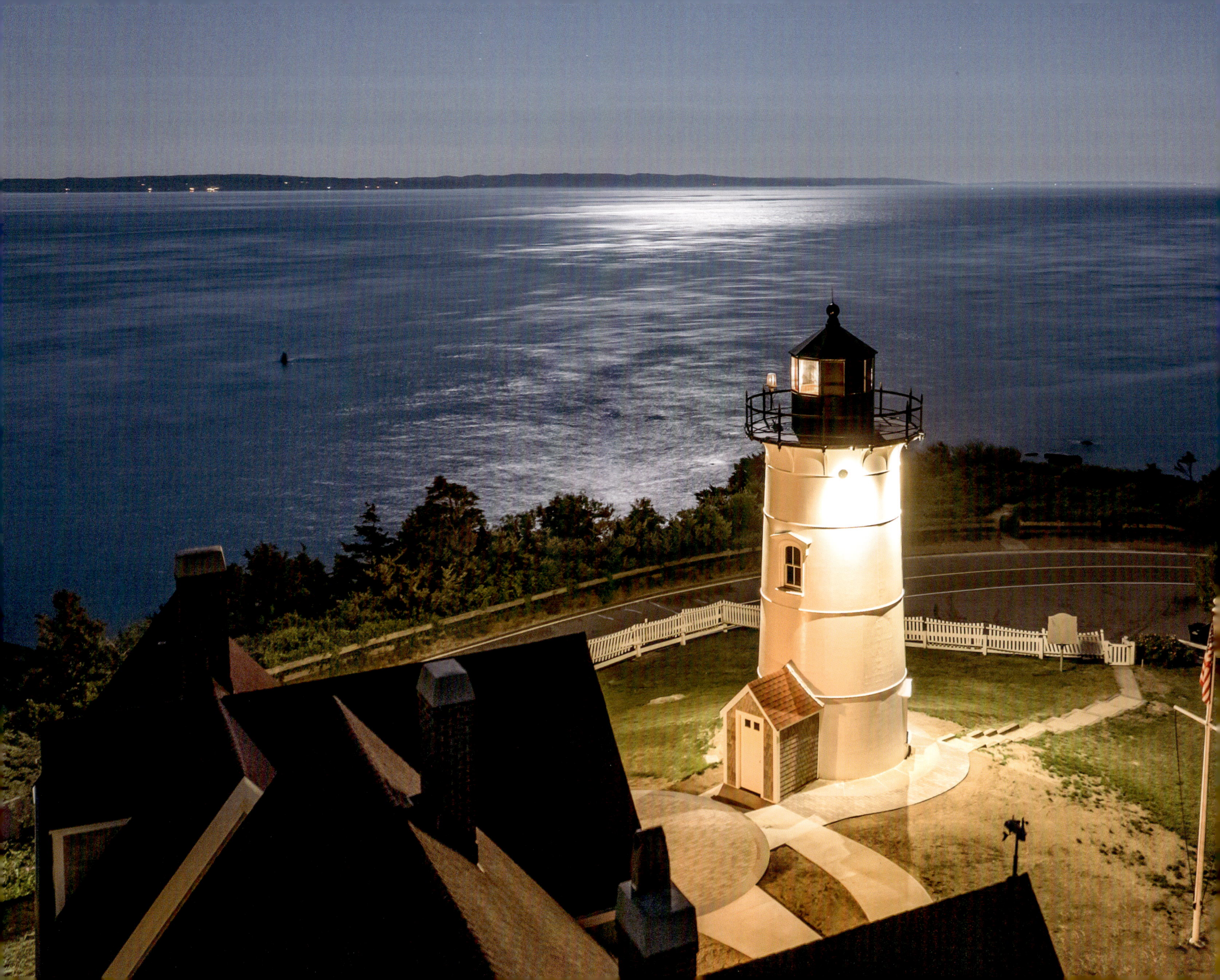

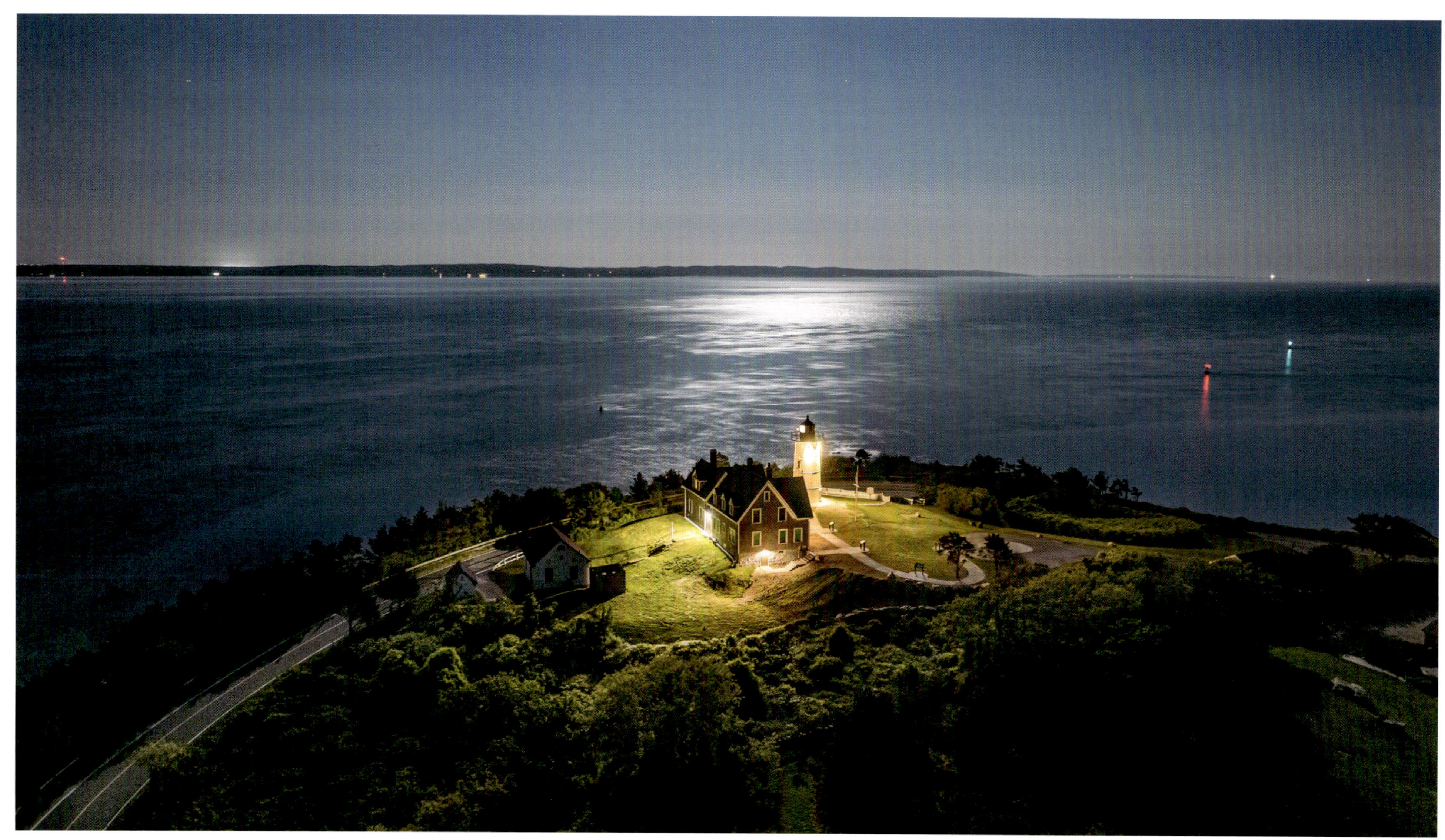

I waited several months for the right conditions to capture these images of Nobska Light from above. Most importantly, a completely windless night was required for the long exposures. A full moon helped illuminate the areas outside the lighthouse ground, including the water and the sky. Each photograph was the result of several images shot at different exposure levels to properly capture the tower, the ground lighting, and the background.

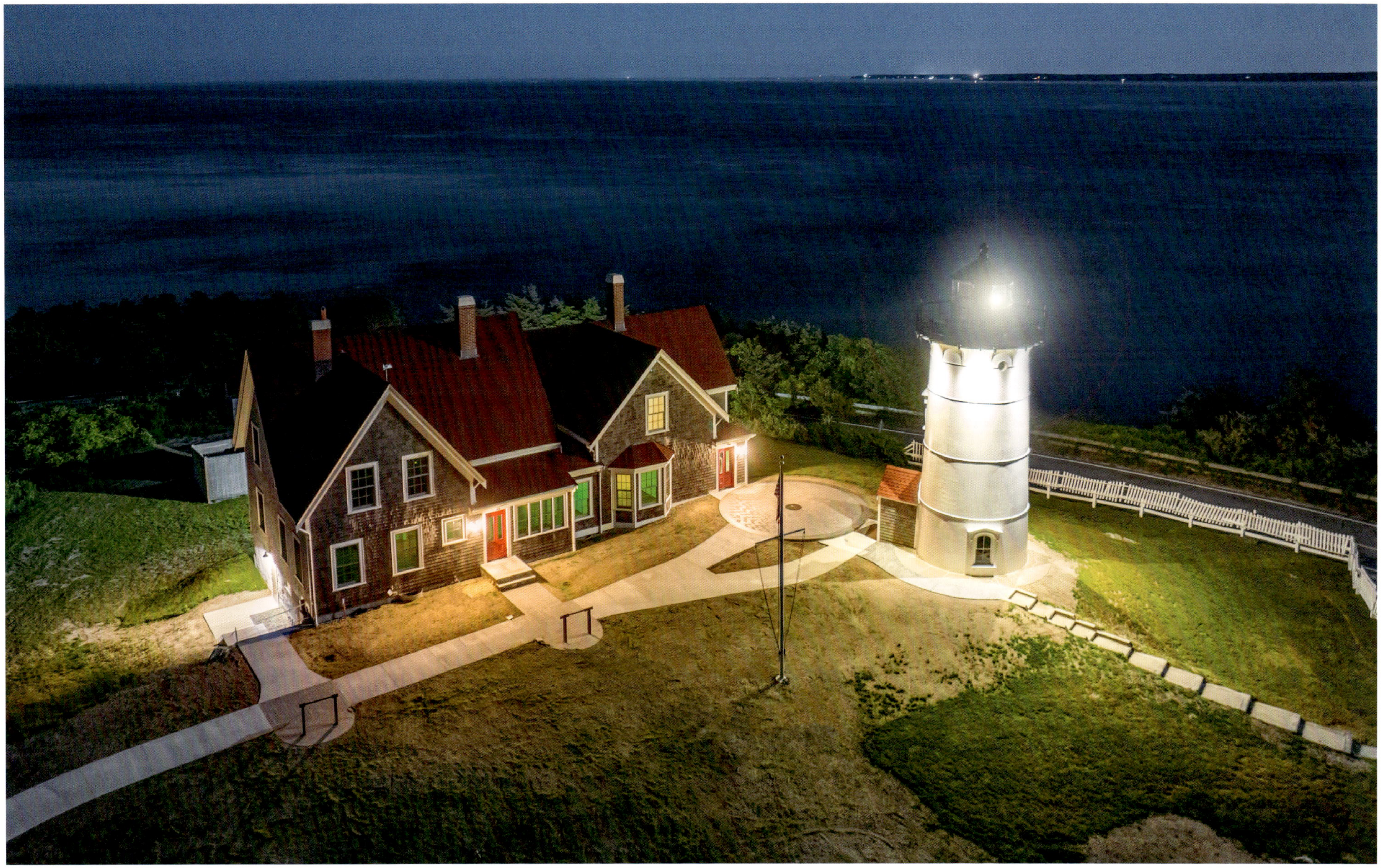

This image was taken at the end of the grounds restoration project. Hoses, ground stakes, and construction tape all were removed in the postproduction process. Photographing on the night of the full moon allowed the distance to be illuminated, which would otherwise have appeared completely black.

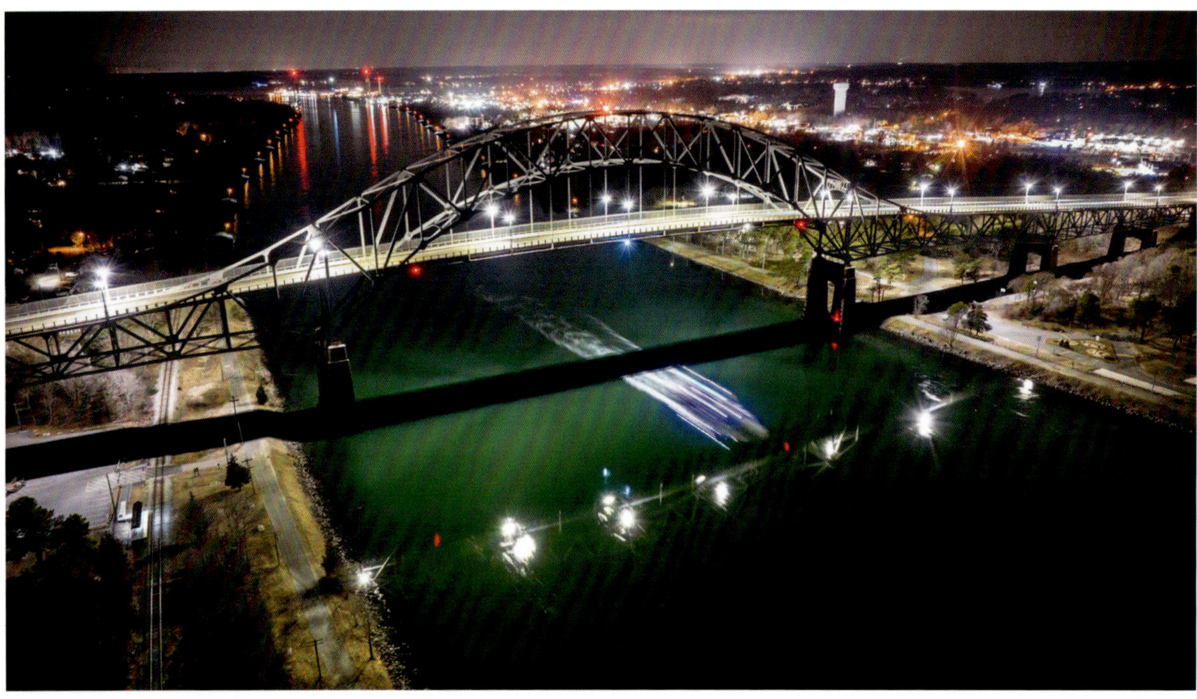

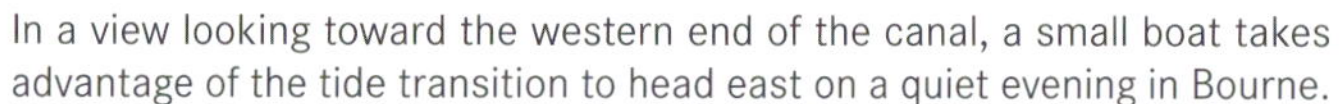

In a view looking toward the western end of the canal, a small boat takes advantage of the tide transition to head east on a quiet evening in Bourne.

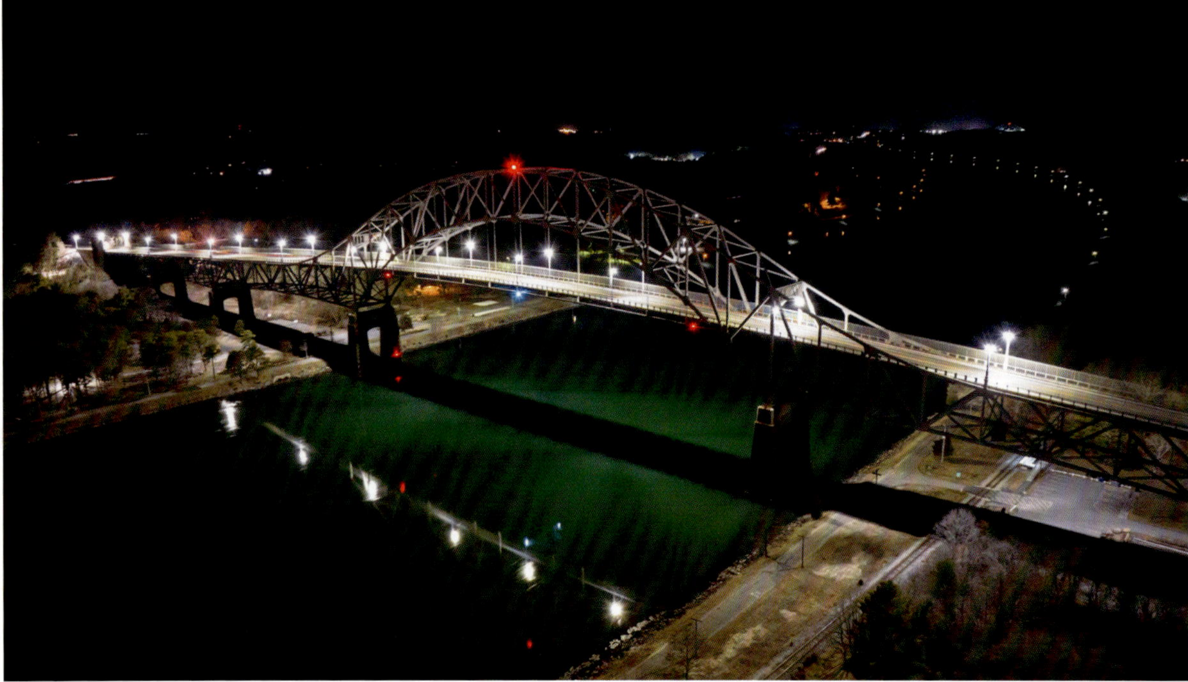

A momentary transition in tide direction is commonly referred to as a "slack tide." During this time, the water comes to a stop, creating a mirrorlike surface before reversing direction. Here, the warm-colored downward lighting from the Bourne Bridge mixes with the blue water below to create the green glow. This is an eight-second exposure, during which any cars passing over the bridge become invisible as they move through the exposure, leaving only their lights behind.

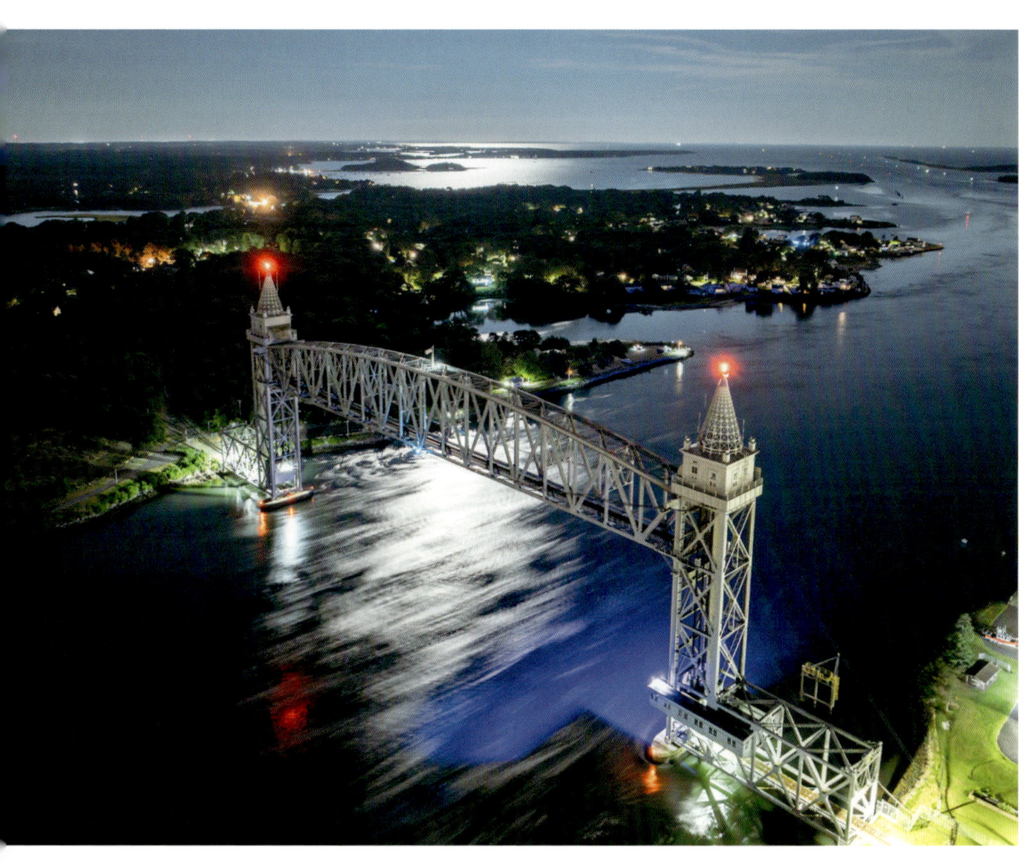

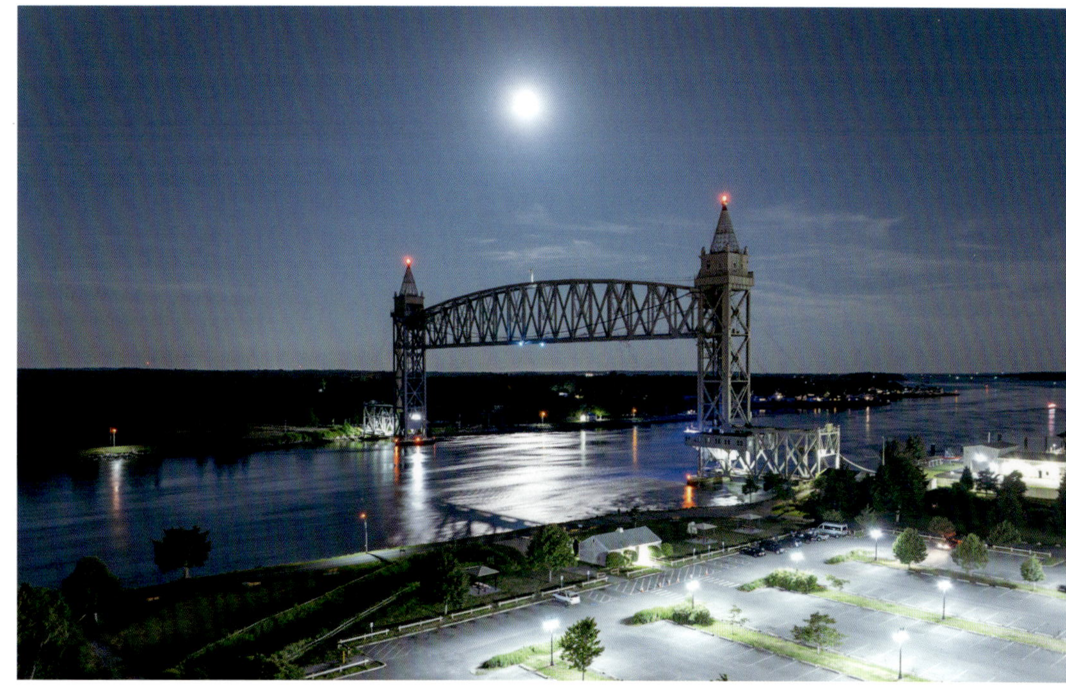

Moonlight shines across the waters below the canal's railroad bridge. Photographed at an altitude of nearly 400 feet, this six-second exposure took several attempts to capture since the drone kept moving slightly. An image like this would have been impossible without the ambient moonlight to help illuminate the sky and distant horizon.

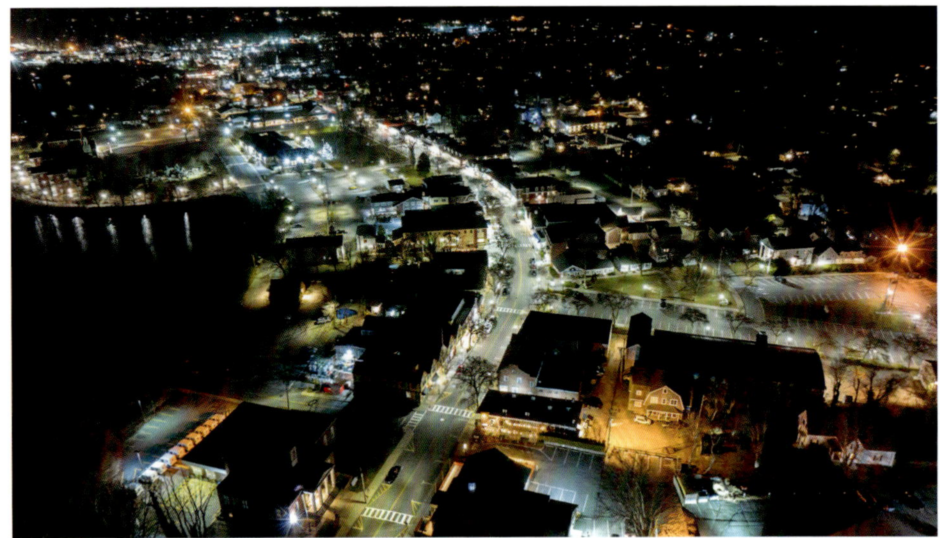

Falmouth's Main Street as seen from the air, looking from the Falmouth Green toward the public library. This was one of my first night flights, so I chose a well-lit environment with which to experiment.

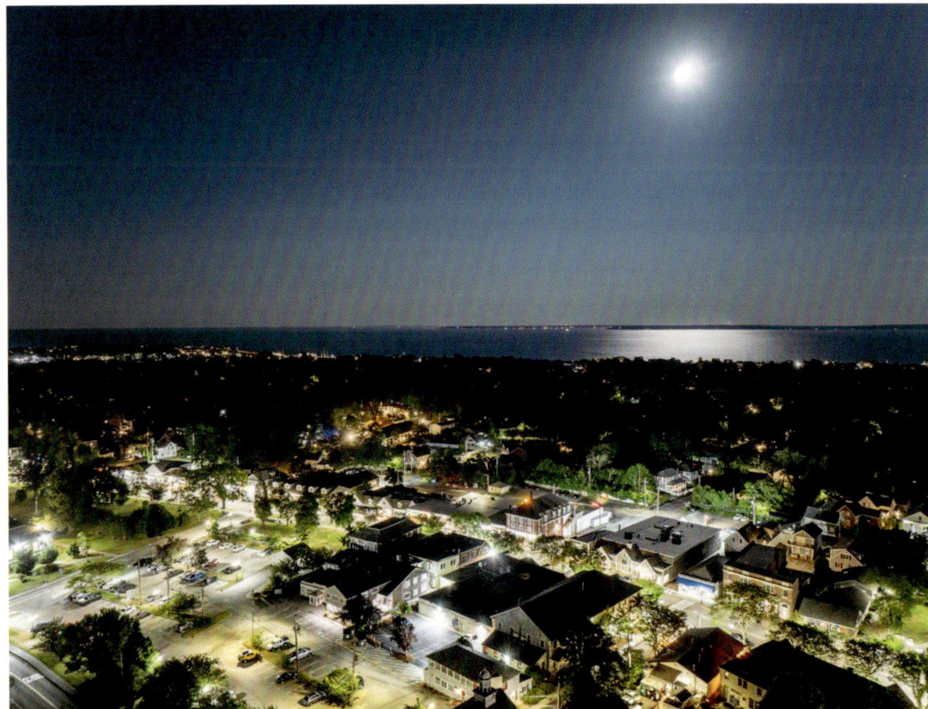

What looks like a quiet, moonlit night on Falmouth's Main Street was filled with music and laughter in the late hours of July 19, 2024.

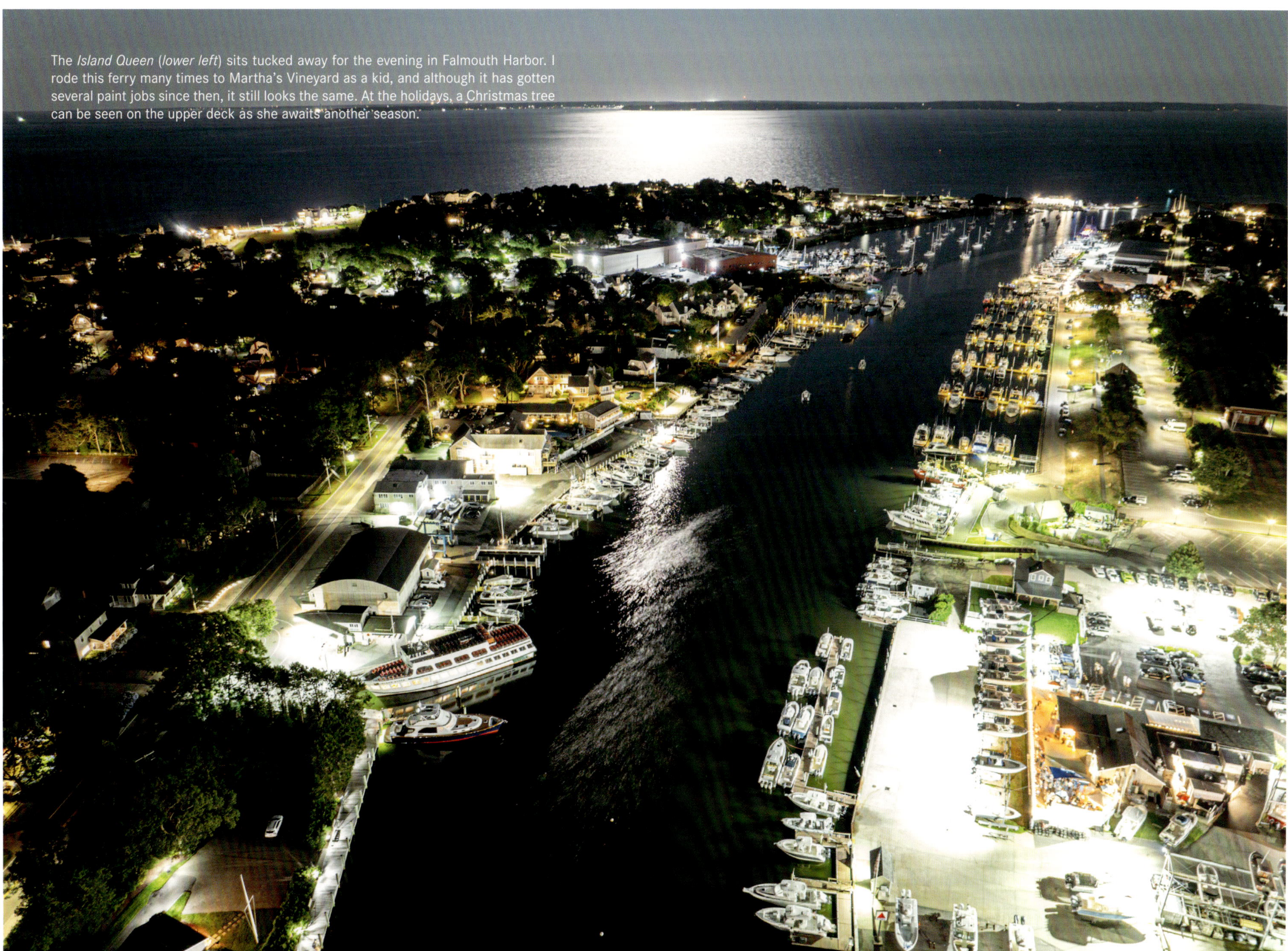
The *Island Queen* (*lower left*) sits tucked away for the evening in Falmouth Harbor. I rode this ferry many times to Martha's Vineyard as a kid, and although it has gotten several paint jobs since then, it still looks the same. At the holidays, a Christmas tree can be seen on the upper deck as she awaits another season.

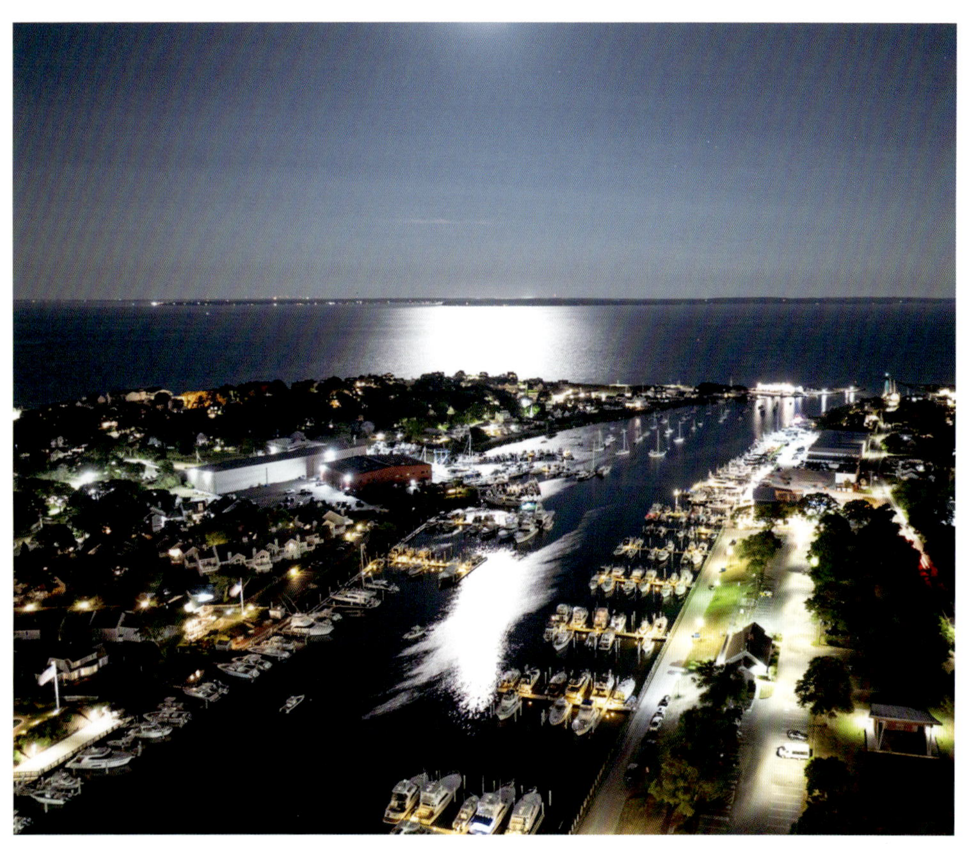

The entrance to Falmouth Harbor couldn't support one more boat in the summer of 2024. The area is a great place to watch boats parade out to the islands and is full of activity all day.

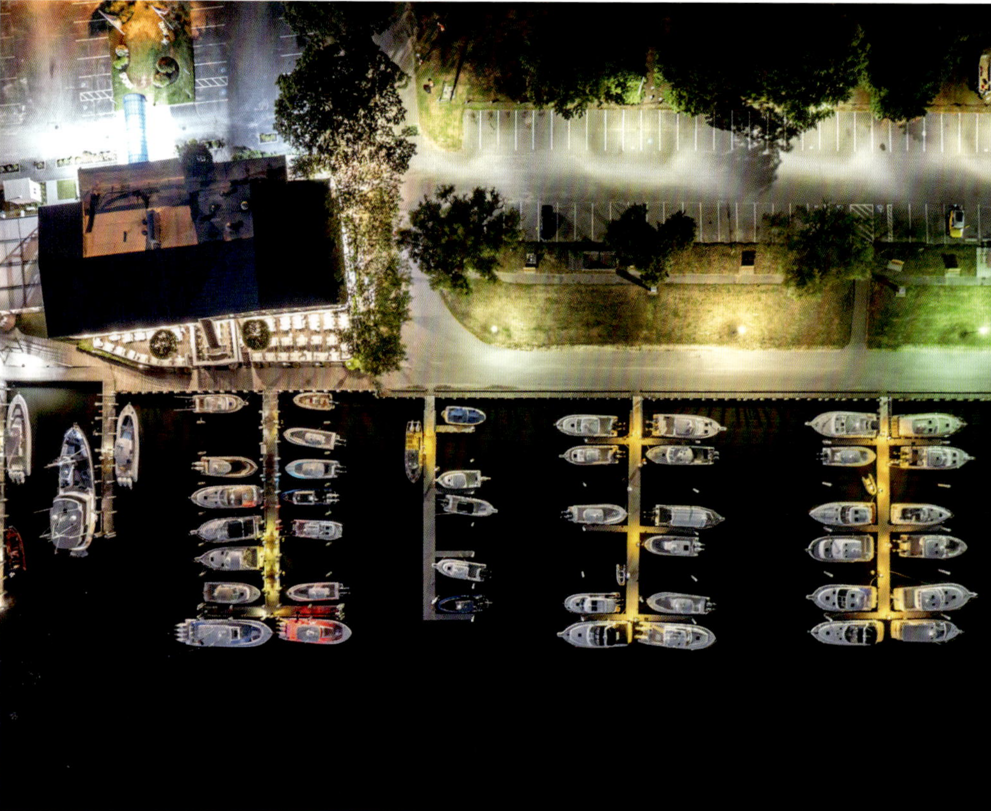

A view of the Flying Bridge restaurant and moorings at Marine Park in Falmouth.

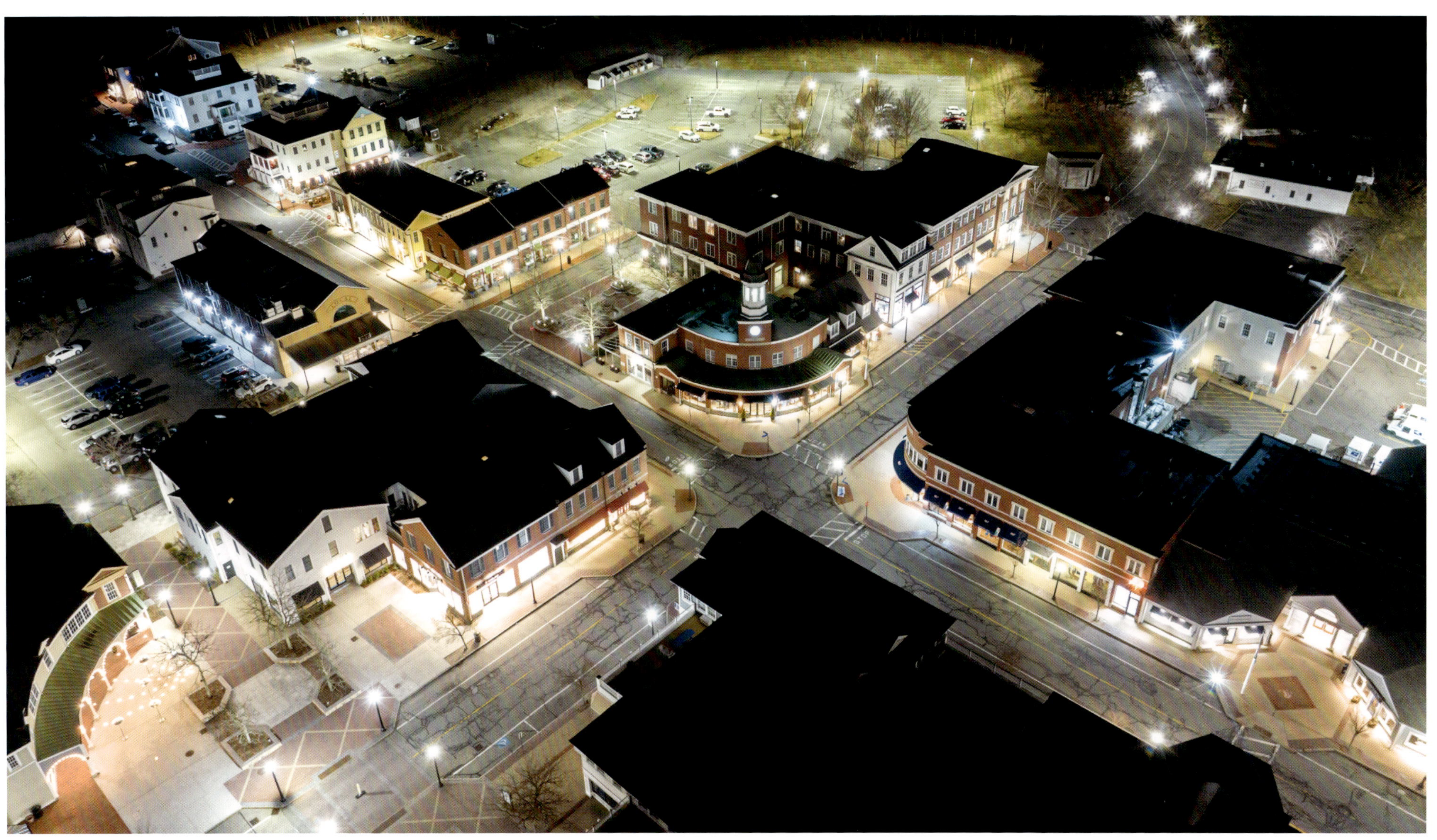

An aerial view of Steeple Street and the clocktower in Mashpee Commons.

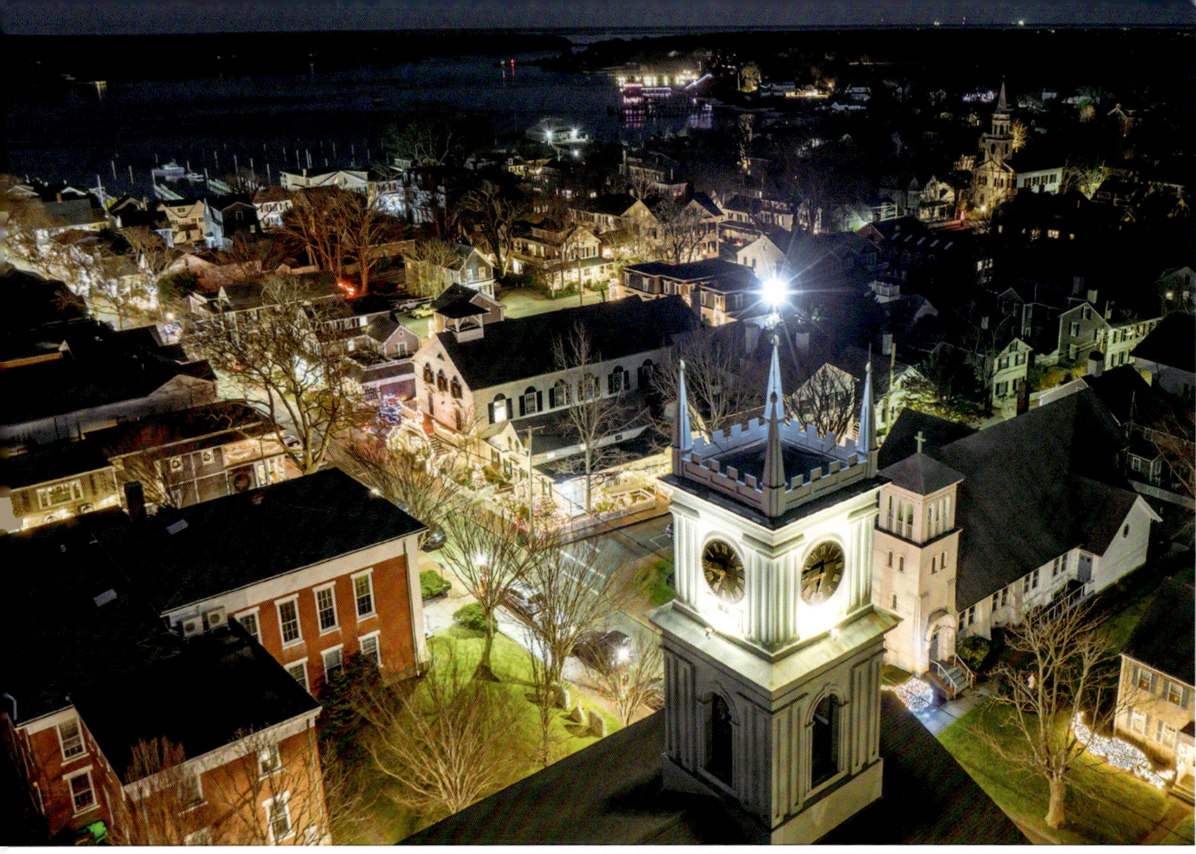

Built in 1843, the Old Whaling Church in Edgartown is adorned annually with a "Christmas star." The church steeple is likely one of the highest points in the town, making it—and the star—easily seen from several vantage points, as shown in these photographs from December 2023.

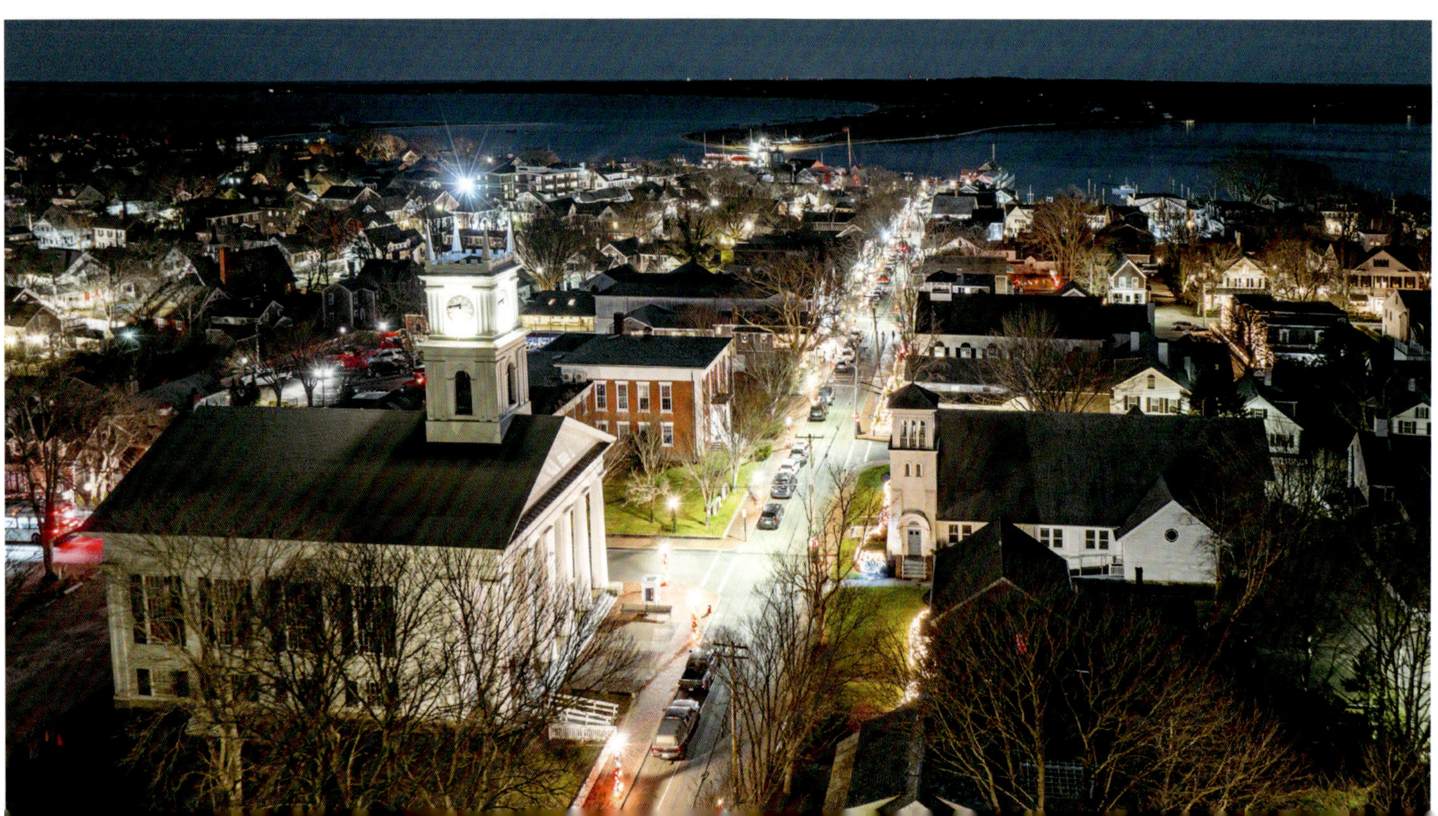

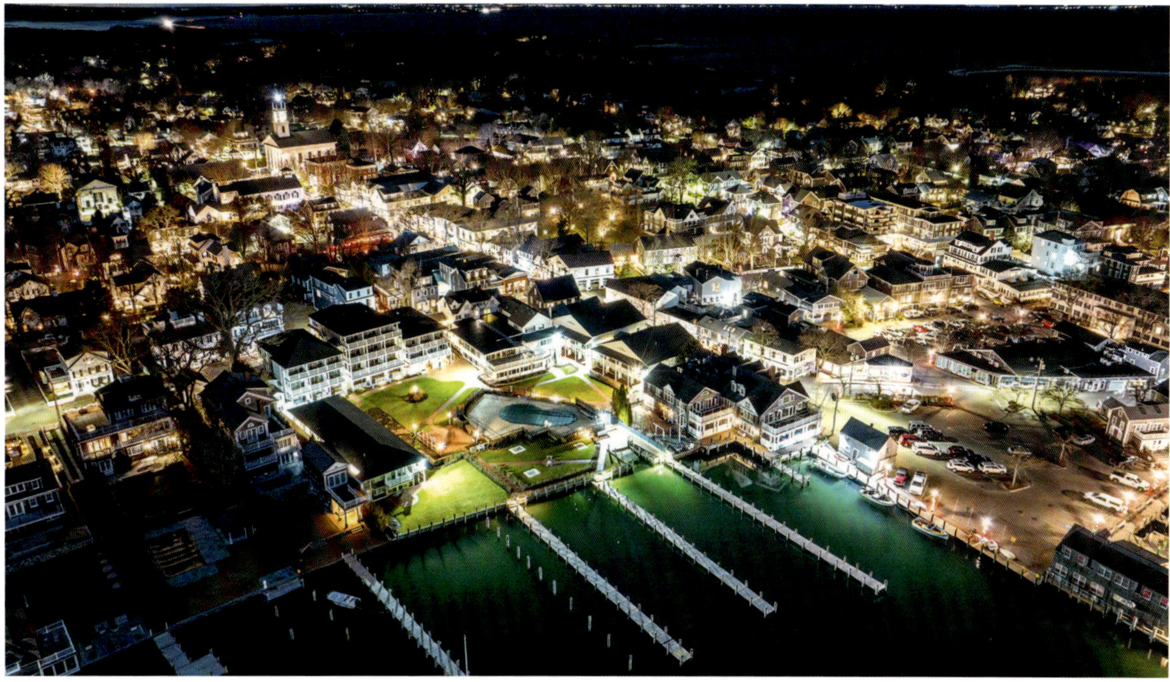

The shoreline near Main Street in Edgartown. Visit here on any summer's day and you'll spot a virtual traffic jam of fancy boats whose passengers are looking for easy access to town, a great meal at one of the several restaurants, or just a place to relax for the day. In the winter, only the docks and walkways remain. Look toward the far end of Main Street to see the Christmas star atop the Old Whaling Church.

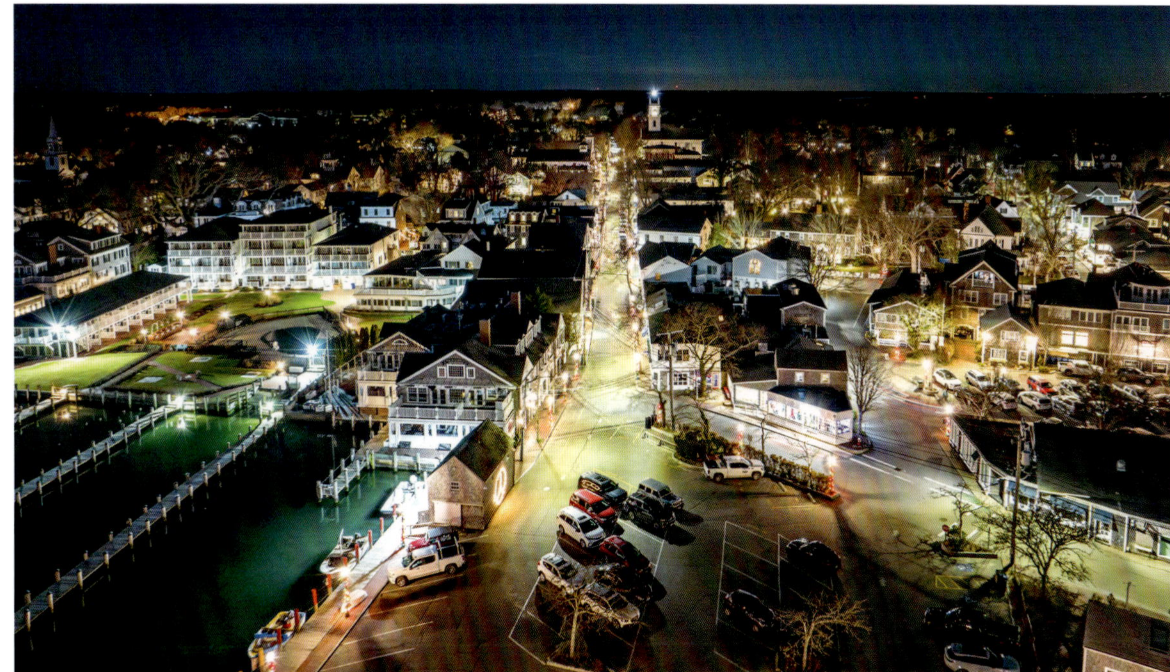

Main Street in Edgartown, looking west. Decorated lampposts outline the parking lot and stretch into the distance. Despite the colder temperatures, plenty of people are out and about, presumably attending holiday get-togethers a few nights before Christmas.

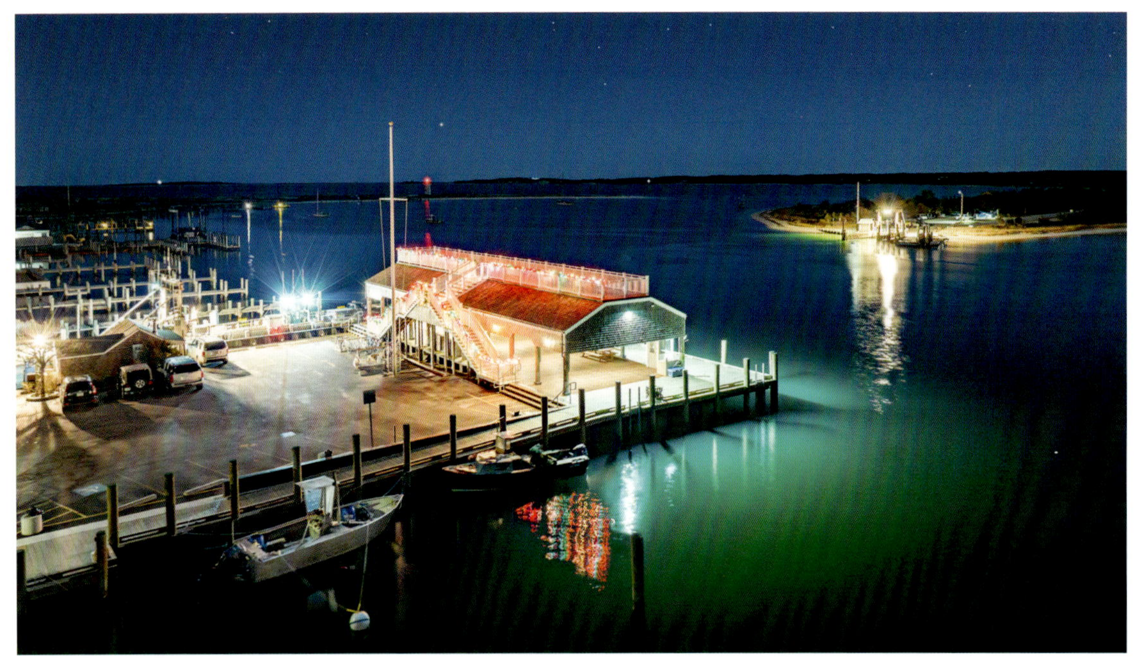

Memorial Wharf in Edgartown as seen at an altitude of about 75 feet. Photographed in mid-December 2023, the viewing platform had been adorned with colorful lights. This area went through an extensive refurbishment over the last few years. If you visit, be sure to climb the steps to the top to enjoy a great view of harbor activity and to watch the "Chappy Ferry" moving cars back and forth. In the distance is the signature red glow of Edgartown Light.

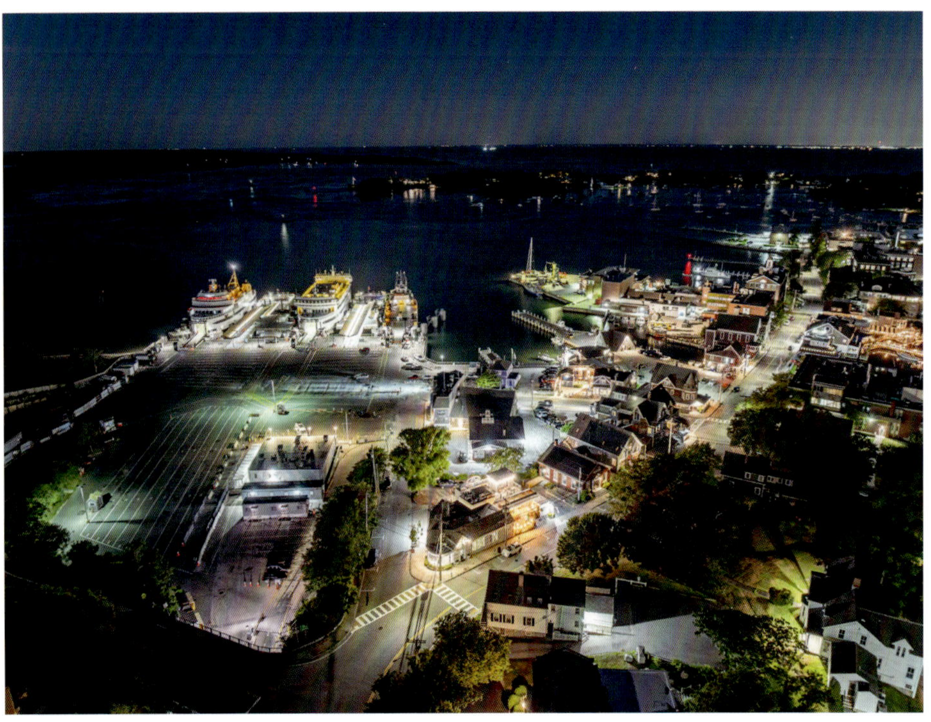

JUST PASSING THROUGH

Woods Hole could be classified as a place on the way to nowhere if thinking in terms of driving. However, it is one of just a few gateways to the Vineyard, making it a destination on its own. Here, ferries operated by the Steamship Authority work hard to move people and vehicles back and forth all year long, from early in the morning until late at night. Over the last several years, the docks have been rebuilt and expanded to accommodate the ever-increasing traffic. On most nights, these ships await the first trip of the day, while similar vessels docked at the Vineyard do the same.

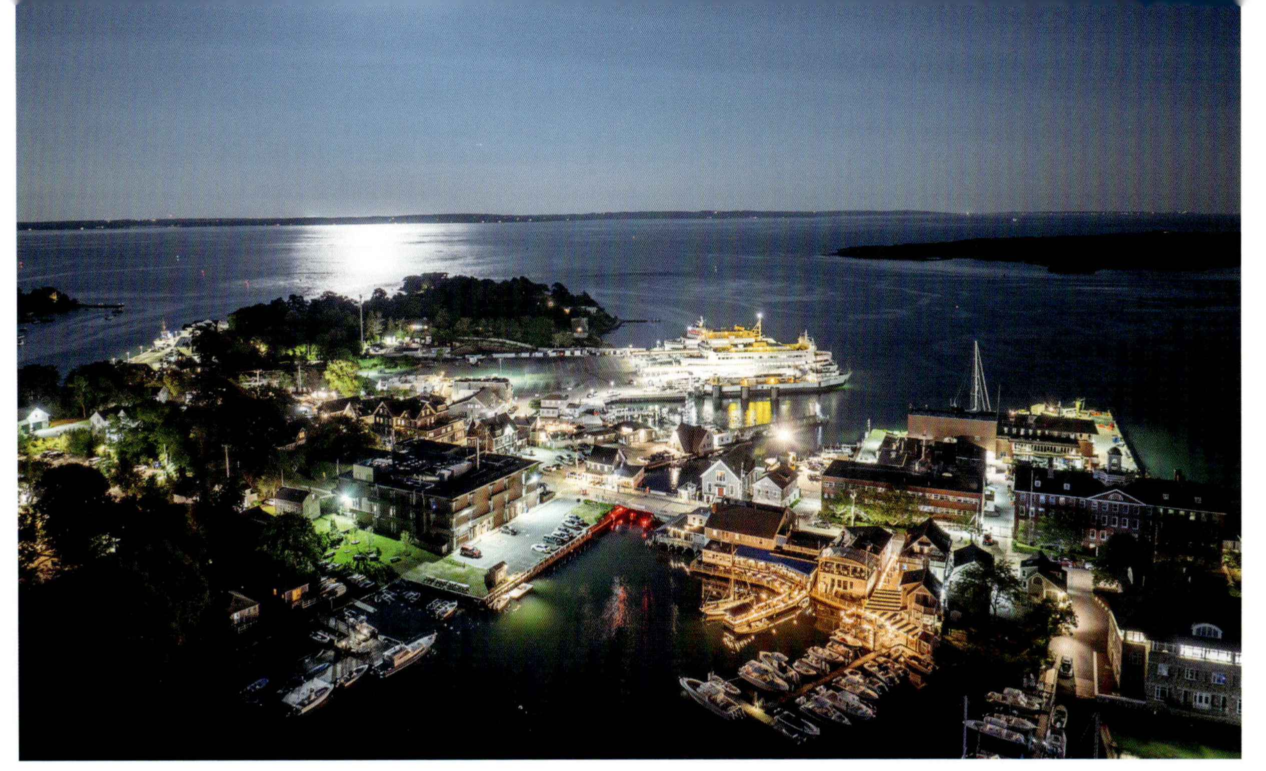

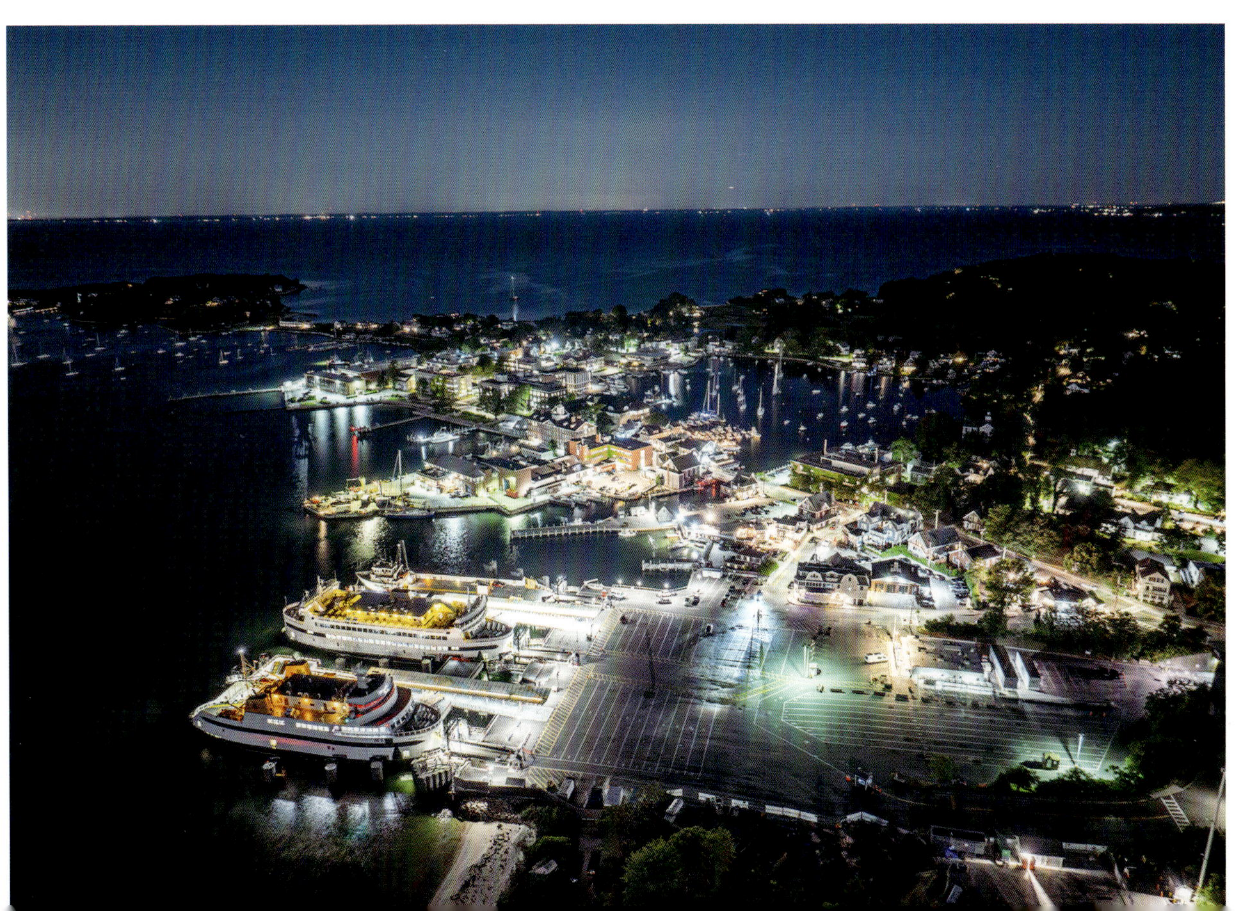

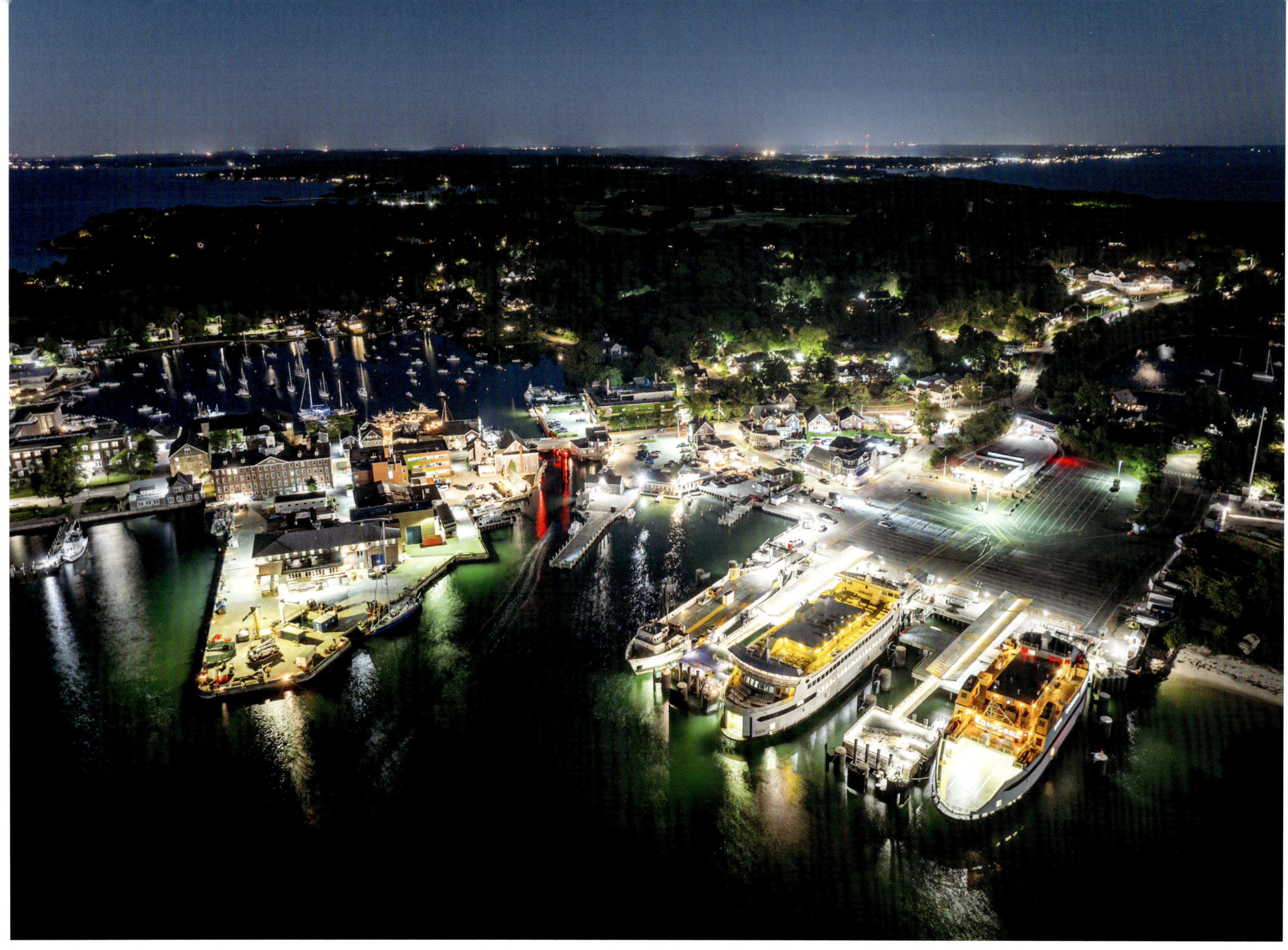

From left to right are the *Gay Head*, *Island Home*, and *Woods Hole*.

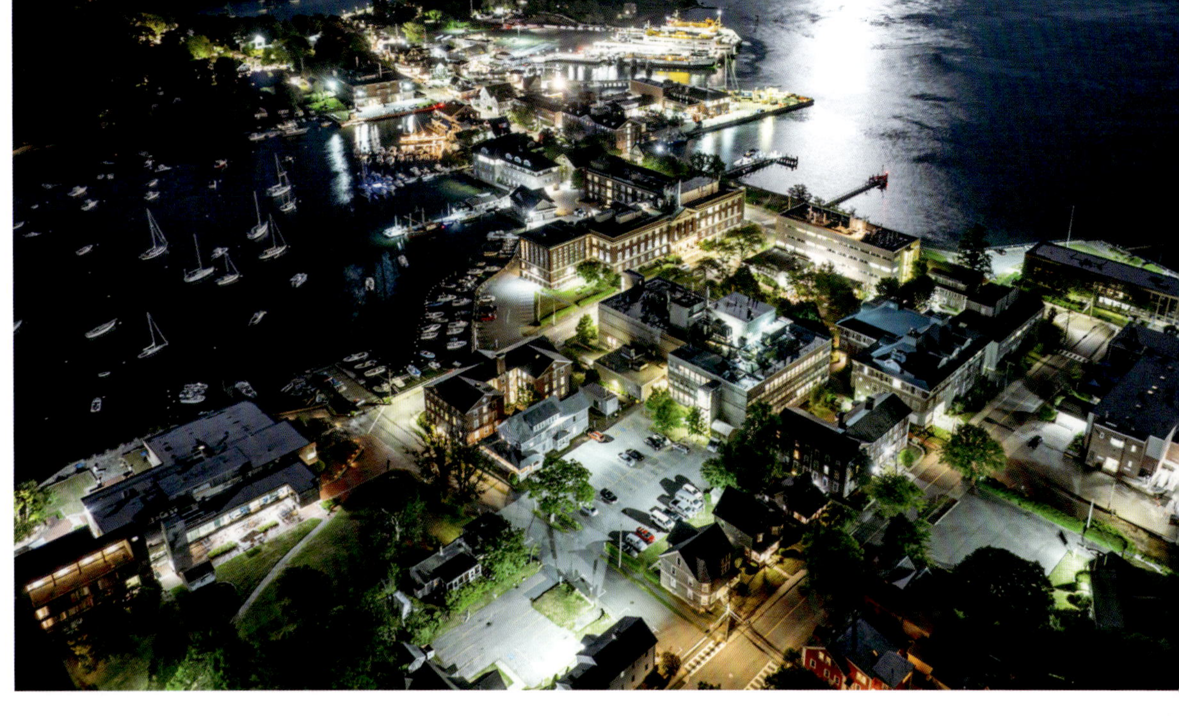

Woods Hole's Marine Biological Laboratory brings a lot of people to town. Whether it be for research or internships, hundreds of staff and faculty fill the multiple buildings that abut Eel Pond.

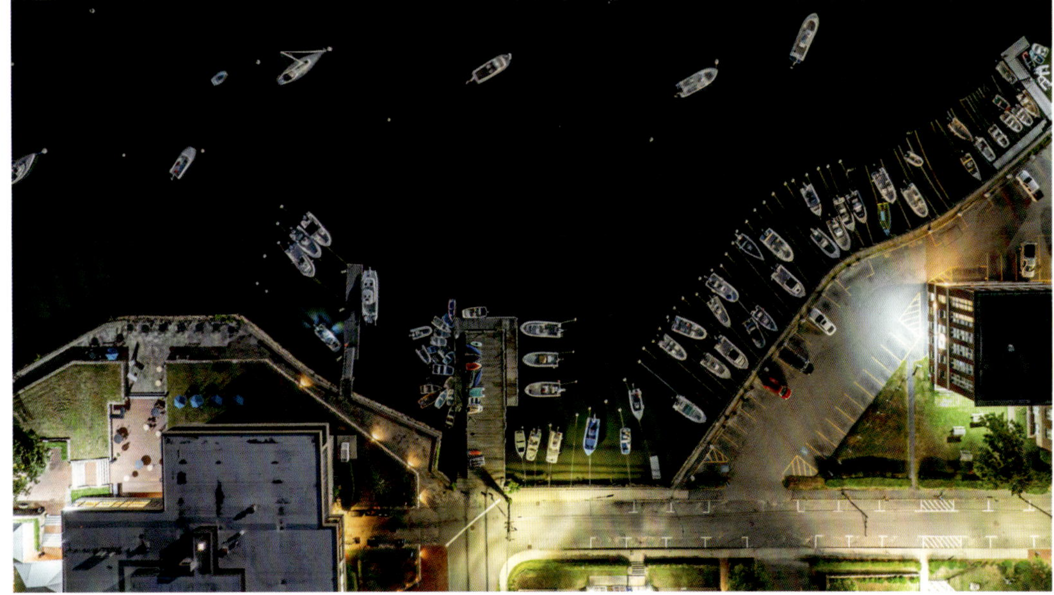

Many of these dinghies sit here year-round but see the most use in the summer months, when they are used to bring sailors out to their larger boats moored at buoys throughout Eel Pond. From here, the boats exit the pond toward Vineyard Sound and other destinations. A small bridge leading into town is raised and lowered to accommodate the tall masts of sailboats.

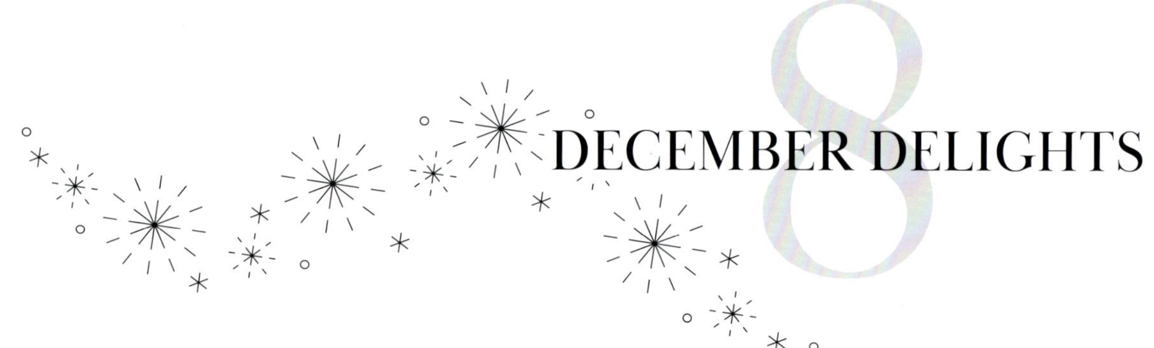

8 DECEMBER DELIGHTS

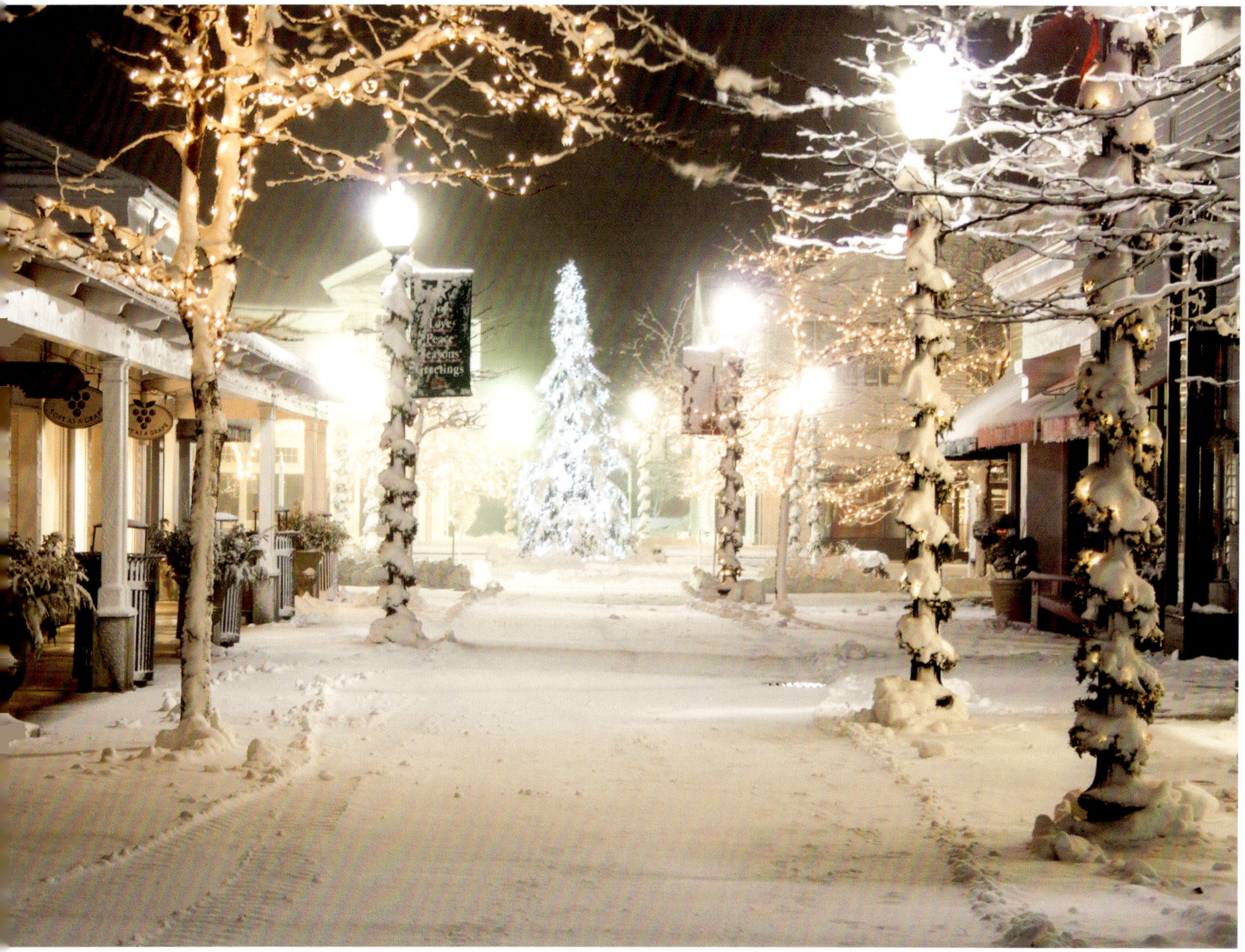

Unless you live in the area, there is a good chance you are not planning a trip to Cape Cod or the Islands this winter or next winter. The three main reasons that most people visit (ice cream, summer fun, and beach days) are not in abundance in December. Still, the Cape has a lot to offer for a photographer who brings a winter hat and a pair of gloves.

In December 2008, the Cape was hit with quite the snowstorm. It started in the afternoon and went on through most of the evening. I had worked late that night and was driving by Mashpee Commons when I thought I would stop in to see if there were any photo opportunities. Here I discovered a very rare trifecta of conditions: fresh snow lit by holiday lights at night. This was the first time I had stopped to appreciate something like this, and it resulted in several great compositions, one of which would become my most popular to this day. Realizing I had struck "night photography gold," I set course for Main Street in Falmouth, where a parking ban left the area devoid of cars. I always had very fond memories of that night, and I suspected it would be a once-in-a-lifetime opportunity to have all these things align. But I was ever hopeful.

Flash forward to 2020—just a few nights before Christmas, it looked like the same conditions were slowly on track to come together again. As with most forecasts these days, I took the predictions with a grain of salt. Predictions of snow accumulations on Cape Cod rarely meet expectations. But this night seemed like it was off to a good start. I began to gather up what I thought I'd need to make it through a few hours of photographing in the snow: big boots, double socks, long underwear, a long-sleeve T-shirt, a sweatshirt, a winter jacket, gloves, and so on. Sure enough, it did look as though history would repeat itself. At 11:30 p.m., I left for Mashpee Commons again, hoping to get a few more cracks at a fresh snowfall.

When I arrived, it was like stepping back in time. Suddenly it was 2008, and although some of the lights had changed since then, the feel was the same. Now I was equipped with a better camera and more experience. I immediately got to work, starting with a few of the same compositions I had shot back then and moving on to other areas I suspected would make good images.

Meanwhile, I could hear the idling engines of the snowplows warming up. My time would be shorter than I would like if I wanted to capture undisturbed snow sitting on the Commons' streets. Within fifteen minutes, I heard that telltale sound of plows moving along the pavement, scraping up the snow and pushing it into piles. And the sound was getting closer. No time now to take multiple images from one spot: shoot, move, repeat.

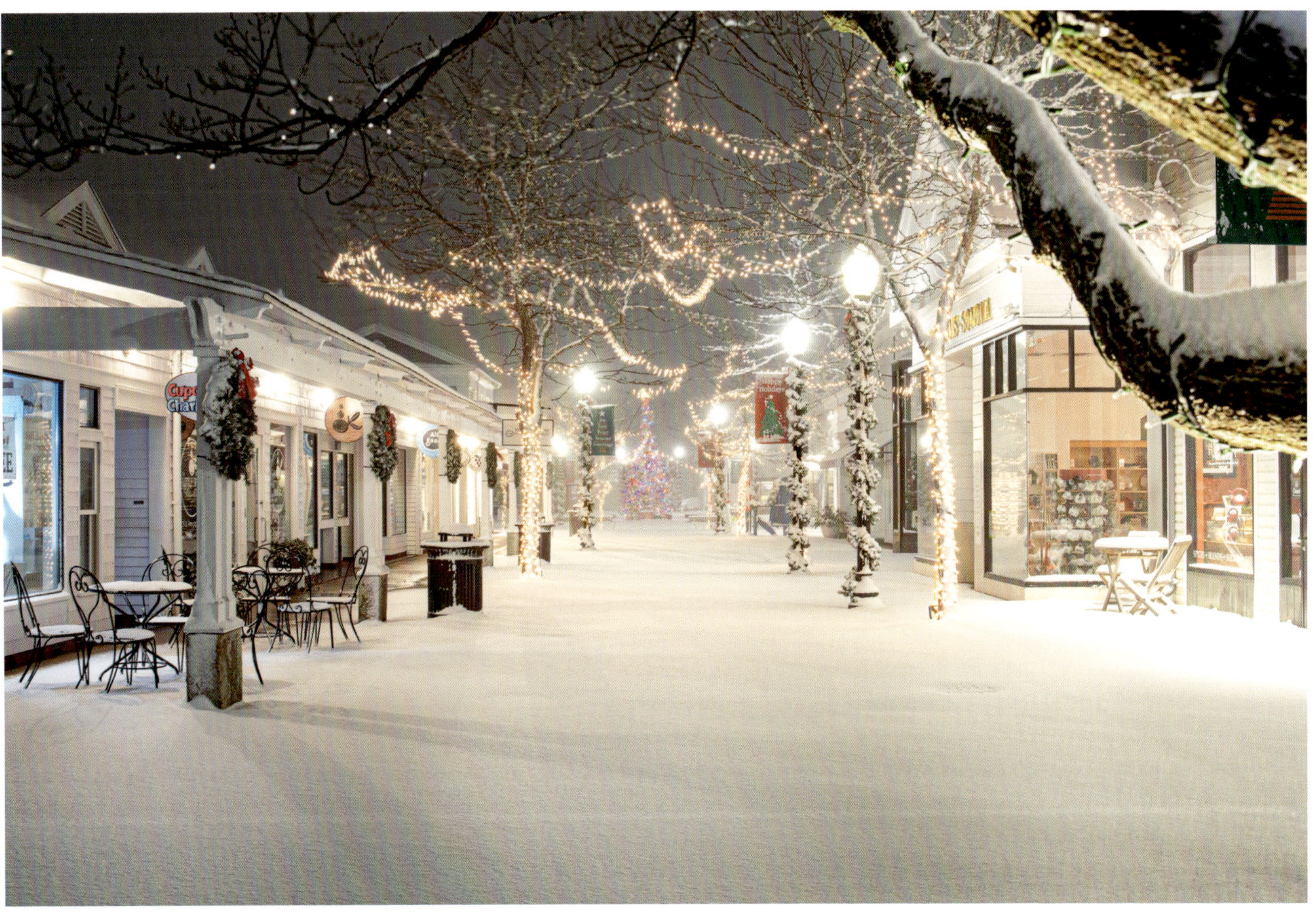

Fresh snow coats the Commons like frosting before shovels and plows soon arrive to clear it away.

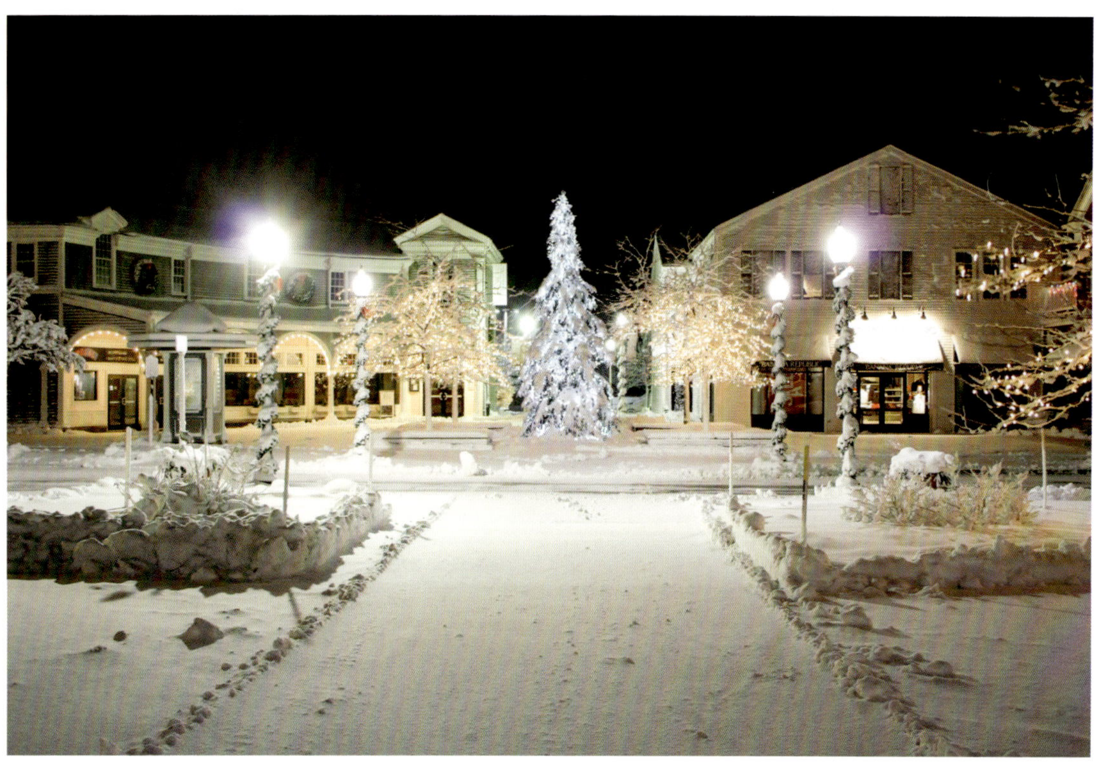

A view of the courtyard tree in Mashpee Commons as it appeared in 2008, one of the only years the white LED bulbs were used. In the following seasons, multicolored lights would replace them.

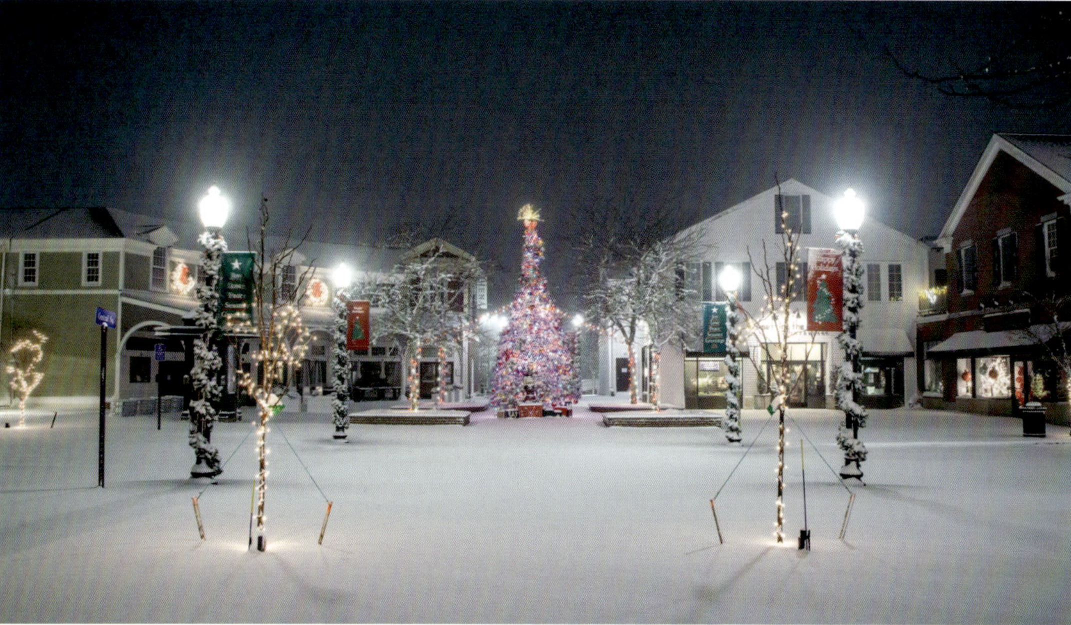

The same area in the winter of 2020.

If you didn't know this was primarily a shopping center, you might think this was the main street of a small New England town. Steeple Street is typically a busy road connecting Route 28 and Jobs Fishing Road via Mashpee Commons. I was excited to have this opportunity to photograph untouched snow, but I knew my time was short as I could hear the plow trucks warming up.

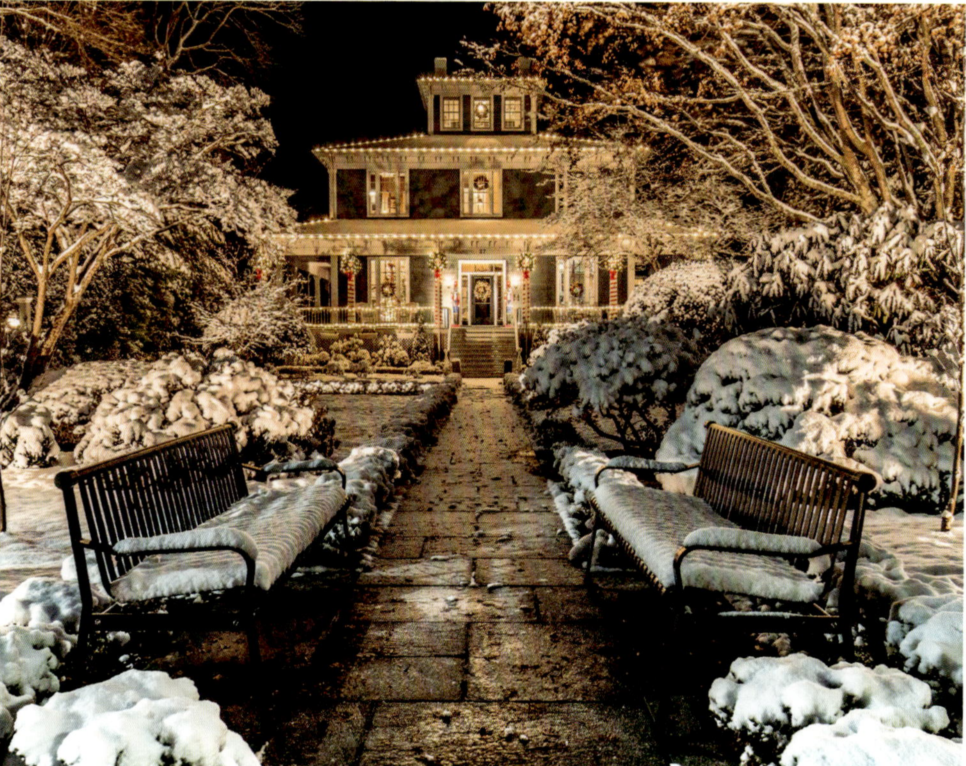

A fresh snowfall welcomes visitors to the Captain's Manor Inn along Main Street in Falmouth. This bed-and-breakfast is one of the best-decorated properties around and has been consistently lit throughout December each year.

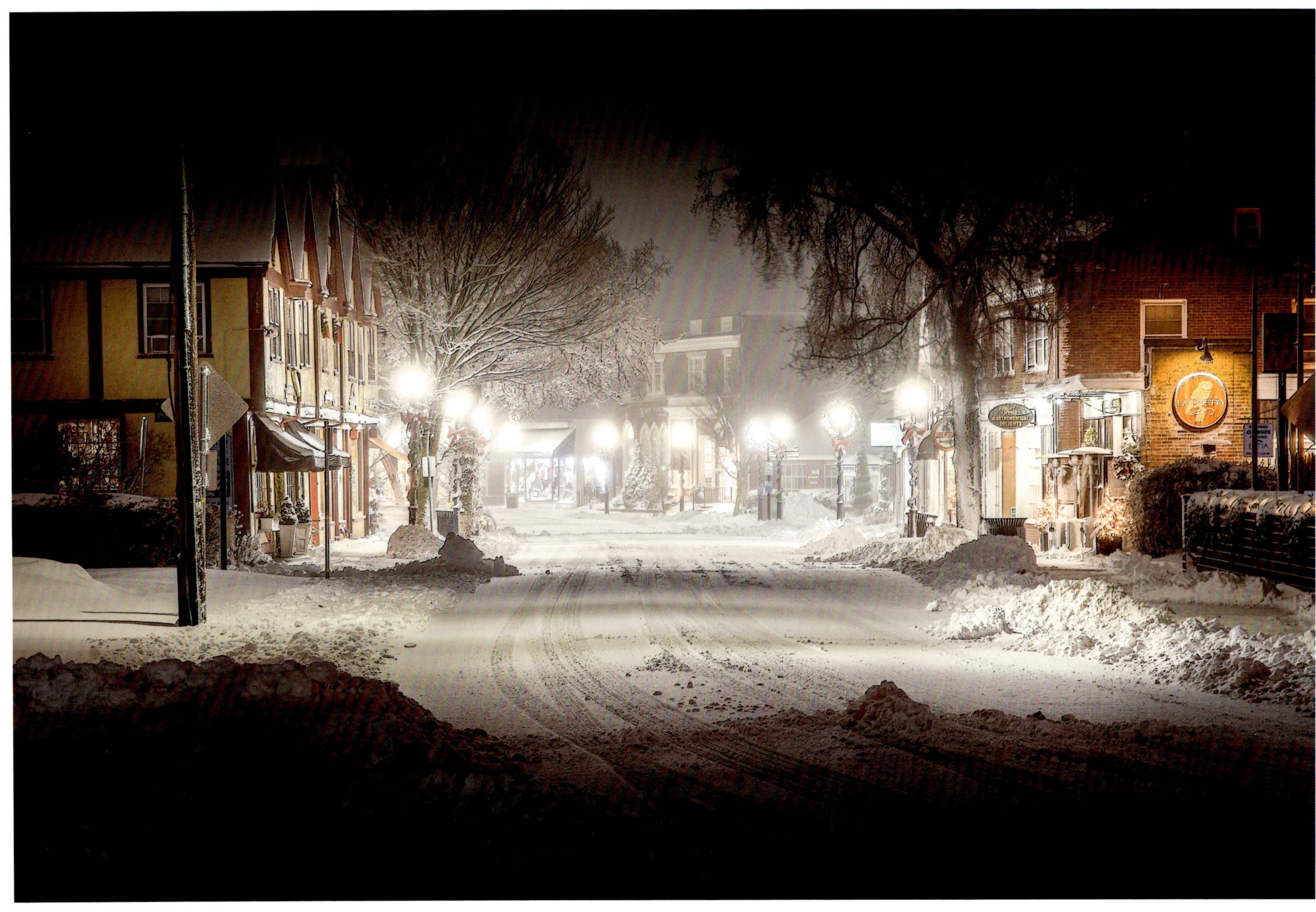

The Snowy Owl, 2020

BOOKENDS IN A WINTER DREAM

A decade earlier, I had photographed one end of Main Street, looking down toward the gentle curve of the road. The sidewalks were mostly untouched; the plows had made a few passes, but it still retained that holiday movie feel. This time, I was hoping to photograph Main Street from the opposite end, showing the same gentle curve from that angle. It would create a visual bookend between the earlier image and this one.

I parked behind an old bank and planted my tripod in the snow, about 8 feet from where I thought the curb might have been. My only worry would be the approach of a plow. I'd have plenty of time to get out of the way, but my image would be ruined and the snowy foreground would be altered. Thankfully, I was given the time I needed. It took about ten minutes to get it just right, and then I moved across the street to shoot the church. By now it was 2 a.m., it was cold and windy, and snow was blowing in every direction. I loved every minute of it.

The Cape at the holidays is underrated. Each year that goes by, the decorations throughout the neighborhoods seem to get more and more elaborate.

The Snowy Owl (*opposite*), named for the owl that appears on the Osteria La Civetta sign seen on the right side of the image, was an instant hit with Falmouth residents and tourists alike. For many, it represents the quintessential New England holiday. It's an inviting scene despite the obvious cold conditions. The blowing snow created a soft glow around the streetlamps during this long exposure, and more than one person has told me that it has a Kincade style to it, which is a high compliment. In order to draw your eyes into the scene, I darkened the top, bottom, and corners of the image to make it seem like you were entering a snowy oasis after a drive on a very dark road.

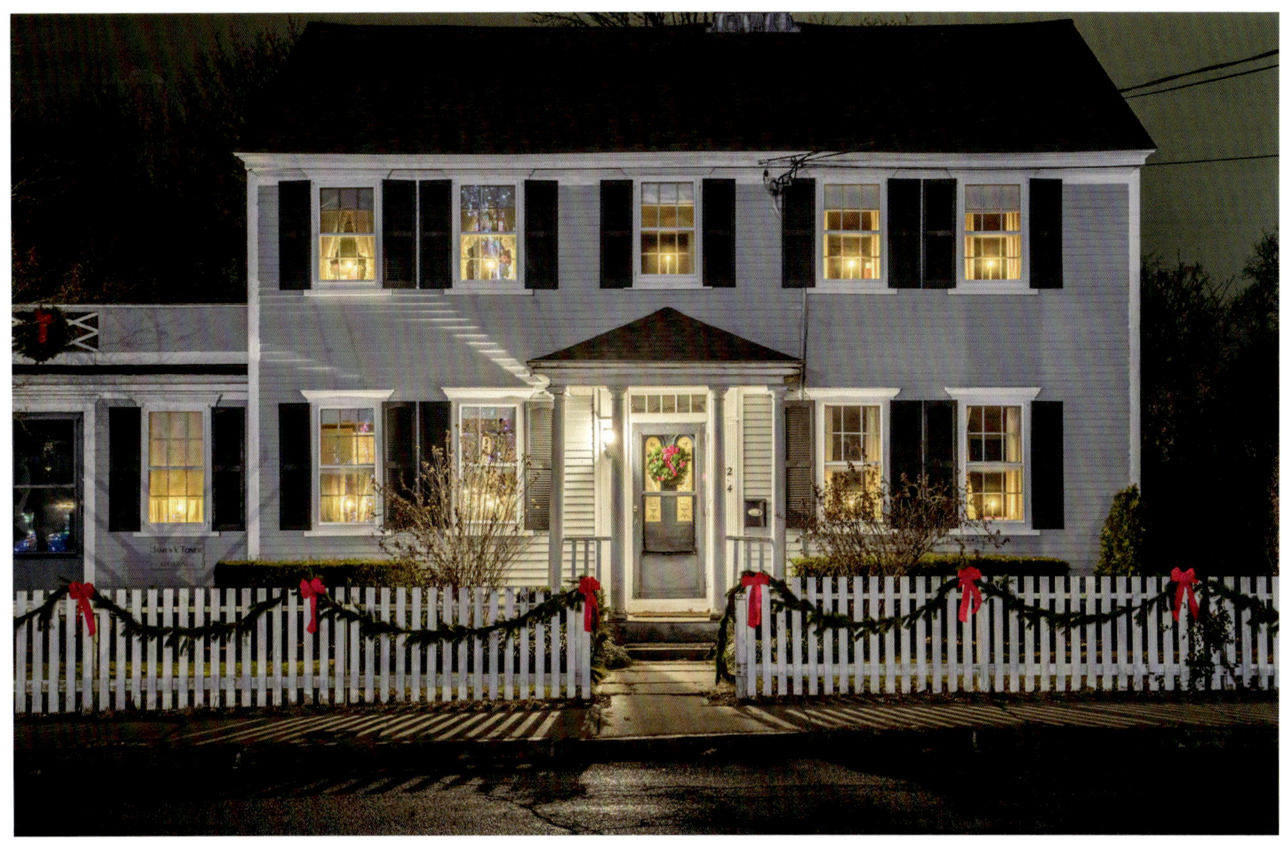

Several of the homes lining the Falmouth Green are given the "classic New England" treatment at the holidays.

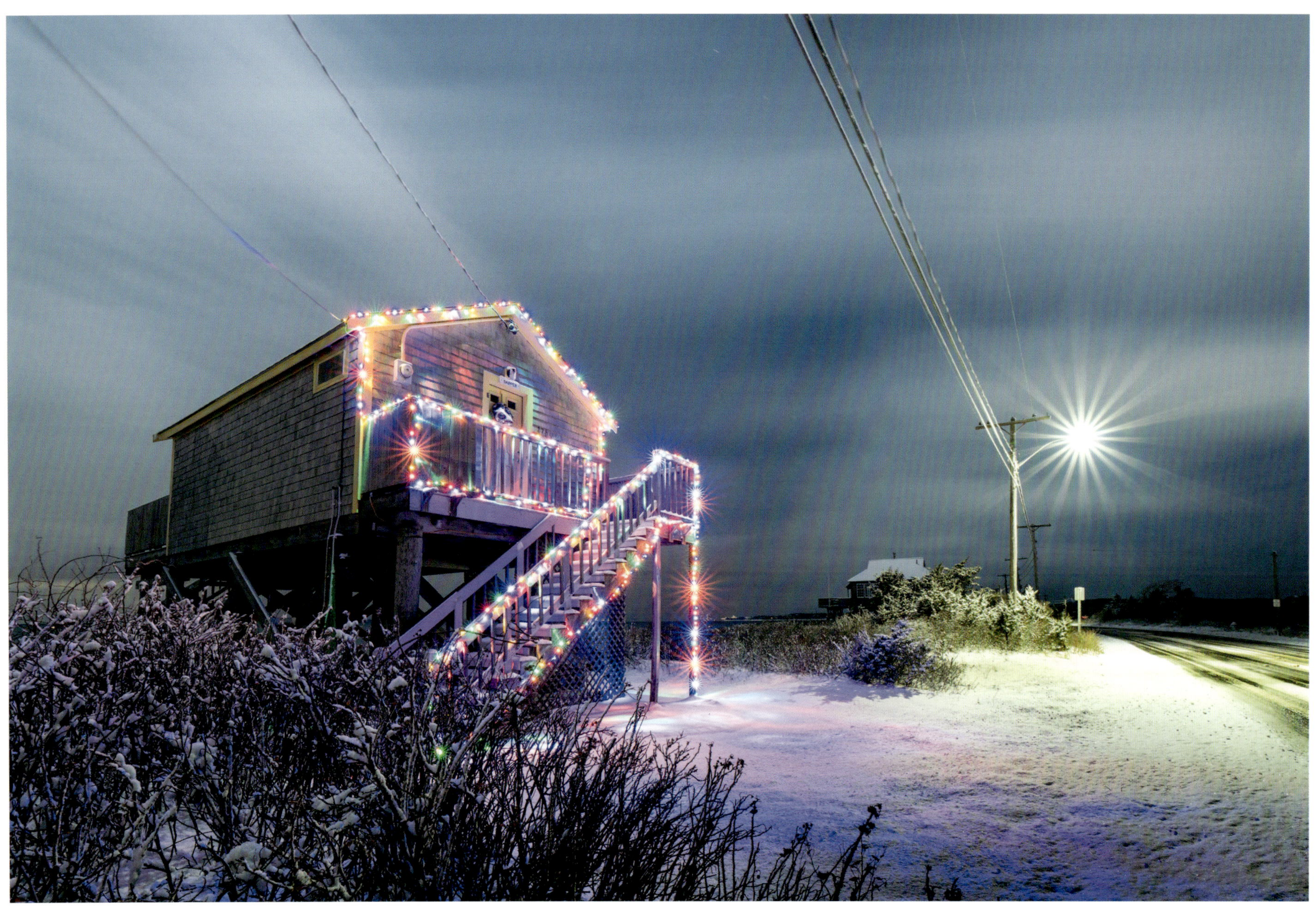

This stilt house was the only one lit along Surf Drive in Falmouth in December 2016. If you weren't suspecting it, the sudden appearance of this brightly lit holiday beacon after driving past several dark houses becomes a pleasant surprise. While I was photographing here, several cars slowed down as they approached. The fresh snowfall further accentuated the colored lights.

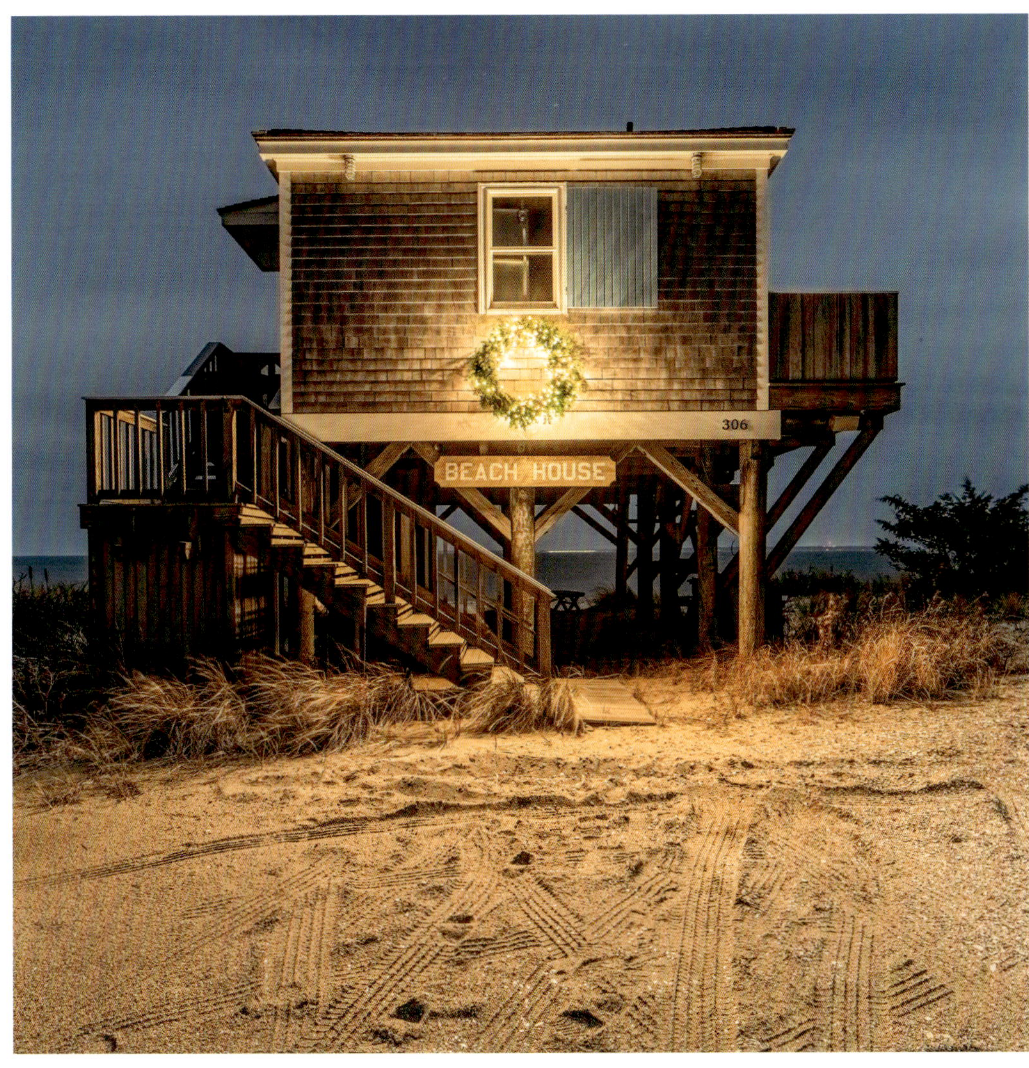

With the first house no longer being decorated, another shack took center stage along Surf Drive. A brightly lit wreath creates a minimalistic but striking display.

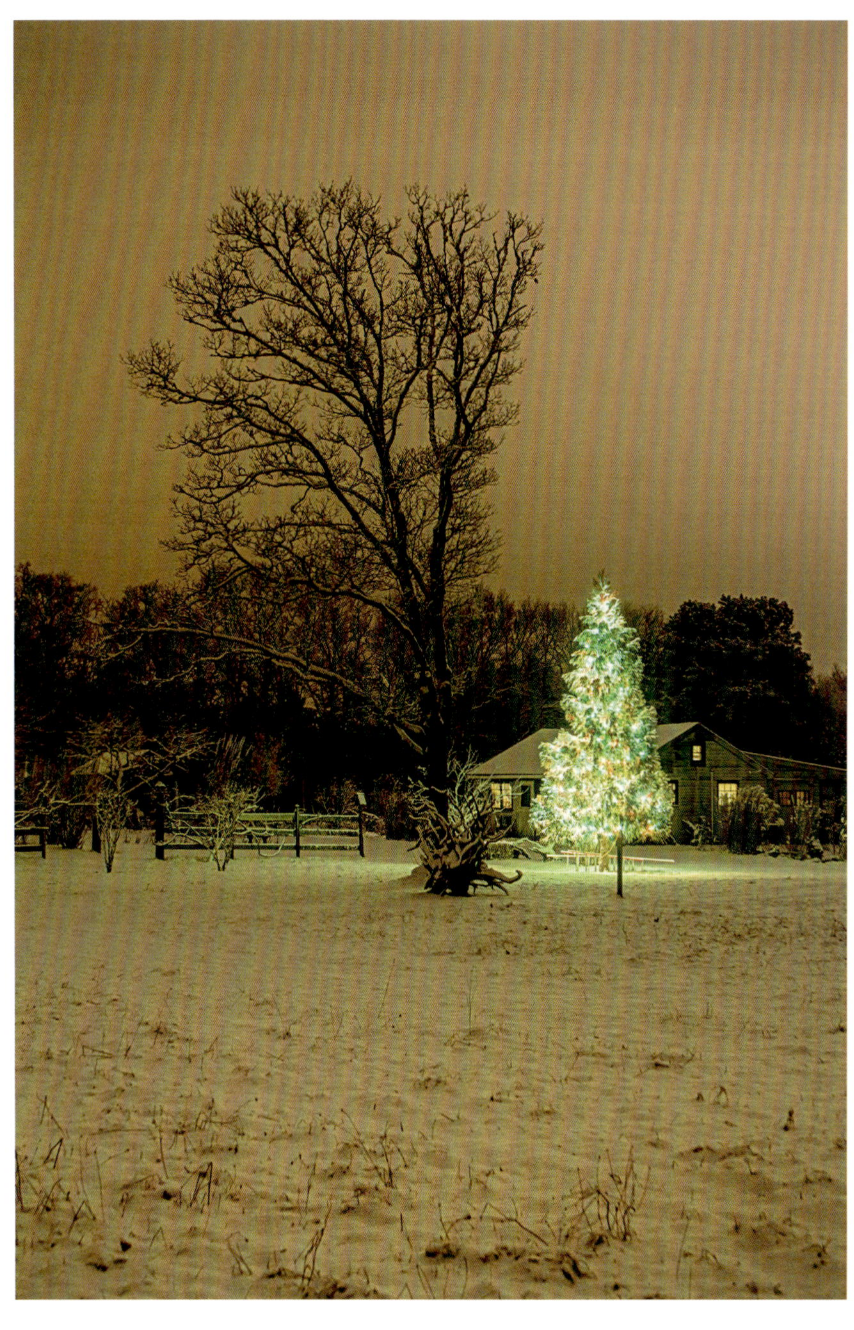

Sepia skies caused by the nearby lights of Falmouth contrast against this vibrant tree in February 2013. I drove by here on the way to dinner and decided to return later in the evening with my camera to photograph it from the side of the road.

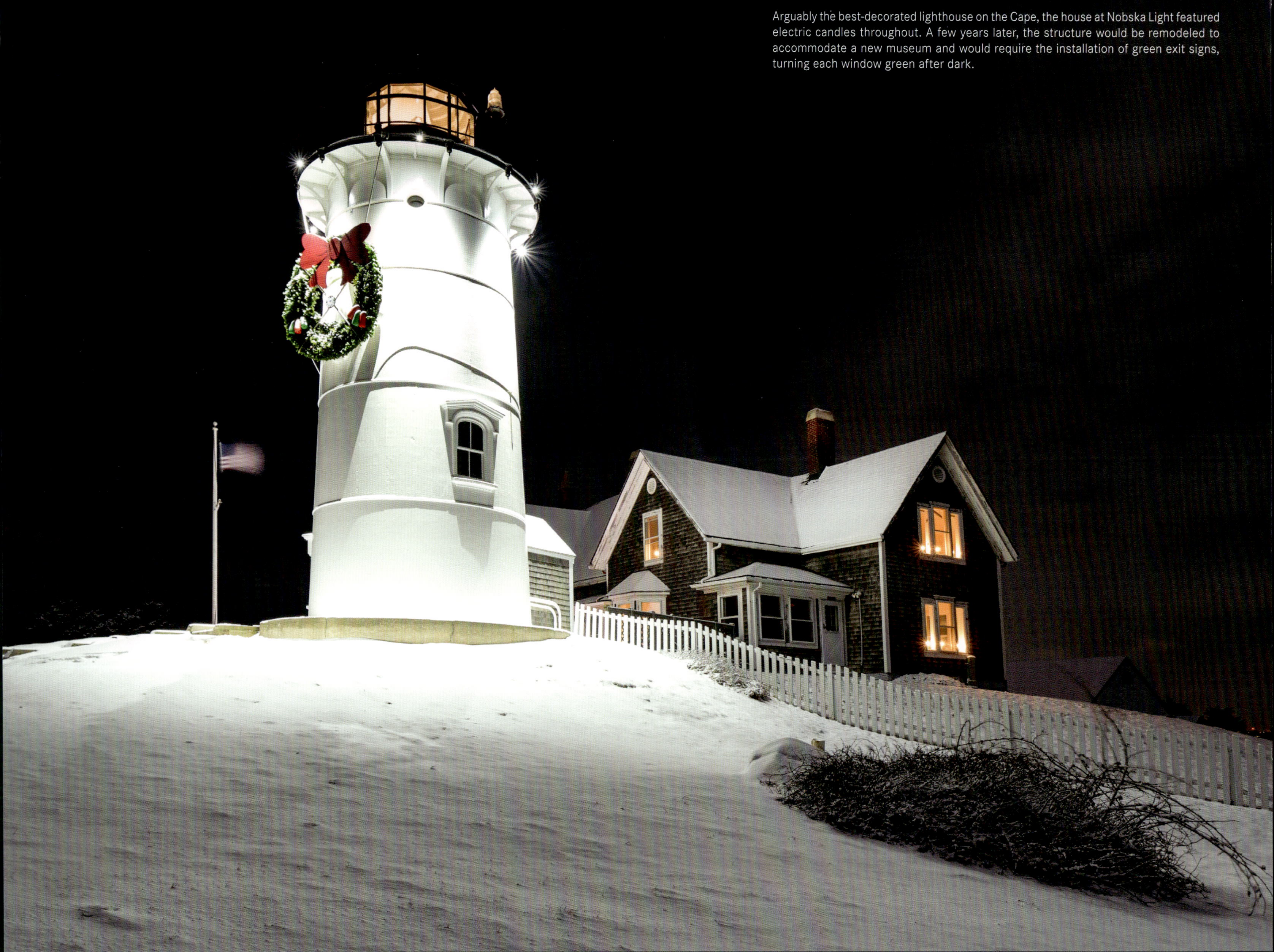

Arguably the best-decorated lighthouse on the Cape, the house at Nobska Light featured electric candles throughout. A few years later, the structure would be remodeled to accommodate a new museum and would require the installation of green exit signs, turning each window green after dark.

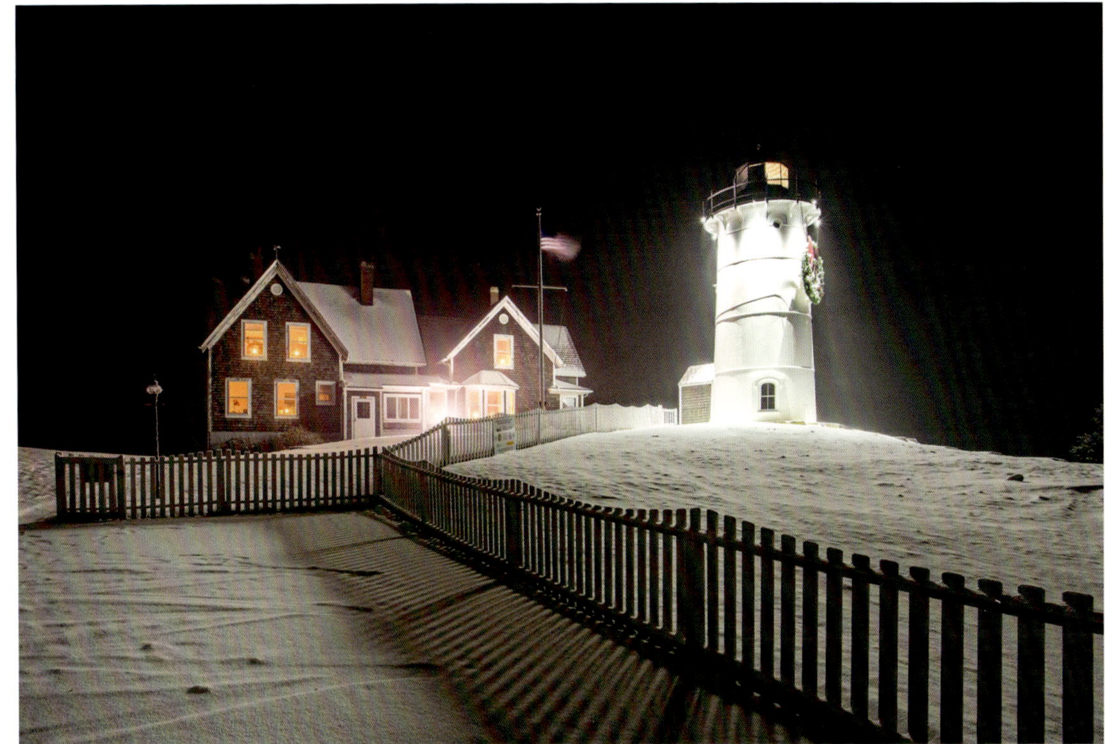

White snow and warm lights combine on a windy winter's night as the flag barely holds on.

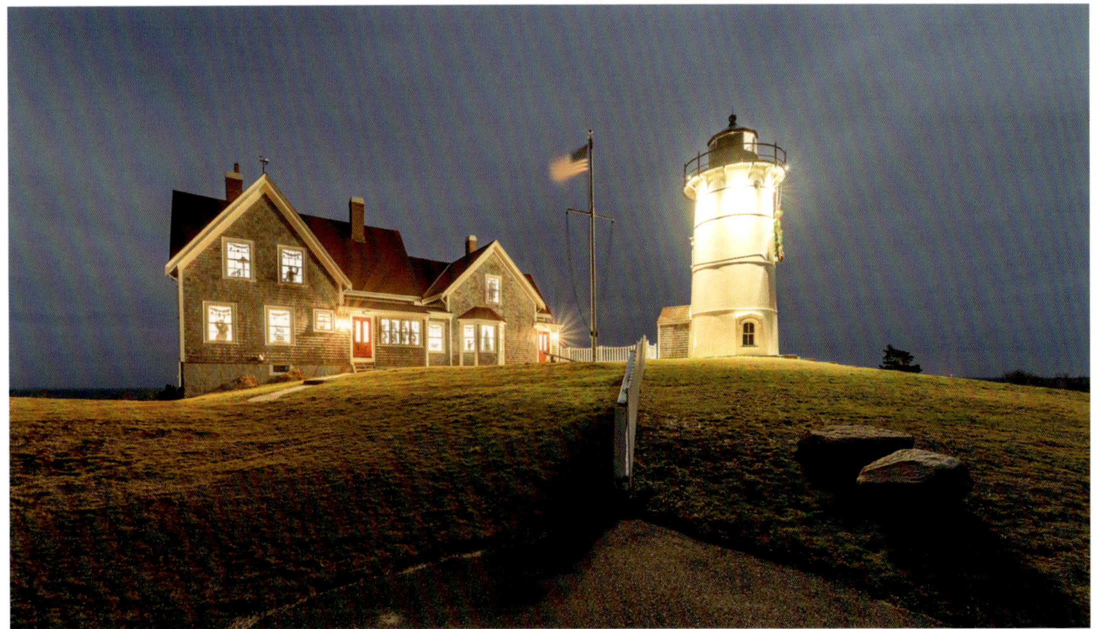

For a few years in a row, the windows of the house at Nobska were frosted over and backlit to show the silhouettes of various characters, such as dancers, carolers, and even Santa. It was a truly unique and interesting way for visitors to experience the property at the holidays.

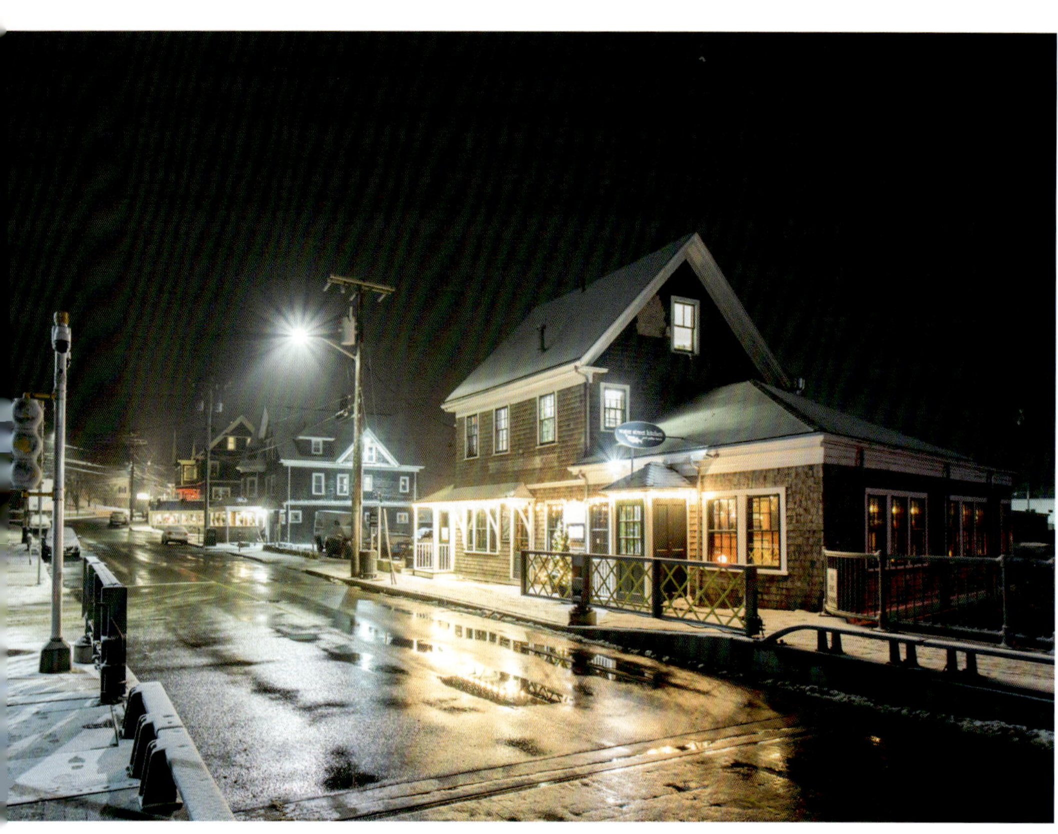

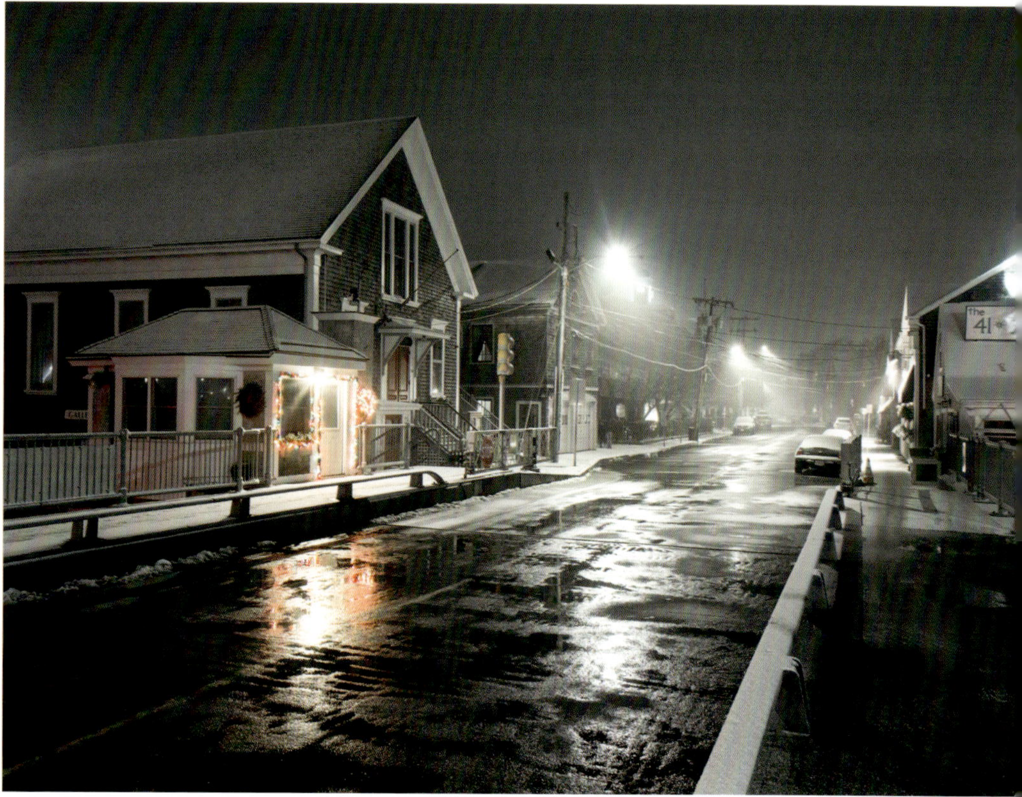

Light snow begins to fall on a quiet December night in 2017. The town seemed empty, with the exception of the occasional partygoer strolling down Main Street and eventually heading home.

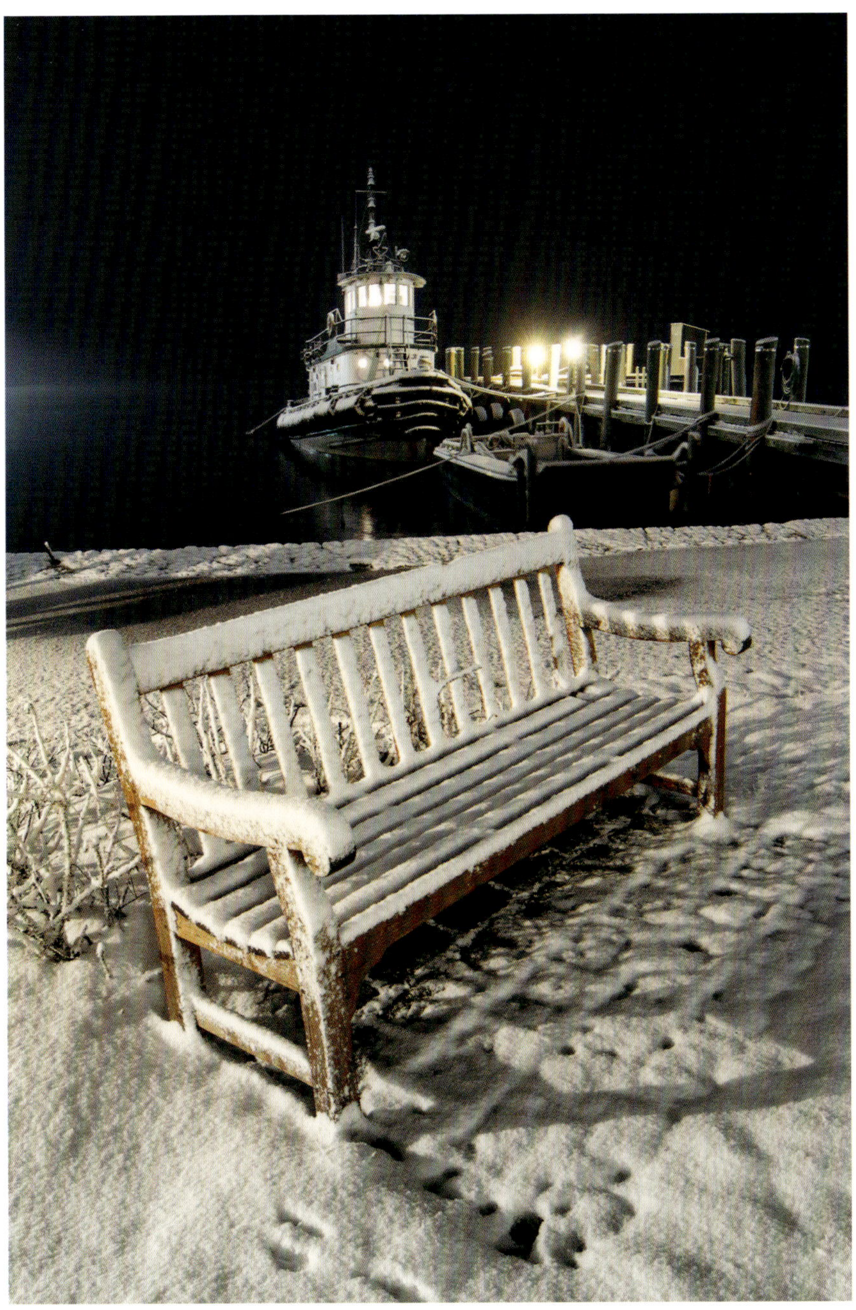

It's a night off for this tugboat caught slumbering in the waters of Woods Hole during the winter of 2009.

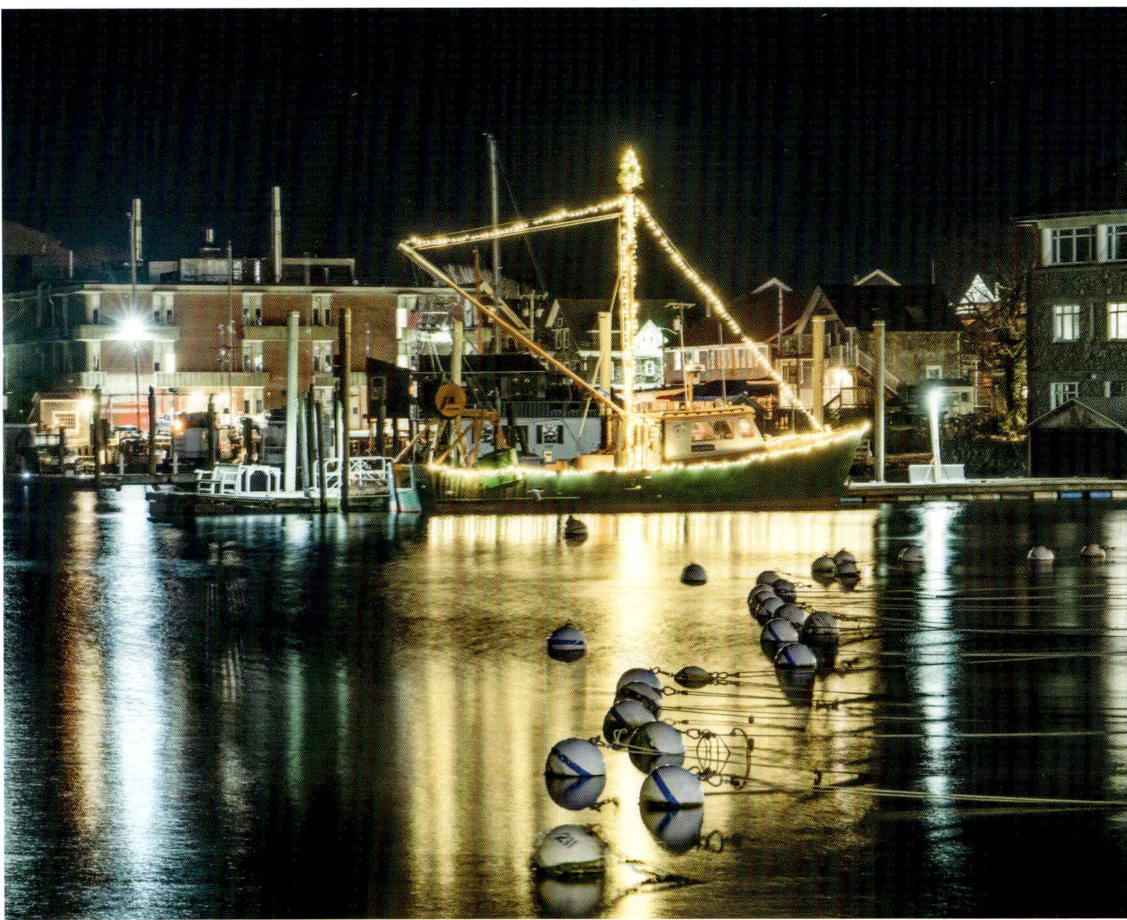

The *Gemma* is a staple of Eel Pond and is sometimes decorated like this for the holidays. It's also one of the only boats in the pond at that point in the year. Photographing boats is difficult at night because they will blur with movement during longer exposures. However, since this area is brightly lit, a shorter exposure was possible, allowing for the movement to be minimized.

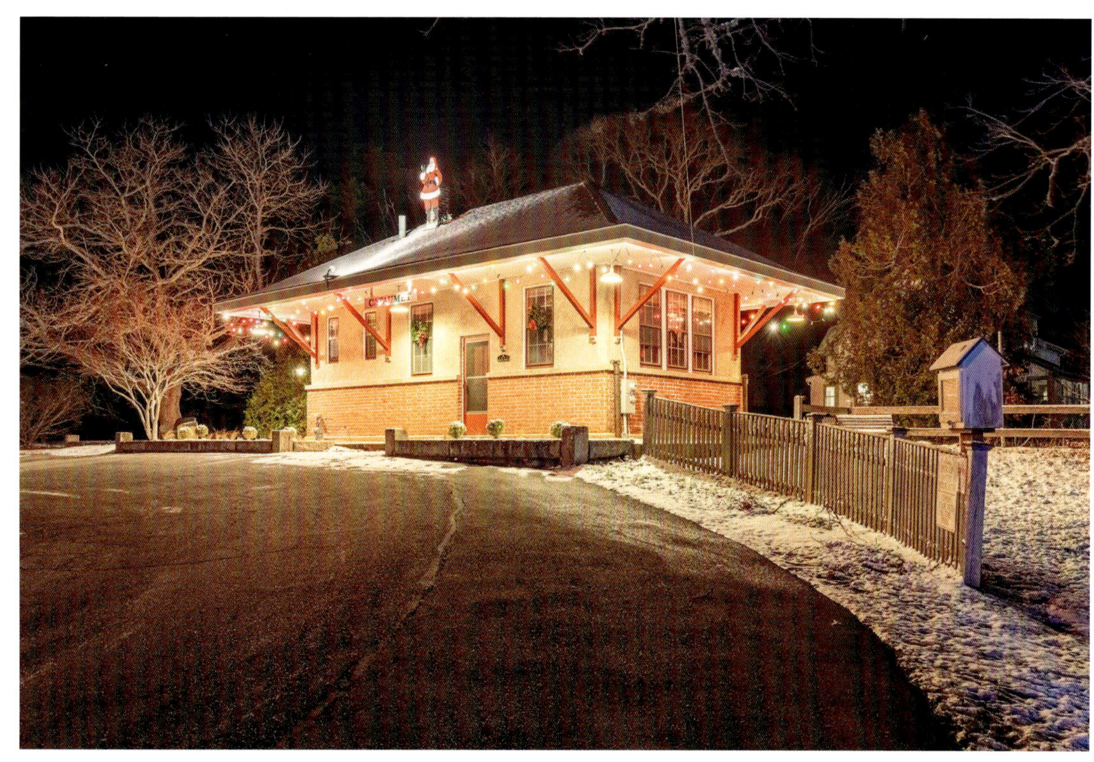

Out of service since the mid-1980s, this old railroad station was the second to be constructed here after a fire nearly sixty years earlier. Now privately owned, it gets decorated just like this annually. Even Santa makes an appearance on the roof. A semiactive rail line remains. You can find this station next to Post Office Square, and it is worth the visit!

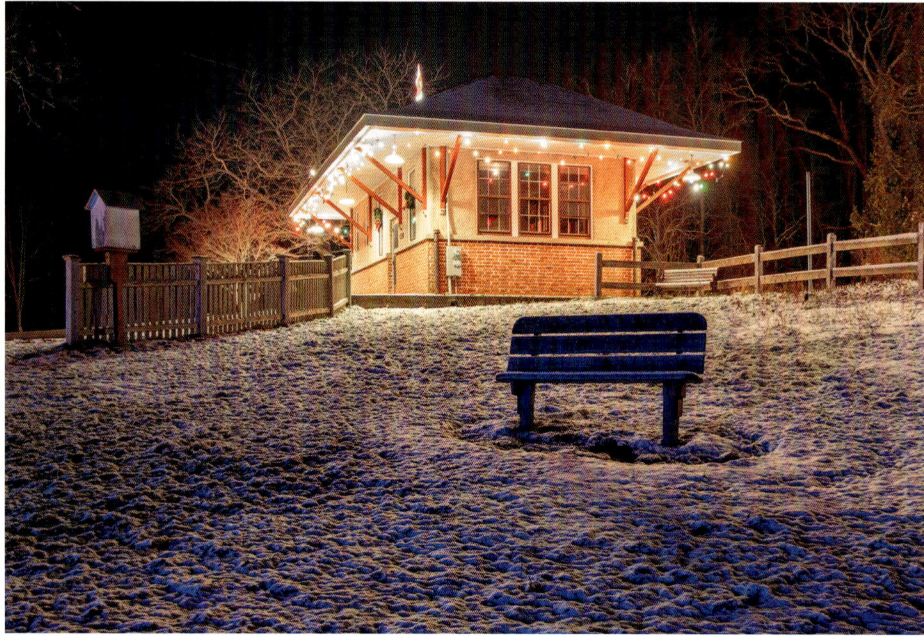

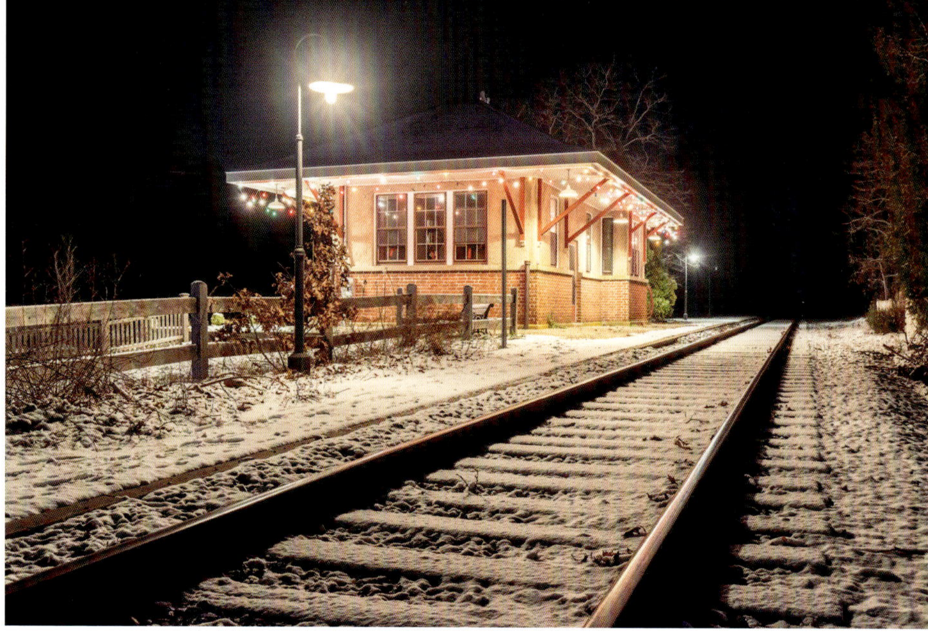

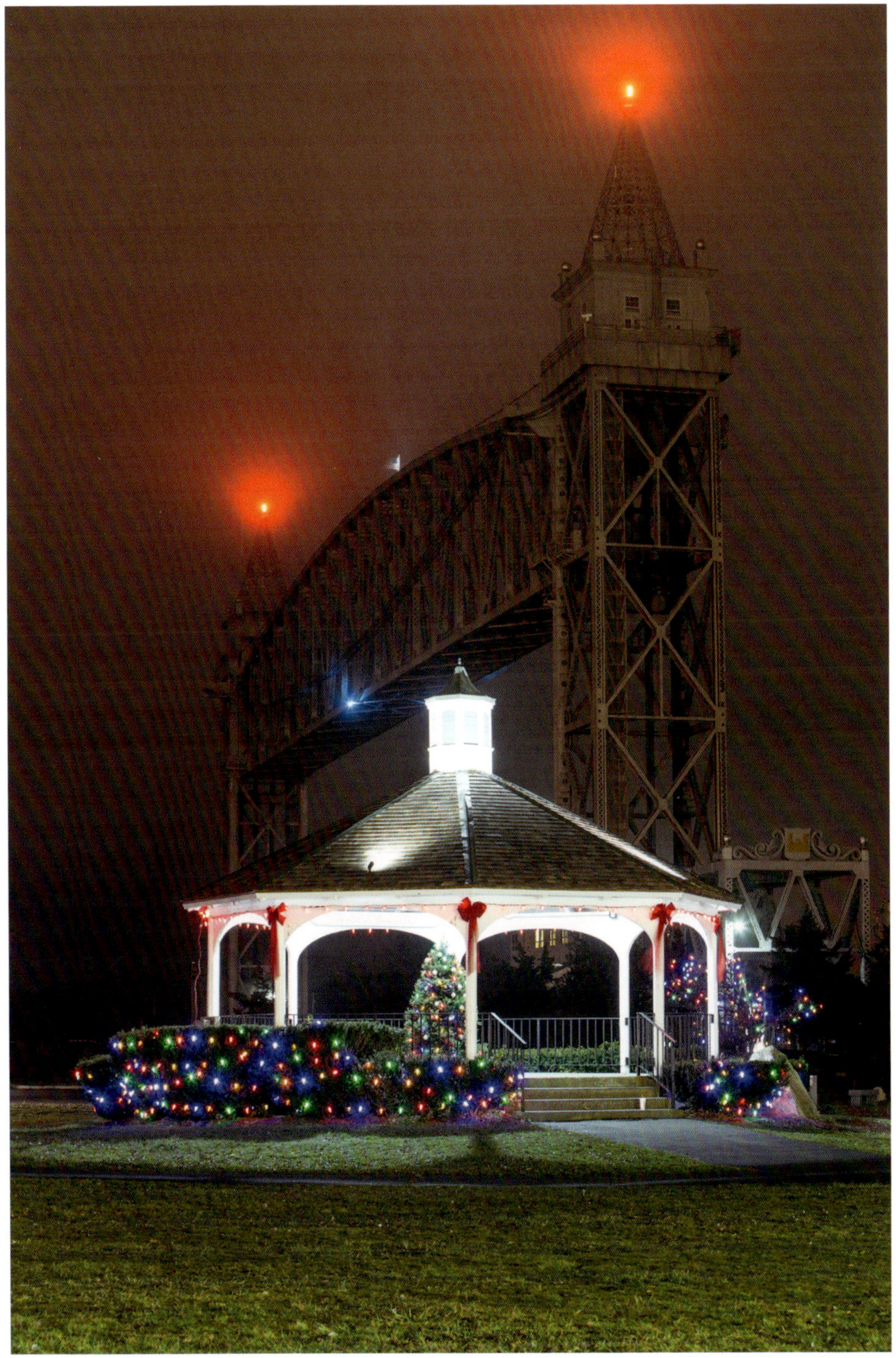

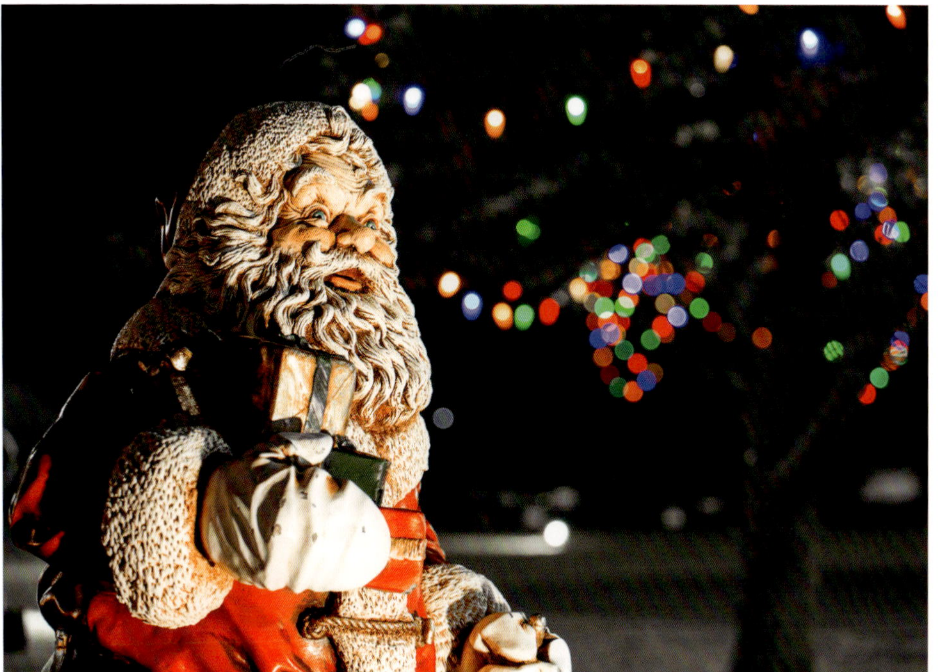

For several years, the park was decorated with figurines like this one, woodcut characters, and small displays. But after the area was refurbished, the only decorations that would return were the lights at the gazebo. We hope Santa has since found a good home!

The gazebo at Buzzards Bay Park gets the holiday treatment every December. The area fills with cars and kids on the weekends, as this is the launching point for the nearby train station's "Polar Express."

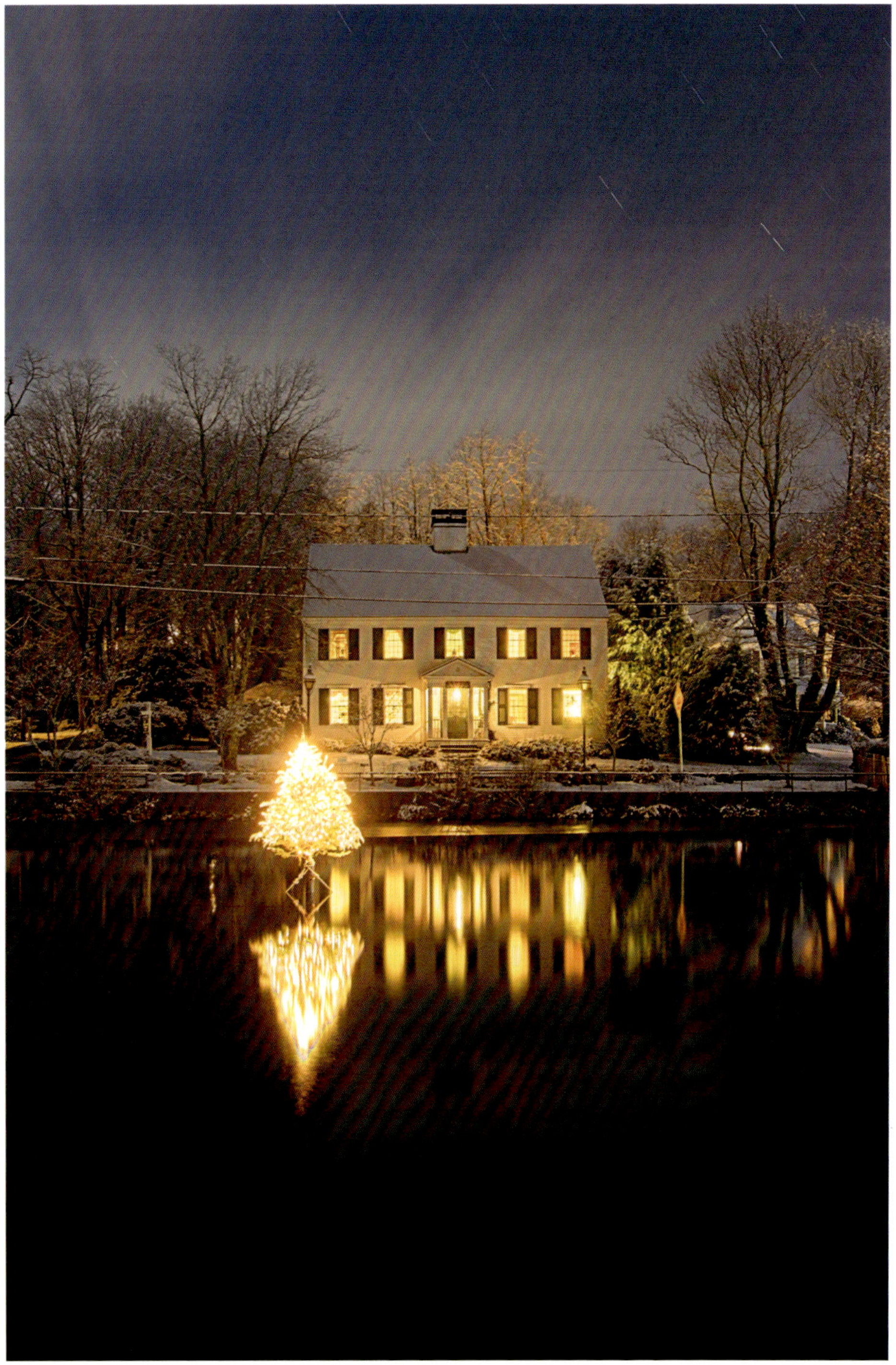

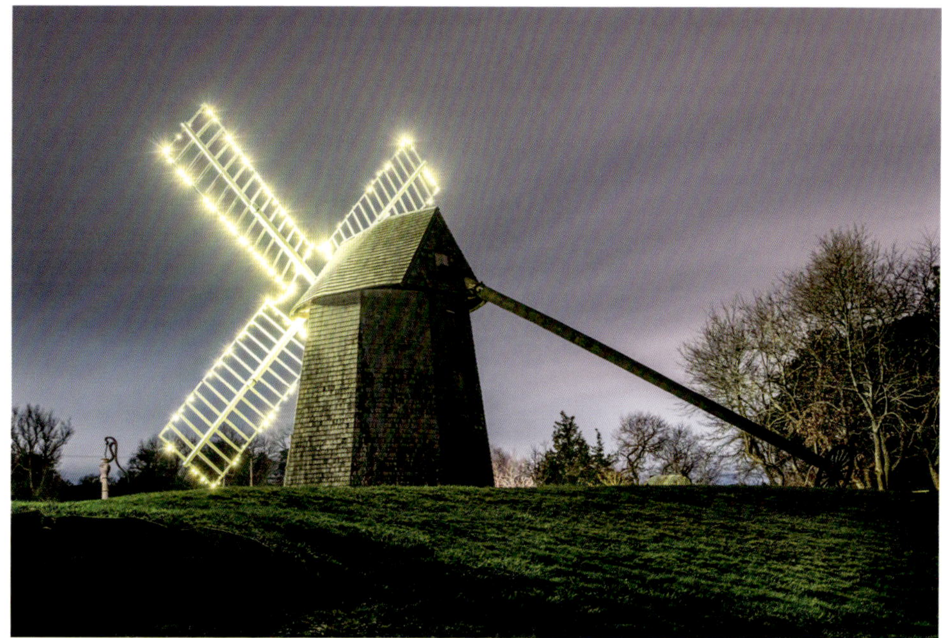

The Old Higgins Farm Windmill at Drummer Boy Park in Brewster is easy to spot from Route 6A during the holidays, thanks to the very bright lights adorning the blades. The windmill was built around 1795 and was last used to grind grain in 1900.

An old colonial home photographed across Shawme Lake in Sandwich. The lit tree on the floating platform is an annual occurrence and an eye-catching subject at the holidays. A major snowstorm had just cleared the area, revealing a bright winter moon. It was an icy, slippery walk to this vantage point but well worth it.

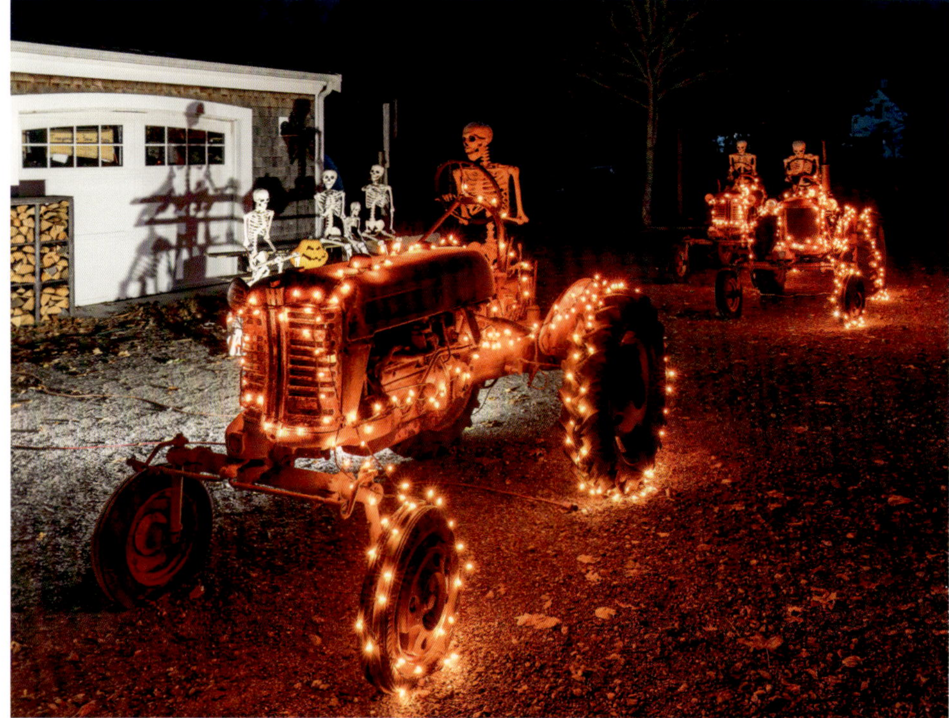

You may have noticed that more and more people tend to decorate at Halloween. This farm tractor race appeared along Route 6 at Log Cabin Farm in Eastham. Notice the "spectators" cheering on the racers. October 2020 was the only time I saw this display.

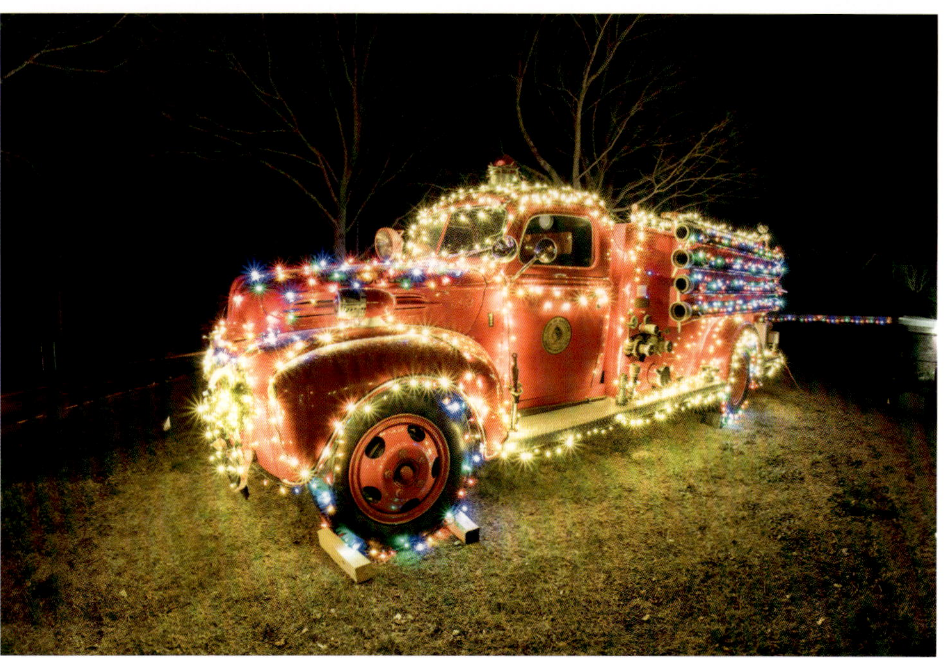

Every year, the Eastham Fire Department lights up their vintage truck along Route 6. It is impossible to miss and sits across the street from the Eastham Windmill.

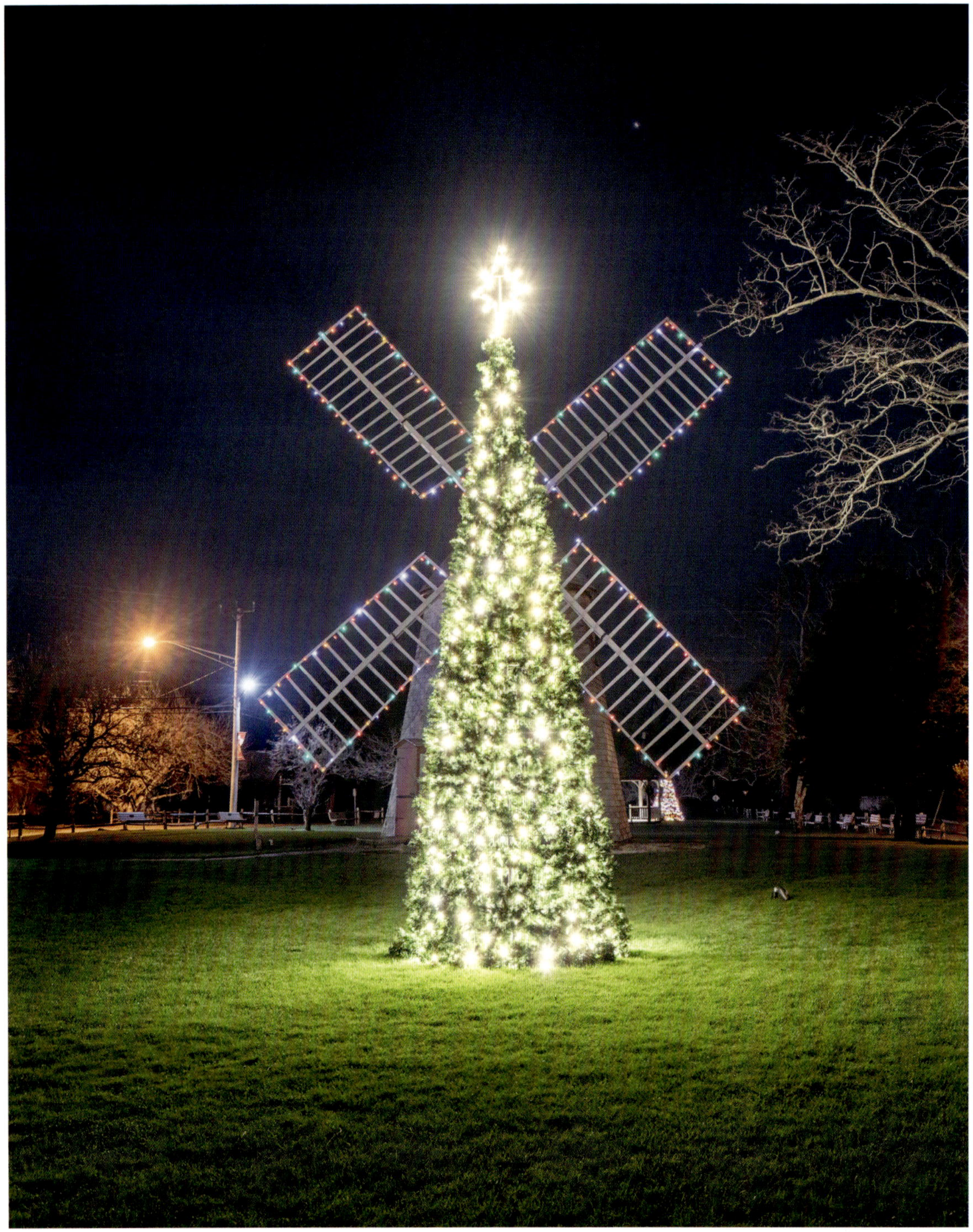

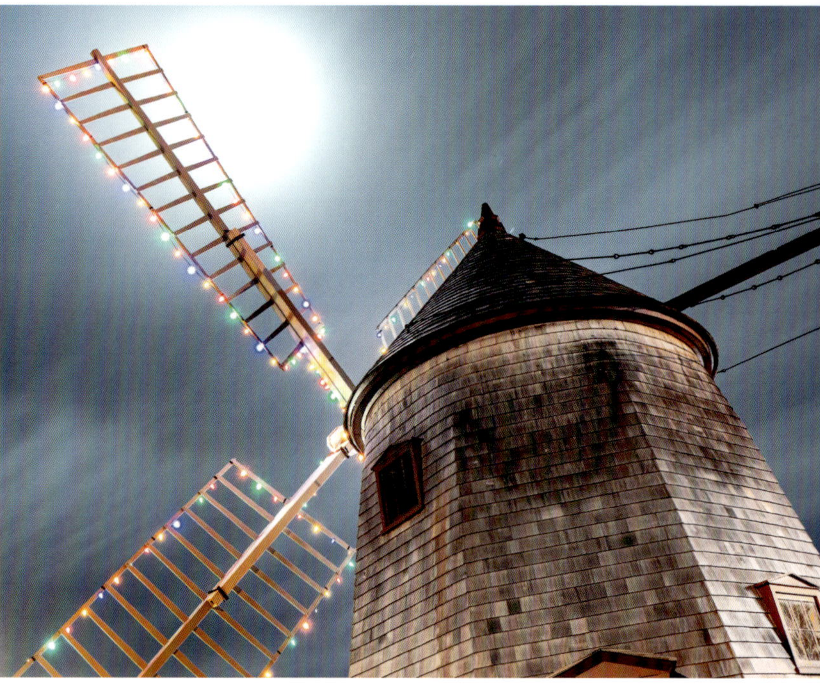

The Eastham windmill property hosts a holiday display that includes this tree and the decorated blades on the structure.

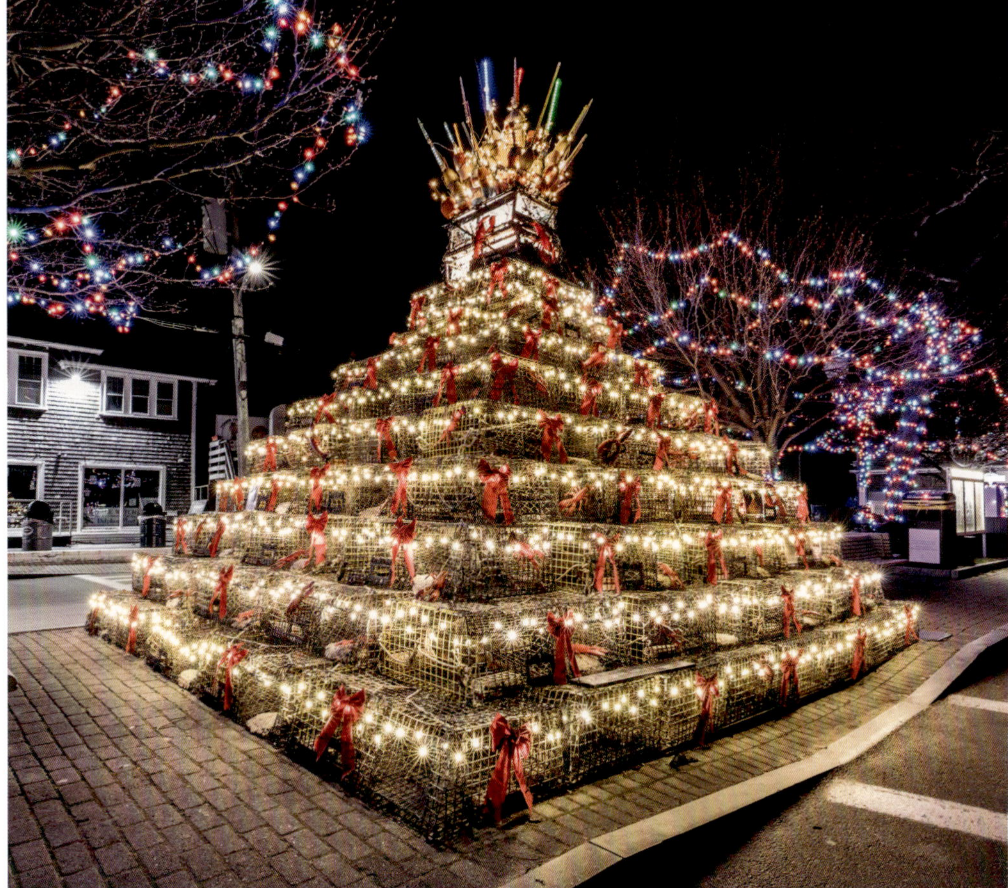

Photographing from this position would have been impossible in the summer months due to the amount of traffic passing through the wharf area. But in the middle of December, I was able to shoot several images without fear in the middle of the road for almost an hour. During my session, I encountered only one person: a woman who was walking back and forth across the street, staring at the ground. I asked if she needed help, and she responded by telling me she had lost her glove earlier. I was able to find it for her. If you lose something after dark, a night photographer can usually help!

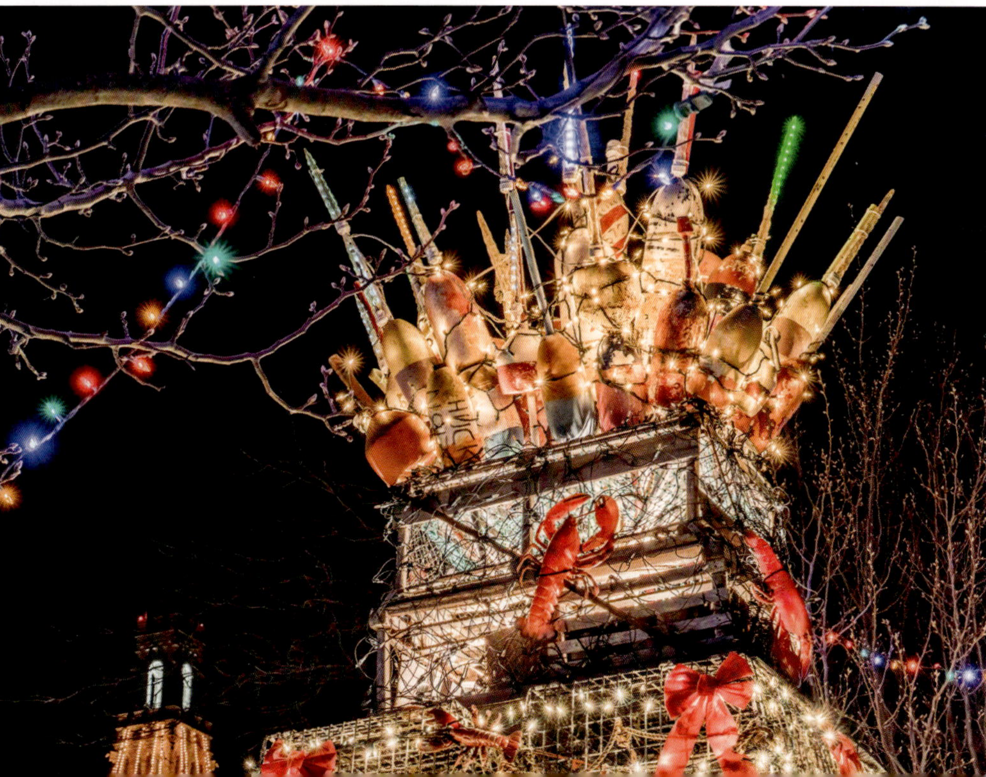

Plastic lobsters try to claw their way to the top of the "tree."

9

VINEYARD NIGHTS, HOLIDAY LIGHTS

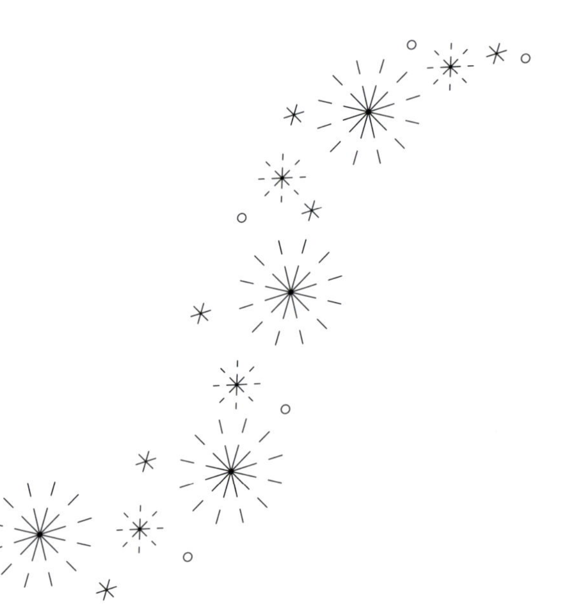

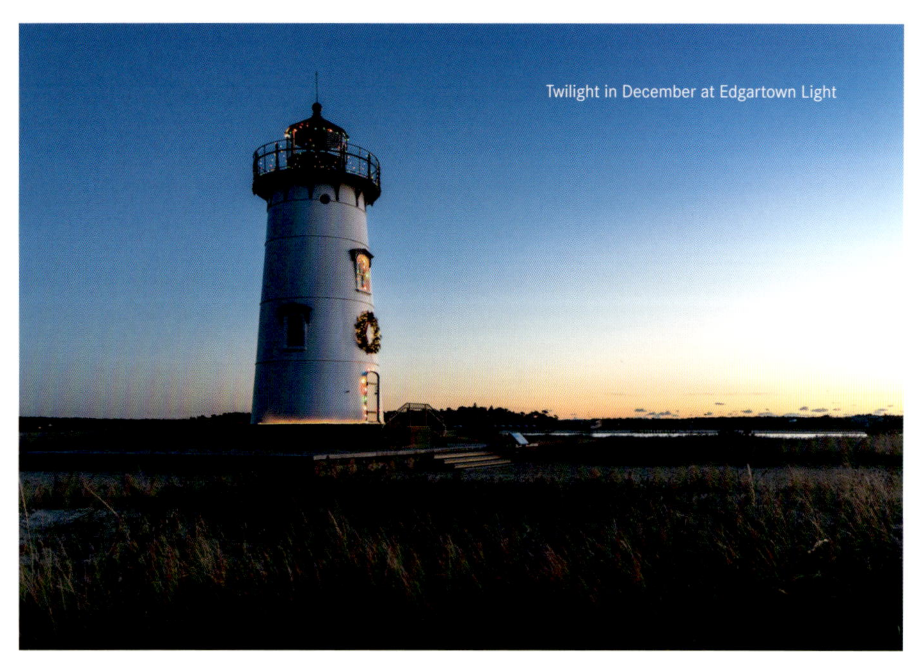

Twilight in December at Edgartown Light

If you search online for the term "Martha's Vineyard holiday displays," as I did, you will likely be shown a series of images from Edgartown's annual Christmas festival. These decorations would include lampposts wrapped in those fat, frosted Christmas lights some of us enjoyed while growing up in the 1970s, along with wreaths, cartoon characters, and even a lobster pot tree not unlike what you'd see in other coastal towns but with its own unique design. Up until around 2018, I had no idea this festival existed.

Despite the promise of cold weather, I decided to bundle up and grab the ferry out to Vineyard Haven. I hopped a bus to Edgartown early enough to eat at the Wharf Pub before sunset and then walked from Main Street down to Edgartown Light. If I told you it was like walking through the set of a holiday movie, this would be no exaggeration. It didn't feel real. It had the magic of a perpetual Christmas Eve. I planned to spend about three hours photographing here, and I used up every last minute of it to do just that. After strolling from the lighthouse, back down Water Street, along the docks, and up Main Street to catch the bus, I left town with more great shots from a single night than I had ever captured anywhere on any other night.

And if that wasn't enough, I stopped at Oak Bluffs to photograph the gazebo at Ocean Park, followed by a short walk into Trinity Park, where some of the small houses dazzled with colorful displays.

Since that night, I have returned every year to recapture the magic. Some things change; some things stay the same. It's part of a new holiday tradition. In 2020, I added a single night shoot as a workshop experience for a small group, and it has sold out every time. Best of all, you can get a lot of great images and still be home by 10:30 p.m. thanks to the early sunsets.

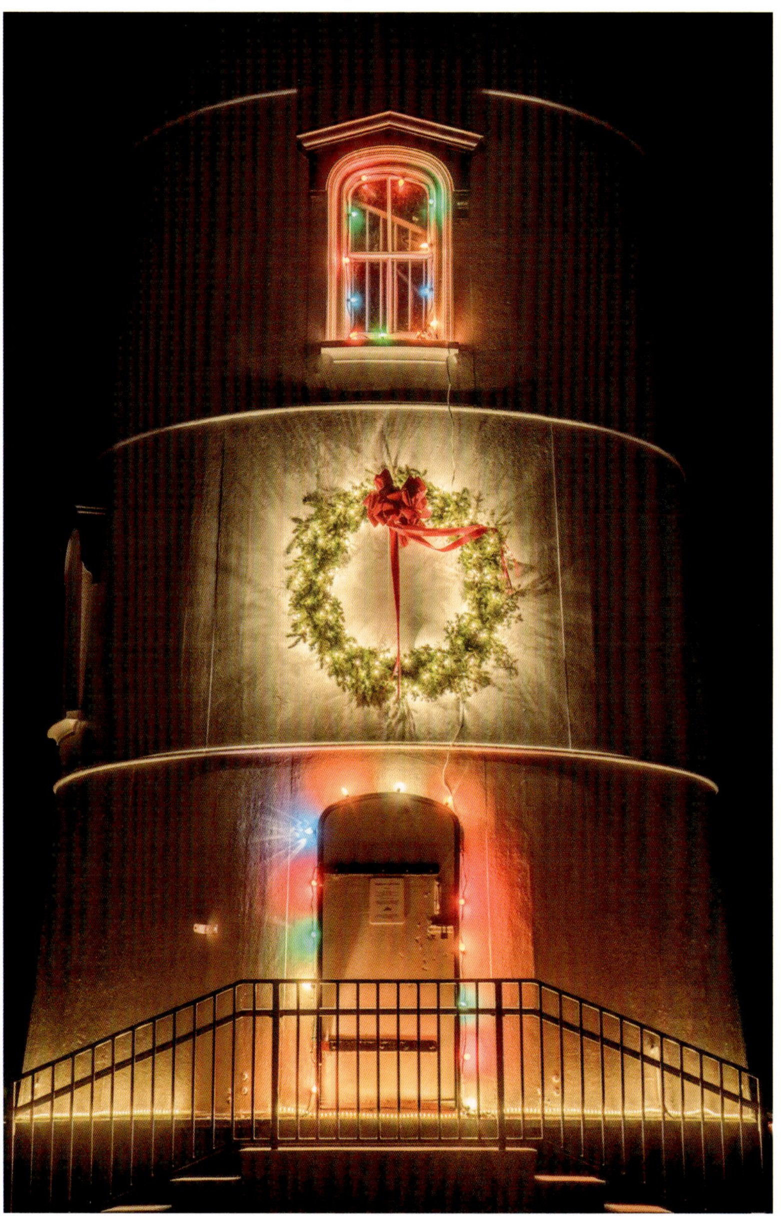

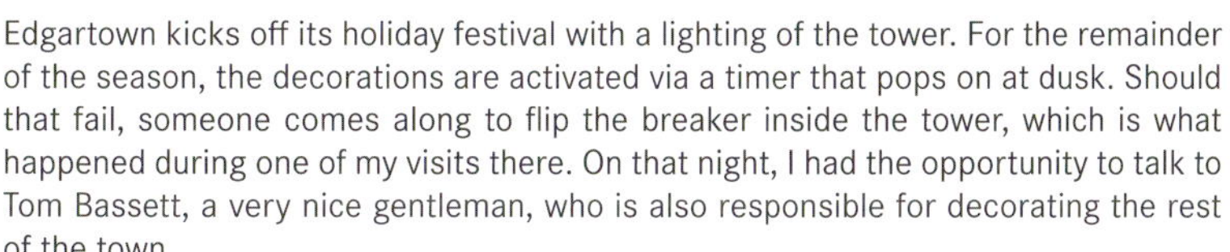

Edgartown kicks off its holiday festival with a lighting of the tower. For the remainder of the season, the decorations are activated via a timer that pops on at dusk. Should that fail, someone comes along to flip the breaker inside the tower, which is what happened during one of my visits there. On that night, I had the opportunity to talk to Tom Bassett, a very nice gentleman, who is also responsible for decorating the rest of the town.

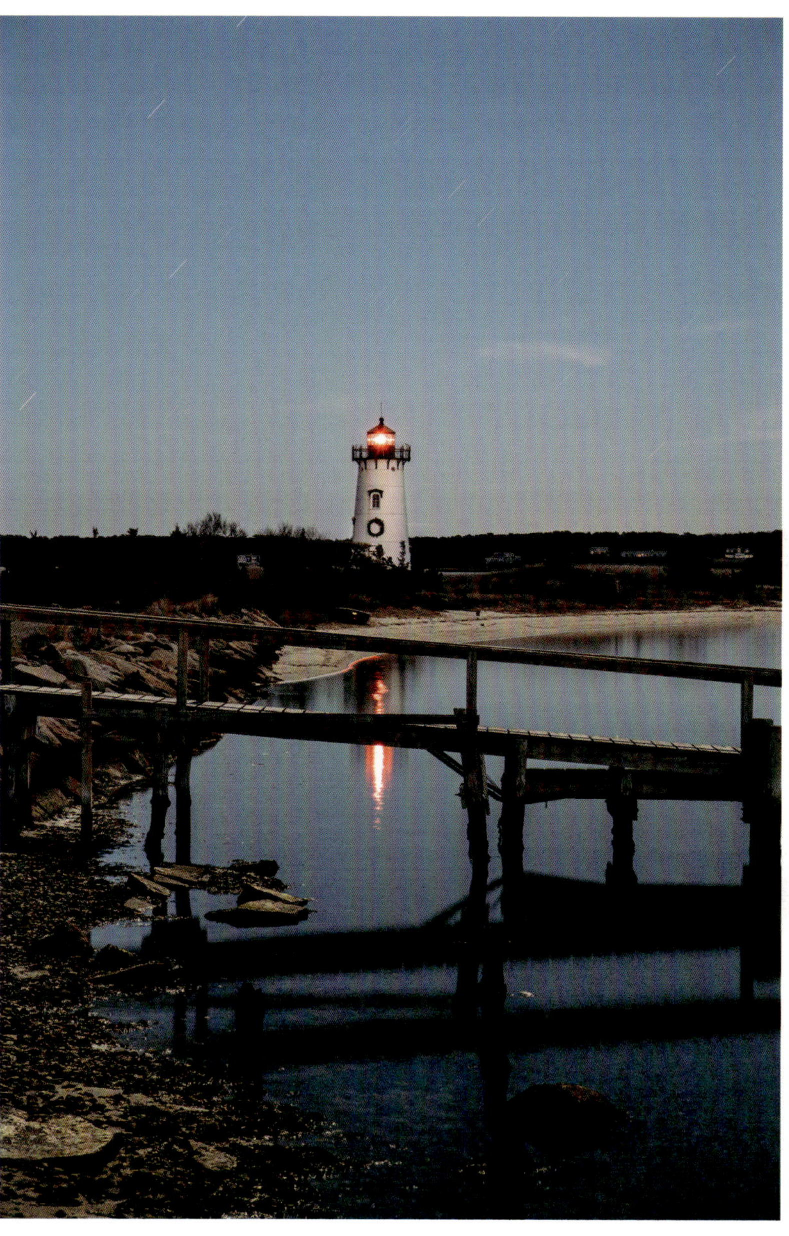

As twilight fades, stars begin to appear and move across the skies over Edgartown Light in December 2023. A few moments later, a timer would activate the decorations on the tower.

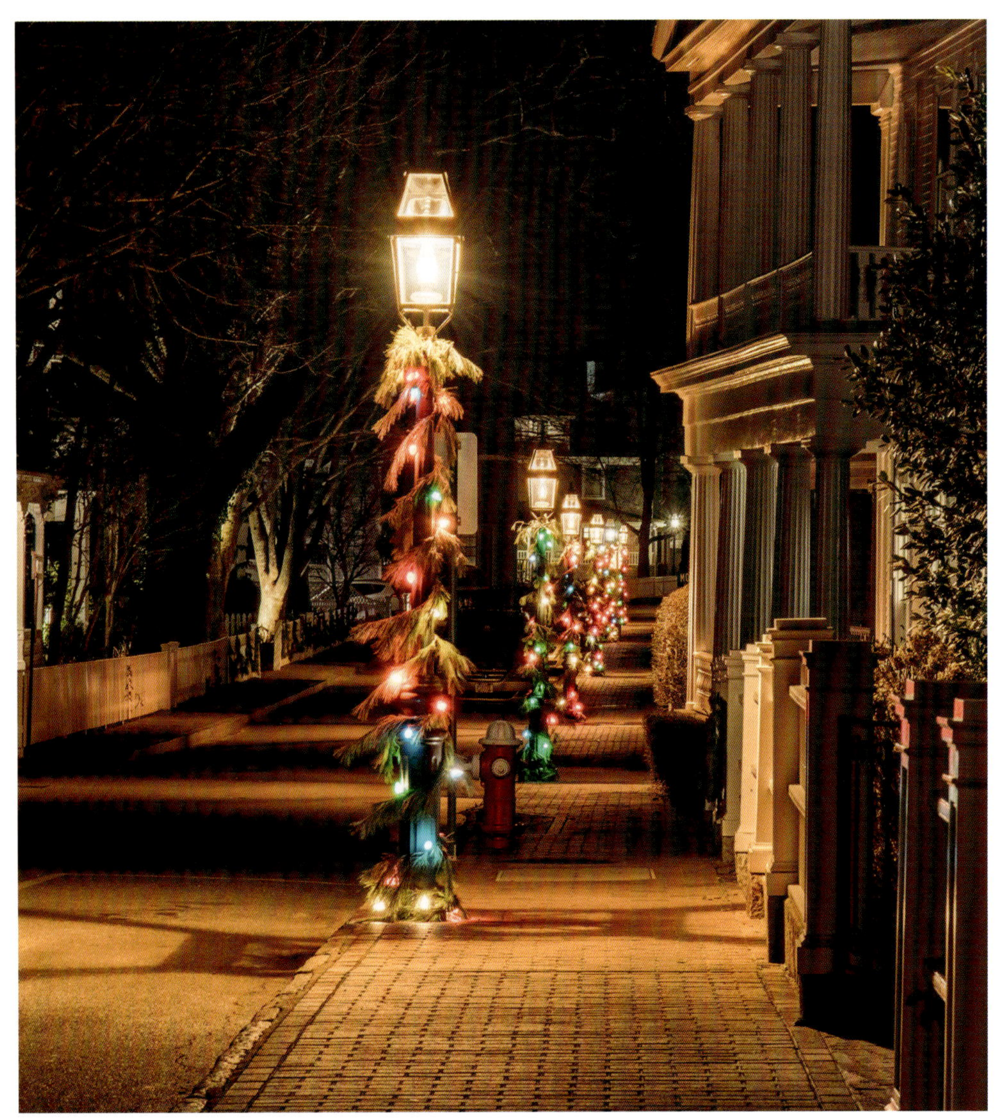

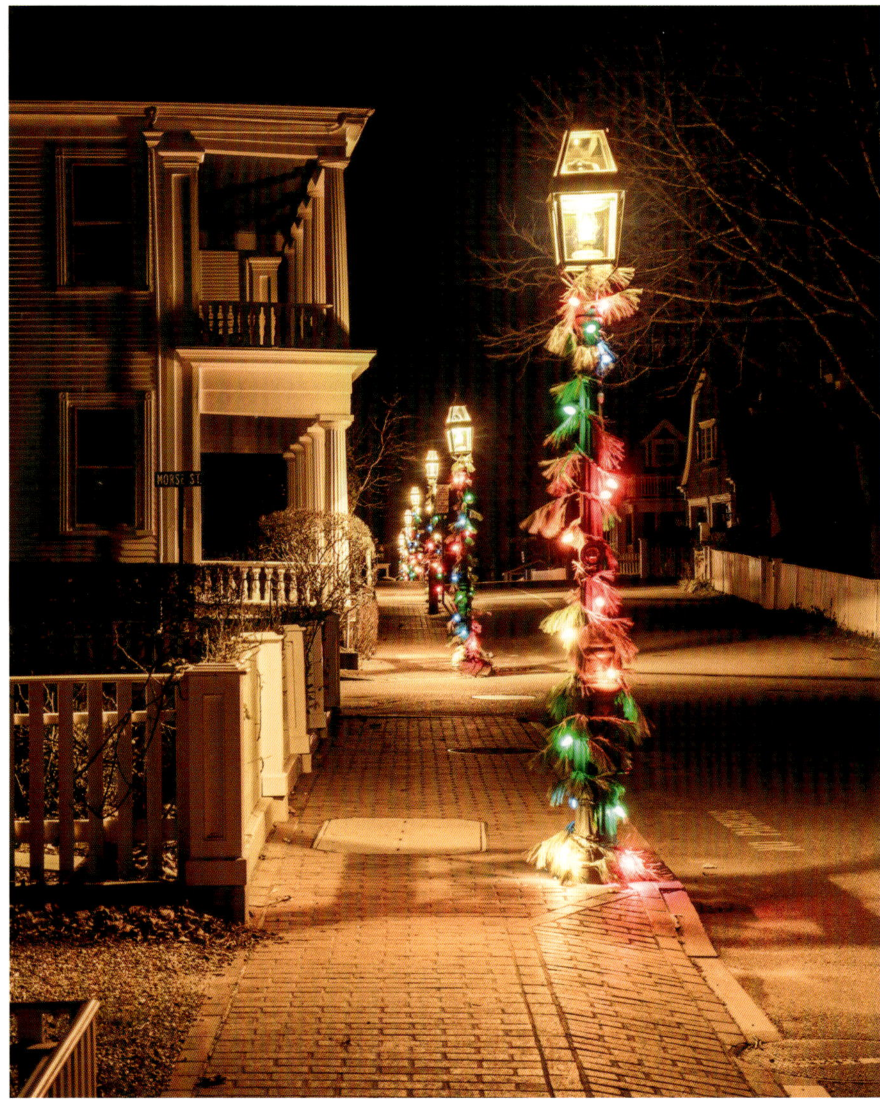

There is no experience more magical than a stroll down Water Street during the holidays. Each lamp has been carefully decorated with pine garland and the big, painted vintage bulbs that many of us remember seeing on our own trees when growing up.

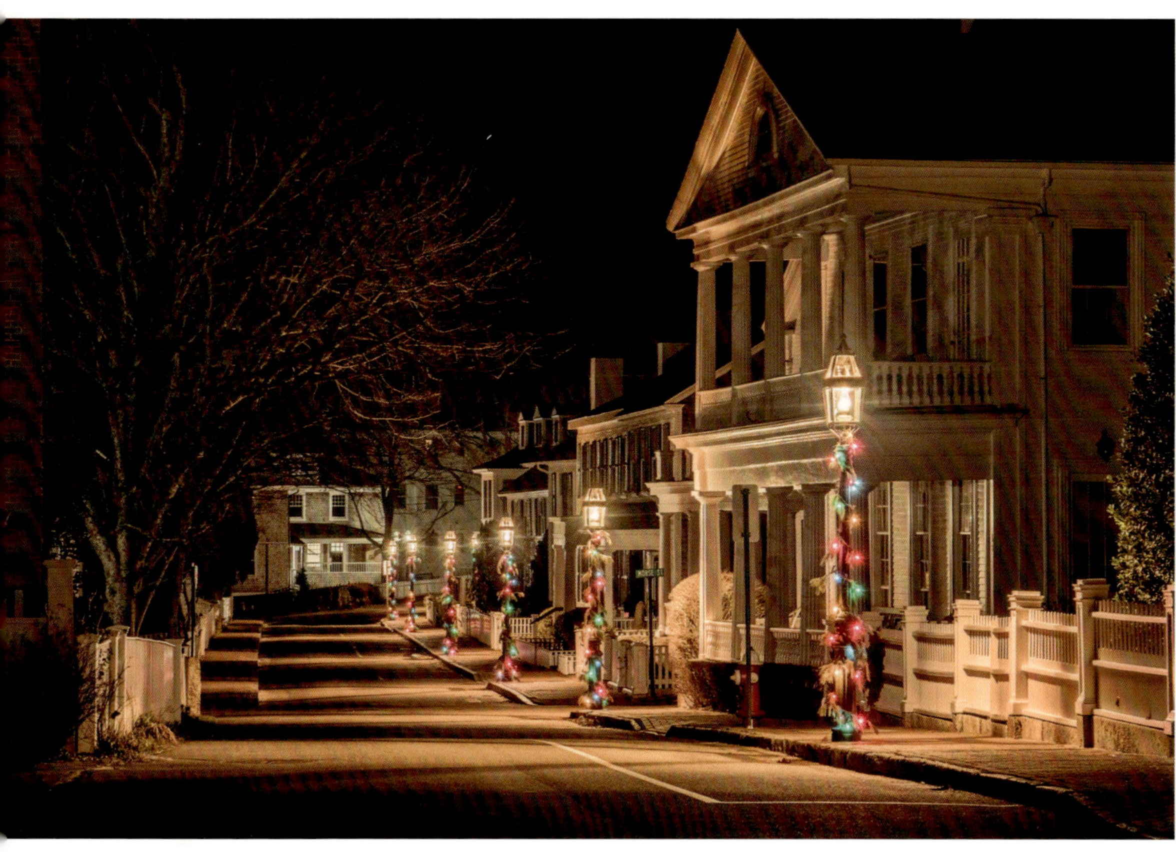

The Water Street lampposts looking toward Main Street. In the few weeks leading up to Christmas, this becomes a popular street to cruise and enjoy the decorations. It sometimes can take several minutes before there is enough time to get a photograph from the middle of the road without a car approaching.

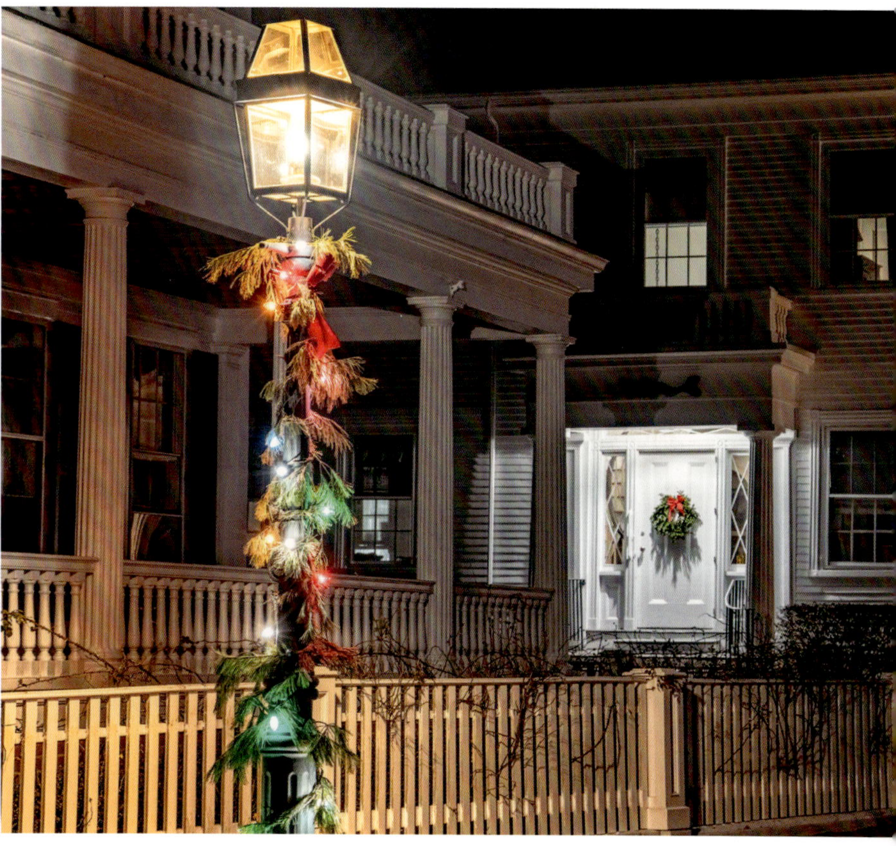

A mermaid keeps guard over a holiday wreath on the corner of Morse and Water Streets.

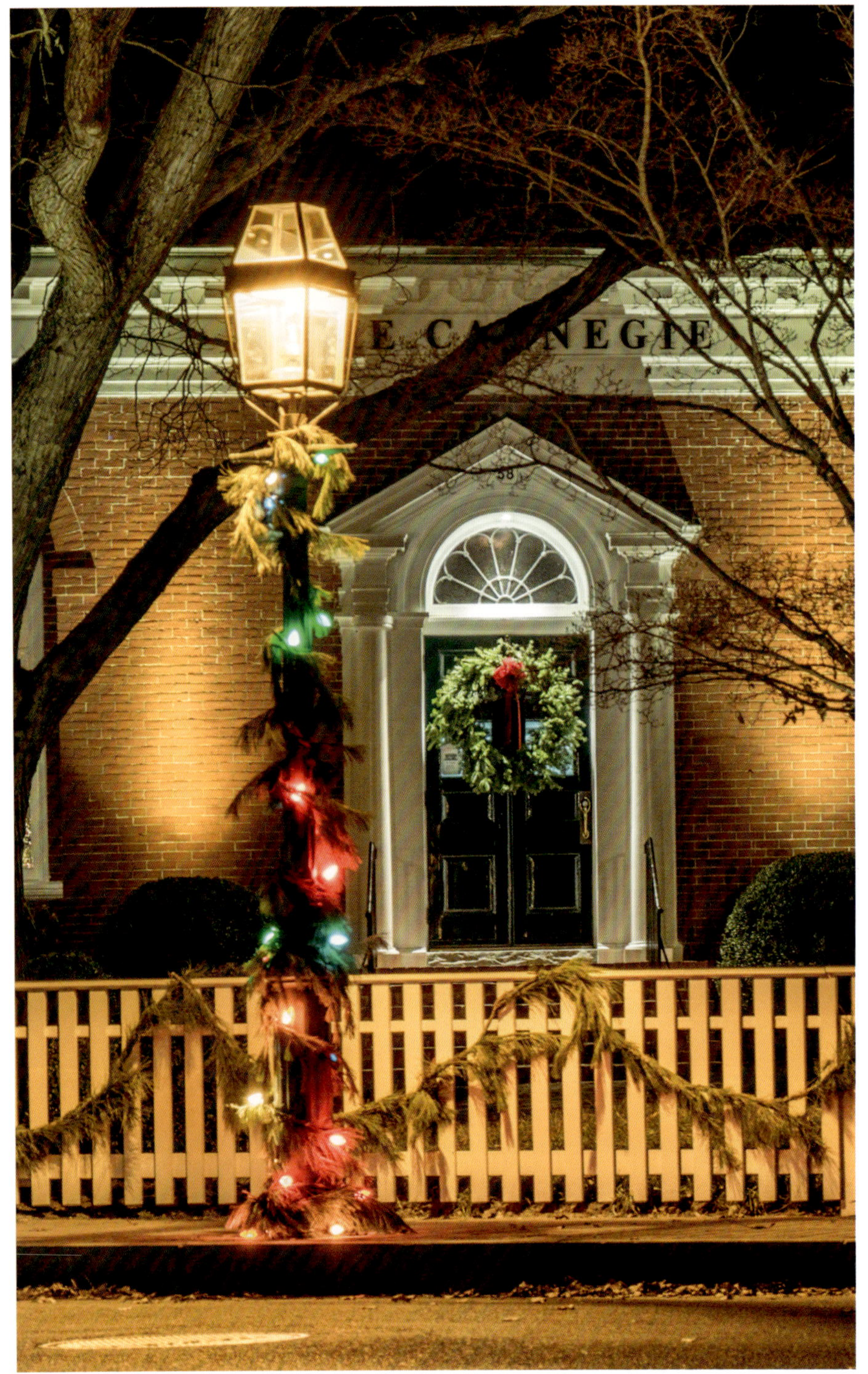

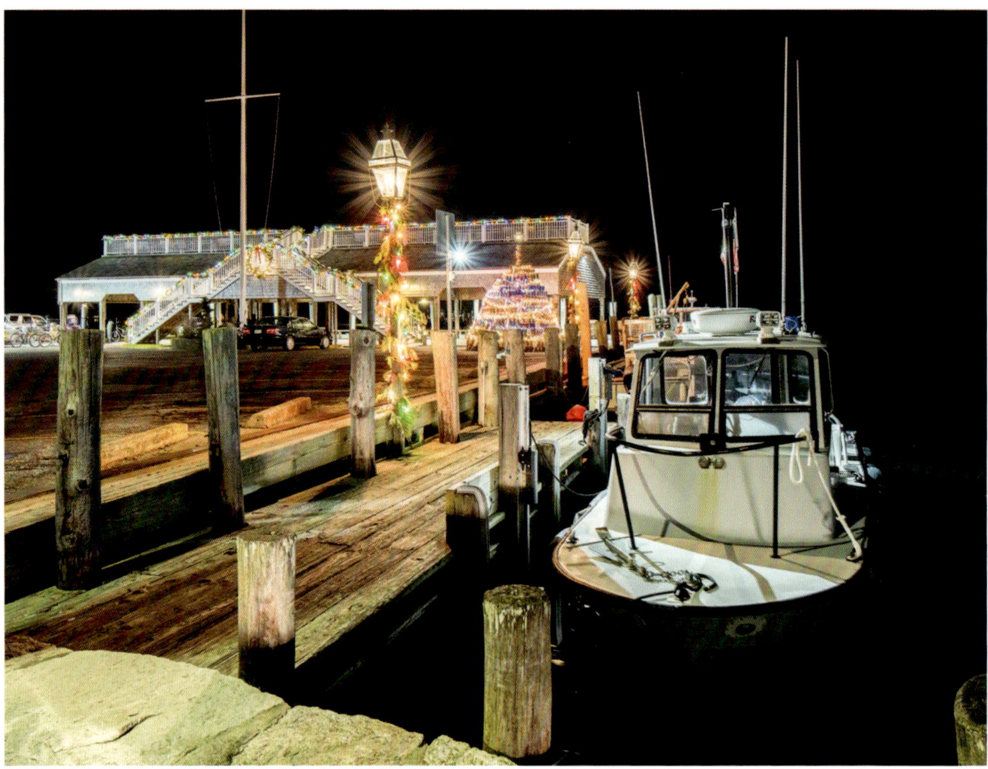

Lampposts near Memorial Wharf. Look behind the boat and to the right to see the lobster pot Christmas tree.

Now the Carnegie Heritage Center, this classic brick building was opened as a library in 1904. In its current form, the building now serves as an exhibit center showcasing the area's rich history, offering programs and an artisan shop. Like the nearby Sculpin Gallery, it is part of the Vineyard Preservation Trust system.

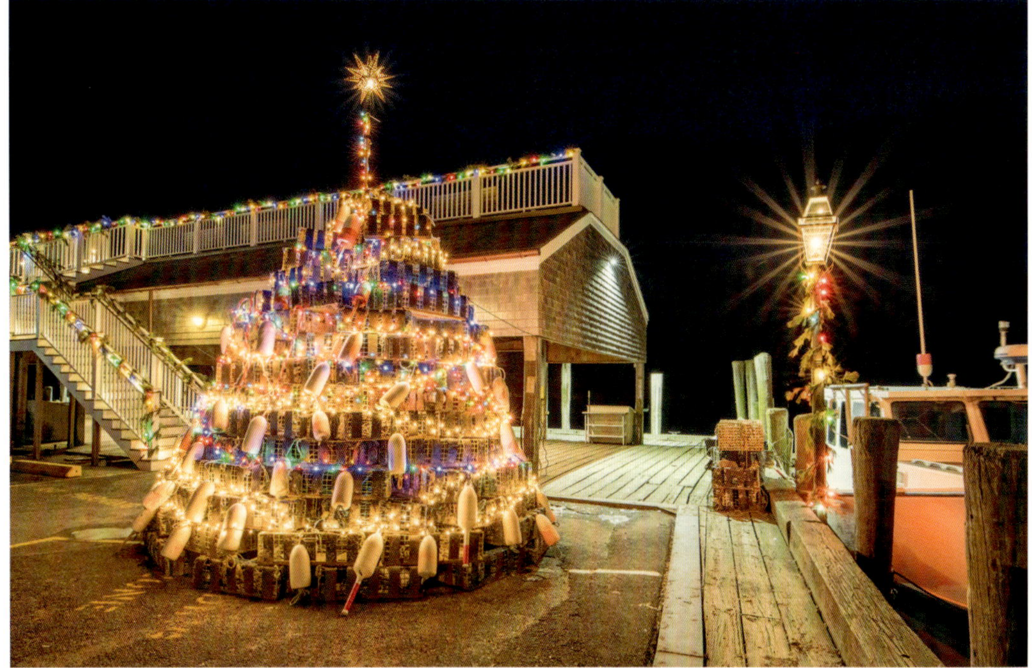

The complete lobster pot stack as it appeared in December 2019. That year, the lights were a combination of warm and colorful lights, which was a change from the previous season.

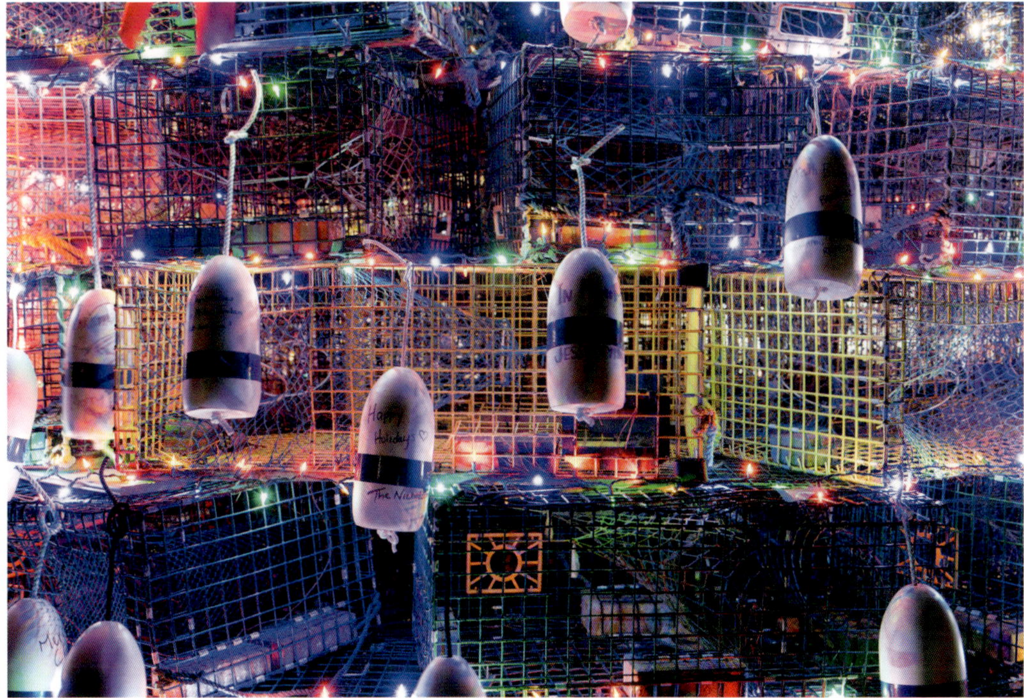

A closeup of the lobster pots stacked into a holiday display as it appeared in December 2018. For that season, the "tree" appeared near the harbor-viewing platform, but it was later moved to the space next to town hall to accommodate the platform's refurbishment.

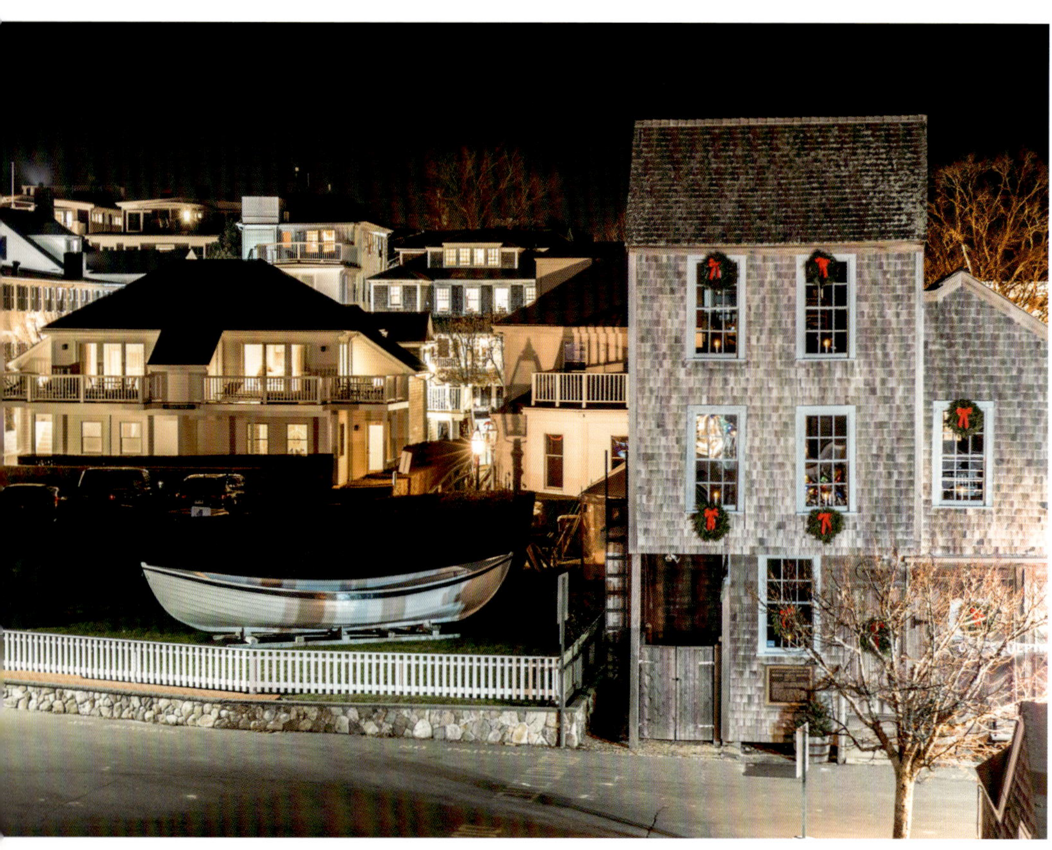

The Old Sculpin Gallery as seen from atop the viewing platform. This building was originally located 50 yards away and is now part of the Vineyard Preservation Trust, serving as an art gallery and educational space for the Martha's Vineyard Art Association. Keen-eyed movie viewers can spot this building, along with the viewing platform, in a certain shark movie filmed on location in the 1970s.

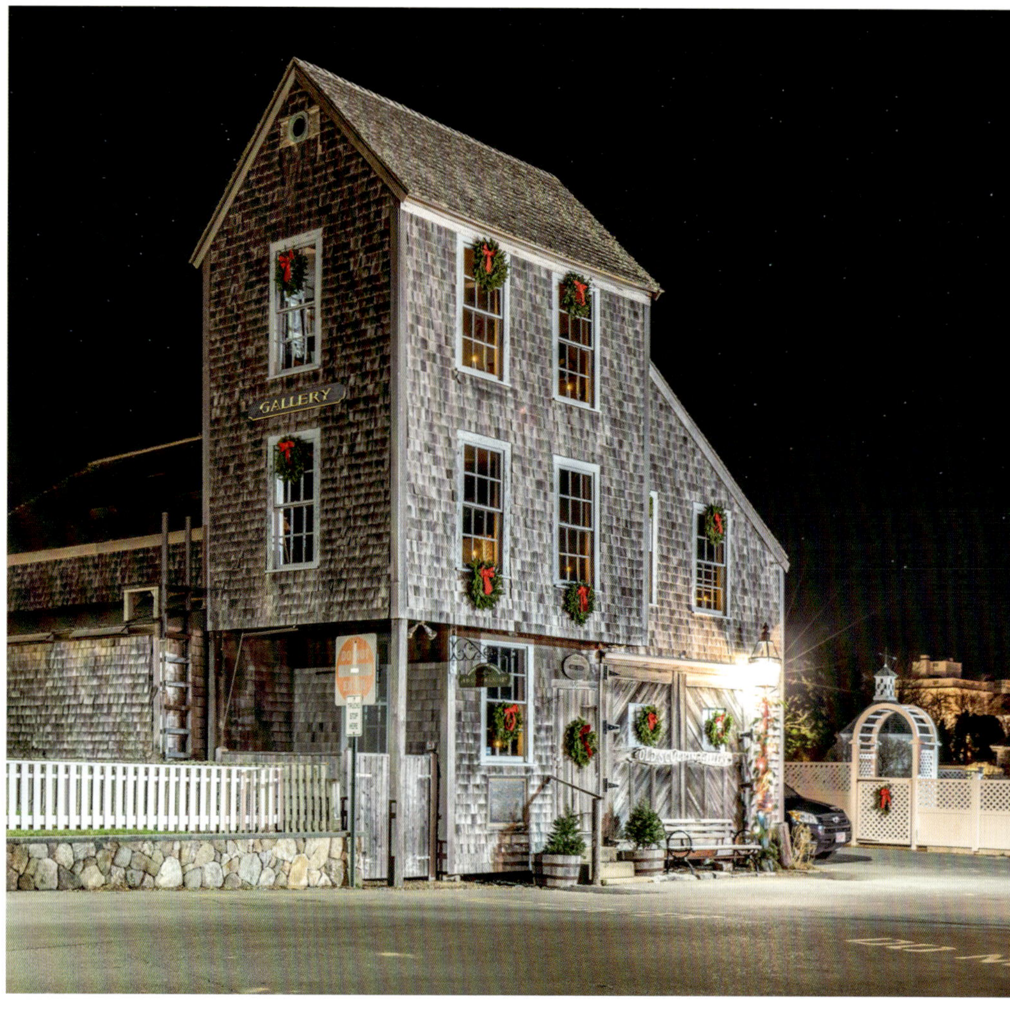

Electric candles and simple wreaths make for a classic New England holiday display. It is along the side of this building where cars line up to await their trip across the harbor via the Chappy Ferry.

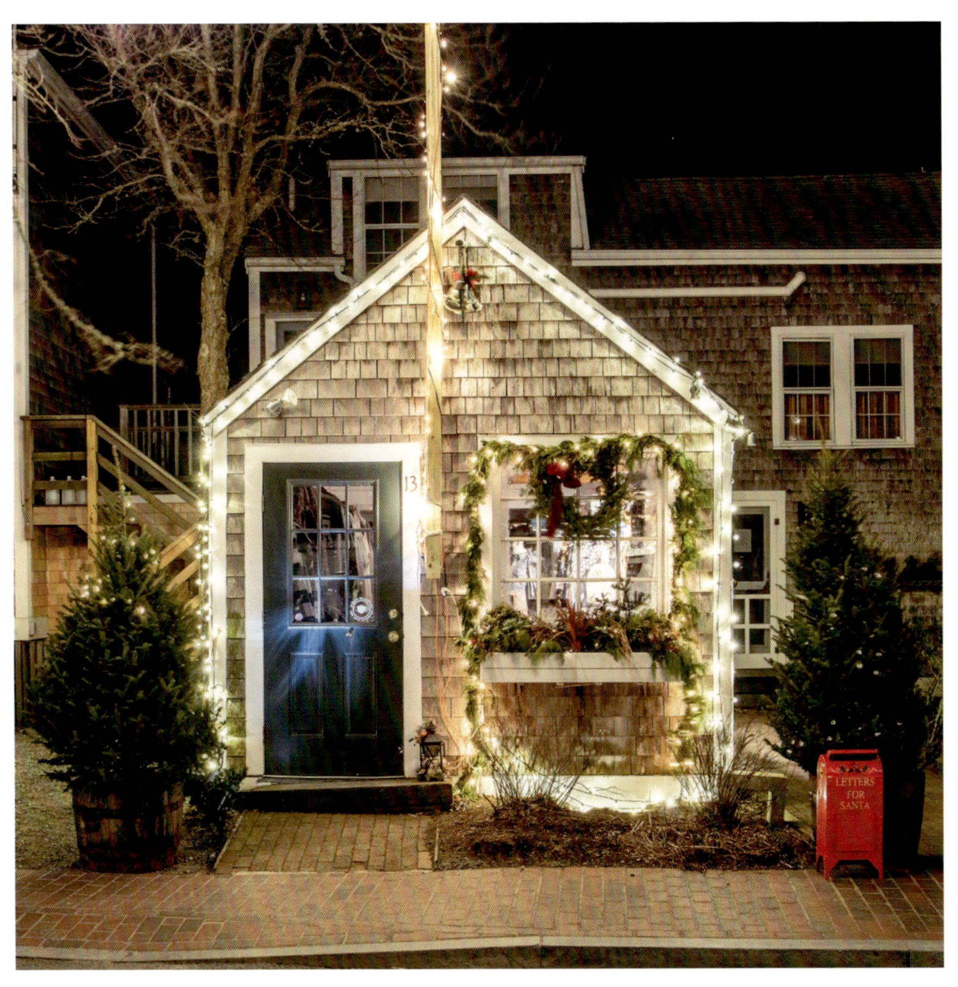

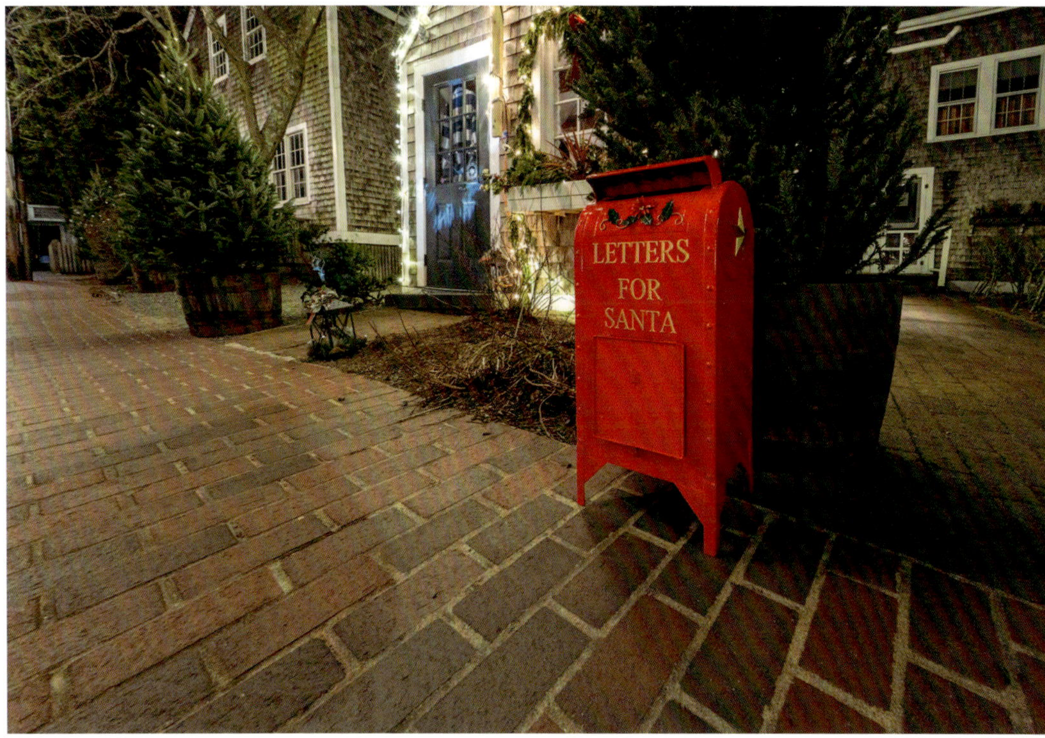

This tiny red mailbox is easy to miss. I imagine this is the perfect size for Vineyard-dwelling elves needing to forward their gift requests to Santa.

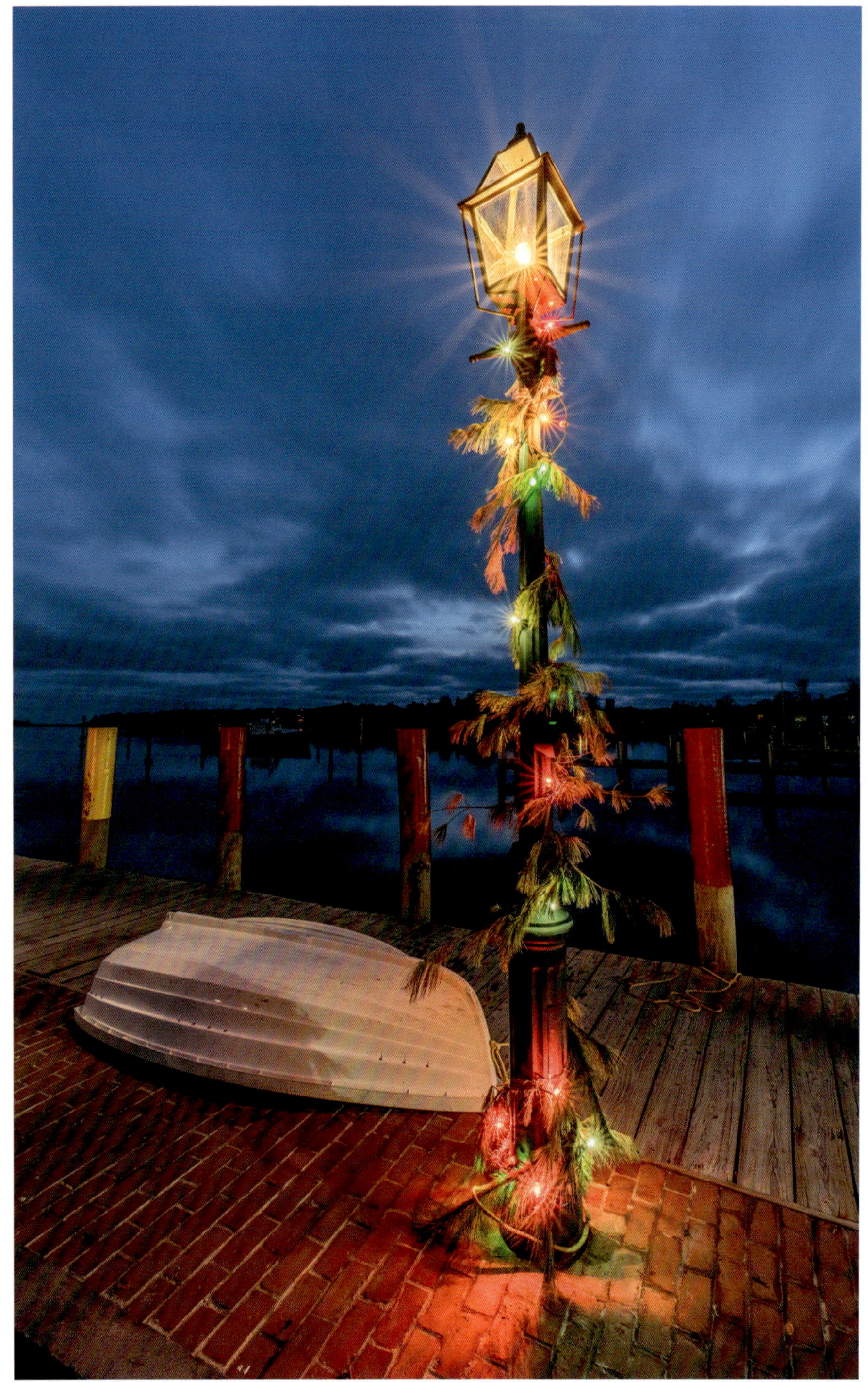

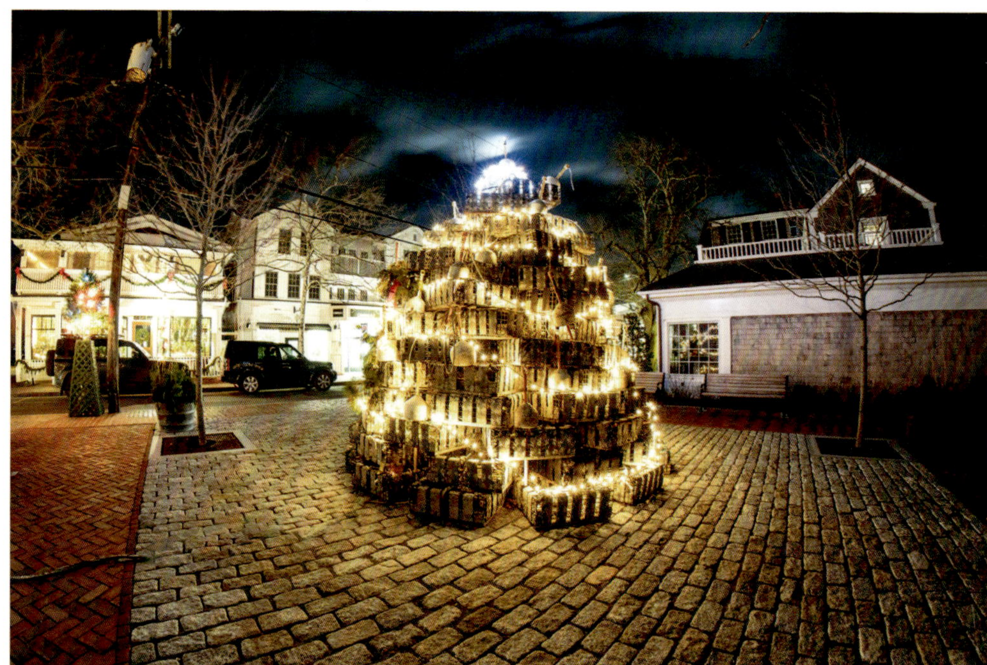

Now located next to the town hall in Edgartown, the lobster pot tree may physically look the same every year, but the lighting varies. In 2023, it was a string of white lights that randomly cycled through twinkle patterns.

One of Edgartown's beautifully decorated lampposts provides an anchor point for this small fiberglass dinghy near the Main Street parking lot. The boat seems to be there year-round.

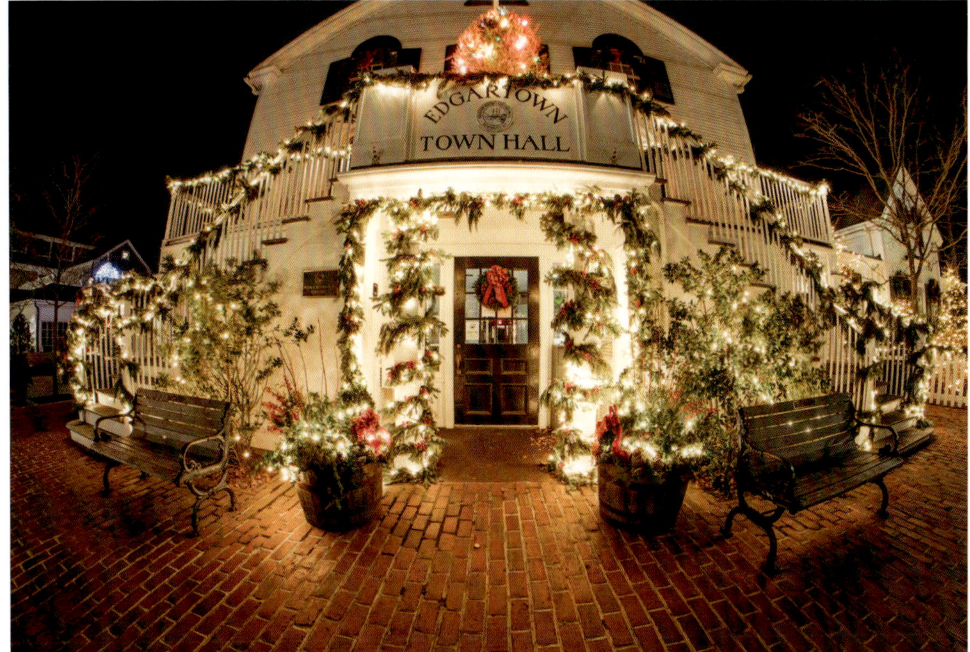

Edgartown Hall is the most festive building you'll see on Main Street. Here it is photographed using a fish-eye lens, so the entire front facade could fit into the composition despite the tight space.

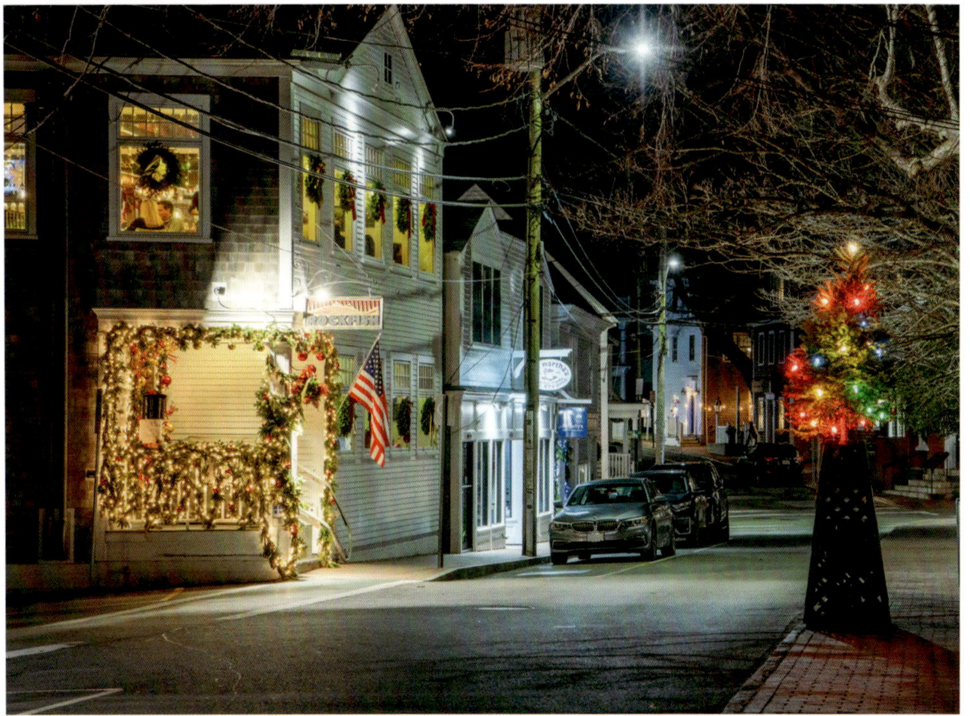

Laughing, dinner plates clanging, car doors closing: the sounds of dinners out at Christmas on Martha's Vineyard.

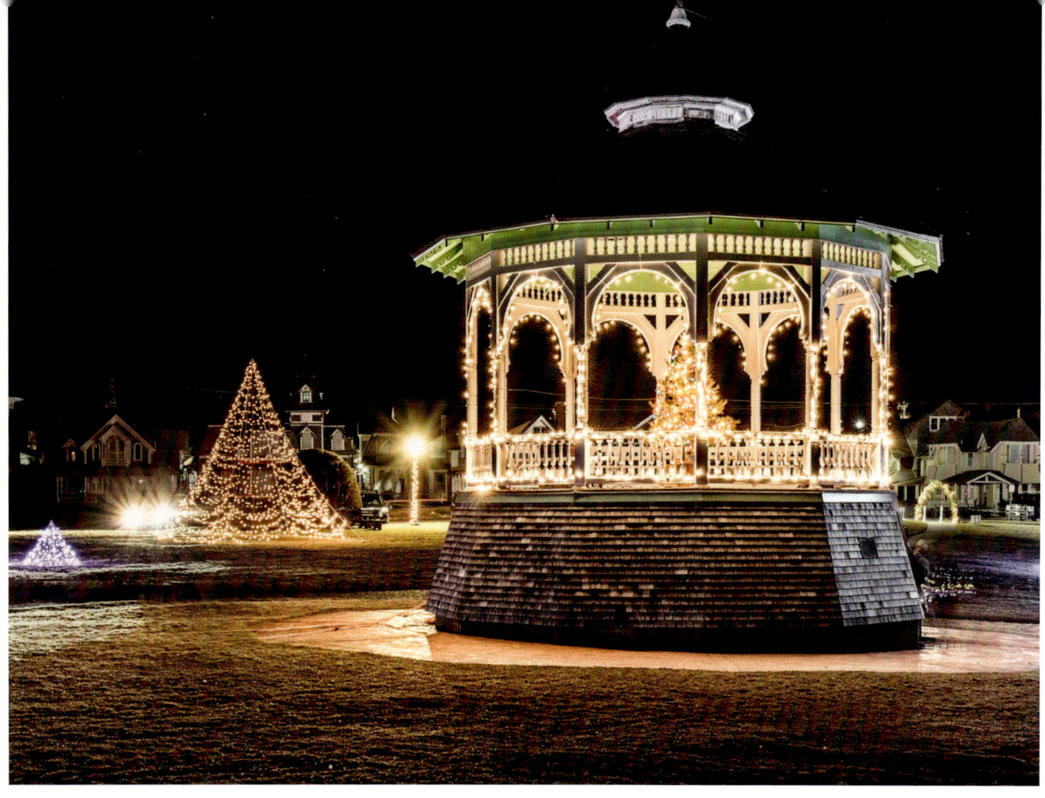

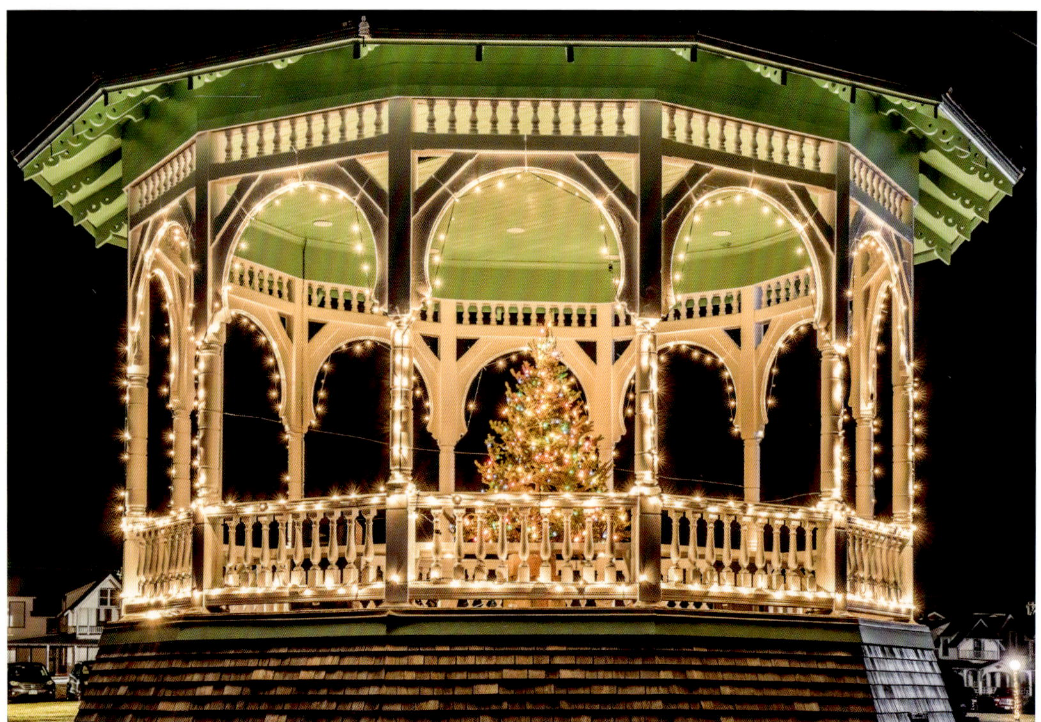

The Oak Bluffs Gazebo is the center point of Ocean Park's holiday decorations. Surrounding it are several light sculptures that appear in the shapes of triangular trees. For a few years, these sculptures were accompanied by music and timed to twinkle and flash along with it.

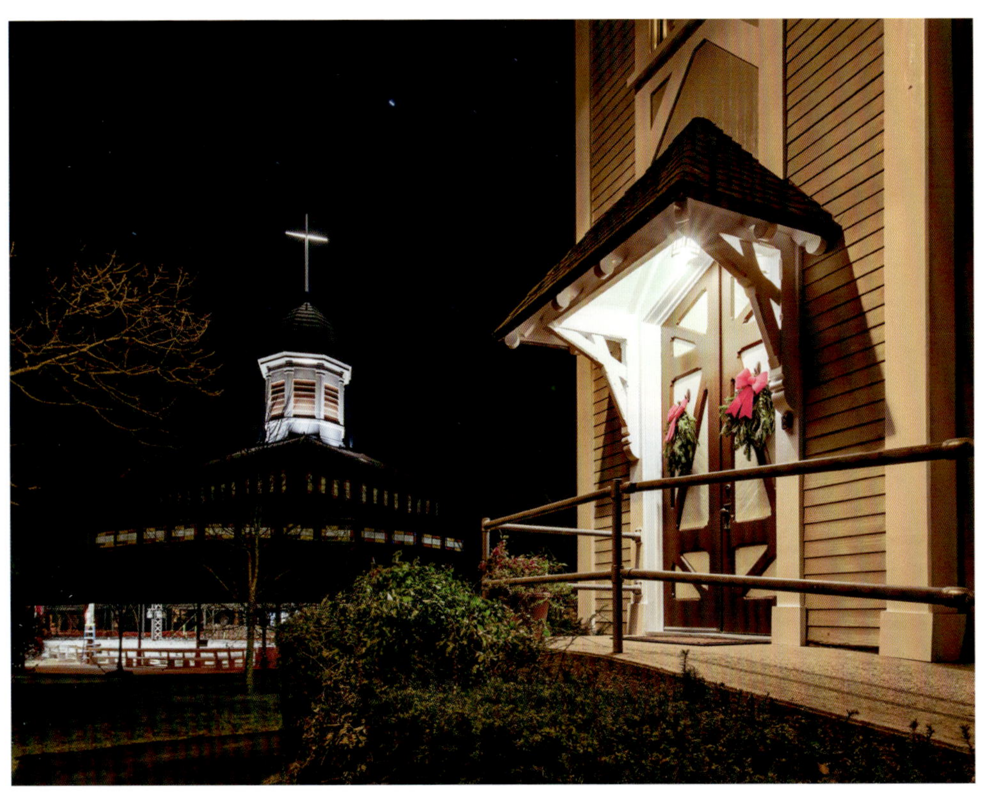

A view of the Tabernacle steeple from the Methodist Church. The brightly lit cross can be seen well above the treeline when approaching Oak Bluffs via boat. This is the center point of the Martha's Vineyard Camp Meeting Association (MVCMA) property and regularly hosts worship, community events, and activities throughout the year.

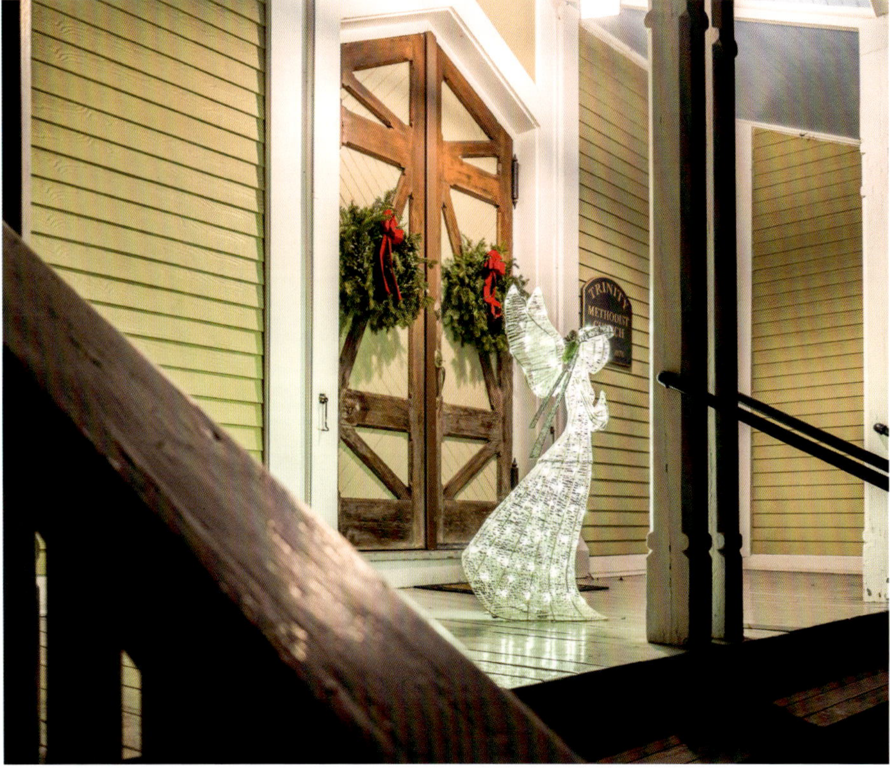

A lone angel welcomes visitors to Oak Bluffs' Trinity Methodist Church in December 2018. This year was the first and last in which I spotted her during the holidays.

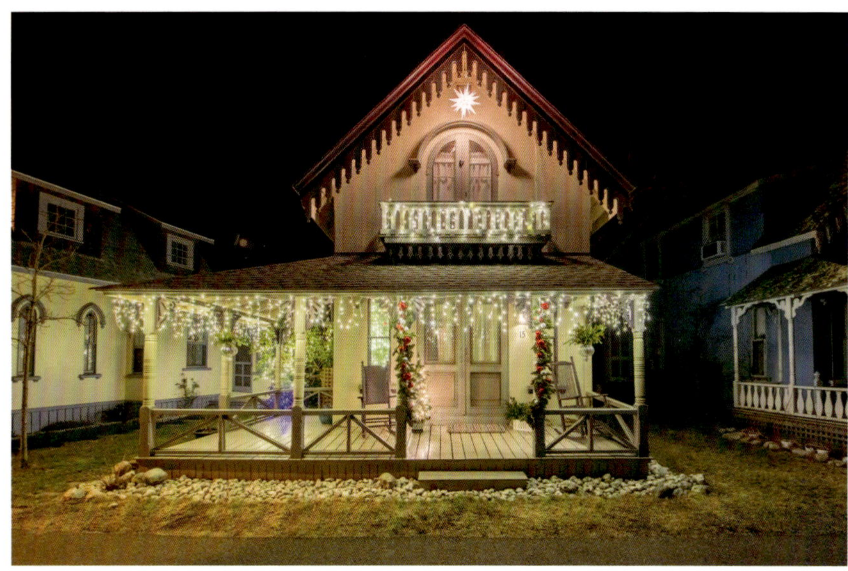

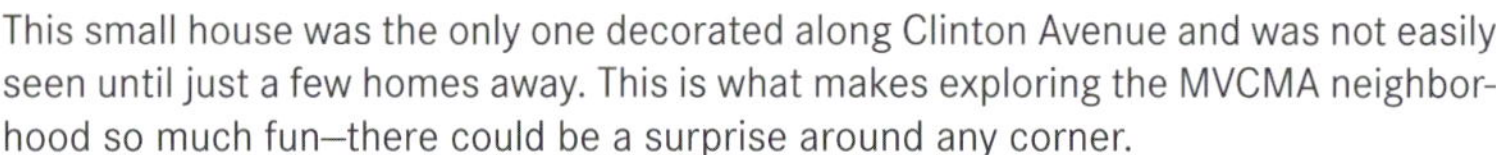

This small house was the only one decorated along Clinton Avenue and was not easily seen until just a few homes away. This is what makes exploring the MVCMA neighborhood so much fun—there could be a surprise around any corner.

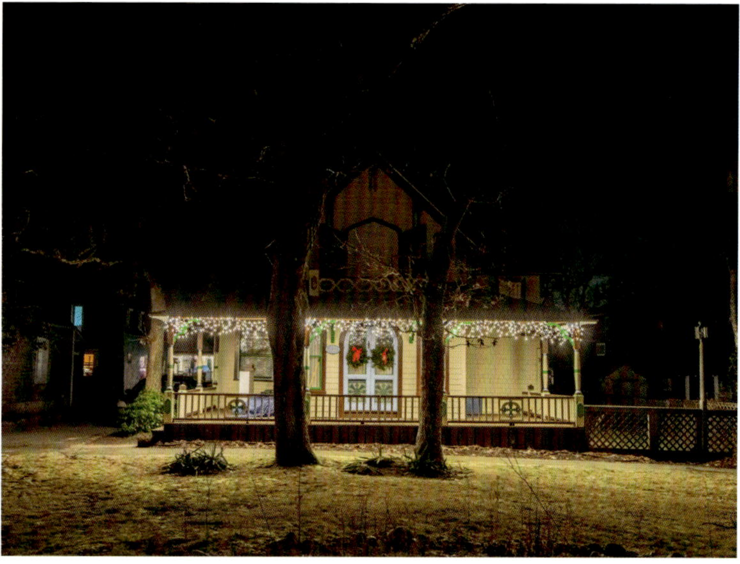

This one was located on Faith Avenue and was also the only home lit on its street. There was something unique about how the trees framed the doorway, which is what caught my eye when deciding how to photograph it. I returned the following year, but it was not decorated again.

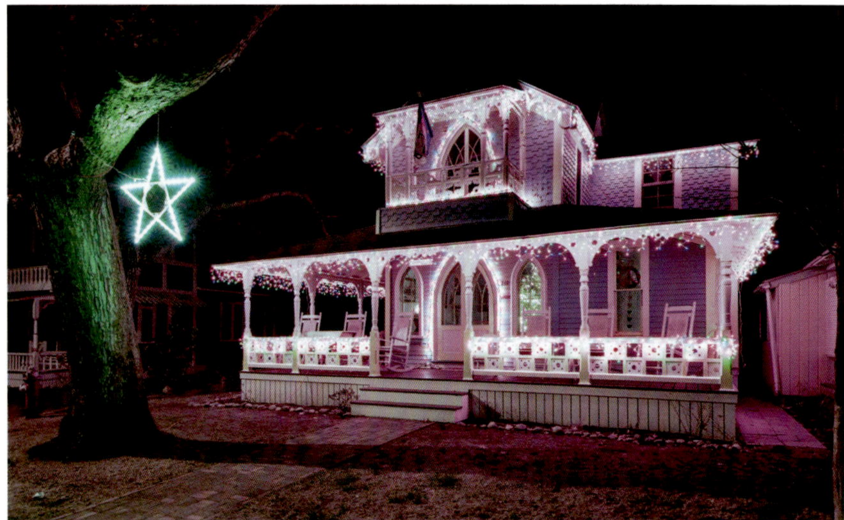

A home near Rural Circle beams a pink-purple glow across the neighborhood. As of 2022, this was a new addition to the area's decorations.

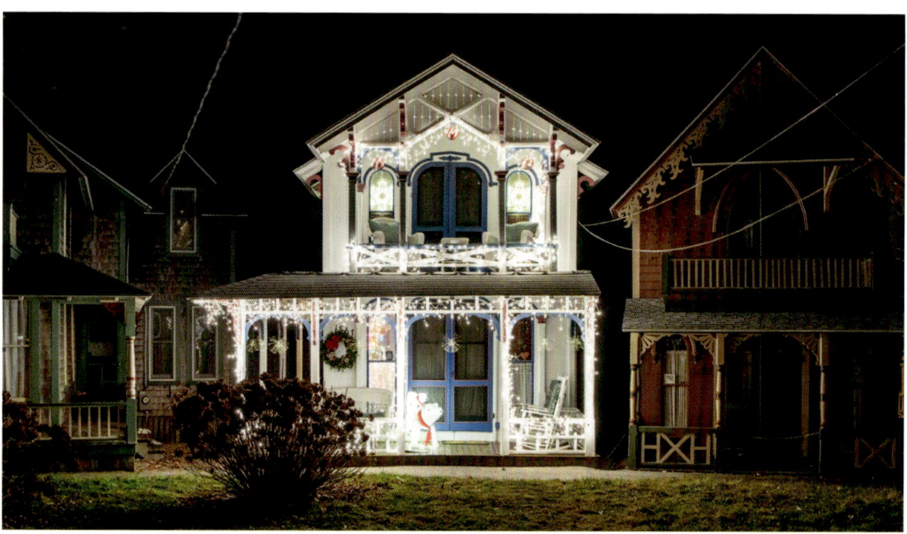

This house is a pitstop for polar bears, and its white paint helps to radiate light in all directions, easily illuminating several nearby houses along Wesleyan Grove in Oak Bluffs.

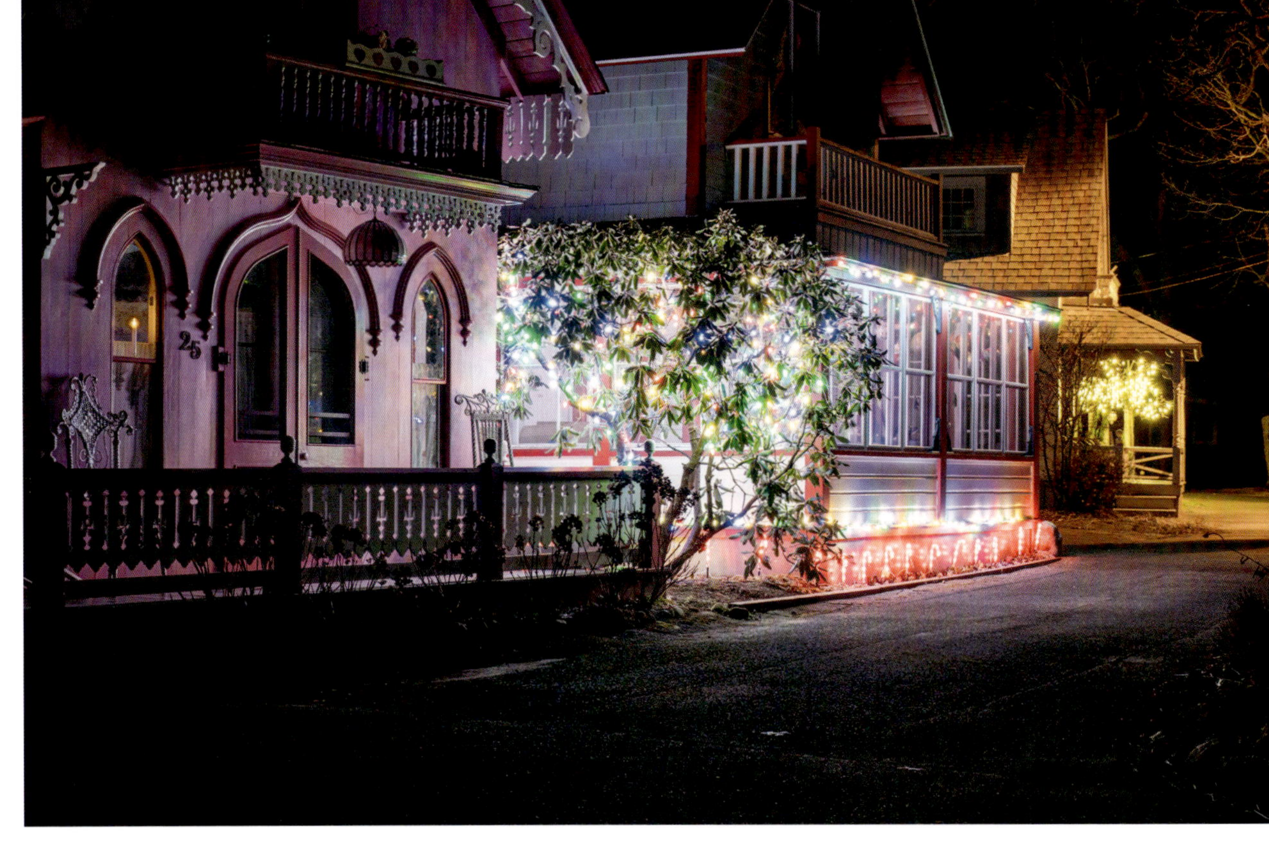

Lots of colorful lights and candy canes make this home feel like a life-sized gingerbread house.

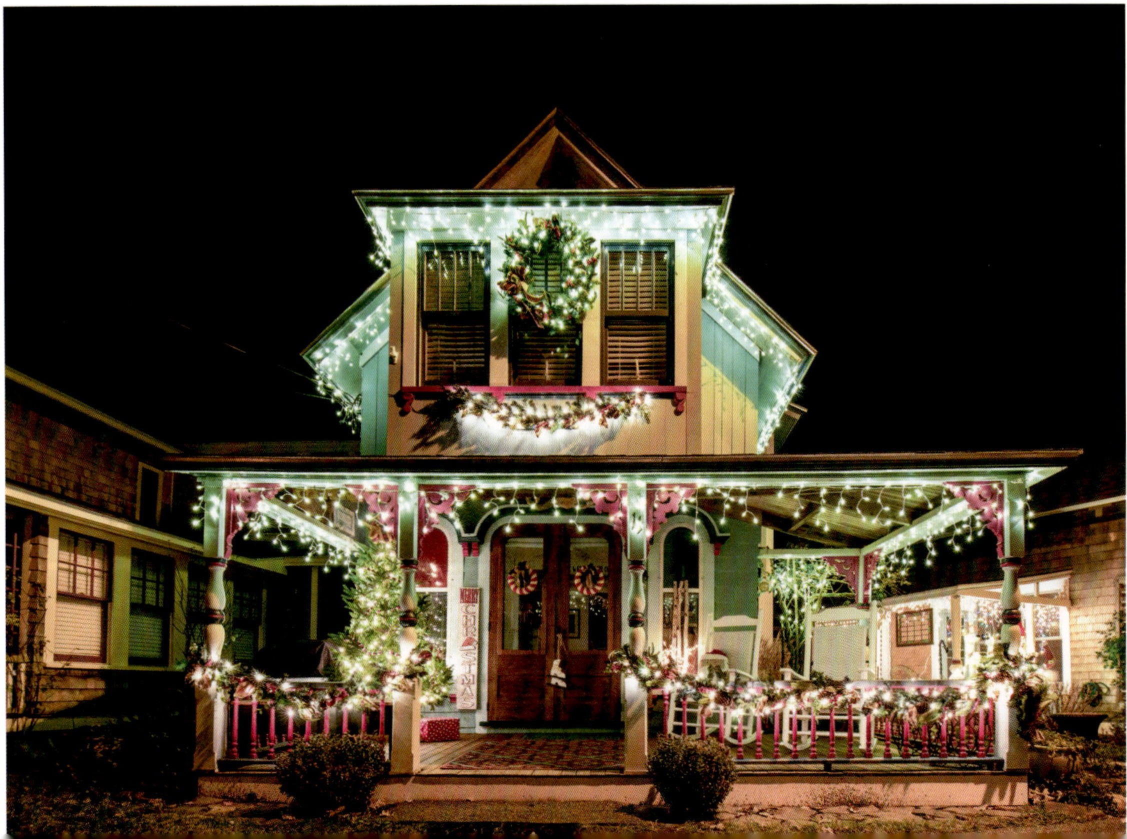

If Santa had a winter home on Martha's Vineyard, this likely would be it.

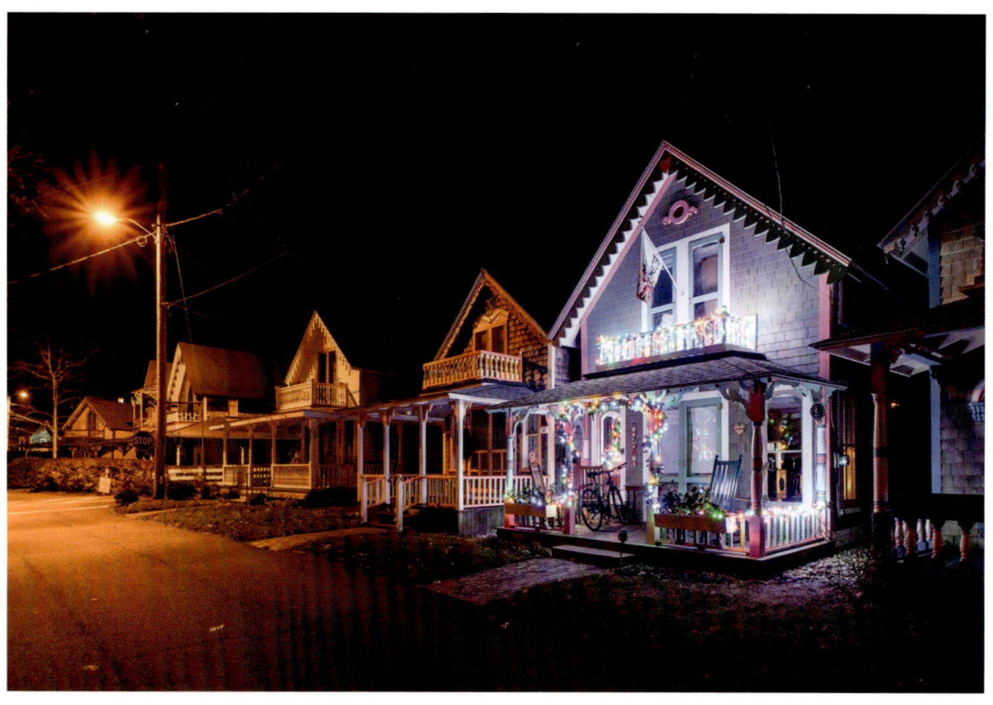

The orange cast of a nearby streetlamp can't overpower the holiday energy being produced by this tiny home.

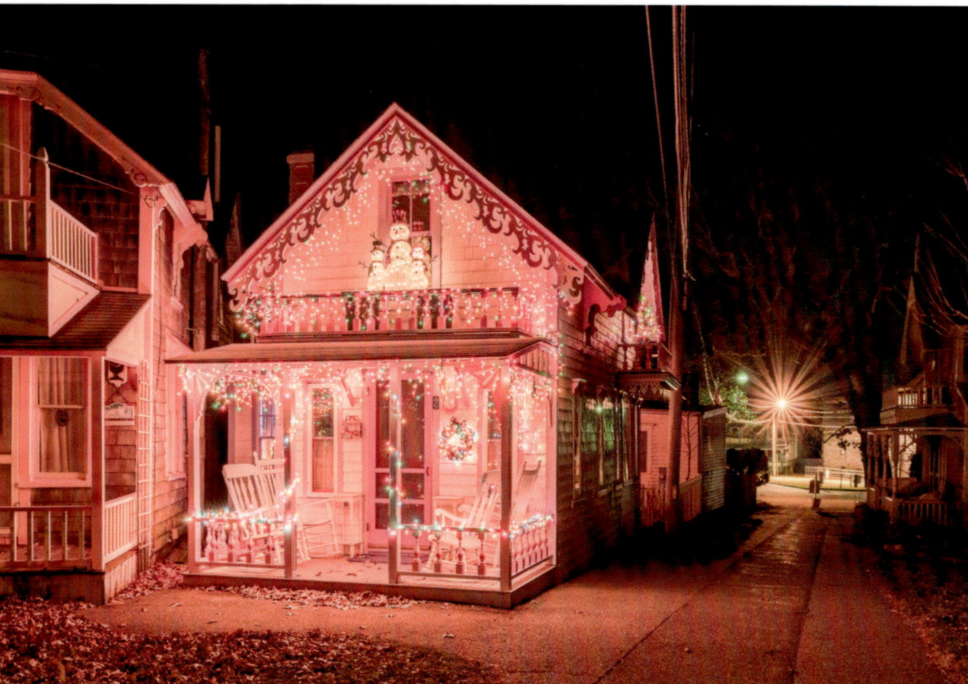

The Martha's Vineyard Camp Meeting Association gets very quiet in the winter, making decorated houses like this even more striking by contrast. There are several homes nearby that participate in holidays, but this one easily overpowers them. A family of snow people is always supervising, making sure you look but don't touch!

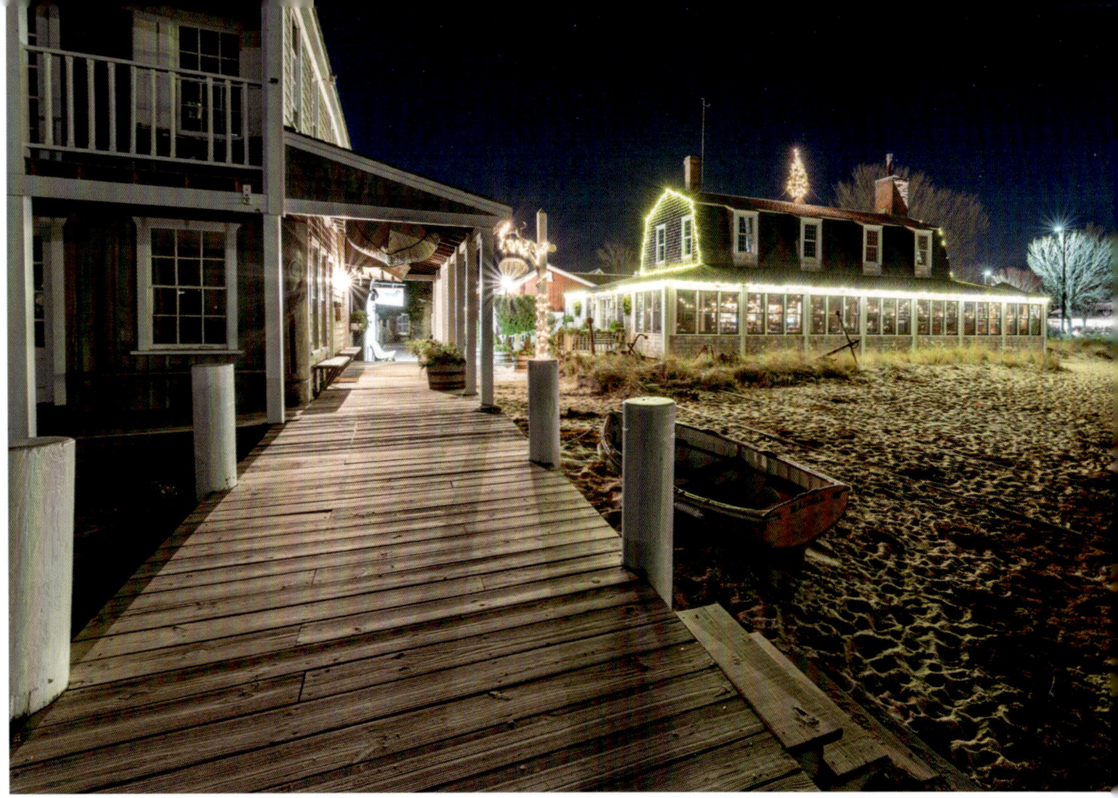

Looking back from the Black Dog Wharf in Vineyard Haven toward the restaurant. Strings of lights cast shadows across the beach while a tree on the roof reaches toward the stars on a chilly December night.

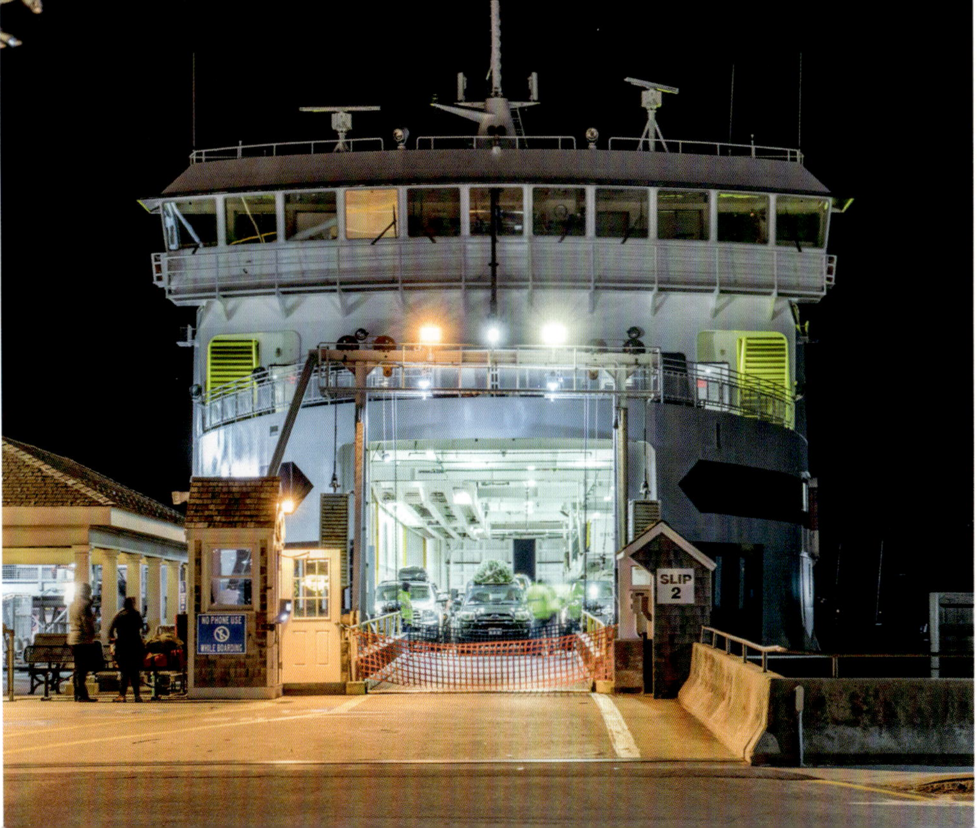

A vehicle waits to disembark the last ferry of the night into Vineyard Haven, having successfully procured a tree from somewhere on the mainland. It wouldn't be the only one to emerge with one.

CONCLUDING THIS BOOK, STARTING YOUR OWN STORY

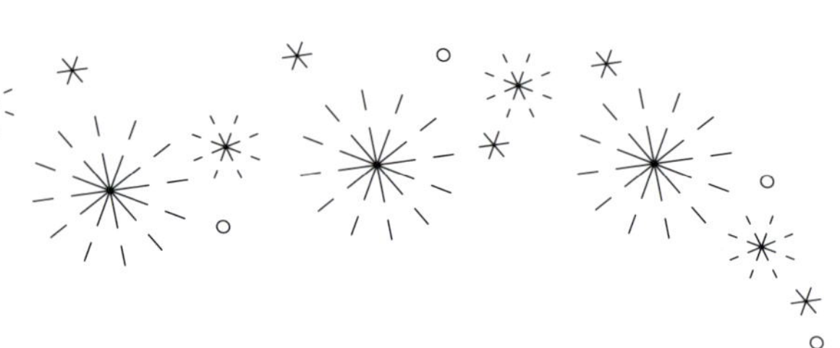

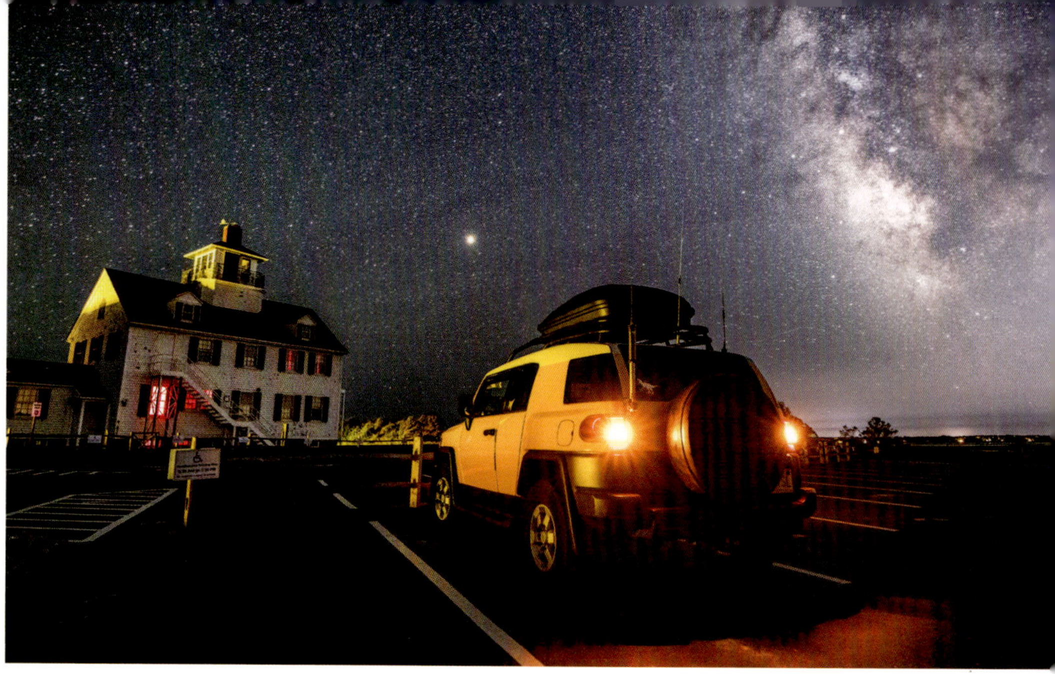

UP ALL NIGHT

Staying up late isn't for everyone, but through this book you experienced the Cape after dark from the comfort of wherever you are right now and on your schedule! You saw starry skies over beaches, moonlight shining onto harbors, holiday decorations lining the streets of Edgartown, and even the northern lights shimmering over the Cape Cod National Seashore.

Curating the images for a book like this is a lot of work, and I sincerely hope you enjoyed seeing what I selected. Did one of them stand out to you? Every photograph featured here is available for purchase in a variety of sizes and formats, and I am more than happy to help get one to you. You can contact me via my website at www.capenightsgallery.com.

HOW TO SEE IN THE DARK

Did you know that nearly 80 percent of Americans and one-third of the world's population cannot see the Milky Way band from where they live? There's a lot of light pollution, but even a short drive out of town can help connect you with the stars.

Taking time out of life to enjoy the night sky, with or without a camera, is good for the soul. And it's easy to get started! Any opportunity to share this experience with a friend or loved one is a moment that won't soon be forgotten. Children of all ages will enjoy a chance to learn about the universe, view a meteor shower, or spot a planet.

Astronomy is a hobby that is best enjoyed in the company of others. Joining a local astronomy club or society can provide valuable opportunities to learn from experienced astronomers, participate in star parties, and gain access to telescopes and other equipment. Many clubs offer introductory programs for people interested in learning even more. Online communities, such as forums and social media groups, are also great places to ask questions, share experiences, and stay updated on astronomical events. Do you have a college nearby? I bet they have a planetarium that they open up to the public for shows hosted by astronomy students. It's also possible there's a museum in your area with a planetarium that has a variety of programs to enjoy.

Numerous apps and websites, such as Stellarium or SkySafari, provide interactive star maps that can help you identify objects in real time. Books such as *NightWatch: A Practical Guide to Viewing the Universe* by Terence Dickinson (a personal favorite of mine) are excellent resources for beginners and are packed with incredible deep-sky images. Understanding celestial movements and the phases of the moon will enhance your stargazing. Even a simple book of constellation maps such as *Observing the Constellations* by John Sanford is a great place for the casual viewer to start. Visit your local used bookstore, where such books can be had for just a few dollars.

FOR PHOTOGRAPHERS

What about creating images like the ones you've seen in this book? Well, there are a lot of resources to help you with that, including some of the information that I have included here.

While you can learn quite a bit online, there's no substitute for going out with an experienced photographer who can help guide you. Workshops and tours offer opportunities for hands-on learning and to meet like-minded people who also have an interest in photography and the night sky. It also helps advanced photographers who don't want to travel alone at night to enjoy the safety of photographing with others. Photography events aren't just about capturing memories; they are also about experiencing them.

If you already own camera equipment, you're well on your way. You don't need the newest, bestest camera that money can buy. The most recent image featured in this book, photographed in December 2024, was taken with an eight-year-old camera. The point is that digital camera technology has been up to the task for more than a decade. If you have an interest, you will succeed. When I started photographing at night, I learned through a lot of trial and error, well before hundreds of tutorial videos and websites were just a few clicks away. New photographers have more resources and equipment choices than ever before, making it a great time to start your own journey.

Should you find yourself on Cape Cod with a camera, you now know where some of the best spots are to see the night sky or to photograph the area after dark. Better yet, book a tour or workshop experience with me! I'll show you these places in person and help you get great images under starry skies! I might even have a story or two to share about the images you've seen here, but couldn't include in the book.

Thank you for exploring Cape Cod with me once again. I had a great time, and I hope you did too! Let's do it again sometime.

See you out there, after dark!

Tim Little
Cape Nights
www.capenightsgallery.com

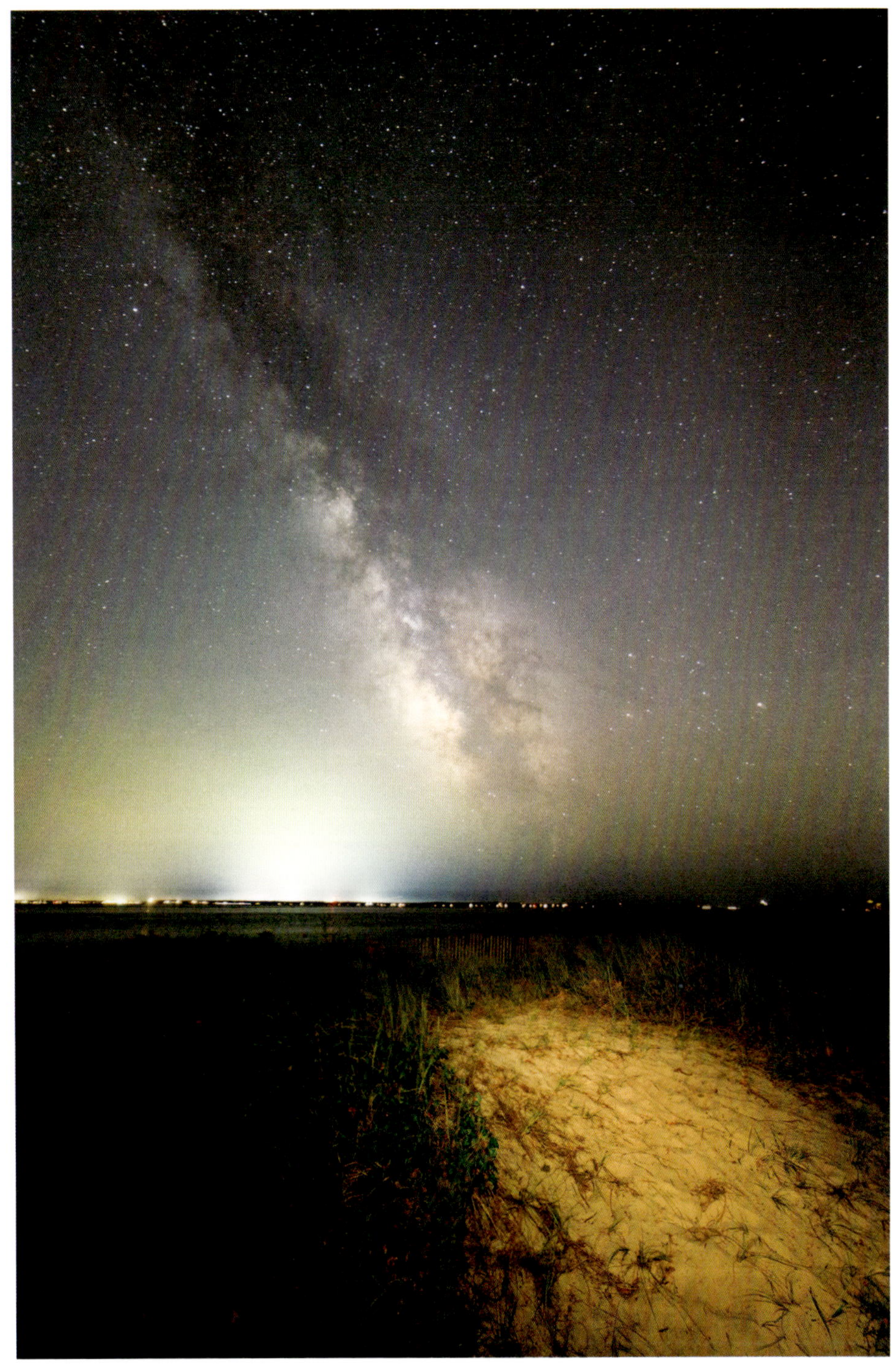

ABOUT THE AUTHOR

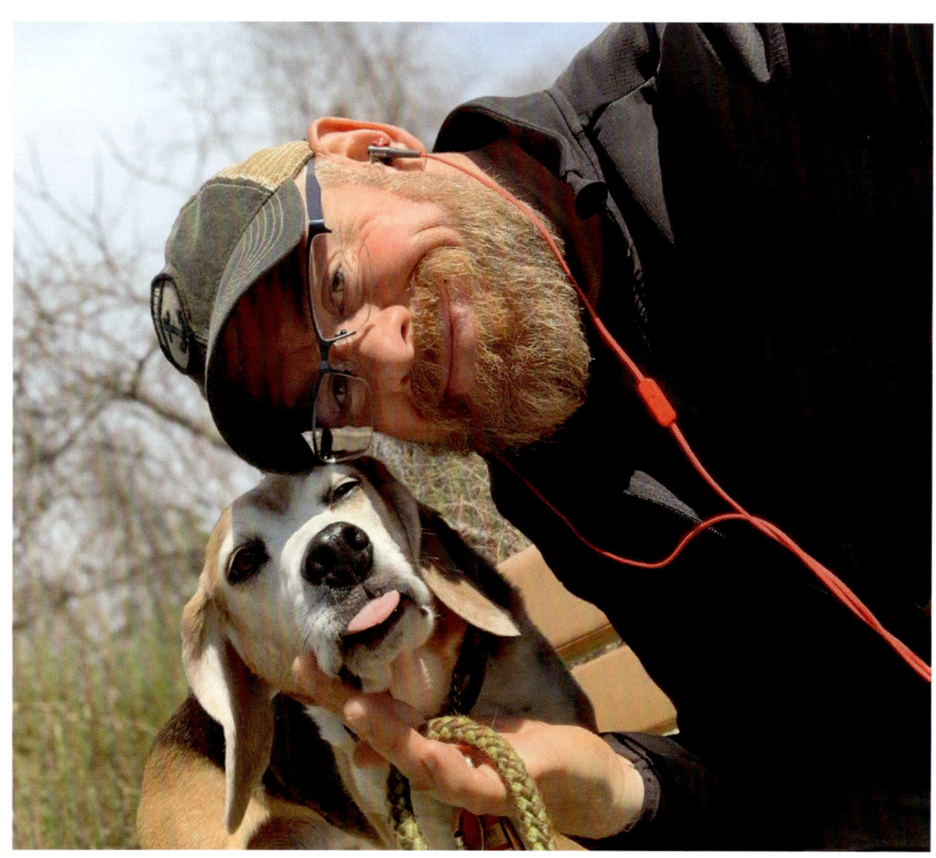

Timothy Little is an artist and educator living on Cape Cod, with a passion for photographing landscapes after dark. For nearly two decades, he has trekked into the night to capture starlight and moonlight over some of the area's most beautiful locations. In 2011, he began leading night photography workshops and tours across Cape Cod, sharing his techniques with thousands of visitors. His award-winning artwork has been featured in regional and national publications and has become synonymous with night photography in New England.